THE FASHION READER

Edited by

Linda Welters

and

Abby Lillethun

Oxford • New York

English edition
First published in 2007 by
Berg

Editorial offices:
First Floor, Angel Court, 81 St Clements Street, Oxford OX4 1AW, UK
175 Fifth Avenue, New York, NY 10010, USA

Berg is the imprint of Oxford International Publishers Ltd.

Library of Congress Cataloging-in-Publication Data

The fashion reader / edited by Linda Welters and Abby Lillethun. — English ed.
    p. cm.
    Includes bibliographical references and index.
    ISBN-13: 978-1-84520-485-3 (cloth)
    ISBN-10: 1-84520-485-9 (cloth)
    ISBN-13: 978-1-84520-486-0 (pbk.)
    ISBN-10: 1-84520-486-7 (pbk.)
  1. Clothing and dress. 2. Fashion. I. Welters, Linda. II. Lillethun, Abby.

TT507.F3545 2007
646'.34—dc22

2006037870

British Library Cataloguing-in-Publication Data

A catalogue record for this book is available from the British Library.

ISBN 978 1 84520 485 3 (Cloth)
        978 1 84520 486 0 (Paper)

Typeset by JS Typesetting Ltd, Porthcawl, Mid Glamorgan
Printed in the United Kingdom by Biddles Ltd, King's Lynn.

www.bergpublishers.com

CONTENTS

PART X: THE FASHION BUSINESS

PART XI: FUTURE OF FASHION

LIST OF FIGURES

ACKNOWLEDGMENTS

This book could not have happened without the contributions and assistance of many individuals and organizations. Our greatest debt goes to the authors who wrote pieces specifically for this reader as well as the numerous authors and publishers who granted permission to reprint published work. We appreciate the suggestions from the anonymous reviewers. Several authors were also instrumental in locating images and securing permission for images to illustrate their essays and articles, specifically Kimberly Chrisman-Campbell, Susan North, Cynthia Cooper, Tiffany Webber-Hanchett, Maureen Molloy, Sonnet Stanfill, Yuniya Kawamura and Vandana Bhandari.

We are also grateful to a number of helpers: Joy Emery for providing images from the Commercial Pattern Archive, Special Collections, University of Rhode Island; Jennifer Penswick, Sarah Smith and Danielle Malone for research assistance; Sarina Wyant, Special Collections, University of Rhode Island Library for photography assistance; Kevin Jones and Christina Johnson at the Fashion Institute of Design and Merchandising for the Rudi Gernreich image; and Lisa Long at the Redwood Library for picture research. For providing photographs from private collections, we thank Kathryn Lillethun, Irma Robey, Charles Reed Jr., Sara Kennedy, Stephanie Taylor, Yvette Harps-Logan and Wilburn Logan. For assistance at *Harper's Bazaar*, we thank Neha Gandhi. For help in obtaining permissions from a Parisian contributor, we salute Claire Kapstein. Valerie Morgan Addison assisted with processing permissions. For critically reading a draft of the introduction to the cultural geography section, we thank Nedra Reynolds. For moral support, we thank Art Mead and Fafar Bayat.

Finally, we thank Tristan Palmer, our editor at Berg, for quickly answering a steady stream of questions and shepherding us through the process of compiling a reader.

Linda Welters and Abby Lillethun
Kingston, RI

NOTES ON CONTRIBUTORS

Teri Agins is a Senior Special Writer covering fashion and retailing at the *Wall Street Journal*, New York

John Andrews is Bureau Chief at *The Economist*

Lisa Armstrong is Fashion Editor, *The Times*, London

Julia Fein Azoulay (1959–2006) was a freelance writer based in Florence

Roland Barthes (1915–1980) was a French social and literary critic

Vandana Bhandari is Professor of Fashion and Textiles at the National Institute of Fashion Technology, New Delhi

José Blanco is Assistant Professor in the Department of Textiles, Merchandising and Interiors at the University of Georgia

Andrew Bolton is Associate Curator at the Metropolitan Museum of Art, Costume Institute, New York

Thérèse Bonney (1894–1978), former Second World War correspondent and photojournalist, and Louise Bonney (d. 1968), wrote guides for Americans visiting Paris

Michael Boodro is a journalist covering art and style, and lives in New York

Susan Bordo holds the Otis A. Singletary Chair in the Humanities in the Department of English at the University of Kentucky

Christopher Breward is Deputy Head of Research at the Victoria and Albert Museum, London

Colleen R. Callahan is Curator Emerita of Costume and Textiles, Valentine Museum, Richmond, VA. Currently, she consults as a partner in Costume and Textile Specialists

Katy Chapman is Design Technologies Director, CHF Industries, a distributor of home furnishings located in New York City

Kimberly Chrisman-Campbell is Andrew W. Mellon Curatorial Fellow in French Art at The Huntington Library in San Marino, CA

Shaun Cole is Curator of the Contemporary Programme at the Victoria and Albert Museum, London

Nicholas Coleridge is Managing Director of Condé Nast Publications

Stuart Cosgrove is a Scottish journalist and broadcaster, and Head of Programmes at Channel 4, a public service television broadcaster in the UK

Jennifer Craik is Associate Professor teaching cultural studies at Griffith University, Australia

Philip Crang is Professor of Cultural Geography at the Department of Geography, Royal Holloway, University of London

Kathleen Craughwell-Varda works as a museum consultant and lecturer on historic textiles and women's history in New York and Connecticut

Cynthia Cooper is Curator of Costume and Textiles at the McCord Museum, Montreal

Sybil DelGaudio is Professor and Chair of the Audio, Video and Film Department, School of Communication, Hosftra University, Hempstead, Long Island, New York

Claire Dwyer is Lecturer in Social and Cultural Geography in the Department of Geography, University College, London

Joanne Entwistle is Senior Research Fellow at the London College of Fashion

Caroline Evans is Reader in Fashion Studies at Central Saint Martins College of Art and Design, London

David Gilbert is Professor of Urban and Historical Geography in the Geography Department at Royal Holloway, University of London

Alison Goodrum is Senior Lecturer in Fashion Theory, Manchester Metropolitan University

Karen Halttunen is Professor of History at the University of Southern California

William Hamilton is a freelance writer based in New York

Dick Hebdige is Professor of Film Studies and Art Studio and Director of the Interdisciplinary Humanities Center at the University of California, Santa Barbara

Anne Hollander is an art historian and writer living in New York City

Peter Jackson is Professor in the Department of Geography at the University of Sheffield

Yuniya Kawamura is Assistant Professor at the Fashion Institute of Technology, New York

Robin D. G. Kelley is Professor of Anthropology at Columbia University, New York

Anna König is an Associate Lecturer at the London College of Fashion

Kurt Lang and **Gladys Engel Lang** are Professors Emeriti of Sociology, Communication and Political Science at the University of Washington, Seattle

Wendy Larner is Head of Graduate School and Professor of Human Geography and Sociology at the School of Geographical Science, University of Bristol

Graham Lawton is a science journalist for *New Scientist*

Michelle Lee is Executive Editor of *In Touch Weekly*

Abby Lillethun is Assistant Professor in the Textiles, Fashion Merchandising and Design Department at the University of Rhode Island

Richard Martin (1946–1999) was Curator at the Metropolitan Museum of Art, Costume Institute, New York

Grant McCracken is author of several books, including *Culture and Consumption II*. He is a private marketing consultant

Richard McIntyre is Professor of Economics and Director of the Honors Center at the University of Rhode Island

Angela McRobbie is Professor of Communications at Goldsmiths College, University of London

Arthur C. Mead is Professor of Economics at the University of Rhode Island

Maureen Molloy is Professor of Women's Studies at the University of Auckland, New Zealand. She is co-director of The Fashion Project, which is studying the globalization of the New Zealand fashion industry

Cathy Newman is a Senior Writer for *National Geographic*

Sandra Niessen is an anthropologist and is a Professor at the University of Alberta, Canada

Susan North is Curator of Seventeenth- and Eighteenth-Century Fashion, Victoria and Albert Museum, London

Alexandra Palmer is the Fashion and Costume Curator at the Royal Ontario Museum, Toronto

Jo B. Paoletti is Associate Professor of American Studies at the University of Maryland

Claudia Brush Kidwell is Curator Emerita of Costume and Textiles at the National Museum of American History at the Smithsonian Institution, Washington, DC

Ted Polhemus is a writer, photographer and youth marketing, style trends and brands consultant, living in the UK

Yngve Ramstad is Professor and Chair of the Economics Department at the University of Rhode Island

Simona Segre Reinach is a Professor of Fashion Studies, Department of Geography, Libera Università di Lingue e Comunicazione (IULM), Milan

Pietra Rivoli is Associate Professor of Finance and International Economics at McDonough School of Business, Georgetown University, Washington, DC

Jennifer Ruark is Editor of Research at *The Chronicle of Higher Education*

Juliet B. Schor is Professor of Sociology at Boston College, Boston, MA

Debora Silverman is Professor of History and Art History at University of California, Los Angeles

Sonnet Stanfill is Curator of Contemporary Fashion at the Victoria and Albert Museum, London

Hugh Trevor-Roper (1914–2003) was formerly Regius Professor of Modern History at the University of Oxford.

Tiffany Webber-Hanchett is Part-time Faculty, Parsons, The New School for Design, New York

Linda Welters is Professor, Graduate Director and Chair of Textiles, Fashion Merchandising and Design at the University of Rhode Island. She was formerly (1998–2006) Editor-in-chief of *Dress*, the scholarly journal of the Costume Society of America

Elizabeth Wilson is Visiting Professor in Cultural and Historical Studies at the University of the Arts, London

Daniel Wojcik is Associate Professor of English and Folklore Studies at the University of Oregon

Olivier Zahm, editor and co-founder of the magazine *PURPLE*, presented *Rose Poussière* at the 2006 *La Force de L'Art*, at the *Galeries nationales du Grand Palai*s

LINDA WELTERS AND ABBY LILLETHUN

Introduction

Fashion. Style. *La mode*. The word "fashion" evokes different meanings for different people. For some, being "in fashion" means being well dressed in the latest styles. For others, it means dressing in more than "just clothes." Often fashion has a feminine connotation, and is linked to young women. In Greece circa 1900, peasants referred to the styles they saw filtering in from Paris as "European clothes." In India, where draped garments, the sari and dhoti, have been used for over a millennium, fashionable clothes are called simply "Western clothes." Whatever it is called in the world's many languages, fashion is now a global phenomenon amounting to nearly four percent of world trade.

FASHION DEFINED

What is fashion? We are defining fashion as changing styles of dress and appearance that are adopted by a group of people at any given time and place. This definition is contested, as the reader will see in this book. One of the key elements is the concept of *change* over time. In ancient Greece, considered the birthplace of Western humanistic thought (e.g., politics, philosophy, aesthetics and the arts), fashion, as we know it, did not exist. The draped and wrapped clothing of the ancient Greeks, while elegant, changed little from generation to generation. Fashion historians propose that fashion began when prevailing styles changed within someone's lifetime. People started discarding their clothes based on style, not because they were worn out.

Change in fashion involves change in *styles* of dress and appearance. Fashion has its own vocabulary, and it is worthwhile to take time to master the terms. A *style* is a combination of silhouette, construction, fabric and details that distinguishes an object from other objects in the same category. Short-lived styles are termed *fads*. A *classic* is a style that enjoys long-term acceptance. *Haute couture* is high-priced, custom-made women's clothing originally from Paris. It is mostly handmade. Ready-to-wear (Fr. *prêt à porter*) is factory-made fashion in a range of sizes. A *trend* is a direction in which fashion may be heading. Someone who is *fashionable* is conforming to current fashions.

Styles begin in many ways. The world's leading designers try out new ideas for an elite clientele at the Paris haute couture shows; some of these styles eventually become adopted in modified form. Fashion directors, editors and others in the business of fashion attend these shows to observe trends. Ready-to-wear designers develop lines from which buyers select certain styles for their retail stores. Fashion leaders, people who are among the first to wear a new style, inspire others to adopt new looks. New styles also come from subcultural groups; these are referred to as "street" fashions. Styles from the past can be recycled too: actual old clothes are currently called "vintage" fashion while new clothes inspired by past fashions are part of a process termed "historicism."

How is fashion different than clothes, apparel, costume or dress? Yuniya Kawamura (2004) argues that clothes are just clothes—a tangible material product—while fashion is much more: it is a symbolic product. "Apparel" is a term used by the industry to differentiate products from each other; for example, apparel is one type of product, while footwear is another. The history of "clothes" has often been labeled "costume history." Yet the term "costume" is associated with theatrical dress, or dressing up in costume (e.g., Halloween costumes). Many of the older titles about fashion history are called "costume history." The term "costume" has fallen out of favor lately. Today, "dress" is preferred when referring to all forms of attire.

According to Mary Ellen Roach-Higgins and Joanne Eicher, dress involves more than just clothes; it includes body modifications and body supplements (1992). Thus, a definition of fashion involves hair, makeup, accessories, posture and other aspects of personal appearance.

Fashion, the verb, means "to make or form something," as in "fashioning a hat." The new use of the word as a noun occurred when humans started cutting into cloth and fashioning it, or tailoring it, into clothes fitted to the body. Ancient Greeks, Romans and Egyptians did not cut their cloth; instead they wore it draped on the body. It was artful and graceful, but not fashionable in the true sense of the word—because it did not change significantly over time. Now fashion writers describe classical-inspired styles as "timeless," implying that such styles are outside fashion's whimsical nature.

In the eighteenth century, fashion often had a negative connotation. Social critics satirized fashion, such as this French response to the introduction of sack-back gowns and hoops in the 1720s:

If we don't follow her,
People will think we're crazy...
Not to put too fine a point on it,
Fashion enslaves us.
We must worship her in spite of ourselves.
She demands to be served,
Since she alone is law
And takes Reason prisoner.

      (as quoted in Benhamou 2001: 17)

"Taste" appears regularly in eighteenth-century writing. Good taste was a quality that many men and women of means aspired to possess, as opposed to being a slave to fashion.

Another key element of the definition of fashion is its *adoption* by groups of people. Designers present many new styles every season and fresh looks are also generated by subcultures. Not all of these are accepted, or become widespread. For more than a century, many scholars have attempted to define fashion and to explain its quirky nature. Thorstein Veblen interpreted fashion as conspicuous consumption. Georg Simmel saw it as trickling down to the masses from the elites. Roland Barthes viewed it as a silent form of communication. More recently, scholars such as Joanne Entwistle have begun to investigate the bodily experience of fashion.

Understanding the culture of fashion is an interdisciplinary venture involving many perspectives. Sociologists view fashion as a form of group behavior. Psychologists see it as presentation of self. Artists use dress as a form of creative expression. Economists chart the fashion industry for employment, import and export data. When people are disadvantaged by fashion, it becomes political. Many of these perspectives are represented in the readings in this book.

The third key element of fashion is that it is *place*-specific. Fashion was born in Europe and it developed there in urban areas. People living in small towns and villages did not have the means to follow fashion, but evolved slow-changing regional dress styles called "folk" or "peasant" dress. Folk dress developed a political agenda when it became a tool to reinforce national goals in the nineteenth century, even as rural dwellers could afford to participate in fashion. As the world industrialized, communications opened up, and fashion spread to all the places that Europeans colonized. Fashion has already taken root in North America and Australia, thanks to European settlers. In the past century, fashion has gradually become a worldwide phenomenon as even the farthest reaches of the globe became accessible to fashion's reach.

Our definition of fashion—changing styles of dress and appearance that are adopted by a group of people at any given time and place—allows fashion to exist among multiple cultures simultaneously. The book examines fashion as it is rooted in Westernized cultures—Europe, North America, parts of South America such as Brazil and Argentina, South Africa, Australia and New Zealand—and increasingly produced and worn in other traditionally non-Western cultures where fashion exists alongside regional or national dress. We recognize that fashion cycles occur in non-Western dress (e.g., the Indian sari), but this aspect is beyond the scope of this book. Some theoreticians argue for expanding the traditional geographical and chronological boundaries of fashion. We agree that scholars should examine the notion of fashion in the history of dress of non-European cultures, for example the Ching dynasty of China, and in western hemisphere cultures prior to the Middle Ages (e.g., Mayan dress).

Fashion exists on multiple levels ranging from the local to the global. Some styles transcend boundaries, becoming transnational. The man's shirt and trousers are an example of a transnational style. These days world fashion capitals include not only Paris, London, Milan and New York, but also Sao Paolo, Johannesburg, Tokyo, Seoul and Hong Kong. All the key elements that define fashion are still in place: the changing form of dress, accepted by a majority at any given time and place. The only difference is that now that place is the world.

Regardless of how one thinks of fashion, it is a central component of modern life. Modernity is constantly referenced in association with fashion. Christopher Breward and Caroline Evans, in the introduction to *Fashion and Modernity* (2005: 1), explain the terms *modernization*, *modernity* and *modernism*. Modernization "refers to the processes of scientific, technological, industrial, economic and political innovation that also become urban, social and artistic in their impact." Modernity, then, is "the way that modernization infiltrates everyday life and permeates sensibilities." Modernism names a series of artistic movements, from the early twentieth century onwards, which responded to cultural changes of modernity, for example, Dadaism, Cubism and Abstract Expressionism. The emphasis on individual experience is an expression of modernity that emerges in the material aspects of modern life. Fashion, involved as it is with production and consumption, becomes a perfect expression of modernity. *Postmodernism* is a term sometimes used to describe the time period since the late 1960s. Its relationship to fashion is discussed at many points throughout this book.

There is some debate about when fashion started. While most historians point to European courts in the 1350s as the beginning of a fashion system, others claim that it is a phenomenon that came to fruition in the latter half of the nineteenth century (Lipovetsky 1994). Advancements in production and diffusion—the birth of the couture system, industrialization of apparel assembly and development of department stores—brought fashion to the majority of the population in Western countries, starting in the 1860s.

Certain components are necessary for a society to have a fashion system. These include a market economy that provides wealth, adequate technology to make apparel items, a distribution system that disseminates both ideas about fashion and the products themselves, and a system of fashion innovation and adoption. The last component involves some form of fashion leadership where styles are first introduced. Our position is that fashion began in the early Middle Ages.

One aspect of fashion we did not cover, although we would have liked to, is fashion in literature. Proust's description of a Fortuny dress in *Remembrance of Things Past* is often quoted. Edith Wharton and others included rich descriptions of fashion in their writings. Some scholars have begun to address fashion in both fiction and non-fiction. Colin McDowell (1998) has assembled a literary anthology of fashion writing; Claire Hughes (2006) analyzes fashion in key fictional texts. Some writers are developing plots around fashion: *The Devil Wore Prada* is a best-selling book, which is now a feature film. Our personal favorite is Steven Millhauser's story—"A Change in Fashion"—because it draws on many of the themes in *The Fashion Reader*: innovation, adoption, media, body, art and memory.

OVERVIEW AND RATIONALE FOR *THE FASHION READER*

Fashion is a complex phenomenon that is difficult for the novice to understand. This book aims to address these complexities. It is designed to serve as a reader for students and scholars. Additionally, others interested in the history, culture and business of contemporary fashion will find it useful in comprehending the nature of fashion.

The book's tripartite approach to fashion encompasses history, culture and business in equal measure. Commissioned essays on fashion history from the eighteenth century until the present combine with extracts and readings. This format introduces readers to the interdisciplinary aspects of fashion studies. We argue that it is important to have some knowledge of the history of fashion, because historicism is rampant in postmodern life. We study history to understand the present and to anticipate the future. We repeat that fashion today is produced and consumed globally. It is dependent on a rapidly changing infrastructure influenced by art, popular culture, technological innovations, politics, trade regulations, and more. Fashion constantly references ideas and cultures from around the world, both past and present.

The book includes an overview of the culture of fashion from the early modern period to the present. The volume introduces key theories of dress and emphasizes current discourse on dress and the body, dress and identity, and the geography of dress. The politics of fashion are also discussed. Fashion and its relationship to art is explored, as is fashion's presentation in the media. One section examines fashion from the beginning of haute couture in the 1850s to current Japanese street fashions. The business of fashion—the industry, the technology, marketing and the role of innovation in stimulating new fashion—appears in several sections as well as in a lengthy section of its own. Each section in Part II through Part X includes one extract with a historical perspective. Because of the international nature of fashion, extracts touch on fashion in regions around the globe. We attempt to keep a balance between women's fashion and men's fashion. The children's market is also addressed.

Comprised of eleven parts, each begins with an introduction and is followed by a set of readings. Part I differs from the others in that it provides a brief history of fashion from 1700 to the current day, during which time Europeans successfully spread their culture to the Americas, South Africa, Australia and now Asia. The five essays in this section were contributed by recognized specialists whose approach to fashion history introduces culture of the period as well as major style changes. Parts II–XI each consist of a set of readings. These are either extracts of previously published work or invited pieces based on papers or lectures delivered at conferences or seminars. Readers are presented with a range of writings—cultural theory, historical essays, scholarly research papers, exhibition catalogs, fashion analysis, selections from book-length studies, and magazines—so that a variety of sources for reliable information about fashion are included. Extracts also vary in length, which is designed to expose readers to longer theoretical pieces as well as shorter topical pieces. Appropriate, but limited, images illustrate the text. We selected images from a variety of sources on purpose: real garments, portraits, photographs, engravings, printed textiles, prints, drawings, dress patterns and advertisements. All sections conclude with an annotated guide to further reading.

In selecting readings for the book, we observed that some extracts might fit in more than one section. The sections overlap in many cases because fashion is interdisciplinary. It is our hope that the reader will make connections from one section to another.

In extracting the readings from published works, we occasionally noticed discrepancies in the bibliographical details of the references: for example, the year of publication, or the location of a publisher. We changed these inconsistencies to match the information available in World Cat, the online database. Likewise, we corrected obvious spelling errors. Brackets indicate editorial intervention. For the purpose of uniformity, the publisher has Americanized all spellings, e.g., "-ise" changed to "-ize."

The reader need not read consecutively. But we do recommend that novices start with Parts I and II before delving into any of the subsequent sections.

PART I

A Brief History of Modern Fashion

LINDA WELTERS

Introduction

Costume historians claim that fashion began in Europe in the middle of the fourteenth century (Boucher 1967; Breward 1995; Laver 1995; Tortora & Eubanks 2005). In the preceding millennium, both men and women wore simple T-shaped tunics and mantles. Inner tunics were made of linen or hemp, while outer tunics were made mostly of wool. Basic shapes and a loose fit characterized these garments, whether for king or for serf. Jewels, furs and rich fabrics signified rank.

About 1340, clothing began to depart from this formula. The pace of change quickened, with major silhouette changes occurring approximately every fifty years (Piponnier and Mane 1997: 65). Tailors began cutting into precious cloth to create garments fitted to the body. Unusual forms and certain extremisms appeared, such as shoes with long, pointed toes called *poulaines*, and very abbreviated garments for men known as *pourpoints* and doublets.

Elements of fashionable behavior existed before the fourteenth century, however. Surviving texts from the early Middle Ages describe recognizable components of fashion: style, innovation and sexual attractiveness. Around 1100, young noblemen started manipulating their appearance by growing their hair long, wearing elongated, tight-fitting tunics and pointed shoes. This happened because of changes in inheritance laws, leaving some young men with only their wits to secure themselves a position in life. They resorted to fashion and courtly manners to gain attention. Young women soon followed suit, wearing dresses "well cut through the body." Both sexes wore tunics fitted to the human form through the use of curved seams, inset gores and lacing at the sides. Sometimes the lacing exposed the linen undergarments or, in hot weather when undergarments were dispensed with, the bare skin underneath. The epics and ballads of the period have explicit sexual overtones. One romance describes a young woman in a silk dress "tightened with laces over her torso, which is well shaped," causing an admirer to tremble with desire (*Prise d'Orange* as quoted in C. Waugh 1999: 7). The new fashions were criticized by clerics as immoral, particularly the effeminate nature of the young men's appearance.

Regardless of whether or not it is possible to pinpoint the date that fashion began, the race was on. During the Renaissance, fashion became a pervasive component of European culture, with ever-changing novel ways for dressing the human body. Fantastic headgear emanated from French, Flemish, Burgundian, German and English courts in the 1400s—horned headdresses, high pointed hennins and padded caps. In Italy, high platform shoes called *chopines* elevated fashionably dressed men and women from the residue of the streets. Soon the forerunner of the corset appeared, continuing as a mainstay in women's wardrobes until the twentieth century. The pace of change accelerated during the sixteenth century, bringing such oddities as the codpiece (a penis sheath) and the ruff (a rigid, sometimes platter-sized, collar). The seventeenth century saw a surfeit of laces and bows, and swashbuckling men in knee-high boots. Indeed, men appeared more fashion-conscious than women with their long, curled hair, abundant lace, and colorful doublets and breeches.

Fashion is often linked to the female gender, but history shows that until the early nineteenth century, elite men were often the first to adopt new ideas in fashion. Their clothes were made from the newest, most luxurious materials. They showed off more of their bodies than women. Societal attitudes toward women placed them in more restricted roles than men; they were idealized as chaste wives and mothers. Once married, women entered into a cycle of maternity. Because women's hair was viewed as seductive, they covered it after marriage. Upon reaching a certain age, they dressed in a conservative, dignified manner. Men, on the other hand, did not abandon fashion as they aged (Piponnier and Mane 1997).

Fashion in the past involved practices that its critics deplored. People deliberately cut, or *dagged*, the edges of their clothing in the Middle Ages. They meticulously *slashed* fine silk to reveal lightweight linen underclothes. Fashion history is replete with examples of how the body has been distorted through restriction (e.g., corsets) or padding, such as stuffing the front of a man's doublet to make the *peascod belly*, or wearing a tube-like *bum roll* around the hips to extend a woman's skirt into a drum-like shape.

The study of fashion history reveals astonishingly beautiful textiles used in dress. Tailors exploited the best new fabrics for their creations—velvet, lace, satin, damask—all produced by hand by skilled artisans. Innovative fabrics and new colors often inspired fashion. At the upper levels of society, cloth was sometimes embellished with gold and silver thread, or encrusted with real jewels in a display of wealth and power. Queen Elizabeth I (1533–1603), for example, was reputed to have had a wardrobe of over 1,900 items of clothing, some of which had pearls as embellishment (Arnold 1988: 174).

Textiles, a vital contributor to fashion, have been important to international commerce throughout history. The rich textiles of the Byzantine and Islamic worlds found their way to Europe during the Middle Ages, as did Indian printed and painted cottons in the seventeenth century. Demand for such "foreign" textiles often created a drain on a nation's economy, resulting in legislation to restrict imports or encourage domestic production.

To have fashion, a society needs a certain level of disposable income to go beyond merely being dressed. Logically, then, fashion innovation follows power and money. The rise of fashion is associated with the emergence of capitalism in Western Europe. As feudalism faded, a merchant class emerged, and it became possible for ordinary people to amass great wealth through commerce. Both the landholding aristocrats and the new bourgeoisie displayed their status through dress. The most powerful courts established trends that were picked up by other courts through royal visits and intermarriage. For example, when the Spanish Armada controlled the seas, the black and gold color schemes favored in the Spanish court appeared in France, the Netherlands and England. The bourgeois merchants imitated court fashions, with basic styles filtering down the ranks to artisans, farmers and fishermen.

Fashion requires a means of spreading news about innovations. Royalty expected courtiers to dress in the latest styles, often gifting fashionable clothing to them. The high value attached to fashionable goods ensured a lively market for used clothing, further extending fashion's influence. Shortly after the invention of the printing press in the 1450s, books about the fashions of various countries became available.

Fashion participation was restricted to the elite prior to the eighteenth century, although this did not prevent people lower on the socioeconomic scale from lusting after new fashions. Legislators enacted sumptuary laws to prevent people from dressing above their social station. Despite the laws, demand for consumer goods spread to all social classes by the late seventeenth century. Court records reveal that servants stole from their masters and mistresses, items went missing at laundries, and drunks were rolled in alleyways outside taverns for their clothes—all in the pursuit of fashion (Lemire 1990). Most sumptuary laws were repealed by 1700 because they were ineffectual.

Occasionally, history provides examples of styles emanating from the ranks of common working people. Queen Marie Antoinette of France (1755–1793) famously wore the attire of milkmaids and shepherdesses when she resided at Le Petite Trianon, her rural retreat. After the French Revolution, working men's trousers became the latest mode.

We begin "A Brief History of Modern Fashion" in 1700 for several reasons. First, historians observe that a consumer culture developed in Europe at this time. Second, society grew less rigidly stratified, and it became possible to move up the social ladder by "looking the part." Last, it is in the eighteenth century that the first of many technological advances that accelerated the making of textiles occurred; the mechanized spinning of yarn, invention of devices to speed up the weaving of cloth, and development of new ways of applying color and design to linen and cotton. Thus, by the early 1800s, inexpensive textiles—the raw material for fashion—were widely available, allowing all but the poorest members of society to wear fashionable clothing.

Why study fashion and dress history? Fashion designers reference styles from many previous time periods, not just the eighteenth, nineteenth and twentieth centuries. Furthermore, they do not restrict themselves to just Euro-American culture. Africa, India, and Native America also are tapped for inspiration. Nevertheless, a review of the last 300 years provides a background for the key themes of culture, technology and business, showing how fashion has developed in the Western world to become the expression of modernity that it is today.

Kimberly Chrisman Campbell covers the eighteenth century, when European courts still determined fashion innovations, to the French Revolution of 1789. Susan North picks up the thread, emphasizing the separate trajectories for men's and women's fashion that emerged in the early nineteenth century. Cynthia Cooper treats the period from 1860 to 1910, when mass manufacturing made fashion widely available in industrialized nations. Tiffany Webber-Hanchett discusses the rapid changes of the years from 1910 to 1960, during which the world experienced two world wars. José Blanco treats the media-driven culture of the years since 1960.

1

KIMBERLY CHRISMAN-CAMPBELL

From Baroque Elegance to the French Revolution: 1700–1790

The eighteenth century saw the birth of fashion as we know it today: that is seasonal, international, corporate, media-driven, and constantly changing. Then as now, fashion was a major industry, centered in Paris but drawing clients, materials and inspiration from all corners of the globe. The invention of the fashion magazine during this period ensured that new styles had a wide and immediate impact. Mass production and ready-to-wear clothing were being pioneered on a small scale, though the technology necessary to realize their full potential did not yet exist. It was an experimental, transitional period between the staggeringly luxurious (if stagnant) fashions of Louis XIV's *Ancien Régime* and the diversity, disposability and accessibility of fashion in the modern age.

In previous centuries, governments regulated dress according to the wearer's social status, through sumptuary laws. From the early eighteenth century, these laws—never very effective—ceased to be regularly renewed. For the first time, people of all classes were permitted to wear fashionable, luxurious dress, provided that they could afford it. "Clothes were no longer an accurate indicator of class or rank" (Delpierre 1997: 113). The introduction of innovative technologies (such as the flying shuttle for weaving fabric) and textiles (such as copperplate-printed cottons and linens) in this period made never-worn clothing more affordable than in the past. Previously, only the very wealthy bought new clothing and almost everyone else settled for used

garments. As these traditional social, legal and economic barriers disintegrated, fashion's influence spread from the court and aristocracy to the middle and lower social strata. Fashion was still driven by the elite, but it was produced—and, increasingly, imitated—at all levels of society.

Before the Industrial Revolution of the nineteenth century, when mechanization transformed the fashion industry, clothing was a major financial investment; fashionable clothing, which had an unnaturally short lifespan, was an extraordinary luxury. Although labor was cheap in the eighteenth century, fabric was expensive. The cost of a garment lay almost entirely in the cloth and trimmings, with labor making up a fraction of the price. Trimmings were often even more expensive than the fabric onto which they were sewn. Lace, for example, was handmade and could cost as much as gems; like jewelry, it would be passed down from generation to generation. Metallic trimmings such as gold or silver braid contained real precious metals, and they were sold by weight rather than length. Silk, wool and linen were the basic textile fibers, with cotton growing in importance later in the century. Cheap, manufactured imitations of these textiles did not exist; however, those who could not afford high-quality fabric could wear lesser-quality fabrics, or used fabrics. Rough/fine and plain/complex fabrics corresponded to social rank.

Most of the clothing worn in the eighteenth century was bought secondhand, if not third- or fourth-hand. Clothing was so valuable that it was frequently stolen. Fashionable clothing had a finite lifespan; after it went out of fashion, it was given to a servant or sold to a secondhand clothes dealer who might alter or update the garment. This cycle of redistribution would continue until the garment was not just outmoded but threadbare. Even the wealthy frequently had garments refurbished, remodeled or otherwise updated, rather than buying everything new. New clothing was the exception, not the rule. However, farmers and laborers had access to fashionable, high-quality clothing through the used clothing market. The same types of garments—and frequently the very same garments—were worn across the social spectrum.

Both sexes wore a layer of white linen next to their skin, which protected the expensive outer garments of wool or silk from perspiration and protected the body from dirt and vermin. Cleanliness was determined by the state of one's linen—visible at the collar, cuffs and hem—rather than one's outer garments or body. Though an aristocratic lady might bathe daily, this was a rare luxury; clean water was scarce, and many people considered bathing to be hazardous to one's health. Men wore T-shaped linen shirts with long tails, which they tucked between their legs; women wore long linen chemises or shifts and additional layers of underskirts. Although some men wore underpants, it was not a common practice. Women did not wear underpants at all; ironically, they were considered immoral, as bifurcated garments were traditionally reserved for men. It was considered improper for a woman to show her legs, beyond the tip of her foot. Likewise, women kept their elbows covered, and wore low-cut gowns only at night or on the most formal occasions. By the end of the century, however, all these rules would be obsolete.

BAROQUE SPLENDOR, 1700–1730

The first years of the eighteenth century did not witness dramatic changes in the ornate dress of the previous century. The baroque style of the

seventeenth century—characterized by heavy, formal, lavishly ornamented dress—remained dominant. Women continued to wear the *mantua*, a simply tailored T-shaped dress—inspired by Middle Eastern attire—that had been introduced in the 1680s. It opened down the front and was often gathered up at the sides to reveal the coordinating petticoat (the eighteenth-century term for a skirt, whether an outer garment or underskirt) worn underneath. A separate, triangular piece of fabric called a stomacher filled in the bodice opening. Most eighteenth-century gowns owed their three-piece construction to the mantua. The mantua had elbow-length sleeves; although long sleeves would be popular in the late eighteenth century, short sleeves did not become acceptable for women until after the French Revolution. The mantua had been an informal gown when it was first introduced, but the informal dress of one era typically becomes the formal dress of the next. By the eighteenth century, the mantua was considered formal attire, and its simple construction had evolved into a more complex design.

For informal dress, the mantua was replaced by the loose-fitting *robe à la française* (also called

Figure 1. Floor Decorations of Various Kinds. John Carwitham (1739), London. Gift of Guy F. Cary. Redwood Library and Athenaeum, Newport, RI.
The lady is dressed in a mantua (gown), stomacher and decorative apron. The gentleman wears a three-piece suit.

the sack-back gown). This elegant style featured a swathe of fabric falling from pleats at the shoulders to the back hem. Elegant and impractical, it was worn only by upper-class women. Today, it is sometimes called a Watteau gown, for it appears in several paintings by the artist Jean-Antoine Watteau.

Another major development in early eighteenth-century fashion was the introduction of the hoop petticoat. First appearing in England in about 1709, the hoop was adopted in France by 1718, and from thence spread throughout the fashionable world. Though its size and shape varied over time, the hoop remained in fashion until the end of the eighteenth century and defined the female silhouette. The earliest hoops were bell-shaped and consisted of a sturdy linen petticoat stiffened with three or more graduated hoops of baleen, called whalebone, which was also used to stiffen stays (the eighteenth-century term for corsets). Though the great expense of baleen limited hoops to high fashion and formal wear, middle-class and serving women imitated the effects of baleen using cheaper materials such as cane. Despite its sometimes inconvenient size, the hoop was considered comfortable and modern, for it was cool and allowed more freedom of movement than multiple layers of petticoats.

Stays provided support for the breasts as well as creating a fashionable silhouette. Over the course of the eighteenth century, this silhouette varied from angular (in the early eighteenth century) to squared and flattened (mid-century), to softly rounded (by the 1780s).

Men wore the three-piece suit, a Persian style adopted by Charles II in 1666 consisting of a collarless coat, waistcoat and breeches, worn with a linen shirt fastened at the neck by a stock (a strip of linen) or a cravat. The knee-length coat was fitted to the torso and flared over the hips. Although details such as the volume of the sleeves, the fullness of the coat, the length of the waistcoat and the arrangement of the buttons and pockets would change, the suit would be the standard uniform for all classes of men until the end of the eighteenth century. Indeed, it was the ancestor of today's three-piece suits.

Figure 2. *Mrs. Charles Willing* (Ann Shippen). Robert Feke, Philadelphia, 1746. Oil on canvas. Courtesy of the Winterthur Museum, Winterthur, DE (1969.0134A).
Mrs. Willing, well supported by stays, wears a mantua made from silk damask woven at Spitalfields, England. Anna Maria Garthwaite, a textile designer, created this pattern in 1743. Mrs. Willing's portrait was painted in Philadelphia just three years later, illustrating how quickly fashionable textiles became available in the American colonies.

In bad weather, a voluminous greatcoat or cape protected men's clothing from the elements. The tricorn (three-cornered) hat was the most common style worn in the eighteenth century, although some versions were designed to be carried under the arm rather than worn. It became smaller over the course of the century as the wigs it adorned shrank in size. At home, men doffed their wigs and covered their shaved heads with colorful caps; long, voluminous robes called *banyans* made of yards of fabric served the same

Figure 3. Henry Collins. John Smibert (American), ca. 1729. Oil on canvas. The Gladys Moore Vanderbilt Széchényi Memorial Collection. Redwood Library and Athenaeum, Newport, RI. *Henry Collins, a Newport merchant and patron of the arts, wears the standard coat, waistcoat and breeches of the eighteenth century with a fine linen or cotton shirt. The coat is made of a red pile fabric, possibly velvet, which would be suitable for a man of his position. His wig is also a status marker.*

function as the smoking jacket would in the following century.

Boys and girls wore ankle-length gowns called frocks. The fabric varied according to the season and the wearer's social rank, but as cotton fabrics such as chintz and muslin became more readily available, they were preferred for children's clothing, for they were comfortable and washable. Rows of tucks at the hem allowed the skirts to be lengthened as the child grew; colorful

Figure 4. Man Reading. Engraved by Jacobus Gole, Amsterdam, Holland, 1693. 1990-170, 1.1. The Colonial Williamsburg Foundation.
Men of certain occupations—artists, writers, musicians and scientists—often wore banyans for their portraits. Banyans, or morning gowns, were considered "undress."

sashes often concealed corresponding tucks at the waist. Leading strings attached to the shoulders helped children learn to walk; padded caps called "puddings" protected the head in case of a tumble. Girls often wore decorative vestiges of leading strings into adolescence. Boys were "breeched" at about the age of five; they traded their sexless frocks for breeches in the adult style. This was a symbolic turning point in a boy's life, marking his transition from the nursery to the schoolroom. From that time on, he wore clothes very similar to those worn by adult men; girls adopted adult garments such as hoops and gowns in early adolescence.

ROCOCO ELEGANCE, 1730–1770

The term "rococo" was invented by nineteenth-century art historians to describe the art and interior decoration that flourished in France (and was imitated everywhere else) during the mid-eighteenth century. The term is derived from *rocaille*, the French word meaning "rockery" or "rubble," a reference to the shell and serpentine patterns that characterize the rococo aesthetic. Rococo art and theatrical productions were populated by nubile nymphs and playful shepherdesses, and fashion evoked these bucolic fantasy worlds with flowers, aprons, straw hats, and other elegant interpretations of rustic dress. Real peasant women wore short, fitted jackets and petticoats or simple gowns, with a *fichu* (a triangular scarf or shawl) around the neck for modesty. The excavation of Roman ruins at Herculaneum, beginning in 1738, and at Pompeii, beginning in 1748, aroused popular interest in classical art and mythology, and fashion borrowed motifs and inspiration from antiquity. Rococo art was criticized as being unnatural, frivolous and morally corrupting. But its supporters were attracted to its escapist sentimentality, its theatricality and its emphasis on three-dimensional ornament, all of which were easily translated into fashion.

France, with its opulent court at Versailles and its long-established, state-supported textile industries, continued to dominate the international fashion scene as it had under the Sun King, Louis XIV. Madame de Pompadour, mistress to Louis XV, was instrumental in popularizing rococo art, and her exquisite taste in dress helped to define the rococo aesthetic's expression in fashion. Her signature fashion statements included a deep shade of pink nicknamed "rose de Pompadour," three-tiered lace sleeve ruffles called *engageantes*, and small ornaments dubbed "pom-poms" after their inventor—worn in closely curled, powdered hairstyles called *têtes de mouton* (sheep's heads). Fashion's focus shifted from structure to surface decoration. Small, delicate patterns—many of them featuring the Chinese motifs Madame de Pompadour adored, or painted silks imported directly from China—replaced the large-scale, stylized designs of baroque silks. The stiff, three-dimensional lace collars and cuffs of the seventeenth century were replaced by delicate ruffles of tissue-thin lace. Trimmings and accessories—ruffles, ribbons, lace edgings, caps, collars, stomachers, tippets—determined, rather than cut or cloth, whether or not a gown (or a suit, for that matter) was *à la mode*. These light, fragile materials, buoyed up by hoops of an enormous width, contributed to the careless, frivolous feel of rococo dress.

Figure 5. Anne (Archer) Garth-Turnour, Baroness (later Countess) Winterton. Allan Ramsay II (British), 1762. Oil on canvas. Courtesy of the Huntington Library, Art Collections, and Botanical Gardens, San Marino, CA.
The delicate trimmings, lace engageantes and the gown's pink color reflect the rococo aesthetic.

Milliners supplied these trimmings and accessories, and thus from the mid-eighteenth century milliners (who were usually female) began to eclipse male mercers (who sold cloth), male tailors (who cut and sewed men's suits), and female seamstresses (who cut and sewed women's gowns) in fashion's labor hierarchy. Previously, milliners had been indistinguishable from mercers and seamstresses; this was due to the shifting demands of fashion as well as strict French labor laws, which lumped the clothing trades together and prevented any one branch from dominating the market. Milliners dressed men as well as women, breaking through the traditional gender barrier in the fashion trades.

The eighteenth-century milliner bore little relation to the "milliner" of today. In France, milliners were called *marchandes de mode* (fashion merchants)—a more accurate description of their activities and importance than the modern definition of "hatmaker." Milliners were more akin to modern-day fashion designers, exercising degrees of imagination and autonomy denied to prosaic mercers and seamstresses. The term "milliner" was originally used to denote a native of Milan, but in the early sixteenth century it came to mean anyone who sold the fashionable trifles and accessories for which Milan was famous, including—but not limited to—hats and bonnets (*Oxford English Dictionary* 2nd ed., s.v. "milliner"). By the eighteenth century, clothing was barely visible under the profusion of feathers, ribbons, tassels, lace, artificial flowers and other ornaments with which it was adorned. And no ensemble was complete without accessories. For men, these might include hats, cravats, jeweled buttons, swords, sword belts, sword knots and knee buckles. For women, headdresses, shawls, capes, *engageantes*, fans, pockets (which could be highly decorative despite being worn beneath one's gown, on a ribbon around one's waist), embroidered garters, and pattens and clogs (overshoes that protected shoes from the horrors of eighteenth-century streets). Both sexes wore hair powder and ribbons, brightly colored silks, embroidery, gold and silver fringes, cosmetics, lace, gloves, muffs, jewelry, decorative shoe buckles

and high-heeled shoes. (It was the last time in history that men would rival women in sartorial splendor, and already some hints of change were evident, as their hairstyles became less elaborate and their coats and cuffs less voluminous.) A complete suit or gown actually consisted of many separate garments and ornaments that could be taken apart and rearranged according to the wearer's taste. Similarly, rococo jewelry was characterized by its versatility: often, pieces were detachable and interchangeable, so a brooch might be worn alone, dangling from a necklace or nestled in a headdress. Never before had fashion been so individual or so imaginative.

EXCESS AND EXOTICISM, 1770–1780

The milliner's influence grew as ladies' petticoats swelled to new extremes and their headdresses

Figure 6. "The Spruce Sportsman, or Beauty and the Best Shot." Mezzotint, London, 1780. 1958–36. The Colonial Williamsburg Foundation.
The exaggerated hairstyles and millinery of the 1770s and 1780s are lampooned in this English print.

grew ever higher. The vast hoops and mountains of false hair that amplified the female silhouette of the 1770s and 1780s provided the ideal canvas for the milliner's art. In the artist Elisabeth Vigée-Lebrun's famous phrase, "Women reigned then" (Vigée-Lebrun 1986: I.122). Their power found expression in their dress and in their ability to influence dress. In the seventeenth century, men and women had worn equally ornate clothing; now, women began to take the leadership role in fashion (Fukai 1989: 109). Thanks to hoops and elaborate hairstyles and hats, women occupied more space than men, and furniture, vehicles and buildings had to be altered accordingly. The sartorial sexual dimorphism that would become so pronounced in the nineteenth century was already present in the eighteenth: women had more clothes, which were more ornamental and more valuable than men's clothes. This was true

at all levels of society, in part because male servants wore livery while their female counterparts wore their mistresses' fashionable castoffs (Roche 1989: 99). Men still dressed ostentatiously by modern standards, but they no longer dictated or popularized new styles as, for example, Louis XIV had. As the female silhouette expanded, the male silhouette contracted, as if in compensation; coats were shorter and more fitted, with very narrow sleeves and tiny standing collars.

The *robe à la polonaise*, which first appeared in 1776, was an ankle-length gown equipped with a pair of internal tapes that allowed the wearer to draw the skirt up into three distinct sections. Typically, the middle section was longer than the two side sections. The short *polonaise* was convenient for walking, as many fashion plates attest. The name is thought to allude to the partition of Poland between its three neighbors (Russia, Austria and Prussia) in 1772, but the style probably evolved from the common practice of wearing gowns *retroussé dans les poches* (with the corners of the overskirt tucked into the pocket openings), a practical solution to the problem of trailing petticoats undoubtedly invented by working women.

In its ceaseless quest for novelty, fashion moved beyond Europe and raided the globe. Garments inspired by the comfortable, sensual dress of the Middle and Far East—previously reserved for theatrical costume or masquerade dress—began to infiltrate female fashion. Turbans, striped silks, exotic furs, fringes and gowns cut in the wraparound style of traditional Turkish or Chinese dress appeared in Europe. "With their fluid lines, their soft drapery crossing over the chest without squeezing it, their loosely belted waits, these gowns prepared the way" for the radical, body-conscious fashions born of the French Revolution (Delpierre 1997: 68).

Figure 7. Sortie at the Opera. *Monument du costume physique et moral de la fin du dix-huitième siècle ou tableaux de la vie* (1789). Gift of Mrs. Beatrice Greenough, Redwood Library and Athenaeum, Newport, RI. *The woman's silhouette is extended by hoops worn underneath the petticoat and gown.*

FASHION AND REVOLUTION, 1780–1789

The French Revolution marked a turning point in fashion history. But long before 1789,

Figure 8. Polonaise. *Monument du costume physique et moral de la fin du dix-huitième siècle ou tableaux de la vie* (1789). Gift of Mrs. Beatrice Greenough, Redwood Library and Athenaeum, Newport, RI.
Internal tapes draw up the skirt, creating the fashionable polonaise of the 1770s and 1780s.

European fashion embraced the principles of liberty and equality, taking its cues from rural and sporting dress rather than from royals and celebrities. The American Revolution (American War of Independence) of 1776 filled Paris with hairstyles *à la Philadelphie* and gowns of *gris Americain* (American gray), named for the color of Benjamin Franklin's hair. More significantly, it got people talking about freedom and democracy, and a general trend toward egalitarianism in dress in the 1780s reflected those sentiments. Hoops, wigs and hair powder virtually disappeared from fashionable circles; women's towering hairstyles relaxed into soft, rounded clouds of curls. Fashion magazines advertised jackets and petticoats for informal dress. Rather than matched three-piece suits, men began to wear jackets, waistcoats and breeches of contrasting colors and fabrics. Men's coat collars grew higher, and waistcoats grew shorter. They ended at the waist, and were almost always white, to show off elaborate, sometimes whimsical, embroidery. Only at the courts of Europe did formal styles persist, frozen in time by strict etiquette.

America was not the only political and sartorial bellwether in the 1780s. The taste for practical, informal clothing distinguished by expert tailoring and plain, high-quality fabrics was just one of many principles and pastimes exported from England in the late eighteenth century, along with gambling, afternoon tea, English gardens, English novels, horseracing and the idea of a constitutional monarchy. Though the island nation was physically remote, the English were intrepid travelers. They carried several unique styles to the Continent via the Grand Tour, the extended European vacation traditionally taken by young English noblemen (and occasionally noblewomen) to complete their education. Although English tourists often adopted foreign styles in deference to local tastes and climates, they also introduced typically English fashions such as the male frock coat, identifiable by its close fit and turned-down collar, and the female

Figure 9. Copperplate-printed toile, Historic Textile and Costume Collection, University of Rhode Island. 1952.99.161.
This toile illustrates several new fashions: jacket, shorter waistcoat and collared frock coat. The men no longer wear wigs.

Figure 10. Redingote, 1780s, Italian, 106-1884. V&A Images/Victoria and Albert Museum. *The redingote was inspired by English men's riding clothes.*

riding habit, a masculine-looking gown or jacket-and-skirt combination with a large collar and lapels, which was practical for riding but increasingly worn as all-purpose casual dress. The restrained, sober elegance of English dress—a marked contrast to the brightly colored, heavily embroidered and embellished garments worn by both sexes elsewhere in Europe—made a powerful impression long before it began to appear in Continental fashion magazines in the 1770s.

While the French set the standard of elegance for all of Europe, the English perfected what we now call sportswear. The English taste for the outdoors and physical activity produced a distinctive wardrobe of functional, comfortable garments. Many of these garments originated as rural dress, including straw hats, aprons, gaiters and frock coats. Hats, boots and jackets based on jockey dress (which looks very similar today) were also popular. "Jacket" comes from "*jacquet*," a French corruption of "jockey." In England, of course, jackets were only worn while actually on horseback; in France, they were worn indoors, as high fashion, to the horror of English visitors. These casual fashions—worn in England by both the landed gentry and the peasants who worked their estates—defied the French tradition of formality and luxury. Nevertheless, they found favor in the most elite circles in Europe.

French fashions often distorted the natural shape of the body; English fashions accentuated it. In France, gorgeous surface embellishment masked haphazard tailoring; English garments were characterized by their flawless cut and construction, unspoiled by superfluous ornament. Long, narrow sleeves and closely fitted bodices and coats created an elegant, distinctly English line while allowing efficient movement. The difference is best illustrated by contrasting the *robe à la française*, with its picturesque but unwieldy

Figure 11. Susannah, Philip Lake, and Maria Godsal: The Godsal Children. John Hoppner (British), 1789. Oil on canvas. Adele S. Browning Memorial Collection, gift of Mildred Browning Green and Honorable Lucius Peyton Green. Courtesy of the Huntington Library, Art Collections, and Botanical Gardens, San Marino, CA.
The Godsal girls are fashionably dressed in frocks, which resemble adult women's chemise gowns, while the boy wears the new skeleton suit.

pleats, with the *robe à l'anglaise*, a gown with a form-fitting bodice, introduced in the middle of the century. Both gowns were worn throughout Europe for much of the eighteenth century. By the 1780s, however, the *robe à l'anglaise* triumphed; even in France, the *robe à la française* appeared only on very formal occasions, when freedom of movement was unnecessary.

Similarly, the era witnessed a transformation in children's dress. In his 1762 novel *Emile* and other writings, the philosopher Jean-Jacques Rousseau popularized the view that children should be dressed in comfortable, practical clothing allowing freedom of movement, rather than wearing miniature versions of adult garments such as breeches, hoops and stays (which were considered beneficial to the posture of growing girls and boys alike). Rousseau's theories prompted several dramatic developments in childrearing practices and children's dress, which are evident in late eighteenth-century portraits of children. Frocks became less fitted around the torso and hairstyles more natural. Girls continued to wear frocks until their teen years instead of adopting adult-style gowns. Instead of breeches, boys began to wear the so-called skeleton suit, a transitional style between the frock and adult clothing, consisting of a shirt—made like an adult man's shirt but with an open, ruffled collar—worn with a jacket and long trousers which buttoned together to form a one-piece garment. (Though trousers were worn by laborers in place of breeches, they would not enter the fashionable adult wardrobe until after the French Revolution.) Older boys continued to wear open collars even after relinquishing the skeleton suit for coats and breeches. The already-controversial practice of swaddling infants in bands of cloth virtually disappeared between 1760 and 1780; instead, enlightened mothers dressed their babies in loose shirts and caps.

Children's clothing followed and, often, directed fashion trends in the 1780s (L. Baumgarten 2002: 173). By the early 1780s, adult women began to take fashion inspiration from the innocent, youthful frock, following Rousseau's advice to return to a state of nature, free from the physically and spiritually confining bonds of fashion. The "chemise" gown (so called because it resembled a woman's undergarment) owed more to a child's frock than underwear; unlike traditional adult gowns, it was put on over the head and had gathered sleeves. Usually made of white muslin, its shape was not distorted by hoops or stays. The chemise achieved lasting popularity (and notoriety) when Marie-Antoinette wore it in a portrait of 1783. Although the casual, revealing style—often worn with very simple, pastoral accessories such as straw hats, aprons and colored sashes—was the height of fashion, it was considered too informal for a queen, and her less fashion-conscious subjects were shocked by the idea of wearing a "chemise"—an undergarment—as outerwear. According to Lady Craven, an English aristocrat who traveled to France in 1785, a rumor went around Paris that the queen had been painted "in a chemise," and the general public misunderstood this as an undergarment, which caused a scandal; those who saw the portrait recognized it as a fashionable gown rather than an undergarment (Craven 1814: 24–25).

The chemise gown could not have become fashionable if not for the new availability of fine muslin. In 1721, Britain's Parliament had banned the sale of Indian cottons under pressure from the long-established wool industry and the thriving silk industry based in Spitalfields in London, which was already facing formidable competition from the French silk industry in Lyon. In France, Indian block-printed cottons were also banned until 1759, although they were frequently smuggled into the country illegally. By the 1780s, Britain had relaxed its ban, and France was importing muslin from its colonies in the West Indies. In addition, Britain had a thriving domestic cotton industry, which flourished in the wake of the ban. Cotton was not as strong as leather, or as warm as wool or as luxurious as silk, but it was washable and relatively inexpensive. For the first time, the lower classes could afford new coarse cotton for clothing; meanwhile, the upper classes enjoyed fine cotton textiles that had been laboriously block-printed and copperplate-printed.

Ironically, Britain's American colonies were exempt from the ban and thus enjoyed imports of Indian cotton throughout the eighteenth century. Though the colonists prided themselves on their simplicity and self-reliance, they were highly fashion-conscious and heavily dependent on imported textiles; indeed, it was cheaper to import textiles from Britain than to produce them locally (L. Baumgarten 2002: 76–79). Fashion magazines and life-sized fashion dolls sent abroad from Paris helped them to keep abreast of what was being worn in London and Paris. From the seventeenth century, European settlers in North America were scandalized by the nakedness of the natives they met, and encouraged them to cover up in European-style clothes or blankets. Disapproval also came from the fact that Indians used skins, which were not tailored to fit the body, and to Europeans this indicated "primitive," "uncivilized" and "pagan" behavior. By the late eighteenth century, if not earlier, Christianized Native Americans in the American colonies were wearing tailored clothes and living on reservations.

Few Frenchwomen suspected, when they donned hairstyles *à la Philadelphie* and gowns of *gris Americain*, that the patriotic fervor surrounding the American Revolution would have catastrophic consequences for France, and for aristocratic fashion. The French Revolution of 1789 produced not just a new set of garments but a more relaxed definition of elegance. The most obvious manifestation of this phenomenon was the term "*sans-culottes,*" which described manual laborers and the urban poor, who generally wore utilitarian long trousers rather than the knee-length breeches (*culottes*) favored by aristocrats and the bourgeoisie, paired with short jackets called *carmagnoles*. On both sides of the political divide, "*sans-culottes*" became shorthand for revolutionaries. Along with breeches, the *sans-culottes* rejected lace, embroidery, diamonds, rouge, silk, swords, shoe buckles, hair powder and non-patriotic jewelry. Fashion was no longer "in fashion" in France, and this change had a ripple effect throughout Europe. Fashions based on military dress and the clinging, austere robes of the ancient Greeks (the originators of democracy) replaced the elegant disorder of the rococo; flowing flowered silks gave way to patriotic stripes and severe tailoring.

As discussed above, however, nearly a decade before the *sans-culottes* condemned luxurious dress, the most fashionable members of society had already renounced it in favor of informal fashions inspired by English sporting dress, the Orient and pastoral simplicity. Rather than starting a revolution in fashion, the French Revolution simply accelerated and accentuated changes already underway (Roche 1989: 146). But the Revolution effectively destroyed the French fashion industry, which employed an estimated 25,000 people in Paris alone (Roche 1989: 266). Stripped of official government recognition and regulation, fashion workers lost much of their social status and financial security. The last of the original French fashion magazines ceased to publish in April 1793. The French textile industry, already hurt by fierce competition with England, degenerated into chaos. Some fashion workers joined the army; others emigrated to England, Italy, Germany, Russia, Switzerland and North America, as they could no longer make a living in France.

Symbolism replaced style; instead of looking forward, French fashion began to look back to an idealized past. Jacques-Louis David and other Revolutionary dress reformers promoted "timeless" dress based on classical and Renaissance models, the antithesis of changeable fashion. Though neoclassical white muslin gowns and sober black suits were considered acceptably "democratic," the luxurious trimmings and accessories so characteristic of eighteenth-century fashion were deemed politically incorrect. The dynamics of the international fashion market had changed forever.

2

SUSAN NORTH

From Neoclassicism to the Industrial Revolution: 1790–1860

The history of fashion from 1790 to 1860 presents several divergences in the narratives of style, culture, technology and business. Key developments for the period include an abrupt change in style during the 1790s and the deviation in the influences affecting the aesthetics of men's and women's dress. Historical revival continued to shape female fashions throughout the early nineteenth century. By the 1850s, women's dress had become so ornate and cumbersome that a movement for its reform and rationalization was founded. Men's dress, after 1790, began to follow an entirely new direction in style and ornament, so that by 1860 it is increasingly difficult to speak of fashion as a whole in any sense. The industrialization of textile manufacture, along with wider dissemination of fashion plates, made the latest styles available to a broader audience, geographically and socially. The production of clothing itself diversified, with a greater range of ready-made garments at one end of the market, and the development of more exclusive styles for the elite.

TECHNOLOGICAL CHANGES— TEXTILES AND IMAGERY

The economic and social impact of the mechanization of textile manufacture occurring earlier in the eighteenth century had its greatest effect during the period 1790 to 1860. Machine spinning, power weaving, and new decorative techniques such as cylinder printing greatly decreased the cost of fabrics. This made fashionable styles and larger, more varied wardrobes available to not just the wealthy, but also to the expanding middle-class populace, and to a growing number of the working class as Sunday best.

The industry that disseminated imagery of the latest styles also increased to include much wider markets, aided by faster, cheaper printing processes and rising levels of literacy. French fashion magazines maintained their dominance, although key English titles such as *The Lady's Monthly Museum*, *La Belle Assemblée* and *The Repository of Arts, Literature, Commerce, Manufactures, Fashion and Politics* are significant for their longevity and distribution throughout the British Empire. Both French and English fashion magazines circulated widely in the United States and American journals, such as *Godey's Lady's Book* and *Graham's American Monthly Magazine of Literature, Art and Fashion*, soon appeared. As the dissemination of fashion became the preserve of women's magazines, a new genre serving men evolved, although an enduring format did not appear until publications such as *The Gentleman's Magazine of Fashions, Fancy Costumes and the Regimentals of the Army* in 1828, and *The Gentleman's Herald of Fashion* in 1851. More successful were the journals targeting the tailoring industry, emphasizing the fact that most men relied on their tailors for the latest styles rather than seeking them out themselves. By 1860 fashion journalism was a global industry, well in advance of the factory production of clothing.

IMPACT OF THE FRENCH REVOLUTION

Most changes in fashion occur fairly gradually: a new cut of sleeve, an increase or diminution of petticoat width or coat skirt, the graduation of an informal style of morning dress into formal daywear. The 1790s are an exception with regard to women's fashions, marked by a distinct rise in the waistline of all female styles in 1794. It is also one of the rare occasions when fashionable change can be attributed to political events. As the previous essay has indicated, elements of neoclassical dress had been evolving since the 1760s. The advent of the Terror in France in 1793 suddenly meant that clothing imitating the unadorned linen and wool garments of the working classes could save one's life. With the execution of Louis XVI and Marie Antoinette in 1793, any sign of aristocratic status, particularly luxurious dress and jewelry, marked its wearer as an enemy of the new state. To survive in France during this time, men adopted trousers, plain wool coats and waistcoats. Women wore simple linen jackets and petticoats or the cotton chemise dress, echoing not only nonelite dress but also the classical garments that visually embodied the Revolution's political ideals. During the eleven months of the Terror, fashion journalism in France ceased and there was little communication with the rest of Europe. With the establishment of the Directorate and a more moderate political regime, however, this brave new look was soon communicated to those parts of the world where European dress was worn and it was adopted with astonishing speed. By 1795, the high waistline and slender silhouette for women was almost universal in urban centers and dominated all styles of dress, including the riding habit.

MEN'S DRESS, 1790–1820

While the neoclassical gown was a modification of garments already existing in the female wardrobe, men's fashions adapted less readily to Greek and Roman dress. Given the strictures of eighteenth-century etiquette, the sight of bare-legged men in short tunics was unacceptable on the street and even on stage. Jacques-Louis David's 1794 designs featuring the Roman toga in uniforms for both citizens and government officials were never adopted (Ribeiro 1995: 150). Pantaloons, a compromise between aristocratic breeches and working-class trousers, came into fashion. These were close-fitting garments of mid-calf length, often made of knitted silk or cotton.

A particularly exaggerated cut of coat was popular from 1795 to 1800. It was called the *Incroyable*, after the flamboyant young men who adopted it in France immediately after the Terror. With a very high turndown collar and extremely wide revers or lapels, the coat had long, tight sleeves extending over the wrist. The side pleats of the coat skirts were reduced to narrow pleats at the center back, and the front was cut straight across at the waist. Mirroring the new dimensions of women's dress, the waistline of the cutaway coat rose between 1790 and 1795. Shirt collars and cuffs deepened to accommodate these new dimensions. The advent of tightly fitting knitted pantaloons required a change in the drawers worn underneath; these too lengthened and were frequently made of knitted cotton. From 1790 to 1860, shirts remained as underwear—to be seen only at the neck and wrists. Along with drawers, the shirt's function in bodily hygiene continued unchanged from the eighteenth century, as a lack of running water made regular bathing the prerogative of only the very wealthy.

Until the 1790s, men's and women's fashions had responded more or less equally to the same aesthetic stimuli. Fashionable garments for both sexes encompassed embroidery, lace and textiles

Figure 12. "Incroyable" coat and waistcoat, 1795–1805, French. T.769-1919, T.14-1995 & T.745A-1913. V&A Images/Victoria and Albert Museum.

Industrial Revolution occurring in Britain, saw a rejection of the aristocratic gentleman as the epitome of male comportment. The new man of the 1790s and early nineteenth century prided himself on his honesty, sobriety and industriousness; the sartorial expression of which was the plain, dark, unadorned suit of the middle-class businessman.

This does not mean that there were no similarities or connections between men's and women's clothing. In terms of silhouette, the dress of each sex continued to mirror the other and a close examination of the masculine wardrobe reveals that the sobriety of neoclassical dress distinguished formal daywear only. Court dress continued the eighteenth-century tradition of luxurious silks and velvets embellished with colorful floral embroidery; these sartorial conventions were upheld by George IV of Great Britain and actively revived by Napoleon Bonaparte upon becoming Emperor of France (1804). Patterned silks and colorful Indian cottons remained popular fabrics for the informal banyan or nightgown throughout the nineteenth century, while the red "pink" coat characterized formal riding and hunting dress.

The increased use of unadorned fabrics for men's daywear put an emphasis on the quality of the cut and skill of the tailor. Wool was preferred for coats because of its greater capacity for shaping and molding during construction. The publication of the first English tailoring manual in 1796, *The Taylor's Complete Guide*, introduced a flood of such texts throughout the nineteenth century. Widespread use of the tape measure, by 1818, advanced the precision of measuring and cutting of both men's and women's clothing (N. Waugh 1964: 130; L. Johnston 2005: 158).

Knitted pantaloons and double-breasted, cutaway coats continued as fashionable men's dress during the first decade of the nineteenth century, with a gradual return of the waistline of the coat to the natural level. Although not as wide as the *Incroyable* style, revers and high turndown collars remained distinctive features of formal coats, the intersection of these two elements characterized, from 1800, by an M-shaped notch. Fashionable

of similar patterns and luxury, and color was not gendered in any sense. The failure of men's dress to respond to the neoclassical influence marks an important departure in the evolution of fashion. From this point, its history can no longer be treated as a whole, for the dress of men and women now responded to different aesthetics, a divergence that can be attributed to changing ideals of masculine behavior and appearance. The American and French Revolutions, and the focus centered on the neck, with a deep shirt collar and elaborately tied linen neck cloth.

Much of the simplicity of men's dress is attributed to the influence of George Bryan Brummell, "Beau Brummell," the first masculine fashion icon of the nineteenth century. Although sometimes labeled a dandy, he only fitted the description in his obsession with his appearance. Unlike later dandies favoring flashy patterns and accessories, Brummell's emphasis was on understated perfection: the expertly cut dark coat, uncreased buff-colored pantaloons, gleaming boots and pristine linen. His brief but dominating

Figure 13. Chevelure à la François 1er, chapeau en barque, charivari de breloques." Horace Vernet, 1814, French. V&A Images/ Victoria and Albert Museum.
Pantaloons, high-collared shirts, and short haircuts with long sideburns became fashionable for men in the early nineteenth century.

influence on English fashion—from about 1798 to 1816—continued neoclassical minimalism. Young men had abandoned the wig in the 1790s and adopted the "Titus" haircut featuring short, tousled curls. This remained in style between 1800 and 1820, with the addition of long sideburns, the first fashionable facial hair since the seventeenth century. In 1807, the Prince of Wales (the future George IV) began wearing trousers for informal wear at his seaside retreat in Brighton; the young men in his circle, who like the rest of their generation had worn trousers as boys, soon followed suit. By the second decade of the nineteenth century, trousers were widely accepted for informal dress.

About 1815, a new style of informal coat emerged to replace the cutaway style; the new "frock coat" was a smarter version of the greatcoat, with knee-length skirts. The long period of the Napoleonic wars introduced into men's dress decorative elements inspired by military uniform. The uniforms of Polish regiments featured braid arranged in elaborate patterns, forming buttons and button loops, decoration which soon appeared on frock coats and the waists of pantaloons. By 1817, a style of trouser with full gathering at the waist had come into fashion, called the "Cossack" after the Russian regiments. Increased fullness at the top of the coat sleeve reflected the high puffed sleeve fashionable in women's dress. Surviving dress in museum collections and contemporary descriptions both reveal a range of fashionable coat colors including navy blue, forest green, maroon and a variety of browns such as bronze and fawn.

MEN'S DRESS, 1820–1840

By the 1820s, the frock coat and trousers had become accepted formal daywear and pantaloons had replaced breeches for evening dress. Reflecting the changes in the female silhouette, the skirts of the frock coat became fuller, accentuating the waistline. To accommodate this new style, tailors began to cut a dart, or "fish" as it was known, at the waistline for better shaping

Figure 14. Brown wool coat and blue striped tan silk "Cossack" trousers, 1820s, English, T.683-1913 & T.197-1914. V&A Images/ Victoria and Albert Museum.

of the coat. By the middle of the decade, this had become a full waist seam with coat torso and skirts cut separately. The un-notched "shawl" or "roll" collar appeared on the coat as well as on the waistcoat. The latter remained the most decorative element of the formal wardrobe for men and

featured a more standardized construction, with glazed white or brown cotton back and buckled adjusters.

The frock coat continued to dominate the day wardrobe in the 1830s; the cutaway style was by now only for evening dress. Waistcoats were made of brightly colored silks in a variety of embroidered, brocaded, figured and velvet weaves and remained the ornamental focus of the masculine ensemble. The fall-front style of closure of eighteenth-century breeches carried over into nineteenth-century pantaloons and trousers, but had been narrowing in width during the 1820s. It was gradually replaced with a fly-fronted, buttoned closure, a style frequently accompanied with braces or suspenders.

MEN'S DRESS, 1840–1860

During the 1840s, the waistline of men's dress lengthened and coat skirts widened, echoing the silhouette of women's fashions. The sleeves of men's coats were more tightly fitting in the 1840s, while the padded "pigeon breast" shape of the coat front remained. Although not frequently seen in portraiture or accurately reproduced in monochrome fashion plates, the waistcoat's vibrancy of color and design is evident from the many examples that survive in museum collections. Striped and checkered trousers characterized the decade. There was yet no trend for the waistcoat, coat and trousers to be made of the same material, although good taste required them to harmonize in shade. Not all men conformed to such etiquette and the 1840s dandy was likely to wear a decorative waistcoat with checkered trousers, non-matching coat, accessorized with gloves and cravat of contrasting and sometimes clashing hues.

A new version of coat for morning or informal daywear appeared in the 1850s. Not as full as the frock coat, nor as cut away as the evening coat, the morning coat remained a distinctive style well into the twentieth century. Another significant addition to the male wardrobe during this decade was the lounge or sack coat

Figure 15. "Three Gentlemen," The Gazette of Fashion, October 1852, English. V&A Images/ Victoria and Albert Museum.
The two men on the left are dressed in daytime ensembles of frock coats and plaid trousers. The tailcoat, shown on the right, had become formal wear. All three men have top hats.

almost water-repellant properties of their compact weave.

In general, new fashions in menswear developed first in informal dress; however, garments such as trousers and jacket had been working-class clothing in the eighteenth century. In both cases, they were made "respectable," and therefore fashionable, for aristocratic circles when adopted by royalty, after which they were taken up by the rest of society. Within the plain and sober boundaries of the business suit, men's fashion demonstrated considerable variety, emphasizing fine fabrics and a wide range of well-crafted accessories. Brightly patterned cravats, pastel-hued gloves, loudly checkered sportswear and exotic banyans provided colorful relief in the masculine wardrobe.

WOMEN'S DRESS, 1790–1820

The neoclassical style introduced to women's fashion the influence of historical revival, which, with a few chronological exceptions, continues today. From 1790 to 1860, each decade featured elements of dress borrowed from past centuries and exotic places. The plain white gown, accessorized with imported Indian shawls woven of cashmere goat hair from the Kashmir region, dominated fashion plates and portraiture of the 1790s, although documentation and surviving dress suggest a greater variety in color and textiles. For winter months and harsh climates, wool and cotton printed in a range of bright and dark shades were worn. Evening dress featured light silks embroidered with metal threads in neoclassical motifs. Examination of dress surviving from 1795 to 1800 demonstrates that their construction carried on traditions of dressmaking established in the eighteenth century, but adapted to the new waistline. One version remained open at the front like the sack-back gown, while a new variation known as the round gown closed front and back, fastened with a bib-fronted opening.

The marked change in silhouette and waistline forced adjustments in women's underwear, with a shortening of the stays and a reduction

(equivalent to the modern suit jacket). Cut loose and short to just below the hip, the lounge coat had no waist seam. First introduced for informal morning wear by yet another Prince of Wales, the future Edward VII, the lounge coat with trousers is the direct antecedent of today's business suit. The decorative waistcoat disappeared during the 1850s with a trend toward making the coat, waistcoat and trousers of the same fabric, although embroidered silk waistcoats, usually white on white, remained part of evening dress. Scottish tweeds and tartans became the latest style for sporting dress, due to the durability and

Figure 16. Gown made from a printed shawl, 1795–1800, English. T.217-1968. V&A Images/Victoria and Albert Museum.
High waistlines were the most noticeable change in women's dresses in the decade following the French Revolution.

may have been a short-lived "elastic" alternative to boned stays (Steele 2001: 31). The bum roll of the 1780s was reduced to a small pad worn at the back of the gown. While the chemise continued its primary hygienic function, the sheer fabrics and reduced layers of women's dress focused attention on bodily shape in a manner not encountered since the fifteenth century. Drawers or pantalettes became essential garments for preserving modesty.

The neoclassical style prevailed for about a decade, before new historical influences appeared. Reference to Greek and Roman dress

Figure 17. "Costume Parisien," *The Fashions of London & Paris During the Years 1804, 1805 & 1806*, London: Richard Phillips. Historic Textile and Costume Collection, University of Rhode Island.
White high-waisted gowns and rectangular shawls reflect the neoclassical taste of the early nineteenth century.

in boning. Documentation on stays during the period 1795 to 1810 is somewhat contradictory, although evidence indicating that stays were abandoned has been judged unreliable (Cunnington 1992: 115; Steele 2001: 30). A longer style of stays reappeared during the first decade of the nineteenth century, for those figures not naturally suited to a slender silhouette. Knitted tubes extending from underarm to thigh was always fairly broad and open to a wide range of "exotic" inspirations including Egyptian and Etruscan art. For example, turbans inspired by the Middle East were a popular style of evening headwear. Various victories during the Napoleonic wars in Egypt and the Mediterranean were often celebrated by the addition of an appropriately named accessory. By 1810, women's fashions had begun plundering sixteenth- and seventeenth-century dress for inspiration, borrowing "Vandyke" lace trim, paned sleeves, fake slashing and a high-necked style of collar known as the "Medici." These historical references introduced

Figure 18. "Fashionable dresses for June 1818," Historic Textile and Costume Collection, University of Rhode Island.
The fashion plate shows dresses with more decorative elements than those from 1800–1810. The figure on the left wears a spencer.

a variety of dark colors and heavier fabrics such as velvet. Fashion plates indicate that plain materials dominated evening and formal day dress, while surviving garments feature the patterned cottons favored for morning attire. The predominately close-fitting style of women's dress allowed the addition of garments such as the spencer (a short jacket) and coat-styled pelisse for outerwear. Formal dress grew increasingly decorative during the period 1810–1820, with flounces at the hem of the skirt and elaboration of the bodice and sleeves. The flowing train of the 1790s shortened to ankle length; the fullness of the skirt now concentrated in gathers at the back waist.

WOMEN'S DRESS, 1820–1840

During the 1820s, the silhouette changed from the vertical orientation of the previous three decades. The waistline lowered, returning to the natural level by the end of the decade. Skirts increased in volume and sleeves grew wider at the shoulder, creating an X-shaped silhouette. This emphasis on the horizontal extended to hats and bonnets featuring wide brims. The embellishment of dress featured a wide variety of piped and padded trims applied in complex patterns. Dressmaking finally broke free of eighteenth-century traditions with the introduction of the bust dart for bodice shaping. By now the bodice and skirt were usually cut separately and seamed together. Most dresses fastened at the back with buttons or hooks and eyes, although the pelisse or coat-style dress opened down the front, neck to hem. With increasingly ornate sleeves, women's dress required far more cutting and shaping than in the previous century, an indication that conserving expensive fabrics was no longer a dressmaking priority. Underwear reflected the changing profile, with corsets (the French term for stays, which comes into English use from 1800) more firmly boned to shape the newly accentuated waist. The introduction of the metal eyelet, first patented in 1823, proved a sturdier alternative to the traditional thread-bound holes

Figure 19. "Evening Dress" and "Ball Dress," 1828, English. V&A Images/Victoria and Albert Museum.

Figure 20. "Public Promenade Dress," *The Ladies' Cabinet of Fashion, Music & Romance*, Vol. VI, London: G. Henderson, 1834. Historic Textile and Costume Collection, University of Rhode Island.
Extremely wide sleeves characterize dresses of the mid-1830s.

through which corsets were laced (L. Johnston 2005: 170). The growing volume of the skirts required more petticoats of thicker fabrics underneath.

The 1660s provided the historical influence for women's dress in the 1830s, which imitated its wide, off-the-shoulder neckline, and a hairstyle featuring a bun at the back of the head, with clusters of curls over the ears. Sleeves became very full at the top of the arm early in the decade, encompassing the whole sleeve by mid-decade, with the volume moving to the lower arm while the shoulder tightened by 1839. The applied decoration of the 1820s eventually gave way to fabrics with printed, woven or embroidered designs. Cartridge pleating at the waist accommodated the increasing amount of material in the skirt, which was now supported with a crescent-shaped bum roll along with starched, quilted or flounced petticoats for added volume. The expanding proportions of women's dress required fairly shapeless garments such as cloaks and capes for outdoor wear. For prolonged outdoor activity the riding habit remained essential; it too reflecting the adjusted waistline, full sleeves and skirts of the 1830s.

WOMEN'S DRESS, 1840–1860

Fashion in the 1840s moved away from the flamboyance of the previous decade. The *gigot* sleeve vanished, replaced by a very close-fitting style, and the waistline extended to a sharp point in front. Such a vertical emphasis encompassed hairstyles, now featuring a center part with the hair smoothed down and falling into ringlets in front of the ears. The Gothic revival dominated the arts in France and England during the 1840s and elements of the style can be seen in women's dress, particularly in textile design, as well as in trefoil and quatrefoil motifs in applied braid. Reflecting another strand of influence, renewed interest in eighteenth-century textile design (although not in any other branch of the decorative arts at this time) introduced neorococo silks and saw the remaking of many eighteenth-century sack-back gowns into contemporary styles. Printed cottons imitated the geometric effects of the woven wool shawls that were so popular, creating remarkably abstract patterns that prefigure twentieth-century design. By the 1840s, the long rectangular Indian shawl had evolved into a much larger square with the intricate patterning covering a deep border and center motif. From about the 1790s, Paisley, Norwich and London manufactured imitations of the Kashmir original in sheep's wool and silk to meet European and

Figure 21. "Latest Fashions, July," *Graham's Magazine*, 1841. Historic Textile and Costume Collection, University of Rhode Island.
The men are in frock coats and pantaloons. The woman on the left illustrates eveningwear; the woman on the right is dressed for day. Evening dresses typically exposed a woman's arms and neck, which were covered during the day.

North American demand. The 1840s skirt grew ever more voluminous, supported by quilted, starched and flounced petticoats as well as the "crinoline," made of woven horsehair.

There was no change in the waistline at the beginning of the 1850s, remaining pointed in front below the natural level. The tight fit of the sleeve relaxed into a bell shape known as the pagoda sleeve. New fashions included the addition of flounces of fabric to the skirt; these were often made of textiles woven or printed *à disposition* to present a decorative border on each tier. Gothic influence was on the wane, with the introduction of fashionable "oriental" and "exotic" details, based on Turkish and Russian dress, in the wake of the Crimean War. This was expressed

Figure 22. Sarah Taintor Waterman, ca. 1853, daguerreotype. Augustus Washington. The Connecticut Historical Society, Hartford, CT.
Sarah Waterman, who vanished with her sea captain husband after becoming shipwrecked, wore a silk dress with a V-waistline and pagoda sleeves to sit for her photograph.

in embroidery design, tasseled braids and a taste for rich colors and fur trimming.

Technology came to the rescue of the expanding skirt with a variety of experimental alternatives to the crinoline in the late 1840s and early 1850s. Whalebone, cane and inflatable india rubber tubes were commercially unsuccessful, but the "cage crinoline" was made of fabric-covered steel springs, such as that patented in Britain by C. Amet in 1856 (L. Johnston 2005: 128). It proved light, flexible and fairly inexpensive, liberating women from the heavy layers previously worn, with the immediate result of an even greater expansion of the circumference of the skirt.

REFORM DRESS

In the decades following 1810, women's fashions had undergone a striking change in the overall silhouette and a marked increase in decoration. By the late 1840s, even before the advent of the crinoline, there was criticism of contemporary fashion, primarily on the grounds of health. The genesis of dress reform occurred in the United States in the 1830s, with new attitudes regarding health and alternative forms of medicine (Fischer 2001). Women's dress was singled out as counterproductive to well-being: tightly laced corsets inhibited breathing and movement, as did long skirts, which also trailed in the dirt and grime of the streets. Practitioners of alternative treatments advocated a type of reform dress: shortened skirts and no corsets or tightly bound clothing.

This radically non-fashionable style was taken up by those involved in the fledgling women's rights movement. Inspired by the health reform example and the dress of Turkish women, the activists Elizabeth Smith Miller, Elizabeth Cady Stanton and Amelia Bloomer devised a reform style with a shortened skirt, worn to just below the knee, over loose trousers (Fischer 2001; Cunningham 2003). Amelia Bloomer described the outfit in *Lily*, the feminist journal she edited, and her name became associated with the ensemble.

Reaction to the Bloomer costume was immediate and fairly hostile; the mainstream press in particular and men in general objected. Reform dress was not taken up by British feminists, but saw considerable use in the US with a very small minority of women continuing to wear it all their lives. In relation to fashion, however, trousers for women would have to wait many more decades.

CHILDREN'S DRESS

Children's dress, which had been so influential on eighteenth-century developments in fashion, played a secondary role in the early nineteenth century. Once walking, all children wore short dresses and pantalettes. Boys were usually breeched between the ages of three and seven, when they began wearing trousers, shirts and jackets. Girls' clothes reflected the styles of adult women's dress in silhouette and decoration, as did young boys' suits until they reached puberty. In 1846, the five-year-old Prince of Wales (later Edward VII) was dressed in a miniature version of a sailor's suit, setting a fashion for boys that continued for decades. Queen Victoria's enthusiasm for all things Scottish introduced the kilt for little boys in the 1840s, an appropriate transition from skirt to trousers.

READY-MADE CLOTHING

New developments in the manufacture of ready-made garments were first seen in the production of men's dress during the early nineteenth century. Slops, ready-made clothing for soldiers and sailors, had been produced in Britain since the 1660s and the eighteenth-century slop trade also provided for the working classes. A new sartorial genre evolved in the early nineteenth century with the growth of industrialization and banking, and their need for armies of office staff. The clerk, whether working privately or for government, was a long-standing occupation; but it was the expansion of this profession that characterized the period. Traditional working-class garments of rough, ill-fitting linen and wool were not appropriate dress for office work. The clerk emulated his employer—banker, merchant, insurance agent, lawyer—whose sober black wool suit had its origins in the early seventeenth century. On a clerk's salary however, a bespoke tailor's suit was out of the question.

The mass production of ready-made, middle-class men's clothing began in the United States in the 1820s, primarily in New York but also in other cities along the eastern seaboard states (Zakim 2003). Available cheap labor, good transportation systems and an insatiable demand for appropriate business dress provided the necessary resources and markets for the ready-made industry several decades before the invention of the sewing machine.

TECHNOLOGICAL DEVELOPMENTS, 1840–1860

Important technological advances occurred during these decades, which were to have significant impact on fashion in the late nineteenth century. The invention of the sewing machine marks the first steps in the mechanization of the making of clothing. There had been several attempts to speed up hand sewing, but it was the American inventor, Elias Howe, who perfected and patented a successful model for a sewing machine in 1846. Five years later, Isaac Merritt Singer patented an improved model that he sold on the installment plan, which made sewing machines commercially viable for the average household. Developments in the use of rubber in the 1830s led to the introduction of the "Mackintosh" raincoat and waterproof boots, but the unpleasant odor of this new material inhibited its extensive use until later decades. The introduction of wood pulp paper in the 1850s, providing cheap and plentiful paper, led to the expansion of all printing and publishing industries including fashion journalism.

The centuries-old methods of harvesting and processing various natural dyestuffs were completely transformed by William Perkin in 1856 (Garfield 2000). He was trying to find a practical use for the by-products produced by the distillation of coal to generate gas for lighting. By accident he extracted a brilliant purple substance and discovered the first synthetic dye. The resulting "Perkin's mauve" became one of the first color fads and for a brief few years, almost every woman in Europe and North America had an aniline mauve dress. Aniline magenta was developed in 1858 and dozens more new synthetic dyes were discovered after 1860, ruining the long-established trades in cochineal, madder, indigo and other traditional dye plants.

Photography was patented when Louis Daguerre fixed an image on a silver-coated copper plate in 1839 and William Henry Fox Talbot did the same on paper a year later. The medium's potential as a truthful visual record was immediately recognized, but the unrelenting veracity of the photograph at first severely limited its use in fashion imagery. The distinct genre of fashion photography would not develop until the camera learned to idealize the dressed body as flatteringly as the illustrator's pen, but as a tool for dress history, the portrait photograph remains an invaluable resource.

In the eighteenth century, fashion had been the prerogative primarily of the wealthy and social elites, but industrial developments increased its availability to a much wider section of society between 1790 and 1860. Given the association of fashionable dress with social status however, such a democratizing process was unlikely to continue indefinitely. Fine clothing was not to be relinquished to the middle and working classes without a new movement toward more luxurious fashions for the privileged. Sometime during the fall/winter of 1857–58, Charles Frederick Worth and his partner Otto Bobergh established an exclusive dressmaking business in Paris and founded the haute couture industry (Coleman 1989: 12). Savile Row tailoring was to become the pinnacle of male fashion, starting in the 1840s. James Poole, an ambitious military tailor on the London street known as Savile Row, dressed his son Henry in the latest fashions and sent him to the races to attract the custom of the sporting set. Their first royal customer, the future Emperor Napoleon III of France, placed an order in 1846 and by 1860, the Prince of Wales, the future Edward VII of Britain, was amongst Henry Poole's exalted clientele (Howarth 2003: 34, 55).

Thus, the *ancien régime* that the 1790s sought to banish from politics and fashion was firmly reinstated by 1860, but now princes and emperors dressed as soberly as bankers and engineers. In contrast, the simple, elegant style of women's neoclassical dress inevitably succumbed to more elaborate historical influences. The Industrial Revolution continued to transform the making of clothing as well as the iconography of style, with new inventions heralding more radical developments in dress and the role of fashion in society.

3

CYNTHIA COOPER

The Victorian and Edwardian Eras: 1860–1910

The democratization of fashion took shape as the second half of the nineteenth century unfolded (Kidwell 1974). Magazines aimed at the growing middle class proliferated, disseminating fashion information more widely. Mass manufacturing sped up and improved the quality of clothing production; department stores and mail order ensured the widespread distribution of ready-made clothing. Fashion became increasingly affordable for growing numbers of people. To separate themselves from the fashionably dressed middling sorts, elite women patronized the new haute couture.

In women's fashion, major stylistic changes occurred regularly. Extant clothing from the period frequently shows signs of alterations and additions to keep up with constantly changing modes. Fashion in men's clothing evolved more slowly however, and style changes were subtle. Children's clothing mimicked adult fashion, yet had distinctive features. The Western world made a clear distinction between male and female, and public and private spheres, and dress was a vehicle for enforcing these boundaries. As consumption became an increasing motivation in Western society, critics saw fashion followers as frivolous. Society demanded that women show their family's standing through their good taste and fashionable clothing, while at the same time their character was judged by how well they appeared to uphold high moral and nonmaterialistic standards. Balancing these contradictory ideals was an ongoing preoccupation for women, as evidenced by literature from the period.

Women's periodicals grew in number and circulation; they carried extensive advice on how to behave in specific contexts—from leaving a calling card at a neighbor's house to accepting an invitation to a ball—revealing tensions in what was considered proper etiquette and the conflation of propriety with gentility. Much of this etiquette advice concerned clothing. In fashionable society, different clothes were required for specific social situations such as visiting, formal balls, undress (leisure clothing worn in the home), fancy-dress or costume balls, sports, bathing and working, as well as for mourning deceased relatives. Fashion illustrations, the most lavish of which were hand-colored fashion plates, were included in the American *Godey's Lady's Book*, the British *Englishwoman's Domestic Magazine*, the French *Journal des Demoiselles,* the German *Der Bazar*, and many others. Tailoring guides and periodicals such as *The Cutter's Monthly Journal* provided up-to-date information for those who produced men's fashion. Newspapers began to devote special pages to fashion, which eventually included illustrations.

Visual information about fashion from this period is abundant. People flocked to portrait photography studios, which had begun appearing in the 1840s. Paintings by the French Impressionist artists Monet, Manet and Renoir provide interesting documentation of garment styles of this period (Steele 1988: 123–32).

This time period is widely known as Victorian (1837–1901) and Edwardian (1901–1911), bearing witness to the dominance of Britain as a world power and its expanding colonial presence in Africa, India and Australia. Western dress followed colonists into all parts of the British Commonwealth, where it was adapted to local climates and circumstances. At the same time, fashion opened to a wide variety of cultural influences, thanks to international exhibitions and world fairs where many countries and their colonies displayed material culture admired for its craftsmanship and exoticism. Victorian culture also placed a high value on technological progress. Many new inventions facilitated daily life, including central heating, electric lighting and indoor plumbing, not to mention telephone communication and the automobile.

MEN'S DRESS

Throughout the entire period men wore a sober, standardized form of clothing in public, which changed very little over the decades. Status and fashionability in men's dress was expressed through the quality of the fabric and cutting. Late nineteenth-century men have been aptly referred to as "hidden consumers" whose interest in clothing was carefully circumscribed and yet manifested in subtle ways (Breward 1999). In public, only a colorful handkerchief or an ornate walking stick might denote a man's interest in dress. In the domestic sphere, men could indulge an interest in fashion to a much greater extent. Indoor caps, also known as smoking caps, and dressing gowns were colorful and embroidered or otherwise embellished. Military and occupational uniforms, and fancy-dress costumes allowed public opportunities for sartorial display.

England set the trends for men's clothing. Tailors made coats and trousers with the help of standard pattern drafting and measuring systems. Standard sizing progressed when statistical data on soldiers' measurements were made available to manufacturers after the US Civil War (Kidwell 1974: 103–5). Other items of menswear were well suited to mass production; shirts, which had straight seams, were well adapted to factory production. All men could be dressed

adequately once clothing had become so affordable. Detachable collars were available by the 1880s in several styles, allowing a fresh-looking shirt without laundering, starching and pressing the entire garment, all of which were very time-consuming and strenuous activities prior to the invention of automatic washing machines and steam irons. Neckties worn with these shirts included the long knotted tie known as the four-in-hand, the string tie, and the bow tie.

Throughout the period, the fashionable male silhouette was straight. The skirted frock coat in a dark color was worn with plaid, striped or plain contrasting narrow trousers in the 1860s. In the later decades, matching trousers became more common. Over the remainder of the century, the frock coat increasingly signified formality and conservatism; by 1900 it was mostly favored

Figure 23. Hon. V. Yorke in frock coat with top hat, 1864. I-12545.1. McCord Museum, Montreal.

by older men. The standard color was black, but in the last decades of the century a man with an extensive wardrobe might own a frock coat in a color such as gray. For formal daywear the frock coat was gradually supplanted by the cutaway or morning coat, which curved back from the waistline, exposing the lower part of the waistcoat. As a foil for dark coats and plain trousers, colored and patterned waistcoats continued to allow men an outlet for sartorial self-expression. The less-fitted sack coat, with its working-class origins, came to be worn with matching trousers and waistcoat. Seen firstly as an outfit for young men, the three-piece sack suit gained popularity until it was the most prevalent form of male ensemble for day and business wear at the end of this period.

The tailcoat—formerly a day garment—became de rigueur for formal evening occasions. A starched shirt, black or white bow tie, and white waistcoat were requisite accompaniments. In the

Figure 24. J. H. Gettings and friend in sack suits, 1886. II-82079. McCord Museum, Montreal.

1880s, a sack coat with a satin-faced shawl collar was introduced for semiformal wear; known as the tuxedo or dinner jacket, it gradually became accepted for formal events.

Hats were a wardrobe necessity. The top hat is perhaps the most enduring form common in the 1860s; but like frock coats, they gradually became more associated with formality as the century progressed. Silk plush supplanted the beaver fur felt, which had been the material of choice at the beginning of the century. The bowler, a stiff hat with a rounded crown, known in the US as a derby, was another option as were the softer fedoras and homburgs. Straw boaters were worn for sports and casual wear. A cloth cap with a soft crown and small, stiff peak at the front distinguished a working man.

Full hairstyles were common at the beginning of the period, with heavy beards, mustaches and dundrearies or full sideburns. Bear grease or macassar oil was used to slick the hair back, giving rise to the need for antimacassars, the linen scarves draped over the backs of upholstered chairs to prevent the oil from staining the chair. Later, hair was cut short and layered, and mustaches remained popular, while beards were associated with older men.

Outerwear options included a frock-style overcoat, a Chesterfield (with velvet collar), or the tweed Inverness coat with a cape covering the shoulder area and sleeves. For popular sports, such as golf or tennis, the tweed Norfolk jacket, with its self belt at the back, and vertical pleats on the side front and back, worn with knee-length breeches or knickerbockers, was suitable; variations were adapted for hunting. As mixed bathing became popular, men's one-piece wool bathing suits were available ready-made. Of woven or knitted wool, they had elbow-length sleeves and knee-length pant legs, and usually buttoned at the front.

WOMEN'S DRESS

Women's fashion changed more rapidly than men's throughout this period. Because of the careful fitting required of Victorian dresses, they were difficult to mass-manufacture. City directories everywhere listed hundreds of dressmakers; extant garments reveal a wide range of skill levels. Home dressmaking was another option and many women possessed sewing skills. Many anonymous "sewing girls" were hired who stayed with families periodically for a few days or weeks at a time for the purpose of updating their wardrobes.

Some aspects of women's fashion remained constant through the entire Victorian and Edwardian periods. A corset gave the waist and torso an hourglass shape. The practice of tight lacing gave rise to much journalistic and medical controversy in the later years of the century. Fueled by these concerns, the corset shape altered in about 1900 but it did not disappear. Attempts to restrict or replace the corset did not gain currency (Steele 2001). Drawers had become common and were required for decency; the chemise continued to act as an easily laundered buffer between the body and the outer clothing.

Upper body garments fitted closely over the corset, but varied according to the occasion. For daytime, sleeves were long and necklines were high. At balls and formal evening occasions, low necklines and short sleeves exposed more of the torso. Until about 1900, formal dresses were made of silk satin, crisp taffeta or other ribbed silks of varying weights. Legs were always fully covered by floor-length skirts except for sports. Likewise, certain accessories remained in common use, such as boots that covered the ankles. A fair complexion was a mark of gentility and parasols were carried to shield the face from the sun. Gloves, usually white kid, were worn for social occasions. Fans were used for balls and formal events. Women wore their hair swept up and back off the face.

The most characteristic feature of women's fashion in the early to mid-1860s was a wide, elliptical skirt silhouette created by a hoop or cage crinoline. It remained fashionable in spite of being recognized as a hindrance to traveling, walking and sitting, and was the subject of derision in cartoons in the popular press (Breward 1995:

157–61). Drawers worn as undergarments were lengthened to cover the ankles, now at risk of being exposed with the sway of the hoops as the wearer moved. Low-heeled ankle boots known as Adelaides also addressed this perceived need. For sports such as walking, skating, croquet or tennis, skirts might be looped up to expose the lower legs. The sewing machine, now common in homes, made it possible to add masses of decorative detail to emphasize the fullness of these skirts, rather than simply speeding up production.

Bodices were cut with very low scyes (armholes), giving the impression of an extended shoulder-line. Day bodices, trimmed with small lace collars and perhaps a ribbon necktie, usually had center front closures. Sleeves, at the beginning of the decade, were either the flared pagoda style worn with an undersleeve, or the loosely fitted coat sleeve, which was shaped at the elbow. As the decade progressed, the latter sleeve style prevailed and the scye returned to the natural shoulder point. The waistline was emphasized with either a deep V-point in the bodice, a small belt, or (on an evening dress) a sash tied in a bow at the back. Red blouses with full, cuffed sleeves—known as Garibaldis, after the leader of Italian unification whose army wore red shirts—became fashionable mid-century, worn with a contrasting skirt.

The color palette of the 1860s and following decades was given a previously unheard-of range of possibilities with the appearance of the first synthetic dyes. While Perkin's mauve had been marketed in France since 1858, a new range of bright blues, pinks and then dark greens followed. Plaid fabrics inspired by Scottish tartans also enjoyed wide popularity.

Oblong shawls woven in France or Paisley, Scotland, imitated shawls originally handwoven in Kashmir, India; these so-called "paisley" shawls enjoyed their final decade of popularity in the 1860s. Short jackets, known as Zouaves in imitation of those worn by the French-Algerian "Zouave" troops, had curved front edges. Outdoor clothing included flared short jackets and bonnets or small pillbox hats worn perched on

Figure 25. Miss Beaufield in evening dress, 1864. Photograph. I-10559.1. McCord Museum, Montreal.
The dress required a cage crinoline to create the desired silhouette.

the front of the head, and perhaps tied under the chin. Typically, hair was center-parted and pulled toward the back of the head with a small net *sac* known as a snood, which retained the hair at the nape of the neck.

Empress Eugénie of France, wife of Napoleon III, provided international fashion leadership until the fall of the Second Republic in 1870. Remembered in fashion history as the preferred client of the British-born Parisian couturier

Charles Frederick Worth, she secured his couture house a following that lasted for several decades. Worth's innovativeness resided in the way he merchandised his garments. In an era when dressmakers were women, his gender was unusual. He maintained a showroom where clothes were modeled for clients under gaslight; he dictated styles and colors to his best clients, eliminating the expected negotiation over style details, and also carried his image as an artist to an extreme with eccentric dress that included a velvet beret. The Chambre Syndicale de la Couture Parisienne was founded in 1868, establishing haute couture as a strictly regulated big business (Palmer 2001: 13–4). Over the decades, Worth became known for the extravagance of his designs, as well as his use of historicism, a popular Victorian aesthetic trend favored by the Pre-Raphaelite artists. Inspiration from the Middle Ages and Renaissance was frequently found in Worth's creations.

Moral debates about women and fashion in the 1860s centered around the archetype dubbed "The Girl of the Period," after an article by Eliza Lynn Linton in the *Saturday Review* (Lynn Linton 1868: 339–40). Linton was concerned about the low moral standards of bold young followers of fashion, who wore makeup and flirted with men. The "Girl" stood in sharp contrast to the "Angel in the House," another archetype, whose submissiveness to her husband and devotion to her household were Victorian ideals.

Through the latter part of the 1860s, skirts became flatter in front and fuller in the back. By 1870, the bustle silhouette—shaped by semicircular hoops or stiff, ruffled pads (also called bustles)—distended the skirt just below the waist. An overskirt or apron trimmed with ruffles, fringes or ribbon bows further emphasized the silhouette. A separate hip-length bodice frequently had long tails or drapery at the sides and back, which also emphasized the bustle area.

A second phase of the bustle silhouette developed in the later 1870s. Bodice styles become longer and more fitted. The "cuirass" bodice of 1880 required an especially long corset, with a spoon busk at the center front that curved over

Figure 26. Miss Cook in day dress, 1872. I-69019.1. McCord Museum, Montreal.
This day dress exemplifies the bustle silhouette in its first phase.

the abdomen. Skirts were narrow, and back drapery dropped to hip level or below. While fashion plates often illustrated this style, few portrait photographs show it. Burgundy and rust shades were popular in the fashions of the 1870s and early 1880s.

The princess line, named after the Princess Metternich, also a Worth client, appeared in the 1870s. This style referred to a one-piece dress with continuous vertical seams from the bustline to the hip, or lower, without a waistline seam. The one-piece wrapper, a similar style intended for informal at-home wear, usually fastened down the center front.

The fashionable 1870s hairstyle was a chignon, sometimes with ringlets dangling from the back; hairpieces could be added to increase volume. Small, high hats were worn well toward the back of the head.

Ready-made clothing was becoming more available as manufacturing advanced. Emmigration to England and North America stepped up in the 1880s. Jewish emigrants from Eastern Europe entered garment manufacturing in large numbers. Factory work was criticized for imposing long hours and poor working conditions, a practice known as "sweating." Improvements appeared slowly, but were bolstered in the United States by the founding of the International Ladies' Garment Workers' Union in 1900. At the same time, the quality and output of ready-to-wear, for both women and men, improved.

Clothing produced in factories was available across North America through mail-order catalogs. Throughout the Western world ready-to-wear clothing was offered by new department stores, the most well known being Bon Marché

in Paris. This new retail format enabled customers to browse and shop for various types of specialty items under one roof, elevating shopping to a leisure activity. Dressmaking and tailoring departments within these stores offered custom services (Steele 1988: 147–50). Ready-made corsets, petticoats, drawers, hats and bonnets, outerwear and bathing costumes were advertised with prices in local papers. Beginning in the 1880s, a typical bathing costume consisted of a navy blue or black wool serge dress with full skirt worn over mid-calf-length trousers. Stockings, shoes and a cap completed the bathing costume.

Options for assistance with home dressmaking increased with sophisticated publications such as *Mme Demorest's Mirror of Fashion*, which illustrated and described sewing patterns available by mail order. These were easier to use than

Figure 27. "Her First Appearance," *Pictures of People*, Charles Dana Gibson, 1896, New York: R. H. Russell & Sons.
Bathing costumes, quite revealing for their time, consisted of knee-length dresses worn over bloomers and stockings.

patterns printed with many pieces superimposed on a single sheet of paper, distributed in publications such as *Harper's Bazaar* in the US and *Der Bazar* in Germany.

A few years into the 1880s, high bustles became fashionable again. At its largest in 1885, the new bustle was substantially different than that of ten years earlier. This silhouette featured a shelf-like projection outward from the back waistline, with the skirt falling straight to the floor without a train. Horizontal rows of pleated ruffles adorned narrow skirt fronts. Tight, waist-length bodices had fitted sleeves and a slightly pointed waistline in front, which along with numerous required undergarments contributed to an upholstered look. Day bodices usually had

Figure 28. "Latest Paris Fashion. Stylish Fete and Race Toilettes," *The Queen*, 1887. M2001X.6.1.15. McCord Museum, Montreal.
These dresses illustrate the high bustle of the 1880s.

a front button closure and a small band collar, while short-sleeved, low-necked evening bodices closed at the back.

The dolman, a fitted, cape-like garment, was the most fashionable outerwear option. Ranging from hip- to floor-length in front, it accommodated the bustle at the back where it was either waist-length or split. Its sleeves, which began at elbow level, allowed very little arm movement. The tweed Ulster, a floor-length coat with a full or half-belt, was a practical yet fashionable utilitarian outerwear option.

Women increasingly selected black for their clothing, as it was ideally suited to hide the dirt generated by coal dust in large, overcrowded urban centers. Also, the color black adapted easily to the requirements of mourning dress, which was prescribed for the proper expression of bereavement. For mourning, crape, a crinkled black fabric with no luster, was the fabric of choice. Women's periodicals carried advice on the length of time mourning dress had to be worn, based on the proximity of the deceased. Queen Victoria assured the longevity of this practice as she continued to wear mourning dress for the forty years from the death of her husband in 1861 to her own death in 1901.

The chignon hairstyles continued in the 1880s, but bangs or fringes distinguished them. Bonnets worn outdoors were slightly conical and truncated at the top.

Increasingly, stage actresses popularized through photography were becoming fashion leaders. Lily Langtry, one of the mistresses of Queen Victoria's son, the Prince of Wales, received widespread publicity and became a trendsetter in her own right. Known as the "Jersey Lily," she once sported a knitted tennis ensemble, which resulted in the term "jersey" being applied to weft knits.

At this time, several schools of thought held that women's dress was unhealthy. Dr. Gustav Jaeger, based in England, began a health movement promoting the hygienic benefits of wool undergarments, claiming that vegetable fibers were dangerous to health, and that silk was the excrement of a worm (Newton 1974). Leading intellectuals of the day backed his premises. The stores he established in England today sell upscale women's apparel. The Aesthetic dress movement grew out of the ideals of the Pre-Raphaelite art movement, which also influenced the Arts and Crafts movement in England. Aesthetic dress favored a specific color palette inspired by those of vegetable dyes. The Aesthetes and their most flamboyant member, playwright Oscar Wilde, were frequently derided in popular cartoons and in the press. The famous Liberty of London store, founded in 1875, sold Aesthetic dress. Though Aesthetic dress never became mainstream, it eventually influenced dress designers. Another movement, the Rational Dress Society, advocated looser garments and no corseting, a move that very few women were tempted to make as it meant renouncing the desirable small and defined waistline, long considered a mark of femininity.

"The Gay Nineties" is also referred to as "*la belle époque*" in the French-speaking world. These names allude to a lessening of the repressiveness of Victorian morality, at least in the lives of trendsetting elite society. Edward, the Prince of Wales, and his wife Princess Alexandra, though both already of mature years, became fashion leaders with a lifestyle far more colorful than Queen Victoria's had ever been. Wealthy American women who married titled British heirs were among the most prominent international trendsetters. Consuelo Vanderbilt, who suffered an unhappy union with the Duke of Marlborough, was the most celebrated of these international beauties.

In 1899, Thorstein Veblen wrote *The Theory of the Leisure Class*, a social critique. He coined the term "conspicuous consumption" to explain Western culture's propensity to display a family's wealth through material objects, particularly women's clothing. Society women's social calendars required several changes of clothing for the various activities in their day, resulting in extensive wardrobes. Exemplifying this trend was the increased popularity of a garment for women known as the tea gown, a dress appropriate only for receiving guests at home in the afternoon.

Though still a decorative garment, the tea gown had a loose front. Similar less ornate garments, wrappers, had been in existence for several decades; but tea gowns brought this seemingly casual form of dress into the public sphere, albeit in a limited way.

The most iconic aspect of women's fashion in the 1890s is the leg-of-mutton sleeve, which was at its largest in 1895. Day bodices typically had high collars, often with boning at the sides to keep them up. Lapels, yokes and shoulder detailing drew the eye outward to the wide sleeves. Bodices were generally slightly pointed at the front waistline. Trumpet-shaped skirts fitted smoothly over petticoats with the waistline softly gathered at center back. A variety of shades of pale mauve and yellow were popular in the 1890s. Fashionable outerwear included black waist-length capes, often trimmed in jet.

Women's presence in the workforce increased dramatically in the 1890s as they took positions as nurses, telephone operators and secretaries, as well as the traditional jobs associated with dressmaking and millinery. The "New Woman" was the archetype of the ambitious young working woman who enjoyed increased social freedom and eschewed traditional ideas of femininity. She wore a two-piece suit with a blouse. These "tailor-made" suits were initially custom-made of wool by men's tailors rather than dressmakers. Other appropriate wear for the working woman was a skirt and ready-made shirtwaist, a new blouse style based on men's shirts and which allowed more freedom of movement than a boned bodice.

Increased access to active sports, particularly bicycling, led to the appearance of the avant-garde bicycle suit. Based on the tailor-made suit, these cycling outfits had fitted jackets and the first accepted form of trousers for women, which covered the knee. A skirt may nonetheless have hidden these trousers. A straw boater, a hat with a flat crown and slightly wide brim, was worn with a bicycle suit and with daywear for work.

Art nouveau was a style prevalent in the 1890s and early 1900s, whose influence was felt in fashion as well as in a variety of other forms

Figure 29. Mrs. Robert Reford in tailor-made and shirtwaist, and Master Robert Bruce Reford in dress, 1897. II-119236. McCord Museum, Montreal.

ranging from jewelry to architecture. It can be understood as a bridge between traditional nineteenth-century art styles and those of the new twentieth century. The Paris exhibition of 1900, where this decorative art style predominated, featured couture fashions by the two sons of Charles Frederick Worth and other important couturiers including Doucet, Paquin, Callot Soeurs and Redfern. The latter had expanded from England into New York and Paris. Lucile, also known as Lady Duff Gordon, was another well-known couturier.

The silhouette of women's clothing from 1900 to 1908 echoed the S-curve of the art nouveau style. The fashionable, straight-fronted corset tilted the upper body forward and thrust the hips backward. A corset cover or camisole covered the corset, adding fullness to the bodice front. Drawers were narrower and seamed closed at the crotch where they had been open before. Some undergarments, known as combinations, combined the drawers and corset cover.

Bodices featured fullness just above the center front waistline, creating a sort of pouch effect. This style is sometimes called the monobosom, as the breasts appeared very low with no visible separation between them. Collars continued to be high and boned. Sleeve styles ranged from the bishop, fitted on the upper arm, puffed into a fitted cuff, or the leg-of-mutton, which reemerged about 1905, though with nowhere near as much fullness as in the previous decade. Silk chiffon, as well as lightweight cottons such as batiste, lawn and voile were popular new dress fabrics, which created a soft, light effect. Skirts fitted over the

Figure 30. "The Enthusiast," *The Social Ladder*, Charles Dana Gibson, 1902, New York: R. H. Russell.
The woman's bodice has a monobosom. Her upswept hairdo and large hat are typical of the Edwardian period. The men wear the popular sack suit.

hips in front then flared with gathers into the center back waistline and emphasized the strong backward thrust of the hips. *Passementerie*, a soutache braid applied in curvilinear designs, adorned tailor-mades and dresses of heavy wool fabrics. The Gibson Girl, the strong, independent young woman illustrated by American artist Charles Dana Gibson, and incarnated in actress Camille Clifford, was often depicted in the popular shirtwaist.

Face-framing hairstyles incorporated a topknot with fullness on the sides, a style sometimes called a Pompadour after the eighteenth-century courtesan. Wide hats decorated with flowers and ostrich plumes echoed these hairstyles. The use of plumage from exotic birds in millinery expanded quickly; birds were being hunted and killed for this purpose in increasing numbers. In the last decade of the nineteenth and first decade of the twentieth centuries, the Audubon Society was established in an attempt to quell this practice.

This decade saw the rise of Paul Poiret, the new century's first modern couturier. He is reputed to have freed women from the corset by creating simple tunic dresses that did not require the body to be molded with boned understructures. His empire-waisted dresses dominated high fashion by 1909.

The new pastime of automobiling introduced the duster, or motorcoat, worn to protect drivers and passengers from the clouds of dust raised on unpaved roads. These long coats with full sleeves were typically of beige linen. Accessories included a wide-brimmed hat with a veil that completely covered the face and hair. Men also wore dusters.

CHILDREN'S DRESS

Children of both sexes were dressed identically in dresses until about the age of five, although as the decades progressed, boys donned trousers increasingly earlier. Dresses facilitated diapering and toilet training, and the white cotton fabrics favored for toddlers were among the easiest options for laundering.

Figure 31. Mrs. Fulton's children, 1886. Boy in sailor outfit; girl in white dress. II-80673.1. McCord Museum, Montreal.

The popular late nineteenth-century passion for dressing up in costume at fancy-dress balls extended to the aesthetics of children's dress, which often had historical or exotic references. A common boy's costume was a trouser suit with a cropped jacket known as an Eton suit. The Little Lord Fauntleroy suit, a velveteen outfit with knee-length trousers and usually a ruffled white collar, named after a novel, was widely known. Nautically inspired sailor suits enjoyed continued popularity, often worn with a hat with the name of a ship embroidered on the band. The Russian suit, a belted tunic with a side or center front closure, worn over knee-length pants, was offered in infinite varieties in mail-order catalogs from 1900 and on through the teens.

Girls' dresses were shortened versions of fashionable adult women's styles. In the teenage years, girls gradually lengthened their skirts until around the age of sixteen to eighteen, when they adopted the adult length. In the 1860s, pantalettes were seen under the short skirts of very small girls, covering their lower limbs. Older girls wore crinolines and bustles in keeping with adult women's fashion. The mode for a white cotton dress accented with a sash of pink, blue, plaid or striped ribbon remained constant over the decades. The popular Kate Greenaway illustrations of girls dressed in styles of the early nineteenth century had some influence on girls' dress. By early adolescence, girls wore boned corsets; earlier in childhood, a stiff cotton waist was found appropriate for both sexes.

Photographs of children in the 1860s show girls wearing their hair at chin length, with a center part, and tucked behind the ears. Later images show boys with adult hairstyles, although occasionally, in keeping with the Little Lord Fauntleroy style, boys had a full head of long ringlets, or long, wavy tresses. Girls wore their hair long and loose, perhaps with a bow on top of the head, until late adolescence. Wearing the hair up was a sign of their coming of age.

The Edwardian era ended in 1911 with the death of King Edward; this marked the close of a period also known as the long nineteenth century because of the way its culture remained consistent through the first decade of the twentieth century. By 1911, however, society and fashion were on the cusp of radical changes. A new "modern" era began.

4

TIFFANY WEBBER-HANCHETT

The Modern Era: 1910–1960

Fashions of the first half of the twentieth century, like other art and design media, broke with past conventions. Production, marketing, distribution and consumption of fashion expanded. Modernization of dress reflected the liberating and devastating social, political and technological changes in Europe, Asia and North America. Two world wars and the Great Depression interrupted the supremacy of French couture, prompting British, American and Italian designers to forge identities within international fashion. Expanded mechanization and standardization within the ready-to-wear industry, and developments in the quality and variety of synthetic fibers, required simplified styles and made decently constructed, inexpensive clothing widely available. Women's suffrage and prominence in the workforce, as well as the increased participation of both men and women in travel, sports and leisure activities, facilitated development of versatile, practical dress. Popular magazines, radio, movies and, finally, television quickly disseminated fashion information. Royalty, celebrities and the emerging youth culture set the fashion trends.

1910–1913

The 1910s saw the breakdown of traditional hierarchical social and political systems. The First World War collapsed "old world" empires, while Vladimir Lenin and his circle of revolutionaries led millions of frustrated Russian workers in the Bolshevik Revolution of 1917, culminating in the institution of a communist regime. Women continued to agitate for the vote in Europe and North America. Sigmund Freud's psychoanalytical thought altered ideas about the subconscious.

In the years leading up to the First World War, conventional sartorial codes, such as multiple clothing changes in a given day, began to relax, and the fashionable female silhouette shifted from the structured S-curve of Edwardian styles to a straight one simulating Empire styles. It also incorporated the cut and drape of Asian garments, such as the Japanese kimono, which had been a popular *fin de siècle* at-home garment. Although seen in the collections of Jeanne Paquin and others, Paul Poiret, self-proclaimed "king of fashion," claimed the new silhouette. His high-waisted gowns, voluminous wrap coats, headbands and turbans were made in lush, brightly colored fabrics and embellished with Poiret's signature rose (Iribe 1908). Shorter and less rigid corsets, worn with "combinations"—camisole and petticoat in one—created the desired shape.

Poiret's designs, along with those of Mariano Fortuny, who in 1909 patented his pleated Delphos gown, and the Aesthetic fashions sold in stores such as Liberty of London, contrasted with the proportions and muted, pastel tones of Edwardian dress. They corresponded with Leon Bakst's vibrant costume designs for Sergei Diaghilev's *Ballets Russes*, which premiered in Paris in 1909 and in London in 1911. Bakst's costumes drew inspiration from the harem pants, tunics, rich fabrics and vibrant colors of Persian

Figure 32. Design by Paul Poiret, French, 1879–1944. Illustrated by Paul Iribe, French, 1883–1935, *Les Robes de Paul Poiret racontées par Paul Iribe*. French, 1908. Pochoir. Museum purchase with funds donated by Mrs. Roberta Logie. 1998.2. Photograph © 2007 Museum of Fine Arts, Boston.

dress. His designs eventually affected mainstream fashion by raising awareness of the dress of antiquity and non-Western traditions. Women in avant-garde literary and artistic circles—many of whom had given up corsets—wore styles based on European peasant dress. Ballroom dancer Irene Castle, who with her husband Vernon helped to spread the tango craze across America and Europe, sometimes wore a tunic overdress and harem pants, reflecting the orientalism vogue (Mendes and de la Haye 1999: 41). Luxurious eveningwear also showed off the orientalism and exoticism evident in the arts. Gowns, such as those by Lucile, consisted of frothy layers of delicate tulle embellished with beads, lace

and appliquéd flowers, floating over sumptuous silks.

Prewar daytime styles for women included dresses or two-piece ensembles of jackets or tunics over underskirts. Bodices buttoned at the front, had kimono-like sleeves and open necklines. A short-lived fashion trend—the appropriately named "hobble" skirt—was a peg-top skirt that narrowed at the ankles. Outerwear included three-quarter- and full-length wrap coats. Large, ornamented hats topped softly waved hair pulled to the back. Tailor-mades continued to be practical wardrobe staples, particularly for college students and working women.

Paris remained preeminent in setting the fashion standards; women of means relied on Parisian couturiers and private dressmakers for their wardrobes. The Chambre Syndicale de la Couture Parisienne promoted French fashions. Mass manufacturing of womenswear continued to expand and working conditions improved in both Britain and the United States; trade publications such as the American paper *Women's Wear* appeared. Merchandise available in department stores and mail-order catalogs, and the variety of commercial patterns for home sewers both increased, allowing a broader cross-section of people to obtain knockoffs of the latest fashions. Fashions were artfully depicted in publications such as *Gazette du Bon Ton* and endorsed by stars of the stage and screen in magazines.

Post-Edwardian men's fashions also followed a straight, slim line that lasted through the war years, and London's Savile Row remained the style source for menswear. The sack suit was a wardrobe essential, and from about 1912, blue wool serge dominated three-piece suits. Suit jackets buttoned high and indented slightly above the natural waistline. Moderately sized notched lapels accentuated a snug shoulder-line. Shirts were white, pale colored or printed with small motifs. Easily laundered and starched detachable high collars and cuffs provided the modern man's crisp, clean look. Center-creased trousers were slim and tapered to the ankle, with cuffs. Oxford shoes with perforated designs, available in two tones, were introduced. The double-breasted

Ulster was a popular overcoat, and hats included the fedora, boater and derby. Short, pomaded hair and a clean-shaven face completed the new look. Special daytime events such as weddings still required the morning coat or frock coat.

Eveningwear consisted of "white tie" or "black tie." Formal white tie included a tailcoat worn with white piqué waistcoat (vest) and bow tie. Less formal occasions called for black tie; the tuxedo or dinner jacket was worn with a black satin cummerbund and bow tie. In summer the jacket was often white. For leisure and resort wear, a dark blazer worn with light-colored trousers was appropriate for tennis or yachting while Norfolk jackets with knickerbockers, stockings and shoes suited golf. Men and women enjoyed motoring as a new recreational activity, and driving gear consisted of dusters and goggles, and caps for men.

Childrenswear generally followed adult silhouettes and changed little. Girls of all ages wore lingerie dresses embellished with lace, smocking or embroidery, sashed with a ribbon at the hips. Schoolwear consisted of navy wool serge sailor dresses with hats; pinafores were worn to protect dresses. Physical education uniforms included sleeveless, square-necked tunics belted over blouses. Dark stockings and ankle boots were worn, but flat, ballet-like slippers or ankle-strap shoes were worn with "best" dresses. The practice of dressing toddler-aged boys in skirts diminished after 1910, as they wore rompers, then

Figure 33. Men's Norfolk jackets, "American Fashions, Spring & Summer, Jno. J. Mitchell Co.," *The Sartorial Art Journal,* February, 1913: 361. Commercial Pattern Archive, Special Collections, University of Rhode Island Library.

knickerbockers. Popular boys' styles included sailor suits and Eton and Norfolk jackets worn with shorts, knickerbockers or trousers.

1914–1918: THE FIRST WORLD WAR

All of Europe was at war by 1914; however, the United States did not enter the fray until 1917. European and American women contributed to the war effort in numerous ways by taking jobs once held by men and joining relief organizations such as the Red Cross. For practicality, their dress for manual labor included bloomers, coveralls and trousers. Normal daywear was the one-piece dress tied loosely at the waist or a khaki suit with military detailing. Lingerie dresses with ribbon cummerbunds, worn for "dressy" daytime events, offset this restrained style. During the war years, both daywear and eveningwear was cut in an amorphous, barrel-shaped silhouette. Loose V-shaped or square-necked bodices and blouses gave little or no bustline definition. A loose belt at, or just above, the natural waist suggested a waistline. Skirts were wider, fuller and shorter than before. The number of undergarments declined; they supported, rather than shaped, the body. Some adventurous women began to "bob" their hair. Hats now had a deep crown, often without a brim.

A number of the practical and protective garments worn by servicemen were integrated into civilian dress after the war. Most notably, Burberry and Aquascutum water-repellent "trench" coats—belted, double-breasted, and with a convertible collar—were appropriated by men and, eventually, women. Shirts with attached soft collars, and pullover sweaters, all originally worn by working-class men, were adopted into mainstream fashion. Wristwatches and abbreviated undergarments replaced old-fashioned pocket watches and "long johns" (one-piece, full-length underwear).

1919–1929

Prosperity, significant social changes, and a vibrant artistic milieu followed the upheaval of the First World War. King Tutankhamun's tomb was

Figure 34. Ladies' undergarments. Left: combinations. Right: teddy and drawers. Butterick pattern, 1916. Commercial Pattern Archive (1916.6.BWS), Special Collections, University of Rhode Island Library.

discovered in 1922, spawning "Egyptomania." Along with gaining the right to vote, women cut their hair short and showed off their legs.[1] The youthful, adventurous flapper of F. Scott's Fitzgerald's *The Great Gatsby* (1925), and caricatured in John Held's *Life* magazine illustrations, partied into the wee hours of the night. Prohibition of alcoholic beverages in the United States gave rise to the speakeasy, where jazz music and the Charleston emerged. Charles Lindbergh made the first nonstop transatlantic flight, becoming an instant hero. The increased affordability of mass-produced automobiles brought greater mobility to the average family. Radio programs broadcast accessible entertainment and news. Film "talkies" (1926) entertained and provided new means of fashion dissemination, especially via star actors.

The "modern" world was on display at the 1925 Paris Exposition Internationale des Arts Décoratifs et Industriels Modernes, which demonstrated Europe's triumphant emergence from the war; the United States did not exhibit, citing a lack of modern talent. The Expo reinforced France's preeminence in luxury goods; department stores sponsored pavilions, couturiers showed fashions, and the displays featured new artist and designer collaborations. Diverse artistic influences, which now define art deco style, included the ancient cultures of Egypt, Asia, Central and South America.

Two contrasting styles were popular in women's fashion for the first half of the 1920s. The feminine, mother-daughter designs of Jeanne Lanvin epitomized the romantic, eighteenth-century-inspired style. Lanvin is remembered for the *robe de style,* a gown with a boned, tubular bodice and an ankle-length, full skirt. The second style, the modern *garçonne,* typified in the personal style and fashions of the young Gabrielle Chanel, defined the period. Chanel opened her first shop in 1909 and introduced or popularized jersey knits, menswear-inspired ensembles, the little black dress, and suntanned skin.

The tubular, dropped-waist chemise dress that characterized the *garçonne* look was simple in cut and construction, making it easy to

Figure 35. Top: "Two Youthful Suits for Spring Wear." Bottom: "Two Graceful Models for the Robe de Style." *Vogue Fashion Bi-Monthly,* June–July 1926. Historic Textile and Costume Collection, University of Rhode Island.

mass-manufacture; ready-to-wear knockoffs of Parisian styles escalated in Britain and America. The simple chemise shape also made the perfect canvas for the elaborate embellishment that defined the dazzling eveningwear of the decade. Bodices cut straight to the hipline were long-sleeved or sleeveless and had low, V-neck or rounded front and back necklines. Skirts were cut in several ways including straight, on the bias, gathered or pleated, often with scalloped or handkerchief hems, as seen in the work of Madeleine Vionnet. Hemlines shortened to the knee in the second half of the decade, before lowering again by 1929. The silhouette required a slim shape, maintained through diet and exercise and by soft undergarments—brassieres, teddies and slips—and flattening corsets fastened by a separating zipper (patented in 1917). Blouses or sweaters—such as those by Italian designer Elsa Schiaparelli that featured *trompe l'oeil* bows—worn over pleated skirts were popular daywear ensembles, as was Chanel's cardigan suit. The newly developed "artificial silk," renamed and marketed as rayon, was used in both daywear and eveningwear by mid-decade. However, the most luxurious evening dresses were made of delicate silk chiffon, satin and velvet, heavily beaded and embroidered with Cubist shapes and motifs borrowed from "exotic" sources.

With shortened skirts came an emphasis on hosiery, available in colors and sheers. Footwear included T-strapped Cuban-heeled pumps, Oxford tie shoes and untied galoshes, which were popular among college girls. The galoshes flapped when the girls walked, giving them the name "flappers." Large wrap coats were held closed, or fastened at the hip with decorative pins. Cloche hats and bandeaus were worn over bobbed haircuts, often with a Marcel wave, or radically short Eton crops. Facial features were emphasized with rouge, Egyptian-inspired kohl eyeliner and dark red lips—the look advertised and endorsed by aristocrats and celebrities such as Louise Brooks. Art deco motifs embellished fashionable accessories such as cigarette and cosmetic cases.

Britain's stylish Prince Edward VIII set fashion trends for menswear. He helped boost the Scottish knitting industry when he wore a golf ensemble of patterned sweater, plus fours (knickerbockers) and argyle socks. The Jay Gatsby look—a light-colored flannel or linen suit—became associated with refined, upper-class summer style, as did the brass-buttoned navy blazer worn with regimental striped tie and white pants. Tuxedo and dinner jackets, now available in "midnight blue," were popular, and tails were reserved for the most formal occasions.

Three fads influenced men's fashions, including jazz suits composed of tight trousers and fitted jackets with long back vents for dancing. Oxford bags were wide-legged trousers worn by college boys, originally over knickerbockers, to facilitate changing for sports after class. Another fad among the collegiate set was the raccoon coat. Mainstream classic suits consisted of single- and double-breasted jackets with a natural shoulder-line, cut narrow through the torso and ending just below the hip. Shirts were still white, colored or patterned with a narrow attached collar pinned together under the necktie.

Tennis and swimming were popular recreational activities for men and women. Tennis stars such as Suzanne Lenglen, dressed by Jean Patou on and off the court, set sports clothing trends. Her look included a menswear-inspired sweater vest over a white pleated dress, stockings, tie shoes, and a bandeau. René Lacoste, nicknamed "The Crocodile," designed a short-sleeved knitted polo shirt with a long tail at the back to keep his shirt in while playing. Couturiers such as Chanel and Patou, along with manufacturers such as Jantzen, provided unisex-looking swimwear of one- or two-piece knitted tank suits worn with swim caps and sunglasses.

Girls' dresses were straight, loose and unfitted like those of adult women. Coats also tended to be straight and narrow. Sailor suits were still common for boys, as were long and belted jackets for special occasions. Commonly worn sweaters included pullovers, cardigans and turtlenecks. Play clothes for boys and girls included costumes, for example cowboy outfits, policemen's and nurses' uniforms.

1930–1938

The stock market crash of 1929 and the ensuing Depression ended the jazz age and ushered in the "machine age," with its streamlined aesthetic epitomized in the skyscraper. The United States severely limited imports to reduce trade imbalances. European textile and clothing manufacturers reduced production as demand diminished. Although Paris labels were coveted, ready-to-wear designers in New York and California gained recognition. To stimulate American consumers, retailers promoted domestic talent. Hollywood movies, a vital source of entertainment and escape, also exported fashion trends. Prince Edward VIII, crowned king in 1936, abdicated the throne shortly afterward to marry Wallis

Figure 36. Man's trench coat, woman's suit with shawl collar, and girl's raglan-sleeved coat. *Beyers Modenblatt*, 1932. Commercial Pattern Archive, Special Collections, University of Rhode Island Library.

Simpson, an American divorcee. As the Duke and Duchess of Windsor, they set fashion trends. Fashion-conscious men could also follow the latest styles in newly published magazines such as *Apparel Arts* (later named *Gentleman's Quarterly*, now *GQ*) and *Esquire*.

The female silhouette emphasized the bust, natural waistline, hips and legs with an elongated and curvilinear aesthetic, best created by cutting fabrics on the bias, as perfected by Madeleine Vionnet. Undergarments employed the newly developed rubberized cotton yarn, Lastex, providing a smooth figure line. Hemlines, which had already begun lengthening at the end of the 1920s, grew longer in the first half of the decade.

Women's daywear included lightweight dresses made from plain or printed silk or rayon crêpe, often with self-fabric belts at the natural waistline. Pumps or tie shoes accompanied wool suits with shawl collars—like those promoted by the dress reform company Jaeger. Hairstyles, longer and often permanent-waved, were complemented by cloche hats, berets, and caps worn close to the head. Neck treatments such as fur scarves, tieclips and rhinestone brooches accented outerwear. Elaborate sleeve treatments—popularized by Gilbert Adrian's widely copied *Letty Lynton* dress (1932) worn by Joan Crawford—peplum waist treatments, and just-below-knee hemlines defined the silhouette. Tailored influences, as seen in fashions by Elsa Schiaparelli, continued later in the decade with an exaggerated shoulderline. She collaborated with Surrealist artists such as Salvador Dalí to create themed collections and quirky accessories, and used zippers and buttons in obvious, innovative ways.

Eveningwear emphasized glamour and overt sexiness, captured in photographs by Horst and Hoynigen-Heune, and partly drawn from movie star Jean Harlow's "blonde bombshell" look of bleached curled hair, shaped eyebrows and dark lips. Silk charmeuse backless gowns, cut along the same lines as swimwear to avoid conspicuous tan lines, demonstrated the impact of recreational dress on fashions. Late in the decade, romanticism in eveningwear referenced eighteenth- and

Figure 37. Evening dresses inspired by *Gone With the Wind*. Hollywood pattern, 1940. Commercial Pattern Archive (1940.108.BWS), Special Collections, University of Rhode Island Library.

the waist and narrow through the hips. Double-pleated trousers with a zipper fly, instead of buttons, were pegged to the hem. Waistcoats were not necessary, as wristwatches had replaced the pocket watch. Shirts had wide collars, complementing the jacket's blade lapel and accommodating the new Windsor knot; bow ties were alternative neckwear. For evening, tuxedo or dinner jackets were worn. Undergarments included boxer shorts or knitted Jockey briefs and athletic-style undershirts, although undershirt sales dropped sharply when Clark Gable appeared without one in *It Happened One Night (*1934). Hair was short, waved and parted on the side, and mustaches were common. Hats, with wide snap brims that flipped down, complemented the drape suits.

Sportswear, worn for leisure and informal occasions and closely associated with casual American style, became an increasingly important clothing category for men and women in

nineteenth-century corset-like bodices and full skirts—seen in gowns by American couturier Charles James and by Cristobal Balenciaga, who drew upon court portraits from his native Spain. Evening and wedding styles of the late 1930s and early 1940s were influenced by period movies like *Gone with the Wind* (1939), a story set in the 1860s during the American Civil War.

The English drape suit, made in lightweight worsted wool gabardine, Glen plaid, or linen, introduced a relaxed fit to men's suiting. The jacket was cut wide in the shoulders, narrow at

Figure 38. Beach pajamas, man in trunks and striped tank, woman in dressmaker swimsuit, *Vanity Fair*, 1932. Historic Textile and Costume Collection, University of Rhode Island.

the 1930s. The buttoned shirtdress and versatile separates—sweaters, loose lounge pants with matching tops—showed the further appropriation of menswear elements into women's fashions. Women matched hats to ensembles and often wore sandals or wedge-heeled shoes. The men's sports jacket, often with an emblem on the chest pocket and worn with an ascot, was sold separately and not meant to match trousers. Cotton khaki safari suits like those worn by explorers and British military officers in Africa were adopted as leisurewear, particularly among upper-class gentlemen. Polo shirts and sports shirts, worn tucked in or left out, and patterned with Hawaiian or Indian bandana motifs, were popular. Casual jackets such as parkas and goatskin leather jackets were worn, as were moccasin-style shoes and sandals. As beach rules loosened, swimwear revealed more skin. Cole of California advertised its women's two-piece "Swoon Suit" in 1939, and men's suits included bare-chested styles. The newly popular sport of skiing had its own set of garments, including wind-resistant jackets worn with full long trousers gathered at the ankle.

Girls' fashions followed adult female fashion trends. Dresses had puffed sleeves and natural waistlines, often accentuated with a sash. For school, skirts and blouses were common. Hairstyles mimicked child actor Shirley Temple's ringlets. Outerwear included raglan-sleeved coats and princess-seamed styles with fur-trimmed collars. For boys, jackets were shorter and less often belted. Polo shirts, sweaters and sweatshirts topped daywear trousers. Outdoor dress included boxy coats as well as parkas. Play clothes for boys and girls included denim jeans and costumes of favorite cartoon and film characters. Retailers placed more emphasis on "College Shops" and "teenage" dress, which would become a bigger merchandising trend in the decades to follow.

1939–1945: THE SECOND WORLD WAR

In 1939, the Germans invaded Poland, starting the Second World War. The German occupation of Paris in June 1940 effectively cut off French couture from the rest of Europe and America. Many couture houses closed or decreased their output, although others remained open to serve an elite Nazi clientele. As news of the latest fashions no longer came from Paris, British couturiers such as Hardy Amies and Norman Hartnell, and American ready-to-wear designers including Norman Norell and Claire McCardell, gained recognition. American retailers, publicists and politicians stepped up efforts begun in the 1930s to promote a distinctly American look of casual elegance. Wartime clothing rations in effect in Britain, and regulations in the United States, limited civilian use of wool, silk, leather and the newly patented nylon, which were employed for war efforts. The restrictions led to creativity on the part of designers and consumers, who found inventive ways to "make do and mend." As in the First World War, women joined the workforce, filling jobs once held by men, and trousers, worn during previous war work and as leisurewear in the 1920s and 1930s, became indispensable in women's wardrobes.

An inverted triangular silhouette—broad shoulders and narrow waist—defined both men's and women's styles. Women's daywear included wool suits with padded shoulders and slightly flared, knee-length skirts. The 1930s shirtdress with puffed sleeves, button front, defined waist and knee-length skirt became a wardrobe basic. This spare style was made in printed cotton, rayon and acetate, available with patriotic patterns and accented with shirring, pleating or appliqué. Claire McCardell's inventive denim popover dress, with a convenient pocket for an oven mitt, became popular at-home wear. Her baby doll dresses, halter top and midriff-baring ensembles, cotton eveningwear, swimsuits and playsuits were hallmarks of her timeless, practical, economical style.

Looking good during the war helped to keep spirits high. Hair was worn shoulder length or piled high in front and topped with a creative hat. Hats were often elaborate, as they required only small amounts of material. Gloves were worn. Red lipstick defined the lips, and women

Figure 39. Dorse and Beaulah Glass on a trip to Niagara Falls, New York, 1947. Glass family collection.
The styles popular during the Second World War continued to be worn in 1946 and 1947.

pleated pants pegged at the ankle. Usually a collared shirt and fedora-like hat finished the style. Wartime regulations banned the zoot suit because the extra-wide cut used too much fabric.

Men's wartime jackets were elongated with padded shoulders, wide lapels, and narrow waist and hips. Ties might include patriotic prints. Sports jackets and printed shirts remained popular leisure garments. As in the First World War, military gear influenced civilian clothing. Short "lumberjack" or utility jackets, double-breasted pea coats worn by sailors, waist-length Eisenhower jackets with a self-fabric belt, fur-lined leather bomber jackets worn by fighter pilots, and servicemen's T-shirts became popular after the war. Children's clothing picked up on military wear as little boys wore smaller versions of the Eisenhower jacket.

1946–1960

Paris was liberated in 1944, the war ended in 1945, and within two years clothing rationing and regulations were lifted. The Chambre Syndicale de la Couture Parisienne, under the leadership of Lucien Lelong, organized the Théâtre de la Mode, consisting of small-scale wire mannequins wearing the latest Parisian fashions, which toured Europe and America to rekindle interest in French couture. Although French couture rose again, New York City was firmly established as the sportswear fashion capital, with many American ready-to-wear designers becoming household names. British designers, such as Norman Hartnell, who designed Princess Elizabeth's wedding dress in 1947, as well as a group of Italian designers who organized a fashion show at the Pitti Palace in 1951, grew more prominent, leading to a plurality of fashionable styles in the postwar years. Dressmakers faded into the past as department stores and boutiques became increasingly popular shopping destinations.

Both optimism and unrest marked the postwar years. Europe rebuilt as the United States experienced prosperity, with families expanding and migrating to the suburbs. Women returned

drew false hosiery seams on the back of their legs to simulate stockings. Leather shortages led to shoes with cork soles or with wooden heels. Ballet slippers and espadrilles were worn, particularly for summer.

The zoot suit of the early 1940s was a menswear fad begun by working-class African-American and Mexican-American teens. The exaggerated sack suit had wide shoulders and lapels, and to the home, fulfilling traditional gender roles as depicted in television shows such as *Leave it to Beaver* (1957–1963). Advertisements showed smiling, well put together women in compliant poses amid a plethora of colorful domestic products made from new synthetic materials such as plastic. However, the devastation of the

Figure 40. The "New Look" by Christian Dior, "First Notes from the Paris Collections," *Harper's Bazaar*, April, 1947.
Harper's Bazaar's fashion writer emphasized the long skirts and round, padded hips of Dior's new silhouette.

war, the beginning of the Cold War, the suspicion spawned by McCarthyism, and the seeming artificiality of the designed world instigated disorientation and disillusionment, which was captured in Abstract Expressionist art and the poetry of the Beat generation.

Christian Dior's 1947 "New Look" was arguably the most influential trend to emerge from postwar Paris and helped to reestablish the preeminence of French couture. The hyper-feminine New Look—soft, rounded shoulders, cinched waist, padded hips and full, below-knee skirts—permeated female fashions of the 1950s. Although not entirely new, the look starkly contrasted with the austere styles of the war years. Dior, along with Jacques Fath and Cristobal Balenciaga, showed a second, slimmer silhouette with a straight, narrow skirt. Confining foundation garments including "uplift" bras, "merry widows" and waist cinchers, and elasticized girdles shaped women's bodies. Full skirts were held away from the body with layers of stiff nylon net or ruffled petticoats. In addition to New Look suits, daywear included shirtdresses, sheath dresses worn with bolero jackets, and skirts worn with sweater sets, commonly made from acrylic. Eveningwear was opulent and structured during this period, as seen in Charles James's architectural "Abstract" dress. Full, ballerina-length gowns with strapless boned bodices predominated. Skirts might also be slim with "fishtail" drapery at the back. Long fur coats, or short versions called toppers, were worn with long gloves.

Another silhouette was a less-fitted chemise style, seen in Balenciaga's loosely fitted suit jackets with stand-away collars and sack dresses, Dior's A-line dresses, and Yves Saint-Laurent's 1958 "trapeze" dress from his debut line for the House of Dior. This loose silhouette coexisted with the New Look until the early 1960s, when it became the dominant shape. Evening dresses might be long or short, often with strapless bodices or embellished overblouses worn over long skirts.

In the early 1950s, hair was often chin length, curled and worn close to the head. Hats and

Figure 41. Dress, Claire McCardell. Spadea pattern, 1955. Collection of Abby Lillethun. *This pattern by American designer Claire McCardell reflects the continued popularity of Dior's full-skirted "New Look" silhouette.*

breaking. Mascara and dramatically dark-lined eyes were in style, and colored eyeshadows became accepted by the end of the decade.

Sportswear in "wash-and-wear" fabrics such as polyester included narrow pants, varying in length—the mid-calf "pedal pushers" for bike-riding, capri pants introduced by Italian designer Emilio Pucci, or Bermuda shorts for summer. Tops included printed shirts, knitted tops or close-fitting sweaters. Moccasins, loafers, ballet slippers, sandals and canvas sneakers were common casual shoe styles, and the car coat became basic suburban wear. Beachwear included playsuits and swimsuits, both one- and two-piece. The bikini, introduced in 1946 and named after the atomic testing at Bikini Atoll in the Pacific Islands, was widely accepted in Europe, but not immediately in the conservative United States.

The men's equivalent of the New Look was the "Bold Look" of the late 1940s, which, like the women's style, was not new; rather, it reintroduced prewar styles such as the English drape suit with its wide cut through the shoulders and chest. Jackets were cut long and broad-shouldered with elongated, rolled lapels; double-breasted styles predominated, worn with cuffed pants. Shirts of nylon or cotton had wide collars.

By the 1950s, British Teddy Boys' Edwardian-inspired dress was evident in mainstream men's suits, leading to less shoulder padding. Single-breasted styles made of dark gray or charcoal wool flannel were celebrated in the novel and movie *The Man in the Gray Flannel Suit* (1955–56). Polyester came into widespread use in the 1950s, blended with cotton to make "wash-and-wear" dress shirts. By the late 1950s, the gray flannel suit had diminished in popularity in favor of the "continental" suit, with shorter jackets cut closer through the torso and rounded, cutaway fronts, popularized by Italian tailors whose growing influence challenged the preeminence of British tailoring. Hairstyles remained short just after the war, as some men continued to wear the crew cut or flattop, although they grew longer over the course of the decade. The fedora was the most common hat.

gloves were worn for most occasions; close-fitting pearl necklaces were popular. By the end of the decade, bouffant hairstyles were fashionable and the pillbox hat was introduced. Nylon came back into use for stockings, now called nylons or hose, which were seamed. Pumps, slingbacks and flat-heeled shoes were common; Roger Vivier is credited with introducing the stiletto, which utilized a steel rod to prevent the skinny heel from

The white dinner jacket was popular for evening, particularly in the summer, as were French blue jackets. Sports jackets of tartan plaid and textured fabrics such as corduroy fitted the relaxed trend. Casual trousers or slacks were slim and straight, and Bermuda shorts were worn. Sports shirts included brightly colored Hawaiian prints, Indian madras, T-shirts and knitted polos. For the beach or pool, men wore swim trunks, often with matching beach jackets.

Postwar styles of youth and subcultural groups were distinct and influential. The Ivy League look included chinos and button-down shirts, and crewneck or letter sweaters for college boys. For adolescent and college-aged girls, a mid-1950s fad was wearing large, loose sweaters known as sloppy joes, or cardigan sweaters backward. Poodle skirts—circle skirts appliquéd with poodle dogs—worn with ankle socks and saddle shoes or loafers, white shirts or sweater sets and a scarf tied around the neck were popular. Another teen look was a pair of jeans worn with saddle shoes and a loose-fitting shirt. The actors James Dean and Marlon Brando popularized "rebel" styles such as T-shirts, jeans and leather jackets. Longer hairstyles, including feathered "DAs" (hair combed back like a "duck's ass"), like those worn by the Teddy Boys and Elvis Presley, also caught on. The style of the Beats included chinos, jeans and flannel shirts. *Funny Face* (1957) popularized a stereotyped beatnik look of dark glasses, black beret and turtleneck, with jeans for guys and black leotard for girls. The fashions of youth and countercultures would increasingly dominate clothing trends of subsequent decades.

NOTE

1. Women's suffrage was achieved in seventeen countries from 1919 to 1929. IPU, Inter-Parliamentary Union, "Women's Suffrage." <www.ipu.org/wmn-e/suffrage.htm>. Accessed June 6, 2006.

5

JOSÉ BLANCO

The Postmodern Age: 1960–2006

In the last half of the twentieth century, the globalizing economy and increased communication outlets dominated changes in the fashion system. The globalization, and often standardization, of fashion was already evident in the 1960s with the worldwide impact of denim jeans and casual T-shirts. By the 1970s, ethnic styles had appeared in both haute couture and street fashion. The 1980s saw the emergence of designers from countries as diverse as Japan, Hong Kong, New Zealand and Venezuela. By the start of the twenty-first century, a number of free trade agreements were in place and Western apparel manufacturers outsourced production to developing countries, creating concerns about proper care for the environment and labor conditions.

Constant social change also defined clothing preferences in the later twentieth century: modes of dressing might reflect identity politics, subcultural or ethnic identity. In the 1960s, African-Americans fighting for civil rights in the United States used African-inspired garments to symbolize unity. The sexual revolution spurred the appearance of items such as miniskirts and hotpants. Opposition to, and subsequent acceptance of, pants/trousers for women in the 1960s, and a limited designer trend incorporating skirts for men in the 2000s, framed a tendency toward unisex fashion. In the gay community, fashion served as a subtle code for identification but later radical drag added shock value to the mix. At the end of the twentieth century, gay styles often stood as the model of masculine elegance. Punk, goth, grunge and other music-based movements used fashion to express rebellion, and exerted a powerful influence on street styles and casual clothing; but it was the urban wear of American hip hop that represented the most successful story in the globalization of a music-based style.

The other major influence in late twentieth-century fashion was the media. Marshall McLuhan (1962) announced the future "Global (Electronic) Village" where time and space collapse allowing humans easy, fast communication. The fashion industry took advantage of new technologies affecting media—from television in the 1960s to the Internet in the 1990s—promoting styles and products targeting specific markets based on age, gender or lifestyle. E-commerce became a successful mode of retail when websites made retailer and designer brands and styles available to consumers globally. Movies, television and music were strong influences on the taste of the general public, from the hippie-inspired looks of the late 1960s to the impact of television shows such as *Sex and the City* in the early 2000s. From the work of 1960s avant-garde designers inspired by art, to the rise in the following decades of the art-to-wear movement and the historicism of 1990s postmodern styles, a debate ensued about the legitimacy of fashion as an art form. By the early twenty-first century, museums around the world welcomed fashion as a cultural artifact and attracted new patrons with retrospective exhibits for designers such as Giorgio Armani (2001), Elsa Schiaparelli (2003), Vivienne Westwood (2004) and Coco Chanel (2005).

THE 1960s

The 1960s were marked by political conflict and social change including the communist revolution in Cuba, political struggles in Ireland, increased tension in the Middle East, the Vietnam War and student protests from Paris to rural America. Television and other media around the world closely followed these struggles. This visibility, and increased travel, created the global awareness announced by McLuhan. The popularity of European peasant-style blouses and dresses, American patchwork, embroidered Indian tunics and Mexican wedding shirts translated into an eclectic mix of styles in Western fashion. Innovations also affected fashion: the invention of pantyhose (1959), combining stockings, garters and panties into one garment, made dressing simpler.

Paris continued to claim the title of world fashion capital by providing a balance between the elegant styles of early 1960s haute couture and the dynamism of avant-garde designers such as Paco Rabanne, Pierre Cardin and Yves Saint-Laurent. London, the "swinging city," provided fertile ground for the "youthquake" that originated in Carnaby Street with designers and fans of mod (modern) fashion. Miniskirts, go-go boots and hotpants spread from London to the rest of the world. Mary Quant, high priestess of mod and often quoted as the inventor of the miniskirt, used boldly colored and patterned fabrics. Twiggy, the first supermodel, embodied the boyish look associated with mod fashion. Austrian Rudi Gernreich, a former modern dancer, developed form-fitting swimwear lines and created a publicity firestorm with his topless bathing suit and "no-bra" looks. The American ready-to-wear industry ushered in a new "democratization of fashion," producing apparel and accessories easily afforded by the middle classes.

Broadcast television changed the world in the 1950s by initiating access to hours of visual information about popular culture and celebrities. In the 1960s, television popularized the "twist" dance craze and fashions that flattered it—slim, shift-style dresses and narrowly cut suits showed off hip movement, and pointed shoes accentuated the cigarette-snuffing foot twist. The appearance of the Beatles on the small screen in 1964 incited young people to emulate the mop-top hairstyles and collarless jackets worn by the Liverpool group. Television fascinated viewers with the exploration of space, perhaps the clearest symbol of the power struggle between the United States and the Soviet Union. Space shows such as *Star Trek* (1966–9) played an important part in the popularity of space age and futuristic merchandise. Space-age design crystallized in fashion in 1964 when André Courrèges showed his *Moon Girl* collection and Pierre Cardin launched his space-age line. Movies popularized several fashion items, particularly the bikini, featured in beach movies staring Annette Funicello and Frankie Avalon. Audrey Hepburn, admired for her elegant style on and off the silver screen, often wore designs by Hubert de Givenchy, the man behind the classic dresses in *Breakfast at Tiffany's* (1961).

American First Lady Jackie Kennedy became a world fashion influence with her boxy suits and trademark pillbox hat. Working in collaboration with Oleg Cassini, she developed her style based on solid colors in simple shapes. After her warm reception in Paris while wearing Cassini in 1961, American fashion stood in the international limelight. She widely influenced the fashions of American women.

Television and press coverage of protests against the Vietnam War, from 1964 onward, made the world aware of the hippies and their resistance to "the establishment," including its dress. Hippies embraced denim jeans, which symbolized solidarity with the working classes. Hippie style also incorporated a mix of long "granny" dresses, colorful psychedelic prints, ethnic elements and long hairstyles. Young people personalized clothing items with tie-dye, embroidery or patches, often with the peace sign or "flower power" motifs. Rock stars Jimi Hendrix, Carlos Santana and Janis Joplin represented the ultimate in hippie style. The aesthetic gained exposure through the Broadway musical *Hair* (1968) and the Woodstock music festival (1969).

Figure 42. Left: Dress modeled after Yves Saint-Laurent's famous Mondrian dress of 1965 (1970.23.01). Middle: Courrèges-inspired coat dress by Bugnand of New York, ca. 1965 (1991.15.33). Right: Dress by Emilio Pucci of printed silk jersey, late 1960s (1995.07.17). Historic Textile and Costume Collection, University of Rhode Island.

From the graphic, psychedelic-inspired prints of Italian designer Emilio Pucci to the op art (optical art) prints created by Ossie Clark in England, art was a powerful fashion influence.

Some clothing designers and manufacturers incorporated Andy Warhol's pop art images of ordinary objects such as the famous Campbell's soup can. The art of Piet Mondrian inspired a famous dress by Yves Saint-Laurent. Saint-Laurent also created narrow, no-waist, A-line silhouettes and other geometric shapes, while also experimenting with nontraditional materials including wood beads and raffia. Paco Rabanne used plastic discs, leather pieces and metal rings to make his innovative outfits.

The 1964 Civil Rights Act signaled the end of the fight for legislated racial equality in America, but hardly an end to social and political inequality. Restlessness in the American political environment was evident after the assassinations of President John F. Kennedy in 1963 and Dr. Martin Luther King, leader of the Civil Rights movement, in 1968. The Black Power movement adopted black berets, African garments such as dashikis and caftans, and Afro hairstyles as symbols of resistance.

Many women saw fashion as limiting choices and forcing them to comply with accepted images of femininity. The sexual revolution of the 1960s and 1970s, attributed partly to the legalization of contraceptives in several Western countries, relaxed social conventions and attitudes toward sex, and as a result toward some aspects of gendered fashion. Changes in women's attitudes toward fashion were influenced in part by Betty Friedan's *The Feminine Mystique*, the 1963 book credited with jump-starting the feminist movement. Both Yves Saint-Laurent and André Courrèges designed trouser suits for women; Saint-Laurent's androgynous tuxedo look, dubbed "le smoking," appealed to independent young women. In many places, trousers/pants for women were accepted by the early 1970s, but trouser-sporting females were also denied employment, service in public spaces or admittance to school. Women boldly adopted the use of body-revealing swimwear, fitted leotards and loose T-shirts.

A dramatic change in male fashion originated in Carnaby Street, London when young men incorporated color, bold patterns and decorative details such as frills and cravats into their attire; *Esquire* magazine called it the "peacock revolution." Although most of this extreme experimentation with fashion diminished after the

Figure 43. Nehru jacket. Spadea "boutique" pattern, 1968. Commercial Pattern Archive (1968.413.URI), Special Collections, University of Rhode Island Library.
The Nehru jacket, named after Prime Minister Nehru of India, featured a stand-up collar and shaped body. It was a short-lived fad of the late 1960s.

1960s, the freedom of style and sense of individuality developed during the period dominated mainstream Western fashion for the rest of the century.

THE 1970s

Movies, television and music continued influencing fashion in the 1970s. George Lucas's film *Star Wars* (1977) revived interest in futuristic

RUDI GERNREICH

SAMPLE:
BLACK

#8
FALL 1970

391

ALL
OTHER COLORS:

BLACK
OR
YELLOW
VINYL
HIP BELT

Figure 44. Drawing by Rudi Gernreich for #391—"Unisex5a," Fall 1970. Courtesy of the Fashion Institute of Design and Merchandising/FIDM Museum, Los Angeles, California. Photo credit: Christina Johnson. *Rudi Gernreich designed this ribbed body suit for his "Future People" statement.*

fashion, but that year's *Saturday Night Fever* became one of the decade's most influential movies by bringing disco dancing and clothing to the mainstream. Men around the world imitated John Travolta's look—bright shirts, pastel polyester suits, gold chains and platform shoes—while women wore tricot knit dresses and spandex tops similar to those in the film. American designer Halston incorporated disco fashion in designs

for halter tops, jumpsuits and other sportswear. Other trends influenced by movies included Diane Keaton's androgynous look for Woody Allen's *Annie Hall* (1977), and African-American styles in blaxploitation films.

"Glam" rock perfectly combined epic music, psychedelic experiences and a sense of playfulness to create outrageous fashion. Elton John's striking eyewear collection, Gary Glitter's shiny outfits and the costume characters created by David Bowie and Alice Cooper inspired fans. Punk rock, the music and cultural rebellion exported from London and New York to the rest of the world, was highly influential on street styles with its distressed and leather garments, body piercing, mohawk hairstyles and anarchist imagery. Designer Vivienne Westwood, the "queen of punk," closely associated with the musical group The Sex Pistols, integrated the anarchist spirit of punk subculture in deconstructed leather and vinyl fetish garments. She also explored historic influences ranging from seventeenth-century pirates to nineteenth-century Romantics. Bob Marley and other reggae musicians wore garments featuring red, green and yellow, the Jamaican flag colors. Reggae fans were recognized by their dreadlocks, crocheted tricolor caps and necklace medallions with maps of Africa.

Consumers responded to increasingly active and individualized lifestyles. Pants that flared at the bottom were popular. Along with the loose-fitting midi (calf-length) and maxi (ankle-length) skirts, young women wore body-revealing fitted items. Hotpants, worn with pantyhose and tank tops, were often paired with the platform shoes or clogs. Rules for men's fashion relaxed in comparison to the past. Men wore closely fitted garments and mixed colors freely. Choices included tight designer jeans, polo shirts, bomber jackets, trench coats, windbreaker jackets and leisure suits—with shirt-like jackets based on casual, western styles and often made in new polyester fabrics. T-shirts evolved into social statements and advertising tools, promoting ideas, brands and products. Unisex styling used such T-shirts with hip-hugger bell-bottom pants and wide belts, a style held over from the late 1960s. By

Figure 45. African Americans ca. 1974 in blaxploitation fashion. Photograph courtesy of Garth Taylor.

the late 1970s, children's casualwear displayed colorful logos and cartoon characters on T-shirts, jackets and midi and maxi skirts worn by girls. Designers explored a range of styles and materials: Sonia Rykiel created monochromatic "total look" knitwear ensembles, Laura Ashley worked with cotton florals and Betsey Johnson created bold print fashions. One of the biggest trends was "dressing for success," through which corporate employees met conservative business

YVES SAINT LAURENT   2727

Figure 46. Pantsuit by Yves Saint-Laurent. Vogue, 1972. Commercial Pattern Archive (1972.116.URI), Special Collections, University of Rhode Island Library.
Yves Saint-Laurent's trendsetting pantsuits of the 1960s became widely accepted by the early 1970s.

standards while still being fashionable. John T. Molloy, self-proclaimed as "America's first wardrobe engineer," wrote the influential *Dress for Success* books; one for men (1975) followed by a version for women (1977).

Rachel Carson's 1962 book *Silent Spring* drew attention to the increasing danger of the industrial abuse of nature. In the 1970s, the fashion industry responded by manufacturing with natural fabrics, developing fake furs and implementing stricter measures for the proper disposal of textile by-products. Some young people embraced environmentally responsible goods. Environmental consciousness prompted a variety of ethnically inspired styles. Japanese surface patterning, origami structures, and South American and Scandinavian motifs appeared in the work of the Japanese designer Kenzo. Other designers incorporated non-Western influences, including the American Mary McFadden, collector of ethnic and historic textiles, and the British Zandra Rhodes, known for exotic fabric designs. The Italian design team Missoni created elaborate knitwear designs using patterns ranging from op art to African imagery.

The market for haute couture had declined during the last part of the 1960s as the mass consumer turned to casual comfort. By the end of the 1970s, designers created ready-to-wear lines, licensed products and designed for mass merchants (e.g., Halston for J. C. Penney). The consumerist spirit of the following decade presented them with an ideal platform.

THE 1980s

The year 1982 marked the end of a recession in the United States and the start of Ronald Reagan's presidency. Reagan's domestic policy eased regulations for corporations, lowered taxes for the upper classes, and reduced government spending. His anticommunist foreign policy resulted in a strengthening of the military budget. He shared ideology with Margaret Thatcher, the only woman ever elected prime minister in Britain. Thatcher held office from 1979 to 1990, becoming the longest-serving British prime minister of the twentieth century.

American economic stability facilitated the worldwide boom of American casualwear designers including Donna Karan, Perry Ellis and Ralph Lauren. Calvin Klein marketed designer jeans at affordable prices and turned men's underwear into a fashion item worldwide. Denim products enjoyed popularity, particularly slashed, torn embroidered and decorated items in a variety

of finishes, including acid-wash. Hong Kong, Taiwan and South Korea emerged as powerful manufacturers of textile and apparel goods. Japan's economic growth facilitated the success of its designers: Yohji Yamamoto's collection of loose, asymmetrically shaped garments surprised Paris in 1981, Rei Kawakubo's Comme des Garçons label explored alternative body shapes and asexual imagery, and Issey Miyake experimented with garment shapes, pleating, textures and dyes, aiming for balance between Eastern and Western aesthetics.

A fitness craze brought Lycra® spandex workout clothes to casual streetwear and into designer fashion lines. In imitation of dance studio styles in the 1983 movie *Flashdance*, young women cut neckbands off sweatshirts for the off-the-shoulder look and wore other garments—bright leotards, leggings and bike shorts—that fitted the body tightly. Both men and women wore sweaters tied around the waist. Men wore athletic shoes with everything: jeans, formal pants and multipleated trousers. Baseball hats became a staple item among young men and, along with the popularity of jogging, running, aerobic dancing and other athletic activities, gave market share to sports brands such as Body Glove, Converse, Nike and Adidas. In general, branding for apparel emerged as an important feature of 1980s fashion. Underwear, for instance, surfaced as a fashion item when brands such as Calvin Klein and Joe Boxer aggressively promoted their products and prominently displayed their labels. The elastic waistband on men's underwear became a successful advertisement, since it often showed above men's pants worn at the hip. Also important was the trend of underwear as outerwear. Popularized by Madonna with the help of Jean-Paul Gaultier, corsets or bustiers, camisoles and brassiere tops sexualized casualwear.

The wealthy, once again, became fashion leaders. Lady Diana Spencer's wedding to Prince Charles in 1981 was a major influence on bridal fashion. Nancy Reagan was recognized as the most fashion-conscious first lady in America since Jackie Kennedy. Technology rapidly changed the lives of the affluent, with the rise of

Figure 47. Jordache/Sergio Valente jeans, 1980. Photograph courtesy of Sara Kennedy and family.
Popular designer jean labels included Calvin Klein and Gloria Vanderbilt, in addition to Jordache and Sergio Valente.

computers and high-tech gadgets. It also affected production of clothing, streamlining the process from concept to the consumer.

Yuppies, or young urban professionals, led trends in business attire, adopting double-breasted suits inspired by Italian designer Giorgio Armani's lean creations. Armani's business received a boost after Richard Gere wore his suits in the movie *American Gigolo* (1980). His innovative tailoring techniques were applied to mass manufacturing and the success of his ready-to-wear lines were also instrumental in the label's role as a fashion powerhouse into the twenty-first century.

The archetypal look of the 1980s was the broad padded shoulders and wide lapels of men's and women's "power suits." Female business suits epitomized the modern businesswoman's spirit—free to alternate between skirts and pants, and comfortable flats or high-heeled pumps. Preppies—affluent high school students—created their own dress for success with fine wool blazers, classic sweaters, formal trousers and brand-name loafers or boat shoes. Both yuppie and preppie males wore short, neatly groomed hair, a clear contrast to the mullet and rat-tail styles popular with rebellious male youths and their athlete and musician role models.

The 1980s has often being dubbed the "decade of the designer," due to increased activity in haute couture, and brand labeling on the outside of clothes. Experimental wearable art, street styles and deconstruction, once considered antifashion, appeared in many top designers' collections. Postmodern style combined influences from the past, non-Western elements, high fashion, street and popular culture trends. Haute couture designers enjoyed the freedom of postmodernism in a number of ways: Italian Franco Moschino used symbolism and surrealist imagery; Marc Jacobs merged classic cashmere and mohair, beaded jeans and incorporated hippie influences; and Christian Lacroix created asymmetric outfits in striking colors and prints. Even with this experimentation many designers also focused on classic looks, such as Thierry Mugler's well-constructed feminine power suits and Gianni Versace's embroidered, appliquéd and beaded evening gowns. Karl Lagerfeld, who became head designer at Chanel in 1983, reworked her classic styles. Several designers reinterpreted Dior's mid-century New Look, adding volume to skirts with bows, poufs and ribbons, and giving rigid support structures to bodices.

The powerful influence of Hollywood on fashion around the world continued. *Top Gun* (1985) popularized crewcut military hairstyles. Fine, custom-tailored business suits exemplified the philosophy that "greed is good" as touted in *Wall Street* (1987). American television programs

Figure 48. Chanel and Chanel-inspired suits, 1960s–1990s (2001.02.01, 2002.07.02, 96.06.02). Historic Textile and Costume Collection, University of Rhode Island.
The suit on the left from the 1970s is Chanel couture; the middle suit is a Chanel boutique style from the 1990s; the suit on the right is a 1960s knockoff of a classic Chanel suit.

Figure 49. Linda Evans. Nolan Miller's Dynasty TV Series Collection, 1984. Commercial Pattern Archive (1984.19.URI), Special Collections, University of Rhode Island Library.

Dallas (1978–91) and *Dynasty* (1981–9), set in Texas, displayed glamorous evening gowns and western attire. Designer jackets matched with white pants, pastel T-shirts and loafer shoes worn without socks, as seen in *Miami Vice* (1984–9), become widespread in men's fashion. Televised fashion shows and celebrity-obsessed programming turned Cindy Crawford, Linda Evangelista and others into fashion supermodels. MTV (Music Television, established 1981) presented fans with the perfect marriage between television, music and fashion: music videos allowed them to emulate the wardrobe of their favorite rock stars. Influential styles from musicians included Prince's colorful and revealing outfits, Boy George's feminized appearance with ethnically inspired dreadlocks and animal prints, and Cindy Lauper's artificially colored hair and layered jewelry. The torn clothes and deconstructed thrift store garments of punk rockers became fashionable in the streets. Their T-shirts sometimes displayed outrageous messages, matching the outlandish hairstyles, tattoos and body piercings often seen in this subculture. The urban breakdancers' (B-boys') style—baggy, low-riding pants, and sweatshirt and tracksuit over fitted gym wear—spread to global capitals and rural American settings.

Most of the oversized styles and bright colors of the 1980s diminished during the next decade, when fashion tended toward minimalism.

THE 1990s

The map of Europe changed dramatically at the end of the 1980s and beginning of the 1990s with several events including the fall of the Berlin Wall in 1989, the reunification of East and West Germany in 1990, the official dissolution of the Soviet Union in 1991 and the subsequent end of communism in most of Eastern Europe. Meanwhile, amid continued attempts at negotiating peace in the Middle East, the 1991 Gulf War increased tension between the United States and Iraq. The United States and the European Community led the world in a movement toward a global liberalized economy. In 1993 Canada, Mexico and the United States signed NAFTA (North America Free Trade Agreement). In 1995, the World Trade Organization was created to promote further trade agreements. Apparel makers in industrialized counties outsourced manufacturing to developing countries where lower wages were paid. So-called "sweatshops" often had poor working conditions. Ultimately, industrialized nations experienced an abrupt drop in domestic manufacturing.

Global communications were crucial as the world population reached 6 billion in 1999. Millions of Internet users had access to online magazines, store catalogs, designers' websites and fashion shows. Manufacturers and retailers customized, or "glocalized" their products for a variety of global markets. Among the most successful global retail enterprises were the American mass merchandising giant Wal-Mart and the Spanish specialty store Zara. Computer technology applied to retail merchandising allowed better pricing control and fast inventory replenishment. Computer-aided design (CAD) became extensively used in apparel product development. Computerized body scanning offered alternatives to improve fit and therefore customer satisfaction. Cyber and techno fashion styles, generally futuristic in nature, explored new materials and used fiber and finish innovations.

Clothing reflected personal taste as lifestyle retailing became a powerful marketing tool. Music styles continued to exert influence on worldwide fashion during the 1990s. Members of Seattle's grunge music scene, distinguished by mosh pit dancing, were clad in flannel shirts with loose camouflage cargo pants, denim jeans or corduroys. Female fans wore baby doll and vintage dresses, paired with fishnet stockings. A second-generation Chinese-American, Anna Sui, was the designer most associated with grunge. Those who were into the goth subculture wore black outfits with lace and netting details, often with black eyeliner, white makeup, hair extensions, spiked dog collars and platform shoes. Body modification—piercing, tattooing and scarification—spread beyond this subculture. Hip-hop musicians and producers successfully promoted their distinctly American urban fashion around the world, launching their own lines, such as Phat Farm by Russell Simmons in 1992 and Sean John by Sean "Puffy" Combs in 1998. Hip-hop fans embraced the oversized denim garments, T-shirts or sweaters, which often incorporated bold graffiti prints and brand logos. Other hip-hop styles included branded sneakers, Kangol caps, do-rags and large gold jewelry for men, while women wore close-fitting tops matched with short, form-revealing skirts or pants. Hip hop claimed Nike's Air Force One basketball shoe, in all its variations, providing Nike with a best-selling product without marketing costs; word of mouth maintained its exclusivity.

Another crucial consumer trend was the search for comfortable clothes. The "casual Friday" practice in business offices demonstrated victory for comfort over formality: classic polo shirts and khaki pants remained a staple. On college campuses, students further relaxed their style, incorporating shorts, easy-fitting tops and flip-flop sandals.

In 1994 the British actress Elizabeth Hurley wore a low-cut black Versace dress, held together by safety pins, to the premiere of one of Hugh Grant's movies. The dress gathered enough attention to skyrocket her career and further popularize the Versace design house. News of the tragic murder of Gianni Versace, however, shocked the fashion world in 1997. The Versace apparel empire moved into the twenty-first century under the leadership of Donatella Versace.

Minimalist tendencies in architecture, art and interior decoration also dominated fashion. Classic, simple styles in evening and formalwear dominated, with black the color of the decade; yet the fashion mix also incorporated non-Western dress, subcultural looks, street styles and historic influences in haute couture and casualwear collections. A postmodern tendency to appropriate and reinterpret religious and magical symbols in body art and jewelry also marked the 1990s. Deconstruction and the recycling of materials and entire garments was common among designers. Austrian Helmut Lang mixed

Figure 50. Emanuel Ungaro, Vogue, 1991. Commercial Pattern Archive (1991.16.URI), Special Collections, University of Rhode Island Library.
The minimalist shape is aided by the large shoulder pads so characteristic of the early 1990s.

expensive and cheap fabrics. In Belgium, Martin Margiela incorporated nontraditional materials such as plastic bags and duct tape. John Galliano's collections delved into historic periods such as ancient Egypt, the French Revolution and the Edwardian era while also exploring ethnic elements from a variety of countries including Russia, Scotland and Japan. Englishman Alexander McQueen incorporated a strong erotic sense in his rebellious postmodern look. The designs of Turkish-born Rifat Ozbek used Asian and New Age influences to create sophisticated, exotic items. Dolce & Gabbana, created by Domenico Dolce and Stefano Gabbana, started in 1982 and grew to international fame in the 1990s. Hispanic designers Oscar de la Renta and Carolina Herrera incorporated styles inspired by Caribbean dance music. Gucci and Prada, old Italian leather firms, reinvented themselves as fashion houses. American designers Tom Ford and Isaac Mizrahi achieved celebrity status and dabbled in television, film and theater. Tommy Hilfiger became an icon of urban casualwear based on hip-hop style through connections to the music industry. Brazil, a world leader in swimwear, received international coverage for Sao Paulo's fashion week, joining other non-traditional fashion centers such as Auckland, New Zealand and Vancouver, Canada. Designers and stylists promoted vintage fashion, turning secondhand and consignment stores into hot shopping venues around the world.

THE NEW MILLENNIUM

Terrorist attacks in the United States (2001), Madrid (2004) and London (2005) indicated that the world balance had changed, resulting in increased airport security and stricter immigration and visitor regulations. The United States responded to the attacks by removing the Taliban regime in Afghanistan in 2001 and allying with other nations to invade Iraq in 2003. American consumers demonstrated their patriotism by incorporating the American flag and other symbols into their wardrobes.

In 1999, adoption of the Euro as currency by several members of the European Union was designed to strengthen Europe's economy. The growth of China as an economic power accelerated apparel-manufacturing competition, with Latin American, Southeast Asian and Middle Eastern countries suffering as a result. Asian fashion stores such as Shanghai Tang flourished in large Western capitals while in Asia, Western styles became more prevalent. Fashion as a system had permeated the entire globe, with fashion shows in New Delhi and Shanghai. Fashion designers came from diverse backgrounds such as Cuban-born Narciso Rodriguez, who used Latin American influences in his tailored feminine lines, Lebanese Elie Saab, who utilized Middle Eastern influences in silk gowns with elaborate embroidery, and Chinese-American Vera Wang, famous for her wedding gowns. Adding to the potpourri were new young American designers such as Zac Posen, and designer partnerships such as Proenza Schouler and Heatherette. Prominent European enterprises in the new millennium included British designers such as Stella McCartney and Hussein Chalayan, and the Italian groups Diesel and Etro.

Technology and the media, and their relationships to celebrity culture grew as powerful forces in the fashion world. New devices such as MP3 music players, iPods and cellular phones entered the market and promptly became fashion accessories. In 2006, for instance, Levi Strauss announced the introduction of iPod-ready jeans. Developments in textiles continued with UV protection and specialized fabrics for sports performance. Digital design was used to create camouflage, algorithmic and fractal patterns. Apparel was successfully sold through E-commerce at online designer stores, retailer websites and magazines. Digital video disks (DVDs) replaced video cassettes, allowing customers to obtain detailed information about costume designs and products featured in movies and on television. Product placement became a successful marketing tool in video games. Characters such as Lara Croft from *Tomb Raider* (1996) became digital fashion icons. *Sex and the City* (1998–2004), perhaps the most fashion-oriented television show in recent memory, actively promoted designers such as Manolo Blahnik, Prada and Roberto Cavalli. Makeover television shows provided viewers with information about fashion, grooming and

Figure 51. Hip-hop group Adrenalyn Rush from Cleveland, OH. Courtesy of Charles Reed, Jr. *The musicians wear oversized jeans, T-shirts, sneakers and caps. Their prominent belt buckles reflect the trend for "bling."*

cosmetic surgery while reality programs showcased the design process as hopeful designers competed for prizes and exposure. Fashion choices of teenage pop singers, for example Britney Spears and Christina Aguilera, who exposed their tattooed and pierced midriffs, were emulated in the teen market. Surf, skate and extreme board sports influenced youth styles that incorporated destroyed denim, board shorts, sandals, caps and branded sunglasses. "Ghetto-fabulous fashion" grew out of hip hop and showcased expensive urban apparel, fur and conspicuous jewelry or "bling bling." Also popular in 2003–5 was the boho chic look, inspired by gypsy and bohemian clothing. Music and fashion were so closely related that musicians such as Gwen Stefani, Jennifer Lopez and Justin Timberlake turned their individual styles into business opportunities by creating clothing lines.

Influences were varied and fast-moving in the new fast fashion era. Jeans remained a trendy fashion item with treatments including stonewashing, distressing, discoloring and painting. Low-rise jeans, originally developed for the female market, were also worn by men. Sheer fabrics were part of a trend for revealing outfits that included backless dresses, spaghetti straps, camisoles, corset tops, fluffy miniskirts and hotpants with letters on the derrière. Retailers embraced the commercial appeal of the "metrosexual," a term applied to men willing to spend time and money on grooming, cosmetic products and apparel. British soccer player David Beckham was lauded as the poster boy for metrosexuals. Garment layering became a trendy practice when T-shirts and dress shirts were combined with hoodies, suit jackets, corduroy coats and velvet blazers. Flat-front trousers were predominant in businesswear and casualwear, while drawstring pants, cargo shorts and capri pants were also worn. Stylish casual footwear included fine leather sandals, designer rubber flip-flops and colorful bowling-inspired shoes.

Stiff competition ensued after the 2005 elimination of almost all quotas. China and India displaced late twentieth-century manufacturing centers like Mexico, Indonesia and Sri Lanka. Full digitization of the supply chain allowed manufacturers to manage, modify and customize products efficiently and quickly around the world. Customers regularly waited for sales, markdowns and clearances to obtain apparel at bargain prices, especially in America, resulting in a glut of product.

Awareness of the costs and benefits of apparel production in the social and environmental landscapes increased. Sectors of the fashion industry committed to the creation of "green" or environmentally responsible products and promotion of sustainable fashion styles. The impact of fair trade initiatives, aiming to educate consumers and empower small manufacturers, grew. Companies, including Nike, responded to pressure for corporate social responsibility concerning pollution and fair labor in apparel production. By the end of the twentieth century, fashion theory flourished as a research field. The power of appearance was recognized as a critical force in the construction of individual and social identities, including shaping subcultures and music movements, and in the struggles for racial, sexual and gender equality.

ANNOTATED GUIDE TO FURTHER READING FOR PART I

The quality of the literature on fashion history varies greatly. While some books are merely inaccurate, others romanticize the styles of the past, creating myths that are difficult to dispel. Enduring titles are based on research using *primary sources*, meaning original documents and artifacts. C. Willet and Phillis Cunnington, early collectors of women's fashionable dress in the United Kingdom, authored numerous authoritative books based on object study; these are available in many libraries and thus are widely cited.

Reprints of older "costume history" titles, some of which have stood the test of time, provide good surveys. François Boucher's *20,000 Years of Fashion,* first published in 1967, was expanded and reprinted in 1987. James Laver's *Costume and Fashion: A Concise History* (1969) has been revised, expanded and updated several times, most recently in 1995.

The cultural studies approach to fashion history involves more than a chronology of stylistic changes. Scholars from humanistic disciplines paved the way, providing new insights into how we understand fashion history (Taylor 2002). Beverly Lemire (1992; 1997), an economic historian, broke new ground by directing her attention to the consumption of fashion rather than its production. Christopher Breward's *Culture of Fashion* (1994) was the first survey to marry cultural studies to fashion history. Since then, Berg's *Dress, Body, Culture* series has published many books on the culture of fashion, drawing on a wide range of disciplines. *Clothing and Fashion*, a

three-volume encyclopedia edited by Valerie Steele, covers many aspects of the "new" fashion history. Among textbooks, Tortora and Eubanks' *Survey of Historic Costume* (2005), now in its fourth edition, is preferred because it synthesizes the latest research.

Fashion scholars often ignore menswear. David Kuchta's *The Three-Piece Suit and Modern Masculinity: England, 1550–1850* investigates the cultural origins and development of the man's suit. Farid Chenoune's *A History of Men's Fashion* (1993), a study restricted to the period 1760–1990, is an invaluable source.

For the study of twentieth-century dress, see Valerie Mendes and Amy de la Haye's profusely illustrated *20th-Century Fashion* and *Twentieth-Century American Fashion*, a collection of case studies edited by Linda Welters and Patricia Cunningham.

Several journals dedicated to fashion history publish peer-reviewed articles on fashion. These are *Costume*, the journal of the UK-based Costume Society; *Dress*, published by the Costume Society of America; and *Fashion Theory*. The journal *Textile History* occasionally includes fashion history articles.

Catalogs of museum costume exhibitions are a valuable guide to extant artifacts. While some consist mainly of illustrations, others are based on years of research by museum curators. *What Clothes Reveal: The Language of Clothes in Colonial and Federal America* (2002) draws on Linda Baumgarten's knowledge of the vast collection at Colonial Williamsburg. A few catalogs, groundbreaking for their time, have altered the way fashion history is taught; one example is *Suiting Everyone: The Democratization of Clothing in America* (Kidwell and Christman 1974), which was published to coincide with the Smithsonian Institution's celebration of the United States' bicentennial. Unfortunately, museum catalogs are printed in small runs and are not widely available.

PART II
*F*ashion Theory

ABBY LILLETHUN

Introduction

Fashion theory provides concepts used by scholars, people in the fashion business and other observers to understand, explain and predict fashion. Academic disciplines engaged in theorizing fashion include, but are not limited to, humanities (art and design history), social sciences (anthropology, area and ethnic studies, cultural studies, economics, geography, history, psychology and sociology), business (marketing, merchandising and retailing), and fashion programs, which are interdisciplinary by nature. Cultural critics and analysts also write theoretical pieces on fashion. Not only do observers from many fields currently examine fashion, but theoretical writing on fashion dates at least to 1575 (Johnson, Torntore and Eicher 2003). Therefore, the body of literature reflects diverse perspectives. Yet, only in recent years has fashion theory gained any degree of prominence. This is due to the increased number of museum exhibitions on fashion, broader awareness of fashion as a social process, more recognition of the personal, social and ecological implications of fashion, and the greater attention paid to fashion in academia as a result of fashion's role in globalization. This section is not a comprehensive examination of fashion theory, but introduces key fashion theories.

What is fashion theory? A theory consists of a conceptual network of propositions that explain an observable phenomenon. While fashion is an "observable phenomenon," at this time no comprehensive theory of fashion has been universally accepted. Instead, concepts and propositions

concerning fashion have been suggested from a variety of disciplinary perspectives. This condition in knowledge development is normal: as knowledge grows, the foundational theories in the field of study reconfigure to encompass new discoveries.

We understand fashion theory as inquiry into fundamental questions about fashion with the objectives of understanding, explaining and predicting fashion change. Among these questions are: What is fashion? What conditions cause or allow fashion to occur? Who has fashion? Does fashion have a purpose or fulfill a specific role in individual lives? In societies? What are the roles of individuals, groups and cultures in fashion? How is fashion disseminated? Obviously, the definition of fashion—the answer to "What is fashion?"—is key to any discussion of fashion. Theorists agree that fashion is inherently about "change" (Sapir 1931; Simmel 1904, 1957; Spencer 1966 [1879]).

DIRECTIONAL FLOWS

Specific cultural conditions observed by fashion theorists influence and shape their theoretical propositions. Perhaps a unifying fashion theory has not developed because the very place that fashion exists—within culture—transforms swiftly and continuously. For example, Thorstein Veblen, an economist and sociologist, wrote *The Theory of the Leisure Class* (1899) during unprecedented industrial expansion that resulted in a visible class of wealthy, powerful elites whose lifestyle contrasted sharply with those of lower socioeconomic status. Influenced by Marxist philosophy, Veblen critiqued this so-called "leisure class" for its "conspicuous consumption" and waste of goods, including dress (M. Carter 2003: 43). Soon, Georg Simmel (1904), a philosopher and sociologist, postulated that fashion occurs in stratified societies with the potential for social mobility (i.e., a person may move between strata), and theorized that lower-status groups emulated the fashions of adjacent higher-status groups. As lower-status groups appropriated their fashions, the higher-status groups would move on to new styles to differentiate themselves. This directional process of imitation (or conforming) and subsequent innovation of new styles (differentiation) forms the basis of the *trickle-down theory*; innovation disseminates from the elites down the status hierarchy.

In contrast, G. A. Field (1970) observed a reverse phenomenon, calling it the "status float phenomenon." By the mid-twentieth century, technology was transforming communication and many cultural attitudes shifted from past ones. These included the "youthquake," the sexual revolution, the struggle for civil rights and acknowledgement of cultural diversity. In this unstable atmosphere, affiliation with a subgroup or ideological cause found symbolic expression in appearance and was not necessarily associated with socioeconomic status. Mass culture and elites appropriated aesthetics developed within subgroups, but not the meaning originally attached to them. Inevitably, subgroups innovated new looks in order to maintain meaning and therefore uniqueness: they purposefully differentiated themselves from imitators. These innovations emerged outside the elites, and often from lower-status groups. Thus, Field's proposition is widely called the *trickle-up theory*, characterizing upward vertical flow in opposition to the trickle-down theory's downward vertical flow. Ted Polhemus, an anthropologist, called the process "bubble up." He found that in the late twentieth century, an "insatiable craving for authenticity"

motivated subgroups (goths, punks, etc.) to create their unique styles; authenticity also motivated people who copied their looks (1994: 7). (See extract 46 by Polhemus.)

C. W. King (1963) observed a horizontal flow of fashion change called the *trickle-across theory*, as styles emerged and disseminated simultaneously across each stratum. This happened as mass manufacturing produced at many quality levels and price points, and marketing increased consumer awareness of fashion change through promotion and advertising across media. These combined forces helped to accelerate fashion change. Fashion influentials of each subgroup, or stratum, led this fashion change process.

FIVE MODELS OF CYCLICAL CHANGE

In my comprehension of the fashion process, five models based on cyclical behavior are apparent. They assist in characterizing and understanding factors influencing fashion change. First, *historical continuity* plays a part in the development of fashion. In this model, new fashions logically develop from immediately preceding styles (Robinson 1975). The second is *shifting erogenous zones*. James Laver, an art and fashion historian and critic, wrote that "The erogenous zone is always shifting, and it is the business of fashion to pursue it, without ever catching up" ([1937]1973: 383). The idea is that part(s) of the body are considered erotic, but lose their allure over time and erotic value shifts to another body part. This model is easily recognized looking back in history: 1930s slinky, low-backed gowns followed the 1920s boyish, rectangular silhouette that exposed the leg.

The third model, the *pendulum swing*, describes the fashion process as swinging from one extreme to its antithesis in repetition. Once a style reaches full development, the pendulum moves toward an opposite or alternate aesthetic. For example, 1990s minimalism—an unadorned aesthetic with limited and subdued hues—gave way to multiple ornamentations and multiple bright colors by the following decade. Following this model, one could expect minimalism to return in the near future.

The fourth model observed in fashion is a *recurring wave* or *dynamic cycle*. Several researchers have investigated this concept, claiming that fashion is predictable due to a recurring wave of change. In investigations of skirts across time, researchers found that widths and lengths recur (Kroeber 1919); that skirts cycle from wide to narrow (Richardson and Kroeber 1940); and that shapes cycle from back fullness to tubular to a bell shape across thirty or more years (Young 1937). This model failed to explain fashion's cyclical nature after the 1960s due to increased variation across time (Lowe and Lowe 1982, 1984, 1985), and increasing speed within the fashion cycle (Weeden 1977).

The fifth model is widely known as *retro* or *vintage style*. The scholarly term is *historicism*, which describes the appearance of style elements from the historical past as themes or elements in contemporary fashion. Historicism is not the same as historical continuity, since it picks and chooses among all past forms of dress. An example is the reinterpretation of ruffs, which originated in the sixteenth century and reappeared in early nineteenth-century women's fashion.

The essayist Walter Benjamin observed modern fashion's historicism in his (unfinished) study of nineteenth-century Parisian shopping arcades (Benjamin 1999). His metaphor for fashion's leap into the past for elements used in new fashions was *tigersprung* (German for "tiger's leap"). With this term, Benjamin linked the wild tiger's energy and unpredictability to the modern fashion process (Lehmann 2000). His work has influenced many contemporary scholars writing about fashion (Evans 2003; Lehmann 2000; Wilson 2003, 2004).

SEEKING ORIGINS

The nineteenth century witnessed the development of disciplines seeking to explain human origins and behaviors. Anthropology emerged from the natural sciences to study humans and culture. Charles Darwin's *The Origin of Species* (1859) served as a springboard for postulating the development of human beings. From the perspective of *Social Darwinism*, humans and their cultures developed on a hierarchical evolutionary scale. "Primitive" people at the bottom of the scale, typically dark-skinned, were from tribal or colonized cultures. At the top were white, Western capitalists, the so-called "civilized" and superior race. The hierarchy also coded the value of dress and appearance practices. Of course, the West's styles of dress—tailored and sewn—were the pinnacle, while the dress of "primitive" people, such as hand-loomed lengths of cloth draped on the body, or garments of unprocessed fibers and grasses, was uncivilized.

Assignation of a hierarchy to cultures and their products affected early fashion theorizing in two ways. First, the assumption of an evolutionary hierarchy implied that the origin and function of dress might be discoverable. Several options were offered; perhaps humans adorned themselves to appropriate the power of an animal, or attract a mate, or for protection from nature, and so forth. We can only speculate. Second, the definition of fashion encompassed only Western, capitalist, socially mobile cultures: traditional and noncapitalist cultures could not meet the definitional standards, and so they did not have fashion.

STRUCTURALISM

A prominent research paradigm used in fashion and dress research is *structuralism*, a perspective used in sociology, anthropology, semiotics, marketing and other fields. With this approach, researchers systematically analyze relationships in order to discover and interpret meanings of cultural acts and products. Among the readings for the section, the extracts by Grant McCracken and Roland Barthes follow structuralism.

Sociology, a field that studies social groups and interaction, has contributed concepts that continue to resonate with contemporary fashion theorists working outside the confines of structuralism. Simmel observed two oppositional, yet critical, processes. First, that the psychological drive to imitate, or conform to the socially prescribed mode could be satisfied, and second, that differentiation offered individuals opportunities for respite from the monotony of conformity. Herbert Blumer noted that the fashion process occurs through *collective selection*, a group process of style selection that both responds to a desire to be in fashion and reflects the emerging taste, rather than through class differentiation (1969a: 282). According to Blumer, fashion has a social role of "enabling and aiding collective adjustment to and in a moving world of divergent possibilities" (289). It also functions to orient individuals toward the future and the modern social order (289–90). Simmel's and Blumer's concepts converge with Benjamin's understanding of fashion.

In "The Power of Fashion," sociologists Lang and Lang analyze relationships between the fashion system and consumers. They examine the promotion and adoption of the New Look after the Second World War, which resonated in fashion for many years. They also evaluate reported resistance to the style. The Langs account for taste change—from women's wartime tailored styles with broad shoulders to the new hourglass shape—from two influences: the visibility of the New Look before it was mass-produced, and the dual desire for novelty and conformity in the collective will.

Semiotics, the study of *signs* and what is *signified* (their meaning), is used to decode the underlying meaning of cultural products. Signs may be linguistic or another mode of communication, including dress (Bogatyrev 1976; Morgado 1993a; 1993b). Roland Barthes, a French intellectual, decoded fashion magazine images and texts using semiotics (1969). In "Written Clothing," Barthes dissects the interaction of clothing (the technological object) and representations of clothing (both iconic and verbal). Among Barthes's contributions to fashion theory are an emphasis on the process of meaning-making and recognition that a variety of meanings occur.

Grant McCracken, an anthropologist, is a marketing consultant whose blog[1] reflects his interest in contemporary consumer culture. In "The Fashion System" McCracken examines the three ways the fashion marketing system acts as an instrument of meaning-making in fashion products. McCracken emphasizes that the instability of the meanings of the West's cultural products lies in the West's social imperative for change and its tolerance of revisions and disruptions to norms. Contrasting Barthes, McCracken suggests that although clothing communicates, the process is not comparable to language since assigning, changing and understanding meanings of language and dress are not the same.

Blumer (1969b), who coined the term "symbolic interaction," argued that human society forms, through meaning, structures developed in interactions between and among individuals and groups. Susan Kaiser et al. (1991, 1995), proposed a symbolic interaction theory of fashion, emphasizing the ambivalence experienced by individuals in contemporary culture, the ambiguity of symbolic content (such as fashion items) and the negotiation process inherent in creating meaning. Symbolic interactionist Erving Goffman (1959) proposed *role theory*, explaining that, akin to theatrical roles, people perform social roles in everyday life, based on expectations for their roles.

NEW DISCIPLINARY APPROACHES

In the second half of the twentieth century, the *cultural turn* resulted in the development of new approaches to understanding culture (Jameson 1998). This shift toward meaning focuses on processes within culture, how people practice their culture, and the objects of culture. The historical development of the new approaches is complex, involving many cultural critics and scholars of the nineteenth and twentieth centuries. This section provides a succinct, "flash card" version of these developments to serve as background for the remaining readings.

Basic definitions of four key terms provide conceptual grounding. The first is *postmodernism,* which names both a condition of existence and the current historical era. Jean-François Lyotard, a French theorist, articulated postmodernity in the 1970s, explaining that a rupture, or gap, had occurred between modernity and the new era, *postmodernity* (1984 [1979]). Postmodernity is marked by an end to belief in meta-narratives and universal truths, history as an inevitable march toward progress, and science as absolute knowledge. It questions myths, the power of authority, and recognizes that cultural assumptions, such as bias, underlie all social interaction.

Second is *deconstruction,* which characterizes a philosophy. From 1966 through the early 1980s, Jacques Derrida developed deconstruction to aid literary criticism (2004 [1967]). Deconstruction requires attention to the omitted, forgotten or marginal in cultural constructions and understands hierarchies as self-defining and preserving social structures dependent upon oppositional or binary organization.

Third is *poststructuralism,* a research paradigm that moved away from structuralism to recognize cultural context as central to human action, and therefore to the production of meaning. Fred Davis (1985) suggested that clothing is encoded with meanings in cultural context. Thus, meanings change in the fashion process due to their instability within changing contexts.

Fourth is *cultural studies,* a research perspective with the objective of reforming society and its power structures. Practitioners emphasize individual everyday experiences, often using ethnographic methods. Notions used in cultural studies include *"the other"*—referring to a group or person that another group attempts to control, and to people who are not allowed to fit into a society; and *"performativity"*—referring to how meaning is created in discourse and its relationship to creating identity (Butler 1997). Michel Foucault's work on power and knowledge relationships is often cited in cultural studies (Rabinow and Rose 2003). Since people construct their appearance daily, and participate

in fashion, it is easy to understand fashion's appropriateness as research material for cultural studies.

The reading by Joanne Entwistle (2003) is from a cultural studies perspective that also references the work of Umberto Eco, a semiotician. Entwistle charges scholars to account for *embodied practices* when theorizing fashion. A sociologist, Entwistle focuses on the experiences of dress and dressing, including the roles of textiles and dress in mediating the body's relationships—as a *situated object*—to the social world. Entwistle develops an argument for increased attention to the interrelationships of social order, the body, its presentation and the experience of dress.

In "Re-Orienting Fashion," Niessen (2003) echoes the observation that Eurocentric assumptions and interests shaped the study of dress (Baizerman et al. 1993; Craik 1994). It follows that a Eurocentric paradigm also dominated the study of fashion. Niessen questions the assumptions that fashion is a Western phenomenon and that non-Western dress is not fashion. Pointing out that previous definitions of fashion privileged one societal form—Western hierarchical capitalism—Neissen prods fashion theorists to develop an inclusive fashion definition reflective of global fashion contexts. Research supporting this position includes observation of localized fashion processes in post-Mao China (Li 1998), and analysis of an incipient fashion system among eighteenth- and nineteenth-century northeastern fur traders and Native Americans (Cannon 1998).

The reading by Caroline Evans (2003), "Fashion at the Edge," hinges on the understanding that modernity is fragmented and fleeting, drawing on Benjamin. Charles Pierre Baudelaire, the nineteenth-century French poet and critic, influenced Benjamin. Baudelaire wrote about the sense of contingency experienced in commodity culture and modernity, using character types— *"flâneur"* and *"flânerie"*—who strolled Paris streets (Baudelaire 1964 [1863]). Evans argues that 1990s experimental fashion design captured the ambiguity, anxiety and gender instability of contemporary life. Fashion not only makes these conditions visible through textiles and designed artifacts, but it transforms the body and the psyche to cope with worldly environments. Invoking historical precedents of eighteenth- and nineteenth-century consumption, Evans examines fashion's use of *tigersprung* as a foil to illuminate contemporary anxiety.

SUMMARIZING REMARKS

This brief historiography of key fashion theories demonstrates a shift occurred in fashion theory after Veblen. Nineteenth-century writings often assumed a hierarchy of human cultures and directed attention to the origins of dress. Today, there is wide recognition of fashion's salience across the globalized world. Theorists grapple with the complex matrix of cultural forces acting on and within the fashion system in diverse cultures. We recognize that contemporary fashion reflects the contingent, changing nature of social worlds. We understand that meanings—subject to interpretation—are negotiated in social processes and coded into perceptions of fashion items. We acknowledge that the directional flow of fashion change is not unidirectional, but multiple. We know that the fashion process hinges on differentiation and conformity, allowing the individual to be expressive and to belong.

The definition of fashion has been called into question. Will an inclusive definition reflective of diverse social systems and evolving globalized context(s) emerge? "Where does fashion occur?" and "Who has it?" are open questions. Due to the cultural turn to interpretive research based on context and lived experience, contemporary fashion researchers have innumerable locales, individuals and contexts to analyze in the search for answers.

NOTE

1. McCracken's blog is "*This blog sits at the intersection of anthropology and economics*" <www.cultureby.com/>.

6

KURT LANG AND GLADYS ENGEL LANG

The Power of Fashion

From K. Lang and G. E. Lang (1961), "The Power of Fashion," in Collective Dynamics (New York: Thomas Y. Corwell), 466–71. Reprinted by permission of the authors.

Fashion is here treated as an elementary form of collective behavior, whose compelling power lies in the implicit judgment of an anonymous multitude. This view is questioned by persons who point to a well-organized industry which, through its advertising campaigns, foists on a gullible public what one critic called "the overwhelming flood of cultural sewage that is manufactured especially for the taste of the lowbrow and middlebrow" (Sargeant 1949: 102). There are, of course, fashion industries and formal communication systems which promote the products of these industries. In view of this, can one call the sway of fashion spontaneous?

It is a basic question whether public taste is first manufactured and then disseminated through organized channels and foisted upon the mass *or* whether changes in the moods and life conditions lead to irrational and widespread changes of taste even without promotion. To what extent the tastemakers merely cater to the changing whims of the great public and to what extent they manipulate changes which are thereafter legitimated by mass acceptance will be illustrated by reference to the "New Look."

THE NEW LOOK: AN EXAMPLE

The collective resistance to the New Look in 1947 is often cited as an example of the limits beyond which women will not be dictated to by fashion. Actually the natural history of the New Look provides a first-rate illustration of the compelling nature of fashion innovation.

THE FASHION IS PLANTED

The New Look involved two major changes in women's dress: the shape was to be radically altered, and the skirt noticeably lengthened. According to fashion publicists, after two decades of the "American Look," marked by slim hips, casual appearance, reasonably short skirts, etc., the female was to cloak herself in hourglass fashion: round shoulders (no more exaggerated padding), sucked-in wasp waist, and, most important, very long skirt.

This new round-shouldered, hourglass fashion, like other major style innovations, was planted. "Months ago," wrote *The New York Times* on September 7, 1947, "the Western world learned that skirts this autumn would be full and longer, hips padded, waists waspishly thin, shoulders daintily rounded..." Among the style planners or norm creators responsible were "a bunch of Paris and New York designers," the custom designers, like Christian Dior, Sophie Gimbel, and Hardy Amies. The first to adopt the New Look were the chic clientele of these designers. Thereafter the fashion received public legitimation by those who customarily are named best-dressed women by the style planners and the style communicators. It was legitimated also by royalty and Hollywood movie stars, who traditionally have acted as style leaders and thereby give something in the nature of official status to projected fashion innovations. For instance, Princess Elizabeth of England was reported to be ordering her wedding trousseau in calf-length skirts.

The New Look also had to be disseminated to a wider audience. A full-scale, well-organized publicity campaign aimed at familiarizing people everywhere with the New Look well ahead of the time dresses in the style were available for sale in stores catering to the general trade. First, there had to be pictures. Women not only had to hear about the New Look; they had also to see it. The first to wear a new fashion are not necessarily the members of the smart international set who order from the top couturiers. Mass fashions are "tested" by professional *modistes* who appear at racetracks, theaters, parties, and other public gatherings to display newly created apparel. *Vogue* and *Harper's Bazaar* featured the New Look, and by the time it reached other magazines of the fashion press—*Mademoiselle, Seventeen*, etc.—the New Look seemed familiar indeed.

Publicity and production must go hand in hand. Through their advance publicity, volume manufacturers, who had secured models from Paris, assured themselves of a demand for the new models. Newspaper ads for the smarter stores began to feature the change. *Women's Wear Daily*, the garment trade paper, began to talk of the new styling, and style consultants for the small shops and large department stores everywhere catering to mass taste began to order the new dresses.

In other words, the New Look was promoted and sold to the public through certain tested and well-organized channels. These networks of communication existed long before the New Look and would long survive it. Through them, the New Look was planted. The change in styling was the initial result of an idea germinated in the fashion industry and nourished by publicity and organization.

THE NEW LOOK MEETS RESISTANCE

How strong was collective opposition to the proposed change? Newspapers and magazines publicized the advent of the change, but it was dramatized even more by the isolated instances of organized resistance reported concurrently. College students protested to the New York Dress Institute. A rumor had it that the J. Arthur Rank Organization in England would continue to dress its film stars in short skirts. *Time* (September 1947) said: "The furor over the new fashions rose to a fine, shrill pitch. Across the land, women by the *hundreds* [sic]—and city editors too—flocked to the banners of resistance." Most publicized was the resistance of a group of women in Dallas, Texas, who demonstrated against the new style. According to one report (*Collier's*, October 11, 1947), thirteen hundred women in that city "formed the 'Little Below the Knee Club,' sworn to hold the hemline at that elevation…" Meanwhile a legislator in Georgia announced that he would soon introduce a bill banning long skirts. That summer of 1947 the polls showed that a majority of American women disliked the new styles—but would wear them anyway.

The most singular, and certainly the most drastic, effort to halt the New Look occurred in England. In September, 1947, the Labour government was reportedly considering a decree governing the length of women's skirts. The postwar period found Britain continuing some of its rationing restrictions to regulate the use of scarce materials and to fight the black market and inflation. Moreover, England was hoping to promote its export market and achieve a more favorable balance of trade. Behind the opposition to the fashion innovation was the legal force of government.

Here is a puzzle. Can Sir Stafford Cripps (or anyone else) prevent women's skirts being longer if Fashion decrees that they shall be? That the ruling [fashion's ruling for the New Look] is idiotic and anti-social at a time when we need to save every yard of material is obvious. Nor does anyone, outside the trade, want skirts longer. Men find short skirts more comely than the half-length style that flops around the woman's calf. Women find the short skirt much more comfortable and women's organizations in America and Paris are protesting against the dictatorship of Paris... Anyway, whatever the reason, I find no one bets on Sir Stafford winning this battle if he engages in it. You may plan peace and war, but women's clothes are like the weather—beyond the control of government. (Critic 1947: 225)

What resistance developed outside official government undoubtedly was not a matter of dwindling national dollar reserves. Nor was it a matter of taste or a deliberate effort to resist the crowd. An English girl summed up the dilemma common to women everywhere:

I know from daily contact with working girls who take a pride in their clothes, that they are thrown into a quandary. I heard one of them saying "I don't know whether to try to scrounge a lot of coupons [rationing] and sell off my clothes or just appear dowdy." (Letter to the Editor 1947: 270)

She went on to cite George Orwell's observation that fashions, by making working girls almost indistinguishable from the wealthy, were helping to break down class barriers. Might not the New Look, she asked, in this period of scarcity and hardship, again widen the gulf between the classes?

While there was some annoyance and concern over the command to change wardrobes and isolated, if well-publicized, instances of deliberate opposition, the New Look caught on and had a lasting effect on women's dress styles. If by the season of 1948, one year after the New Look was "sweeping the country," most skirts did not quite reach the decreed ten or eleven inches from the floor, they were nevertheless considerably nearer the floor than they had been for decades. Also gone were the huge padded, mannish shoulders which had so long seemed natural to women.

We have, then, to account for the success of the New Look by considering two aspects of fashion change: first, why women everywhere conform to a change and, second, why there is any change at all. Consideration of both may clarify what is meant by the "compelling nature of fashion."

THE COMPELLING NATURE OF FASHION

The fashion world plans and makes available clothes, and, where the major source of supply is ready-made, women must for practical reasons go along. Yet to follow a major change in fashion means for most women a complete turnover in wardrobe. Had women everywhere in 1947 simply replenished their current wardrobes, bought one new dress or one new suit, this would not have constituted a major turnover in fashion. If fashion were a mere caprice in what is available, the styles of yesteryear would not be altogether inappropriate after the change. For instance, when the sack dress, the trapeze, and the chemise were promoted in 1957, many women bought one of the new creations, but the older, more closely fitted dresses did not thereby seem inappropriate. It is unlikely that any, save the most modish, felt compelled to discard or alter entire wardrobes. Fashion induces a change in mass taste. The short skirt, which one season seems aesthetic and appropriate, comes to look ugly and out of place—somehow improper.

In this context, we are using taste to designate the subjective preference for which there are no objective standards. We are not concerned here with aesthetic judgment—that is, with the cultivation in the individual of a standard of beauty and truth which secures the gentleman, the scholar, and the aesthete from the influences of the vulgar. Fashion is a collective phenomenon and has an objective existence apart from any individual. It makes attractive what often seems outrageous and bizarre to the preceding generation as well as the next. The standard set by fashion is, according to Sapir (1931: 139–44), "accepted by average people with little demur and is not so much reconciled with taste as substituted for it." In the mass, most are "average," and taste becomes what fashion is all about. Taste implies a purely subjective judgment with which there is no arguing, but aesthetic judgment requires a certain consistency with aesthetic principles as well as an evaluation of the functional relevance of an object.

How the fashion process operates to produce a simultaneous change in the personal taste of individuals all over is well illustrated in this letter by an American returning in 1947 to the United States after a year abroad:

> At every airport where we stopped on the way back from China I started watching the women coming the other way. At Calcutta the first long skirt and unpadded shoulders looked like something out of a masquerade party. At the American installations in Frankfurt (also in Vienna) a lot of the newer arrivals were converted and were catching everyone's attention. At the airport in Shannon I had a long wait; I got into a conversation with a lady en route to Europe. She was from San Francisco, and told me that there they still hadn't been completely won over—just as many were wearing the long skirts as not. But as she flew East, she found that just about everybody in New York had gone in for the new styles and she was happy she wasn't staying or her wardrobe would have been dated. By the time I took the train from New York for home, my short skirts felt conspicuous and my shoulders seemed awfully wide! Two weeks now and I am letting down hems, trying to figure out which of all my China-made clothes can be salvaged, and going on a buying spree!

The operations of the bandwagon and the way in which it snowballs are well illustrated. When the first few fashion leaders adopt a new style, they identify themselves as members of an elite apart from the rest of the world. In this age of rapid communication, the news of their adoptions soon spreads and helps to make the new mode familiar. The first few to dress in it are objects of interest and excitement; they are different; strange. A few more follow, impelled to be *à la mode* by the need to assert their difference from those less fashionable. The bandwagon is gradually on and soon it begins to roll. In the end no one can afford to be different. The final blow comes when the woman standing aside appears ridiculous even to herself. "They" are no longer odd; she herself is. Popular taste, even one's own, has changed. But in the meantime the fashion innovators may already be striking out in new directions.

Thus, the collective change in taste—an objective trend—is dictated not by an organized fashion industry but by the nature of fashion itself. The essence of fashion lies in its caprice: the transitory shift in some trivial area toward novelty for the sake of novelty. Fashion, then, is a process by which the taste of a mass of people is collectively redefined.

7

ROLAND BARTHES

Written Clothing

From R. Barthes (1983 [1967]), "Written Clothing," in **The Fashion System** *(London: Jonathan Cape), 3–7. Reprinted by permission of The Random House Group Ltd. Translated by Matthew Ward and Richard Howard. Translation copyright © 1983 by Farrar, Strauss and Giroux, LLC. Reprinted by permission of Hill and Wang, a division of Farrar, Strauss and Giroux, LLC.*

A leather belt, with a rose stuck in it, worn above the waist, on a soft shetland dress.

I THE THREE GARMENTS

1.1 Image-Clothing and Written Clothing

I open a fashion magazine; I see that two different garments are being dealt with here. The first is the one presented to me as photographed or drawn—it is image-clothing. The second is the same garment, but described, transformed into language; this dress, photographed on the right, becomes on the left: *a leather belt, with a rose stuck in it, worn above the waist, on a soft shetland dress;* this is a written garment. In principle these two garments refer to the same reality (this dress worn on this day by this woman), and yet they do not have the same structure,[1] because they are not made of the same substances and because, consequently, these substances do not have the same relations with each other: in one the substances are forms, lines, surfaces, colors, and the relation is spatial; in the other, the substance is words, and the relation is, if not logical, at least syntactic; the first structure is plastic, the second verbal. Is this to say that each of these structures is indistinguishable from the general system from which it derives—image-clothing from photography, written clothing from language? Not at all: the Fashion photograph is not just any photograph, it bears little relation to the news photograph or to the snapshot, for example; it has its own units and rules; within photographic communication, it forms a specific language which no doubt has its own lexicon and syntax, its own banned or approved "turns of phrase."[2] Similarly, the structure of written clothing cannot be identified with the structure of a sentence; for if clothing coincided with discourse, changing a term in the discourse would suffice to alter, at the same time, the identity of the described clothing; but this is not the case; a magazine can state: "Wear shantung in summer" as easily as "Shantung goes with summer," without fundamentally affecting the information transmitted to its readership. Written clothing is carried by language, but also resists it, and is created by this interplay. So we are dealing with two original structures, albeit derived from more general systems, in the one case language, in the other the image.

1.2 Real Clothing

At the least we might suppose that these two garments recover a single identity at the level of the real garment they are supposed to represent, that the described dress and the photographed dress are united in the actual dress they both refer to. Equivalent, no doubt, but not identical; for just as between image-clothing and written clothing there is a difference in substances and relations, and thus a difference of structure, in the same way, from these two garments to the real one there is a transition to other substances and other relations; thus, the real garment forms a third structure, different from the first two, even if it serves them as model, or more exactly, even if the model which guides the information transmitted by the first two garments belongs to this third structure. We have seen that the units of image-clothing are located at the level of forms, those of written clothing at the level of words; as for the units of real clothing, they cannot exist at the level of language, for, as we know, language is not a tracing of reality;[3] nor can we locate them, although here the temptation is great, at the level of forms, for "seeing" a real garment, even under privileged conditions of presentation, cannot exhaust its reality, still less its structure; we never see more than part of a garment, a personal and circumstantial usage, a particular way of wearing it; in order to analyze the real garment in systematic terms, i.e., in terms sufficiently formal to account for all analogous garments, we should no doubt have to work our way back to the actions which governed its manufacture. In other words, given the plastic structure of image-clothing and the verbal structure of written clothing, the structure of real clothing can only be technological. The units of this structure can only be the various traces of the actions of manufacture, their materialized and accomplished goals: a seam is what has been sewn, the cut of a coat is what has been cut;[4] there is then a structure which is constituted at the level of substance and its transformations, not of its representations or significations; and here ethnology might provide relatively simple structural models.[5]

II SHIFTERS

1.3 Translation of Structures

There are, then, for any particular object (a dress, a tailored suit, a belt) three different structures, one technological, another iconic, the third verbal. These three structures do not have the same circulation pattern. The technological structure appears as a mother tongue of which the real garments derived from it are only instances of "speech." The two other structures (iconic and verbal) are also languages, "translated" from the mother tongue; they intervene as circulation relays between this mother tongue and its instances of "speech" (the real garments). In our society, the circulation of Fashion thus relies in large part on an activity of *transformation:* there is a transition (at least according to the order invoked by Fashion magazines) from the technological structure to the iconic and verbal structures. Yet this transition, as in all structures, can only be discontinuous: the real garment can only be *transformed* into "representation" by means of certain operators which we might call *shifters,* since they serve to transpose one structure into another, to pass, if you will, from one code to another code.[6]

1.4 The Three Shifters

Since we are dealing with three structures, we must have three kinds of shifters at our disposal: from the real to the image, from the real to language, and from the image to language. For the first translation, from the technological garment to the iconic garment, the principal shifter is the sewing pattern, whose (schematic) design analytically reproduces the stages of the garment's manufacture; to which should be added the processes, graphic or photographic, intended to reveal the technical substratum of a look or an "effect": accentuation of a movement, enlargement of a detail, angle of vision. For the second translation, from the technological garment to the written garment, the basic shifter is what might be called the sewing program or formula: it is generally a text quite apart from the literature of Fashion; its goal is to outline not what is but what is *going to be* done; the sewing program, moreover, is not given in the same kind of writing as the Fashion commentary;

it contains almost no nouns or adjectives, but mostly verbs and measurements.[7] As a shifter, it constitutes a transitional language, situated midway between the making of the garment and its being, between its origin and its form, its technology and its signification. We might be tempted to include within this basic shifter all Fashion terms of clearly technological origin (a *seam, a cut),* and to consider them as so many translators from the real to the spoken; but this would ignore the fact that the value of a word is not found in its origin but in its place in the language system; once these terms pass into a descriptive structure, they are simultaneously detached from their origin (what has been, at some point, sewn, cut) and their goal (to contribute to an assemblage, to stand out in an ensemble); in them the creative act is not perceptible, they no longer belong to the technological structure and we cannot consider them as *shifters.*[8] There remains a third translation, one which allows the transition from the iconic structure to the spoken structure, from the representation of the garment to its description. Since Fashion magazines take advantage of the ability to deliver *simultaneously* messages derived from these two structures—here a dress photographed, there the same dress described—they can take a notable shortcut by using elliptical *shifters:* these are no longer pattern drawings or the texts of the sewing pattern, but simply the anaphorics of language, given either at the maximum degree (*"this" tailored suit, "the" shetland dress*) or at degree zero (*"a rose stuck into a belt"*).[9] Thus, by the very fact that the three structures have well-defined translation-operators at their disposal, they remain perfectly distinct.

NOTES

1. "It would be preferable to have only objects to define and not words; but since so much is expected today from the word *structure,* we will assign it here the meaning it has in linguistics:

'an autonomous entity of internal dependencies'" (L. Hjelmslev, *Essays in Linguistics,* 1959*).*

2. We touch here on the paradox of photographic communication: being in principle purely analogical, the photograph can be defined as a *message without a code;* yet there is actually no photograph without signification. So we must postulate a photographic code which obviously operates only on a second level which we shall later call the level of connotation. ("Le message photographique," *Communications,* no. 1, 1961, pp. 127–38, and "La rhétorique de l'image," *Communications,* no. 4, 1964, pp. 40–51.) In the case of Fashion illustration, the *question* is simpler, since the *style* of a drawing refers to an openly cultural code.

3. A. Martinet, *Elements of General Linguistics, 1.6.*

4. Provided, of course, these terms are given in a technological context as, for example, in a program of manufacture; otherwise, these terms of technological origin have a different value.

5. For example, A. Leroi-Gourhan differentiates clothing that hangs straight with parallel edges, clothing which is cut and open, cut and closed, cut and double-breasted, etc. (*Milieu et techniques,* Paris, Albin-Michel, 1945, p. 208).

6. Jakobson reserves the term *shifter* for the elements intermediary between the code and the message (*Essais de linguistique générale,* Paris, Editions de Minuit, 1963, chap. 9). We have broadened the sense of the term here.

7. For example: "Place all the pieces on the lining you are cutting and baste. Baste a vertical fold three cm. wide on each side, one cm. from the ends of the shoulders." This is a transitive language.

8. We might regard the catalog garment as a shifter, since it is intended to effect an actual purchase by means of the relay of language. In fact, however, the catalog garment obeys the norms of Fashion description altogether: it seeks not so much to account for the garment as to persuade us that it is in Fashion.

9. Anaphora, according to L. Tesnières (*Eléments de syntaxe structurale,* Paris, Klincksieck, 1959, p. 85), is "a supplementary semantic connection without a corresponding structural one." There is no structural link between the demonstrative "this" and the photographed skirt, but rather, so to speak, a pure and simple collision of two structures.

GRANT McCRACKEN

The Fashion System

Originally published as G. McCracken (1986), "Culture and Consumption:
A Theoretical Account of the Structure and Movement of the Cultural Meaning
of Consumer Goods," in Journal of Consumer Research 13(1): 71–84.
See also G. McCracken (1988) Culture and Consumption
(Bloomington: Indiana University Press), 79–83.

Less frequently observed, studied, and understood as an instrument of meaning is the fashion system. Yet this system, too, serves as a means by which goods are systematically invested and divested of their meaningful properties. The fashion system is a somewhat more complicated instrument for meaning movement than advertising. In the case of advertising, movement is accomplished by the advertising agency and its effort to unhook meaning from a culturally constituted world and transfer it to a consumer good through the means of an advertisement. In the case of the fashion system, the process has more sources of meaning, agents of transfer, and media of communication. Some of this additional complexity can be captured by noting that the fashion world works in three distinct ways to transfer meaning to goods.

In one capacity, the fashion system performs a transfer of meaning from the culturally constituted world to consumer goods that is remarkably similar in character and effect to the transfer performed by advertising. In the medium of a magazine or newspaper, the same effort to conjoin aspects of the world and good is evident, and the same process of glimpsed similarity is sought. In this capacity, the fashion system takes new styles of clothing or home furnishings and associates them with established cultural categories and principles. Thus does meaning move from the culturally constituted world to the good. This is the simplest aspect of the meaning-delivery capacity of the fashion system and the one, ironically, that Barthes (1983) found so perplexing and difficult to render plain.

In a second capacity, the fashion system actually invents new cultural meanings in a modest way. This invention is undertaken by "opinion leaders" who help shape and refine existing cultural meaning, encouraging the reform of cultural categories and principles. These are "distant" opinion leaders: individuals who by virtue of birth, beauty, celebrity, or accomplishment, are held in high esteem. These groups and individuals are sources of meaning for those of lesser standing. It is suggested in fact that their innovation of meaning is prompted by the imitative appropriations of those of low standing (Simmel 1904). Classically, these high-standing groups are a conventional social elite: upper-upper and upper-lower classes. These are, for instance, the origins of the "preppie look" that has recently "trickled down" so widely and deeply. More recently, these groups are the unashamedly nouveau riche who now predominate on evening soap operas such as *Dallas* and *Dynasty* and who appear to have influenced the consumer and lifestyle habits of many North Americans.

Motion picture and popular music stars, revered for their status, their beauty, and sometimes their talent, are also the occupants of this relatively new group of opinion leaders. These groups all invent and deliver a species of meaning that is largely fashioned by the prevailing cultural coordinates established by cultural categories and cultural principles. These groups are also permeable to cultural innovations, changes in style, value, and attitude which they then pass along to the subordinate parties who imitate them.

In a third capacity, the fashion system engages not just in the invention of cultural meanings but also in its radical reform. Some part of the cultural meaning of Western industrial societies is subject to constant and thoroughgoing change. The radical instability of this meaning is due to the fact that Western societies are, in the language of Claude Lévi-Strauss (1966: 233–34), "hot societies." They willingly accept, indeed encourage, the radical changes that follow from deliberate human effort and the effect of anonymous social forces (Braudel 1973: 323; Fox and Lears 1983; McKendrick et al., 1982). As a result the cultural meaning of a "hot," Western, industrial, complex society is constantly undergoing systematic change. In contradistinction to virtually all ethnographic precedent, they live a world that is not only culturally constituted but also historically constituted. Indeed it does not exaggerate to say that hot societies demand this change and depend on it to drive certain economic, social, and cultural sectors of the Western world (cf. Barber and Loebel 1953; Fallers 1961). The fashion system serves as one of the conduits for capture and movement of this category of highly innovative meaning.

The groups responsible for this radical reform of meaning are usually those that exist at the margin of society: hippies, punks, or gays (Blumberg 1974; Field 1970; Meyersohn and Katz 1957). These groups invent a much more radical, innovative kind of meaning than their high-standing partners in diffusion leadership. Indeed all of them represent a departure from the culturally constituted conventions of modern North American society and all of them illustrate the peculiarly Western tendency to tolerate dramatic violations of cultural norms. Each of these groups generated new cultural meaning, if only through the negative process of violating cultural categories of age and status (hippies and punks) or gender (gays). Their redefinitions of these cultural categories and a number of attendant cultural principles then entered the cultural mainstream. Innovative groups of this sort become "meaning suppliers" even when they are devoted to overturning the established order (as were hippies) and even when they are determined not to allow their cultural inventions to be absorbed by the mainstream (as were punks, cf. Hebdige 1979; B. Martin 1981).

If the sources of meaning are more dynamic and numerous, so are the agents who gather this meaning up and accomplish its transfer to consumer goods. In the case of the fashion system, these agents exist in two main categories. The designers of products are one. These are sometimes the very conspicuous individuals who establish themselves in Paris or Milan as arbiters of clothing design and surround themselves when possible with a cult of personality. Architects and interior designers sometimes assume a roughly comparable stature and exert an equally international influence (Kron 1983). More often, these designers are less well known and indeed most are anonymous to all of those outside of their industry (Clark 1976; Meikle 1979; Pulos 1983). The designers of Detroit automobiles are a case in point here, as are the product developers of the furniture and appliance industries. The second category consists of fashion journalists and social observers. Fashion journalists may belong to print or firm media and may have a high profile or a low one. Social observers are sometimes journalists who study and document new social developments (e.g., Birnbach 1980; Fraser 1981; Wolfe 1970; York 1980), and sometimes they are academics who undertake a roughly similar inquiry from a somewhat different point of view (e.g., Barthes 1972; Lasch 1979). Market researchers are beginning to serve in this capacity as well (e.g., Naisbitt 1982; Mitchell 1983; and, possibly, Molloy 1977).

Both of these groups are responsible for meaning transfer. Normally, they establish a relatively equal division of labor. Journalists perform the first part of a two-part enterprise. They serve as gatekeepers of a sort, reviewing aesthetic, social, and cultural innovations as these first appear, judging some as important and others as trivial. They resemble in this respect the gatekeepers in the world of art (H. Becker 1982) and music (Hirsch 1972). It is their responsibility to observe, as best they can, the whirling mass of innovation and decide what is fad and what is fashion, what is ephemeral and what will endure. After they have completed their difficult and often mistaken process of winnowing, they engage in a process of dissemination with which they make their choices known.

It must be admitted that everyone in the diffusion chain (E. Rogers 1983) plays a gatekeeping role and helps to discourage or encourage the tastes of those who look to them for opinion leadership. Journalists are especially key in this process because they make their influence felt even before an innovation has passed to the "early adopters" (S. Baumgarten 1975; Meyersohn and Katz 1957; Polegato and Wall 1980).

When journalists have served to discriminate certain innovations from others, designers begin the task of drawing meaning into the mainstream and investing it in consumer goods. The designer differs from the advertising agency director insofar as he or she is transforming not just the symbolic properties of the consumer good but also its physical properties. Apart from fashion and trade shows through which only some potential consumers can be reached, the designer does not have a meaning-giving context like the advertisement into which he or she can insert the consumer good. Instead, the consumer good will leave the designer's hands and enter into any of the contexts the consumer chooses for it. So the designer must transform the object in such a way that the viewer/possessor can see that the object so designed, possesses certain cultural meaning. The object must leave the designer's hands with its new symbolic properties plainly displayed in its new physical properties.

The designer, like the director, depends upon the viewer/possessor to supply the final act of association. The designer depends on the viewer/possessor to effect the transfer of meaning from world to good. But there is a special difficulty here. Unlike the director, the designer does not have the highly managed, rhetorical circumstances of the advertisement to encourage and direct this transfer. The designer cannot inform the viewer/possessor of the qualities intended for the good. These must be self-evident to the viewer/possessor. The viewer/possessor must be able to supply the new meaning for him or her self. It is therefore necessary that this viewer/possessor have access to the same sources of information about new fashions in meaning as the designer. The viewer/possessor must have been given prior acquaintance with new meaning so that he or she can identify the cultural significance of the physical properties of the new object. In short, the designer relies on the journalist at the beginning and then again at the very end of the meaning-transfer process. The journalist supplies new meaning to the designer as well as to the recipient of the designer's work.

In short, both advertising and the fashion system are instruments for the transfer of meaning from the culturally and historically constituted world to consumer goods. They are two of the means by which meaning is invested in the "object code." It is thanks to them that the objects of our world carry such a richness, variety, and versatility of meaning and can serve us so variously in acts of self-definition and social communication.

9

JOANNE ENTWISTLE

The Dressed Body

From J. Entwistle (2003), "The Dressed Body," in M. Evans and E. Lee (eds.),
Real Bodies: A Sociological Introduction (New York: Palgrave), 133–50.
Reprinted by permission of the author.

Dress has an intimate relationship to the body. The materials we hang at the margins of our body—fabric, jewelry, paint or feathers—enjoy a close proximity to the flesh, outlining, emphasizing, obscuring or extending the body. Choosing leather as opposed to silk, Lycra as opposed to cotton, denim rather than wool, will affect the way the body looks and feels. Umberto Eco captures this close relationship between dress and the body very well when he describes wearing jeans, which are still too tight after losing some weight. He describes how the jeans feel on his body, how they pinch and restrict his movement, how they make him aware of the lower half of his body; indeed, how they come to constitute what he calls an "epidermic self-awareness" which he had not felt before:

> As a result, I lived in the knowledge that I had jeans on, whereas normally we live forgetting that we're wearing undershorts or trousers. I lived for my jeans and as a result I assumed an exterior behavior of one who wears jeans. In any case, I assumed a demeanor... Not only did the garment impose a demeanor on me; by focusing my attention on demeanor it obliged me to live towards the exterior world. (Eco 1986: 192–4)

Dress, then, forms part of our epidermis—it lies on the boundary between self and other. The fact that we do not normally develop epidermal self-awareness tells us a lot about our routine relationship to dress, that is, that it forms a second skin which is not usually an object of consciousness. Our consciousness of dress is heightened when something is out of place—when either our clothes do not fit us, as Eco describes, or they do not fit the situation, for example, when we find ourselves dressed too casually at a formal situation or too formally at a casual situation. In the first instance, when clothes do not fit us, the experience is very private and sensual—an experience of the body. To understand the relationship between dress and the body one must acknowledge the very private and very visceral nature of dress which imposes itself on our experience of the body, expressing or constraining it, making us aware of the girth of our waist as Eco describes, or the breadth of our shoulder blades, the length of our arms or legs, and so on. In the second instance, the experience is about the relationship of dress to the social world. It tells us that our dress does not only belong to our bodies but to the social world as well. Thus, any understanding of the dressed body must acknowledge the social nature of it—how it is shaped by techniques, attitudes, aesthetics and so on, which are socially and historically located.

Different techniques of dress produce different bodies. A body dressed in *Comme des Garçons* is very different to a body dressed in a Vivienne Westwood corset and skirt. Many Japanese designers have, in recent years, deconstructed the dressed body familiar to the West, draping it in garments of fluid cloth, which do not conform to the conventions of Western tailoring. In contrast, Westwood plays with the conventions of traditional English tailoring by exaggerating them. In each case, the dressed body takes on very different shapes and forms, largely as a result of the tailoring of the cloth: *Comme des Garçons* clothes often obscure the line of the body, creating space between the body and the fabric, while Westwood's tailoring exaggerates the body's lines and curves. Cloth, and the tailoring practices that shape it, give form to the body's presentation in culture. These practices are always historically and culturally located: the fact that we can locate a particular "Japanese" as opposed to "English" style of tailoring is indicative of this. Such labels are, of course, imaginary in the way that Benedict Anderson (1986) suggests—constructive of national communities rather than unproblematically reflecting them. Nevertheless these imaginary constructions, once in place, have an historical, political and cultural reality to them.

What I hope these examples suggest is that dress and the body exist in dialectic relationship to one another. Dress operates on the phenomenal body; it is a very crucial aspect of our everyday experience of embodiment, while the body is a dynamic field, which gives life and fullness to dress (Entwistle and Wilson 1998). Dress is a ubiquitous aspect of our social embodiment, a basic fact of all social life. The social world demands that we appear dressed and there are no examples of cultures that leave the body unadorned, although what constitutes "dress" varies from culture to culture. Bodies can be dressed in a variety of ways with fabric, body paint, tattoos, jewelry and makeup being some of the more common forms of adornment. Any number of these might be worn by bodies within a culture, since what is considered appropriate dress will vary according to the situation or occasion.

[...]

I want to explore this relationship between dress and the body, examining how each shapes the other. As a sociologist, I examine the dressed body as a *situated object* within the social world. The dressed body is not only a uniquely individual, private and sensual body, it is a social phenomenon too, since our understandings and techniques of dress and our relationship to cloth, are socially and historically constituted. However, I posit that the dressed body is a fleshy, phenomenological entity that is so much a part of our experience of the social world and so thoroughly embedded within the micro-dynamics of social order, as to be entirely taken for granted. While it would seem obvious that dress cannot be understood without reference to the body, and while the body has always and everywhere to be dressed, there has been a surprising lack of concrete analysis of the relationship between them. With the exception of anthropology, which has long investigated the body's centrality to culture, much social theory has ignored or repressed the body.

Classical social theory failed to acknowledge the significance of dress because it neglected the body and the things that bodies do (B. Turner 1984). The emergence of studies of the body in sociology, cultural studies and other fields in the last twenty years or so, would seem an obvious place to look for literature on dress and fashion, but this research has also tended not to examine dress. The reasons for this are not clear, but it may perhaps have something to do with a long-felt antipathy towards fashion and dress which are seen as frivolous and not worthy of serious, scholarly attention (see, for example, Veblen 1953). This absence of the dressed body within classic and modern social theory is surprising considering the importance of dress to bodily social order. Questions of social order are, in essence, questions of bodily order.

This point is made forcefully by Bryan Turner in his now classic study *The Body and Society* (1984). Turner's book helped to establish the "sociology of the body" and place it firmly on the academic map within contemporary social theory. He argues that all societies, however large or small, have to control, contain and manage bodies, and the mechanisms and techniques for coordinating bodies are many and varied. He argues, therefore, that much classic social theory, which has typically been concerned with social order, can be reframed to consider the body as the thing that is controlled and managed. He notes, in particular, the influence of French theorist Michel Foucault as crucial to the inauguration of sociology of the body.

[...]

Foucault (1977, 1978, 1980) argues that the institutions and disciplines of modernity were centrally concerned with the control and manipulation of bodies and his work therefore provides for a historical account that renders visible the body in social life. However, to date, there has been little consideration of the role played by techniques of dress in the establishment and maintenance of social order. Turner does not consider the role of dress in social order, nor does Foucault, although, as I will argue below, the latter's work can be utilized to analyze the dressed body.

There is another absence too in the literature on fashion and dress produced by history, cultural studies and other fields. This has, until relatively recently, paid little attention to the body, focusing instead on the communicative aspects of dress and adornment, sometimes adopting the rather abstract and disembodied linguistic model of structural linguistics (see, for example, Barthes 1985; Hebdige 1979; Lurie 1981) and examining the spectacular, creative and expressive aspects of dress rather than the mundane and routine part it plays in reproducing social order (for example, J. Clarke et al. 1992; Polhemus 1994).

Between these bodies of literature, between the theorists of the classical tradition and theorists of the body who tend to overlook fashion and dress as trivial, and those theorists of fashion and dress who have focused rather too much attention on the articles of clothing, the *dressed body* as a discursive and phenomenological field

vanishes and dress is disembodied. Either the body is thought to be self-evidently dressed (and therefore beyond discussion) or the clothes are assumed to stand up on their own, possibly even speaking for themselves without the aid of the body. And yet, the importance of the body to dress is such that encounters with dress, divorced from the body, are strangely alienating. Wilson (1985) grasps this when she describes the unease one feels in the presence of mannequins in the costume museum and, likewise, the clothes of dead relatives are often the most poignant of objects left behind, particularly when the shape of the arm or the imprint of the foot is still visible. These encounters with clothes, haunted by the bodies of the dead, point to the ways in which we "normally" experience dress as alive and "fleshy": once removed from the body, dress lacks fullness and seems strange, almost alien, and all the more poignant to us if we can remember the person who once breathed life into the fabric.

[...]

I therefore want to flesh out some ways of thinking about the dressed body, which capture the dynamic relationship between body and dress—in other words, an account that tries to embody dress. In doing so, I am arguing for ways of thinking about the dressed body which bridge the gap between theories of the body, which often overlook dress, and theories of fashion and dress, which too frequently leave out the body. I want to explore a number of ways of thinking through the body in culture and I suggest how these may be extended to the analysis of dress. I discuss the work of a number of theorists whose work sheds some light on the relationship between the body and dress. In most cases, these theorists have not recognized the role of dress but I want to draw out the implications of their analysis for understanding the dressed body. However, I hope to avoid giving an overly theoretical and abstract discussion by illustrating these theories through a number of examples, some of them drawn from my own research, as well as that of others.

THE TWO BODIES

As I have already suggested, the body is both an intimate and social object: intimate in that, as Fred Davis (1992) puts it, it comes "to serve as a kind of visual metaphor for identity"; social in that it is structured by social forces and subject to social and moral pressures. It is no surprise to note, therefore, that the body's margins and boundaries are rich in symbolic meaning and the focal point of cultural and individual anxieties. The body, as we know, is subject to moral pronouncements and social regulations from the macro to the micro level. As Foucault (1977, 1978, 1980) argues, Church, state and other modern institutions, such as prisons, hospitals and family, seek to control and coordinate bodies, rendering them meaningful and productive in the process. Other aesthetic and moral practices, such as tailoring and the fashion system, also operate on the body, coordinating, managing bodies and imposing ways of being on the body that come to constitute the common sense of our everyday embodiment. Since all cultures "dress" the body in some way or another, it is therefore no surprise either to find individuals concerned with what to hang at the body's margins. Thus, as the historian and theorist Mikhail Bakhtin (1984) and the anthropologist Mary Douglas (1973, 1984) have demonstrated, the body's physiological properties and boundaries are a rich repository of cultural meaning. The boundaries of the body are potentially dangerous since they are "leaky"—the body is semipermeable, open and therefore must be managed by culture.

Douglas (1973, 1984) has provided a most compelling account of what she calls the "two bodies" which constitute the totality of our experience of embodiment—the physical body (the biological, individual body) and the social body (the body demanded by our culture). The latter gives meaning to the former, shaping our understandings of our embodiment. She summarizes the relationship between them in *Natural Symbols*:

The social body constrains the way the physical body is perceived. The physical experience of the body, always modified by the social categories through which it is known, sustains a particular view of society. There is a continual exchange of meanings between the two kinds of bodily experience so that each reinforces the categories of the other. (1973: 93)

In other words, our experience of embodiment is thus always mediated by the culture we live in. According to Douglas, the body is a highly restricted medium of expression that expresses the social pressure brought to bear on it. Our ways of being in the body are crucially shaped by the social practices of our culture. Thus, the social situation imposes itself upon the body and constrains it to act in particular ways. Indeed, the body becomes a symbol of the situation. Douglas gives the example of laughing to illustrate this. Laughter is a physiological experience, which starts in the face but can infuse the entire body. Douglas asks, "What is being communicated?" by laughter and says, in answer, "Information from the social system" (Douglas 1979: 87). To put it another way, she is arguing that the social situation determines the degree to which the body can laugh: the looser the social constraints, the freer the body is to laugh out loud. In this way, the body and its functions and boundaries symbolically articulate the concerns of the particular group in which it is found and, indeed, become a symbol of the situation: the social imprints itself onto the body in such a way that the individual body symbolically expresses that situation. Groups that are worried about threats to their cultural or national boundaries might articulate this fear through rituals around the body, particularly pollution rituals and ideas about purity (Douglas 1984). These rituals have a strong moral component to them. If we follow them, we demonstrate ourselves to be respectful citizens of our culture, if we fail to meet them, we risk censure, criticism, condemnation or exclusion.

In the work of the sociologist Erving Goffman (1971, 1972), the moral dimension of embodiment is brought to the fore. For Goffman, as for Douglas, the body is both the property of the individual and the social world: it is the vehicle of identity but this identity has to be "managed" in terms of the definitions of the social situation which impose particular ways of being on the body. Thus, the individual feels a social and moral imperative to perform their identity in particular ways and this includes learning appropriate ways of dressing. Learning to keep our clothes on while in public is something parents have to enforce upon unruly young children who are so fond of taking them off, especially if there is an audience. Preschool toddlers can get away with stripping in public, but as they approach school age, parents may become anxious to ensure that children learn shame and do not risk ridicule in public by stripping off at school. Obvious though this seems, it is a taken-for-granted aspect of social life that illustrates the centrality of dress to our experiences of embodiment and to the moral order of the social world. Like so much bodily behavior, codes of dress come to be taken for granted and are routinely and unreflexively employed, although some occasions, generally formal ones (like weddings and funerals) set tighter constraints around the body, and lend themselves to more conscious reflection on dress. I will return to this point below.

Dress is the way in which individuals learn to live in their bodies and feel at home in them. Wearing the right clothes and looking our best, we feel at ease with our body, and the opposite is true also: turning up for a situation inappropriately dressed, we feel ill at ease in our bodies, out of place and vulnerable. Dress is, therefore, a fundamentally moral phenomenon. Goffman's work thus adds to Douglas's account of the "two bodies" by bringing actual bodily practices into the frame, describing how individuals manage their bodies in concrete settings—on the street, in bars and restaurants, asylums and hospitals.

Douglas and Goffman do not talk in detail about dress in their analysis of bodily practices, but their ideas can be extended to the interpretation of dress and adornment. Goffman's ideas can be extended to discussion of the ways in which dress is routinely attended to as part of the "presentation of self in everyday life." Most situations, even the most informal, have a code of dress and these impose particular ways of being on bodies in such a way as to have a social and moral imperative to them. Quentin Bell gives the example of a five-day-old beard, which could not be worn to the theater without censure and disapproval "exactly comparable to that occasioned by dishonorable conduct" (Bell 1976: 18–19). Indeed, clothes are often spoken of in moral terms, using words like "faultless," "good," "correct." Few are immune to this social pressure and most people are embarrassed by certain mistakes of dress, such as finding one's flies undone or discovering a stain on a jacket.

However, the embarrassment of such mistakes of dress is not simply that of a personal faux pas, but the shame of failing to meet the standards required by the moral order of the social space. When we talk of someone's "slip showing" we are, according to Wilson, speaking of something "more than slight sartorial sloppiness—the exposure of something much more profoundly ambiguous and disturbing ... the naked body underneath the clothes" (Wilson 1985: 8), and such nakedness is closely associated with our feelings of shame. A commonly cited dream, for many people, is the experience of suddenly finding oneself naked in a public place: dress, or the lack of it in this case, serves as a metaphor for feelings of shame, embarrassment and vulnerability in our culture as well as indicating the way in which the moral order demands that the body be covered in some way. These examples illustrate the way in which dress is part of the micro-order of social interaction and intimately connected to our (rather fragile) sense of self, which is, in turn, threatened if we fail to conform to the standards governing a particular social situation.

Thus, as Bell puts it, "our clothes are too much a part of us for most of us to be entirely indifferent to their condition: it is as though the fabric were indeed a natural extension of the body, or even of the soul" (Bell 1976: 19). Thus, in the presentation of self in social interaction, ideas of embarrassment and stigma play a crucial role and are managed, in part, through dress.

If we extend Douglas's analysis we can understand dress as expressive of the concerns of the particular cultural milieu and social situation in which it is found. Dress conveys information about a situation, providing what Douglas calls "feedback" about that situation. Formal events, such as weddings, funerals and job interviews, impose themselves more forcefully on the body, making more demands of it than do informal ones and this generally translates into a more highly regulated body in terms of dress. At a wedding one must not wear white unless one is the bride and it would be inappropriate to dress in jogging pants or jeans to a job interview. Such rules are relaxed in more informal situations, although they are not without any rules. Informal situations, such as a party, require a casual appearance, and not being dressed in clothing that is in keeping can generate embarrassment. For example, in the film, *Bridget Jones's Diary*, the central character, Bridget Jones, turns up for a party she thinks is on the theme "tarts and vicars," dressed in a skimpy bunny-girl outfit, only to find out that this theme has been dropped and everyone is in regular clothes. Her embarrassment is shared by other party members and made worse by the fact that she is dressed in a sexually provocative way. What these examples highlight is that the dress we wear in different situations is to some extent governed by the codes of that situation, to such an extent that, as Douglas suggests, the dressed body can symbolize the rules of each.

Let me illustrate Douglas's point with my own research on career women. In my analysis of the dress practices of career women, this contrast between formal and informal situations and the way the body articulates these implicit rules of such situations, becomes very apparent. The women I interviewed all spoke of two different bodies, one appropriate to work, the other to home. These two bodies were very much defined in terms of a sharp distinction between tailored or structured dress worn to work and untailored or unstructured dress at home. The dressed body at work, described by my respondents, was a public body, dressed for the formal conditions of the professional workplace. This formal body was more tightly constrained in terms of its visual appearance, its contours firmly demarcated by tailored clothing, especially by the tailored jacket which marks a clear boundary around the body in much the same way as a man's suit jacket does. I have argued elsewhere (Entwistle 1997, 2000) that this structured dress gives visible form to the professional woman, marking her out as a businesswoman, lawyer, and manager, as opposed to a secretary or other clerical worker. Thus, the sharp skirt or trouser suit articulates a very particular kind of body: one that is feminine *and* professional at the same time. Such a public body is a relatively recent historical invention since only recently have women become visible as professional women. This is not to say that women had never before been seen in tailored clothing. The appearance of tailored dress for the professional woman in the 1970s and 1980s can be compared to the first fashions in tailored dress worn by women at the end of the nineteenth century and early twentieth century. This dress reflected the increasing visibility of women in public in the late Victorian era, as sportswomen in riding garb or on bicycles and, later, as clerks and secretaries in offices. These ancestors of the career woman adopted tailored jackets and waistcoats, mannish hats and neckties similar to those worn by men at the time. It marked a new fashion for women, adapted to meet newly expanding opportunities for women to appear in public. Similarly, in the late 1970s and early 1980s, the growth of professional and businesswomen in relatively male-dominated occupations and spheres of work required a new way of dressing for increasing visibility at work as professionals. This resulted in the adaptation of the male business suit, known as the "power suit," because of its associations with a new breed of career-orientated and increasingly powerful women in the professions, powerful symbolically, and to some extent, in real economic terms too.

This particular female, dressed body was articulated in a number of sites: in new self-help manuals on how to "dress for success" and by a relatively new group of "experts" or dress consultants who gave advice on how to "dress for success." This female body was also articulated in the design and manufacture of dress for working women, most notably by designers such as Donna Karan, Georgio Armani, as well as by retailers such as Jigsaw and Next during the 1980s, and she figured in a whole range of representations in magazines (*Cosmopolitan*), newspapers, film (*Working Girl*, 1988) and television (*Thirtysomething*). The tailored, female body, found in increasing numbers since the 1980s, thus constituted a new kind of public body which took shape against the backdrop of very particular social, economic and political circumstances.

In contrast to the tailored body at work, the professional women I spoke to described a very different body at home. This was a body dressed not for *visibility* in sharp suits in clear, tailored lines but for *comfort* in jeans, jogging pants and T-shirts. This dressed body, unlike the professionally dressed body, was defined in terms of unstructured clothing, loose as opposed to tailored.

To return to Douglas's notion of the body as symbolic of the social situation, it would seem, from these examples, that the body in the formal situation at work and the informality of the home becomes a symbol of the implicit "rules" or norms of the situation. The formal conditions of work require a formality in the body and set tighter constraints around it. The body at work, then, is a more formal, highly structured body and sharply outlined in tailored dress. At home, bodily constraints are loosened and this quite literally is expressed in terms of "loose" clothing, such as jeans and T-shirts, designed for comfort and movement. In this way, we can see how fabric gives form to the body, producing it as formal or informal, tailored or casual.

FABRIC AND EMBODIMENT

As this example illustrates, the cut and shape of cloth, and the overall practices of tailoring, constitute an important part of the social and historical context of the dressed body. These practices frame the meanings given to cloth and mediate the relationship between dress and the body. As Christopher Breward (1999) has argued, the introduction of new techniques in tailoring from the 1820s, such as the tape measure and developing standardization in measuring and cutting techniques, can be correlated very closely to emerging ideas about the fashionable male and, to a lesser extent and a little later perhaps, to emerging ideas about the female body in public. Tailoring techniques articulate cultural attitudes to the body which are historically and culturally specific and which have a moral imperative to them, since any practice that works so closely on the body touches on questions of morality.

I want to say a little more about the relationship between fabric and embodiment and how these relate to one another to constitute part of our experience and understanding of embodiment. Relatively recent developments in fabric production can be analyzed in relation to ideas and ideals of the body. Let me illustrate with some examples. Our relationship to fabric has a historical dimension to it. If we examine evidence as to fabric fetishism, it would seem that different fabrics have been endowed with erotic content. The early twentieth-century psychoanalyst William Sketel (1930) documented some rare examples of female fetishism, many of which focused on fabrics such as silk and satin. For these women, the sensual properties of silk were the focus of intense sexual pleasure, leading one young woman, a silk weaver's daughter, to steal silk from shops. However, as Valerie Steele (1996) has noted in her analysis of fetishism, the "soft" fabrics like silk, satin and also fur, popularly fetishized in the nineteenth and early twentieth century, have been supplanted by the emergence of new technologies for the production of "hard" fabrics in recent years, such as leather, PVC and rubber. Today's fetishists are more likely to focus on plastic, PVC, rubber or leather than satin or fur. The erotic content of these softer fabrics has not, of course, been emptied out, since lingerie, often the focus of fetishistic desires, is still largely made from soft fabrics like silk. However, there are few documented cases of silk or satin fetishists today: fetishists are more likely to eroticize the feeling and smell of rubber or leather. This would seem to suggest that the eroticism of fabric and the relationship of fabric to the sexual and sensual body, is in part historically constituted as well as culturally variable. In other words, our understandings of dress and the relationship of fabric to the body, are the products of our time.

New technologies of fabric production are also altering other relationships between cloth and the body and are indicative of the dynamic relationship between the dressed body and broader social and cultural developments. For example, Lycra has the ability to mold the body in such a way as to promote a body that looks fit, lean and muscular, enabling the production of a more streamlined body. Initially used in sportswear, Lycra has become so popular that it is now used in a wide range of garment production. It suggests how bodily matters, such as comfort, flexibility and movement, are important aspects of the modern dressed body, as is the aesthetic concern to look fit and toned. Compared to the dressed bodies of the nineteenth and early twentieth century, the contemporary body dressed in Lycra is an altogether different body. In the realm of sportswear, new intelligent fabrics are utilized to produce bodies that look leaner and more lithe and have helped to promote new body aesthetics. Similarly, the "fast skins" worn by the Australian swimmers at the last [2000] Olympic games promoted a new kind of swimming body, one that provoked considerable controversy as to whether or not such a totally encasing suit of special fabric constituted inappropriate technology or apparatus. It also changed the image of the swimming body, which is conventionally dressed in the tiniest piece of fabric, in such a way as to threaten understandings of the Australian body, so closely associated with sport, and especially

with the image of the swimmer. Fabric then, in its close proximity to the body, carries enormous social, cultural, political and moral weight. It is closely bound up with individual anxieties and broader social and historical concerns about the regulation of bodies in social space.

If fabric can be said to constitute a "technology," then the work of anthropologist Marcel Mauss (1973) is pertinent here, for he describes how the physical body is shaped by culture when he elaborates on mundane "techniques of the body." Mauss's work has some potential for understanding the situated nature of the dressed body. The techniques he outlines are not "natural" but the product of particular ways of being in the body, which are embedded within culture, and his examples also point to the ways in which these are gendered. Ways of walking, moving, making a fist, and so on, are different for men and women because, in the making of "masculine" and "feminine," culture inscribes the bodies of men and women with different physical capacities. Mauss's "techniques of the body" has obvious application to dress and the way in which dress modifies the body, embellishing it and inflecting it with meanings, which, in the first instance, are gendered. Although he says little about dress, he does note how women learn to walk in high heels, which would be difficult and uncomfortable for men who are generally unaccustomed to such shoes. Mauss's idea of "techniques of the body" is therefore useful for understanding how dress works on the body, requiring particular forms of knowledge, skills and producing various sorts of body movement which gender the body in the process.

Haug et al. (1987) provide ample evidence of the ways in which femininity is reproduced through various techniques, bodily and sartorial. They argue that the female body and its ways of being and adorning are the product of particular discourses of the body, which are inherently gendered. Take for example the fact that women learn to pluck their eyebrows while men shave their faces; both these techniques are far from "natural" (that is, there is no reason why men and women have to do either) and thus point to the cultural meanings and practices surrounding the male and female body. Other techniques include the various skills required to apply makeup or style one's hair, all of which are gendered, as are various other techniques of dress such as knotting a tie or walking in short or tight skirts. All of these have to be learned, but the chances of one learning one or other technique is largely dependent upon our gender.

This argument that techniques of the body are closely bound up with the reproduction of gender is taken much further in the work of Judith Butler (1990, 1993). Butler's notion of gender performativity argues that it is in, and through, techniques of the body that sex/gender is reproduced. In other words, there is no prior "natural" sex, only performances of male and female that are always cultural. In this way, as previous chapters [*Real Bodies*] have explained using examples other than dress, according to Butler, sex is the product of cultural inscriptions and discourses that constantly call upon us to act as "masculine" or "feminine" through techniques and strategies of the body/dress. Drag artists draw attention to the artificiality of such codes by adopting the dress of the opposite "sex," many of them successfully "passing" as the opposite sex, but if all such acts of the body are "unnatural," that is, in no way determined by some essential qualities of our "sex," then we are all wearing "drag."

DRESS, SOCIAL STRUCTURES AND BODILY ORDER

Butler draws much inspiration for her analysis of performativity from the work of Foucault. Foucault, as argued earlier, has been very influential in demonstrating the social significance of the body to the social world. In *Discipline and Punish*, Foucault (1977) argues that bodily practices are part of the capillary-like operations of power which work to render bodies docile and obedient. His concept of power is novel in that it argues that modern power works not by repressing or forbidding things, but by inducing ways of acting and being, so that individual

bodies come to manage themselves. In this way, power is productive of subjectivity: modern prisons produce the "criminal," psychoanalysis produces the "hysteric" and so on. Power is at work in discourses which, in turn, are put into practice: so, for example, the eighteenth-century discourse of liberalism was important in producing the idea of the "criminal" as reformable and was put into practice through the building of prisons. This discourse and system of punishment was enforced through panoptical surveillance and had obvious implications for bodies, which were incarcerated. The panopticon was a design for a prison produced by social theorist and reformer, Jeremy Bentham. The cells of the prison were organized around a central watchtower which remained in darkness. The design enforced the principle of self-surveillance: since prisoners could not know when they were being observed, they would be forced to monitor their behavior at all times. This prison, though never built in this form, has informed the design of many modern institutions, such as the hospitals, schools and indeed prisons that we may have all encountered at some point in our lives.

While feminists such as McNay (1992) and Diamond and Quimby (1988) argue that Foucault ignores the issue of gender, they point out that his theoretical concepts can provide feminists with a framework for understanding the ways in which the body is acted on by power/knowledge. Indeed, Foucault's notion of discourse can enable the analysis of fashion as a discursive domain which sets significant parameters around the body and its presentation. Fashion (defined here as a system of continually changing styles), which sets out an array of competing discourses on image and is the dominant system governing dress in the West, has been linked to the operations of power, initially marking out class divisions but, more recently, playing a crucial role in policing the boundaries of sexual difference. For example, fashion magazines frequently proclaim "*Vive la différence!*" when fashions for men and women conform to dominant stereotypes of "masculine" and "feminine," but this can and does get replaced from time to time by proclamations about androgyny. However, even androgynous fashions rely on the idea of some a-priori sexual difference for their clothing, even while they appear to unsettle or challenge fixed ideas about male/masculine, female/feminine.

Although utilized by Wilson (1992), Foucault's work on the body has not been usefully employed in the analysis of fashion as a textual site for the construction of the body, although it would seem that it would have some application. Fashion, particularly as it is laid out in the fashion magazine, is "obsessed with gender" (Wilson 1985: 117) and constantly shifts the boundary between the genders. This preoccupation with gender starts with babies and is played out through the life cycle so that styles of dress at significant moments are very clearly gendered (weddings and other formal occasions are the most obvious examples). Such styles enable the repetitious production of gender, even when gender appears to break down as with androgynous fashion, and are aided, in part, by the repetition of gendered styles of bodily posture routinely reproduced in fashion magazines. While these styles of being reproduce gender as a body style, they are also open to subversion through exaggeration and parody, as Butler (1990, 1993) has forcefully suggested.

Foucault's insights into the ways in which bodies are subject to power and discursively constituted can also be utilized to show how institutional and discursive practices of dress act upon the body, marking it and rendering it meaningful and productive. The idea of surveillance through self-surveillance is one that has also been extended to describe the emergence of a new modern self who is increasingly called upon to monitor behavior, often by technologies of the body, such as, diet, exercise and plastic surgery, to name but a few. It can also be used to describe technologies of dress and how they are one means of managing bodies in public. Institutions and corporations often use dress codes and uniforms as part of the establishment of a corporate discipline. Carla Freeman (1993, 2000) describes how a smart dress code was utilized by one data-processing corporation in Barbados as part of the surveillance and discipline of its largely female staff. Similarly, institutions such as prisons and hospitals impose uniforms which erase the individual features of the wearers' bodies and produce a uniform image of the institution or corporation. Likewise, some shops may also enforce a dress code or require their workers to wear a uniform to project an appropriate image: indeed, to ensure that workers embody the image the corporation seeks to project. On the other hand, professional occupations, by and large, do not lay down a specific uniform, but they generally expect professional staff to have inculcated a "professional" dress and wear smart, suited dress. In this way, Foucault's ideas about the relationship between institutions and the discipline of the body can be extended to the examination of dress in a wide range of social settings.

However, while Foucault's insights on the body and the way it is shaped by society are useful, there are limitations to his analysis. In particular, he has been criticized for seeing bodies as "passive" and thereby failing to explain how individuals may act in an autonomous fashion (see McNay 1992, 1999).

[...]

His analysis might, therefore, lead to the discussion of fashion and dress as merely constraining social forces and neglects the way individuals can be active in the choices they make from fashion discourse in their everyday experience of dress. His overly poststructuralist perspective produces an account of bodies as if they were texts, acted upon by social forces, rather than the flesh and blood material of our embodied existence. If the dressed body is to be understood not only as always situated and structured by culture, but also as an intimate aspect of embodied experience, we have to look elsewhere for a fuller account of dress as a "fleshy" practice, that is, one that involves real flesh and blood bodies. How can one begin to understand the experience of choosing and wearing clothes that forms so significant a part of our daily practice, a crucial experience of our body/self? Thomas Csordas (1993, 1996) argues that the structuralist and poststructuralist paradigm of Douglas and Foucault is inadequate because it does not tell us what people do with their bodies in daily life—it neglects to account for embodiment. He posits a "paradigm of embodiment," which examines *what the body does* to supplement the "paradigm of the body" which examines, as do Douglas and Foucault, *what is done to the body*. He looks to the phenomenology of Maurice Merleau-Ponty and the sociologist Pierre Bourdieu as offering ways of thinking about embodiment. Merleau-Ponty puts embodiment at the centre of his philosophical approach. Embodiment is an a-priori fact of existence and it is through the body that we come to know and act in the world. This philosophical tradition does not easily lend itself to application but has been translated into a more sociological approach through the work of Bourdieu, as Csordas suggests, and also Goffman, as Nick Crossley (1995a, 1995b, 1996) has argued. In his account, Goffman describes how people embody space, how they improvise within space, much like actors do. Thus, while space imposes itself on us to some extent (the spaces of work dictating how we should dress/appear), we are active in producing this space and can transform space through our active engagement with it. As a symbolic integrationist, Goffman sees space as something produced through the actions of individuals, not as something a priori to them.

Pierre Bourdieu's (1984, 1989) work has also demonstrated how embodied social agents orientate themselves to situations. Although he ultimately produces a rather too structuralist account of embodiment, that is, one that focuses rather too much attention on social structure rather than agency in his account of the world, Bourdieu's methodological framework does lend itself to an account of embodiment in everyday life. There is much potential in his idea of the "habitus" as a concept for thinking through embodiment. The habitus is used to describe the way we come to live in our bodies and how our body is both structured by our social situation, primarily our social class, but also produced through our own embodied activities. It is, therefore, a concept that can provide a link between the individual and the social. According to Bourdieu, our social class structures our "tastes," which are themselves bodily experiences, but these structures are only brought into being through the embodied actions of individuals. Once we have acquired the appropriate habitus, we have the capacity to generate practice. The important point is that these practices or embodied activities are constantly adaptable to the conditions it meets. Class taste, then, is something that is reproduced through our intimate relationships to the body.

This analysis seems far removed from dress but, as with the other theorists I have discussed here, it is possible to extend Bourdieu's analysis to dress. It can be argued that the habitus predisposes individuals to particular ways of dressing: for example, the middle-class notion of "quality not quantity" generally translates into a concern with quality fabrics such as cashmere, leather and silk which, due to cost, may mean buying fewer garments. On the other hand, working-class dress may favor quantity not quality. Our class position may therefore orientate us to particular kinds of cloth, for example, silk as opposed to nylon, and to particular styles of dress, such as the middle-class style of Laura Ashley.

CONCLUSION

To conclude, I have tried to suggest how understandings of the dressed body need to explore the dynamic relationship between the body and dress, rather than abstract the body from dress. I have drawn on the work of a number of theorists who examine the body in the social world and sought to extend their analysis to the study of the dressed body. I have argued that the dressed body is a crucial component in micro-social order and that, in order to understand the forces at work in dressing the body, a range of theoretical resources are needed. Although I have discussed theorists of the body, rather more than theorists of dress, I have done so in order to bring these theoretical resources to bear on how we dress the body in the social world. I have also used them to examine the role that dress plays in the production and reproduction of bodily and social order. I would argue that the close relationship of fabric and flesh is one that can be explored through the analysis of the attitudes to cloth and tailoring practices that shape it. There is not the space to give anything more than a glimpse at some of the possibilities for analyzing the dressed body and it is hoped that future research might extend the preliminary thoughts laid down here.

10

SANDRA NIESSEN

Re-Orienting Fashion Theory

From S. Niessen, A. M. Leshkowich and C. Jones (eds.) (2003),
Re-Orienting Fashion: The Globalization of Asian Dress
(Oxford: Berg), 243–66.

That fashion is a global phenomenon is indisputable. We need only look at the labels in our closets to assure ourselves that this is so. That there is persistent momentum in the perception of fashion as a Western phenomenon, however, is equally indisputable. An unquestioned, popular understanding of what fashion is can be found in any fashion magazine, on the fashion page of any newspaper, on the fashion channel of any satellite package, indeed, on any city street or in any social scene anywhere in the world. And it is reflected in a century of writings by sociologists, anthropologists, art historians, and students of popular culture. It is also realized in the fashion world on haute couture runways. Fashion's presence and its forms are largely taken for granted. That fashion is a Western phenomenon is a central component in the package of assumptions about fashion.

Fashion: global but Western. A complex, ambiguous, and not just a little bit murky relationship exists between Western fashion and other clothing systems, especially non-Western, found throughout the world. Given fashion's global systems of production and marketing to which our labels testify, and given that fashion is Western, to what, then, does the relatively recent recognition of "fashion globalization" refer? What is fashion and what is not fashion? What are fashion's criteria for inclusion and exclusion? What do the criteria tell us about fashion,

fashion theory, fashion theorists, and also about the social machinery that renders fashion so unquestionable a force?

Fashion's definition has long been in need of review and revision, but this challenge has not been taken up sufficiently. As a result, the Orientalist momentum[1] that resides in the conventional definition of fashion as a uniquely Western phenomenon has not been properly addressed, leaving both primary and concealed the power relations that I contend are central to fashion's processes.

In 1978 Polhemus and Proctor proposed the term "anti-fashion" to designate all systems of dress in the world, both Western and non-Western, that do not fall under the definition of fashion. While I argue below that this dichotomous understanding of the world's dress systems illustrates the false historicism characteristic of Orientalist thought, I also claim that, because the Orientalist understanding of fashion reifies itself throughout the world, Polhemus and Proctor's model has incipient value for understanding global fashion processes. By examining the relations of power that operate between fashion and anti-fashion—precisely that which fashion theorists have neglected on the conviction that fashion's distinctiveness is empirically founded—the dichotomous model is useful for explaining the dynamics of dress on both sides of the great divide between what is considered to be fashion and what is not. Non-fashion refers to indigenous/local Asian dress forms.

I am searching for a definition of fashion that will illuminate the dusky theoretical gap between fashion and its non-fashion foil. The fashion process is about the creation of oppositions through time: that which is (conceived as) current and that which is (conceived as) past. I contend that the definition of fashion is too limited when it focuses only on one side of the process, and it must be broadened to acknowledge the systemic interdependence of the oppositions generated by the fashion process.

EUROPE AND THE PEOPLE WITHOUT FASHION

...ideas, cultures, and histories cannot be seriously understood or studied without their force, or more precisely their configurations of power, also being studied. (Said 1979: 5)

Because the word "fashion" is accorded only to select dress phenomena, the word implies a division of the world's adornment into that which is fashionable and that which is not. Logically, the dichotomous reach of the denotation is global. Who decides, and how the decision is made, is primary to the definition of fashion, but almost invariably the definition is given exclusively in terms of the material characteristics of dress. I make the claim that fashion has been defined a priori as a Western phenomenon, and that, in this way, fashion has been a function of "the enormously systematic discipline by which European culture was able to manage—and even produce—the Orient..." (Said 1994 [1979]: 3). Who has, and who does not have fashion is politically determined, a function of power relations. To paraphrase Said, what was "discovered" to be *without fashion* was *what could be made* to be without fashion.

It is perhaps inevitable that temporal distinctions were invoked as the key attribute separating fashionable from non-fashionable bodily adornment. During the Enlightenment,

the West prided itself on its rapid progress toward a more ennobled state. By contrast, Other societies outside the West were static. Encompassing everything from depraved to noble savages, they had in common that they possessed tradition, but not history; they were members of "cold societies" (Lévi-Strauss 1966: 233–4). The clothing of such societies was constant, stable, and unchanging; designed for "the maintenance of a particular way of life and a stable tribal identity" (Polhemus and Proctor 1978: 16). There appears to be unequivocal agreement on this point among early fashion theorists:

Fashion does not exist in tribal and classless societies. (Simmel 1904: 541)

Any area of social life that is caught in continuing change is open to the intrusion of fashion. In contrast, fashion is scarcely to be found in settled societies, such as primitive tribes, peasant societies, or caste societies, which cling to what is established and has been sanctioned through long usage. (Blumer 1968: 342)

"Fixed" costume changes slowly in time... "Modish" costume, on the other hand, changes very rapidly in time, this rapidity of change belonging to its very essence. (Flügel 1930: 129–30)

In custom-bound cultures, such as are characteristic of the primitive world, there are slow, non-reversible changes of style rather than the often reversible forms of fashion found in modern cultures. (Sapir 1931: 141)

By contrast, the clothing in the West reflected the rapid passage of time, the constant need for improvement, the climb toward higher social echelons. Garments that just would no longer do could be cast aside so that garments could be donned that depicted the more admirable social position to which one aspired. Social hierarchy was a second requisite to the possibility of fashion. The definition of fashion was designed and assigned within the crucible of social Darwinism by those who *could*. In addition, descriptions of the system of dress found in the West were used as the definition of fashion, a projection of "our clothing system."

The consistency in the above definitions of fashion is seductive, but its persistence is what is more remarkable. As recently as the mid-1990s, Anne Hollander wrote:

Fashionable dress thus has a built-in contingent character quite lacking to all ethnic and folk dress, and to most clothes of the ancient world. Traditional dress, everything that I call non-fashion, works differently. It creates its visual projections primarily to illustrate the confirmation of established custom. All non-fashion primarily conveys an ideal of certainty, and demonstrates a link to a fixed cosmology. In traditional societies without our sort of uneasy self-propelling fashion, clothing may have immediately readable meaning in its forms, in its methods of wear, and in the character of adornments, all directly linked to the character of customary life, and staying relatively still to do so. (1994: 17–8)

These propositions seem to have been received without consternation or controversy. The truth appears to be self-evident, and the fashion-defining mantra has been handed down intact in academe for a century.

Furthermore, alternative uses of the word "fashion" do not seem to have inspired a review of its accepted definition. New directions of theoretical inquiry that have been launched within the study of dress have not led to a critical retrospective of the field, and a division of analytical labor in clothing studies appears to have stuck, whereby anthropologists continue to study non-Western "dress," and Western fashion remains the focus of fashion studies. A quick statistical review of the relevant library shelf reveals the strong predilection to use the word "dress" for anthropological works, and "fashion" for analyses of Western dress. Disciplinary boundaries appear to support the West/Rest fashion dichotomy even while, as a theoretical issue, the distinction of who does and who does not have fashion is no longer a burning one. But there does still appear to be a need to distinguish Western dress from the dress of other peoples. Popular fashion literature maintains the dichotomy and the central chambers of high fashion ensure that admission is limited and carefully screened.

The conventional, evolutionarily dichotomized definition of fashion seems to coexist with alternative visions, descriptions, and approaches. That this coexistence of different trains of thought has not been more critically evaluated is all the more remarkable given the theoretical directions taken in some partner disciplines that study fashion, as well as the diversity of findings from the study of fashion itself.

In anthropology, for example, the incorporation of a historical paradigm exposed Western, imperialist bias in the assignation of which societies have history and which do not. When anthropologists became aware that their assignation of the Other as being "without history" was a projection of a Western conceptual system, it sparked a thought revolution with much fertile energy being spent on rethinking the subject matter of the field (e.g., E. Wolf 1982; Hobsbawm and Ranger 1983; Dominguez 1986), changing forever the way anthropologists go about their work. The ethnographically irresponsible "lumping" of non-Western dress in undifferentiated contrast to Western clothing systems is symptomatic of the kind of false historicism with which anthropologists began to concern themselves. The characterizations of fashion cited above as exclusively Western were not constructed inductively on the evidence of exhaustive, cross-cultural study of non-Western clothing systems—only since the latter decades of the twentieth century have these begun to be a more popular (and acceptable) academic pursuit. Furthermore, the anthropologists in the first half of the twentieth century who *did* study "dress," did so in a non-Western, ethnographic setting and did not participate in the discourse about (Western) fashion. In addition, their studies of clothing were synchronic, in part due to the nature of fieldwork as a temporary drop-in affair, and in part because anthropologists accepted that they were studying societies "without history." Later twentieth-century anthropological study of systems of dress approach the subject matter differently. Such study is consistent with a discipline that has been transformed by a historical paradigm (e.g., Hendrickson 1996; Kondo 1997; Tarlo 1996; Schneider 1978). Nevertheless, they have not resulted in a revision of the conventional, evolutionary, imperialist definition of fashion (Craik 1994), nor have they confronted the issue.

In a second instance, art history has been squarely confronted with the problem of what is art, by whom is it defined, and using which criteria? The pressure to accord non-Western art forms the designation "art," showed up the evolutionist intellectual framework that had dominated the field: only the West could have true art. The close company kept by fashion design(er)/analyst with art(ist)/art historian is partly to blame for the exclusively Western definition of fashion. Costume historians borrowed the parameters of their study of costume (history of dress was once referred to as the history of costume) from the historical study of art, with the result that the trajectory of Western costume is the same as that of Western art, beginning with ancient civilization through Medieval and Renaissance Europe, and ending in industrialized Western Europe and North America. In reconsidering their subject matter in such a way as to include non-Western art and women's art, and even to throw a glance at "craft," the "new" art history that emerged from the fray was founded on a reorientation of the definition of art. They rejected the assumption that "a universal history of art ... evolves in a linear progressive fashion and culminates in the art of Western Europe," and adopted new research strategies to approach the proliferation of art forms that had now fallen under their purview (R. Phillips 1989: 5).

At first glance, fashion studies would do well to once again take a page from the field of art history. At second glance, much of the work seems to have been done already. In pointing to the need for a "model for studying dress in the modern, globally interconnected world," Baizerman et al. (1993) have conducted a critique of the costume historian's evolutionary model for its bias of Western superiority. Second, in the journal *Fashion Theory*, contributions to Western and non-Western dress phenomena are juxtaposed, an important step in developing a global model. Third, studies of non-Western dress systems are burgeoning, and fourth, some students of Western fashion, such as Jennifer Craik, acknowledge fashion as a "cultural technology that is purpose-built for specific locations" (1994: xi), and therefore multiple, various, and unencumbered by a West/Rest dichotomy. Fifth, the tools of analysis are available. While art historians turned to anthropological methods to approach non-Western art (R. Phillips 1989: 8), anthropological methods for the study of dress have never been absent. Furthermore, recent emphasis on the process of dressing above the study of dress forms[2] (e.g., Wilson 1985; Butler 1990; Kondo 1997) facilitates global comparisons of dress phenomena.

In the world of art, one of Picasso's legacies was his recognition that Africans and other non-Western peoples produce art (Rubin 1984). Within the fashion world, such a vanguard stimulus has emerged in the person of designer Yves Saint-Laurent, known for incorporating the ethnic in haute couture. The fashion world also had its analogue to the Primitivism exhibition with the "invasion" of Japanese design on European runways.[3] The empirical grounds on which to continue the claim that fashion is a Western phenomenon are anything but firm.

Finally, within the study of Western fashion, all has not been illusion and falsity. Sound, detailed descriptions of "the" Western fashion system abound. Simmel, for example, described a hierarchical social system in which fashion forms worn by a higher class of higher means were desired by a lower class of higher aspirations, and thus appeared to "trickle down" as their wearers tried to ascend the social ladder. His work reveals the relationship between the dynamics of clothing systems and the extant social structure in his time. Roche (1994), to cite a more recent example, provided a minute analysis of the fashion system of the *ancien régime* in France. When fashion began appears to be as unclear as whether it might have constant features, and which they might be. Elizabeth Wilson discerns the rudiments of fashion in fourteenth-century Europe in "a proliferation of styles" and the increased means to acquire them (1985: 16). For other scholars, fashion began when Western technological capacities allowed for mass production and expanded consumption. However, even this usage obfuscates the tremendous variety of systems of Western dress that have come into being, one succeeding the other at an accelerating rate, or coexisting in different locations at the same time, since the industrial revolution (D. Crane 2000). While few describe identical phenomena, the definition of the word "fashion" (as noted above) has persisted.

In addition, fashion has been assaulted by counter-expressions. These have been variously termed anti-fashion, oppositional fashion, and non-fashion, and are the looks of protest meant to displace the fashion elite, or to provide an ideological alternative to what fashion stands for. In the nineteenth century, for example, dress styles were developed to protest "against the artificiality and waste of fashionable attire" (Ash and Wilson 1992: xv). In the twentieth century, the dress of feminists and counterculture youth is best known for shaking the status quo. Reactions to war, and against bourgeois affluence and middle-class morality (König 1973), have all registered in anti-fashions.

> The Royal Family, at least in public, wear anti-fashions; my mother wears anti-fashions; Hell's Angels, hippies, punks and priests wear anti-fashions; Andy Capp and "the workers" wear anti-fashions. (Polhemus and Proctor 1978: 16)

Anti-fashion trends have become so prevalent that they are symptomatic of what is often referred to as a "crisis" in fashion (e.g., Ash and Wilson 1992). This is because they have been picked up off the street and placed on the fashion runway, thereby defusing them of their power of protest, but also weakening fashion's elite image (Hebdige 1979). The international, the ethnic, the subcultural, and the day-to-day have all paraded down Europe's most important runways. Some fashion theorists have considered whether to pronounce fashion "dead" (Polhemus and Proctor 1978: 17; F. Davis 1992; König 1973:

200). Steele is representative of the majority decision when she reassures her readers that fashion is alive and well:

> As the culture of fashion has changed, so also has the fashion industry and the image of fashion. But fashion itself remains alive and well, always new, always changing. (2000: 20)

While it is reassuring that regardless of how Western clothing systems change, fashion does not die, logically it does make the issue of fashion's definition more pressing. The accuracy of Simmel's and others' time-bound sociological definitions of fashion demanded that, upon social change, the definition of fashion not just be reconsidered, but also problematized. If defined relative to a single social form, what becomes of fashion when that social form changes? Or, to approach the problem in another way, how should or may fashion be defined if it is changeable and not exclusively linked to a particular social form or forms? The problem of the unfailingly mutating, but nevertheless constantly present and always exclusively Western fashion system is particularly critical when assigning who does and who does not have fashion on a global scale. How can it be that such a proliferation of fashion forms can exist in the West but that the non-West still does not have fashion? Is there a qualitative difference in the variety of Western dress systems compared to non-Western dress systems? This problem needs to be taken up. By not doing so, fashion theorists forfeit the ability to compare fashion systems. Early fashion theorists oriented themselves entirely toward Western fashion, and the momentum of their thought persists unconsciously, perhaps, and perhaps with subconscious intent, but certainly anachronistically. Even if evolutionary thought were no longer providing momentum to fashion studies, this would need to be addressed. A great divide between the studies of Western fashion/clothing processes and the universal phenomenon of dress/adornment still obtains. As a result, global dress events of profound implication for fashion theory are kept either hidden or barred from scrutiny.

EDITORS' NOTES

1. Orientalism, according to Said (1994), is viewing non-Western societies as "the other" and objectifying them as less culturally advanced than the West. Nevertheless, they are considered "exotic." Unequal power relations result.

2. Niessen is referring to artifact analysis, the study of the object by itself.

3. The Primitivism exhibition was staged in the Museum of Modern Art in New York in 1984 (Rubin 1984).

11

CAROLINE EVANS

Fashion at the Edge

From C. Evans (2003), **Fashion at the Edge: Spectacle, Modernity, and Deathliness** *(New Haven: Yale University Press), 4–14.*
Reprinted with permission © *Yale University Press.*

From "heroin chic" to Alexander McQueen, the distressed body of much 1990s fashion exhibited the symptoms of trauma, the fashion show mutated into performance and a new kind of conceptual fashion designer evolved. These are just three examples of fashion "at the edge," fashion which exists at its own margins. While becoming more vivid in its presentation, many of its themes became correspondingly darker in the 1990s. Often permeated by death, disease and dereliction, its imagery articulated the anxieties as well as the pleasures of identity, alienation and loss against the unstable backdrop of rapid social, economic and technological change at the end of the twentieth century.

Perhaps this new trend marked a paradigm shift in sensibilities but it was also embedded in the tradition of Western consumer capitalism. Rather than examining the experimental fashion of the 1990s merely as a series of rapid style changes, I consider it as part of a broader historical and philosophical trajectory that has a relationship to concepts not always associated with fashion: modernity, technology and globalization. We speak of "edgy" fashion to suggest fashion that is sharp, urban, knowing, experimental, unsentimental. We are at the edge of centuries, and on the edge of technological transformation. Such epochal change requires its participants to embrace a knowledge economy, turn their backs on the old age of industrial modernity and begin to make sense of the revolution in communications of the last thirty years. The fashion design discussed here was at the edge commercially, of the big global brands and of mass production. Its themes were on the edge too, at the borders of beauty and horror, where sex and death intersected with commerce. Conceptually as well as stylistically experimental, this strand of fashion design addressed contemporary anxieties and speculations about the body and identity.

These were legitimate concerns for cultural practitioners at the turn of the millennium, set as they were against the backdrop of the dark history of the twentieth century (holocaust and genocide, the rise of totalitarianism, and two world wars), the collapse of older epistemological certainties in the West, the rapid development of information technology since the first satellite was sent into space in 1957, the demise of the old Soviet Union in 1991, the consequent spread of globalization and the intensification of an ideological divide between Islam and the secular West. Yet, although it is the business of cultural practitioners to speculate about questions of identity and community in a changing world, such concerns have not been the traditional domain of the fashion designer. Despite this, in periods in which ideas about the self seem to be unstable, or rapidly shifting, fashion itself can shift to center stage and play a leading role in constructing images and meanings, as well as articulating anxieties and ideals. The time and place could be *fin de siècle* Vienna, Paris of the 1930s, or 1990s London: each has a relationship to modernity and to technological change and its impact on sensibilities. These sensibilities may be described as the "decentered subject" of the interwar years (Dean 1992), or the "emergent identities" of 1990s cyber-culture (Haraway 1997; Plant 1997). What is significant in each case is the role which fashion plays in articulating contemporary concerns about the self and the world. Jonathan Dollimore has argued that the decentered self, far from being a singular product of contemporary thought, is simply a reiteration of the idea of the disintegration of human nature after the Fall: "the 'crisis' of the individual is less a crisis than a recurring instability" (Dollimore 1998: xix). He argues that the individual has always been in crisis in the Western tradition, driven forward by the destabilizing forces of mutability and death. But if this "crisis" has been formally sanctioned in the Western tradition of tragedy, as Dollimore argues, it has also concealed itself, *en travesti*, at the heart of fashion, that discourse of youth, frivolity and lightness. The surface of fashion, like Watteau's *fêtes galantes*, conceals a core of melancholy (Evans 1999). The leitmotif of mutability, with all its perils and excitements, is ultimately its real, if fugitive, subject.

Many of the features of Western fashion today have their origins in the development of European mercantile capitalism from the fourteenth century, and in what Norbert Elias (1983) called "the civilizing process." For Elias, the evolution of manners since the Middle Ages involved the suppression of aggressive and instinctual behavior in favor of the development of a reflexive, modeled and nuanced self. It is in this sense that fashion "speaks," both as a discourse which articulates what we are, might be or could become, and as a kind of etiquette or style book for the "care of the self" (Foucault 1984). The late twentieth-century articulation of the idea of the self as culturally constructed has important implications for fashion. Gilles Lipovetsky has argued that fashion is socially reproductive, training us

to be flexible and responsive to change in a fast-changing world: "Fashion socializes human beings to change and prepares them for perpetual recycling" (Lipovetsky 1994: 149). The kinetic, open personality of fashion is the personality which a society in the process of rapid transformation most needs. No longer derided as superficial, frivolous or deceitful, fashion thus has an important role to play, not merely in adorning the body but also in fashioning a modern, reflexive self (Giddens 1991).

However, if fashion is part of the "civilizing process," in the form of conventional and mainstream fashion design, it is also and equally, in its experimental and avant-garde manifestations, capable of providing a resistant and opposing voice to that process. On the edge of discourse, of "civilization," of speech itself, experimental fashion can act out what is hidden culturally. And, like a neurotic symptom, it can utter a kind of mute resistance to the socially productive process of constructing an identity. As we produce a disciplined and controlled self, via the "technology" of manners for example (Foucault 1984), what is repressed comes back as a trace, under the weight of some cultural trauma, of which experimental fashion can function as a telltale memory. Seen thus, fashion is hysterical. It can be a symptom of alienation, loss, mourning, fear of contagion and death, instability and change. Like psychoanalysis, it "investigates the domain and configuration of incoherence, discontinuity, disruption and disintegration" (Abraham and Torok 1994: 1).

In arguing, however, that experimental fashion, like the psychoanalytic model of the unconscious, acts out repressed desires and fears, I do not suggest that these are the desires and fears of the designers themselves. If fashion speaks, it speaks independently of its creators. My work seeks to locate it in the context of historical rather than personal trauma, by relating it to the larger questions of history, rather than to the designers' motives and intentions. Its "symptoms" are wide-ranging and diffuse: death (or its corollaries mourning, trauma and shock), gender instability and free-floating anxiety. The memory traces invoked here are historical fragments of instability and transience from earlier centuries. These traces come back as fragments under the weight of a cultural trauma which has been expressed by earlier twentieth-century writers on modernity as "shock" and "neurasthenia," and by writers about contemporary culture as "trauma" or "wound culture" (Simmel 1903; Benjamin 1939; H. Foster 1996; Seltzer 1998).

Fashion, with its affinity for transformation, can act out instability and loss but it can also, and equally, stake out the terrain of "becoming"—new social and sexual identities, masquerade and performativity (Rivière 1929; Apter 1992; Butler 1990, 1993). One of my concerns is to contrast a cynical and knowing decadence on the one hand with a more passionate and hopeful approach on the other. If the imagery of late twentieth-century fashion seemed dark or bleak, it may be because it signaled an attempt to chart new social identities in a period of rapid change, while reflecting contemporary concerns with death and decay. Much fashion from the 1990s appeared, in the glossy closure of its luxurious designs, to shore up and contain anxieties about cultural continuity, the body and mortality. And this was particularly so among the "big players" and global brands of international fashion. But a small proportion of designers, many of them Japanese, Dutch, Belgian or British, rather than French, Italian or American, were among those whose work articulated the experience of cultural discontinuity, transforming "negative" ideas into critical and questioning designs. In the small and commercially less lucrative hinterland in which they worked, new ideas were able to form, grow and spread. Many of the designers of the 1990s regarded it as hypocrisy simply to present happy, shiny images, rather than exploring the entire range of human emotion and experience. For them, it went without saying that fashion was an appropriate arena in which to investigate the complexities of modern life. And out of this questioning and experimental tendency in contemporary art and fashion emerged new images, of which some were bleak but others were curiously optimistic.

SEGUEING BETWEEN PAST AND PRESENT

Contemporary sensibilities echo earlier moments of modernity, from the growth of mercantile capitalism in seventeenth-century Europe to the accelerated consumption of commodity culture in the industrialized nineteenth-century city. In the course of looking at contemporary fashion, I have made comparisons with other periods of change and instability in European history, and drawn on the imagery of these periods to explain that of the present.

In order to do so, I have relied on the sometimes problematic and perhaps overused concept of modernity, albeit with some reservations (Wilson 1985). Definitions of modernity are as many as they are contradictory, particularly between the social sciences and the humanities traditions. A number of historians, for whom the idea of modernity is bound up with an analysis of industrial capitalist society as a form of rupture from the preceding social system, have used the term to designate the enormous social and cultural changes which took place from the mid-sixteenth century onwards in Europe (B. Turner 1999). For the sociologist Max Weber, the origins of capitalism lay in the Protestant ethic; its leitmotifs were modernization and rationalization but also, and crucially, ambiguity (B. Turner 1999). This sense of ambiguity underlies an important presumption that there is an intimate connection between opposites—such as despair and optimism, beauty and horror, fashion and mortality.

I have followed Marshall Berman (1983) and used the term "modernity" as one of a triumvirate of terms: modernization, modernity and modernism. "Modernization" refers to the processes of scientific, technological, industrial, economic and political innovation that also become urban, social and artistic in their impact. "Modernity" refers to the way that modernization infiltrates everyday life and permeates sensibilities. And "modernism" refers to a wave of avant-garde artistic movements that, from early in the twentieth century, in some way responded to or represented these changes in sensibility and experience (Tickner 2000).

In 1903 Simmel related fashion to the fragmentation of modern life and discussed its neurasthenia, that is, the overstimulation and nervous excitement that came with the growth of the metropolis. He associated fashion with the middle classes and with the city, as well as with the stylization of everyday objects, and he pointed to the close relation of art, fashion and consumer culture, connections which became topical again in the 1990s, for example in the work of Comme des Garçons, Martin Margiela and Viktor & Rolf. In 1939, Walter Benjamin described a change in the structure of experience whereby modern life was characterized by violent jolts and dislocations, a feature of many accounts of postmodern experience at the close of the century. Urban encounters with telephones, cameras, traffic and advertising are experienced as "a series of shocks and collisions" and the fractured and dislocating experience of modernity is made formal in the principle of montage in early modernist cinema.

Among the many writers on modernity, only Ulrich Lehmann (2000) and Elizabeth Wilson (1985) have addressed the role of fashion in modernity by making it central rather than peripheral to their accounts. Both assert the continuing relevance of nineteenth-century modernity to the present, Lehmann in general terms and Wilson in more specific ones. Wilson pinpointed the moment of dissonance in the modern city as being key to twentieth-century style; the "hysteria and exaggeration of fashion" expressed "the colliding dynamism, the thirst for change and the heightened sensation that characterize the city societies particularly of modern industrial capitalism [that] go to make up this 'modernity'" (10). Unlike other writers on modernity, she traced a connection to today's fashion. Wilson described postmodern fashion in 1985 as enacting "the most hallucinatory aspects of our culture, the confusions between the real and the not-real, the aesthetic obsessions, the vein of morbidity without tragedy, of irony without merriment, and the nihilistic critical stance towards authority, empty rebellion almost without political content" (63). Although from the 1980s many academics differentiated the present from the past by identifying postmodernism as a moment of absolute rupture, Wilson's analysis suggested that she too saw a connection with moments of instability in the past that were reprised in present-day fashion.

With Wilson and Lehmann, I argue that modern fashion sits on the bedrock of nineteenth-century commercial relations, urbanization and technological developments, and the impact of these upon sensibilities; further, that modern fashion continues to bear a relationship to them, for all the specific differences of its recent development. While modern modes of fashion production, along with the idea of inbuilt obsolescence, developed largely in the twentieth century, many features of the modern fashion industry and of modern consumption are traceable to the eighteenth and nineteenth centuries, if not earlier. However, it is not my aim to plot a precise and structural genealogy of the connection between Western fashion and modernity by tracking back through European culture. Furthermore, such an enterprise might construct a linear history which, in a sense, runs counter to my project. I have instead drawn on Benjamin's metaphor of fashion as a "tiger's leap," the metaphor that provides the title to Lehmann's book on fashion and modernity, and on Benjamin's concept of dialectical images, with the aim of juxtaposing the more spectacular manifestations of the consumer explosion of the nineteenth century against those of the late twentieth-century fashion show to illuminate the way that the past can resonate in the present to articulate modern anxieties and experiences. And from Benjamin's references to urban space and time (1985), I have developed the metaphor of history as a labyrinth.

The metaphor of history as a labyrinth allows the juxtaposition of historical images with contemporary ones; as the labyrinth doubles back on itself what is most modern is revealed as also having a relation to what is most old. Distant points in time can become proximate at specific moments as their paths run close to each other. Although there is no repetition without difference, nevertheless the conditions of postindustrial modernity are haunted by those of industrial modernity when fashion designers dip into the past for their motifs and themes. These traces of the past surface in the present like the return of the repressed. Fashion designers call up these ghosts of modernity and offer us a paradigm that is different from the historian's paradigm, remixing fragments of the past into something new and contemporary that will continue to resonate into the future. They illuminate how we live in the world today and what it means to be a modern subject.

The effect of developments in communications and information technology of the last thirty years of the twentieth century, and their acceleration in the final ten, as well as their impact on social relations, is still to be quantified. Rapid technological change alters the way we experience the world, from our social relations to the way we inhabit cities and make sense of our lives in them. Consequently, meaning frequently seems to mutate to the surface of things; and clothing functions as a metaphor for the instability and contingency of modern life. Many of the fashion designers I studied intuitively and inexorably drew on earlier images of disruption and instability from the past to interpret present concerns.

I am not, however, making a claim for any crude historical equivalence between past and present. On the contrary, my historical examples are selective and are chosen for what they can tell us about fashion today. In comparing, for example, a John Galliano dress with a turn-of-the century vamp, the visual link uncovers interesting things about the present that has echoes in the past. If I have chosen to focus more on contemporary links with specific centuries, it is not because I am making a wider historical claim for similarities between periods but because what designers take from particular periods in the past tells us about our anxieties and concerns in the present. When designers hark back to such periods they are simply providing interesting instances that crystallize the use we make of history in the present. Hence the "tiger's leap" and the "dialectical image" are tools to map the modern, rather than to chart the past. For if there are stylistic similarities between the excesses and sleights of hand of late twentieth-century fashion spectacles and those of an earlier century, that does not in itself imply a lineage. Such labyrinthine returns could equally bring two other historical moments into proximity, such as Calvin Klein and Donna Karan's evocations of a modernist aesthetic in the sleek and streamlined elegance of American fashion.

There are risks attached to a form of interpretation that moves apparently irresponsibly across centuries to construct meaning in the present. Perhaps in the 1990s the imagery of death, decay and dereliction came to stand for mutability more than for mortality. Perhaps it sketched a contemporary sense of change, instability and uncertainty that had more to do with rapid technological and social transition than with death itself. The impact of the information revolution of the late twentieth century had particular force and velocity from the late 1980s. Sony Walkmans, mobile telephones, closed-circuit television novelties altered the experience of space, time and the body, changed the notion of privacy and affected work and leisure practices in varying ways that seemed to some exhilarating and to others profoundly destabilizing.

RAGPICKING

If late twentieth-century fashion looped back to earlier moments of modernity in specific formations, it was not because the moments of past and present were the same but because a visual link between them uncovered interesting things about the present that echoed the past. Fashion designers can elucidate these connections visually in a way that historians cannot do without falsifying history. For designers, it is precisely through the liberties they take that contemporary meaning can be constructed.

The labyrinthine relay between past, present and imagined future in the work of designers surveyed here is at odds with the idea of linear history, and their design methods approximate more to those of the nineteenth-century rag-picker.

Ragpicking, as well as describing fashion designers' methods, is also a useful tool for the cultural historian in thinking about fashion today. Bringing together two moments in the labyrinth, it gives cultural historians a method of conceiving of the experimental fashion design of the late twentieth century as historically located in the context of, for example, nineteenth-century capitalism. Contemporary fashion has fastened on the themes of instability and alteration, selecting past images of mutability which resonate in the present. Fashion imagery, itself semiotically unstable, thus fixes images of instability and change, but in ways that destabilize conventional history, and run counter to the idea of coherent narrative. It demands, rather, a reevaluation of the imagery of the past in the light of the present, something that characterizes the work of Michel Foucault as well as that of Walter Benjamin.

For Foucault, the breaks, ruptures and discontinuities of history serve to unravel the straightforward relationship of causes and effects over time. All history is written about from the perspective of the present, in the sense that the present throws up the themes to be studied historically. Since the present is always in a state of transformation the past must constantly be reevaluated; and the past takes on new meanings in the light of new events in the present. This is "genealogy"—history written in the light of current concerns (Foucault 1973). It is also closely similar to the actual process of fashion design as it reveals complex historical relays between past and present. In such collections, fragments and traces from the past reverberate in the present. Reversing Foucault's idea of "genealogy," that is, of history written in the light of current concerns, one might use the idea of the historical fragment to uncover traces from the past and to read the present through them. Contemporary fashion images are bearers of meaning and, as such, stretch simultaneously back to the past and forward into the future. Not just documents or records but fertile primary sources, they can generate new ideas and meanings and themselves carry discourse into the future, so that they take their place in a chain of meaning, or a relay of signifiers, rather than being an end product of linear history.

Benjamin's concept of the trace, from his Arcades project (Buck-Moss 1991), could be used in a new kind of cultural analysis, more fragmented and less coherent than the historian's, in which the fashion historian and the designer alike are scavengers, moving through cultural history like the figure of the ragpicker sifting rubbish in the nineteenth-century city. The historical fragment, or trace, can illuminate the present. Here history turns into detective story, with the historical trace as a clue. The figures of the collector, the ragpicker and the detective wander through Benjamin's landscape. Thus the historian's method, like that of the designer, is akin to that of the ragpicker who moves through the city gathering scraps for recycling.

In the process, the distinction between past and present is almost imploded. In exactly the same way, the fashionable moment that constantly collapses into the outmoded realigns the present as it goes, transforming it into a past that it will one day revive as it trawls through it for new motifs. The modern fashion designer rummages in the historical wardrobe, scavenging images for reuse just as the nineteenth-century ragpicker scavenged materials for recycling. And, in turn, I do something similar, scavenging images from the past to examine and reinterpret those of the present. I have assumed an equivalence here between the historian and the designer. Perhaps, however, the designer is better equipped. It is the task of designers to take liberties and poeticize, suborning ghosts to speak to contemporary concerns (Zenderland 1978). My own descriptions of the historical to-ings and fro-ings of contemporary fashion are not properly cultural materialism at all but, rather, examples of how the traces of the past can be woven into the fabric of a new story to illuminate the present. Yet they serve as something more than a mere hermeneutic tool to interpret the work of a few designers. They unlock the way in which the work of these designers—fragmented, episodic and emblematic—helps us to make sense of contemporary culture and its concerns.

Walter Benjamin's historical rummagings in the archive moved among the Middle Ages, the Reformation and the reverberations of the nineteenth century in the twentieth. In them all he saw periods of mourning or decline. The decline of pagan antiquity, the Thirty Years' War, the devastation of the First World War and the threat of the Second World War all caused a heightened sense of transience or, in Benjamin's words, of history as a desolate "place of skulls" (Buck-Moss 1991: 169–70). Perhaps the experience of transience in Benjamin's own historical period, as well as in his personal life, led him to track a comparable sense of transience in earlier periods. And, by the same token, one could argue for a sense of transience, impermanence and anxiety in the modern period which results in fashion images leaping back to comparable ones in the past.

I hope that my own crisscrossings may produce new and unexpected connections by writing about ephemera, images and traces in such a way as to invoke a poetics of history rather than solid historiography. Jacques Derrida described the architecture of the uninhabited or deserted city, "reduced to its skeleton by some catastrophe of nature or art," as "a city haunted by meaning and culture." This state of being haunted keeps the city from returning to nature (Derrida as quoted in Rossi 1982: 3). To extend Derrida's analogy of the city as skeleton, late twentieth-century fashion can function, like urban building types that are not neutral but experimental structures, as armatures for ideas, as well as skeletons of history. Looking back at history from the vantage point of contemporary fashion, like Benjamin's angel of history we are blown backwards into the future. As we go, history becomes a kind of haunting, the haunting that keeps nature at bay from the ruined city, so that we may refashion the skeletons of history into armatures for ideas.

ANNOTATED GUIDE TO FURTHER READING FOR PART II

The original books containing the extracts in this section are recommended as a means to flesh out each author's full intent. In addition, Grant McCracken's (2005) "Celebrities" presents an analysis of social-psychological theories applicable to marketing using celebrities, a topic relevant to contemporary fashion. Herbert Blumer's (1969a) article "Fashion: From Class Differentiation to Collective Selection" is recommended. Erving Goffman's (1959) book *Presentation of Self in Everyday Life* articulates role theory. Articles by Susan B. Kaiser, Richard H. Nagasawa, and Sandra S. Hutton (1991; 1995) on the symbolic interaction theory of fashion explain the theory in detail and provide a succinct review of symbolic interaction.

Recent publication of three compilations on fashion theory—two are edited collections of excerpts from theorists—provide a well-rounded historiography of fashion theory. The books are: Kim K. P. Johnson, Susan J. Torntore and Joanne B. Eicher's (2003) *Fashion Foundations: Early Writings on Fashion and Dress*, containing English language excerpts from 1545 to 1940; Daniel Leonard Purdy's (2004) *The Rise of Fashion: A Reader,* an anthology spanning the years 1724 to 1969, with English translated readings including Baudelaire; and Michael Carter's (2003) *Fashion Classics from Carlyle to Barthes*, which contextualizes and critically analyzes selected fashion theories.

For valuable reading in critical and cultural studies, see Ulrich Lehmann's *Tigersprung* (2000) where Walter Benjamin's *Arcades Project*, fashion and modernity are examined. Peter Wollen, author of *Raiding the Icebox*, has offered his cogent thoughts on Benjamin in "The Concept of Fashion in the *Arcades Project*" (2003). Fredric Jameson's (1998) *The Cultural Turn: Selected Writings on the Postmodern 1983–1998*, is imperative for serious students of contemporary theory. The same is true of Jean-François Lyotard's (1979) *The Postmodern Condition: A Report on Knowledge*. Elizabeth Wilson's seminal work *Adorned in Dreams* has been updated from the 1985 version (2003*).

Social-psychological fashion theories are covered in the textbook *Changing Appearances* by George B. Sproles and Leslie Davis Burns (1994). An informative chapter "A Theory of the Fashion Process" merges diffusion of innovations theory and consumer decision-making process. Another textbook, Evelyn L. Brannon's (2005) *Fashion Forecasting,* presents fashion theory in "The Direction of Fashion Change."

For discussion of fashion outside hegemonic Western culture, see Jennifer Craik's (1994) groundbreaking book *The Face of Fashion*, and *Consuming Fashion: Adorning the Transnational Body* by Anne Brydon and Sandra Niessen. Karen Tranberg Hansen's (2004) report "The World in Dress: Anthropological Perspectives on Clothing, Fashion, and Culture" informs on the status of dress research within the anthropological field and encourages wider use of recently developing perspectives from that discipline, including acknowledging fashion's presence in "ethnic" dress.

PART III
*F*ashion and Identity

ABBY LILLETHUN

Introduction

Identity reflects a person's location within social context. As Gregory Stone explained, "When one has identity, he is *situated*—that is, cast in the shape of a social object ..." (Stone [1962] in Roach-Higgins et al. 1995: 23). Appearance is part of identity: the individual presents himself or herself in social contexts and others perceive and assign meaning to his or her presentation. People *manage their appearance*: each person participates to some degree in appearance norms or else suffers social consequences (e.g., a person who fails to meet bodily cleanliness norms risks being ostracized) (Goffman 1959). People develop a *self-image*, or internal representations of their identity. Role theory suggests that since people may have multiple *roles* they fulfill, they may have a variety of identities, constructed, in part, through appearance (Sarbin 1943, 1954; Goffman 1959).

All of the *body supplements* (garments, hats, jewelry, etc.) and *body modifications* (grooming practices, tattoos, plastic surgery, etc.) utilized by a person comprise their *dress* (Roach-Higgins and Eicher 1992). In addition, the *situated body* and its attributes, such as age, health, skin color, stature, mood, and more, combine with dress to form one's *appearance*. All five senses discern appearance. Vision is the predominant sense: through sight the individual perceives silhouette, color, mass and texture. Touch is critical in understanding appearance. If a tactile experience is not possible, sense memory informs the viewer. Rough woolen tweed and a smooth silk

satin are distinctly understood without touching. Through the olfactory sense, the scent of another person is detected. Hearing also informs about appearance. For example, footfalls may indicate snow boots or stiletto heels. Taste comes into play through grooming practices such as oral hygiene. Dress has been defined as a form of nonverbal communication contingent upon social contexts where it is presented (Barnard 2002; Damhorst 2005). Thus, the totality of dress and the situated body—appearance—also constitutes a nonverbal communication system.

Multiple identities for various life roles contribute to the total self (Roach-Higgins and Eicher 1992). Occupation, kinship, religion and marital status are among the aspects of identity that may be shown through dress and appearance. Identities can include public, private and secret selves that may have many dimensions such as cultural, ethnic, subcultural, gender, sexual and others. While people manage their appearance in order to present identities they perceive as congruent with their objectives and goals, others may perceive the presentation differently than intended. Since meanings are negotiated in social interaction, the meanings underlying an appearance may be diffuse, undetermined or unclear. In the postmodern condition, shifting, contingent and overlapping meanings result in *ambiguous* and misunderstood identities (multiple meanings are possible). According to symbolic interaction theory, in modernity and postmodernity, *ambivalence* concerning appearance contributes to ambiguous meanings in presentation of the self (Davis 1992; Kaiser et al. 1991). Ambivalence leads to taking contradictory positions and experiencing vacillating states. Fred Davis suggested that collective identity ambivalence is "fashion's fuel." Subcultural identities, such as mods, punks, and Japan's various fashion *otaku*, evolve in urban settings where the speed of negotiating and revising subcultural style leads to overlapping and changing meanings, even to those within the subculture. Outsiders cannot accurately read, or decipher the underlying meaning of the looks; the styles and meanings change before they are decoded.

J. C. Flügel discussed desire for decoration as one of the fundamental origins of dress (1930: 15–38). Archaeologists recently reported the oldest known shell beads, dated to 100,000 years old, and interpreted them as evidence of symbolic behavior—use of ornamentation—that may have signaled social and cultural identity (Vanhaeren et al. 2006). Perhaps little has changed, since humans continue to symbolically signal their identity through managed appearances that both include decorative adornments and proclaim identity. The readings in this section span the mid-nineteenth century to the late twentieth century to examine fashion and gender, class, ethnicity, sexual and subcultural identity.

The first three selections treat gender identity. Colleen R. Callahan's and Jo B. Paoletti's *Is it a Girl or a Boy? Gender Identity and Children's Clothing* details shifts in gender-coded meanings of infants' and children's dress in Western culture. Nineteenth-century boys and girls were dressed alike, and color, such as pink for girls and blue for boys, was not associated with a child's sex. Today, rigid color conformity for the sexes often encircles babies from birth. In addition, in the nineteenth century, dresses served as the unisex garment of childhood; today it is trousers. While today's toddler may have greater physical freedom in trouser outfits, they experience stronger gender socialization earlier, since sexual identity is symbolically communicated through color. The second reading, by Karen Halttunen,

is from a classic book-length study of middle-class America in the nineteenth century. The excerpt "Sentimental Culture and the Problem of Fashion" explains how fashion became a social tool for middle-class Americans who sought to move up the social ladder. The mobile class structure, based on economic success instead of heritage, and the pursuit of fashion, led to a crisis in identity. The middle class used fashion as a dual-purpose tool: on one hand they followed fashion to enter higher status; on the other they used fashionability to exclude those beneath their status from the middle class. Further complicating negotiation of the social role of fashion, and the tenuous line trodden by female fashion followers, was the perception of fashion as an impediment to a moral life. From a twenty-first century perspective, these middle-class American fashion followers experienced a state of high ambivalence! The third reading—"Gender Symbols or Fashionable Details?"—by Jo B. Paoletti and Claudia Brush Kidwell, discusses gendered fashions up to the 1980s. In Western fashion, feminine dress borrows or uses elements from masculine dress extensively, while the opposite is not true.

Life stages can imply or dictate appearance within a culture: they may be strictly coded by age, as suggested by Callahan and Paoletti. Sexualized dress, improper in some cultures at any point in life, is not appropriate in Western cultures until later teen years, although this is changing to younger ages. As humans age, interest in dress and appearance often diminishes, but not always. As the baby boomer generation ages, it is expected that interest in fashion will be greater than in the previous generation. Women try to stay young-looking well past menopause. Men also increasingly strive for a youthful appearance. Body techniques such as diet, exercise and body modifications are used to maintain a youthful appearance.

The unmistakable zoot suit style originated among Mexican American and Black city youths. Encountering racism and the concomitant economic pressures of the Second World War, these two ethnic subcultures developed a distinctive suit style to express their ethos. It also immediately signaled their ethnic and minority identity to the dominant culture. Stuart Cosgrove provides a detailed historical account of the cultural forces that created the zoot suit, fostered its dissemination to associated communities in American cities, and resulted in ethnic conflict called the *zoot suit riots of 1943*, which were symbolically localized on young men wearing zoot suits.

Before the current era of increased openness toward gay lifestyles, homosexuals employed a variety of strategies to pass unnoticed in their workplaces, while simultaneously signaling their identity to those within gay culture. In "Invisible Men?," Shaun Cole uses extensive testimonial accounts to examine twentieth-century homosexual identity and its coded appearance practices in North America and Britain. This extract, from a book-length account, details changing covert and overt symbols of gay sexual identity, and the carefully strategized techniques of dressing for specific social contexts. Cole offers equal treatment to bodily nuances (mannerisms), garment colors, textiles, and to speech behaviors, informing the complete presentation of appearance and identity.

Occupations take up the better part of the daily life of adults and play a critical part in identity. Social structures are stratified based on income and the status of occupations. Workplace appearance contributes to performance and perceptions such as status, competence and appropriateness. Many roles in the workplace demand specific narrowly coded appearances. Lawyers and business people avoid sexualized dress at work. Those at the top rungs of status construct looks to communicate refined attributes such as quality and taste. Soldiers are recognizable through standardized grooming and identical functional uniforms. Professional athletes wear sport-specific garments to facilitate athletic performances. Gender, sexual and ethnic identity can influence evaluations of work performance and therefore advancement, because stereotypes can negatively affect perceptions. As a result, people often manage their appearance to counteract potential stereotyping, as shown in Cole's "Invisible Men."

Dick Hebdige's book *Subculture: The Meaning of Style* is considered a seminal cultural studies treatise on late industrial subcultures. According to Hebdige, age and class act as organizing forces around which hybridized styles evolve as the subculture searches for an identity that signifies *difference* from the fractured dominant culture. In this context, subculture is both about ideology and consumption: for example, innovations in punk style that expressed an ideology of anarchy and rupture necessarily meant acquiring new fashion products to create the next look. In "Subculture: The Unnatural Break," Hebdige presents the emergence of the mods (1964) and punks (1977) and their ambivalent receptions by media. Punks were praised and vilified at once; they were recognized as innovative while they were reviled as "other," repugnant and nonhuman. Hebdige recounts the encoding of their styles with ideology and the swift commodification of the styles into retail products. Fashion designer Vivienne Westwood, "The Queen of Punk," continues to design today.

Organized religion and spiritual beliefs may affect identities presented through dress. Belief systems that expect high standards of grooming and conscious attention to self-presentation, in honor of the worshipped, encourage fashion participation. Getting dressed up in "Sunday best" is a common occurrence in Western culture. Others abjure fashion participation, requiring strict dress conformity. Many religions have well-defined dress codes for officiates; the Pope and cardinals have wardrobes for specific holy days; mullahs wear robes that are not worn by the Muslim populace; Southeast Asian Buddhist monks wear draped, saffron-colored robes.

Consumer fashion products with hybrid and multiple identities are in the globalized fashion arena. Salient examples are the accessory designs by artist Takashi Murakami for Louis Vuitton. These began in 2003 with Murakami's logo designs "Monogram Multicolore" and "Eye Love Superflat" of pink and yellow smiling-face flowers. The products combine European luxury (a consistent fashion trope) with two specific Japanese identities. One Japanese identity is Murakami the artist. The other, drawing on *kawaii*, or Japan's "cute" subculture, resonates with Japanese fashion consumers. Superflat, the style of the logo art, is Murakami's conceptualization of Japanese art after the Second World War. Murakami's articulation of Superflat also recognizes a "'heritage of eccentricity' that runs from the seventeenth-century Edo Mannerists and the nineteenth-century *ukiyo-e* masters [woodblock artists] to the creators of Japanese animation" (Murakami [2000] in Matsui 2005: 226). Thus, Louis Vuitton accessories with Murakami-designed logos, sold worldwide by luxury retailers, can deploy an array of meanings based on the context of ownership, use, and the knowledge of the viewer. These accessories may merely identify luxury goods' fashionability, however; to those familiar with Japanese culture they can signal the global reach of *kawaii* subculture and even promote Murakami's Superflat program for Japanese art and its heritage of eccentricity.

Identity is such a key issue in contemporary fashion that other relevant extracts appear in subsequent sections, including Part VI: Fashion and the Body and Part IX: High/Low: From Haute Couture to the Street. The notion that identity is associated with a geographical location is examined in relation to fashion in Part IV: Geography of Fashion.

12

COLLEEN R. CALLAHAN and JO B. PAOLETTI

Is it a Girl or a Boy? Gender Identity and Children's Clothing

From C. Callahan and J. B. Paoletti (1999), Is it a Girl or a Boy?
Gender Identity and Children's Clothing, *exhibition catalog
(Richmond, VA: Valentine Museum).
Reprinted by permission of the Valentine Richmond History Center.*

To modern eyes, the most striking feature of nineteenth-century children's clothing is that both boys and girls wore dresses from birth through early childhood, leading to the perception that boys were dressed like girls. It is more accurate, however, to say that boys and girls were dressed alike. At the time, dresses and skirt outfits were merely seen as clothing appropriate for small children, regardless of gender. Babies and young children were considered innocents who, in their sexual immaturity, did not need specifically male or female clothing. In contrast, standard adult attire was gender-specific—only men wore trousers and only women wore skirts. Clothing modeled on female attire seemed proper for little boys because boys spent their first years within the feminine sphere of home and hearth, culturally and legally subordinate to men.

The first outer garments a nineteenth-century baby wore were white cotton dresses, called "long clothes." These dresses extended a foot or more beyond the child's feet, the extra length considered necessary for warmth and often tucked up around the infant to protect from drafts. For a layette—the diapers, shirts, petticoats, caps, pinafores, dresses, etc. constituting a baby's wardrobe—white cotton was used because it was easily washed and could be bleached

without fading. Between the ages of four and eight months, as a child began more active movement, it was dressed in "short clothes" or short white dresses.

Because many nineteenth-century baby dresses were ornately trimmed with embroidery and lace, today they are often mistaken as special-occasion attire. Actually, children wore these standard baby "uniforms" every day until about age two, with no distinction made between boys' or girls' outfits. Older toddlers continued to wear similar short dresses in light colors and, by mid-century, colorful prints were worn until the age of three or four.

Breeching, the occasion when a nineteenth-century boy put away the skirts and dresses of babyhood and donned his first pair of trousers, was a significant event in his life. When a boy assumed that most exclusive element of male dress, trousers, society viewed him as symbolically beginning the process of becoming a man. The age at which a boy was breeched depended on parental influence (for example, a mother might delay dressing her son in pants, signaling his continued dependence on her); the boy's maturity, defined as how masculine he appeared and acted; and his physical size. Another important factor determining breeching age was the period in which he was born during the century, because the average age for breeching changed over time.

At the beginning of the century, boys of about three traded their dresses for a fitted outfit called a *skeleton suit*—a jumpsuit-like garment that fitted close to the body, hence its name. Initially introduced in the 1770s, skeleton suits were significant as the first garments especially designed for little boys between three and six—older boys and men did not wear skeleton suits. A knee-length tunic dress over long trousers began to replace skeleton suits for three- to six-year-olds in the late 1820s; girls also wore versions of this style. The tunic and trouser outfit remained in fashion through the 1850s, with boys wearing trousers without the tunic overdress for the first time at six or seven.

The *knickerbocker* or *knicker suit*, named for its knee-length trousers, was introduced about 1860. As with skeleton suits, boys went from wearing dresses to knicker suits at around age three, but wore knickers for a longer time, to about age twelve. There were, however, noticeable differences between the outfits worn by younger and older boys. In the 1890s, boys as young as two were wearing knickers matched with blouse-like belted tunics or short velvet jackets, accessorized with large draping bow ties and lace-trimmed collars and cuffs—the famous "Little Lord Fauntleroy" look. Their older brothers from six to twelve wore knickers with tailored wool jackets, stiff-collared shirts and four-in-hand ties, indications the older boys were moving closer to adult status.

Most outfits for schoolboys younger than thirteen included features not found in men's clothes, implying the boys were not yet ready for the replicas of men's attire worn by teenage boys. For example, early in the 1800s, when men wore cutaway frock coats with knee-length tails, boys' jackets were cropped at the waist without tails. From the 1870s to 1940s, the major difference between men's and boys' clothes was that men wore long trousers and the boys short ones. By the end of the 1800s, when the breeching age had dropped from the mid-century high of about age six to between two and three, the point at

SUIT FOR BOY FROM 4 TO 6 YEARS OLD.

Figure 52. "White Duck Suit for Boy From 4–6 Years Old," *Harper's Bazar*, 1868. Commercial Pattern Archive (1868.2.BWS), Special Collections, University of Rhode Island Library.

which boys began wearing long trousers, usually between twelve and fourteen, was often seen as a more significant event than breeching.

The clothing of nineteenth-century girls did not undergo dramatic transformation as they grew—girls wore skirted garments as toddlers and as adults, but these differed in cut and style details. Children's dresses were shorter than women's gowns, gradually lengthening to reach adult length by a girl's mid-teen years. At the beginning of the nineteenth century, neoclassical fashions with high waists and narrow columnar skirts were worn by young boys and females of all ages, with the shorter length of children's dresses distinguishing them from adult attire.

Fitted waist-length bodices and full skirts in various styles dominated women's fashion from 1830 to the 1860s. During this time, the dresses worn by little boys and pre-adolescent girls were more similar to each other than to women's dresses. The characteristic "child's" dress of this period featured a wide off-the shoulder neckline, short puffed or cap sleeves and a full skirt. When fashioned for one-year-olds, these dresses were made up in white cotton, and in colored or printed fabrics for older children.

With the advent of bustle styles in the late 1860s, children's dresses became more streamlined, and many were cut without a waist seam, using princess seaming for shaping. Although young children usually did not wear bustles, throughout the bustle period (late 1860s to 1890) children's dresses often reflected women's styles with additional back fullness or trim. Between ten and twelve, girls began wearing dresses with fitted bodices and skirts draped over small bustles that were essentially women's garments, differing only in their length.

At mid-century, children's dresses were slightly below-knee in length and both young boys and girls wore ankle-length trousers, called pantaloons or pantalettes, under their skirts. When pantalettes for girls were introduced in the 1820s, they provoked controversy. Trouser-wearing females, even little girls, were seen as undermining society's natural order because trousers were such important icons of masculinity and male power. Pantalettes (later called drawers) gradually became accepted as underwear for both girls and women and, as "private" feminine garments, no longer posed a threat to the male privilege symbolized by trousers.

Subtle changes occurred during the second half of the 1800s, blurring some of the strict distinctions between male and female clothing. While girls and women did not wear trousers as outer garments in formal public situations, they did wear outfits with short gathered skirts over long full pants for exercise in the privacy of gymnasiums and as bathing costume. These full pants, called bloomers, were first seen in public without overskirts as part of women's bicycling attire in the 1890s. While disputes still raged about women wearing trousers, bicycle bloomers were one step toward trousers becoming accepted as standard items of female attire in the twentieth century.

Around 1900, new concepts of child rearing, which emphasized children's developmental stages, began to influence young children's clothing. Newborn infants still wore long white dresses, but a new one-piece garment called *creepers* or *rompers*, with short, full bloomer-like pants, became available for the crawling or toddling child. Contemporary research about children's development supported crawling as an important step in physical growth. Initially called "creeping aprons," rompers were devised in the 1890s as cover-ups for the traditional short white dresses worn by crawling infants. Before long, active babies were wearing rompers without dresses underneath. Despite earlier disputes about women and girls wearing pants, rompers were accepted without controversy as the first unisex pants outfits. By the 1920s, long white baby dresses were relegated to ceremonial occasions, although the short versions continued to be worn by newborn infants of both sexes into the 1950s.

The first rompers' solid colors and gingham checks provided a lively contrast to traditional baby white. With child-rearing experts advocating the use of color in young children's surroundings, both color and child-centered design motifs became integral elements of twentieth-century infants' clothing. In the 1920s, whimsical floral and animal motifs began to appear on children's clothing. At first these designs were as unisex as the rompers they decorated, but gradually certain motifs were associated more with one sex or the other. These designs had links to nineteenth-century depictions of children; dogs and drums, for example, were more often paired with boys, and kittens and flowers with girls.

Similar sex-typed motifs now appeared directly on children's clothing, thereby designating even unisex styles as a "boy's" or a "girl's" garment.

As infants' clothing gradually became more sex-typed, certain colors and trims also took on gender symbolism. Today this is most universally represented by blue for boys and pink for girls. Yet it took many years for this color code to become standardized. People are often surprised to learn that little boys wore pink as recently as the 1940s. Pink and blue were associated with gender as early as the 1910s, but the colors were typically used interchangeably for boys and girls until after the Second World War. There were early efforts to codify the colors, especially for newborns, with pink favored for girls and blue for boys. But, as late as 1939, a *Parents' Magazine* article argued that pink, a pale tint of red, was appropriate for boys because of red's connection with Mars, the god of war, while blue's association with Venus and the Madonna made it the color for girls. By 1950, a combination of public opinion and manufacturers' clout ordained just the opposite—pink for girls and blue for boys.

Even with this mandate, blue continued to be permissible for girls' clothing, although that "pale shade of red" was rejected for boys' attire. This exception to the "pink for girls, blue for boys" rule illustrates an important trend begun in the late 1800s. Over time, garments, trim or colors once worn by boys, yet traditionally equated with female clothing, have become unacceptable for boys' clothing. In the mid-nineteenth century, there was little difference in trim on dresses worn by children under three, but dresses for boys over that age sometimes had more "manly" details such as braid trim instead of lace, or more subdued colors. This effect became more pronounced after 1900 as boys' garments shed much of their elaborate trimming and ornamental details, and masculine outfits such as sailor suits were favored for younger and younger boys. By the 1970s, parents involved in the "nonsexist" child-rearing movement pressed manufacturers for children's clothes they considered gender-free. Interestingly, the resulting pants outfits were only "gender-free" in the sense that they incorporated styles, colors and trims currently acceptable for boys, eliminating any "feminine" adornment such as the color pink or ruffles.

Boys' attire grew progressively less "feminine" during the twentieth century, and in the 1990s, boys wear items associated with females only under special circumstances, such as a lace-trimmed heirloom christening dress worn at baptism. Conversely, female clothing became more "masculine," with those formerly male-only—trousers—gradually accepted for women and girls in nearly every social situation. By the 1940s, girls of all ages wore pants outfits at home and for casual public events, but they were still expected—if not required—to wear only dresses for school, church, parties and even shopping. About 1970, trousers' strong masculine connection had eroded to the point that school and office dress codes finally sanctioned trousers for girls and women. Although pants attained unisex status, many pants outfits continued to be strongly sex-typed through decoration and color.

A person from the 1830s, 1890s, or even the 1910s would be bewildered by the sight of males and females of every age wearing pants today, and very surprised little boys do not wear dresses. In these eras, the concept of unisex clothing applied only to young children whose unisex styles—dresses—were "feminine" in character. In contrast, today's dominant unisex styles—pants and T-shirts—are worn by all ages and both sexes, even though they were initially viewed as "masculine" styles. The shift in children's clothing from unisex dresses to unisex pants over the last century and a half signals society's constantly evolving definition of ideal feminine and masculine looks and behavior.

13

KAREN HALTTUNEN

Sentimental Culture and the Problem of Fashion

From K. Halttunen (1982), **Confidence Men and Painted Women:**
A Study of Middle-Class Culture in America, 1830–1870
(New Haven and London: Yale University Press), 61–5.
Reprinted with permission © Yale University Press.

Before the Industrial Revolution fashion was primarily the province of the court-based aristocracy: the nobility set fashions in dress and determined the rigid rules of "courtesy" for the European upper classes (König 1973). In colonial America, aristocrats imitated the fashions set by the London court. But over the course of the eighteenth century, the increasing power of the middle classes gradually undermined the court's domination of fashion. In England, a wealthy and powerful oligopoly accepted the worldly advice of that wily diplomat, the Earl of Chesterfield, and began to imitate aristocratic dress and etiquette (Wildeblood and Brinson 1965: 30–8). Even as fashion was becoming the aristocrat's only possible means to distinguish himself from the wealthy but untitled bourgeois, fashionable forms of dress and conduct were increasingly adopted by the middle classes. The aristocracy endeavored to stay one step ahead of the fashion-conscious middle classes, and the rate of fashion change accelerated. But with the coming of the French Revolution, according to sociologist René König, fashion at last became "a universal formative principle of society" (1973: 146). Once the revolution had abolished the distinctions of birth as illegitimate, the middle classes seized upon fashion as a means to segregate themselves from the less deserving lower classes. Nowhere was this phenomenon more pronounced than among the American middle classes in the Age of Jackson. The vociferous egalitarianism of the republic apparently made middle-class aspirants all the more anxious to pursue fashion in an effort to distinguish themselves from the democratic mob. As Alexis de Tocqueville insightfully observed:

> In democracies, where the members of the community never differ from each other and naturally stand so near that they may all at any time be fused in one general mass, numerous artificial and arbitrary distinctions spring up by means of which every man hopes to keep himself aloof lest he should be carried away against his will in the crowd. (1945: 227)

For the rising middle classes of the nineteenth century, fashion served both as a barrier which had to be surmounted by those entering the more privileged bourgeois circles and as a standard which could be applied to the claims of those seeking admission from below (König 1973: 158). According to European observers of democratic manners and morals, the social conduct of the American middle classes clearly demonstrated the first function of fashion as barrier. In their eagerness to enter the more privileged bourgeois circles above them, middle-class Americans strived to pass the fashion barrier by dressing stylishly and practicing ceremonial etiquette to a degree condemned by many visitors as absurd. The social supremacy of the Chestnut Street set within Philadelphia society, reported Harriet Martineau, her tongue in cheek, rested on the practice of rising thrice on the toes before the curtsey; Arch Street residents rose only twice (1837: 34). American efforts to enter higher social spheres often led them to imitate European fashions, with what foreign travelers regarded as ridiculous results. Francis Grund was struck, for example, by the efforts of a beautiful sixteen-year-old social aspirant who,

> throwing her head back and her breast forward, imitated by a sudden jerk of her body one of those ludicrous bows which the Gallo-American dancing-masters have substituted for the slow, graceful, dignified courtesies of old; and which fashionable women in the United States, who are generally in advance of the most grotesque fashions of Paris, are sure to turn into a complete caricature. (Grund 1959: 33)

Charles Dickens scornfully reported that fashionable young ladies in America "sang in all languages—except their own. German, French, Italian, Spanish, Portuguese, Swiss; but nothing native; nothing so low as native" (Dickens 1861: 302). Worst of all, Americans anxious to crash the fashion barrier assumed false titles, lionized or cultivated titled nobility, and engaged in "toad-eating" or "toadying," the obsequious flattering of their social superiors.

Fashion-conscious behavior among middle-class Americans also demonstrated the importance of fashion as a standard that might be applied to the social claims of the less fortunate. The middle-class American who succeeded in crossing the fashion barrier, in other words, could then use fashion to exclude applicants who followed. Americans were merciless, according to European observers, in their scrutiny of the parvenu seeking admission to what was called society. "Claims are canvassed and pretensions weighed," wrote Thomas Hamilton; "manners, fortune, tastes, habits and descent undergo a rigid examination" (1833: 206). To distinguish

themselves from the egalitarian masses below them, Americans wielded invitations and calling cards to barricade the vulgar from their social presence. Above all, they learned to "cut" former acquaintances as they improved their social status. Good manners in America, wrote Francis Grund, were aimed at making their victims "as uncomfortable as possible" to prove their inferiority. "In order to be 'genteel,'" he observed, "it is necessary, in the first place, to know nobody that is *not* so; and our fashionable women and girls have a peculiar talent for staring their old friends and acquaintances out of countenance, as often as they take a new house" (1959: 146, 55).

Many of the European visitors who attacked the follies of American fashion-hunters revealed at least as much about their own sense of social superiority as they did about the snobbery of the American middle classes. Francis Grund's contempt for the fashionable American was not untypical: "This aristocracy here is itself nothing but a wealthy overgrown bourgeoisie, composed of a few families who have been more successful in trade than the rest, and on that account are now cutting their friends and relations in order to be considered fashionable" (1959: 10). Grund, along with many other European visitors to the United States, criticized the middle-class pursuit of fashion primarily for its ridiculous pretentiousness. But for American middle-class moralists, such as the writers of advice to young men, the problem of fashion was far more serious. In the view of men such as Rufus Clark, young men and women of fashion led:

> a mere butterfly existence, sporting from flower to flower, and chasing one shadow after another, with no adequate views of the responsibilities and duties of life. Their greatest excitement is derived from the most trivial sources. The changes in the weather, the last novel, a new fashion, afford them the highest mental stimulus. (1853: 50)

The life of fashion, in other words, undermined all moral self-improvement. Fashion was regarded as the art of surface illusion, and the youth who mastered this art was advised sternly "to turn himself inside out and see the vile arid empty chambers of his soul, and then put on his airs" (Todd 1850: 126). Young men and women of fashion were learning to cultivate a showy appearance at the expense of moral character: they "put on the tinsel" to emulate the "show and glitter" of the wealthy; they struggled hard "to *seem* to be what they really are not*" (Waterbury 1852: 112–13). In the view of American moralists, the middle-class pursuit of fashion was not merely a ridiculous pretension; it was an act of hypocrisy. The greatest evils of fashion were symbolized in the "bland, smooth-tongued, genteel, fashionable companion," the confidence man (R. Clark 1853: 167).

Fashion, in short, seemed to be infecting middle-class parlor society with the immoral practices of the worldly confidence man. The figure of the confidence man served to focus the anxieties of middle-class Americans concerning upward social mobility. For the advisers of youth recognized that behind the fashion impulse lay the middle-class American's desire to set himself or herself apart from the democratic masses by establishing artificial social distinctions. With less sophistication than Tocqueville, William Alcott essentially echoed the French critic's theory: a peculiarly American "*shame of being thought poor*" fueled the American pursuit of fashion, and the "dread of what is called falling in the scale of society" was so great that many Americans were driven to insanity and even suicide (Alcott 1834: 145, 149). Alcott thus confronted what he considered to be a grave crisis: the pursuit of fashion, by which middle-class Americans attempted to establish their claims to gentility, was simply a parlor version of the confidence game that was poisoning social relations in the world outside the home.

Worst of all, the fashionable confidence game was being played primarily by that group of Americans most responsible for preserving the parlor as a sacred realm of sincerity: women. Of fashion-hungry women, Alcott wrote despairingly that "dress, personal appearance, equipage, style of a dwelling or its furniture, with no other

view, however, than the promotion of mere physical enjoyment, is the height of their desires for self-improvement!" (Alcott 1834: 266). Freed from many of the productive economic tasks performed by women in the earlier agricultural households, and often released from many domestic responsibilities by servants, the middle-class woman in the nineteenth century assumed the responsibility of elevating her family's social position as her husband struggled up the ladder of economic status (Davidoff 1973). It was she who worked to gain admittance into the finer bourgeois social circles by crossing the fashion barrier, and it was she who excluded the less deserving from her own set by raising the fashion standard. The American woman, whose highest moral responsibility was to preserve sincerity in the parlor, threatened to poison parlor society with the hypocrisy of fashion.

Middle-class women were thus caught in a conflict between two important social roles: how were they to act both as keepers of sincerity and as arbiters of fashion in the parlor? Fashion was condemned by sentimentalists as a form of hypocrisy, but fashion was increasingly viewed as a necessary evil in a society established on the promise of social mobility. This conflict between the sincere ideal and the growing power of fashion over middle-class life was a powerful force shaping the conventions of polite parlor conduct in the three major areas of sentimental culture: dress, etiquette, and social ritual. Of the three the most obvious area was women's dress: no other aspect of middle-class conduct was so completely shaped by the capricious dictates of fashion. The task of mediating the conflict between sentimental sincerity and fashionable hypocrisy thus had to be confronted in the pages of America's leading fashion magazine, *Godey's Lady's Book,* which began publication in 1830. By 1860, at least 150,000 women were regularly consulting *Godey's* to learn how to dress in the latest styles (Kunciov 1971: 1). Significantly, even *Godey's Lady's Book* expressed great anxiety about the moral evils of the fashionable life: throughout the 1830s and 1840s, and into the 1850s, the fashion columns, articles, and short

Figure 53. "Godey's Paris Fashions Americanized," *Godey's Lady's Book*, 1849. Historic Textile and Costume Collection, University of Rhode Island.
The editors at Godey's Lady's Book *often toned down the fashion plates they copied from* Les Modes Parisiennes.

stories of *Godey's* were dominated by the moral critique of fashion as hypocrisy. In embracing the sentimental critique of fashion, the editors and contributors to *Godey's* set themselves two very difficult tasks: they had to articulate a sentimental rationale for a woman's attention to fashion, and they had to explain how particular dress styles conformed to the sentimental ideal by enhancing woman's sincerity.

EDITORS' NOTE

The remainder of the chapter details how *Godey's Lady's Book* consistently claimed that character mattered more than appearance, and that women who assumed the "mask of fashion" were social hypocrites. This attack on fashion by the Philadelphia-based magazine, edited by Sarah Josepha Hale from 1837 to 1877, "revealed a powerful republican bias" against "the fashionable excesses of the Old World aristocracy" (67). Yet the magazine recognized that fashion was here to stay, having become "an active force in middle-class social life" (70). "*Godey's* began to advise readers to observe these inescapable laws of middle-class social life" (70).

14

JO B. PAOLETTI and CLAUDIA BRUSH KIDWELL

Men and Women: Dressing the Part

From J. B. Paoletti and C. B. Kidwell (1989), in C. B. Kidwell and V. Steele (eds.),
Men and Women: Dressing the Part
(Washington, DC: Smithsonian Institution), 158–61.
Reprinted by permission of the authors

How does fashion express gender? While dress can reinforce the physical differences between men and women, padded shoulders, for example, have been perceived as both feminine and masculine. Dress also reflects social differences between the sexes, such as women's more restricted public lives, the need for men to project authority, and the emphasis on physical attractiveness as the measure of a woman's value. As women entered occupations previously dominated by men, they have adopted more or less masculine styles. But despite these changes, men's and women's appearance is almost never identical. There is continuing pressure to retain some distinguishing features.

Certain symbols resist change stubbornly. Consider the time required for women to adopt trousers for everyday dress. In the process new feminine forms of trousers appeared, as if to mitigate the extent to which a potent male symbol was being usurped. Skirts are another rigid symbol. Their use for children in the nineteenth century was acceptable only insofar as infants and young children did not need to be identified publicly by gender. Distinctions between male and female dress have been maintained both by keeping a few symbols tightly bound to masculinity or femininity and by transforming borrowed symbols.

The overwhelming direction in the borrowing of gender symbols is from the men's to women's dress. Nor is this a twentieth-century phenomenon, as women's adoption of hats during the sixteenth century reveals. Examples of men imitating women's dress are rare. Even when apparently feminine symbols are borrowed, justification is offered by citing examples of men's earlier use of the style. Long-haired youths in the late 1960s countered criticism by pointing out that Jesus had long hair.

What does it mean when gender symbols change or are challenged? Fashion change is a complicated activity, involving individual choice and a vast manufacturing and distribution complex. The biggest gap in our understanding becomes evident when we attempt to find the motivation behind a fashion change. Consider the round-shouldered suit in the style of the New Look, for example. Did individuals see it as more feminine than previous styles, or as a welcome change from years of regulated sameness? There is a temptation to attach too great a significance to changes in gender symbols. When potent symbols of one gender are adopted by another (such as the introduction of trousers for women or long hair for men), the public reacts as if basic gender conventions are being threatened. But not all fashion changes have significant meaning.

Clothing styles are influenced by more factors than gender, and they change more frequently than do accepted definitions of masculinity and femininity. To read gender significance into the nuances of fashion would be oversimplifying a complex form of communication. A brief vogue for three-inch heels does not foreshadow a repeal of the nineteenth amendment.

The period from approximately 1880 to 1920 was a time when gender conventions and gender images changed. Men, women, and children of the 1920s looked significantly different than their parents. But we must be accurate in interpreting the new look, since the connection between role and appearance is not usually simple and direct. Women's clothing of the 1920s had become lighter in weight and much less restricting, allowing more physical freedom. The new body-skimming silhouette represented important changes: the acceptance of female athleticism and the introduction of a slimmer ideal of feminine beauty. In general, the options for women's and girls' clothing increased a great deal in the span of a generation, mostly by the appropriation of formerly masculine-style features. At the same time, women and girls did actually begin to enjoy more options in education, sports, and work, although these social changes were well underway in the late nineteenth century. In contrast, the changes that affected men's and boys' clothing did not reflect corresponding changes in conventional masculinity, but instead represented a new expression of the traditional masculine image.

Controversial fashion changes such as women adopting trousers can only take place after women's roles in society have altered. The mass acceptance of a style may accompany a change in public opinion, but does not precede it. Dress reformers were correct in seeing the connection between women's roles and their clothing, but erred in believing that by changing the costume, changes in gender conventions would automatically follow.

Do differences between men's and women's dress imply the existence of sexual inequality? Women's clothing prior to the twentieth century was usually more restricting than men's and there are still women's styles that hamper natural movement or distort the body. But men's clothing is hardly perfect: women's legs have been liberated since the 1920s, while men continue to suffer through the summer heat in long trousers, suit coats, tight collars, and neckties. Women enjoy a much larger range of choices than men, including personal styles drawing almost entirely from men's clothing.

It would appear that truly androgynous dress, if it existed, could eliminate the disadvantages of feminine and masculine dress, while combining their advantages. Yet styles that combine male and female characteristics that are worn by men and women have never been widely accepted. Women have incorporated almost every conceivable masculine element into their dress, but for men to adopt potent feminine symbols raises questions about their masculinity. Why is it more acceptable for women to copy men's clothing than for men to adopt women's clothing? Could it be, in part, because masculine symbols are valued more highly? If this is true, then women's adoption of trousers represents an important readjustment of the definition of femininity, but not necessarily a change in the existing balance of power.

Will distinctive masculine and feminine apparel ever become obsolete? If there isn't distinctive clothing, what might be worn? In 1970 the avant-garde designer Rudi Gernreich predicted that by 1980 male and female dress would be interchangeable. From his vantage point amidst the upheavals of the 1960s, Gernreich envisioned men and women in unisex or styles with their appearance differentiated by anatomy alone. His clothing was functional, devoid of gender symbolism. Yet the differences in young masculine and feminine bodies were celebrated. Gernreich's view was radical even for his time. But Gernreich could not exorcise traditional patterns of gender imagery from his vision of an egalitarian future. His man and woman dressed identically but posed in the familiar stances of angular, erect male and curving, submissive female. Gernreich's designs are no less radical today than they were twenty years ago.[1]

Men and women will never be the same, but their differences need not give them unequal status. It is possible that someday women and men will be valued equally, for all their differences. The clothes we wear today do not indicate that this will happen soon. If and when equality comes, both men and women will be free to express their unique individuality drawing from the broad vocabulary of masculinity and femininity.

EDITORS' NOTE

1. In 1989, when *Men and Women: Dressing the Part* was published, Western men did not wear skirts on an everyday basis. Since then, the MUG (male unbifurcated garment) movement has challenged the notion expressed here that men do not adopt clothing styles considered to be feminine. Both the 1995 movie *Braveheart* and the 2003–2004 exhibition "Bravehearts: Men in Skirts" broadened awareness of historical and contemporary cultures in which the wearing of skirts does not threaten masculinity.

15

STUART COSGROVE

The Zoot Suit and Style Warfare

From S. Cosgrove (1984), "The Zoot Suit and Style Warfare,"
**History Workshop Journal *18*: 77–91. Reprinted by
permission of Oxford University Press.**

INTRODUCTION: THE SILENT NOISE OF SINISTER CLOWNS

What about those fellows waiting still and silent there on the platform, so still and silent they clash with the crowd in their very immobility, standing noisy in their very silence; harsh as a cry of terror in their quietness? What about these three boys, coming now along the platform, tall and slender, walking with swinging shoulders in their well-pressed, too-hot-for-summer suits, their collars high and tight about their necks, their identical hats of black cheap felt set upon the crowns of their heads with a severe formality above their conked hair? It was as though I'd never seen their like before: walking slowly, their shoulders swaying, their legs swinging from their hips in trousers that ballooned upward from cuffs fitting snug about their ankles; their coats long and hip-tight with shoulders far too broad to be those of natural Western men. These fellows whose bodies seemed—what had one of my teachers said of me? "You're like one of those African sculptures, distorted in the interest of design." Well, what design and whose? (Ellison 1947: 380)

The zoot suit is more than an exaggerated costume, more than a sartorial statement; it is the bearer of a complex and contradictory history. When the nameless narrator of Ellison's *Invisible Man* confronted the subversive sight of three young and extravagantly dressed blacks, his reaction was one of fascination not of fear. These youths were not simply grotesque dandies parading the city's secret underworld, they were "the stewards of something uncomfortable" (1947: 381), a spectacular reminder that the social order had failed to contain their energy and difference. The zoot suit was more than the drape-shape of 1940s fashion, more than a colorful stage-prop hanging from the shoulders of Cab Calloway; it was, in the most direct and obvious ways, an emblem of ethnicity and a way of negotiating an identity. The zoot suit was a refusal: a subcultural gesture that refused to concede to the manners of subservience. By the late 1930s, the term "zoot" was in common circulation within urban jazz culture. "Zoot" meant something worn or performed in an extravagant style, and since many young blacks wore suits with outrageously padded shoulders and trousers that were fiercely tapered at the ankles, the term "zoot suit" passed into everyday usage. In the subcultural world of Harlem's nightlife, the language of rhyming slang succinctly described the zoot suit's unmistakable style: "a killer-driller coat with drape-shape, reet-pleats and shoulders padded like a lunatic's cell." The study of the relationship between fashion and social action is notoriously underdeveloped, but there is every indication that the zoot suit riots that erupted in the United States in the summer of 1943 had a profound effect on a whole generation of socially disadvantaged youths. It was during his period as a young

DRAPE SHAPE WITH A REET PLEAT
AND NO PLACE TO GO
↓

Figure 54. Zoot suit, 1943, *The Grist* (Rhode Island State College Yearbook), Providence: Roger Williams Press.
A college student sports a zoot suit for the 1943 yearbook.

zoot-suiter that the Chicano union activist Cesar Chavez first came into contact with community politics, and it was through the experiences of participating in zoot suit riots in Harlem that the young pimp "Detroit Red" began a political education that transformed him into the Black radical leader Malcolm X. Although the zoot suit occupies an almost mythical place within the history of jazz music, its social and political importance has been virtually ignored. There can be no certainty about when, where or why the zoot suit came into existence, but what is certain is that during the summer months of 1943 "the killer-driller coat" was the uniform of young rioters and the symbol of a moral panic about

juvenile delinquency that was to intensify in the postwar period.

At the height of the Los Angeles riots of June 1943, the *New York Times* carried a front-page article which claimed without reservation that the first zoot suit had been purchased by a black bus worker, Clyde Duncan, from a tailor's shop in Gainesville, Georgia ("Zoot Suit Originated in Georgia" 1943: 21). Allegedly, Duncan had been inspired by the film *Gone with the Wind* and had set out to look like Rhett Butler. This explanation clearly found favor throughout the USA. The national press forwarded countless others. Some reports claimed that the zoot suit was an invention of Harlem nightlife; others suggested it grew out of jazz culture and the exhibitionist stage costumes of the bandleaders, and some argued that the zoot suit was derived from military uniforms and imported from Britain. The alternative and independent press, particularly *Crisis* and *Negro Quarterly*, more convincingly argued that the zoot suit was the product of a particular social context (Turner and Surace 1956). They emphasized the importance of Mexican-American youths, or *pachucos*, in the emergence of zoot suit style and, in tentative ways, tried to relate their appearance on the streets to the concept of *pachuquismo*.

In his pioneering book, *The Labyrinth of Solitude*, the Mexican poet and social commentator Octavio Paz throws imaginative light on pachuco style and indirectly establishes a framework within which the zoot suit can be understood. Paz's study of the Mexican national consciousness examines the changes brought about by the movement of labor, particularly the generations of Mexicans who migrated northwards to the USA. This movement, and the new economic and social patterns it implies, has, according to Paz, forced young Mexican-Americans into an ambivalent experience between two cultures:

What distinguishes them, I think, is their furtive, restless air: they act like persons who are wearing disguises, who are afraid of a stranger's look because it could strip them and leave them stark naked ... This spiritual condition or lack of a spirit, has given birth to a type known as the pachuco. The pachucos are youths, for the most part of Mexican origin, who form gangs in southern cities; they can be identified by their language and behavior as well as by the clothing they affect. They are instinctive rebels, and North American racism has vented its wrath on them more than once. But the pachucos do not attempt to vindicate their race or the nationality of their forebears. Their attitude reveals an obstinate, almost fanatical will-to-be, but this will affirms nothing specific except their determination ... not to be like those around them. (Paz 1967: 5–6)

Pachuco youth embodied all the characteristics of second-generation working-class immigrants. In the most obvious ways they had been stripped of their customs, beliefs and language. The pachucos were a disinherited generation within a disadvantaged sector of North American society; and predictably their experiences in education, welfare and employment alienated them from the aspirations of their parents and the dominant assumptions of the society in which they lived. The pachuco subculture was defined not only by ostentatious fashion, but by petty crime, delinquency and drug-taking. Rather than disguise their alienation or efface their hostility to the dominant society, the pachucos adopted an arrogant posture. They flaunted their difference, and the zoot suit became the means by which that difference was announced. Those "impassive and sinister clowns," whose purpose was "to cause terror instead of laughter" (Paz 1967: 8), invited the kind of attention that led to both prestige and persecution. For Octavio Paz the pachuco's appropriation of the zoot suit was an admission of the ambivalent place he occupied. "It is the only way he can establish a more vital relationship with the society he is antagonizing. As a victim he can occupy a place in the world that previously ignored him; as a delinquent, he can become one of its wicked heroes" (Paz 1967: 8). The zoot suit riots of 1943 encapsulated this paradox. They emerged out of the dialectics of delinquency and persecution, during a period in which American society was undergoing profound structural change.

The major social change brought about by the United States' involvement in the war was the recruitment to the armed forces of over four million civilians and the entrance of over five million women into the wartime labor force. The rapid increase in military recruitment and the radical shift in the composition of the labor force led in turn to changes in family life, particularly the erosion of parental control and authority. The large scale and prolonged separation of millions of families precipitated an unprecedented increase in the rate of juvenile crime and delinquency. By the summer of 1943 it was commonplace for teenagers to be left to their own initiatives whilst their parents were either on active military service or involved in war work. The increase in night work compounded the problem. With their parents or guardians working unsocial hours, it became possible for many more young people to gather late into the night at major urban centers or simply on the street corners.

The rate of social mobility intensified during the period of the zoot suit riots. With over fifteen million civilians and twelve million military personnel on the move throughout the country, there was a corresponding increase in vagrancy. Petty crimes became more difficult to detect and control; itinerants became increasingly common, and social transience put unforeseen pressure on housing and welfare. The new patterns of social mobility also led to congestion in military and industrial areas. Significantly, it was the overcrowded military towns along the Pacific coast and the industrial towns of Detroit, Pittsburgh and Los Angeles that witnessed the most violent outbreaks of zoot suit rioting (Nelson 1971).

"Delinquency" emerged from the dictionary of new sociology to become an everyday term, as wartime statistics revealed these new patterns of adolescent behavior. The pachucos of the Los Angeles area were particularly vulnerable to the effects of war. Being neither Mexican nor American, the pachucos, like the black youths with whom they shared the zoot suit style, simply did not fit. In their own terms they were "24-hour orphans," having rejected the ideologies of their migrant parents. As the war furthered the dislocation of family relationships, the pachucos gravitated away from the home to the only place where their status was visible, the streets and bars of the towns and cities. But if the pachucos laid themselves open to a life of delinquency and detention, they also asserted their distinct identity, with their own style of dress, their own way of life and a shared set of experiences.

THE ZOOT SUIT RIOTS: LIBERTY, DISORDER AND THE FORBIDDEN

The zoot suit riots sharply revealed a polarization between two youth groups within wartime society: the gangs of predominantly black and Mexican youths who were at the forefront of the zoot suit subculture, and the predominantly white American servicemen stationed along the Pacific coast. The riots invariably had racial and social resonances, but the primary issue seems to have been patriotism and attitudes to the war. With the entry of the United States into the war in December 1941, the nation had to come to terms with the restrictions of rationing and the prospects of conscription. In March 1942, the War Production Board's first rationing act had a direct effect on the manufacture of suits and all clothing containing wool. In an attempt to institute a 26 percent cutback in the use of fabrics, the War Production Board drew up regulations for the wartime manufacture of what *Esquire* magazine called "streamlined suits by Uncle Sam" (Schoeffler and Gale 1973: 24). The regulations effectively forbade the manufacture of zoot suits and most legitimate tailoring companies ceased to manufacture or advertise any suits that fell outside the War Production Board's guidelines. However, the demand for zoot suits did not decline, and a network of bootleg tailors based in Los Angeles and New York continued to manufacture the garments. Thus the polarization between servicemen and pachucos was immediately visible: the chino shirt and battledress were evidently uniforms of patriotism, whereas wearing a zoot suit was a deliberate and public

way of flouting the regulations of rationing. The zoot suit was a moral and social scandal in the eyes of the authorities, not simply because it was associated with petty crime and violence, but because it openly snubbed the laws of rationing. In the fragile harmony of wartime society, the zoot-suiters were, according to Octavio Paz, "a symbol of love and joy or of horror and loathing, an embodiment of liberty, of disorder, of the forbidden" (Paz 1967: 8).

The zoot suit riots, which were initially confined to Los Angeles, began in the first few days of June 1943. During the first weekend of the month, over sixty zoot-suiters were arrested and charged at Los Angeles County jail, after violent and well-publicized fights between servicemen on shore leave and gangs of Mexican-American youths. In order to prevent further outbreaks of fighting, the police patrolled the eastern sections of the city, as rumors spread from the military bases that servicemen were intending to form vigilante groups. The *Washington Post's* report of the incidents, on the morning of Wednesday June 9, 1943, clearly saw the events from the point of view of the servicemen:

> Disgusted with being robbed and beaten with tire irons, weighted ropes, belts and fists employed by overwhelming numbers of the youthful hoodlums, the uniformed men passed the word quietly among themselves and opened their campaign in force on Friday night.
>
> At central jail, where spectators jammed the sidewalks and police made no efforts to halt autoloads of servicemen openly cruising in search of zoot-suiters, the youths streamed gladly into the sanctity of the cells after being snatched from bar rooms, pool halls and theaters and stripped of their attire. ("Zoot-Suiters Again on the Prowl as Navy Holds Back Sailors" 1943: 1)

During the ensuing weeks of rioting, the ritualistic stripping of zoot-suiters became the major means by which the servicemen reestablished their status over the pachucos. It became commonplace for gangs of marines to ambush zoot-suiters, strip them down to their underwear and leave them helpless in the streets. In one particularly vicious incident, a gang of drunken sailors rampaged through a cinema after discovering two zoot-suiters. They dragged the pachucos onto the stage as the film was being screened, stripped them in front of the audience and as a final insult, urinated on the suits.

The press coverage of these incidents ranged from the careful and cautionary liberalism of the *Los Angeles Times* to the more hysterical hate-mongering of William Randolph Hearst's west coast papers. Although the practice of stripping and publicly humiliating the zoot-suiters was not prompted by the press, several reports did little to discourage the attacks:

> Zoot suits smoldered in the ashes of street bonfires where they had been tossed by grimly methodical tank forces of servicemen ... The zooters, who earlier in the day had spread boasts that they were organized to "kill every cop" they could find, showed no inclination to try to make good their boasts ... Searching parties of soldiers, sailors and Marines hunted them out and drove them out into the open like bird dogs flushing quail. Procedure was standard: grab a zooter. Take off his pants and frock coat and tear them up or burn them. Trim the "Argentine Ducktail" haircut that goes with the screwy costume. (quoted in Menefee 1943: 189)

The second week of June witnessed the worst incidents of rioting and public disorder. A sailor was slashed and disfigured by a pachuco gang; a policeman was run down when he tried to question a carload of zoot-suiters; a young Mexican was stabbed at a party by drunken Marines; a trainload of sailors were stoned by pachucos as their train approached Long Beach; streetfights broke out daily in San Bernardino; over 400 vigilantes toured the streets of San Diego looking for zoot-suiters, and many individuals from both factions were arrested.[1] On June 9, the *Los Angeles Times* published the first in a series of editorials designed to reduce the level of violence, but which also tried to allay the growing concern about the racial character of the riots:

> To preserve the peace and good name of the Los Angeles area, the strongest measures must be taken jointly by the police, the Sheriff's office and Army and Navy authorities, to prevent any further outbreaks of "zoot suit" rioting. While members of the armed forces received considerable provocation at the hands of the unidentified miscreants, such a situation cannot be cured by indiscriminate assault on every youth wearing a particular type of costume.
>
> It would not do, for a large number of reasons, to let the impression circulate in South America that persons of Spanish-American ancestry were being singled out for mistreatment in Southern California. And the incidents here were capable of being exaggerated to give that impression. ("Strong Measures Must be Taken Against Rioting" 1943: 4)

THE CHIEF, THE BLACK WIDOWS AND THE TOMAHAWK KID

The pleas for tolerance from civic authorities and representatives of the Church and State had no immediate effect, and the riots became more frequent and more violent. A zoot-suited youth was shot by a special police officer in Azusa, a gang of pachucos were arrested for rioting and carrying weapons in the Lincoln Heights area; twenty-five black zoot-suiters were arrested for wrecking an electric railway train in Watts; and 1,000 additional police were drafted into East Los Angeles. The press coverage increasingly focused on the most "spectacular" incidents and began to identify leaders of zoot suit style. On the morning of Thursday, June 10 1943, most newspapers carried photographs and reports on three "notorious" zoot suit gang leaders. Of the thousands of pachucos that allegedly belonged to the hundreds of zoot suit gangs in Los Angeles, the press singled out the arrests of Lewis D. English, a 23-year-old black, charged with felony and carrying a "16-inch razor-sharp butcher knife"; Frank H. Tellez, a 22-year-old Mexican held on vagrancy charges; and another Mexican, Luis "The Chief" Verdusco (27 years of age), allegedly the leader of the Los Angeles pachucos ("Zoot Suit Fighting Spreads On the Coast" 1943: 23).

The arrests of English, Tellez and Verdusco seemed to confirm popular perceptions of the zoot-suiters widely expressed for weeks prior to the riots. Firstly, that the zoot suit gangs were predominantly, but not exclusively, comprised of black and Mexican youths. Secondly, that many of the zoot-suiters were old enough to be in the armed forces but were either avoiding conscription or had been exempted on medical grounds. Finally, in the case of Frank Tellez, who was photographed wearing a pancake hat with a rear feather, that zoot suit style was an expensive fashion often funded by theft and petty extortion. Tellez allegedly wore a colorful long drape coat that was "part of a $75 suit" and a pair of pegged trousers "very full at the knees and narrow at the cuffs" which were allegedly part of another suit. The caption of the Associated Press photograph indignantly added that: "Tellez holds a medical discharge from the Army" ("Zoot Suit Fighting" 1943: 23). What newspaper reports tended to suppress was information on the Marines who were arrested for inciting riots, the existence of gangs of white American zoot-suiters, and the opinions of Mexican-American servicemen stationed in California, who were part of the war effort but who refused to take part in vigilante raids on pachuco hangouts.

As the zoot suit riots spread throughout California to cities in Texas and Arizona, a new dimension began to influence press coverage of the riots in Los Angeles. On a day when 125 zoot-suited youths clashed with Marines in Watts and armed police had to quell riots in Boyle Heights, the Los Angeles press concentrated on a razor attack on a local mother, Betty Morgan. What distinguished this incident from hundreds of comparable attacks was that the assailants were girls. The press related the incident to the arrest of Amelia Venegas, a woman zoot-suiter who was charged with carrying, and threatening to use, a brass knuckleduster. The revelation that girls were active within pachuco subculture led to consistent press coverage of the activities of two female gangs: the Slick Chicks and the Black Widows ("Zoot-Girls Use Knife in Attack" 1943: 1). The latter gang took its name from the members' distinctive dress: black zoot suit jackets, short black skirts and black fishnet stockings. In retrospect the Black Widows, and their active part in the subcultural violence of the zoot suit riots, disturb conventional understandings of the concept of pachuquismo.

As Joan W. Moore implies in *Homeboys* (1978), her definitive study of Los Angeles youth gangs, the concept of pachuquismo is too readily and unproblematically equated with the better-known concept of machismo. Undoubtedly they share certain ideological traits, not least a swaggering and at times aggressive sense of power and bravado, but the two concepts derive from different sets of social definitions. Whereas machismo can be defined in terms of male power and sexuality, pachuquismo predominantly derives from ethnic, generational and class-based aspirations, and is less evidently a question of gender. What the zoot suit riots brought to the surface was the complexity of pachuco style. The Black Widows and their aggressive image confounded the pachuco stereotype of the lazy male delinquent who avoided conscription for a life of dandyism and petty crime, and reinforced radical readings of pachuco subculture. The Black Widows were a reminder that ethnic and generational alienation was a pressing social problem and an indication of the tensions that existed in minority, low-income communities.

Although detailed information on the role of girls within zoot suit subculture is limited to very brief press reports, the appearance of female pachucos coincided with a dramatic rise in the delinquency rates among girls aged between twelve and twenty years old. The disintegration of traditional family relationships and the entry of young women into the labor force undoubtedly had an effect on the social roles and responsibilities of female adolescents, but it is difficult to be precise about the relationships between changed patterns of social experience and the rise in delinquency. However, wartime society brought about an increase in unprepared and irregular sexual intercourse, which in turn led to significant increases in the rates of abortion, illegitimate births and venereal diseases. Although statistics are difficult to trace, there are many indications that the war years saw a remarkable increase in the numbers of young women who were taken into social care or referred to penal institutions, as a result of the specific social problems they had to encounter.

Later studies provide evidence that young women and girls were also heavily involved in the traffic and transaction of soft drugs. The pachuco subculture within the Los Angeles metropolitan area was directly associated with a widespread growth in the use of marijuana. It has been suggested that female zoot-suiters concealed quantities of drugs on their bodies, since they were less likely to be closely searched by male members of the law enforcement agencies. Unfortunately, the absence of consistent or reliable information on the female gangs makes it particularly difficult to be certain about their status within the riots, or their place within traditions of feminine resistance. The Black Widows and Slick Chicks were spectacular in a subcultural sense, but their black drape jackets, tight skirts, fishnet stockings and heavily emphasized makeup were ridiculed in the press. The Black Widows clearly existed outside the orthodoxies of wartime society, playing no part in the industrial war effort, and openly challenging conventional notions of feminine beauty and sexuality.

Towards the end of the second week of June, the riots in Los Angeles were dying out. Sporadic incidents broke out in other cities, particularly Detroit, New York and Philadelphia, where two members of Gene Krupa's dance band were beaten up in a station for wearing the band's zoot suit costumes; but these, like the residual events in Los Angeles, were not taken seriously. The authorities failed to read the inarticulate warning signs proffered in two separate incidents in California: in one a zoot-suiter was arrested for throwing gasoline flares at a theater; and in the second another was arrested for carrying a silver tomahawk. The zoot suit riots had become a public and spectacular enactment of social disaffection. The authorities in Detroit chose to dismiss a zoot suit riot at the city's Cooley High School as an adolescent imitation of the Los Angeles disturbances ("Zoot Suit Warfare Spreads to Pupils of Detroit Area" 1943: 1). Within three weeks Detroit was in the midst of the worst race riot in its history.[2] The United States was still involved in the war abroad when violent events on the home front signaled the beginnings of a new era in racial politics.

OFFICIAL FEARS OF FIFTH-COLUMN FASHION

Official reactions to the zoot suit riots varied enormously. The most urgent problem that concerned California's State Senators was the adverse effect that the events might have on the relationship between the United States and Mexico. This concern stemmed partly from the wish to preserve good international relations, but rather more from the significance of relations with Mexico for the economy of Southern California, as an item in the *Los Angeles Times* made clear. "In San Francisco Senator Downey declared that the riots may have 'extremely grave consequences' in impairing relations between the United States and Mexico, and may endanger the program of importing Mexican labor to aid in harvesting California crops" ("Zoot Suit War Inquiry Ordered by Governor" 1943: A). These fears were compounded when the Mexican Embassy formally drew the zoot suit riots to the attention of the State Department. It was the fear of an "international incident" that could only have an adverse effect on California's economy, rather than any real concern for the social conditions of the Mexican-American community, that motivated Governor Warren of California to order a public investigation into the causes of the riots. In an ambiguous press statement, the Governor hinted that the riots may have been instigated by outside or even foreign agitators:

As we love our country and the boys we are sending overseas to defend it, we are all duty bound to suppress every discordant activity which is designed to stir up international strife or adversely affect our relationships with our allies in the United Nations. ("Warren Orders Zoot Suit Quiz" 1943: 1)

The zoot suit riots provoked two related investigations: a fact-finding investigative committee headed by Attorney General Robert Kenny and an un-American activities investigation presided over by State Senator Jack B. Tenney. The un-American activities investigation was ordered "to determine whether the present zoot suit riots were sponsored by Nazi agencies attempting to spread disunity between the United States and Latin-American countries" ("Tenney Feels Riots Caused by Nazi Move for Disunity" 1943: A). Senator Tenney, a member of the un-American Activities committee for Los Angeles County, claimed he had evidence that the zoot suit riots were "Axis-sponsored," but the evidence was never presented. However, the notion that the riots might have been initiated by outside agitators persisted throughout the month of June, and was fueled by Japanese propaganda broadcasts accusing the North American government of ignoring the brutality of US marines. The arguments of the un-American activities investigation were given a certain amount of credibility by a Mexican pastor based in Watts, who according to the press had been "a pretty rough customer himself, serving as a captain in Pancho Villa's revolutionary army" ("Watts Pastor Blames Riots on Fifth Column" 1943: A). Reverend Francisco Quintanilla, the pastor of the Mexican Methodist Church, was convinced the riots were the result of fifth columnists. "When boys start attacking servicemen it means the enemy is right at home. It means they are being fed vicious propaganda by enemy agents who wish to stir up all the racial and class hatreds they can put their evil fingers on" ("Watts" 1943; A).

The attention given to the dubious claims of Nazi-instigation tended to obfuscate other more credible opinions. Examination of the social conditions of pachuco youths tended to be marginalized in favor of other more "newsworthy" angles. At no stage in the press coverage were the opinions of community workers or youth leaders sought, and so, ironically, the most progressive opinion to appear in the major newspapers was offered by the Deputy Chief of Police, E. W. Lester. In press releases and on radio he provided a short history of gang subcultures in the Los Angeles area and then tried, albeit briefly, to place the riots in a social context:

> The Deputy Chief said most of the youths came from overcrowded colorless homes that offered no opportunities for leisure-time activities. He said it is wrong to blame law enforcement agencies for the present situation, but that society as a whole must be charged with mishandling the problems. ("California Governor Appeals for Quelling of Zoot Suit Riots" 1943: A3)

On the morning of Friday, June 11, 1943, the *Los Angeles Times* broke with its regular practices and printed an editorial appeal, "Time For Sanity," on its front page. The main purpose of the editorial was to dispel suggestions that the riots were racially motivated, and to challenge the growing opinion that white servicemen from the Southern States had actively colluded with the police in their vigilante campaign against the zoot-suiters:

> There seems to be no simple or complete explanation for the growth of the grotesque gangs. Many reasons have been offered, some apparently valid, some farfetched. But it does appear to be definitely established that any attempts at curbing the movement have had nothing whatever to do with race persecution, although some elements have loudly raised the cry of this very thing. ("Time for Sanity" 1943: 1)

A month later, the editorial of July's issue of *Crisis* presented a diametrically opposed point of view:

> These riots would not occur—no matter what the instant provocation—if the vast majority of the population, including more often than not the law enforcement officers and machinery, did not share in varying degrees the belief that Negroes are and must be kept second-class citizens. ("The Riots" 1943: 199)

But this view got short shrift, particularly from the authorities, whose initial response to the riots was largely retributive. Emphasis was placed on arrest and punishment. The Los Angeles City Council considered a proposal from Councilor Norris Nelson, that "it be made a jail offense to wear zoot suits with reet pleats within the city limits of LA" ("Ban on Freak Suits Studied by Councilmen" 1943: A3), and a discussion ensued for over an hour before it was resolved that the laws pertaining to rioting and disorderly conduct were sufficient to contain the zoot suit threat. However, the council did encourage the War Production Board (WPB) to reiterate its regulations on the manufacture of suits. The regional office of the WPB, based in San Francisco, investigated tailors manufacturing in the area of men's fashion and took steps "to curb illegal production of men's clothing in violation of WPB limitation orders." Only when Governor Warren's fact-finding commission made its public recommendations did the political analysis of the riots go beyond the first principles of punishment and proscription. The recommendations called for a more responsible cooperation from the press; a program of special training for police officers working in multiracial communities; additional detention centers; a juvenile forestry camp for youths under the age of sixteen; an increase in military and shore police; an increase in the youth facilities provided by the Church; an increase in neighborhood recreation facilities and an end to discrimination in the use of public facilities. In addition to these measures, the commission urged that arrests should be made without undue emphasis on members of minority groups and encouraged lawyers to protect the rights of youths arrested for participation in gang activity. The findings were a delicate balance of punishment and palliative; it made no significant mention of the social conditions of Mexican laborers and no recommendation about the kind of public spending that would be needed to alter the social experiences of pachuco youth. The outcome of the zoot suit riots was an inadequate, highly localized and relatively ineffective body of short-term public policies that provided no guidelines for the more serious riots in Detroit and Harlem later in the same summer.

THE MYSTERY OF THE SIGNIFYING MONKEY

The pachuco is the prey of society, but instead of hiding he adorns himself to attract the hunter's attention. Persecution redeems him and breaks his solitude: his salvation depends on him becoming part of the very society he appears to deny. (Paz 1967: 9)

The zoot suit was associated with a multiplicity of different traits and conditions. It was simultaneously the garb of the victim and the attacker, the persecutor and the persecuted, the "sinister clown" and the grotesque dandy. But the central opposition was between the style of the delinquent and that of the disinherited. To wear a zoot suit was to risk the repressive intolerance of wartime society and to invite the attention of the police, the parent generation and the uniformed members of the armed forces. For many pachucos, the zoot suit riots were simply high times in Los Angeles when momentarily they had control of the streets; for others it was a realization that they were outcasts in a society that was not of their making. For the black radical writer, Chester Himes, the riots in his neighborhood were unambiguous: "Zoot Riots are Race Riots" (1943). For other contemporary commentators the wearing of the zoot suit could be anything from unconscious dandyism to a conscious "political" engagement. The zoot suit riots were *not* "political" riots in the strictest sense, but for many participants they were an entry into the language of politics, an inarticulate rejection of the "straight world" and its organization.

It is remarkable how many postwar activists were inspired by the zoot suit disturbances. Luis Valdez of the radical theater company, El Teatro Campesino, allegedly learned the "chicano" from his cousin the zoot-suiter Billy Mirand.[3] The novelists Ralph Ellison and Richard Wright both conveyed a literary and political fascination with the power and potential of the zoot suit. One of Ellison's editorials for the journal *Negro Quarterly* expressed his own sense of frustration at the enigmatic attraction of zoot suit style:

A third major problem, and one that is indispensable to the centralization and direction of power is that of learning the meaning of myths and symbols which abound among the Negro masses. For without this knowledge, leadership, no matter how correct its program, will fail. Much in Negro life remains a mystery; perhaps the zoot suit conceals profound political meaning; perhaps the symmetrical frenzy of the Lindy-hop conceals clues to great potential powers, if only leaders could solve this riddle. (Neal 1974a: 67)

Although Ellison's remarks are undoubtedly compromised by their own mysterious idealism, he touches on the zoot suit's major source of interest. It is in everyday rituals that resistance can find natural and unconscious expression. In retrospect, the zoot suit's history can be seen as a point of intersection between the related potential of ethnicity and politics on the one hand, and the pleasures of identity and difference on the other. It is the zoot suit's political and ethnic associations that have made it such a rich reference point for subsequent generations. From the music of Thelonious Monk and Kid Creole to the jazz-poetry of Larry Neal, the zoot suit has inherited new meanings and new Mysteries. In his book *Hoodoo Hollerin' Bebop Ghosts*, Neal uses the image of the zoot suit as the symbol of Black America's cultural resistance. For Neal, the zoot suit ceased to be a costume and became a tapestry of meaning, where music, politics and social action merged. The zoot suit became a symbol for the enigmas of Black culture and the mystery of the signifying monkey:

But there is rhythm here
Its own special substance:
I hear Billie sing, no Good Man, and dig Prez, wearing the Zoot suit of life, the Porkpie hat tilted at the correct angle; through the Harlem smoke of beer
And whisky, I understand the mystery of the Signifying Monkey. (Neal 1974b: 9)

ACKNOWLEDGMENTS

The author wishes to acknowledge the support of the British Academy for the research for this article.

NOTES

1. Details of the riots are taken from newspaper reports and press releases for the weeks in question, particularly from the *Los Angeles Times, New York Times, Washington Post, Washington Star* and *Time Magazine*.
2. Although the Detroit Race Riots of 1943 were not zoot suit riots, nor evidently about "youth" or "delinquency," the social context in which they took place was obviously comparable. For a lengthy study of the Detroit riots, see R. Shogun and T. Craig (1964), *The Detroit Race Riot: A Study in Violence*, Philadelphia and New York: Chilton Books.
3. El Teatro Campesino presented the first Chicano play to achieve full commercial Broadway production. The play, written by Luis Valdez and entitled *Zoot Suit,* was a drama documentary on the Sleepy Lagoon murder and the events leading to the Los Angeles riots. (The Sleepy Lagoon murder of August 1942 resulted in twenty-four pachucos being indicted for conspiracy to murder.)

16

SHAUN COLE

Invisible Men?

From S. Cole (2000), "Don We Now Our Gay Apparel": Gay Men's Dress in the Twentieth Century (Oxford: Berg), 59–69.

From the turn of the century right up until the 1960s, when changes in attitudes toward sexuality and men's fashions began to alter perceptions of homosexuality, the effeminate queen was the dominant public image of male homosexuals. This could mean two things. On the one hand the flamboyant stereotype diverted attention from other more guarded men and made it relatively easy to "pass" as straight. On the other it threatened to overwhelm any other images people had of anyone they discovered to be homosexual (Steward 1982; Chauncey 1994: 103). Just as there were men who expressed their homosexuality through the adoption of an effeminate appearance in both the gay and the straight worlds, so there were men who would not or could not express their sexuality in this way. They did not identify with the feminine, and regarded themselves as homosexual but not as "fairies." As early as 1881 John Addington Symonds had noted that while "a certain class of people are undoubtedly feminine, the majority do not differ from 'normal' men. They are athletic, masculine in habits, frank in manner." These "normal" homosexuals are "passing through society year after year without arousing a suspicion of their inner temperament" (Symonds 1881: 251–2).

For most homosexuals the 1930s through to the 1950s were characterized by the very real fear of exposure, blackmail and imprisonment. In both Britain and America the police were conducting a virtual witch-hunt of homosexuals (Weeks 1990; Marcus 1992; Loughery 1998; Bérubé 1990). In Britain this led to events such as the Montagu trials. [Lord Montagu and others were accused of indecent assault in 1953.] Gay men also had to contend with the threat of vigilante anti-gay violence and strove to remain invisible in public (Brighton Ourstory Project 1992: 37). In 1948 the following "Don'ts" were suggested as "sane and useful advice for male inverts" in England:

> Don't commit to writing any admissions as to your inclinations; don't masquerade on any occasion whatsoever in women's clothes, take female parts in theatrical performances or use makeup; don't be too meticulous in the matter of your own clothes, or affect any extremes in color or cut; don't wear conspicuous rings, watches, cufflinks, or other jewelry; don't allow your voice or intonation to display feminine inflection—cultivate a masculine tone and method of expression; don't stand with your hand on your hip, or walk mincingly; don't become identified with the group of inverts which form in every city ... (Anomaly 1948; Margin 1955)

Dress for these gay men broadly followed conventions of fashion: they wore "dark suits, three pieces, very quiet shirts" that would not elicit comment or notice from outsiders (Porter and Weeks 1992: 62). Dudley Cave, for example, tended to wear "grey flannels, a sports coat and an extremely butch belt, an ex-army belt, a tie."

He "wouldn't have dreamt of going into town in those days without wearing a tie and usually a sports jacket. Generally speaking we kept our heads down and tried to avoid being seen as what we were (Author interview with Dudley Cave, 1997). John Hardy echoes the fact that everyday dress for most gay men followed conventions of fashion: "When you were out and about in the streets and going about your ordinary day-to-day business you *wouldn't* think of wearing anything really outrageous. You tended to dress down and look like everyone else (Author interview with John Hardy, 1995). In America gay men were also at pains not to express their *sexual* orientation through their dress. Bill Miller, owner of Village Squire (a shop with a large homosexual clientele in New York) said that covert or closeted homosexuals do not wish to be identified as homosexual and dress accordingly: "They will fight fashion completely. They will want to wear a uniform, get lost in the rush. I'm willing to guess that Brooks Bros. has more homosexual customers than all the Village boutiques put together" (Lukey 1970: 82). In a novel written in 1958, a "self-confessed fairy" decides to move away from the town he has lived in and start a new life as a *"normal"* man. He changes his image from the camp, effeminately dressed queen to what he perceives as "respectable," for which we can read *not* queer.

> He thought of dyeing his hair black, of buying a tweed suit to fill out his figure, and of honoring his fingers with rings, big solid knots which were the emblems of athletic trophies. With square, heavy soled, box-toed shoes he would be just another Southerner in search of Manassas ... he snipped his ringlets to the nubbin and looked almost respectable, he thought. (Talsman 1966: 207)

Adhering to normative dress codes was seen as an important factor in the progression of the early gay rights movements. Frank Kameny, one of the leaders of the Mattachine Society, insisted that a strict dress code was enforced on all participants in gay demonstrations. Men were to wear suits, shirts and ties and women skirts. "If we want to be employed by the Federal Government," Kameny intoned, "we have to look employable to the Federal Government." Kameny and his allies felt that it was important to look ordinary, to get bystanders to hear the message rather than be prematurely turned off by appearances (Duberman 1994: 111).

Writing in 1965, Douglas Plummer observed that in one smart members-only London gay club, "it would be difficult, if not impossible, to judge any of these men as being homosexual if they were seen individually in a crowd" (1965: 54–6). Stratton Ashley observed a similar clientele in New York bars, where the men were all "young and well groomed. On the whole they looked like a bunch of clean-cut college boys." They were, one of them told him, "most interested in those qualities regarded as masculine in each other. We cultivate those qualities in ourselves and look for them in others. No one is more 'out' in our group than the queen who swishes" (Ashley 1964: 5). Other journalistic accounts of gay life in New York and San Francisco made reference to the smart and inconspicuous style of dress of many of the men in gay bars and clubs, where no one "looked" homosexual (Helmer 1963: 85–92).

In the light of society's and the law's attitudes toward gay men, they devised a variety of tactics that allowed them to move about freely, to appropriate for themselves spaces that were not marked as gay, and to construct gay space in the midst of, yet invisible to, the dominant culture. They were aided in this effort, as always, by the disinclination of most people to believe that any "normal"-looking man could be anything other than "normal." In "The Sexed Self: Strategies of Performance, Sites of Resistance," David Bell and Gill Valentine discuss the "managed self" in relation to lesbian identity, noting how lesbians create apparently asexual identities by avoiding reference to their personal life but bearing discreet signals that can be read by "those in the know." This theory can equally be applied to those gay men who remained invisible in heterosexually defined public spaces while revealing their hidden identity to those in the know through a series of sartorial or behavioral signifiers. Thus in Bell and Valentine's words they were "putting on or taking off different 'masks,'" sometimes maintaining multiple identities in one space at different times or in different spaces at the same time (Bell and Valentine 1995; Finch diary in Chauncey: 273). Men who dressed conventionally in public did not necessarily continue this practice once inside their own home or in accepted gay spaces, such as pubs or clubs (Gidlow 1980: 122). Grant remembered that in Brighton (which had a large and often visible gay population in the 1950s): "The only time you saw a gay man was probably at the weekend. During the week, you would have passed him by with his bowler hat, navy suit and black shoes with a paper under his arm and a rolled umbrella" (Brighton Ourstory Project 1992: 30).

Involvement in the gay world familiarized men with the styles of clothing and grooming, mannerisms, and conventions of speech that had become fashionable in that world, but were not stereotypically associated with effeminate homosexuals. Both gay and straight observers have noted this. Those fashions served as signs "neither masculine nor feminine, but specifically and peculiarly homosexual," observed the writer and gay activist Donald Webster Cory in the early 1950s: "these were difficult for [outsiders] to pinpoint," but enabled men to recognize one another even as they concealed their identities from others (1953: 7–11). Whereas effeminate men used codes that were intelligible to straights as well as to gays, such as flashy dress (Author interview with Daniel 1997; Khan 1937: 217), other gay men developed codes that were intelligible only to other men familiar with the subculture:

Most inverts are practiced at spotting others, whether obvious or not, in all countries in general and their own country in particular. It is partly experience, partly intuition. I suppose I was a little quicker than the average, and fairly good at spotting the middle-class "respectable" homosexual who tries to hide the thing, but who gives himself away by his anxiety to appear normal. (Garland 1995: 159–60)

Accessories, such as red ties or suede shoes, were used to allow these gay men to recognize one another without drawing the attention of the uninitiated. They were so effective that researchers repeatedly expressed their astonishment at gay men's ability to identify each other, attributing it to something akin to a sixth sense:

Sexual perverts readily recognize each other, although they may never have met before and there exists a mysterious bond of psychological sympathy between them ... Instances have been authenticated to me where such perverts when meeting another of the same sex, have at once recognized each other, and mutually become acquainted and have left company with each other to practice together their unnatural vices. (Comstock, 1892: 172)

Suede shoes are perhaps one of the better-known historical signifiers of homosexuality, especially in Britain. Observers in America in the late nineteenth century noted that "fairies" were wearing suede shoes in New York, and Thomas Painter observed that dark brown and gray suede shoes were "practically a homosexual monopoly" (Painter 1941: 168–9, quoted in Chauncey 1994: 52). In Britain in the 1930s suede shoes were a sure sign of deviancy. Stephen "distinctly remember[s] it was a very bad sign for people if they wore camel hair coats and suede shoes! I remember when I bought myself a camel hair coat and suede shoes I thought I was really coming out" (Porter and Weeks: 111; Greenidge 1930: 133). Trevor Thomas was known as "the man who wore suede shoes" and that "it was known if you wore suede shoes and a Liberty (silk) tie you were (homosexual)." His "alibis," to anyone who was not homosexual, were "(a) I was an artist, (b) I worked in a Museum and (c) I acted" (Porter and Weeks: 62l; *Sexual Identity* 1981 in Howes 1994; Author interview with Cave, 1997). By the 1950s, with a relaxing of conventions in men's leisure dress, suede shoes were not automatically a sign of homosexuality. Peter says that "You were classed as 'one of those' but it didn't really mean much. There was no seriousness in it because they didn't really know;

there were a lot of normal people who used to wear brown suede shoes and gray flannel trousers and cravat. But that was the fashion, particularly on the Sunday lunchtime" (Brighton Ourstory Project 1992: 50; Author interview with Robins, 1997). Dudley Cave agreed that as Teddy Boy (influenced) fashions became more popular they lost their connotations of homosexuality, but did retain a certain rebellious or anti-establishment connotation.

The color of a man's clothing was also often an indicator that he might be homosexual. At a time when men's clothing was on the whole somber, certain colors were "suspect." In 1949 Mass-Observation conducted a survey on sexual attitudes, and found that amongst its study group "pale blue was a queer's 'trade color'"— The group studied favored pale blue for short socks, ties and pullovers (Mass-Observation Sex Survey). Barbara Bell noted that in Blackpool the gay men also used traditionally nonmasculine-associated colors to reflect their sexuality: "I remember vividly," she says, "one year it was pink shirts. Nobody ever had pink shirts so if you wore a pink shirt you definitely signaled that you were a gay boy" (quoted in A. Jivani 1997: 50; Brighton Ourstory Project 1992: 52). Green was also a color that had homosexual associations. Writing in the *Urological and Cutaneous Review* in 1916 in an article entitled "Classification of Homosexuality" James Kiernan noted that "inverts are generally said to prefer green" (Kiernan 1916). In his groundbreaking book *Sexual Inversion*, Havelock Ellis had written that homosexuals had a preference for the color green, and in Paris green cravats were worn as a badge. Both these passages reflect the green carnation worn by Wilde and the rent boys of Piccadilly in London in the late nineteenth century. Peter Robins remembers the implications that the color green had, but only because it differed from conventional heterosexual dress of the day:

My first awareness of people actually using dress as a code was in the early fifties in Manchester. By this time I had bought a pair of bottle green trousers, cords, and I was wolf-whistled. In Heaton Park on Sunday afternoon; that's on the north side of Manchester. And I had a perfectly good Harris tweed jacket I was wearing with it and I was going out for tea, quite innocuously, but some local lads certainly thought I went too far, as it were, away from the dreariness of their own clothes. (Author interview with Robins)

Dudley Cave illustrates how despite knowing these signifiers it could often take courage to wear them:

I had read, I think in Havelock Ellis or somewhere, gay men's favorite color was blue or green. So when I had the opportunity, after all it was very difficult to buy clothes, I was in Simpson's and they had a rail of green sports jackets, green Harris tweed. They were so good that I took one. I bought one, but I was very embarrassed about its color but it showed me up, I feared. Though how everybody . . . how the straight community would know this secret coloring I have no idea. (Author interview with Cave 1997)

Often it was not so much the actual clothes that the men wore, but the manner in which they wore them. "If one can only present the visible and nonidentifying aspect of one's identity" Martin Hoffman noted, then "one's physical appearance will be the central aspect that can be displayed to others" (Hoffman 1968: 59). Douglas Plummer noted that "You will observe that the men around you are well dressed. In such clubs the standard and quality of clothes is high. Most 'queers' are concerned about their appearance, revealing the feminine side of their nature in a love of color, carefully made suits, original designs, and a progressive attitude toward dress. Usually they show good taste" (Plummer: 56). The emphasis here is upon how smartly dressed and well turned out gay men were. One of the characters in Rodney Garland's 1953 *The Heart In Exile* describes the men at "the Aldebaran," a gay bar in the West End of London. They "looked queer, well dressed and not tatty and no bright colors, and yet they looked queer, the way they talked and moved about . . ." (Garland: 54). In the 1950s British newspapers reflected a paranoia about the seemingly growing existence of invisible homosexuals by producing articles that offered advice on "how to spot a homo." They often concentrated on an overdeveloped sense of fashion: "When one-, two- or three-button jackets are in he is the first to wear them. His shirts are detergent bright, his tie has the latest knot and is always just so" and personal appearance: "His cheeks are smooth, his hair sparkles, his nails are manicured" (Crane, 1963: 7).

Hoffman described what he observed as the typical dress of middle-class American gay men in 1968. It was:

> the same style of dress that an average college undergraduate might wear. It would consist of a sport shirt, Levi's and loafers or sneakers. In this "typical" middle-class gay bar which I am attempting to describe, extremely effeminate dress and mannerisms are not well tolerated ... There is a tendency toward effeminacy in the overall impression one gets from observing the bar, although this may not be anything striking or flagrant ... Also in spite of the fact that the modal bar costume is very much like that one would see on a college campus, there is a good deal of special attention paid by the bar patrons to their dress, so that they seem almost extraordinarily well groomed ... the majority of individuals in the bar are not identifiable and would not be thought to be homosexual in another setting. (Hoffman: 54–5)

Mannerisms were also vital signifiers at a time when clothing was not an obvious signal. "The 'meanings' of clothes are," John Harvey argues, "constructions placed upon them, and are not readable in a dictionary sense as verbal meanings are. These meanings are based on the perception of specific choices (or abdications of choice) as to the material, color, cut, newness, but there is a high degree of ambiguity as to the purposes of such choices" (Harvey 1995: 12). Consequently, he continues, "Any meaning in the clothes will, moreover, be either corroborated or qualified by posture and movement of the body inside the clothes" (12). If Harvey's argument is correct, then signifiers such as suede shoes are only a "possible" indication of the (homo)sexuality of the wearer: this suspicion is quantified by the mannerisms of the wearer, and so certain behaviors were an essential element of the revelation of the identity of these "invisible queers" to one another. Many gay men who rejected crudely effeminate styles and behavior would not have seemed "masculine" in their interests or demeanor. In the light of this argument, a mincing walk or the tilt of the head could give a man away and "invariably you could find a queer by the way he held his cigarette" (Brighton Ourstory Project: 51). Prior to gay liberation, observers frequently commented on seeming inconsistencies of gay men's behavior. At times they seemed fully manly, while at other times, among themselves, in the safety of the gay bar or party, they could become outrageously effeminate (Kleinberg 1978: March). This was still true into the 1970s. Carol Warren's description of her friend Danny recalls how in gay company he dressed in an overly elegant style in soft, colorful fabrics and behaved in a somewhat "feminine" manner, and how his demeanor changed at a primarily straight company dance (Warren 1974: 95).

In addressing what I have termed the invisible gay man I have concentrated on a number of signifiers and aspects of behavior that gave an indication of homosexuality. There were always and still are many men who regard themselves as homosexual but have no desire to announce this either to other gay men or to straight society through their dress, and continue for all intents and purposes to maintain an invisible appearance. This is not necessarily through fear of exposure as gay, but may be due to their individual perceptions and the relative importance they place upon their sexuality as a defining aspect of their person (Simpson 1996; Sinfield, 1998; Harris 1997). In the 1950s, in attempting to pass as straight, it was possible for men to go to the opposite extreme and to become what Rodney Garland called a Male Impersonator. A male impersonator was "obvious, because he overdoes things ..." One such man:

> assumed an unnecessarily deep voice and adopted gestures that were too big and too heavy for his five

feet ten inches and his thirty-eight chest. Bred in London he became a caricature of a country gentleman, with his tweeds, a concealing moustache and his new vocabulary with the dropped "g's." It didn't need a trained psychologist to see that he was a failure ... touchy and nasty and feminine under the disguise. (Garland: 206–7)

It was exaggerations of masculine behavior such as that described by Garland, coupled with an adoption of work clothes, that were to formulate a new stereotype of the homosexual in both America and Britain in the postliberation years.

17

DICK HEBDIGE

Subculture: The Unnatural Break

From D. Hebdige (1979), **Subculture: The Meaning of Style**
(London and New York: Methuen), 90–9. Reprinted by permission of the author.

I felt unclean for about 48 hours.

> GLC councilor after seeing a concert by
> the Sex Pistols. [*New Musical Express,*
> July 18, 1977]

[Language is] of all social institutions, the least amenable to initiative. It blends with the life of society, and the latter, inert by nature, is a prime conservative force.

> Saussure (1974)

Subcultures represent "noise" (as opposed to sound): interference in the orderly sequence which leads from real events and phenomena to their representation in the media. We should therefore not underestimate the signifying power of the spectacular subculture not only as a metaphor for potential anarchy "out there" but as an actual mechanism of semantic disorder: a kind of temporary blockage in the system of representation. As John Mepham (1973) has written:

> Distinctions and identities may be so deeply embedded in our discourse and thought about the world whether this be because of their role in our practical lives, or because they are cognitively powerful and are an important aspect of the way in which we appear to make sense of our experience, that the theoretical challenge to them can be quite startling.

Any elision, truncation or convergence of prevailing linguistic and ideological categories can have profoundly disorienting effects. These deviations briefly expose the arbitrary nature of the codes which underlie and shape all forms of discourse. As Stuart Hall (1974) has written (here in the context of explicitly political deviance):

> New ... developments which are both dramatic and "meaningless" within the consensually validated norms, pose a challenge to the normative world. They render problematic not only how the ... world is defined, but how it ought to be. They "breach our expectancies." ...

Notions concerning the sanctity of language are intimately bound up with ideas of social order. The limits of acceptable linguistic expression are prescribed by a number of apparently universal taboos. These taboos guarantee the continuing "transparency" (the taken-for-grantedness) of meaning.

Predictably then, violations of the authorized codes through which the social world is organized and experienced have considerable power to provoke and disturb. They are generally condemned, in Mary Douglas's words (1970), as "contrary to holiness" and Levi-Strauss has noted how, in certain primitive myths, the mispronunciation of words and the misuse of language are classified along with incest as horrendous aberrations capable of "unleashing storm and tempest" (Levi-Strauss 1969). Similarly, spectacular subcultures express forbidden contents (consciousness of class, consciousness of difference) in forbidden forms (transgressions of sartorial and behavioral codes, law breaking etc.). They are profane articulations, and they are often and significantly defined as "unnatural." The terms used in the tabloid press to describe those youngsters who, in their conduct or clothing, proclaim subcultural membership ("freaks," "animals … who find courage, like rats, in hunting in packs"[1]) would seem to suggest that the most primitive anxieties concerning the sacred distinction between nature and culture can be summoned up by the emergence of such a group. No doubt, the breaking of rules is confused with the "absence of rules" which, according to Levi-Strauss (1969), "seems to provide the surest criteria for distinguishing a natural from a cultural process." Certainly, the official reaction to the punk subculture, particularly to the Sex Pistols' use of "foul language" on television[2] and record,[3] and to the vomiting and spitting incidents at Heathrow Airport[4] would seem to indicate that these basic taboos are no less deeply sedimented in contemporary British society.

TWO FORMS OF INCORPORATION

Has not this society, glutted with aestheticism, already integrated former romanticisms, surrealism, existentialism and even Marxism to a point? It has, indeed, through trade, in the form of commodities. That which yesterday was reviled today becomes cultural consumer-goods, consumption thus engulfs what was intended to give meaning and direction. (Lefebvre 1971)

We have seen how subcultures "breach our expectancies," how they represent symbolic challenges to a symbolic order. But can subcultures always be effectively incorporated and if so, how? The emergence of a spectacular subculture is invariably accompanied by a wave of hysteria in the press. This hysteria is typically ambivalent: it fluctuates between dread and fascination, outrage and amusement. Shock and horror headlines dominate the front page (e.g., "Rotten Razored,"

Daily Mirror, June 28, 1977) while, inside, the editorials positively bristle with "serious" commentary[5] and the centrespreads or supplements contain delirious accounts of the latest fads and rituals (see, for example, *Observer* color supplements January 30, July 10, 1977; February 12, 1978). Style in particular provokes a double response: it is alternately celebrated (in the fashion page) and ridiculed or reviled (in those articles which define subcultures as social problems).

In most cases, it is the subculture's stylistic innovations which first attract the media's attention. Subsequently deviant or "antisocial" acts—vandalism, swearing, fighting, "animal behavior"—are "discovered" by the police, the judiciary, the press; and these acts are used to "explain" the subculture's original transgression of sartorial codes. In fact, either deviant behavior or the identification of a distinctive uniform (or more typically a combination of the two) can provide the catalyst for a moral panic. In the case of the punks, the media's sighting of punk style virtually coincided with the discovery or invention of punk deviance. The *Daily Mirror* ran its first series of alarmist centrespreads on the subculture, concentrating on the bizarre clothing and jewelry during the week (November 29–December 3, 1977) in which the Sex Pistols exploded into the public eye on the Thames *Today* program. On the other hand, the mods, perhaps because of the muted character of their style, were not identified as a group until the Bank Holiday clashes of 1964, although the subculture was, by then, fully developed, at least in London. Whichever item opens the amplifying sequence, it invariably ends with the simultaneous diffusion and defusion of the subcultural style.

As the subculture begins to strike its own eminently marketable pose, as its vocabulary (both visual and verbal) becomes more and more familiar, so the referential context to which it can be most conveniently assigned is made increasingly apparent. Eventually, the mods, the punks, the glitter rockers can be incorporated, brought back into line, located on the preferred "map of problematic social reality" (Geertz 1964) at the point where boys in lipstick are "just kids dressing up," where girls in rubber dresses are "daughters just like yours" (see Note 8). The media, as Stuart Hall (1977) has argued, not only record resistance, they "situate it within the dominant framework of meanings" and those young people who choose to inhabit a spectacular youth culture are simultaneously *returned,* as they are represented on TV and in the newspapers, to the place where common sense would have them fit (as "animals" certainly, but also "in the family," "out of work," "up to date," etc.). It is through this continual process of recuperation that the fractured order is repaired and the subculture incorporated as a diverting spectacle within the dominant mythology from which it in part emanates: as "folk devil," as Other, as Enemy. The process of recuperation takes two characteristic forms:

(1) the conversion of subcultural signs (dress, music, etc.) into mass-produced objects (i.e., the commodity form);

(2) the "labeling" and redefinition of deviant behavior by dominant groups—the police, the media, the judiciary (i.e., the ideological form).

The Commodity Form

The first has been comprehensively handled by both journalists and academics. The relationship between the spectacular subculture and the various industries which service and exploit it is notoriously ambiguous. After all, such a subculture is concerned first and foremost with consumption. It operates exclusively in the leisure sphere ("I wouldn't wear my punk outfit for work—there's a time and a place for everything" (see Note 8). It communicates through commodities even if the meanings attached to those commodities are purposefully distorted or overthrown. It is therefore difficult in this case to maintain any absolute distinction between commercial exploitation on the one hand and creativity/originality on the other, even though these categories are emphatically opposed in the value systems of most subcultures. Indeed, the creation and diffusion of new styles is inextricably bound up with

the process of production, publicity and packaging which must inevitably lead to the defusion of the subculture's subversive power—both mod and punk innovations fed back directly into high fashion and mainstream fashion. Each new subculture establishes new trends, and generates new looks and sounds which feed back into the appropriate industries. As John Clarke (1976) has observed:

The diffusion of youth styles from the subcultures to the fashion market is not simply a "cultural process," but a real network or infrastructure of new kinds of commercial and economic institutions. The small-scale record shops, recording companies, the boutiques and one- or two-woman manufacturing companies—these versions of artisan capitalism, rather than more generalized and unspecific phenomena, situate the dialectic of commercial "manipulation."

However, it would be mistaken to insist on the absolute autonomy of "cultural" and commercial processes. As Lefebvre (1971) puts it: "Trade is … both a social and an intellectual phenomenon," and commodities arrive at the marketplace already laden with significance. They are, in Marx's words (1970), "social hieroglyphs"[6] and their meanings are inflected by conventional usage.

Thus, as soon as the original innovations which signify "subculture" are translated into commodities and made generally available, they become "frozen." Once removed from their private contexts by the small entrepreneurs and big fashion interests who produce them on a mass scale, they become codified, made comprehensible, rendered at once public property and profitable merchandise. In this way, the two forms of incorporation (the semantic/ideological and the "real"/commercial) can be said to converge on the commodity form. Youth cultural styles may begin by issuing symbolic challenges, but they must inevitably end by establishing new sets of conventions; by creating new commodities, new industries or rejuvenating old ones (think of the boost punk must have given haberdashery!). This occurs irrespective of the subculture's political orientation: the macrobiotic restaurants, craft shops and "antique markets" of the hippie era were easily converted into punk boutiques and record shops. It also happens irrespective of the startling content of the style: punk clothing and insignia could be bought mail order by the summer of 1977, and in September of that year *Cosmopolitan* ran a review of Zandra Rhodes's latest collection of couture follies which consisted entirely of variations on the punk theme. Models smoldered beneath mountains of safety pins and plastic (the pins were jeweled, the "plastic" wet-look satin) and the accompanying article ended with an aphorism—"To shock is chic"—which presaged the subculture's imminent demise.

The Ideological Form

The second form of incorporation—the ideological—has been most adequately treated by those sociologists who operate a transactional model of deviant behavior. For example, Stan Cohen has described in detail how one particular moral panic (surrounding the mod–rocker conflict of the mid-60s) was launched and sustained.[7] Although this type of analysis can often provide an extremely sophisticated explanation of why spectacular subcultures consistently provoke such hysterical outbursts, it tends to overlook the subtler mechanisms through which potentially threatening phenomena are handled and contained. As the use of the term "folk devil" suggests, rather too much weight tends to be given to the sensational excesses of the tabloid press at the expense of the ambiguous reactions which are, after all, more typical. As we have seen, the way in which subcultures are represented in the media makes them both more *and less* exotic than they actually are. They are seen to contain both dangerous aliens and boisterous kids, wild animals and wayward pets. Roland Barthes furnishes a key to this paradox in his description of "identification"—one of the seven rhetorical figures which, according to Barthes, distinguish the meta-language of bourgeois mythology. He

characterizes the petit bourgeois as a person "… unable to imagine the Other … the Other is a scandal which threatens his existence" (Barthes 1972).

Two basic strategies have been evolved for dealing with this threat. First, the Other can be trivialized, naturalized, domesticated. Here, the difference is simply denied ("Otherness is reduced to sameness"). Alternatively, the Other can be transformed into meaningless exotica, a "pure object, a spectacle, a clown" (Barthes 1972). In this case, the difference is consigned to a place beyond analysis. Spectacular subcultures are continually being defined in precisely these terms. Soccer hooligans, for example, are typically placed beyond "the bounds of common decency" and are classified as "animals." ("These people aren't human beings," football club manager quoted on the *News at Ten*, Sunday, March 12, 1977.) (See Stuart Hall's treatment of the press coverage of football hooligans in *Football Hooliganism* (Ingham 1978).) On the other hand, the punks tended to be resituated by the press in the family, perhaps because members of the subculture deliberately obscured their origins, refused the family and willingly played the part of folk devil, presenting themselves as pure objects, as villainous clowns. Certainly, like every other youth culture, punk was perceived as a threat to the family. Occasionally this threat was represented in literal terms. For example, the *Daily Mirror* (August 1, 1977) carried a photograph of a child lying in the road after a punk-ted [Teddy Boy] confrontation under the headline "VICTIM OF THE PUNK ROCK PUNCH-UP: THE BOY WHO FELL FOUL OF THE MOB." In this case, punk's threat to the family was made "real" (that could be my child!) through the ideological framing of photographic evidence which is popularly regarded as unproblematic.

Nonetheless, on other occasions, the opposite line was taken. For whatever reason, the inevitable glut of articles gleefully denouncing the latest punk outrage was counterbalanced by an equal number of items devoted to the small details of punk family life. For instance, the

October 15, 1977 issue of *Woman's Own* carried an article entitled "Punks and Mothers" which stressed the classless, fancy-dress aspects of punk.[8] Photographs depicting punks with smiling mothers, reclining next to the family pool, playing with the family dog, were placed above a text which dwelt on the ordinariness of individual punks: "It's not as rocky horror as it appears" … "punk can be a family affair" … "punks as it happens are nonpolitical," and, most insidiously, albeit accurately, "Johnny Rotten is as big a household name as Hughie Green." Throughout the summer of 1977, *The People* and the *News of the World* ran items on punk babies, punk brothers, and punk-ted weddings. All these articles served to minimize the Otherness so stridently proclaimed in punk style, and defined the subculture in precisely those terms which it sought most vehemently to resist and deny.

Once again, we should avoid making any absolute distinction between the ideological and commercial "manipulations" of subculture. The symbolic restoration of daughters to the family, of deviants to the fold, was undertaken at a time when the widespread "capitulation" of punk musicians to market forces was being used throughout the media to illustrate the fact that punks were "only human after all." The music papers were filled with the familiar success stories describing the route from rags to rags and riches—of punk musicians flying to America, of bank clerks becoming magazine editors or record producers, of harrassed seamstresses turned overnight into successful businesswomen. Of course, these success stories had ambiguous implications. As with every other "youth revolution" (e.g. the beat boom, the mod explosion and the Swinging Sixties), the relative success of a few individuals created an impression of energy, expansion and limitless upward mobility. This ultimately reinforced the image of the open society which the very presence of the punk subculture—with its rhetorical emphasis on unemployment, high-rise living and narrow options—had originally contradicted. As Barthes (1972) has written: "myth can always, as a last resort, signify the resistance which is brought to bear against it" and

it does so typically by imposing its own ideological terms, by substituting in this case "the fairy tale of the artist's creativity"[9] for an art form "within the compass of every consciousness,"[10] a "music" to be judged, dismissed or marketed for "noise"—a logically consistent, self-constituted chaos. It does so finally by replacing a subculture engendered by history, a product of real historical contradictions, with a handful of brilliant nonconformists, satanic geniuses who, to use the words of Sir John Read, Chairman of EMI "become in the fullness of time, wholly acceptable and can contribute greatly to the development of modern music."[11]

NOTES

1. This was part of a speech made by Dr. George Simpson, a Margate magistrate, after the mod–rocker clashes of Whitsun 1964. For sociologists of deviance, this speech has become *the* classic example of rhetorical overkill and deserves quoting in full: "These long-haired, mentally unstable, petty little hoodlums, these sawdust Caesars who can only find courage like rats, in hunting in packs" (quoted in Cohen 1972).

2. On December 1, 1976 the Sex Pistols appeared on the Thames twilight program *Today.* During the course of the interview with Bill Grundy they used the words "sod," "bastard" and "fuck." The papers carried stories of jammed switchboards, shocked parents, etc. and there were some unusual refinements. The *Daily Mirror* (December 2) contained a story about a lorry driver who had been so incensed by the Sex Pistols' performance that he had kicked in the screen of his color television: "I can swear as well as anyone, but I don't want this sort of muck coming into my home at teatime."

3. The police brought an unsuccessful action for obscenity against the Sex Pistols after their first LP *Never Mind the Bollocks* was released in 1977.

4. On January 4, 1977 the Sex Pistols caused an incident at Heathrow Airport by spitting and vomiting in front of airline staff. The *Evening News* quoted a check-in desk girl as saying: "The group are the most revolting people I have ever seen in my life. They were disgusting, sick

and obscene." Two days after this incident was reported in the newspapers, EMI terminated the group's contract.

5. The August 1, 1977 edition of the *Daily Mirror* contained just such an example of dubious editorial concern. Giving "serious" consideration to the problem of Ted—punk violence along the King's Road, the writer makes the obvious comparison with the seaside disturbances of the previous decade: "[The clashes] must not be allowed to grow into the pitched battles like the mods and rockers confrontations at several seaside towns a few years back." Moral panics can be recycled; even the same events can be recalled in the same prophetic tones to mobilize the same sense of outrage.

6. The characters that stamp products as commodities, and whose establishment is a necessary preliminary to the circulation of commodities, have already acquired the stability of natural, self-understood forms of social life before man seeks to decipher, not their historical character, for in his eyes they are immutable, but their meaning (Marx 1970).

7. The definitive study of a moral panic is Cohen's *Folk Devils and Moral Panics.* The mods and rockers were just two of the "folk devils"—"the gallery of types that society erects to show its members which roles should be avoided"—which periodically become the centre of a "moral panic."

> Societies appear to be subject, every now and then, to periods of moral panic. A condition, episode, person or group of persons emerges to become defined as a threat to societal values and interests; its nature is presented in a stylized and stereotypical fashion by the mass media; the moral barricades are manned by editors, bishops, politicians and other right-thinking people; socially accredited experts pronounce their diagnoses and solutions; ways of coping are evolved or (more often) resorted to; the condition then disappears, submerges or deteriorates and becomes more visible. (Cohen 1972)

Official reactions to the punk subculture betrayed all the classic symptoms of a moral panic. Concerts were canceled; clergymen, politicians and pundits unanimously denounced the degeneracy of youth. Among the choicer reactions, Marcus Upton, the late MP for Lambeth North, declared:

"If pop music is going to be used to destroy our established institutions, then it ought to be destroyed first." Bernard Brook-Partridge, MP for Havering-Romford, stormed, "I think the Sex Pistols are absolutely bloody revolting. I think their whole attitude is calculated to incite people to misbehavior ... It is a deliberate incitement to antisocial behavior and conduct" (quoted in *New Musical Express,* July 15, 1977).

8. See also "Punks have Mothers Too: They Tell Us a Few Home Truths" in *Woman* (April 15, 1978) and "Punks and Mothers" in *Woman's Own* (October 15, 1977). These articles draw editorial comment (a sign of recognition on the part of the staff of the need to reassure the challenged expectations of the reader?). The following anecdote appeared beneath a photograph showing two dancing teddy boys:

> The other day I overheard two elderly ladies, cringing as a gang of alarming-looking punks passed them, say in tones of horror: "Just imagine what their children will be like." I'm sure a lot of people must have said exactly the same about the Teddy Boys, like the ones pictured ... and mods and rockers. That made me wonder what had happened to them when the phase passed. I reckon they put away their drape suits or scooters and settled down to respectable, quiet lives, bringing up the kids and desperately hoping they won't get involved in any of these terrible punk goings-on.

9. "The fairy tale of the artist's creativity is Western culture's last superstition. One of Surrealism's first revolutionary acts was to attack this myth ..." (Max Ernst, "What is Surrealism?" quoted in Lippard 1970).

10. "Surrealism is within the compass of every consciousness" (Surrealist tract quoted in Lippard 1970). See also Paul Eluard: "We have passed the period of individual exercises" (quoted in Alexandrian 1985).

> The solemn and extremely reverential exhibition of Surrealism, mounted at London's Hayward Gallery in 1978 ironically sought to establish the reputation of individual Surrealists as artists and was designed to win public recognition of their "genius." For a comparison of punk and Surrealism, see the sections entitled "Style as Bricolage" and "Revolting Style" in *Subculture: The Meaning*

of Style. It is fitting that punk should be absorbed into high fashion at the same time as the first major exhibition of Dada and Surrealism in Britain was being launched.

11. On December 7, one month before EMI terminated its contract with the Sex Pistols, Sir John Read, the record company's Chairman, made the following statement at the annual general meeting:

> Throughout its history as a recording company, EMI has always sought to behave within contemporary limits of decency and good taste—taking into account not only the traditional rigid conventions of one section of society, but also the increasingly liberal attitudes of other (perhaps larger) sections ... at any given time ... What is decent or in good taste compared to the attitudes of, say, twenty or even ten years ago?
>
> It is against this present-day social background that EMI has to make value judgments about the content of records ... Sex Pistols is a pop group devoted to a new form of music known as "punk rock." It was contracted for recording purposes by EMI ... in October, 1976 ... In this context, it must be remembered that the recording industry has signed many pop groups, initially controversial, who have in the fullness of time become wholly acceptable and contributed greatly to the development of modern music ... EMI should not set itself up as a public censor, but it does seek to encourage restraint. (quoted in Vermorel, 1978)

Despite the eventual loss of face (and some £40,000 paid out to the Pistols when the contract was terminated) EMI and the other record companies tended to shrug off the apparent contradictions involved in signing up groups who openly admitted to a lack of professionalism, musicianship, and commitment to the profit motive. During the Clash's famous performance of "White Riot" at The Rainbow in 1977, when seats were ripped out and thrown at the stage, the last two rows of the theater (left, of course, intact) were occupied almost exclusively by record executives and talent scouts: CBS paid for the damage without complaint. There could be no clearer demonstration of the fact that symbolic assaults leave real institutions intact. Nonetheless, the record companies did not have everything their own way. The Sex Pistols received five-figure sums in compensation from both A&M and EMI and when their LP (recorded at last by Virgin) finally did reach the shops, it contained a scathing attack on EMI delivered in Rotten's venomous nasal whine:

> You thought that we were faking
> That we were all just money-making
> You don't believe that we're for real
> Or you would lose your cheap appeal.
> Who?
> EMI—EMI.
>
> Blind acceptance is a sign
> Of stupid fools who stand in line
> Like EMI—EMI. ("EMI," Virgin, 1977)

ANNOTATED GUIDE TO FURTHER READING FOR PART III

The creation and maintenance of identity through dress is the subject of the textbook *Dress and Identity* by Mary Ellen Roach-Higgins, Joanne B. Eicher and Kim K. P. Johnson (1995). Roach-Higgins and Eicher's seminal article, also titled "Dress and Identity" (1992) is the first reading in the book. *Dress and Ethnicity*, edited by Joanne B. Eicher (1999), is a key work for anyone interested in the intersection of identity, ethnicity and dress.

Diana Crane's *Fashion and Its Social Agendas* (2000) compares nineteenth- and twentieth-century social identities as constructed through appearance, from occupational dress to couture and across gender identities.

Material culture studies of fashion and dress include in their scope fabric and its materiality in everyday experience. An excellent piece is Judy Attfield's "Change: The Ephemeral Materiality of Identity" in *Wild Things: The Material Culture of Everyday Life* (2000). *Clothing as Material Culture,* edited by Susanne Kücher and Daniel Miller, aims to transcend the previous dichotomous relations of material culture/cultural studies with the more positivistic research traditions in conservation, design and museum collections. An excellent entry on the ways that contemporary clothing mediates space between women and the world is Sophie Woodward's "Looking Good: Feeling Right—Aesthetics of the Self."

Four recent book-length studies from Berg examine cultural identity shaped through dress and fashion during and after the Second World War. They are Irene Guenther's award-winning *Nazi Chic?*(2004), Eugenia Paulicelli's *Fashion Under Fascism* (2004), Dominique Veillon's *Fashion Under Occupation* (2002) and Judd Stitziel's *Fashioning Socialism* (2005).

On English identity, see *The Englishness of English Dress* edited by Christopher Breward, Becky Conekin and Caroline Cox (2002) and Alice Cicolini's (2005) *The New English Dandy*. On US ethnic identities, see *The Latin American Fashion Reader* by Regina A. Root (2005). See also Gwendolyn S. O'Neal's "African-American Aesthetics of Dress: Current Manifestations," which links aesthetic roots in West African culture and metaphysical beliefs to African-American aesthetics (1998). Guy Trebay wrote an excellent commentary titled "Taking Hip-Hop Seriously. Seriously" (2003).

Dangerous Designs, Asian Women Fashion the Diaspora Economies by Parminder Bhachu (2003) examines the shalwar kameez and its multiple roles in new economic micro-markets, identity and fashionability in the Indian diaspora. *The Sari* by Mukulika Banerjee and Daniel Miller (2003) is an excellent treatise on the embedded meanings of the sari across all castes in India.

For a new treatment of subcultural identity see *Inside Subculture: The Postmodern Meaning of Style* (2000) where David Muggleton uses in-depth ethnographic practices to uncover meanings and examine subcultural relationships to postmodern sensibilities. An important work for anyone interested in subcultures is Stan Cohen's *Folk Devils and Moral Panics* (1972).

PART IV
The Geography of Dress

LINDA WELTERS

Introduction

Geography—the study of the physical features of a place or region, including climate, plant, animal and human life—is new to the study of fashion. The branch of geography that intersects with fashion is called cultural geography. Denis Cosgrove describes cultural geography as a vibrant and contested subfield of human geography with several distinct theoretical positions and methodologies (2000: 134).

Carl Sauer (1889–1975), a former professor at the University of California at Berkeley, is considered the father of cultural geography. His work concentrated on human interaction with nature in certain regions over time. He preferred to work with slow-changing cultures, and he advocated fieldwork as the major methodology. Early cultural geographers produced studies showing that culture operated over time on a natural landscape to produce specific forms, with emphasis on spatial distribution. One example would be the vernacular architecture of a specific region. Sauer and his followers produced maps of bounded cultural areas. Sauer himself studied Mexico, dividing it into two culture areas: the "high culture" of the south and the "ruder culture" of the north. Cultural geography in the United States is still influenced by Sauer's approach and is sometimes referred to as the Berkeley School (Baldwin et al. 1999).

Scholars in Great Britain began departing from this approach by introducing methodologies from the field of anthropology and theoretical perspectives based on Marxism (Baldwin et al.

1999). Together, Peter Jackson and Denis Cosgrove argued for a new approach that was contemporary as well as historical, concerned with space as well as landscape, urban as well as rural, interested in issues of domination and resistance, concerned with representation as well as reality, and committed to the centrality of culture to human life (Cosgrove and Jackson 1987).

At the same time, scholars in cultural studies began incorporating themes from geography, claiming that culture cannot be understood outside the space it inhabits. While cultural studies brought a broad range of issues to cultural geography—identity, class, race, power and representation—cultural geography contributed space–time and city–country distinctions to the developing field of cultural studies. This interdisciplinary interaction resulted in the formation of "the new cultural geography."

THE NEW CULTURAL GEOGRAPHY

The major issues that concern the new cultural geography are cultures of difference and the poetics and politics of representation (Baldwin et al. 1999). In the new cultural geography, culture is a contested domain. Different social groups impose their systems of cultural meaning on the world. These cultures of difference may be embraced (as in the rhetoric of multiculturalism of the 1990s) or resisted through acts of power (as in Judeo-Christian belief systems versus Islamic fundamentalism). The poetics and politics of representation refer to the multiplicity of realities in today's world. Determining an objective reality is irrelevant; rather, understanding how the world is represented in various media is the goal. These representations, in turn, may be contested.

The terms "space," "place" and "landscape" are important in cultural geography. "Space" refers to the distribution of objects and activities, the formation of boundaries and patterns of movements, and their effect on the formation of culture. Postmodernism conceives of space differently than modernism. Space is "produced" through perceptions, conceptions and lived practices (Lefebvre 1991). "Place" refers to the ways in which specific locations contribute to the making of a cultural world. Place is not as abstract a notion as space. "Landscape" means both the area itself and how it appears in representation. While interest in place involves philosophy, landscape draws in art history and literature.

Discourses that interest cultural geographers these days involve the themes of power, resistance and representation. Different places can be examined, ranging from the local all the way to the global. Inevitably, such discourse involves discussion of country versus city, rural versus urban, and their respective representations. How people identify themselves as coming from specific places brings in the notion of identity. Identifying with a place can range from the local, to the regional, to the national. Some people may even think of themselves as global citizens. Nation is an important component of identity, which some claim is an "imagined community." Issues of inclusion and exclusion are affected by the cultural meaning of community. In the areas of the world settled by English emigrants, for example, the white Anglo culture is the dominant one. Wherever the English settled, fashionable Western dress soon took root. Conversely, immigrants to a Western European country often experience exclusion. In France, emigrants from developing countries encounter difficulty negotiating the deep-rooted French culture. For example, in 2004 the French government proposed a ban on the wearing of religious symbols in schools in an effort to protect France's secular culture. This was precipitated by Muslim schoolgirls wearing headscarves in keeping with their religious beliefs. The Islamic community demonstrated against the measure, yet the law was passed easily. As just shown, the theme of power also involves gender.

Globalization and hybridity are concepts that concern cultural geographers. *Globalization* "describes the process of gradually intermeshing world economies, politics and cultures into a global system" (Baldwin et al. 1999: 159). This process is associated with the rise of capitalism in Europe, which gradually spread to areas colonized by Europeans: the Americas, Asia and Africa. Globalization has affected not only trade, but culture as well. *Hybridity* is a term that incorporates the interrelationships and connections between cultures; *creolization* is a related term. Cultural products are involved as objects formed at the intersections of cultures. Thus, geographers are interested in issues of consumption (Mansveldt 2005).

Indeed, the new cultural geography, the new fashion history, and fashion criticism are interested in similar issues in the comprehension of the postmodern condition. It is with this in mind that we elected to include a section on the geography of fashion in this reader.

DRESS AND CULTURAL GEOGRAPHY

Cultural geographers have been slow to consider fashion, and vice versa. Fashion falls into the category of material goods that humans "consume," like food. New Zealand geographer Juliana Mansveldt begins *Geographies of Consumption* with this claim: "Buying, using and disposing of commodities connects us to other people and other places in ways which may be beyond our imaginings. Commodities are more than just objects; they are shifting assemblages of social relations, which take place and assume form and meaning in time and space" (2005: 1). Since dress and appearance are part of commodity culture, it is heartening to see that she covers topics such as shopping (and shoplifting), wardrobes, apparel sweatshops, identity and the body, tourism, and the transnational nature of the second-hand clothing business. She does not, however, include "fashion" as an entry in the index.

Wilbur Zelinsky, a prominent American cultural geographer and a student of Carl Sauer, chastised his colleagues for "the utter absence of systematic scholarship dealing with the geography, much less historical geography, of clothing" (2004). He also chides "the increasingly sophisticated band of fashion scholars for being so oblivious to the spatiality of their material." He views the geography of dress as a "wonderfully promising scholarly terra incognita."

One issue that interests both cultural geographers and fashion scholars is identity. Dress is an important component in negotiating identity—gender, sexual orientation, subcultural affiliation, class, age, etc.—as discussed in Part III. Dress also has the potential to ground the individual with a particular place, or in the case of internationally accepted fashion, to disassociate an individual with a place. We begin the readings with a selection about Scottish Highland tartan. Originally published in expanded form (Trevor-Roper 1983), in this extract the author succinctly unfolds the invention of both the kilt and the clan tartan as noble, long-standing traditions in Scotland. This mythologizing occurred in the eighteenth and nineteenth century as Scotland grappled with its national identity. Themes familiar to the cultural geographer—identity, class, power and resistance, and representation—are woven into the story.

Fashion and national identity is beginning to be explored. The topic of "Britishness" and "Englishness" as expressed in fashion connects subcultures, multiculturalism and pageantry with the concept of nation. Real versus imagined "Englishness" is important to the interpretation (Goodrum 2005; Breward et al. 2002).

A related issue is ethnicity. The piece by Claire Dwyer and Philip Crang investigates multiculturalism in fashion through a case study of the British firm Ghulam Sakina. The designer, Liaqat Rasul, was born in Wales to parents who had emigrated from Pakistan. He considers himself a British Pakistani. As part of his design training, he interned in India with Ritu Kumar. Now he produces his handcrafted creations in India. Here is a British citizen of Pakistani heritage who grew up in Wales designing fashion that is made in India for sale to an international clientele in elite London stores.

An issue that has concerned geographers for decades is now drawing the interest of fashion scholars—the differences between fashion in the city and fashion in the country. Scholars of European folk dress have long recognized the parallel universes of the dress worn by villagers and the fashionable attire of city dwellers. Attention has now turned to the city as a site that embraces the culture of fashion (Breward and Gilbert 2006). Paris, of course, has been a world fashion city for centuries. London, New York and Milan are also recognized as fashion capitals. David Gilbert's piece discusses the key issues revolving around the production and consumption of fashion in urban spaces, particularly Paris, London and New York. But what about Tokyo, Hong Kong, Shanghai, Sydney ... and Auckland? The selection by Goodrum, Larner and Molloy illustrates how government policy, the built environment, and SMEs (small and medium enterprises) are reshaping Auckland, New Zealand as a contender for becoming Australasia's major fashion city.

Globalization and hybridity are expressed in fashion, as discussed by Margaret Maynard (2004). Consumption of Western dress styles in non-Western countries demonstrates creolization, where neither fashion nor tradition dominates, resulting in hybrid dress forms (Maynard 2004: 8). This is a particularly interesting avenue of exploration for fashion, as it embraces spatial and historical distribution as well as cultural meaning. Karen T. Hansen's work on the recycled clothing trade in Zambia is just one example.

Certain styles defy spatial or historical location. Since the nineteenth century, the male suit has been an accepted form of attire. With minor changes in fabric and detail, it has withstood the test of time, becoming the outfit of choice for both men and women in financial and political positions throughout the world. A number of writers from a variety of disciplines have examined this anomaly. Art historian Anne Hollander (1994) proposed it as the ultimate expression of modernity; historian David Kuchta (2002) traced its cultural origins and development; and cultural geographer Wilbur Zelinsky (2004), who labeled it Modern Western Male Attire (MWMA), traced its historical geography. The suit has emerged as the ultimate transnational fashion. In "Suitably Attired," William Hamilton investigates this particularly long-lived sartorial form.

HUGH TREVOR-ROPER

The Highlander Myth

Today, whenever Scotsmen gather together to celebrate their national identity, they wear the kilt, woven in a tartan whose colors and pattern indicate their clan. This apparel, to which they ascribe great antiquity, is, in fact, of fairly recent origin. Indeed, the whole concept of a distinct Highland culture and tradition is a retrospective invention.

Before the later years of the seventeenth century, the Highlanders of Scotland did not form a distinct people. They were simply the overflow of Ireland. On the broken and inhospitable coast of western Scotland, in that archipelago of islands large and small, the sea unites rather than divides, and from the late fifth century, when the Scots of Ulster landed in Argyll, until the mid-eighteenth century, when it was "opened up" after the Jacobite revolts, the west of Scotland, cut off by mountains from the east, was always linked rather to Ireland than to the Saxon Lowlands.[1]

The Gaelic language spoken there was regularly described, in the eighteenth century, as Irish. The native literature, such as it was, was a crude echo of Irish literature. The bards of the Scottish chieftains came from Ireland or went thither to learn their trade. The creation of an independent Highland tradition occurred in the eighteenth century, with a cultural revolt against Ireland or, more precisely, with the usurpation of Irish culture and the rewriting of Scottish

history. The claim that the Celtic, Irish-speaking Highlanders of Scotland were not merely invaders from Ireland but were in fact the Caledonians who had resisted the Roman armies, was of course an old legend. It was reasserted successfully in the 1760s by two writers of the same surname: James Macpherson, the "translator" of Ossian, and the Reverend John Macpherson, pastor of Sleat on the island of Skye. These two Macphersons, though unrelated, were known to each other, and they worked in concert.

The sheer effrontery of the Macphersons must excite admiration. James Macpherson picked up Irish ballads in Scotland and, in 1763, reworked them into an "epic," which he attributed to a legendary third-century Gaelic bard named Ossian; he transferred the whole scenario from Ireland to Scotland, and then dismissed the genuine ballads thus maltreated as debased modern compositions.

John Macpherson, the pastor of Sleat, then wrote a *Critical Dissertation*, in which he provided the necessary context for his colleague's "discovery": He placed Irish-speaking Celts in Scotland four centuries before their historical arrival and explained away the genuine, native Irish literature as having been stolen, in the Dark Ages, by the unscrupulous Irish from the innocent Scots.

Of the success of the Macphersons in literary London, no more need be said than that they seduced even the normally careful and critical Edward Gibbon, author of *The Decline and Fall of the Roman Empire* (1788). He acknowledged as his guides in early Scottish history those "two learned Highlanders" and thus perpetuated what historian M. V. Hay has called "a chain of error in Scottish history."

These two insolent pretenders had achieved a lasting triumph: They had put the Scottish Highlanders on the map.

Previously despised alike by the Lowland Scots as disorderly savages, and by the Irish as their unlettered poor kinsmen, Highlanders were now celebrated throughout Europe as a *Kulturvolk* which, when England and Ireland were sunk in primitive barbarism, had produced an epic poet of exquisite refinement and sensibility, equal (said Madame de Staël) or superior (said F. A. Wolf) to Homer. And even as the Scottish Highlands acquired, however fraudulently, an independent ancient culture, a new tradition sprang up—that of a peculiarity of dress.

INVENTING THE KILT

Since the Scottish Highlanders were, in origin, Irishmen, it is natural to suppose that originally their dress was the same as that of the Irish. And indeed this is what we find. Accounts written in the sixteenth century show that the ordinary dress of the Highlanders was a long "Irish" shirt, which the higher classes—as in Ireland—dyed with saffron; a tunic; and a rough cloak, or "plaid," which, in general, was of a russet or brown effect, as protective coloring in the heather.

Chieftains and great men who had contact with the more sophisticated inhabitants of the Lowlands might wear trews, a combination of breeches and stockings. Trews could be worn outdoors in the Highlands only by men who had attendants to protect or carry them: They were therefore a mark of social distinction. The higher classes' plaids and trews were probably of colorful tartan, a design that seems to have come originally from Flanders and reached the Highlands through the Lowlands.

In the course of the seventeenth century, the Irish long shirt fell into disuse. Accounts of the British civil wars depict Highland officers wearing trews, but the ordinary soldiers with their legs and thighs bare. The name "kilt" first appears in 1727, when Edward Burt, an English officer posted to Scotland, wrote a series of letters, mainly from Inverness, describing the character and customs of the country. In his letters, he gives a careful description of the "quelt," which, he explains, is simply the plaid "set in folds and girt round the waist to make of it a short petticoat that reaches halfway down the thigh, and the rest is brought over the shoulders and then fastened before." This petticoat, Burt adds, was normally worn "so very short that in a windy day, going up a hill, or stooping, the indecency of it is plainly discovered." Clearly he is describing not the modern kilt but a particular method of wearing the plaid, called the belted plaid or *breacan*.

Burt was explicit about the Highland dress because already, in his time, it was the object of political controversy. After the Jacobite rebellion of 1715, the British Parliament had considered banning it by law, as the Irish dress had been banned under Henry VIII, to help integrate the Highlanders into modern British society. The proposed law, however, was not passed. The Highland dress, it was conceded, was convenient and necessary in a country where a traveler must "skip over rocks and bogs and lie all night in the hills."

Ironically, if the Highland dress had been banned after the rebellion of 1715, the kilt, which is now regarded as one of the ancient traditions of Scotland, would probably never have come into existence. Its inventor was an English Quaker ironmaster from Lancashire, Thomas Rawlinson.

In 1727, Rawlinson made an agreement with Ian MacDonell, chief of the MacDonells of Glengarry near Inverness, for a thirty-one-year lease of a wooded area at Invergarry. There he built a furnace to smelt iron ore, which he had shipped up from Lancashire. During his stay at Glengarry, Rawlinson became interested in the

Highland costume, but he also became aware of its inconvenience. For men who had to fell trees or tend furnaces, the belted plaid was "a cumbrous, unwieldy habit." Being "a man of genius and quick parts" Rawlinson sent for a tailor and, with him, set out "to abridge the dress and make it handy and convenient for his workmen."

The result was the *felie beg,* philibeg, or "small kilt," which was achieved by separating the skirt from the plaid and converting it into a distinct garment, with pleats already sewn. Rawlinson himself wore this new garment, and his innovation, we are told, "was found so handy and convenient that in the shortest space the use of it became frequent in all the Highland countries and in many of the Northern Lowland countries also."[2]

The first painting to feature a person wearing a recognizable modern kilt, not a belted plaid, was a portrait of Alexander MacDonell of Glengarry (the son of Rawlinson's friend) and his servant. It is interesting to note that, in this portrait, the kilt is worn not by MacDonell but by the servant—thus emphasizing, once again, its "servile" status.

If this was the origin of the kilt, a question immediately arises. Was a distinctive "sett" or pattern of colors devised for a Lancashire Rawlinson, or did he become an honorary member of the clan of MacDonell? When did the differentiation of patterns by clans begin?

The sixteenth-century writers who first noticed the Highland dress did not remark any such differentiation. They describe the plaids of the chiefs as colored, those of their followers as brown, so that any differentiation of color, in their time, was by social status, not by clan. A carefully painted series of portraits of the different members of the Grant family by Richard Waitt in the eighteenth century shows all of them in different tartans. The only way in which a Highlander's loyalty could be discerned in battle was by the colored cockade in his bonnet; tartans were a matter of private taste.

The great Scottish rebellion of 1745, however, changed the sartorial as well as the social and economic history of Scotland. Acts of Parliament that followed the victory at Culloden not only disarmed the Highlanders and deprived their chiefs of their hereditary jurisdictions but also forbade the wearing of Highland costume— "plaid, philibeg, trews, shoulder-belts … tartans or parti-colored plaid or stuff."

TOUTING THE PHILIBEG

This last draconian measure remained in force for thirty-five years, years during which the whole Highland way of life quickly crumbled. In 1773, when Samuel Johnson and James Boswell made their famous tour of Scotland, they found that they were already too late to see what they had expected, "a people of peculiar appearance and a system of antiquated life." It was during this period that the Macphersons composed their ancient literature and inventive history.

The Highland costume did indeed die out among those who had been accustomed to wearing it. When the ban was lifted in 1782, the simple sheep-raising peasantry of the Highlands saw no reason, after a generation in trousers, to resume the belted plaid or the tartan, which they had once found so serviceable. They did not even turn to the "handy and convenient" new kilt.

On the other hand, the upper and middle classes, who had previously despised the "servile" costume, now picked up, with enthusiasm, the garb discarded by its traditional wearers. During the years when it had been banned, some Highland noblemen had taken pleasure in wearing it and being portrayed in it in the safety of their homes. Now that the ban was lifted, the fashion spread. Anglicized Scottish peers, improving gentry, well-educated Edinburgh lawyers, and prudent merchants of Aberdeen would exhibit themselves publicly, not in the historic trews, the traditional costume of their class, nor in the cumbrous belted plaid, but in a costly and fanciful version of that recent innovation, the philibeg, or small kilt.

Two causes explain this remarkable change. One was the romantic movement in Europe, the cult of the noble savage whom civilization threatened to destroy. Before 1745, the Highlanders had been despised as idle predatory barbarians. In 1745, they had been feared as dangerous rebels. But after 1746, when their distinct society crumbled so easily, they combined the romance of a primitive people with the charm of an endangered species.

ENTER GEORGE IV

The second cause was the formation, by the British government, of the Highland regiments. The creation of the Highland regiments had begun before 1745—indeed, the first such regiment, the Black Watch, had fought at Fontenoy in 1740. But it was during the years 1757–60 that William Pitt the Elder systematically sought to divert the martial spirit of the Highlanders from Jacobite adventure to imperial war. The Highland regiments also helped to establish a new sartorial tradition. For by the "Disarming Act" of 1747, they were explicitly exempted from the ban on Highland dress.

Originally, the Highland regiments wore as their uniform the belted plaid; but once Rawlinson had invented the kilt and its convenience had made it popular, it was adopted by them. Moreover, it was probably their use of the kilt that gave birth to the idea of differentiating tartan by clans; for as the Highland regiments were multiplied to meet the needs of Britain's overseas wars, so their tartan uniforms were differentiated.

At least one Scotsman, from the beginning, raised his voice against the whole process whereby the Celtic Highlanders, so recently despised as outer barbarians, were claiming to be the sole representatives of Scottish history and culture. John Pinkerton was a man whose undoubted eccentricity and violent prejudices cannot rob him of his claim to be the greatest Scottish antiquary since Thomas Innes. He was an implacable enemy of the historical and literary falsification of the two Macphersons. He was also, in the late 1700s, the first scholar to document the history of the Highland dress, terming the philibeg "modern," "grossly indecent," and "effeminate."

He wrote in vain. The Highland takeover, already begun, was given emphatic publicity in 1822 by King George IV's state visit to Edinburgh.

Never before had a Hanoverian monarch appeared in the capital of Scotland, and elaborate preparations were made to ensure that the occasion would be a success. The master of ceremonies entrusted with all practical arrangements was Sir Walter Scott, already the author of eleven novels, including *Waverly* (1814) and *Ivanhoe* (1819). Carried away by romantic Celtic fantasies, Scott was determined to forget historic Scotland, his own Lowland Scotland, altogether. "Do come and bring half-a-dozen or half-a-score of clansmen," Scott wrote to one Highland chief. "Highlanders are what he will best like to see."

The Highlanders duly came, wearing the clan tartans provided by local manufacturers who had a long history of resourcefulness in creating markets for their wares.

The greatest of these firms was that of William Wilson and Son of Bannockburn. Messrs. Wilson had seen early the advantage of building up a repertoire of differentiated clan tartans and thus stimulating tribal competition. For this purpose, they entered into alliance with the Highland Society of London (which had been founded in 1788, and whose early members included both James Macpherson and Sir John Macpherson), thereby throwing over their commercial project, a cloak, or plaid, of historical respectability.

In 1819, when the royal visit was first suggested, the firm prepared a "Key Pattern Book" and sent samples of its various tartans to London, where the Society duly "certified" them as belonging to this or that clan. However, when George IV's visit was confirmed, the time for such pedantic consistency had passed. The spate of orders was now such that "every piece of tartan was sold as it came off the loom."

THE BROTHERS ALLEN

In these circumstances, the first duty of the firm was to keep up the supply and ensure that the

Highland chiefs were able to buy what they needed. So Cluny Macpherson, heir to the discoverer of Ossian, was given a tartan from the peg. For him it was now labeled "Macpherson." Previously, having been sold in bulk to a Mr. Kidd to clothe his West Indian slaves, it had been labeled "Kidd."

Thus was the capital of Scotland "tartanized" to receive its King, who himself came dressed in a kilt, played his part in the Celtic pageant, and at the climax of the visit solemnly invited the assembled dignitaries to drink a toast, not to the actual or historical elite, but to "the chieftains and clans of Scotland."

So we come to the last stage in the creation of the Highland myth: the reconstruction and extension, in ghostly and sartorial form, of that clan system whose reality had been destroyed after 1745. The essential figures in this episode were two of the most elusive and most seductive characters who have ever ridden the Celtic hobbyhorse or aerial broomstick: the brothers Allen.

They came from a well-connected English naval family. Their grandfather, John Carter Allen, had been an admiral. His son, their father, had served briefly in the Royal Navy; their mother was the daughter of a learned clergyman in Surrey.

AN EXCITING DISCOVERY

The early life of the two sons is undocumented. All that we can say of them is that they were both talented artists in many fields. They wrote romantic poems in the style of Scott; they were learned, though evidently self-taught, in many languages; they were skillful draftsmen, wood-carvers, furniture-makers. Their persuasive manners and great social charm enabled them to move at ease in the best society.

The exact occasion of their first appearance in Scotland is unknown, but they were evidently there with their father during the royal visit in 1822. There is some reason to think that the Allen family was in touch with Wilson and Son at this time.

In the following years, the brothers may have spent some time abroad, but they also appeared occasionally in great Scottish houses or at fashionable functions, dressed (as one English observer put it) "in all the extravagance of which the Highland costume is capable—every kind of tag and rag, false orders and tinsel ornaments."

They had now Scoticized their name, first as Allan, then, via Hay Allan, as Hay; and they encouraged the belief that they were descended from the last Hay, Earl of Errol. (As the earl had remained a lifelong bachelor, they presumably credited him with a secret marriage; but their claims were never weakened by explicit assertion.)

Much of the brothers' time was spent in the far north, where the Earl of Moray gave them the run of Darnaway Forest, and they became expert deer hunters. They never lacked aristocratic patrons such as Sir Thomas Dick Lauder, whose wife had an estate in Elgin. To him, in 1829, they revealed that they had in their possession an important historical document. This was a manuscript that (they said) had once belonged to John Leslie, Bishop of Ross, the confidant of Mary Queen of Scots, and had been given to their father by none other than the Young Chevalier, Bonny Prince Charlie.

The manuscript was entitled *Vestiarium Scoticum*, or *The Garde-robe of Scotland*, and was a depiction of the clan tartans of Scottish families, declaring itself to be the work of one Sir Richard Urquhart, knight. Bishop Leslie had inserted his date—1571—but the manuscript could have been, of course, much earlier.

Sir Thomas was very excited by this discovery. Not only was the document important in itself, but it also provided an authentic ancient authority for distinct clan tartans, and it showed that such tartans had been used by Lowlanders as well as Highlanders—a fact very gratifying to Lowland families eager to scramble in on the act. So Sir Thomas made a transcript of the text, which the younger brother obligingly illustrated for him. He then wrote to Sir Walter Scott, as the oracle on all such matters, urging that the document be published to correct the numerous "uncouth, spurious, modern tartans which are every day manufactured, christened after particular names, and worn as genuine."

Scott was not taken in. He did not believe that Lowlanders had ever worn clan tartans, and he suspected a tartan weavers' scheme. At the very least, he insisted that the original manuscript be submitted to experts at the British Museum.

Sir Thomas followed up this suggestion, and the elder brother very readily agreed; but that line of research was blocked when he produced a letter from his father, signed "J. T. Stuart Hay," firmly reprimanding him for even mentioning the document, which (he said)—apart from the futility of seeking to revive a world now irrecoverably lost—could never be exhibited to profane eyes on account of certain "private memorandums on the blank leaves."

SEEING IS BELIEVING

Defeated by the authority of Scott, the brothers retired again to the north and gradually perfected their image, their expertise, and their manuscript. They had now found a new patron, Lord Lovat, the Catholic head of the Fraser family, whose ancestor had died on the scaffold in 1747. They also adopted a new religious loyalty, declaring themselves Roman Catholics and a new and grander identity. They dropped the name of Hay and assumed the royal name of Stuart. The elder brother called himself John Sobieski Stuart (John Sobieski, the hero-king of Poland, was the maternal great-grandfather of the Young Chevalier); the younger became, like the Young Chevalier himself, Charles Edward Stuart.

In 1842, the brothers at last published their famous manuscript, *Vestiarium Scoticum*. It appeared in a sumptuous edition limited to fifty copies. The series of colored illustrations of tartans was the first ever to be published.

John Sobieski Stuart, as editor, supplied a learned commentary and new proofs of the authenticity of the manuscript, including a "traced facsimile" of Bishop Leslie's autograph. The manuscript itself, he said, had been "carefully collated" with a second manuscript recently discovered by an unnamed Irish monk in a Spanish monastery, unfortunately since dissolved. Another manuscript, recently in the possession of Lord Lovat, was also cited, although it had unfortunately been carried to America and there lost; but it was being actively sought...

The *Vestiarium Scoticum,* being of such limited distribution, attracted little notice on its publication. Scott was now dead, and Dick Lauder, though he had remained "a believer," held his peace. Had he scrutinized the printed setts, he might have noted, with surprise, that they had been considerably revised since they had been copied by the younger brother into his own transcript.

But the published *Vestiarium,* it soon appeared, was only a preliminary *pièce justificative* for a far more wide-ranging original work. Two years later, the two brothers published an even more sumptuous volume, clearly the result of years of study. This stupendous folio, lavishly illustrated by the authors, and dedicated to Ludwig I, King of Bavaria, as "the restorer of the Catholic arts of Europe," was entitled *The Costume of the Clans.*

CLAIMING ROYAL BLOOD

The Costume of the Clans is an extraordinary work. It cites the most arcane sources, Scottish and European, written and oral, manuscript and printed. It draws on art and archaeology as well as on literature. It is intelligent and critical. The authors admit the modern invention of the kilt. Nothing that they say can be immediately discounted. On the other hand, nothing can be taken on trust.

Elusive manuscripts cited in *The Costume of the Clans* include "a large copy of the original poems of Ossian and many other valuable Gaelic manuscripts" obtained from Douay by the late chevalier Watson but now, alas, invisible; a Latin manuscript of the fourteenth century found, with other manuscripts, in that Spanish monastery now so unfortunately dissolved; and, of

Figure 55. John Sobieski Stolberg Stuart and Charles Edward Stuart (1892), *The Costume of the Clans*, Edinburgh: John Grant. Special Collections, University of Rhode Island Library.

course, the *Vestiarium Scoticum* itself, now firmly ascribed "on internal evidence" to the end of the fifteenth century.

The thesis of *The Costume of the Clans* is that Highland dress was the fossil relic of the universal dress of the Middle Ages. It had been replaced throughout the rest of Europe in the sixteenth century, but had survived, debased but still recognizable, in that forgotten corner of the world.

For in the Middle Ages (according to these authors), Celtic Scotland had been a flourishing part of cosmopolitan Catholic Europe, a rich, polished society in which the splendid courts of the tribal chiefs were nourished—thanks to the advanced Hebridean manufactures—by the luxuries and the enlightenment of the Continent. Unfortunately, that rich civilization had not lasted: By the close of the Middle Ages, those humming Hebridean looms, those brilliant island courts, that "high intellectual sophistication" of Mull, Islay, and Skye had declined; Highland society had become impoverished and introverted and its costume drab and mean.

Only the *Vestiarium*—that great discovery of the two brothers—by revealing the brilliance of the original tartan setts, opened a narrow window onto that splendid culture now gone forever. For the authors professed no interest in the modern attempt to revive the costume alone, divorced from the Catholic Celtic culture of which it was a part. That was to convert it into mere fancy dress. The only true revival was one in which the whole past lived again—as it was lived by the Stuart brothers, writing poetry, hunting the deer, maintaining their own tribal court on an island in the Beauly River.

Unfortunately, *The Costume of the Clans* never received the criticism, or even the notice, of the learned world. Before that could happen, the authors made a grave tactical error. In 1846, they went as near as they would ever go toward explicitly claiming royal blood. They did this in a series of short stories, which, under romantic but transparent names, professed to reveal historical truth.

The work was entitled *Tales of a Century*, the century from 1745 to 1845. The burden of these tales was that the Stuart line was not extinct; that a legitimate son had been born to the wife of the Young Chevalier in Florence; that this infant, through fear of assassination by Hanoverian agents, had been entrusted to the care of an English admiral who had brought him up as his own son; and that, in due course, he had become the legitimate father of two sons who, having fought for Napoleon at Dresden, Leipzig, and Waterloo, and been personally decorated by him for bravery, had then retired to await their destiny in their ancestral country, and were now seeking to restore its ancient society, customs, costumes.

CREATING PROSPERITY

At this point, a hidden enemy struck. In 1847, under the cloak of a belated review of the *Vestiarium,* an anonymous writer published in the *Quarterly Review* a devastating exposure of the royal claims of the two brothers. The elder brother attempted to reply. The reply was Olympian in tone, but weak in substance.

The household at Eilean Aigas, the romantic residence lent to them by Lord Lovat, suddenly broke up; and for the next twenty years, the two brothers maintained abroad, in Prague and Pressburg, the royal pretensions that had been fatally damaged at home. In the same year, Queen Victoria bought Balmoral, and the real Hanoverian court replaced the vanished, illusory Jacobite court in the Highlands of Scotland.

The Sobieski Stuarts never recovered from the exposure of 1847. But their work was not wasted. The *Vestiarium* might be discredited, *The Costume of the Clans* ignored, but the spurious clan tartans devised by them were taken up, without their damaged names, by the Highland Society of London, and became the means of the continuing prosperity of the Scottish tartan industry. For the rest of the century, numerous books of clan tartans were regularly published. All of them were heavily dependent—directly or indirectly—on the *Vestiarium.*

This essay began with reference to James Macpherson. It ends with the Sobieski Stuarts.

Both imagined a golden age in the past of the Celtic Highlands. Both created literary ghosts, forged texts, and falsified history in support of their theories.

But Macpherson was a sensual bully whose aim, whether in literature or in politics, was wealth and power, and he pursued that aim with ruthless determination and ultimate success. The Sobieski Stuarts were amiable, scholarly men who won converts by their transpicuous innocence; they were *fantaisistes* rather than forgers. They were genuine in the sense that they lived their own fantasies.

Unlike Macpherson, they died poor. The wealth that they generated went to the manufacturers of the differentiated clan tartans now worn, with tribal enthusiasm, by Scots and supposed Scots from Houston to Hong Kong.

NOTES

1. The Jacobites supported the restoration of the Stuart dynasty to the thrones of Scotland and England. James VI of Scotland had become James I of England following the death, in 1603, of his first cousin once removed, the childless Queen Elizabeth. Eighty-five years later, in 1688, James II, a Catholic and the fourth of Britain's Stuart monarchs, was deposed in the Glorious Revolution that brought the Dutch Protestant William of Orange to the throne. Led from France first by the unseated King, then by his son, James Francis Edward, and then by his grandson, Charles Edward ("Bonny Prince Charlie"), the Jacobites sought to achieve their ends by invasion (1708) and insurrection (1715). Jacobite opposition was finally crushed at the Battle of Culloden in 1746.
2. This account, from Ivan Baillie of Aberdeen, was published in the *Edinburgh Magazine*, March 1785.

19

CLAIRE DWYER and PHILIP CRANG

Ghulam Sakina: A Case Study in Transnational Design Production

Reproduced with permission from C. Dwyer and P. Crang (2002),
"Fashioning Ethnicities: The Commercial Spaces of Multiculture,"
Ethnicities 2(3): 419–26. © Sage Publications.

The first Ghulam Sakina collection [by Liaqat Rasul] was entitled "Multicultural Mind Mayhem." Implicated in the promotional text and elaborated on in his work with us are engagements with three different registers of the multicultural. First, we can recognize an engagement with "the multicultural" that might be termed "sociological." This is an engagement that is described partly in familial histories, partly in career terms. Yet this is also a register of engagement with "the multicultural" in terms of the ways in which Liaqat sees his relationships with imagined communities and collective identities. Second, there is an "aesthetic" engagement with the multicultural in terms of the ways in which Liaqat works as a designer and how he thinks about and talks about his clothes. Finally, there is a "commercial" engagement with the multicultural told to us in terms of his relations with buyers and imagined "markets." Together, we suggest that these different registers of engagement with "the multicultural" mark out a terrain in which multiculture is neither simply a commercial invention nor some pure cultural political moment of possibility. To that end, we overlay the three below, moving broadly from the sociological through the aesthetic to the commercial.

Liaqat was born—somewhat distanced from the multicultural centers of Birmingham or Brick Lane—in Wrexham, Wales. He laughs that, "I'm really Welsh," although he describes his identity as British Pakistani. His parents (both born in Pakistan) ran a clothes shop called Guys and Dolls which catered for "Western" fashion—what Liaqat describes as cheap, disposable clothes: "white Lycra, that sort of thing." He often went with his father to the Asian manufacturers and wholesalers in Manchester from whom supplies were garnered. Asked to reflect upon this, he suggests that his interest in fashion was evident even then. He would often point out to his father the poor quality of the clothes that he was buying, noticing where stitching had come undone. He also describes how he would irritate his father by rearranging the window displays to make them "more artistic" and describes the shop as having been "too dark and cluttered." Liaqat reflects that there were only "two or three other Asian families in Wrexham" at that time, and he remembers with pride his mother coming to school to pick him up in her bright and beautiful shalwar kameez while all the other mothers wore "dull jeans." Wrexham was a long way off the beaten path of spectacular urban multiculture. Indeed, even now he enthuses touristically about how amazing "Asian" areas of London, such as Southall and Wembley's Ealing Road, are "like a little piece of India or Pakistan that has just been taken up and dropped in England."

Liaqat studied fashion at Derby University (after a brief period studying fashion at Edinburgh University). As part of his degree, he chose to go to India to study at the National Institute of Fashion Technology (NIFT) in Delhi, enabled by a partnership that Derby had with NIFT. Asked whether he thought about going to Pakistan, he is a little surprised by the question. He jokes that there would have been "too many relatives to visit there" and, on further reflection, judges the fashion scene in Pakistan to be far less open and vibrant and much "more conservative" than that in India. Moving between the two countries has not, however, always been easy for him, and he describes the questioning he faces at the Indian embassy and their concerns about young British Pakistani "militants" coming to India. Reflecting on his unshaven appearance, he laughs "They think I'm a terrorist." During his time at NIFT, Liaqat obtained a work placement with Ritu Kumar. Well known in India, Ritu Kumar is the grande dame of Indian "ethnic chic," characterized by the revival of indigenous handicrafts such as block prints, chikan kari, zardozi, bandhani and kalamkari (see Nag 1991; Tarlo 1996). Kumar has several prestigious shops in major Indian cities and is well known throughout India for her writing on Indian fashion. For Liaqat, Kumar remains "a great influence and inspiration." It was through her that he developed an understanding and appreciation of many Indian textile traditions that have come to be a key element in his own contemporary fashion designs.

When he returned to the UK, Liaqat continued to work with Ritu Kumar in her (now closed) shop off Oxford Street in London's West End, and also helped her in organizing exhibitions. He designed and ran her stand at the first BBC "Mega Mela" exhibition in Birmingham. Kumar has been criticized for her commercial and artistic elitism in relation to the British Asian market (Bhachu 2000). For Liaqat, such critiques were evident when he saw the incredulity expressed by the young British Asian women attending the "Mega Mela" at the prices of Kumar's clothes. Reflecting on this, Liaqat argues that, "The theory behind a designer garment

that had longevity and a strong culture reference in terms of embroidery and fabric technique just did not appeal to the people that attended." He explains this by saying that second generation British Asians have no knowledge of "the cultural aesthetics of India or Pakistan," dependent as they are on "secondhand knowledge, passed down from the older generation." Reflecting that he too "knew nothing about any of this when I was growing up," Liaqat often speaks about the kinds of projects that he would like to undertake to reconnect Kumar's imagined communities of Indian craft traditions and the imagined communities of British Asians. He tried to see if the Crafts Council would fund him to put together a flick book that would show young British Asians the rich heritage of South Asian fashion aesthetics, juxtaposed with reflections on contemporary British multiculturalism. He would also like to open a center where British Asian women could come to sew and learn about traditional embroideries: "It's difficult for them to go out, you know, because of their husbands, but they could come to something like that." As part of his degree he chose to write a dissertation entitled "British Pakistani Culture: What Makes a Modem British Pakistani?" which looked at questions of culture and difference and included an analysis of his experiences at "Mega Mela." Indeed, while Liaqat is acutely aware, as we discuss below, that the commercial value of multicultural aesthetics may ebb, he reflects that they will always be important to him "sociologically if nothing else."

Ritu Kumar went on to sponsor Liaqat's end of degree show, entitled "Observational Composite." Liaqat's collection was spotted at the Graduate Fashion Week Gala Show and he was offered a commission for Liberty. This sold well enough (80 percent) for them to place orders for further collections. Liaqat's first collection was made in workshops in Delhi with which he had made contact through Ritu Kumar and Kiki Siddique. However, his second collection was made in Jaipur in the workshops of the Rajasthan-based company, Anokhi. Anokhi is well established as a block-print-based fashion design and textile company, whose products have been sold in the UK through Monsoon and now through the high-street retailer EAST (Dwyer and Jackson 2001). Liaqat and Anokhi have gone on to collaborate in the production of a new range of clothes for Anokhi—the Anokhi Designer Collection. For Liaqat, the collaboration with Anokhi reflects his appreciation of Anokhi's commitment to the revival of traditional forms of block printing and textile design. His collection for them attempts to rework this tradition of printing in more contemporary designs and using fewer colors than more "traditional" Anokhi prints.

Aesthetically, Liaqat describes his own collections for Ghulam Sakina as being "inspired" by multiculturalism. Asked to reflect on how he relates his clothes to multiculturalism, Liaqat responds by emphasizing an aesthetic of juxtaposition: "just putting things alongside each other … making things jar against each other." For example, in a dress shown in his first collection, Liaqat includes: the packing material used to wrap up Ritu Kumar's clothes when they were sent from Delhi to North Audley Street, London (this is a common motif, the use of cheap georgette fabrics printed with Indian writing that are hand sewn around deliveries of clothes); a cutting taken from a borrowed paisley duvet that a friend had had on his bed; and a decoration based on the Bengali Kantha or running stitch used traditionally to recycle materials by sewing them together. But he has also developed a particular take on this juxtapositional aesthetic opposed to what he calls the cut and mix approach of those who, in this context, become "Western designers." Emphasizing the use of embroidery, natural fibers and color, Liaqat explains that the fabrics used are chosen for their properties of both "longevity and a sense of nostalgia." He stresses again and again the importance of knowing about and appreciating the heritage of the different elements, of not simply appropriating them with no attention to their lineage. As he explains in a promotional interview with *Maya* magazine (I, 2000: 107): "The Ghulam Sakina label reflects the organic and indigenous relationship that clothing

has with heritage." Part of this seems to be about cultural respect, but this is a respect very much filtered through a valuing of cultural production. What is valuable is not so much some immaterial cultural sensibility, but particular craft skills and practices, particular materialities. On the other hand, for Liaqat his clothing is not simply about bringing Indian handicrafts to the West, as he explains: "What I'm doing isn't simply Indian export; it's an intellectual project, if that doesn't sound too pretentious." Such an engagement has not always proved easy and he describes the struggles he had overseeing production in Delhi when he first began, because those undertaking it didn't appreciate his nostalgic aesthetic. Tailors would straighten out a wiggly stitch assuming he had simply mis-stitched it and, on one occasion, they went to the market to buy new ribbon to replace the frayed and old ribbon with which he had supplied them!

Of course, as should have been apparent from the preceding descriptions, also central to Liaqat's aesthetics are constructions of difference and identity that are less directly mapped onto ethnicity than those of the British and the Indian, the Western and the Eastern. There is the emphasis on nostalgia, expressed through the personal geographies of domestic space and childhood material culture as much as through global or regional geographies of modernity and tradition. For example, his press release for the Liberty launch is printed on school graph paper with a house point star stuck on. Elsewhere in his designs, he has used stripy cotton bedding and pillowcase fabrics that remind him of his childhood. He likes to reuse old fabrics and values traditional means of recycling such as Kantha embroidery. There is an emphasis on the reclaiming of sewing as a craft skill (labels on his clothes are printed with a sewing machine logo), and he is also fascinated by traveling objects and the travel of objects (as evoked by using luggage labels as his clothes' labels, incorporating packing materials with addresses in his clothes, and so on). These aesthetic impulses reflect Liaqat's positioning of his work as art, as high culture, as fitting for a gallery space such as the "OOOzerozerozero" exhibition [at Whitechapel Art Gallery in East London, July 1999]. At the same time, he applauds the aesthetic work of popular fashion cultures—highlighting the changing styles within local Asian subcultural styles such as long shalwar kameez tops with flared trousers—even if he has to admit that, in terms of his own aesthetic taste, he does not always admire the outcome!

In turn, all these aesthetic themes are developed in the context of negotiations with a range of commercial organizations and settings, and in the pursuit of some sort of living. As he negotiated his way through fashion college, Liaqat was faced with the dilemma of how commercial his designs should be. He was very conscious, he says, that most fashion graduates who created experimental works in their studies ended up "designing socks for Sock Shop" in their working lives (McRobbie 1998). He took Joe Casely Hayford's advice to be innovative and experimental in his graduate show, perhaps recognizing the paradox that, for him, that strategy might be particularly marketable. Reflecting on the phenomenon of so-called Asian Kool (Garratt 1998), he explains that he is sometimes wary of his incorporation in particular initiatives (such as "OOOzerozerozero") "just because I'm Asian." Although conscious of the visibility and contacts the show created, he argues that, "It should be about the work, not who you are." He is also aware of the ephemeral fashion cycles that mean that the moment for such a multicultural/exotic aesthetic may already have passed. In the spring of 2001, struggling to find new buyers for his collection, he points out that in 1999, when he sold his first collection, the fashion was for styles that were much more textured, much more in tune with his approach: "Even Prada had these little dresses with appliqué on; [now] it's all minimalist, no color."

Commercial considerations also raise questions of cost, of course. As Liaqat reflects, given the labor required and the cost of the fabrics, by the time his clothes reach the customer, "My stuff is just so expensive." While Liaqat is happy that his collection has sold well at Liberty, it means that he needs to engage with their aesthetics and market as he plans for the future. Should he continue to be driven by his understanding of their market or seek new customers? He already feels that he may be pigeonholed, as one of the viewers of his recent collection immediately identified it with Liberty. According to informal conversations with Liberty shop floor workers, customers for Ghulam Sakina are international, particularly from the Gulf States. Liaqat is positioned within Liberty in their "contemporary designers" section, although his first collection for them also included a home furnishing range that was sold in their "Indian gallery" alongside clothes and textiles produced by companies like Abraham and Thakore.

Liaqat's current worries about the commercial future of Ghulam Sakina fit into a more general spatialization of sales and creativity. In London, he tends to feel ground down by the commerce with which he is engaged and worried about his financial fragility. Like most designers, he remains financially pecunious and, when he is not in India overseeing production, he is in London combining casual bar work with trying to develop new customers for his designs. In India, he finds it easier to be optimistic and creative, although here he also worries that he can become too distanced from the commercial world of the market. Yet, although it may sometimes appear that creativity and commerce are opposed, it is more true to say that Liaqat's working life in both London and India is constituted through commercial spaces. So, in his studio in Rajasthan, he was to be found organizing his ideas and designs into categories such as "commercial" or "funky/fusion," acutely aware of how he needs to position his clothes within the marketplace.

20

DAVID GILBERT

World Cities of Fashion

From D. Gilbert (2000), "Urban Outfitting: The City and the Spaces of Fashion Culture," in S. Bruzzi and P. C. Gibson (eds.), Fashion Cultures: Theories, Explanations and Analysis (London: Routledge), 13–19.

One enduring cliché of high-fashion advertising is a list of great cities following a brand or designer name. Two or three city names are permutated from a limited range of possibilities: Paris, New York, Milan, London, and maybe a few others. In extreme cases of this symbolic geography, the city name itself becomes an integral part of branding—DKNY is the most obvious current example. The formula is so familiar that it has become an almost completely transparent sign, absorbed and understood without reflection. But by playing with the elements, the force of this formula becomes clear. Put the name of a mundane high-street brand in front of "Paris, London, New York" and the effect is immediately pretentious and comic. Play this game the other way round, substituting new place-names for one of high fashion's established centers, and the dissonant combinations say much about the inclusions and exclusions of fashion's world order: Paris, London, New York—and Tokyo, Barcelona, Sydney (probably); and Manchester, Seattle, or Hamburg (perhaps, but only for a certain kind of fashion);—and Detroit, Birmingham Alabama or Birmingham West Midlands (almost certainly not).

The construction of this world order of fashion cities has a complex history. There is some overlap with what Saskia Sassen has termed the global cities—those places that play a key role in the world economic system, and which are often marked by extreme concentrations of wealth (Sassen 1991). The emergence of New York as a world city of fashion in the early twentieth century, or the development of Tokyo as an international fashion center from the early 1980s, was not unrelated to the position of those cities in rising economic super-powers. Yet the symbolic and economic geographies of the fashion industry are different from those of finance and business services. Even in cities that are global financial and fashion centers, like London and New York, there is often a distinct spatial and cultural separation between the spaces of finance and those of fashion. This is not to suggest that Wall Street or the City of London has been untouched by fashion. Breward has suggested that through much of its modern history, the City has been a contradictory fashion space. The Square Mile has been characterized by both intense occupational and social differentiation through the detailing and quality of masculine clothing, but also by a culture which associated more overt demonstrations of fashion with effeminacy, creating "particular problems for the communication of masculine values by sartorial means" (Breward 1999: 241). There were some shifts in the 1980s when the Hugo Boss suit became an aggressive symbol of the newly deregulated financial markets of London and New York. The same kind of ungainly compromises between decoration and domineering bulk that were to be found in the new landscapes of Battery Park City and Canary Wharf were matched in the personal architecture of double-breasted facades and reinforced shoulder-padding. As women became more significant in these corporate landscapes, there were uneasy negotiations between different fashion codes. Some senior women began wearing adaptations of masculine conventions ("power dressing") to claim equal status, while others adopted elite designer fashions of the West End or Fifth Avenue to differentiate themselves from women in subordinate secretarial jobs (McDowell and Court 1994).

However, to understand the position of the handful of elite fashion's world centers we need to look beyond what Arjun Appadurai (1990) has described as the finance-scapes of global flows of money and capital. But we also need to look beyond the internal processes of the fashion industry itself, such as the couture and collection systems. If any sense of this geography were to be found in traditional fashion history, it usually entailed an uncritical reference to certain sites of elite fashion design and consumption. In effect, Simmel's trickle-down theory was extended from the social to the spatial. Standard accounts of the fashion process contained an implicit geography of emulation in which elite fashion was simultaneously metropolitan fashion—it's not just that I want to look like someone "better" than me, it's also that I want to look as if I come from a better place. The archetypal example was the couture system, which projected Paris as world fashion's central place—the source of actual designs for a small elite, and of pronouncements on the "look" for the rest of the fashion world. Even at the height of its powers, the claims made for the stylistic influence of the couture system were exaggerated and the relationship between elite design and mass-market fashion was complex. Moreover, this kind of account had little to say about the processes by which Paris and other cities established and maintained their positions. The continuing status of London, New York, Milan, and particularly Paris has to be understood through the long-term intersection of a number of cultural and economic processes bound up with the development of the modern city. In thinking about the long-term development of the geography of fashion's world cities, it is useful to identify five main themes. These can be characterized as:

- the urban consumer revolution of the eighteenth century,
- the economic and symbolic systems of European imperialism,
- the development of rivalries between European fashion cities,
- the influence of an American engagement with European fashion, and
- the development of a symbolic ordering of cities within the fashion media.

Discussions of the emergence of modern consumption now conventionally stress the importance of an urban renaissance and "consumer revolution" of the late seventeenth and early eighteenth centuries, rather than the later Industrial Revolution. Glennie and Thrift (1992) suggest that European and new North American urban contexts were central both to the learning of new consumption practices and to their pursuit. Yet clearly not all cities were equally suited to the development of the fashion process. If knowledge of consumption was essentially practical, acquired less through instruction or advertising than through "quasi-personal contact and observation in the urban throng," then some cities (and particularly London) were more thronging than others (Glennie and Thrift 1992: 430). And if the rise of fashion was dependent on the prioritization of novelty, then some cities (and again particularly London) were in positions in the networks of world trade which enhanced the supply of novel experiences, and encouraged the acceleration of the fashion cycle. Part of the shock-value of the extreme figure of the macaroni on the London streets of the 1770s came not just from the speed at which his fashions changed, but also from the seemingly wasteful and indulgent geographical reach of his clothing.

As Miles Ogborn has suggested, the macaroni was "understood within the international chains of commodities that made London itself a dangerous place through the ways in which its endless varieties of consumption brought together the produce of the world" (Ogborn 1998: 139). These early developments were of vital significance for London's long-term status as a fashion center; while fashions themselves came and went rapidly, the overall spatial ordering of fashion proved remarkably stable.

The "consumer revolution" also shaped London's internal geography, establishing a pattern that appeared in other important fashion centers. In a sense, London's geography remained preindustrial, with an economic structure characterized not by factory production but by small-scale workshops, often involved in the finishing of fashions and luxury goods. Fashion was therefore significant not only in the elite "front regions" of the city, where it was displayed, purchased and worn, but also in "back regions" where it was made, finished and often copied. Despite the development of an international division of labor, where many mass-market fashions are produced for a pittance in the Third World, the existence of a finishing trade has remained an importance feature of fashion's world cities. Indeed, the fashion industry's dependence on an accessible and flexible local manufacturing sector has often encouraged a miniature version of the international division of labor within the metropolis, in sweatshops exploiting immigrant labor. The proximity of these front and back regions remains one of the key characteristics of fashion's world cities, and can produce unexpected crossings and blurrings of the boundaries between different social worlds: modern Parisian shoppers who abandon the Rue du Jour to slum for bargains among the workshops of the Passage du Caire are following a journey made many times before, perhaps in late nineteenth-century Whitechapel, or the Garment District in the 1930s. In a beautiful essay on her childhood as the daughter of a Jewish master tailor in the London rag trade, Ruth Gershon has described how her life was saturated with experiences of the latest styles and cuts: "swaggering around Hendon Central in a copy of a 1961 Cardin suit in a brilliant blue-and-black tweed with a fur collar" (Gershon 1999: 82). Fashion's great centers have long contained overlapping fashion cultures and spaces, in which conventional models of the fashion process—trickle-down emulation or bubble-up street innovation—prove hopelessly inadequate as descriptions of the interlocking circuits of production and consumption, imitation and intimidation.

If in the late eighteenth century London's position as a commercial city created new forms of the fashion process, by the mid-nineteenth century London's imperial centrality was the most significant influence on its development as one of fashion's world capitals. During the nineteenth century, London came to be understood as a site of both innovation and of fashion authority, in the British Empire and beyond. For example, the development of London's department stores in the second half of the nineteenth century was accompanied by a rhetoric and performance of world significance and centrality. Thus Harrods of Knightsbridge was able to style itself as "the most elegant and commodious emporium in the world," while increasingly exotic displays of commodities took place in stores like Liberty and Selfridges (Nava 1996). These stores rapidly became part of an idea and image of London promoted to the provinces and the colonies, developing the established reputation of the West End as a site for the purchase and performance of elite fashion. Shopping, particularly for women's fashions, became one of the essential tourist acts in the city, and guidebooks for those arriving from the colonies stressed the significance of London as a capital of style and luxury (Gilbert 1999).

The modern character of fashion culture in cities like London and Paris cannot be understood without reference to their imperial past and post-imperial presence. Most obviously, the economic ordering of the fashion industry has been shaped around the international divisions of labor established in the imperial age. Imperialism also shaped profoundly the ideological context of fashion, so that the stylistic incorporation of "exotic" elements took place within an imaginative geography that set the imperial cities at the center and the colonized at the margins. A dramatic feature of the fashion culture of these cities in a post-imperial age is the way in which this ordering has been disrupted by recent social and cultural change. While London and Paris have provided homes for non-Europeans for as long as they have been cities, postwar migration has created distinctively new sites of hybridity and cultural fusion. The elite fashion of these cities still regularly creates "new looks" through crass pillaging of stylistic tropes from other cultures, but the 1990s also saw the local development of transcultural fashions, directly related to the emergence of new forms of social and cultural identity. The recent transformation of Brick Lane in London's East End is indicative of this development. One of fashion's archetypal back regions, a district characterized by a long history of immigration, a sweatshop economy, and a huge weekly fleamarket, Brick Lane is gaining a reputation as one of the emerging fashion districts of twenty-first-century London.

Across nineteenth-century Europe, high fashion became part of the promotion of a certain ideology of distinction and distinctiveness, in which constructions of historical depth and cultural superiority were reinforced by the demonstrable political and economic dominance of European "civilization." The age of Empire was marked not only by highly unequal relations between Europe and the rest of the world, but also by intense economic, political and cultural competition between the European powers. Like the magnificence of the architecture of capital cities or the size of the great exhibitions, the influence of high fashion became another of the ways in which European national cultures could measure themselves against each other. As the London fashion industry was only too well aware, it was Paris which proved best able to position itself as the world capital of fashion.

The idea of Paris as the source for the diffusion of high fashion has a history that predates the couture system, stretching back at least as far as the courtly fashion systems and *marchandes de modes* of the seventeenth and eighteenth centuries (J. Jones 1996). Neil McKendrick has argued that the veneration of Paris was a significant dimension of the consumer revolution centered on eighteenth-century London. Fashion that was "expensive, exclusive and Paris-based" was translated into something that was "cheap, popular and London-based" (McKendrick 1983: 43). It was vital that the process of translation from exclusive Parisian fashion to popular London fashion was incomplete, and that a residue of Parisian origins remained on clothes that were intended for consumption outside the traditional elites. There has been a remarkably consistent tension between the fashion cultures of London and Paris; Parisian fashions have long been derided as elitist and decadent, while being copied and incorporated into designs for popular commercial fashion. Similar processes to those identified by McKendrick for the eighteenth century can be found in the example of the appropriation of Dior's "New Look" by British working-class women in the 1940s and 1950s (Partington 1992). While only a small international elite could afford the actual clothes, Parisian designs, and perhaps as importantly, the ideal of Parisian fashion, could be part of the repertoire and dreams of a vast number of distant consumers.

A long tradition in urban guides and topographies has used London and Paris as indicators of the double-sided nature of the modern city (see Hancock 1999). The feminine "capital of pleasure" was routinely contrasted with a more masculine city of work and business. Despite London's incontrovertible economic and political supremacy, it is Paris which is remembered, in Walter Benjamin's phrase, as the "capital of the nineteenth century," not least because its cityscape was remade as a global object of desire and consumption (Hancock 1999: 75). The "Haussmannization" of Paris changed more than its street pattern and its architecture; it also altered the imagined geography of the city, locking together a strong visual trope of the material city with ideas about its cultural life, in which the consumption and public display of high fashion were key elements. International tourism was one of the growth industries of Second Empire Paris, and by the end of the nineteenth century developments in transatlantic travel helped to turn the city into the hub of the European tour for thousands of upper- and middle-class Americans. Guidebooks for Americans increasingly stressed Paris's position at the center of the fashion world. London was slow to respond to these developments, and by the beginning of the twentieth century, English publicity for traveling American women featured rather desperate pleas to support the "English-speaking races" by buying in "tariff-free London" (D. H. Evans & Co. 1902: 25).

This, to put it mildly, was missing the point. Transatlantic tourists were not interested in acts of political or economic solidarity, but in experiencing the pleasures of elite consumption. Very often for middle-class Americans these experiences did not extend to actual purchases of clothing or perfume (which in any case were increasingly available in the major stores of New York or Chicago). The fashion object that was being consumed was the city itself, and the spectacle of high fashion *in situ*. Those Americans who traveled to experience Paris were just part of a wider process of the popular consumption of the idea of Paris as an elite space. As Craik (1994: 74) suggests, the development of fashion in the early twentieth century was schizophrenic, marked by an unprecedented democratization as more and more people had access to fashion clothing and fashion imagery, but also by a concentration of the control of style and design. There was a strong interdependence between Parisian and American fashion. Craik emphasizes what Hollywood did for Paris—"Paris took off as the fashion heart because of Hollywood" (1994: 75)—but Paris, or more accurately the aura of Parisian fashion authority, was a critical feature in the systematization of the American fashion cycle.

In the early twentieth century, New York City itself came to enjoy the status of a new world city of fashion, and became established as another place which existed both as an actual site of elite fashion consumption and as an imagined space of fashion fantasy. Since the late eighteenth century, New York had been the dominant economic city of the United States, and a public culture of socially choreographed displays of fashion, taste and difference on Broadway and Fifth Avenue was well developed by the 1860s (Domosh 1998). By the late nineteenth century, the city was the match of London and Paris in both its scale and its "intensely urban qualities," which stimulated the development of a vibrant commercial culture (Hammack 1991: 37). Like the great European capitals, it also possessed a highly flexible local manufacturing sector able to respond rapidly to changes of style, at least in part due to the heterogeneity of a population in which immigrants formed a majority.

A number of factors pushed New York into the front rank of fashion cites. To some extent, this was a direct reflection of the rise of American political and economic power. The development of New York's international fashion prestige depended on the development of a class of the super-rich resident in the apartments and hotels of the city. As the novels of Edith Wharton and Henry James indicate, this new elite often sought to validate and consolidate their status through connections with established European aristocratic families. High fashion formed part of the performance of this new status; but what was significant was that this performance was increasingly one with a global audience. The image of elite New York consumption was one element in an unprecedented promotion of a city as a spectacle of commercial culture. Alongside the emerging vertical city of skyscrapers, and Broadway's "great white way," the high-fashion shops of Fifth Avenue became a familiar part of a cityscape which was celebrated in film, song and literature. One 1924 tourist guidebook indicated that public displays of fashion were among the sights of the city, and that fashion culture touched parts of the city far beyond the "gorgeous shops of Fifth Avenue":

Another characteristic of New York, and one that applies to all grades of society, is the lavish and conspicuous mode of dress adopted by New York women on the public streets. The styles for street wear change more rapidly and more radically than any other costumes; and no sooner has a new mode found favor on Fifth Avenue than cheap imitations of it make their appearance on Fourteenth Street and the lower East Side. (Rider 1924: xlv)

21

ALISON GOODRUM, WENDY LARNER and MAUREEN MOLLOY

Auckland as a Globalizing Fashion City

From A. Goodrum, W. Larner, and M. Molloy (2004), "Wear in The World? Fashioning Auckland as a Globalizing City," in I. Carter, D. Craig and S. Matthewman (eds.), Almighty Auckland? (Palmerston North: Dunmore), 262–74. Reprinted by permission of the authors.

Auckland provides an interesting and important case study of the relationships between globalization, fashion and cities, even though it does not feature in the formal hierarchy identified in the "global cities" literature. Indeed, the latter point is not surprising. Many international companies formerly based in New Zealand have moved offshore ... together with their support functions, and numerous large multinationals have closed their New Zealand head offices. As Australasia has come increasingly to be seen as a single economic market, so Sydney has come to dominate in the regional hierarchy of cities, throwing doubt on earlier claims that sophisticated communications technologies obviate the need for face-to-face interaction.

Yet Auckland remains key to New Zealand's global aspirations and to the processes through which New Zealand-based activities attempt to insert themselves into global flows and networks. One implication of these changes for New Zealand's economic development policies is particularly significant: small and medium enterprises (SMEs) are increasingly posited as New Zealand's new economic base. However, success for these smaller, locally based businesses will not, it is argued, come from a national focus: they must seek out niche markets in the global economy in order to prosper. New Zealand's new policy emphasis on biotechnology, information and

communications technologies, and cultural and creative industries, underlines this emphasis on interconnectedness. New Zealand firms, people and places are now represented not as members of a self-contained national or urban economy, but as necessarily located within a global socio-economic system (Larner 1998).

In this section we explore the significance of these changes for Auckland's economic base in terms of the city's aspirations to be a global player in the "fashion stakes." We explore the impacts of trade liberalization on the Auckland garment industry. We use the idea of cultural economy to explore how designer fashion exemplifies the new directions in economic development policy to which government has linked New Zealand's future well-being, and the workforce and consumption patterns that enable the growth of this industry. Then we examine how the built environment of Auckland has been influenced by the growth of the industry. Finally we look at the implications of the establishment of a New Zealand Fashion Week for Auckland's positioning in national and international networks.

Until recently the idea that fashion might play a central role in either New Zealand's bid for prosperity or Auckland's efforts to be a globally significant city would have seemed laughable. Ten years ago the New Zealand domestic clothing and apparel industry was moribund—a casualty of the deregulation and tariff-cutting which are hallmarks of the globalization process. Economic liberalization in New Zealand in the 1980s followed international trends for mass- and middle-market apparel to be manufactured in developing countries (especially Southeast Asia and, for New Zealand, Fiji) at greatly reduced costs. As a result, clothing imports to New Zealand rose from NZ$129 million in 1985 to NZ$480 million in 1996 (<www.kiwicareers.govt.nz/industry>). The implications for the domestic industry were dramatic, with mass redundancies ensuing as New Zealand manufacturers' firms relocated to lower wage sites, particularly in Fiji (Harrington 1999). Employment in textile, clothing and footwear industries (TCF) fell from 28,450 to 25,580 between February 1995 and 1997 (Burleigh-Evett Report 2001: 8).

Larson (2001: 49) articulates the paradox that emerged: "Even as mills and manufacturers began moving out or closing down, a subversive little bunch of designers sneaked up on the international couture circuit and sent commentators in London and Sydney scrabbling for their notebooks." Today the designer fashion industry sits quite apart from the remainder of the country's TCF and is the focus of unprecedented attention from media, government and industrialists alike. In keeping with the government policy to promote "knowledge-based and creative" industries, in 2001 Industry New Zealand named "fashion, apparel and textile" one of five areas to

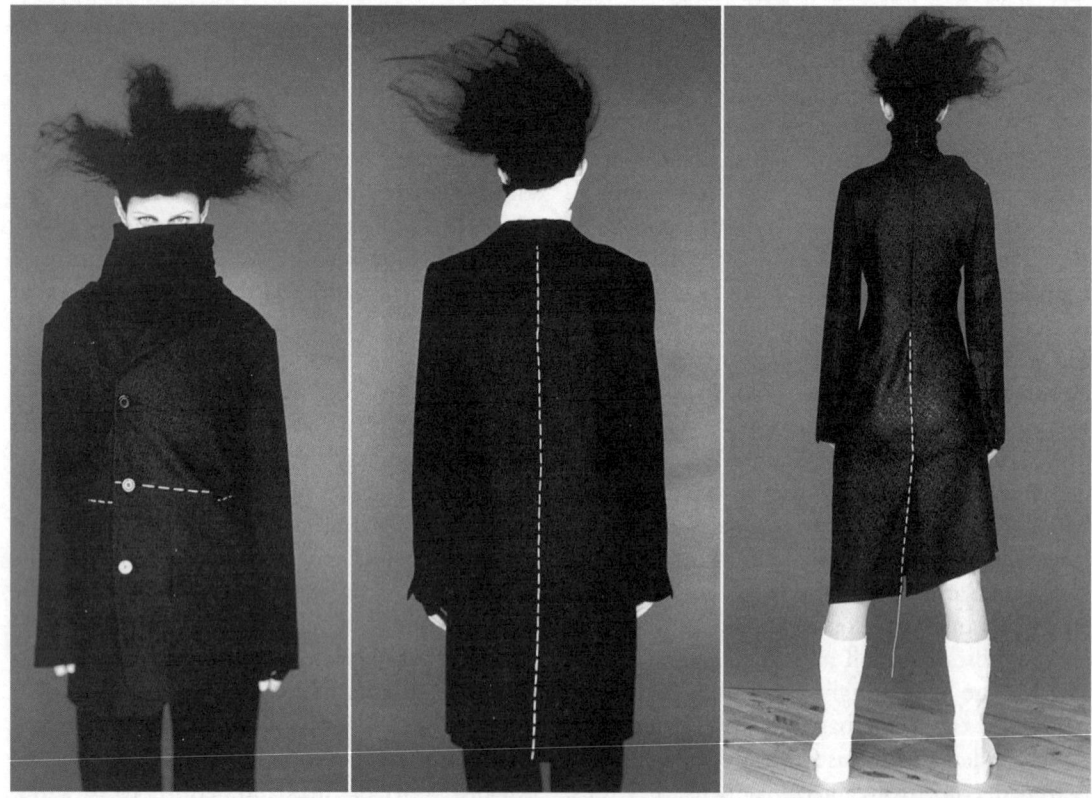

Figure 56. Karen Walker, Auckland, New Zealand, "Daddy's Gone Strange Collection," Hong Kong Fashion Week, 1999. Courtesy of Karen Walker.

be targeted for development, along with music and film production, tourism, light manufacturing, communications and biotechnology. This increased attention is traceable to the milestone year of 1999 when the "New Zealand Four" (a group of four fashion design firms: Zambesi, Karen Walker, World and Nom D) entered into the global fashion scene as participants at London Fashion Week.

Since 1999, the government has repeatedly dubbed designer fashion a "transforming" sector. Like other cultural industries, the fashion industry is seen as having two tasks. The first is the usual task of economic development. The industry is targeted because of its potential for growth, particularly in export earnings, and a section of TradeNZ is devoted to promoting and supporting the development of export markets for fashion design firms. TradeNZ has supported designers' participation in overseas fashion events, as well as the establishment and ongoing costs of L'Oreal New Zealand Fashion Week. But unlike, for example, the biotechnology industry (and like, for example, the film industry), the fashion industry has the additional task of presenting an image of New Zealand in the international marketplace, a function seen as enhancing broader economic development goals of the country as a whole. "Like the film business," says former CEO of the New Zealand Apparel and Textile Federation, Paul Blomfield (quoted in Larson 2001: 51), "high fashion has the ability to gain an international profile for New Zealand, far beyond other industries that may turn over more dollars." Blomfield continues: "A local furniture-maker told me the publicity generated by New Zealand designers at London Fashion Week enabled him to sell into a market that had previously rejected his line." Government policy on the creative industries is thus based on this dual function—that they create export earnings for their sector, and that they enhance the earning capacity of other, more mundane, less symbolic industries.

Seen through this lens of cultural economy, the designer fashion industry has significant implications for Auckland. While fashion design's high profile can be attributed to its cultural exploitability, the current structure of the industry indicates that this particular profile is a perceived requirement for maximizing New Zealand's (and Auckland's) economic development. Fashion design firms are quintessential small and medium enterprises (SMEs), typically employing fewer than ten people and having a relatively low turnover. Furthermore, like many SMEs in other industry sectors, fashion firms typically depend, at least in their initial years, on a high degree of self-exploitation. Young designers often live from hand to mouth, or more aptly, from sewing machine to shop counter, recycling proceeds of sales into new textiles on a week-to-week basis, working long hours for little reward. Also, like many other SMEs, design firms usually depend largely on the commitment of their owners, who are likely to have few business skills and often lack the capital base to make the transition from a small, largely self-employing business to a medium-size sustainable business. Furthermore, New Zealand designers tend to have a high degree of commitment to "place," which includes a refusal to move physically to more lucrative markets, and a commitment to manufacturing their garments in New Zealand. They tend to value creativity, product quality and lifestyle, and thus tend to produce high-quality, innovative garments, and to generate local employment, often at the cost of their personal income.

If the new economic climate in New Zealand provides space for the development of such niche firms, the changing nature of the labor market provides consumption demand. An important impetus in this transformation away from heavily lifestyled and globally ubiquitous fashion branding toward the desire for differentiation and for doing "one's own unique *style* thing" is the continued rise of a female consumer faction (see for example, Bourdieu 1984; Goodrum 2001; McRobbie 1989, 1997; Thornton 1997) who are demanding in their taste for cultural goods. This is the first generation of women who have little time to spend on making clothing (unlike their mothers and grandmothers), but who have plenty of personal disposable income.

They have high levels of cultural capital and are able to reject the "anticipatory" (i.e., unsurprising and mainstream) fashions of larger corporations in favor of something a little bit different or avant-garde. Furthermore, in an employment market that values innovation, youth, flexibility and cultural "savvy," embodiment of these values in one's clothing becomes an asset, indeed an imperative, rather than a lifestyle choice.

Auckland is exceptional for its high quota of locally derived brands and independent, rarer fashions produced by small local companies where uniqueness (of design, sourcing of materials, production and merchandising) is key to sustaining consumer interest. Most designers have an intensely local set-up, often working out of a site that doubles as workroom and salesroom. These labels generally have only a handful of employees who take on a wide range of roles, from finishing the actual product to administration and sales. The emphasis is on flexibility, from specialized production methods that allow consumers to custom-select fabrics, sizing and trims, to adaptable operating practices such as varied opening hours and "lay-by." Even the "stars" who inhabit the top echelon of New Zealand fashion continue to run their businesses as family concerns or husband-and-wife teams and champion a "hands-on" style of doing business in which their professional, creative and personal identities are inextricably linked.

These niche fashion businesses influence both the built environment and urban lifestyles in Auckland. Inner-city High Street is now Auckland's "fashion quarter," usurping longer-established suburban fashion precincts such as Ponsonby Road and Parnell Rise. Of particular note in High Street is the linking of the emergent designer fashion industry with intense forms of urban living (high-density apartments, cafes, hair salons, and homeware boutiques, high-status consumption spaces such as the custom-built, European-styled "Chancery" precinct). In turn, as High Street has become a destination for tourists and locals alike, this has bolstered the profile of the designer fashion industry. We begin to see local versions of interconnections underpinning

the new "cultural economy," which have been explored in studies on other such "alternative" fashion districts: notably, Crewe's work on Nottingham's (UK) Lace Market (Crewe and Beaverstock 1998; Crewe and Forster 1992, 1993; Crewe and Lowe 1995) and Purvis's work on Manchester's pop fashion (1996).

In addition to these local firms, Auckland is the symbolic site through which New Zealand plugs into a geographically extensive designer fashion network. It has a concentration of retail outlets for internationally celebrated, major designers. It thus has been afforded gravitas as New Zealand's key fashion node. Auckland's Galleria, located close to the tourist Mecca of Viaduct Basin, has four storeys dedicated to selling globally iconic brands such as Louis Vuitton, Prada, Burberry, Gucci and Dior; Ralph Lauren recently opened an outlet in Newmarket, and one store, Scotties in High Street, has achieved cult status for its eclectic mix of designs from Belgian and Japanese "fashion packs" and beyond. Hosting well-known designer flagship stores along with administrative offices and a supporting sectoral infrastructure, Auckland forms the hub through which the majority of high fashion flows into the country are marshaled.

Undoubtedly the most significant event in consolidating Auckland's claim to preeminence among New Zealand cities and its international profile as a fashion city is the recent establishment of an official New Zealand Fashion Week modeled on the long-standing, and larger, Fashion Weeks of the northern hemisphere. The politics surrounding this event provide a commentary on the quite conscious manufacture of Auckland's fashion standing, as well as fashion aspirations for Auckland; and the ongoing manipulation of the city's status as a global fashion node. During 2000, two fashion event organizers, Jennifer Souness pitching for Wellington as host city, and Pieter Stewart for Auckland, did battle for the rights to host this event. While Stewart, a former modeling agent and event co-coordinator, attributes her success to superior contacts and business acumen, the Auckland location of Stewart's bid also influenced the proposal's success. The "wannabe" aspirations of Auckland and the notion discussed earlier of Auckland as a fashion "hub," were an influential combination (Linnell 2001:1).

Simon Lock, organizer of Australian Fashion Week, contributes a further twist to this tale. Lock "slammed" (Vidal 2000: 2) attempts to establish a New Zealand fashion week, sending letters to industry members urging them not to support plans for the event for fear that Australian Fashion Week could be jeopardized. Lock's fears reflect the impact New Zealand designers have made at Australian Fashion Weeks since their first showing in 1997, summed up when Maggie Alderson of the *Sydney Morning Herald* wrote that "without the darker, more intellectual view of those New Zealand designers … [Australian Fashion Week] was like eating a meal that was all dessert" (quoted in Larson, 2001: 51). This rivalry between Australia and New Zealand illustrates the mobilization of Auckland as a real fashion "player" capable of threatening Sydney's supremacy as the center for fashion in the southern hemisphere (*The New Zealand Herald*, May 10, 2002). It also underlines the emergence of an Australasian sphere of operations, how this contests earlier nation-state imaginaries, and the rivalry between cities emerging as a consequence. Sydney and Melbourne have hosted Australian Fashion Week, and habitually jostle to be the preeminent Australasian fashion city.

Finally, the perceived need by industry insiders for New Zealand to invent an internationally significant fashion event is itself an interesting development. In order to achieve parity with more established fashion cities, it is widely considered in global fashion circles that an internationally acclaimed event calendared into the "annual round of big city fashion collections" (Gilbert 2000: 7) is a crucial requisite. In the geographically disparate markets of designer fashion, where business is conducted transcontinentally, such events have become essential. The tendency towards disembodied global exchanges has meant that arenas for face-to-face interactions provide a rare opportunity for real-time (and real-place) connections to be made, and for

networks to be forged. It is, therefore, of intense importance to the development of New Zealand fashion generally, and to Auckland as New Zealand's "city of fashion," that a locally embodied and internationally aspiring event has come into being. L'Oreal New Zealand Fashion Week reinforces the notion of Auckland as a fashion hub through which New Zealand's presence in broader networks of global connectivity is negotiated.

[…]

The New Zealand designer fashion industry has become much more than just a relatively successful niche industry. As the city of Auckland has emerged as a "nodal point" for New Zealand and New Zealanders to enter global flows and networks and vice versa, the designer fashion industry has been explicitly positioned as a means for the city—and indeed for the country at large—to brand itself as a more sophisticated, urbane and globalized player in the global marketplace. Auckland is thus peculiarly positioned as a site of what might be termed "in-betweenness," indicating that Auckland inhabits a position both symbolically and geographically on the fashion margins yet at the same time at the center of national fashion and the gateway to the rest of the world. This very in-betweenness lies at the crux of Auckland's fashionability. For Auckland is embedded in a global fashion network, but also has the vibrantly creative and urbane cultural-economic stature with which to inculcate a sophisticated fashion scene. Yet, this scene is also one where provinciality—and an offbeat quirkiness quite purposefully distinguished from the high-fashion crowd—is a characterizing feature.

ACKNOWLEDGMENTS

We are grateful to all of the designers who have contributed to our study, and wish especially to thank Karen Walker for permission to use the image.

NOTE

An important caveat on this idea of New Zealand fashion design as "newly" established is that, while the sector *is* relatively new, it stems from a small base of designers who set up in the 1970s (e.g., Marilyn Sainty, Elizabeth Findlay's "Tart" label which evolved into Zambesi, and Gaye Bartlett) and have slowly grown in size and reputation.

22

WILLIAM HAMILTON

Suitably Attired: Well-dressed Men have Worn the Same Thing for a Century Now—A History and an Appreciation of the Suit

From **The Atlantic Monthly,** *September 2001.*
Reprinted by permission of the author.

"It's hardest on the older guys," the well-tailored captain of an elegant New York restaurant known for the ego-mindful seating of its powerful clientele told me last spring. "They don't know what to wear, and when they try, they just don't look right. Look at Gerald Levin over there—he might as well be carrying a toolbox." Levin is the CEO who sent chills through haberdashery, in January 2000, when he wore khaki trousers and an open-necked shirt to the press conference announcing the merger of his company, Time Warner, with AOL. Levin has scarcely been seen in a necktie since.

Later in the season I stopped by a great Manhattan store to have a look around the men's-suits floor. It was nearly empty of customers, and the ranks of hanging suits brought to mind the terracotta army guarding the Emperor's tomb near Xian. Would souls ever come to fill these silent human forms, or was this spectacle archaeological, an awesome and monumental reminder of a bygone age?

"About three months ago there was some concern," said an executive called in by a manager who had been called over by a clerk. "But the whole formal look is definitely coming back now." Evidently, the possibility that we were gazing at an obsolescent inventory made my question about how suits were selling too hot to handle for anyone less than a vice president. When the executive left, the clerk called my attention to an entering customer, a man in shorts, a backpack, and a baseball cap. This apparent hiker or bird-watcher picked up a sleeve to look at the tag. Before closing in on him as delicately as a fisherman stalking a trout, the clerk said, "It was those damn dot-coms that nearly killed us, but now that they've all crashed, we're going to be just fine again."

"We went casual in the nineties," the senior partner of a mighty New York law firm told me. "We had to compete with the dot-coms for the best and the brightest new talent, and not just with money. The dot-coms didn't wear suits. No ties. Comfortable cottons. They looked like a new way to do business. Some of my partners still wear suits. And you know who else does? The women. The young women lawyers all wear these black suits, with pants. I think it's so they won't be mistaken for secretaries. But none of the young guys wear suits anymore. I still wear a shirt and tie under my sweater. And I keep a blazer in my closet for important meetings."

Who would argue against the proposition that the twentieth century went farther, faster, than any before it? Yet despite the spectacular, transmogrifying effects of electricity and telephones and rockets and nuclear energy and birth control pills, men, at least in their most official capacities, wore nearly the same outfit the whole time. My grandfather, a member of Yale's class of 1896, kept a photo scrapbook of his college life. The haircuts, suits, ties, and shoes—even such accessories as suspenders, cufflinks, fountain pens, and little wire eyeglasses—in these old snapshots indicate that a male time traveler from 1896 would not look very unusual on a present-day city sidewalk (except, of course, for his look of shocked amazement as he took in contemporary transportation, architecture, and women). But in 1896 a man of 1796, in a tricorn hat, powdered wig, knee breeches, buckled shoes, and frock coat, would have looked like someone on his way to a costume party.

The Roman toga and the mandarin robes of Imperial China covered correct officials for years too, but in comparatively static worlds that their wearers were trying to keep that way. The modern men's suit, with its pockets and sleeves and trouser legs and lapels and buttons, and flying that pennant of necktie, was devised and rigged for motion, like a sailboat. But it came from the turf, not the surf. That split in the back of the jacket was originally cut to drape over a saddle. The notched lapels can close the front as sleekly as a cavalryman's breastplate. Trousers, too, were probably first pulled on for horseback riding. The flying skirts of Alexander the Great's legions could cause riders not only sudden gusts of embarrassment but saddle sores.

When conquest became more administrative than heroic, the suit dismounted and gave orders from behind a desk. The outfit never looked smarter or more urban and organized than it did in the nineteenth century, standing against untailored backdrops of crumbling feudalism and spreading colonialism. In counterpoint to the ancient, often buttonless clothing on peasants and muzhiks and natives and slaves, suits were officers' uniforms of the New Authority.

Understandably, such a style of dress would come to the ruling classrooms of Yale in 1896—but what kept such caballero wear in vogue for yet another hundred years? Jackets cut for saddles are cumbersome in cars. In our indoor,

thermostat-steadied atmospheres the suit and tie can feel as monstrously clumsy as the old lead-footed, copper-domed suits in which deep-sea divers were lowered to the muddy bottom. In fine restaurants many chairs containing males are now hung with removed suit jackets. Pilots wear their jackets only in the airport, to look official and able and in charge (and reminiscent of the sea captains they have superseded). Like Clark Kent's boxy double-breasted suit, which had to be removed, in a phone booth or behind a tree, for Kent to function as Superman, ours have become more a transitory disguise than the clothes in which we actually do our work. Could the suit and tie, like the tuxedo, become an example of special-occasion wear? Maybe even a rental?

"Well, the suit per se has no utilitarian value," the senior law partner told me. "It once had a psychological value, but even then it had no actual function. With guys in shirts and jeans working their computers on Microsoft-style campuses, the appearance of a suit just means somebody from outside the hive has arrived—maybe a banker or a lawyer or a mortician. After you've sat in a couple of meetings with billionaires wearing shorts—and drinking water from baby bottles the whole time, by the way—you wonder which is stranger: these new guys, or you in your suit and tie?"

The first suit came into focus as photography did. Freezing actual instants of light and shade, the camera took all the guessing, exaggeration, and rumor out of fashion news. There for all the boys to see on a magazine page was a photograph of Queen Victoria's heir, the Prince of Wales, off duty in reality, smoking a cigar in Paris, in trousers, a frontally buttoning jacket, and a necktie. So this is what a man who could buy anything wore when he wasn't in the ermine! Photography saw through the hundreds and thousands of formerly opaque miles and layers of class between his off-duty Royal Highness and the ambitious miners' and farmers' and grocers' sons who would change the world. It turned the robes of state into antiques reserved for parade wear. For the first time the everyday plumage of the unpecked apogee of the pecking order was available for popular study. Tailors clipped such pictures to show their clients, who obviously liked the idea of wearing what the Prince of Wales—and J. P. Morgan and Oscar Wilde and Caruso—did on the boulevards. Despite differences in quality, the suits on Kafka, in Prague, and Santos-Dumont, in Rio de Janeiro, and Toulouse-Lautrec, in Paris, were strikingly alike—and not that different from what Grandpa and his schoolmates wore in New Haven or, amazingly, what Big Business (Gerald Levin excepted) still wears, at least to shareholders' meetings. In the 1890s the suit and tie spread through haberdashery like Gutenberg's Bible through Christendom.

When it started, the new look had considerable advantages: it united all its wearers in a single anonymous, international, and interacting commercial urban class—modern man. Playing at being human, possibly giggling Japanese emperors stuck their divine hands into their first experience of pockets as courtiers tied their neckties. Scottish kilties lost a familiar updraft off the floor. Turkish rug dealers found it more awkward to lounge on their goods smoking their hookahs in woolen stovepipe trousers than it had been in the old, voluminous Kublai Khan cavalry-style pants; but the advantages outweighed any possibly estranging unfamiliarity. The suit offered every nineteenth-century man an identity beyond the tribe, the class, even the nation, of his birth. At least from a distance, the suit offered nineteenth-century man a new self.

Fashions, however, change—or anyway they used to. With sighs of relief, women climbed out of the Spanish galleons of nineteenth-century bustles and whalebone corsets into one new look after another. Men demurred. Perhaps because the suit and tie of 1896 were ahead of their time, and photographically promoted, and internationally significant, and as flattering as gift wrap on a wide variety of masculine figures, they stayed à la mode. Human males have a tendency to dress defensively. Unlike women, they dress not so much to look fabulous as to look acceptable. Even so, the old horseback-bred suit and tie should have had it by 1950: by then

the future had become a vivid popular fantasy. Men seemed certain to appear eventually in sleek synthetic jumpsuits with magic belts they would use to teleport around the universe, taking an occasional pill to satisfy all their dietary needs. Futuristic tales of 1950 did not picture men of the year 2000 wearing more or less what Sherlock Holmes did.

What kept the suit in style was television. TV changed the visual world as powerfully and profoundly as photography had done before it. Everything on TV looked incredibly new and exciting, even Ed Sullivan in a suit. Little boys lying on the floor watching TV in 1950—and for the next fifty years—were imprinted with the male dress code seen on newscasters, hosts, quizmasters, sportscasters, evangelists, press secretaries, pundits, and even comedians: the coat and tie. For the aging suit, TV was Viagra. When anchormen moored by ties told viewers that Monica Lewinsky had given President Bill Clinton one so that she could see it around his neck when he next appeared on TV, we may have witnessed this totemic accessory's actual climax. Less than two years after this Pirandello/Marshall McLuhan/Danielle Steel moment of medium-message delivery, Gerald Levin, in the process of announcing that Time Warner had been sucked into cyberspace, made no necktie at all look even louder than Monica's notorious Ermenegildo Zegna.

Now it might seem that the eerily private and portable world facing us on our computer screens could drive dress back to loincloths, or at least bathing suits (though telecommuting may mean that you don't have to go out to work, you still have to answer the door). Bringing the world to you but not you to the world, cyberspace is not a dressy place.

But ceremony is a dressy place. Ceremony celebrates rank and order in public. A traditional hallmark of ceremony is the unrelaxed situation of the principals. We nobodies lining the parade route like to know that an uncomfortable effort is being made by those we watch; it's the price they should pay for being so much grander than the rest of us. Kings and popes will tell you that neither the headgear nor the thrones are ergonomic. Standing at attention in uniforms in the army, privates learn they must not twitch or slouch or scratch. Since they must ultimately be prepared to surrender even their lives to their institution, this first submission is a vital paradigm. Something referentially ancient and attractive and *suit*ably irksome must be found for males to wear to the ceremonies indicating (and possibly thereby proving) the existence of organized civilization.

"I don't know—I just don't think we should go around here looking like pizza deliverymen," an annoyed forty-year-old investment banker told me, glaring at the door he'd just shut between us and the elegantly paneled lobby in which some of his colleagues wore golf shirts. "Goddamn it, I think we should look like somebody. Somebody in charge."

Menswear executives I interviewed all agreed that this fall will tell the tale. One said, "If the casual look was a trend, the suit will come back. But if this is evolution, it won't." A well-cut vice president said, "This fall will be the one in which the suit and tie either make a big comeback or become extinct."

Can our great corporations continue half in suits and half in golf wear? How will the future mark off its officers from its enlisted men? Will casual funerals bury the dead in sweaters? Born with photography and regenerated by television, the relic of horsedrawn times may turn out to have been kicked upstairs by the new technology—the same way ermine and embroidered robes were by photography. The suit, if cryogenically preserved in cyberspace, may find a more democratic but equally ceremonial and possibly eternal life.

EDITORS' NOTE

Suit sales have risen steadily for the last few years. While men are not wearing suits as often as in the past, it is still the vestment of choice when dressing up. Women wear feminized versions of pant suits for work. Even aging hip-hop moguls have donned casual-looking suits in place of their baggy jeans and T-shirts, testifying to its longevity as a style.

ANNOTATED GUIDE FOR FURTHER READING FOR PART IV

Understanding the new cultural geography means grasping the concepts associated with both cultural studies and the new cultural geography. *Introducing Cultural Studies* by Elaine Baldwin et al. (1999) helps the novice negotiate unfamiliar territory. Likewise, David Harvey's *The Condition of Postmodernity* lucidly explains the nature of postmodernism and argues that the change in cultural, political and economic practices since the early 1970s has also changed the ways in which people experience space and time.

Journals in the field include *The Journal of Cultural Geography*, which has been published since 1980 in the US. An examination of the table of contents for the first forty-five issues revealed only one article on fashion: Wilbur Zelinsky's essay on Modern Western Male Attire (2004). This article is well worth reading as it includes a state-of-the-art assessment of the link between fashion scholarship and cultural geography. In the UK, starting in 2000, the journal *Social and Cultural Geography* has published "research concerned with the spatialities of society and culture, particularly the role of space, place and culture in relation to social issues, cultural politics, aspects of daily life, cultural commodities, consumption, identity and community, and historical legacies" (<www.tandf.co.uk/journals/titles/14649365.asp>). No articles addressing fashion have been published as of 2006. See also *The Geographical Journal* and *Transactions of the Institute of British Geographers*, the source of the extract from Peter Jackson, which appears in Part V.

It is not surprising that much of the scholarly activity in geography occurs in England. The Royal Geographical Society was formed in 1830, just prior to the start of the Victorian era. Geography is a mandatory subject in the British educational system.

Regional characteristics of American fashion are covered in the *Encyclopedia of American Regional Cultures* (2004). Each of the eight volumes includes a chapter on fashion. The volume on New England, for example, discusses the persistence of Puritanism in the conservative attire of long-time New Englanders.

World fashion cities are an up-and-coming topic. Valerie Steele's *Paris Fashion* (1998), which covers the cultural history of this famous city's involvement with fashion, was one of the earliest titles. More recently *Fashioning London* (Breward 2004) and *Fashion's World Cities* (Breward and Gilbert 2006) have appeared. Breward also included this topic in the book *Fashion* (2003) in a chapter entitled "Fashion Capitals."

Perceptions about representative national fashion are explored for Britain (Goodrum 2005; Breward et al. 2002) and Italy (White 2000). The globalization of fashion is the subject of Niessen's *Re-Orienting Fashion* (2003) and Rabine's *The Global Circulation of African Fashion* (2002). Comprehensive books on the subject of globalization are *Dress and Globalization* (Maynard 2004) and *Global Fashion Local Tradition* (Brand and Teunissen 2005).

PART V
*P*olitics of Fashion

ABBY LILLETHUN

Introduction

What is meant by "politics of fashion"? For some, a definition of politics refers only narrowly to government entities and processes, and those of organizations that interface with governments. This perspective includes trade regulations and agreements, legislation and other government policy matters affecting the textiles and apparel supply chain. To others, all human acts are political because of the nature of living within a society, where conflicts between competing interests are pervasive. From this position, it follows that everything about fashion is political and so the wider definition is used here. Fashion and politics are enmeshed in a relationship that extends from gender socialization to worker rights to the World Trade Organization. The readings in this section—on feminism, globalization, production and consumption, sweatshops and trade regulations—were selected to portray a variety of ways that political interests and power relations are mobilized, both in the intellectual conceptualization of fashion and in the apparel supply chain.

As a political movement and a philosophy, feminism seeks equality between men and women. All forms of discrimination—unequal pay, objectification, oppression, patriarchy and stereotyping—are their targets. Among the oppressive cultural forms that most feminists reject or critique are subservient, sexualized or physically idealized media representations of females. Yet, there are variations and many nuances among feminist viewpoints. A dichotomy arose within feminist ranks toward fashion, which Elizabeth Wilson characterized as "locked in contradiction." The reading by Wilson, titled "Feminism and Fashion," traces the split to two nineteenth-century perspectives. One finds fashion oppressive, a criticism that fashion continues to receive today. The other finds fashion a pleasure, often remarked on by its advocates across history. Wilson rejects feminist ambivalence toward fashion and posits a declaration of fashion's functions and characteristics.

In the early twenty-first century, the textile and apparel industries are globalized. This does not mean that a small entrepreneur cannot manufacture textile products or apparel in local ways. Some still do; however, large companies and multinational corporations are key forces in globalization. Globalization, a theme throughout this book, is explained here in brief to provide background to contextualize the remaining readings in this section.

Following the Second World War, the International Trade Organization (ITO) was established. One component of the ITO was the Global Agreement on Tariffs and Trade, or GATT. Several rounds of talks took place under GATT, and following the Uruguay Round (1989–94) the current World Trade Organization (WTO) was formed in 1995. Currently there are 149 member countries. Its stated functions are: "Administering trade agreements; Forum for trade negotiations; Handling trade disputes; Monitoring national trade policies; Technical assistance and training for developing countries; Cooperation with other international organizations"

(<www.wto.org/>). The purpose is to encourage free trade through agreements between member nations and to improve conditions for the world's poor. The WTO is not the sole force in the globalization trend; however, reductions in trade tariffs and reduced, eliminated or harmonized subsidies to localized entities, have produced marked changes in the flow of goods and finance. Other infrastructure aspects of globalization, but not yet organized by the WTO, include global telecommunications that have led to transnational data flow. This makes global financial systems possible, which facilitates the transactions of large companies and multinationals. Global telecommunications also facilitate outsourcing. These are the basic components of the governmental and business side of globalization.

Globalization and culture have intersected in less straightforward ways. Since the 1944 meeting that established the ITO, cultural exchange and multiculturalism have increased. Travel and tourism have also increased. Through the global telecommunications systems and the World Wide Web, people connect and create communities of common interest. They create digital identities in cyberspace at sites such as <myspace.com>, where images are posted, and <secondlife.com>, where virtual fashions are promoted and sold.

Beyond these perceived benefits, globalization also fosters developments whose effects are highly contested between supporters and critics. Immigration and illegal immigration have increased as people migrate in search of jobs and for political freedom. As companies seek lower production costs in Asia, for example, globalization critics report that the poor and working class in the US, Mexico, Europe and Africa are squeezed. Likewise, the environmental costs of globalization and increased energy consumption are constant news items. In the increased contact between cultures, as social relations are *stretched* in new ways and overlapping *interpenetrations* occur, localized cultures respond (Held 2004). One way they do this is in the creation and management of appearance. They may adopt new clothing or appearance practices, or

transform their dress in new ways to suit their lifestyles. This process is characterized as *hybridization* or *transcultural dress.* To critics, such processes damage indigenous cultures, with some predicting one homogenized culture across the globe.

Peter Jackson conducted interviews with Indian people in London and Mumbai to ground inquiry into East–West dichotomies, in a quest to understand globalization as lived experience. "Local Consumption Cultures in a Globalizing World" first provides an interpretation of globalization as a *site of struggle* rather than a completed process. This is followed by analysis of Indians' experiences of Indian food and fashion in diverse geographical locations.

Oxfam International is a nonprofit organization with global partners. Oxfam America is one of those partners. Its action statement is that it "works to end global poverty through saving lives, strengthening communities, and campaigning for change" (<www.oxfamamerica.org/whoweare>). The Oxfam Briefing Paper "Finding the Moral Fiber: Why Reform is Urgently Needed for a Fair Cotton Trade" is a position statement on the disparity in the global cotton-farming industry. It calls for the WTO to enforce a ruling concerning US cotton-farming subsidies. The US is the top cotton producer in the world and Brazil is second. Brazil sought redress from the WTO because US subsidies to its cotton farmers depressed the global price of cotton. US farmers sold cotton for less than their production costs. They can do this because US government subsidy money guarantees a profit. Oxfam and other nongovernmental organizations (NGOs), rallied around the Oxfam position, seeking to influence action to end US cotton subsidies. While Brazil will benefit, a critical objective is to help African cotton farmers succeed in making any profit at all. This is an example of globalization as a site of struggle: the less powerful NGOs, specifically Oxfam, and Brazil, are contesting the world's superpower, the US, to the potential benefit of some of the world's poorest nations.

Sweating and *sweatshop* are terms that derive from mid-nineteenth-century tailoring industry practices in England. The master tailor did the highly skilled cutting and first phase of preparing the garment pieces (the tailoring techniques) and then sent them to a subcontractor to do the sewing. Subcontractors would further subcontract to people working out of their homes. Payment for this work was below a living wage. The term sweatshop still evokes images of long hours and dark, crowded and unsanitary conditions. In late nineteenth-century America in New York City, many entrepreneurial apparel-makers began by "sweating" in their own tenement homes on the Lower East Side of Manhattan, making ready-made dresses for the new department stores. Later, a tragic fire brought intense focus to garment industry working conditions. In 1911, the Triangle Shirtwaist Factory Fire in Greenwich Village caused the death of 146 garment workers. Most of the garment workers were young women, working for the 2006 equivalent of US$122–204 a week for approximately sixty-five hours of work. A fire broke out in the building and workers on the ninth floor were trapped, as one of two doors was locked to keep the workers from stealing or taking breaks and the other exit filled with smoke. Many jumped from the windows to their deaths on the sidewalks below; photographs of their bodies appeared in newspapers. This factory had resisted unionization in the preceding months. In the aftermath, the International Ladies' Garment Workers' Union or ILGWU was active in establishing safety regulations for factory workers.

Globalization is not the root cause of sweatshops, but they do continue to exist in factory production. One recent example is Jordan's sweatshops, where factories reportedly engage in human trafficking, bringing workers primarily from China and Bangladesh. Jordan has enjoyed a "privileged trade position" with the US ever since a 2001 free trade agreement (Greenhouse and Barbaro 2006). This potentially lucrative position relative to the US apparel market has drawn the apparel industry to Jordan. Charles Kernaghan, Executive Director of the National Labor Committee, said, "These are the worst conditions I have ever seen … You have people

working forty-eight hours straight. You have workers who were stripped of their passports, who don't have ID cards that allow them to go out on the street. If they are stopped, they can be imprisoned or deported, so they're trapped, often held under conditions of involuntary servitude" (Greenhouse and Barbaro 2006). An apparel factory worker reported a working week of one hundred hours. Workers say they make clothes for Wal-Mart, Target, Sears, Gap, Kohl's and J. C. Penney. Factory owners deny the deplorable conditions. Other sweatshop conditions have been reported in China and Los Angeles, California.

In "Not Only Nike's Doing It: Sweating and the Contemporary Labor Market," Richard McIntyre and Yngve Ramstad provide the legal definition of sweating in the US. They argue that outsourcing provides a barrier between manufacturers and the producers of their product: a layer of deniability distances the company from knowledge or accountability for low wages or poor work conditions. This organization of the production of goods means that workers cannot bargain for wages with the entity that actually contracts for and then sells the product they have made. McIntyre and Ramstad observe that globalization is a continuation of past patterns: the problem is destructive competition. To rectify the workers' untenable plight, the authors make a recommendation for imposition of minimum labor standards, to be administered by the International Labor Organization.

Several topics on fashion and politics are not treated here. A critical issue is sustainability within textile production. Most cotton is grown using inordinate amounts of environmentally hazardous pesticides. Most dyes are also toxic and require appropriate procedures to protect the environment, but structural oversight from local, regional or central governments, or from WTO, is not guaranteed. Many textiles use fibers and filaments manufactured from fossil fuels, a source expected to be depleted eventually. Without political action, these critical issues will not be regulated. Without regulation, the environment deteriorates.

People also dress in political ways, to show allegiances or to proclaim status in power hierarchies. In the US, elected officials in the federal government often wear dark suits with light-colored plain shirts or blouses. On their lapels they place small pins indicating affiliations or to make quiet unity statements to constituents. In contrast, the public dresses casually much of the time, and often wears T-shirts that announce associations, concerns or interests.

In 2005 in Bolivia, the socialist President Evo Morales, himself a native Aymara, signaled a strong commitment to the Aymara population through his clothes. Aymara dress, especially for women, is a hybrid of Western and indigenous garments, and textiles that evolved during the Spanish colonial period. He signaled his allegiance to the Aymara by seldom wearing a Western suit in the campaign, and when he was made Supreme Leader of the Aymara, he wore a replica of an ancient cape. At his inauguration in late 2005, he wore a suit of semiprecious alpaca fiber, an indigenous animal of the Andean highlands, with lapels embroidered with Aymara motifs.

23

ELIZABETH WILSON

Feminism and Fashion

From E. Wilson (2003 [1985]), "Feminism and Fashion," in Adorned in Dreams: Fashion and Modernity *(London and New York: I. B. Taurus), 228–47. Reprinted by permission of the author.*

It is difficult to discuss fashion in relation to the feminism of today, because the ideologies about dress that have circulated within the women's movement seem never to have been made explicit. This may be one reason for the intense irritation and confusion that the subject provoked from the beginning of the women's liberation movement in 1970, and still provokes.

One cause for irritation has been that from the earliest days of contemporary feminism the mass media promoted a caricature of feminists—the bra-burning "women's libbers" who hated men but dressed just like them; a caricature virtually unchanged from nineteenth-century *Punch*. It seems that bra-burning was an invention of the media. There were, however, many demonstrations, both in England and in America, against sexism in the media, against the way in which stereotyped ideals of beauty were forced on women, and against the way in which women were seen only as sexual objects, not as people (Morgan 1970: 521; O'Sullivan 1982). This was an important theme in the early years of the contemporary women's movement but the mass media consistently and willfully confused antisexism with being antisex.

Meanwhile, two different ways of understanding culture emerged within feminism. The first of these was a wholehearted condemnation of every aspect of culture that reproduced sexist ideas and images of women and femininity, all of which came to seem in some sense "violent" and "pornographic"; the other, by contrast, was a populist liberalism which argued that it would be elitist to criticize any popular pastime which the majority of women enjoyed, whether it were reading pulp romances or dressing in smart clothes, an approach that was an offshoot of a general intellectual interest in popular culture.

Underlying these two approaches were hidden discourses rooted in the history of culture. On the one hand there was the continuing effect of the nineteenth-century cult of the natural sciences,

[...]

yet simultaneously feminists were influenced by the beliefs of nineteenth-century liberalism and its twentieth-century reinterpretations.

[...]

These two views are mutually inconsistent, although no debate within feminism has fully brought this out. They possibly reflect a deeper division, which, it has been suggested, underlies many current political debates—a division between

on the one hand, those committed to "cultures of identity" and the achievement of true self and expression. On the other hand, those who act on the basis that human interaction depends on dissimulation, who insist on the central value of the city, its unpredictability, the fluidity of its codes and the subversive play with them. (Chalmers 1983)

This division between the "authentic" and the "modernist" can be applied to many of the fashions

[…]

and especially to contemporary countercultural fashions. The hippie, for example, would be "authentic," the punk

[…]

"modernist." The nineteenth-century dress reformers were "authentic," but the dandies, like the courtesans of the French Second Empire, were "modernists"—preoccupied with the creation of an image, not the discovery of the "true" self. The division suggests two radically divergent ways of seeing the world—and fashion—and two radically different kinds of politics. Is fashionable dress part of the oppression of women, or is it a form of adult play? Is it part of the empty consumerism, or is it a site of struggle symbolized in dress codes? Does it muffle the self, or create it?

An unresolved tension between "authenticity" and "modernism" haunts contemporary feminism. The recurring theme of women's relationship to nature, of women's utopias, and of the vision of a wholly other world in which "women's values" hold sway suggests a longing for a more "authentic" world, closely bound to "nature," in which we will find our true selves. Engagement in the political battle, the use of avant-garde art, the appropriation of jazz and rock by women's bands and of an anarchic tradition of humor by women comics, and the belief in the social construction of the gendered self represent the "modernist" approach.

[…]

This unresolved tension marks a number of feminist debates, for example the debate about

heterosexual love, the controversies over pornography and romantic fiction, and the debate about dress and feminist attitudes to personal adornment. Some feminists, for example, have defined men—men at least in so-called "patriarchal society"—as the oppressors of women, and the construction of female sexuality as the core of female subordination; since they have also acknowledged that most women, including most feminists, do wish to relate sexually and emotionally to men, they have set up an insoluble problem. Thesis and antithesis can never dissolve into a synthesis; the dialectic simply leaves a wound. Others, of course, have argued that it is fine for women to pursue their desires in whatever direction they lead; lesbian sadomasochism has been the practice most frequently justified, but the arguments apply equally to heterosexuality in any form (Snitow, Stansell and Thompson 1984).

In the sphere of literature, while some feminists have argued that pornography constitutes actual violence toward women, others have asserted our right to look, and, indeed, to be turned on by it. In discussions about pulp fiction there is a similar dispute between the moralists who denounce it as promoting false values and as being a form of ideological subordination of women, and the hedonists who emphasize its fantasy and erotic potential.

Similarly with dress: the thesis is that fashion is oppressive, the antithesis that we find it pleasurable; again no synthesis is possible. In all these arguments the alternatives posed are between moralism and hedonism; either doing your own thing is okay, or else it convicts you of false consciousness. Either the products of popular culture are the supports of a monolithic male ideology, or they are there to be enjoyed and justified.

A slightly different version of these arguments acknowledges that desires for the "unworthier" artifacts of the consumer society have been somehow implanted in us, and that we must try to resolve the resulting guilt by steering some moderate middle way. To care about dress and our appearance *is* oppressive, this argument goes, and our love of clothes is a form of false consciousness—yet, since we *do* love them we are locked in a contradiction. The best we can then do, according to this scenario, is to try to find some form of reasonably attractive dress that will avoid the worst pitfalls of extravagance, self-objectification and snobbery, while avoiding also becoming "platform women in dingy black."

Susan Brownmiller's *Femininity* exemplifies this false logic. She defines the erotically appealing as being in direct conflict with the serious and the functional, and offers feminists only the choice between the two:

> Why do I persist in not wearing skirts? Because I don't like this artificial gender distinction. Because I don't wish to start shaving my legs again. Because I don't want to return to the expense and aggravation of nylons. Because I will not reacquaint myself with the discomfort of feminine shoes ... Because the nature of feminine dressing is superficial in essence. (Brownmiller 1984)

Yet she finds unshaven legs unappealing, and low-heeled shoes unerotic (although they were certainly *fashionable* in 1984, the year the book was published) and longs for the gracefulness and pretty colors of her discarded gowns.

Neither a puritanical moralism, nor a hedonism that supports *any* practice in the name of "freedom" is an adequate politics of popular culture. The body of theory, or ideology, that I have called "utilitarianism" contributed to the construction of this impasse with the unacknowledged, and unrecognized, influence of its machine philosophy, its glorification of the work ethic and its inability to grant pleasure a proper place in human culture—the influence of Veblen. Later nineteenth-century feminism was marked by this Fabian spirit, which posed use against beauty; the same utilitarianism marks it today. The logic of this view is ultimately that the only justification for clothing is function—utility.

The emphasis on function leads to an image of what is "natural," which is inseparably locked into this debate. The belief that nature is superior to culture was enshrined within the Romantic reaction to the Industrial Revolution. Janet Radcliffe Richards, one of the few writers to have examined feminist attitudes to dress, suggests that underlying feminist contempt for fashion and cosmetics is a "muddle" about "the natural person being the real thing" (Radcliffe Richards 1980). She argues that feminists share what is actually a conservative view: that to try to "make the most of oneself" is to create a *false* impression, somehow to deceive the world.

Human beings, however, are not natural. They do not live primarily by instinct. They live in socially constructed cultures. To suggest, therefore, as Professor Jaegar did, that we would do better to dress as much as possible like sheep, since we, like sheep, are mammals, is to make a fundamental mistake about what human existence is.

To set up the "natural" as superior to the "artificial" (as if the very concept of human culture were not artificial) is a view also influenced by some of the nonconformist, puritan versions of Christianity, which confused the natural with simplicity, and so the uncorrupt. These

[...]

have influenced British and American non-Marxist socialism. Since contemporary feminism, in Britain at least, has been greatly influenced by the socialist tradition, it is hardly surprising that the feminist debate about dress has been marked by this counter-liberatory ideology. One side of the stifled debate about dress has been simply a rerun, in very different circumstances, of the whole nineteenth-century dress reform project: to *get out of* fashion.

It would be wrong to deny the rational aspects of this view: the dreadful exploitation of garment workers throughout the world is a reality, and feminists should support campaigns against it. In the United States, for example, there is a label in clothes made by properly unionized labor stating that fact. Ultimately only progressive economic policies can end this exploitation, and in that sense the clothes we wear are part of a wider struggle that doesn't necessarily imply a rejection of finery as such. There is also the issue of the way in which certain styles of female dress are held to signal sexuality in a way that invites sexual harassment, makes women vulnerable (when they wear high heels, for example, so that they can't run away from a rapist, or to catch a bus) and also punishes them by making them uncomfortable.

Yet these arguments are often used not rationally, but as rationalizations. Exploitation in the electronics industry does not lead feminists to reject the use of videos and word processors; the horrors of the agri-industry in no way restrict their enjoyment of gourmet food. Those who can afford foreign holidays usually take them, notwithstanding the despoliation that international tourism inflicts on the Third World. The quite special rage reserved for fashionable dressing tells us that dress speaks the irrational-unconscious in a special way.

This relates also to an attitude of persistent hostility to the fine arts that has been evident in certain veins of progressive thought. A "progressive" condemnation of fashion can extend to a general denigration of "bourgeois art." Aesthetes are then equated with the degenerate upper classes, and their preoccupations become suspect. To care or know about traditional art, classical music or "high culture" generally is often to be convicted of pretentiousness and a damaging involvement with the norms of bourgeois culture. The ultimate example of such an attitude is the radical feminist who dismisses Tintoretto and Rubens as "all tits and bums" or as "pornography" (Mooney 1984).

The self-righteousness of such attitudes surfaces whenever, as happened several times in recent years, "serious" British newspapers carried articles about feminism and fashion (Wilson 1982a). One correspondent (a man) wrote to *The Guardian* (August 1982) in response to such a piece:

The strength of the feminist movement lies in the fact that they do not need to rely on such superficiality—they gain their sisterhood through being

women in a patriarchal environment. They are fighting the oppression of society—a fight they will never win if they feel obliged to conform to the fashions that society imposes on them.

while a woman responded:

I can't be the only woman who reaches for the first T-shirt and skirt/trousers that come to hand in the morning, adding a jumper (knitted by Mum from age-old patterns) when it looks chilly ... I'm wearing the same summer frocks that I've worn for the past two years. Well, they're not worn out, are they? I have absolutely no idea what is going on in the distant, nonsensical world of fashion. And oddly enough I don't think I'm the one out of touch.

More recently the same issue surfaced in the pages of *Spare Rib,* a feminist magazine. One woman wrote to the letters page (*Spare Rib* no. 139, November 1983):

Recently I have been the target of a lot of criticism from women ... because they do not like the way that I dress and wear my hair (i.e., Mohican, Bondage, etc.). They tell me that I am ignoring its racist and sexist overtones, that it is not "feminist," and that I am allowing myself to be exploited by the fashion market ...

Do you criticize your sisters because they don't wear dungarees and Kickers? Is a woman any less emancipated because she "chooses" to wear make-up and stilettos?

Is not the whole point of feminism to help a woman to realize her right to control her own life and make decisions for herself?

If so, why are we as feminists oppressing women with a new set of rules ... Would anyone with any individuality call that liberation?

Other readers wrote in to agree with her.

This letter shows how, coexisting with a tradition of puritanism (a word not used as a term of abuse, but to indicate a specific historical tradition) is a wholly other ideology of individualism and free choice. While feminists with one voice condemn the consumerist poison of fashion, with another they praise the individualism made possible by dress. "I thought that the feminist ideal was to dress according to personal preference and choice, and not according to a set of rules," wrote a correspondent to *The Sunday Times* (August 29, 1982) in response to an article (*The Sunday Times,* August 22, 1982) in which Adrianne Blue had tried to *describe* feminist styles of dress. Although she made no attempt to tell anyone what to wear, the writers of several letters published appeared to object to the very attempt even to classify "feminist" ways of dressing, perhaps partly because it seemed to confirm stereotypes, but also, I suspect, because it subtly undermined the "free choice" ideology.

Liberated dress, according to this ideology, means "doing your own thing." The idea of free choice has contributed significantly to contemporary feminism. Perhaps feminists should have questioned it more than they have. Perhaps feminists haven't dared to, because the idea of free choice is so powerful in Western societies. Yet "free choice" is really a myth, and is inconsistent with the belief, to which all feminists pay at least lip service, that human beings are "socially constructed." The concept of social construction is based on the view that at birth a baby has the potential to develop in a variety of ways, limited to some extent by genetic heritage, but equally, or more importantly, dependent on the environmental influences that shape its experience and provide a comparatively favorable or unfavorable soil for growth. Many of the most important aspects of this development occur in early childhood. By the time we become adults, therefore, our capacity to choose freely is greatly restricted by the way in which our personality has developed. It is also equally restricted by external circumstances such as class, wealth, gender, age, and where we live.

Despite their apparent acceptance of this "social construction" model, many feminists continue to discuss moral choice as though we were all free agents, as if they had never heard of that well-worn but sensible aphorism: "Men make their history, but they do so in circumstances that are not of their own choosing." In the realm of aesthetics the very idea of "free choice" is inappropriate; styles of dress are not dictated simply by economics or sexist ideology but are, as I have argued, intrinsically related to contemporary art styles.

Insofar as feminists have dressed differently from other women (and most have not) their style of dress has still borne a close relationship to currently circulating styles. The initial "look" of movement women was the countercultural look of the student movement at the end of the 1960s, when miniskirts and Egyptian wig hairstyles (by then slightly out of date) coexisted with hippie robes and curls. Feminists wore floor-length dresses in dusty tints, and long, Pre-Raphaelite hair. Soon, to cut off your hair curtains became a symbol of liberation, and makeup was seldom worn—but then naturalism was fashionable in the mainstream.

If liberated dress meant doing your own thing, no one ever commented on how strange it was that everyone wanted to do the *same* thing. In the early seventies, alternative lifestyle gear varied only within a narrow and predictable range of ethnic blouses, cheesecloth skirts, Biba sleeves, Laura Ashley smocks, bell-bottomed denims and cords and woolly sweaters with that special matted jumble sale finish. (Fifteen years later a different set of aesthetic conventions dictated trousers that are either much baggier or much tighter, bold colors and black and grey instead of Biba greenery-yallery, and hair that is dyed in flashes instead of being hennaed.)

In pioneering thrift-shop styles and retro chic, feminism was innovative rather than anti-fashion. The hacking jacket worn with a flowery skirt (1977), the trilby hat (1979) and the old-fashioned handmade sweaters were fashions that feminism initiated and the mainstream copied.

Some feminists did disdain skirts and high heels, and the popular public stereotype of the feminist was of a stalwart woman in dungarees or boilersuit and Dr. Martens boots. Some feminists did wear such clothes, perhaps partly in order to avoid sexual harassment. Some lesbians had always worn boyish or "butch" styles, and lesbian feminists sometimes took over these styles as a way of proudly proclaiming their sexuality.

Even feminists who never wore a skirt or makeup went crazy about Kickers, or wore beautifully hand-painted boots in rainbow colors; they adorned themselves with rings and long, bright earrings made of feathers, beads or metal—drawing attention with all these, and with their brightly flashed hair, away from the body and toward its periphery. Fashion, banished from clothing, reappeared surreptitiously in forms of adornment that were less obviously feminine or sexualized.

Dungarees and boilersuits can in any case—and have been—redefined as "fashionable" and "sexy." Yet the very idea of them has sometimes seemed to send men into a frenzy of agitation. In the spring of 1979 a debate was staged in London between Arthur Scargill, later President of the National Union of Miners, and Anna Coote, a feminist journalist, following an article in the *Morning Star* which had attacked the *Yorkshire Miner,* the newspaper of the most militant section of the National Union of Miners, for its policy of having "page three" pinups. Maurice Jones, then editor of the *Yorkshire Miner,* who was also on the platform, at one stage in the proceedings worked himself up into an incoherent frenzy at the outrage of women in dungarees (of whom there were none in an audience consisting in large part of feminists). Such irrational rage could only indicate some deep-seated fear, presumably because "dungarees" when associated with "feminists" has become shorthand for rejection of men, for the most menacing (to men) aspect of lesbianism (Wilson 1982b).

The rage of men such as Maurice Jones suggests that it may well be important for women to challenge norms of feminine dress, and even if there is nothing especially political about wearing "whatever you like," women (and men) should be able to choose not to dress fashionably insofar as this is possible—I have argued that it is not really possible. Nevertheless it is mistaken to set up something called "alternative fashion" as a morally superior ideal, as another series of correspondents in *The Guardian* (October 25, 1983) tried to do:

I'm sick of being patronized by … subtle propaganda … It's no news to me and millions of other women who wear bright, cheap clothes, that overalls per se are not revolutionary. What matters is dressing to please ourselves and to say what we want. Men may like "impossible heels"—we want to walk and run, not deform our spines … Let's hear about who runs the fashion industry and why it's there at all.

So wrote one London woman. Another, from Yorkshire, bewailed the absence of alternative fashion in the north of England:

High-street chic is the ultimate fashion goal for young women. The cinched waist, dolman sleeve and three-quarter-length leather boot is more eagerly sought than any amount of [alternative fashion].

Why is it … that despite dwindling incomes and few jobs people want conformist fashion instead of cheaper, imaginative and experimental apparel? Can alternative fashion only exist if it is underwritten by well-established subcultures? Or do people prefer to display the badges of achievement and status in mainstream society, no matter how precarious their own position is?

Some pertinent questions are asked; but the writers seem not to doubt that their own mode of dressing is both freely chosen and rationally superior. They thus manage to collapse together the two opposed traditions of liberal free choice and utilitarianism. This doesn't resolve the contradiction, the ambivalence; it merely expunges it with the false claim that there exists some form of "alternative dress" that *is* both these things.

To the extent that a feminist style does exist, it has to be understood as a subtheme of the general fashion discourse. Boilersuits and dungarees are after all fashion garments, not just a feminist uniform. They are commercially marketed items of casual chic; and the contortions necessary in the lavatory, and the discomfort in cold weather of having to undress completely in order to relieve oneself, should prove conclusively that this form of dress is worn not to promote rational apparel, but to announce the wearer's feminism in public. In urban society, clothes are the poster for one's act. In the preindustrial world clothes were the badge of rank, profession or trade. As classes fragment we revert to a state in which our clothes once more informally define us. Feminism, in evolving a style among these styles, joins the discourse rather than breaking with it, capitulates rather than transcends—which it could in any case never do.

Feminist style relates to a wider social structure. It is the style of dress adopted by intellectuals and white-collar workers of a certain status, what might be called polytechnic dressing (if "polytechnic" wasn't used as a term of abuse along with "feminist"). Anita Brookner again mistakes this form of dressing for an expression of freedom:

> A five-minute survey of my immediate community reveals a preponderance of blue jeans, dungarees, pullovers, tennis shoes, boots, shawls, odd waistcoats, long skirts, plaid blouses ... To be sure academic gatherings are not noted for their elegance, but ... there are several messages to be read here ...
>
> The first is that all degrees of seniority are obliterated in the desire to look as young, as carefree, as natural as possible. The second is that these unreconstructed dressers, although brought together for purposes of work ... are dressed for play ... The rules have disappeared ... there does not seem to be the slightest awareness of the purpose of dressing: there is no disguise, no self-consciousness—and certainly no shame. (*London Review of Books*, April 15–May 5, 1982)

Yet, in the environment described, this form of dress is virtually compulsory, and does conform to a set of unspoken rules, of which one is the pseudo-democracy of 1960s liberal views on education: that it is possible to abolish the hierarchic distinctions between teachers and taught. In reality, the differences in status and power have changed little since the student rebellions; it is simply that now the informal dress of teachers gestures rather placatingly toward

some alternative ideal. Angela Carter is nearer the mark when she suggests that "Jeans have lost their outlaw chic since the class of '68 took them into the senior common room by a natural progression. They are now ... a sign of grumpy middle age" (*New Society*, January 13, 1983).

The casual dress described by Anita Brookner, far from being the inspiration of free spirits, is the latter-day version of the Fabian style, of the vegetarians and socialists in sandals and hairy knickerbockers whom George Orwell used to refer to as "gruff lesbians," "sandals wearers," "orange juice drinkers," "pansies" and other "cranks" unfortunately attracted to socialism. Orwell's caricatures are offensive; moreover these "cranks" *had* been innovative. For example, it *was* liberating when Edward Carpenter wore open sandals. Then he broke a taboo; now casual dress may surely be optional. The idea that casual dress must be both freely chosen and somehow "better" is mixed up with another ideology from the 1960s: that formality is always repressive. We confuse opposition to the repressive rituals of our society with opposition to all ritual.

In relation to dress, some feminists, mostly American, have tried to retrieve fashion as one amongst other traditional female skills. They would argue that women's creativity in the art of dress has been underrated, as have most feminine skills. Lois Banner uses a slightly different argument in suggesting that "the pursuit of beauty and of its attendant features, fashion and dress, has more than any other factor bound together women of different classes, regions and ethnic groups, and constituted a key element in women's separate experience of life" (1983). She offers no evidence for this, and it would be as easy to argue that dress, beauty and fashion have promoted competitiveness and envy among women.

I have suggested that more typical of feminist discourse on dress has been its tendency to set up a kind of syllogism that cannot be resolved. It attempts to address and to resolve the ambivalence that is such a widespread response to fashion; yet the terms of the debate inevitably perpetuate that very ambivalence.

I have argued that to understand all "uncomfortable" dress as merely one aspect of the oppression of women, is fatally to oversimplify; that dress is never primarily functional, and that it is certainly not natural. I have argued, against those who see fashion as one form of capitalist "consumerism," that these critics fail to understand that women and men may use the "unworthiest" items of capitalist culture to criticize and transcend that culture. The disaffected use bizarre dress to thumb the nose at consumerism and to create jeering cartoons of society's most cherished conventions. But the fashionably dressed and the more traditionally glamorous are not therefore to be dismissed as necessarily the slaves of consumerism. Socially determined we may be, yet we consistently search for the crevices in culture that open to us moments of freedom. Precisely because fashion is at one level a game (although it is not *just* a game), it can be played for pleasure.

This perspective on fashion is diametrically opposed to that of those radicals who make a root and branch attack on "consumerism." Many radicals do advocate a return to "use values." We should struggle for a world, they argue, in which we would respect craft-made objects and lovingly *use* them. The beauty of pottery, fabrics and furniture—and of course clothes—resides in their simplicity and functionalism. Such critics contrast this sturdy "use" with modern culture in which we "consume," that is, "use up." Consumerism then comes to have destructive and voracious implications. Theodor Adorno and other cultural critics of the "Frankfurt School" developed a deeply pessimistic view of consumer culture, seeing its very diversity, hedonism and inventiveness as a hidden form of uniformity... But the political implication of this was "repressive tolerance" and the idea that *every* aspect of consumer culture duped and doped the masses: consumer culture was a form of "false consciousness." These critics used psychoanalysis—a theory of the *unconscious,* to try to explain the way in which this false consciousness takes over the individual. Consumerism becomes a compulsive form of behavior, over which we have little conscious control. According to this puritanical view, we are squeezed between the imperatives of the market and the urges of an unconscious whose desires are warped and invalidated by the culture in which we live. Fashionable dressing and our pleasure in it then becomes one example of a mass outbreak of inauthenticity.

I believe that, on the contrary, fashion is one among many forms of aesthetic creativity which make possible the exploration of alternatives. For after all, fashion is more than a game; it is an art form and a symbolic social system:

> Once literacy and a rich vocabulary of visual, aural and dramatic expressions exist, then society has a permanently available ... resource in which all the tabooed, fantastic, possible and impossible dreams of humanity can be explored in blueprint. (B. Martin 1981: 51)

This is a far more democratic view than the elitism of the radicals—whether these are the Frankfurt School, Christopher Lasch, Stuart and Elizabeth Ewen or some feminists—who see consumer culture as nothing more than "false consciousness." Apart from anything else, it is clear that while the modern educational system, based ultimately on elitist principles, has failed many of its pupils, these same young men and women have managed to develop what is often an extremely knowing and sophisticated visual taste and a capacity to use images and the adorned person to make complex—if often cynical and nihilist—commentaries on contemporary life.

The pointlessness of fashion, what Veblen hated, is precisely what makes it valuable. It is in this marginalized area of the contingent, the decorative, the futile, that not simply a new aesthetic but a new cultural order may seed itself. Out of the cracks in the pavements of cities grow the weeds that begin to rot the fabric.

In the sense, therefore, that we can use and play with fashion, we should reject feminist ambivalence as an inappropriate if understandable response. Yet there is another sense in which fashion elicits an ambivalent response, and that has to do with an ambivalence that runs deeper and is more tightly embedded in fashion itself.

Fashion acts as a vehicle for fantasy. The utopias both of right and left, which were themselves fantasies, implied an end to fantasy in the perfect world of the future. There will, however, never be a human world without fantasy, which expresses the unconscious unfulfillable. All art draws on unconscious fantasy; the performance that is fashion is one road from the inner to the outer world. Hence its compulsiveness, hence our ambivalence, hence the immense psychological (and material) *work* that goes into the production of the social self, of which clothes are an indispensable part.

In this sense, ambivalence *is* an appropriate response to dress; and in this sense "modernism" is a more adequate response than the "cult of the authentic," since the later allows for no ambivalence:

> Take the example of nudity as it is presented in … the mass media's discovery of the body and sex. This nudity claims to be rational, progressive: it claims to rediscover the truth of the body, its natural reason, beyond clothing, taboos and fashion. In fact, it is too rationalistic, and bypasses the body … and the true path of desire, which is always ambivalent, love and death simultaneously. (Baudrillard 1981: 97)

This ambivalence is that of contradictory and irreconcilable desires, inscribed in the human psyche by that very "social construction" that decrees such a long period of cultural development for the human ego. Fashion—a performance art—acts as vehicle for this ambivalence; the daring of fashion speaks dread as well as desire; the shell of chic, the aura of glamour, always hide a wound.

Fashion reflects also the ambivalence of the fissured culture of modernity, is only like all modern art in expressing a flawed culture. The dilemma of fashion is the dilemma of all modern art: what is its purpose and how is it to be used in the world of "mechanical reproduction"? Where fashion differs from some forms of art is that whereas in some fields high art and popular culture have veered further and further apart, in dress the opposite has happened. High fashion has become to some extent demotic. All chic is now gutter chic.

Like all art, it has a troubled relationship with morality, is almost always in danger of being denounced as immoral. Yet also, like all art, it is likely to become most "immoral" when it comes closest to the truth. Utilitarian dress, like conventional "good" clothes and academic art, expresses conservatism. The progressive project is not to search for some aesthetically pleasing form of utilitarian dress, for that would be to abandon the medium; rather we should use dress to express and explore our more daring aspirations, while respecting those who use it to disguise personal inadequacies, real or imagined, or to make themselves feel confident or important.

Art is always seeking new ways to illuminate our dilemmas; dress, however tainted a medium—from its association with the body and with daily life and behavior—nevertheless does this too. Fashion is ambivalent—for when we dress we wear inscribed upon our bodies the often obscure relationship of art, personal psychology and the social order. And that is why we remain endlessly troubled by fashion—drawn to it, yet repelled by a fear of what we might find hidden within its purposes, masked by the enigma of its Mona Lisa smile.

24

PETER JACKSON

Local Consumption Cultures in a Globalizing World

Extracted from P. Jackson (2004), "Local Consumption Cultures in a Globalizing World," Transactions—Institute of British Geographers 29: 165–78. Reprinted with permission.

GLOBALIZATION AS A SITE OF STRUGGLE

"Globalization" is a deeply contested concept that has assumed almost talismanic status in recent years. Like other talismanic terms, great claims have been made in its name. According to Peter Dicken, the word entered the social sciences in the 1960s as part of a wider debate about the social impact of new communication technologies. The term was said to herald:

> a world in which nation-states are no longer significant actors or meaningful economic units; in which consumer tastes and cultures are homogenized and satisfied through the provision of standardized global products created by global corporations with no allegiance to place or community. (Dicken 2000: 315)

Often regarded as a key exponent of this view, Manuel Castells argued that information technologies were producing a frictionless world or "space of flows," superseding the previous and familiar "space of places" (Castells 1991, 1996). In other accounts, globalization is held responsible for the erosion of local difference, where the constraints of geography on social and cultural arrangements are receding and where people are increasingly aware that they are receding (Waters 1995).

[Here] I join forces with those who have sought to demonstrate the resilience of "local" cultures against some of the exaggerated claims that have been made in the name of globalization. Following David Held (2004), I prefer to talk about a "globalizing" world rather than to think in terms of a world that is already fully "globalized."[1] While the pace and intensity of social change is impressive, its geographical impact is far from even. There is, then, an urgent need to "ground" the study of globalization through empirical investigation of particular places and to historicize the transformations that have taken place within living memory. So, for example, Hirst and Thompson (1996) remind us that globalization is nothing new and that previous generations have witnessed equally dramatic social transformations following capitalism's earlier expansionary phases. So, too, in Bayly's (2004) magisterial reworking of the history of consumption in light of recent postcolonial critiques, a convincing case is made that the world was far more "globalized" in the eighteenth and nineteenth centuries than is commonly supposed. Such accounts of global interconnection emphasize the multicentered origins of modernity and demonstrate that European power, though increasingly dominant, was fiercely contested. From such a perspective, references to "globalization" in the present era can be understood as a rhetorical device, deployed in support of a specific (neoliberal) political agenda (Larner 2003). But what of globalization's impact on consumer culture? Here, too, it is possible to puncture some of the more inflated claims that have been advanced in the name of global economic transformation. So, for example, recent work has demonstrated the slow advance and uneven penetration of the commodity form, even within Western economies, and the many forms of resistance to its further spread (Williams 2003; Williams and Windebank 2003).

On close examination, the "globalization" thesis looks far less impressive, the forces promoting de-territorialization (whether economic, political, technological or cultural) always being subject to the countervailing forces' re-territorialization. While the balance of forces is often far from equal, globalization might be better thought of as a *site of struggle* rather than as a foregone conclusion. For, as Watts has argued, globalization requires a sensitivity to how location, identity and community are refashioned in incompletely globalized sites: "Globalization does not so much mark the erasure of place but in a curious way contributes to its revitalization" (Watts 1996: 64). From this perspective, globalization emerges as an incomplete, uneven and contested process: an unfinished project whose contours are shaped by locally specific social and cultural practices.

LOCAL CONSUMPTION CULTURES

In this section, I want to consider the resilience of local consumption cultures in the face of "globalization" and to document some of the ways in which these global forces have been "domesticated" (tamed and localized) in specific contexts of consumption. Consumption is clearly a key site in debates over globalization with the apparently limitless reach of brands like McDonald's and Coca-Cola becoming virtually synonymous with the term, and yet there is now extensive ethnographic evidence with which to challenge many of the exaggerated claims made in the name of globalization.[2]

It is now widely appreciated that even the most "global" brands, such as McDonald's or Coca-Cola, have different cultural connotations and are consumed quite differently in different places. D. Miller's (1998) work on consumption practices in Trinidad and Gillespie's (1995) ethnographic study of young Punjabis in Southall, West London are just two of the many examples of this "domestication" of meaning.[3] The wider argument is well put by Appadurai, who argues that "as rapidly as forces from various metropolises are brought into new societies, they tend to become indigenized in one way or another" (1996: 32). So too, for the Swedish anthropologist Ulf Hannerz, the contemporary world is characterized by "an intense, continuous, comprehensive interplay between the indigenous and the imported" (1996: 5). Nor can any single society claim to provide the "authentic" source of meaning for any particular commodity or cultural form. Rather, as Miller argues, there is the growing equality of genuine relativism:

> Central Africans in suits, Indonesian soap operas, and South Asian brands are no longer inauthentic copies by people who have lost their culture after being swamped by things that only North Americans and Europeans "should" possess. Rather there is the equality of genuine relativism that makes none of us a model of real consumption and all of us creative variants of social processes based around the possession and use of commodities. (D. Miller 1995: 144)

If, as Escobar claims, culture still "sits in places," despite the forces of displacement and de-territorialization that have accompanied globalizaton, it does so as a result of what he describes as "subaltern strategies of localization" (2001: 159).

[...]

Our own research sought to extend this work through an exploration of transnational food and fashion cultures in London and Mumbai (Dwyer and Jackson 2003). The project used focus group evidence in order to produce a more "grounded" reading of globalization and to challenge the simple mapping of "tradition" and "modernity" onto "East" and "West" (Jackson et al. 2004). While some of our focus group respondents felt that, "Fast foods, like McDonald's, have taken over Mumbai," the range of foods that were locally available were more usually regarded as a source of pride: "In Bombay we can get anything"; "Actually Bombay is the place where you can get everything and you get a blend of all the cultures"; "We eat everything" (including Thai, Chinese and Mexican food); "Indians are basically adapted to any kind of food."[4] Moreover, our respondents celebrated the city's capacity to absorb and adapt a range of foreign influences: "Bombay absorbs everything."[5]

Several of our focus groups referred to the "Indianization" of pizza (often itself regarded as an Italian-American hybrid), including one group who talked about "Punjabi pizza," with the addition of Indian toppings and ready-made *masalas*. Others referred to the addition of garlic and chili sauces to McDonald's burgers, while Chinese food was commonly regarded as Indian or Indian-Chinese with one person insisting that "Indian people do Chinese food much better than Chinese people." Other culinary traditions, such as eating outside the home (Conlan 1995), have survived the introduction of a range of "global" cuisines. The weekend family outing to a restaurant—most often on a Sunday night— was commonplace among all generations. One retired man spoke about going to restaurants at least once a week and at the weekend, and about the popularity of outdoor eating such as family picnics.

Our work on transnational fashion also challenges simplistic notions about the Westernization of "Asian" dress. We demonstrate, instead, that the pace of change is socially and spatially uneven in both London and Mumbai, with evidence of "multiple modernities," rather than a single East–West gradient. So, for example, many of our Indian respondents were keen to emphasize the modernity of Mumbai, whether in terms of the fast pace of life, the city's ability to absorb a wide range of international influences, or the increased freedom of contemporary consumer choice. The commonly assumed contrast between "Western" modernity and "Eastern" tradition was not only resisted by many of our focus group participants but was, in some cases, reversed. A group of university students in Mumbai insisted that their cousins living overseas were more traditional in terms of dress than they were because, nowadays, "You can get everything in Mumbai." Young women in the fashion industry were also adamant that their relatives in the UK were very much behind the trends in Indian clothing. Members of one of our London-based groups recalled how "They're more clued up" in India and Pakistan than in Britain:

> We never know what the fashions are going [to be] in Pakistan or India, and suddenly we're five years behind them, we're wearing something they wore five years ago and you go over there and you feel, "Oh my God, I'm out of fashion."

Walton-Roberts and Pratt (2004) report similar findings from their work with Non-Resident Indians in Canada and Britain, where India was said to be more modern in terms of fashion and style than Britain, challenging the arrogant assumption that modernity resides exclusively in the West. A group of British Asian students in London described how they sought to "keep up with what's happening in Bollywood films; what the stars are wearing and stuff," acknowledging how this meant that they were "always behind what the style is like": "I'm always out of fashion compared to my cousins."[6]

[…]

While "globalization" has been a dominant feature of our collective geographical imaginations in recent years, this paper has sought to demonstrate that local geography still matters, particularly when mapping the contours of specific consumption cultures.

NOTES

1. Held (2004) suggests that we should distinguish between four "dimensions" of globalization: the *stretching* of social relations, the *intensification* of

global flows, the *interpenetration* of economic and social practices at all scales, and the development of institutional *infrastructure* for governing the global system.

2. See, for example, George Ritzer's various accounts of "McDonaldization" (1993, 1998) and Barry Smart's (1999) collection of essays on *Resisting McDonaldization*.

3. See also Watson's (1998) account of the expansion of McDonald's in East Asia.

4. We follow our respondents in their usage of "Mumbai"/"Bombay."

5. This quotation is reminiscent of Narayan's work on the British appropriation of "Indian" food which argues that "when the British incorporated curry into British cuisine ... they were incorporating the Other into the self, but on the self's terms" (1995: 65). Significantly, in terms of our argument about the local impact of "globalization," Narayan goes on to argue that the influence of the colonies on colonizing powers is as complicated a matter as the impact of the colonizers on their colonies (1995: 68).

6. A similar argument could be made about Indian music (thinking of *bhangra*, for example) where the complex process of cultural borrowing is closely related to constructions of social difference. For an ethnographically grounded study of musical appropriations, see Born and Hesmondhalgh (2000).

25

Finding the Moral Fiber: Why Reform is Urgently Needed for a Fair Cotton Trade

Oxfam Briefing Paper, October 2004. Reprinted with permission.

Cotton has been at the top of the World Trade Organization's (WTO's) agenda for the past two years. However, little has changed so far for small-scale cotton producers in West Africa, who will not survive another major slump in cotton prices. In July 2004, WTO members committed to ambitious and expeditious cotton subsidy reforms. To give African producers a chance, it is urgent to turn these commitments into action. Oxfam calls for the implementation of the Brazil-US cotton panel ruling and a timetable for the elimination of all trade-distorting cotton subsidies by the time of the Hong Kong WTO ministerial conference in December 2005.

SUMMARY

Cotton has become a symbol of the inequities of global agricultural trade. The case of cotton clearly demonstrates how rich-country agriculture subsidies cause harmful impacts on developing-country farmers. Subsidies skew production levels and value, undermining the income of cotton farmers in developing countries. Some of the poorest countries in the world are cotton producers, and they stand to gain significantly from reforming trade and agriculture policies. Yet these countries face a depressed cotton market caused, in part, by rich-country subsidies.

Reform of US cotton subsidies is urgently needed to address the distortions in cotton trade that undermine the value of cotton to developing countries. Every season, poor cotton farmers face reduced incomes. Each year, developing countries which export cotton suffer declining balance of payments due to loss of export revenues. The central issue is US cotton subsidies, and the reforms needed are quite clear. There is no doubt about the unfairness of US trade cotton practices, as the WTO panel has proved. The issue now is how these conclusions are going to be implemented. The USA must agree to eliminate trade-distorting subsidies at the WTO and implement the necessary reforms to its farm programs.

In crop year 2002, the US government provided US$3.4 billion in total subsidies to the cotton sector. To put this figure into perspective, it is nearly the same as the total US foreign aid ($3.5 billion) given to all of sub-Saharan Africa over the same period. It is also more than the GDP of Benin, Burkina Faso, or Chad, the main cotton-producing countries in the region.

US subsidies have led to depressed world cotton prices, which in turn have cost countries in Africa millions of dollars in lost export earnings. This means less revenue, which these countries badly need to fund basic services such as education and healthcare, and to finance debt. Oxfam estimates that sub-Saharan African countries lost $305 million due to US subsidies in crop year 2001. These are some of the poorest countries in the world, and these losses are not a one-time event. For the 2002 crop year, Oxfam estimates sub-Saharan African countries lost $94.6 million.

US agriculture and trade policies also undermine the benefits of US foreign aid. The losses associated with cotton subsidies exceed the value of US aid programs in some of the major cotton-producing countries in Africa. For example, in 2002:

- Burkina Faso: received $10 million in US aid, yet lost $13.7 million in export earnings;
- Chad: received $5.7 million in US aid, but lost nearly the same amount in export earnings;
- Togo: received $4 million in US aid, but lost $7.4 million in export earnings.

Moreover, US cotton subsidies undermine the ability of developing countries to pull themselves out of debt. Lost export revenue due to US cotton subsidies in 2002 amounted to between 21 and 33 percent of total debt service payments for Burkina Faso, Benin, Chad, and Mali.

The impact of US cotton subsidies is not simply on balance of payments or debt service. They cause poverty, and West African farmers are particularly vulnerable. A recent IFPRI (International Food Policy Research Institute) report focused on Benin indicates that a 40 percent reduction in farm-level cotton prices leads to a 21 percent reduction in income for cotton farmers and results in an increase in rural poverty of 6–7 percent.

In the US, cotton production has reached historic highs in recent years. However, US demand for cotton has slumped, so US exports have surged. Export volumes broke records in 2002 and 2003, and will likely do so again in 2004. In crop year 2003, the US exported 76 percent of its cotton production and took a 41 percent share of world exports. These drastic increases could not have been accomplished without government support. According to the US Department of Agriculture, without subsidies the average US cotton farmer would have lost $871 for each acre planted with cotton over the past six years.

All told, between crop years 1998 and 2002, the US spent $14.8 billion on cotton subsidies. This is virtually the same as the total value of cotton produced during that time—$21.6 billion. Harvesting government subsidies is nearly as lucrative as growing cotton in the US. Without subsidies, most US cotton production would not be economical.

Not all US farmers benefit from subsidies. A large majority of farms—67 percent—are ineligible for government support because they do not grow a select group of subsidized commodities. Of the 33 percent of farms that do get subsidies, the top 10 percent receive 52 percent of all government payments. And the subsidies for cotton are particularly concentrated: the top 10 percent of cotton farms receive 79 percent of all payments, and the top 1 percent receive 25 percent of all payments. The average payment in 2002 was $331,000, and 25 farms received more than $1 million each.

Indeed, there are other factors that affect the world market price of cotton. Exchange rates, competition from synthetic fibers, competition from other cotton producers, and China's decreasing consumption and demand for cotton imports contribute to the gloomy forecast for cotton prices in the future. Nevertheless, US subsidies have the effect of depressing prices despite market volatility, as the WTO panel ruled in the case brought against the US by Brazil. And yet West African farmers are well positioned as some of the most cost-efficient producers to compete in this future market if only a level playing field is created.

An improved cotton market has clear potential to help reduce poverty for millions of people. Through the Doha Development Round of negotiations at the WTO, a real opportunity exists to make significant reforms to agricultural trade policies. Cotton is a litmus test to demonstrate that the WTO, and indeed trade itself, can truly serve the interests of less powerful countries and poor people.

The outlook for breaking the deadlock in negotiations on cotton subsidies took a positive turn in the spring of 2004, when a WTO dispute settlement panel found that US cotton subsidies do indeed violate commitments to reduce domestic supports. More broadly, the panel ruling confirms many of the criticisms developing countries have made in recent years: that industrialized countries have not fulfilled their commitments to open their agriculture markets and reduce the farm subsidies that distort trade.

In July 2004, the WTO General Council met to pick up the Doha Round negotiations where they left off after the collapse of the talks in Cancun the previous year. The final text of the July framework agreement reflects a series of compromises that undermine the ambition of reformers and delay action. While it sets no concrete objectives or clear timeframe on subsidy reform for cotton within the agriculture negotiations, a mechanism has been established to continue negotiations.

The next critical deadline for negotiations is the 2005 WTO Ministerial in Hong Kong. It is critical to ensure that the general statements of principle on cotton contained in the July framework agreement are translated into specific measures that will have real meaning for cotton producers in developing countries—particularly those in West Africa.

To ensure that the Doha Round of trade negotiations delivers real opportunities for reform, developed country governments must agree to:

- Implement the findings of the US-Brazil cotton panel fully and expeditiously;
- Eliminate US export subsidies for cotton by July 2005, including use of export credit guarantees and the Step 2 program;
- Commit to phase out the use of trade-distorting farm subsidies for cotton by December 2005, including marketing loan programs and counter-cyclical payments;
- Ensure that direct payments are truly decoupled from production and do not create an implicit encouragement to grow more crops;
- Resolve and enforce that development funding is not conditional on trade negotiating positions or elimination of subsidies;
- Increase development assistance to developing countries' cotton producers to manage the crisis and ensure stability in producer revenues.

EDITORS' NOTE

Since this Oxfam Briefing Paper was written in 2004, measured progress has been made toward the stated goals. Although the US enacted legislation to cut some of its cotton subsidies, implementation had not advanced in July 2006. Here is the sequence of events: In March 2005, the WTO confirmed its September 2004 decision, ruling that the majority of US cotton subsidies are illegal. The US was required to comply with the ruling by July 1, 2005, but did not. Brazil agreed not to seek sanctions entitled through the WTO. In February 2006, The Deficit Reduction Omnibus Reconciliation Act of 2005, S. 1932, passed the US Congress, repealing the Step 2 program effective August 1, 2006. It was enacted upon President Bush's signing the Bill. This means that the US Government must put forward a plan to stop the subsidies. However, in July 2006 WTO negotiations for implementation schedules for these and other tariffs and subsides were reported to be "in crisis" on the WTO website.

26

RICHARD McINTYRE and YNGVE RAMSTAD

Not Only Nike's Doing It: "Sweating" and the Contemporary Labor Market

Extracted and updated from R. McIntyre and Y. Ramsted (2004), "Not Only Nike's Doing It: 'Sweating' and the Contemporary Labor Market," in D. P. Champlin and J. T. Knoedler (eds.), The Institutionalist Tradition in Labor Economics (Armonk, NY: M. E. Sharpe), 297–314.

In 1997, Nguyen Thi Thu Phuong died making Nike sneakers in a factory in Bien Hoa, northeast of Ho Chi Minh City in Vietnam. She was struck in the heart by a piece of shrapnel that flew out of a machine that a coworker was fixing. She died instantly. Nike's response to this (and other similar incidents) was "We don't make shoes" (Larimer 1998: 30). This was technically correct because Nike's core business strategy involves outsourcing *all* manufacturing to subcontractors in poor Asian countries.

In 2003 Immigration and Customs enforcement officers made arrests at sixty Wal-Mart stores in twenty-one states, taking in undocumented immigrants from Eastern Europe, Central America, and Asia. Most of these immigrants worked for cleaning companies contracted by Wal-Mart. Although the criminal indictment alleges that violations of immigration law took place with the "direct knowledge" of Wal-Mart executives, a corporate spokeswoman pleaded ignorance. "No, we did not know," Wal-Mart spokeswoman Mona Williams said. "Our understanding was that these third-party agencies had only legal workers" (Armour and Leinwand 2003).

We perceive the business strategy employed by Nike and Wal-Mart *not* to be unusual. Specifically, each company has adopted the "sweating system" of organizing work. In that regard, Nike and Wal-Mart labor practices exemplify a significant development in the labor market. For the sweating system is now being used not only by producers, like Nike, who outsource production to low-wage countries but also by companies, like Wal-Mart, operating in the United States.[1]

Conventional economics provides no point of entry into the analysis of this development and, equally, offers no ground for attempting to reverse its deleterious consequences for workers. In contrast, the institutional economist John R. Commons *did* develop an interpretation of the labor market providing a fruitful point of entry into this important development. In a report he made to the US Industrial Commission a century ago (Commons 1901), Commons set forth an analysis of the sweating system that comes closer to the essence of how many firms organize the production of the commodities they sell than do many contemporary definitions.

In application to the labor market, the terms "sweat" and "sweating" are generally employed to signify the practice of paying workers inappropriately low wages for long hours of work under conditions that may be unsafe or unsanitary. Consistent with this interpretation, the United States government defines a "sweatshop" as "a business that violates more than one federal or state law governing wages and hours, child labor, health and safety, workers' compensation, or industry registration" (US GAO 1994). This more or less arbitrary definition is important, of course, because the government uses it.

In his report to the US Industrial Commission, Commons provided an alternative definition focused on labor market processes rather than on the actual terms of a wage bargain. "The term 'sweating' or 'sweating system,'" Commons observed, "originally denoted a system of subcontract, wherein the work is let out to contractors to be done in small shops or homes … The system to be contrasted with the sweating system is the 'factory system' wherein the manufacturer employs his own workman" (Commons 1901: 45).

Commons emphasized that contractor control of information is a crucial element of the sweating system. It is worth quoting Commons at length on this point.

> [The labor contractor] deals with people who have no knowledge of regular hours. He keeps them in the dark with regard to the prevailing number of hours people work. The contractor is an irresponsible go-between for the manufacturer, who is the original employer. He has no connection with the business interests of the manufacturer nor is his interest that of his help. His sphere is merely that of a middleman. He holds his own mainly because of his ability to get cheap labor, and is in reality merely the agent of the manufacturer for that purpose.
>
> Usually when the work comes to the contractor from the manufacturer and is offered to his employees for a smaller price than has previously been paid, the help will remonstrate and ask to be paid the full price. Then the contractor tells them, "I have nothing to do with the price. The price is made for me by the manufacturer. I have very little to say about the price." That is, he cuts himself completely loose from any responsibility to his employees as to how much they are to get for their labor …
>
> In case the help form an organization and send a committee to the manufacturer, the manufacturer will invariably say, "I do not employ you and I have nothing to do with you." (Commons 1977 [1901]: 46)

We see the strategy deployed by Nike, Wal-Mart and many other contemporary companies as visible "moments" in an ongoing process of labor market transformation centered on the creation of "social distance," whatever the physical location, between employer and employee so as to subject the latter ever more effectively to destructive competition, that is, to a "race to the bottom." By the phrase "creation of social distance," we are referring to the severing of a direct bargaining transaction relationship between the worker—the actual producer—and the entity for whom the productive activity is substantively expended. We understand this severing to be the crucial step in implementing a sweating system of production.

It is widely recognized that Commons believed regulation, that is, the establishment and enforcement of labor market standards, to be the appropriate remedy for destructive competition. It is, of course, possible that moral and empathic appeals to consumers and employers might provide an alternative method of remedying the problem. Since standard economic theory is premised on the ubiquity of self-interested action within the economic realm, conventional economics provides no insight into the process by which such appeals might alter the transactional behavior of market participants.

In contrast, the founder of conventional market economics, Adam Smith, understood economic actors to exercise restraint in granting dominion to their self-interested impulses. Specifically, Smith submitted that "natural liberty" (or, in contemporary language, the exercise of "free choice") incorporates an appropriate degree of forbearance occasioned by, first, "sympathy" and, second, the moral principles embraced by an "impartial spectator" internal to each individual. If Smith was essentially on target about human nature (admittedly, his terminology is now dated), moral and empathic appeals have the potential to influence how employers will proceed in their unregulated transactional negotiations with workers.

Because moral and empathic appeals have been utilized in some highly publicized recent cases involving sweating, and because we believe Smith's ideas are not without some merit, we will also briefly summarize Smith's conception of self-regulated transactional behavior. We will then explain why we are skeptical that Smithian self-regulation will prove an effective means of reversing the growing reliance on sweating within the realm of production. We conclude by again endorsing Commons's call for labor market regulation as the only viable mechanism for achieving that end.

NIKE DOES IT

Chief Executive Officer Phil Knight formulated Nike's strategy of total outsourcing while he was at Stanford Business School in the early 1960s. The money saved through outsourcing would then be poured into marketing, primarily using high-profile celebrity endorsements. Significantly, "the manufacture of these sneakers was based on an arms-length and often uneasy relationship with low-paid, non-American workers" (Spar and Burns 2000: 2–3). Initially Knight subcontracted with firms in South Korea and Taiwan, but by the early 1990s most production had shifted to lower-cost East Asian countries, especially Indonesia.

The production of Nike shoes in Indonesia coincided with a period of rising labor unrest there. But Nike officials insisted that labor conditions in contractor factories were not their concern. Even if legal violations existed, the company's general manager in Jakarta said, "I don't know that I need to know" (Spar and Burns 2000: 5). Nike did draft a corporate code of conduct for its suppliers in 1992 that addressed working conditions, safety, environmental practices, and workers' insurance. Contractors were required to certify that they were following relevant laws and regulations.

Media attention to conditions in factories in developing countries increased between 1992 and 1996, exploding in the latter year with revelations that the clothing line endorsed by media celebrity Kathy Leé Gifford was made by child workers in Honduras. When Gifford called on other celebrity endorsers to investigate conditions in the factories where the products they endorsed were made, sports celebrity Michael Jordan denied any personal responsibility, saying that the company was responsible. Nike continued to maintain that this was not their problem.

Following congressional hearings in May 1996, President Bill Clinton convened the Apparel Industry Partnership, which was meant to be a meeting ground for the companies and their critics. Nike quickly joined. Later that year Nike formed a new "labor practices department" and also hired the former US ambassador to the United Nations, Andrew Young, to evaluate the effectiveness of its supplier code of conduct. Denial had been replaced by engagement. According to Knight, "In labor practices as in sport, we at Nike believe 'there is no finish line'" (Spar and Burns 2000: 7).

Things got worse for Nike in May 1997 when the popular comic strip *Doonesbury* ran a week's worth of biting criticism of Nike plants in Vietnam. Young's largely positive reports were heavily criticized for failing to address the issue of wages and as methodologically flawed, a celebrity endorsement rather than real research.

In the spring of 1997 Nike aided a team of graduate students at Dartmouth's Tuck School of Business who wanted to conduct a study of "the suitability of wages and benefits" paid by Nike's Vietnamese and Indonesian subcontractors (Calzini et al. 1997: 5). The faculty member coordinating the student group claimed that "workers made enough to eat a good diet, house themselves simply but comfortably, dress nicely, buy basic consumer goods and, primarily in the Indonesian case, save for the future" (Mihaly 1998). He argued that Nike and other multinationals were supporting social progress in these very poor countries and that labor critics actually understood this but were pandering to the self-interests of US trade unionists.

The Dartmouth team had no language skills, so local interpreters had to be used. The students did not look at pay stubs or various deductions from wages, which are often greater than managers' or handpicked workers' memories make them out to be. This leaves us less than convinced that a "living wage" was being paid to Nike workers.

But the more serious problem is a theoretical one. This and other similar studies focus on labor market *outcomes* rather than the social relations of the labor market. Nike's subcontracting network may or may not be a string of sweatshops with the traditional low wages, long hours, and unsafe conditions. Yet Nike's network clearly exhibits the separation of the worker from the price bargain and from a contractual relationship with the manufacturer that was, for Commons, the definition of the sweating system. "We don't make shoes" and "I don't know that I need to know" may make for bad public relations strategy, but they reflect the core of a business model in which the ultimate manufacturer tells the worker, "I do not employ you and I have nothing to do with you."

WAL-MART DOES IT TOO

That Wal-Mart is ruthless in exercising its considerable bargaining power is indisputable. The average salary for store "associates" is below the federal poverty level for a family of three (Monbiot 2004). It ruthlessly forces down prices in its supply chain, leading to systematic abuses of worker rights and giving more and more business to the gigantic Chinese factories that turn out schlock goods with "always low prices." Levi's was happy to get a Wal-Mart contract to supply jeans, but was forced to close its remaining US and Canadian factories to secure cheaper labor (S. Anderson et al. 2005). The owner of a local jewelry firm communicated to us that Wal-Mart contacted him shortly after 9/11 for a large order of American flag lapel pins, but the terms he was offered forced him to source the pins from China.

Wal-Mart has changed the nature of managerial transactions, in its own stores, and as the leading edge of a new type of employer. Common practices at Wal-Mart allegedly include illegal

doctoring of time cards ("time theft"), extensive violation of child labor laws, unequal pay and treatment of workers, illegal use of undocumented workers, violation of state regulations governing time for breaks and meals, and violations of the American with Disabilities and the Occupational Safety and Health Acts (Greenhouse 2004a, 2004b; G. Miller 2004). As the model for retail success, others stores are now following Wal-Mart's lead both in contracting out to labor subcontractors employing undocumented workers and violating labor law (Schneider and ElBoghdady 2003).

In defending itself in the undocumented workers' case, Wal-Mart continued to insist that it was unaware of any violations. While Gus Whitcomb, a Wal-Mart spokesman, said the company was cooperating with prosecutors, he stated, "We reiterate, as we have from day one, that our senior management team knew nothing about the employment practices of the contractors until the government contacted us seeking our cooperation" (Greenhouse 2004c).

REMEDIES

Can we expect the impartial spectator mechanism to be a more effective counterforce to sweating? Nike's "engagement strategy" agreement in response to public criticism, as well as the highly publicized Kathy Lee Gifford call for better supervision of subcontractors, suggests the possibility that moral appeals can play a role in restraining sweating. It is worth noting, however, that by bringing the controlling "impartial" spectator inside the economic actor, Smith was submitting that one responds not to the judgment of an external, actual spectator, who may have only a partial knowledge of the full context within which a transaction is being negotiated, but to one's own judgment.

In other words, an actual spectator may render a judgment regarding what *appears* to be the right—the moral—action, but from Smith's standpoint it is the internalized impartial spectator who judges what is *really* right. The issue, therefore, is: What is the relevant moral code or, more narrowly, the general rule of behavior that present-day owners and managers are internalizing? Judging by the statements made by authorized representatives of the "real" employers in the cases we reviewed, that code or rule decrees: *If someone is not a member or, in Commons's term, a citizen of "our" firm, that is, if we have no direct wage bargain with her, "we" have no responsibility of any kind for the wage bargain under which she works.* In short, we fail to discern any sign of moral objection to the sweating system, as a system, on the part of Nike or Wal-Mart. If they are representative, then it is clear that empathic appeals to "real" employers will fail to elicit corrective action. The sweating system itself, of course, makes it difficult if not impossible for the actual employer—the subcontractor or labor contractor—to respond positively if moral appeals are directed at them.

We recognize that Nike's decision to create a labor practices department, to "investigate" the labor practices of its subcontractors, to publish a list of its suppliers and a corporate responsibility report, and similar nascent efforts at Wal-Mart, may appear to contradict our conclusion. Based upon our reading of that case, however, we interpret Nike's action to be motivated by the goal of safeguarding the goodwill of its customers, some of whom might stop purchasing Nike products due to negative publicity directed at Nike's labor practices, rather than by a moral concern on the part of its owners for the plight of the sweated workers producing those products. This reality would appear to establish that the market ethos preached by the "Chicago School" of economists—that greed is good—has taken very deep root in America's owning and managerial classes. If our inference is on target, those championing empathic appeals as the appropriate strategy for raising labor market attainments would be wise to direct such appeals exclusively at consumers.[2]

Under the present scheme of relatively free global trade in the context of global labor redundancy, destructive competition in the globalized labor market seems likely to persist. We submit that adjustment of the rules governing negotiation of the wage bargain is the only feasible method of actually reversing destructive competition in the labor market—of which the spread of the sweating system is but a discernible symptom.

The decisive step in instituting the sweating system—whether by subcontracting production or through labor contracting—is the legal severing of the worker from the going concern (a business enterprise) that is her "real" employer and thereby to strip her of functional "citizenship." By means of this severing the owners and managers of the original enterprise are able to regard their "real" employee as a non-employee and hence as ineligible to receive the protections or rights enjoyed by enterprise "citizens." Those "real" employees are similarly regarded as having no legitimate role in shaping the working rules of the original concern.

We find it highly implausible that an effective method of reorganizing the realm of production by corporations themselves could ever be implemented. We find it equally implausible that purchasers of products (like Nike and Wal-Mart) will forbear from negotiating agreements that result in "substandard" wages or working conditions. Nor is it likely that subcontractors can be induced to forbear from fully exercising their market power over individual workers. To our mind, the only plausible remedy for sweating, without overthrowing capitalism itself, is the creation by an overarching rule-creating entity—a state, a nation, an international organization—of mandatory minimal labor market standards making it unnecessary for anyone to forbear in order for all workers to obtain "reasonable" wages and enjoy "reasonable" working conditions.

A continuing failure to implement "reasonable" standards will only make the sweating system more prevalent as a form of organizing an enterprise's relationship with its "real" employees. And we might add that while the focus of attention in the Nike and Wal-Mart cases has been on foreign and immigrant labor, it surely is only a matter of time until the institutionalization of sweating via the creation of social distance between the worker and her "real" employer begins to impact the "native" workforce as well.

We arrive at the conclusion, therefore, that the sweating system approach to organizing work, and through it destructive competition, will continue to grow in significance unless a means of imposing minimum labor standards on all enterprises can be instituted by a supra-national "concern" with the sovereign power to command obedience to its laws. We have previously addressed the issue of international labor rights and analyzed some of the difficulties that will be encountered in crafting any set of standards that developed and developing nations alike will find acceptable (McIntyre and Ramstad 2002; 2003). In doing so, we forwarded our judgment that the ILO [International Labor Organization] is best suited among the already created international organizations for moving forward with

the development of reasonable minimal international standards, and we similarly judge the ILO to be the only international body within which an appropriate set of internationally applicable anti-sweating standards has any possibility of being crafted.

NOTES

1. In our original article we argue that these practices are indeed general in the United States, through case studies of higher education and food processing (McIntyre and Ramstad 2004). In a related essay we discuss the "external sweating system" in Wal-Mart's supply chain and characterize Wal-Mart's relations with directly contracted "associates" as a factory system (McIntyre and Ramstad 2005).
2. Even here they are unlikely to succeed. See McIntyre 2006.

ANNOTATED GUIDE TO FURTHER READING FOR PART V

Workers' relationships to the production process and employers draw attention from many scholars. Recommended books are: *Making Sweatshops: The Globalization of the US Apparel Industry* by Ellen Rosen; *Behind the Label: Inequality in the Los Angeles Apparel Industry* by Edna Bonacich, R. P. Appelbaum, Ku-Sup Chin et al.; *Slaves to Fashion: Poverty and Abuse in the New Sweatshops* by Robert J. S. Ross; and *No Sweat: Fashion, Free Trade and the Rights of Garment Workers*, edited by Robert J. S. Ross. At the close of 2004 and the beginning of 2005 *The New York Times* published a series titled "Made Elsewhere" on changes in the global textile and apparel business. The articles are: Elizabeth Becker's "Textile Quotas to End Soon, Punishing Carolina Mill Towns"; Keith Bradsher's "Bangladesh Survives to Export Again: Competition Means Learning to Offer More Than Just Low Wages"; David Barboza's "In Roaring China, Sweaters Are West of Socks City"; James Brooke's "Down and Almost Out in Mongolia; End of Garment Quota System Signals Tough Times Ahead"; and Michael Wines' "Dollar's Fall Silences Africa's Garment Factories." Malcolm Gladwell wrote a *New Yorker* article on Dov Charney, his retail chain American Apparel, and his employment practices for clothes made in the US, which relates Charney's unusual employment practices.

The World Wide Web offers the best way to be informed about trade negotiations and NGO activities. Constant updates at the WTO website (<www.wto.org>) provide up-to-the-minute reports on their initiatives. Websites for national and international movements for workers' rights are informative. Oxfam International (<www.Oxfam.org>) can lead to other national and regional Oxfam sites. For reports from the American Fair Labor Association (FLA) see <www.fairlabor.org/>. Other NGOs are the Council on Economic Priorities (CEP) at <www.cepnyc.org/>; Social Accountability 8000 program (SA-8000) at <www.sa-intl.org/>; the new Workers' Rights Consortium (WRC) at <www.workersrights.org/>; and the Clean Clothes campaign at <www.cleanclothes.org/>.

"Patterns of Culture in Global Fashion" by Lise Skov demonstrates the differing agendas of Hong Kong's Trade Development Council and Hong Kong fashion designers. Margaret Maynard's chapter "Political Dress" in *Dress and Globalization* documents various uses of dress in grass root politics, and examines the important role of dress as worn by politicians.

The following, from feminist authors, are recommended. Naomi Wolf's bestselling *The Beauty Myth* critiques the fashion and beauty industries for promoting unattainable (for the majority) beauty ideals. Linda Scott's *Fresh Lipstick: Redressing Fashion and Feminism* complements Elizabeth Wilson's position that fashion is not merely a means of oppressing women. Gayle V. Fischer's *Pantaloons and Power* carefully plots the sociopolitical and cultural matrix of the nineteenth-century dress reform movement in the US.

The Politics of Appearances by Richard Wrigley is an in-depth historical study of dress in revolutionary France, one of the few times in history when dressing in the garb of a political group, or not keeping up with the shifting meanings, could end in death.

PART VI
*F*ashion and the Body

ABBY LILLETHUN

Introduction

Every morning we manage our appearance in order to participate in the activities of the day. While we may stay in sleeping clothes until going out, we usually reformulate our appearance to meet social standards when in public. What is done to the body (body modifications) and what is put on it (body supplements) create a look that situates the body within the social environment. To meet the fashionable norm, varieties of strategies or techniques are used.

Humans often purposely distort the body from its natural dimensions. In part, body supplements make this possible: stiletto heels thrust the hips forward and make a person taller. People compress and bind parts of their bodies (e.g., tight corsetry). They wear garment structures that enlarge the silhouette of the clothed body (e.g., a 1950s full skirt, or the big shoulder pads of the 1980s). This section explores various modifications to the body such as grooming practices, nutrition, diet and exercise, surgical procedures, and skin markings.

Since the 1990s, there has been increased focus on the body within the study of fashion and dress. Jennifer Craik (1994) and Joanne Entwistle (2000) have both argued for dress researchers to account for the body in their analysis of dress. Dress serves as the mediating tool between the self in the body and the social environment. People conform to deeply internalized social norms: there are expected ways of "being in the body," covering the body and using the body in social space. People also engage in "extreme" body modifications in order to transform themselves, stretching the concepts of normal bodily practices. Scientific advances also bring focus to the body. A constant flow of new information about the aging process, maintaining good health, dealing with illness, and the body's relationship to the environment activates new strategies for creating and managing appearance.

Corsets have helped women to meet social standards of beauty for over 500 years. In the past, corsets were worn over shifts, not next to the skin. Corsets themselves changed at regular intervals to create the desired silhouette. When the corset was tightened, flesh and soft tissue pressed to the top of the corset, causing a soft, "jiggly" décolletage. This was erotically charged, but carefully controlled. Corsets altered the wearer's posture, forcing an erect and less flexible ribcage. A corset's shoulder strap placement limited arm movement. Corsets are just one example of how a garment can change the body, not solely in shape, but how it moves, and what it communicates.

Nineteenth-century dress reformers in Europe and America felt that fashionable corsets impeded good health, instead proffering "health" corsets. But there are other views on corsetry. The reading "A Second Look at the Big Squeeze" provides overviews of six books published between 1998 and 2003 on aspects of body modification or beauty standards for women. Valerie Steele's *The Corset: A Cultural History* inquired if corsets were actually harmful to women's health. Leigh

Summers's *Bound to Please: A History of the Victorian Corset* and Steele agree that women were not "dupes of patriarchy," that is, wearing corsets that restrained and hurt them in order to allow men to control their lives. Instead, the researchers ask, "What was at stake for the women? What do they get out it?" Perhaps corsets enhanced their lives within their specific life contexts. Women were not the only ones to use body-enhancing techniques. Men also used them. From the eighteenth into the nineteenth centuries, men sometimes padded their stockings to make their legs look more muscular. Jennifer Ruark also features Dorothy Ko's book *Every Step a Lotus: Shoes for Bound Feet*. Ko has asked similar questions about the Chinese practice of binding female children's feet to keep the foot tiny, even though it caused deformity.

Body weight is critical to fashion and to health. Fashion, as it is advertised, looks best on thin, young bodies. However, most people cannot attain the ideal. The ideal weight has shifted over time. In the eighteenth and nineteenth centuries, plumpness signified health and prosperity. Partly because they might have been in poor health, thin people were interpreted as lower on the socioeconomic scale. Even in the nineteenth century, thin physiques were not appreciated for similar reasons.

Today *globesity* (a term coined by the United Nation's World Health Organization) is a concern. The world trend toward obesity is predicted to have high costs in terms of healthcare and lost productivity. Since overweight people are increasing in number, it is no surprise that the current Western ideal for men and women is the opposite—thin and healthful, with muscles for men. It was not until the 1930s, when the movie industry had matured into a fully fledged system, that diet and exercise became popular. Movies brought unusually attractive people— movie actors—to local theaters, illuminated "bigger than life" on the silver screen. The 1930s fashions were closely fitted: dresses for women made in a single layer of slinky, bias-cut satin hugged every curve, and every imperfection. Madeleine Vionnet, the famous designer of the period who developed techniques to create bias-cut garments, is reported to have insisted on thin models (Kirke 1998). With the body so exposed, dieting and exercise became important in order to be attractive in the newest styles. Today women strive to meet the ideal type, and to maintain youthful appearance beyond menopause. Since the later twentieth century, severe psychological disorders related to body image (the mental image of one's self) such as bulimia and anorexia nervosa have been observed.

Manipulation of the body through exercise is widely practiced today. Gym memberships and media advertising for exercise machines are ubiquitous. An example of the ways diet and exercise change body dimensions across a culture can be observed in US Army anthropometric studies from 1955 to 1988. They found that compared to men in 1955, men in 1988 had more developed upper bodies. As a result, men's shirts, jackets and coats are cut with additional ease in the shoulder and chest.

The reading "Material Girl" by Susan Bordo is from her widely acclaimed book, *Unbearable Weight: Feminism, Western Culture and the Body*. The reading interprets Madonna's manipulation of her public self, from her body that is molded through extensive exercise regimes, to the control of her press image. Madonna's overt sexuality, gender crossing and seemingly constant transformations, challenge codification of her identity. In many ways, her body is the subject of her career, as she manipulates the "gaze" of the world via ambiguous representation of herself.

Cultural myths about hair are in opposition by gender. Women's hair is sensual and alluring and men's hair signals virility and strength. These myths have been challenged by the recent popularity for men to shave their heads or wear extremely short hair, and by the fashion for plucking hair from eyebrows, and waxing backs and the pubic area. This recent fashion has also extended to women. Women in the West have removed leg hair for decades, and plucked eyebrows and shaved underarms as well; now it is common to reduce pubic hair with a "Brazilian waxing" or have a FBW (full body wax). The practice of genital hair removal did not originate in the West, but has been practiced in warm climate cultures for many years.

Another way humans modify their appearance is dyeing the hair on the head. In the nineteenth century, fashionable women emulated Princess Eugénie by dyeing their hair red. In the late 1970s and early 1980s, the punk movement's exuberant hairstyles of spikes, shaved sections, teased hair, and bright colors not normally associated with hair such as crimson, bright blue, green and shocking pink completed their styles. Today colored hair dye can be purchased in the grocery store.

"Nap Time: Historicizing the Afro" is a historical account of the Afro hairstyle in American culture. D. G. Kelly debunks the myth that the Afro originated with the Black Power movement of the mid-1960s. He places its first appearance among feminist black women in New York City in the 1950s. This study explores how historical memory reshapes the past to suit idealized perceptions.

Graham Lawton's "Extreme Surgery" provides a glimpse into the growth in permanent body modifications through plastic surgery. In the early twenty-first century, media coverage of plastic surgery has proliferated, from magazine cover stories to television programs. Celebrities' surgical adjustments are watched with vicarious interest as they unfold in the popular press. Plastic surgery originated following the First World War, as physicians sought to help disfigured soldiers. Now it has become a voluntary procedure as people search for the "perfect" body or to maintain a youthful appearance.

Body modifications often evolve in the art and subcultural areas. The French artist Orlan undergoes plastic surgeries as performance art (<www.orlan.net/>). She rejects the possibility of perfect beauty and incorporates lumps and mounds into her face. Tattooing, other body marks, and piercing, have transformed in recent years from rebel and renegade meanings to expressions of unity, spirituality and creativity.

27

JENNIFER RUARK

A Second Look at the Big Squeeze

From Chronicle of Higher Education *48(13), November 23, 2001: A12.*
Copyright © 2001, The Chronicle of Higher Education.
Reprinted with permission.

WERE CORSETS—OR EVEN FOOT-BINDING—REALLY SO BAD?

Long before the sexual revolution led women to shed their bras and girdles for physical freedom, early feminists campaigned against a far more restrictive garment. "Burn the corsets!" wrote Elizabeth Stuart Phelps in 1874. "Make a bonfire of the cruel steels that have lorded it over your thorax and abdomen for so many years and heave a sigh of relief, for your emancipation I assure you, from this moment has begun." Doctors, too, inveighed against the popular waist-cinching, bust-lifting contraption that put up to 80 pounds of pressure on every square inch of a woman's torso, squeezing her rib cage in and up and pressing mercilessly on her internal organs. They blamed illnesses and even deaths on it, and at least one nineteenth-century doctor compared corsetry to Chinese foot-binding.

Ever since then, historians and other scholars interested in the ways that beauty standards oppress women have referred knowingly to the corset as the example par excellence. But new research suggests that they've been wrong—and not just about corsets.

"'Fashion' cannot logically be reified as a magic power that causes women to behave in ways contrary to their own best interests," writes Valerie Steele, chief curator of the Museum at the Fashion Institute of Technology, in her book *The Corset: A Cultural History*. It is one of several new studies that revise the history of fashion, insisting that women have had good reasons for squeezing themselves into corsets, bras, and girdles, and even for binding their feet.

THAT GIANT SUCKING SOUND

Worn off and on by members of the upper classes—both men and women—since the early sixteenth century, corsets exploded in popularity in the nineteenth century. Many people considered the corset to be an essential part of proper, modest dress for women, and some women "tightlaced," squeezing their waists down to 15 inches or smaller. Doctors opposed to corsetry said it interfered with women's natural role as child bearers, while doctors who favored the practice said women needed corsets to support their weak bodies. No one questioned that the female sex was weak, but feminist dress reformers blamed corsets for sapping women's strength and keeping them from achieving equality with men.

"Niggardly waists and niggardly brains go together," wrote Frances Willard, a suffragist and dress reformer. "A ligature around the vital organs at the smallest diameter of the womanly figure means an impoverished blood supply to the brain, and may explain why women scream when they see a mouse."

Figure 57. Corset, 1890–1900 (1954.14.01); pair of stiletto-heeled shoes ca. 1960 (1996.12.02); and pair of Chinese lotus shoes (1955.03.08). Historic Textile and Costume Collection, University of Rhode Island.
The corset, stiletto heels and Chinese shoes for bound feet all show signs of having been worn. Each illustrates ways to modify the body to fit cultural ideals.

Dress reformers didn't make much headway, though, in part because their movement was associated not just with women's suffrage but with other dangerous ideas like atheism and free love. (In fact, Ms. Steele points out, some feminists were quite prudish, and opposed corsets on the grounds that they turned women into sex objects.) Even feminists were not unanimous in their opposition; to many, the rigidity of corsets implied self-control and respectability. The editor of *Woman's Suffrage Journal* urged her readers to "stick to your stays."

Contemporary scholars who rail against the corset, Ms. Steele says, have been too willing to believe nineteenth-century medical reports that attributed diseases as varied as tuberculosis, breast cancer, scoliosis, and prolapsed uterus— not to mention hysteria, insanity, and "impure desires"—to tight-lacing. "Historians who would never accept medical accounts of the dangers of masturbation (causes blindness and insanity) or female education (sucks the blood from the uterus to the brain with appalling results) become perversely credulous whenever fashion is the subject of medical anathema," she writes.

Ms. Steele read medical and autopsy reports with a cardiologist to pin down corsetry's actual effects. "When you start investigating all of these claims, they don't stand up," she says. Citing a 1998 reenactment experiment by Colleen Gau, an independent scholar, Ms. Steele says there is no question that corsets reduced women's lung capacity, forcing them to breathe with their upper diaphragms (and creating the heaving bosoms of bodice-ripper fame). Their long-term use must certainly have weakened women's back and abdominal muscles, and may have aggravated uterine problems, she says. But the most serious illnesses caused by corset-wearing were probably indigestion and constipation.

Contemporary feminists, including Mary Daly, Andrea Dworkin, and Helene E. Roberts, who have argued that men found the corset sexy because it inflicted pain on women, have overstated the prevalence of tight-lacing, Ms. Steele says. Published accounts of it, including testimonies of enforced tight-lacing at boarding schools, were most likely the erotic fantasies of a minority of fetishists (who may have included women).

Many women simply liked wearing corsets, Ms. Steele argues. "Certainly, some women perceived the corset as a physical assault, but it's an exaggeration to say that all or even most women perceived it that way. We tend to regard comfort as a very high priority, and they didn't, for a variety of reasons, including the fact that there were so many uncomfortable things going on in your life anyway." She says the corset may have been attractive to many women because it allowed them to express their sexuality in a socially acceptable way: while it controlled jiggly female flesh, the hourglass shape and heavy panting it induced were blatantly erotic.

CIVILIZING MISSION

Leigh Summers, a research associate at the University of New England, in Australia, is much more critical of the corset. In *Bound to Please: A History of the Victorian Corset*, just out from Berg Publishers, she writes that, while extreme tight-lacing may not have been the norm, even the more common goal of a 21-inch waist was dangerously unrealistic. Yes, she concedes, Victorian

medicine had a long way to go, but enormous pressure consistently placed on the pelvic area was undoubtedly harmful. Moreover, "it deadened women's lives by causing fits of depression, uneasy feelings, and a sense of general malaise."

But while Ms. Summers believes corsets were used to police Victorian women's bodies and their minds, she too discredits the notion that women were simply dupes of the patriarchy. Not only did the corset provide women with "culturally sanctioned eroticism," she writes, but (paradoxically) missionary women may have considered the corset an "ideological ally," helping them maintain their identity as "civilized" in remote parts of the world. Moreover, its spread during the Industrial Revolution to working-class women allowed them to challenge the status of their betters: If they could look like their mistresses, how different were they, really?

Certainly, enough women objected to corsets to create a market for alternatives, such as the brassiere, an early version of which was patented in 1863. About a hundred years later, feminists rejected that item of clothing, too. But Ms. Gau and Jane Farrell-Beck, a professor of textiles and clothing at Iowa State University, argue in *Uplift: The Bra in America*, that it is "time to shelve the stereotype of the brassiere as oppressive and to take a more balanced view of its development."

"The brassiere brought women 'uplift' in several facets of their lives, including health, fashion, and economic development," they write. Even as late as the early 1900s, a "bust girdle" meant a break from the corset: It was recommended for sportswomen, for pregnant and nursing women, and for singers and lecturers who needed full use of their lungs. As women moved into factory jobs in the 1940s, bra promoters argued that its physical support relieved fatigue. And it also provided business opportunities for women: They held almost half of the more than 1,230 patents for breast supporters between 1863 and 1969. While the emphasis in the 1960s on "natural" shapes coincided with a downturn in the industry, Ms. Gau and Ms. Farrell-Beck point with satisfaction to the bra's renewed popularity today.

The idea that women ever embraced foot-binding is harder to swallow. You don't have to be a feminist to cringe with sympathy at the hooflike appearance of bound feet in archival photos, and the idea that Chinese men were turned on by the broken bones and stench is repulsive to most contemporary observers. But Dorothy Ko, a history professor at Columbia University's Barnard College, says the practice was neither senseless nor perverted. It was "entirely reasonable" for women, given the time and place in which they lived, she argues in *Every Step a Lotus: Shoes for Bound Feet*. Foot-binding "had less to do with the exotic or the sublime than with the mundane business of having to live in a woman's body in a man's world."

WOMEN'S WORK

Her research dispels several myths about foot-binding, most importantly that it was practiced among the rich as a symbol of leisure. "Foot-binding did not cloister women, because it wasn't meant to cripple them," she says, and indeed, shoes caked with mud and tiny rain boots show that women with bound feet did venture out of their houses. In fact, she says, beginning in the eighteenth century, peasant daughters emulated the upper classes by binding, and although some Chinese people criticized the practice as frivolous, women with bound feet could and did work.

That work might mean collecting firewood or weeding, rather than standing knee-deep among the rice paddies, but even women who stayed inside were always productive, crafting beautiful "Lotus shoes" of satin, silk, and cotton at home or laboring in silk workshops.

Brides with bound feet were desirable not because potential grooms found them sexually alluring but because to potential in-laws their feet signaled modesty and morality, Ms. Ko argues. Women wore slippers even to bed, and until the nineteenth century their husbands were not likely to have seen their naked feet. Ms. Ko also demonstrates that women's feet were usually larger than their three-inch-long shoes suggested. Some shoes were constructed to allow the back of the foot to hang over the edge, where it was hidden by long leg coverings.

A SOURCE OF PRIDE

There's no getting around the fact that the bound foot was deformed, of course. Though Ms. Ko has found no evidence that binding actually broke bones, it did redistribute them. But she says the emphasis for both women and men was on the shoes, not the bound feet, and that is her focus, too. Lotus shoes were a source of pride for the women who made and wore them, she says. "The reason I did not talk about the smell or the pain is we know it all too well. It's time for us to gain a more balanced and accurate historical understanding of the women who were motivated to do it."

Shoes were given as gifts, and the embroidery on them evoked folk tales and puns. In that way, illiterate women used them as a substitute for writing. "A good woman worked with her hands and used her body to display her craft," writes Ms. Ko. "In the end, isn't [foot-binding] also an expression of female labor, diligence, and skills?"

The arrival of Westerners in the mid-nineteenth century, and the shift of shoemaking soon after from the home to the factory, led to the demise of foot-binding. Under the scrutiny of Western missionaries, "foot-binding became a stand-in for everything that was wrong about 'tradition,'" Ms. Ko writes.

But even when the Chinese government waged anti-foot-binding campaigns in the first half of the twentieth century, many women with bound feet refused to be "liberated." They threw inspectors from their bedrooms or fled to the mountains to hide. "Why would they submit to a campaign that derided them as wasted and wasteful, crippled and lazy?" she asks.

On the other side of the world, women were more willing to give up their corsets. But the corset's gradual disappearance in the twentieth century is less a result of feminist reform than of women's "internalization" of the corset through exercise, Ms. Steele argues. It began to be undesirable to need a corset or a girdle: Everything underneath was supposed to be hard and tight.

The corset has made a recent comeback, thanks largely to designers like Jean-Paul Gaultier and the pop star Madonna, but it has been redefined: Now it's worn on the outside, an overt, parodic expression of sexuality.

EXPRESS YOURSELF

The new work on female fashion reflects a broader shift among feminist scholars, many of whom—like Kathy Peiss in her study of makeup, *Hope in a Jar: The Making of America's Beauty Culture* or Debra L. Gimlin in *Body Work: Beauty and Self-Image in American Culture*—are giving credit to women for knowing their own minds.

The new work may be an inevitable result of the turn in scholarship toward material culture and the body as a historical subject. "Once we turn our attention to something as private and perhaps ultimately unknowable as how did someone live in his or her body in a different time and culture," says Ms. Ko, "we are bound to ask new questions that burst the previous frameworks of analysis."

But not all feminists have signed on. Scholars like Ms. Steele and Ms. Peiss "are not skeptical enough about the role of consumerism and merchandising in the experience of American women," says Joan Jacobs Brumberg, a professor of history, human development, and women's studies at Cornell University, who has written about female body image. She appreciates the nuances that the new research brings to earlier feminist accounts, but says "some of this is related to a larger interpretation that … self-expression is the ultimate value, as opposed to a collective activity. But the corset and makeup are not impulses that come from an individual psyche."

THEY MAY HAVE LIKED IT

The divide seems to come down to differences over whether truly independent thought is really possible. The notion that anyone is simply a passive recipient of cultural messages—an idea established in academe thanks to theorists of power like Michel Foucault—is itself losing power.

"You can't possibly argue that for 1,000 years Chinese women were morons and Chinese men were sexual perverts. You have to ask, what stakes did women have?" says Ms. Ko. Her students who pierce, tattoo, and brand their bodies "have no problems dealing with the fact that women might actually have liked their bound feet," she says, "because not only did it alter their gait but it altered the way they perceived the world. They see their navel ring or tongue ring in the same light: No pain, no gain."

28

ROBIN D. G. KELLEY

Nap Time: Historicizing the Afro

From R. D. G. Kelley (1997), **Fashion Theory 1(4): 339–51.**

Whenever I see an Afro, whether in photographs or on live human beings, nostalgic for the days of ghetto rebellion and black counterculture, the CD player in my brain always kicks into an imaginary soundtrack. Sometimes it's the theme from *Shaft* or *Superfly*; other times it's just some generic blaxploitation background music—the funky bass, incessant wah-wah guitar, heavy back beat, screaming saxophone or flute. More than dashikis, platform shoes, black berets and leather jackets, the Afro has clearly been the most powerful symbol of Black Power style politics. Although hair had long been a site of contestation within black communities and between African-Americans and the dominant culture, the Afro, unlike any other style, put the issue of hair squarely on the political agenda. Indeed, the debate over the meaning of the Afro found its way into mainstream newspaper and scholarly journals, involving a diverse array of black intellectuals (Simkins 1982).

Unfortunately, these debates shed little light on the Afro's history or the ways in which its meaning changed over time. On the contrary, the very discourse that endowed the Afro with political meaning has also profoundly obscured crucial aspects of the style's history that might call into question its Black Power roots. The framing of the Afro in popular culture has made it impossible for many contemporary writers to see beyond the raised-fisted militant attired in black turtlenecks or faux African garb. Most commentators repeat the timeworn narrative linking the

Afro to the masculinist rhetoric and iconography of Black Power. As a result, the Afro's long-standing association with post-1966 black militancy

Figure 58. An Afro hairstyle, 1974, Starkville, Mississippi. Courtesy of Yvette Harps-Logan.

has become "common sense" in the world of hair scholarship. Like the Afro itself, the basic contours of the story remain unchanged even if some details differ. The purpose of this brief essay, then, is to explore the perils of a "politics of style" approach that views the Afro through the limited lens of mid-1960s, phallocentric black nationalist politics and offer an alternative narrative that considers the experiments of black women intellectuals of an earlier era as well as the efforts by black hair professionals to write their own histories of the Afro.

Most "cultural politics" approaches start with styles that have radical intentions but are ultimately domesticated and depoliticized by the marketplace. We see this with the zoot suit, ripped and bleached jeans, punk and grunge styles, to name a few (Hall and Jefferson 1976; Hebdige 1979; Cosgrove 1984; Chibnall 1985; Fiske 1988; Budd et al. 1990; Kelley 1994). And, to a certain degree, we can see this with the Afro. As Kobena Mercer points out in his brilliant essay, "Black Hair/Style Politics" (1990: 255):

> Once commercialized in the marketplace the Afro lost its specific signification as a "black" cultural-political statement. Cut off from its original political contexts, it became just another fashion: with an Afro wig anyone could wear the style. Now the fact that it could be neutralized and incorporated so quickly suggests that the aesthetic interventions of the Afro operated on terrain already mapped out by the symbolic codes of the dominant white culture. The Afro not only echoed aspects of romanticism, but shared this in common with the "countercultural" logic of long hair among white youth in the 1960s.

Of course, whether the depoliticization of the Afro is the result of its debt to "the symbolic codes of the dominant white culture" or of capitalism's amazing ability to turn anything into a commodity, is debatable. But the debate itself depends on our accepting the "taming of the bush" narrative. The evidence suggests that the story is a bit more complicated.

The Afro has partial roots in bourgeois high-fashion circles in the late 1950s and was seen by the black and white elite as a kind of new female exotica. Even though the intention, among some circles at least, was toward achieving healthier hair and expressing solidarity with newly independent African nations, it entered public consciousness as a mod fashion statement that was not only palatable to bourgeois whites but, in some circles, celebrated. There were people like Lois Liberty Jones, a consultant, beauty culturist and lecturer, who claimed to have pioneered the Natural as early as 1952! She originated "Coiffures Aframericana," concepts of hairstyling that she practiced in Harlem for several years from the early 1960s. More importantly, it was the early, not the late, 1960s when women like Odetta, Miriam Makeba, Abbey Lincoln, Nina Simone and Margaret Burroughs began wearing the "au naturel" style—medium to short Afros (Jones and Jones 1971). Writer Andrea Benton Rushing has vivid memories of seeing Odetta at the Village Gate long before Black Power entered the national lexicon. "I was mesmerized by her stunning frame," she recalled, "in its short kinky halo. She had a regal poise and power that I had never seen in a 'Negro' (as we called ourselves back then) woman before—no matter how naturally 'good' or diligently straightened her hair was" (Rushing 1988: 334). Many other black women in New York, particularly those who ran in the interracial world of Manhattan sophisticates, were first introduced to the Natural through high-fashion models in "au naturel" shows, which were all the rage at the time (Jones and Jones 1971; King and Ogunbiyi 1963: 68).

Helen Hayes King, associate editor of *Jet*, came in contact with the au naturel style at an art show in New York, in the late 1950s. A couple of years later, she heard Abby Lincoln speak about her own decision to go Natural at one of these shows and, with prompting from her husband, decided to go forth and adopt the 'fro. Ironically, one of the few salons in Chicago specializing in the au naturel look was run by a white male hairdresser in the exclusive Northside community. He actually lectured King on the virtues of Natural hair: "I don't know why Negro women with delicate hair like yours burn and process all the life out of it ... If you'd just wash it, oil it and take care of it, it would be so much healthier ... I don't know how all this straightening foolishness started anyhow." When she returned home to the Southside, however, instead of compliments she received strange looks from her neighbors. Despite criticism and ridicule by her coworkers and friends, she stuck with her au naturel—not because she was trying to make a political statement or demonstrate her solidarity with African independence movements. "I'm not so involved in the neo-African aspects of the au naturel look," she wrote, "nor in the get-back-to-your-heritage bit ..." Her explanation was simple: the style was chic and elegant and in the end she was pleased with the feel of her hair. It is fitting to note that most of the compliments came from whites (King and Ogunbiyi 1963: 69–71).

What is also interesting about King's narrative is that it appeared in the context of a debate with Nigerian writer Theresa Ogunbiyi over whether black women should straighten their hair or not, which appeared in a 1963 issue of *Negro Digest*. In particular, Ogunbiyi defended the right of a Lagos firm to forbid employees to plait their hair (women were required to wear straight hair). She rejected the idea that straightening hair destroys national custom and heritage: "I think we carry this national pride a bit too far at times, even to the detriment of our country's progress." Her point was that breaking with tradition is progress, especially since Western dress and hairstyles are more comfortable and easier to work in. "When I wear the Yoruba costume, I find that I spend more time than I can afford retying the head tie and the bulky wrapper round my waist. And have you tried typing in an 'Agbada'? [*a large caftan-like garment*] I am all for nationalization, but give it to me with some comfort and improvement" (King and Ogunbiyi 1963: 67–8).

Andrea Benton Rushing's story is a slight variation on King's experience. She, too, was a premature Natural hair advocate. When she stepped out of the house sporting her first Afro, perhaps inspired by Odetta or prompted by plain curiosity, her "relatives thought I'd lost my mind and, of course, my teachers at Juilliard stole sideways looks at me and talked about the importance of appearance in auditions and concerts." Yet, while the white Juilliard faculty and her closest family members found the new style strange and inappropriate, brothers on the block in her New York City neighborhood greeted her with praise: "'Looking good, sister,' 'Watch out, African queen!'" She, too, found it ironic that middle-class African women on the continent chose to straighten their hair. During a trip to Ghana years later, she recalled the irony of having her Afro braided in an Accra beauty parlor while "three Ghanaians (two Akan-speaking government workers and one Ewe microbiologist) ... were having their chemically-straightened hair washed, set, combed out, and sprayed in place" (Rushing 1988: 334, 326).

No matter what spurred on the style or who adopted it, however, the political implications of the au naturel could not be avoided. After all, the biggest early proponents of the style tended to be women artists such as Abbey Lincoln, Odetta, and Nina Simone whose work identified with the black freedom movement and African liberation. In some respects, these women were part of what might be called Black Bohemia. They participated in a larger community—based mostly in New York—of black poets, writers, musicians of the 1950s, for whom the emancipation of their own artistic form coincided with the African freedom movement. It was the age of Mau Mau, armed struggle in the Cameroon, independence for Kwame Nkrumah's Ghana, the famous meeting of "Non-Aligned" nations in Bandung, Indonesia, the formation of the American Society of African Culture (AMSAC), the creation of the Organization of African Unity. *Ebony, Jet*, and *Sepia* magazines were covering Africa, and African publications such as *Drum* were being read by those ex-Negroes in the States who could get their hands on them. The Civil Rights movement, the struggle against apartheid in South Africa, the emergence of newly independent African nations, find voice in Randy Weston's *Uhuru Afrika*, Max Roach's *We Insist: Freedom Now Suite* (featuring Abby Lincoln, Roach's wife); Art Blakey's "Message from

Kenya" and "Ritual," Sonny Rollins's "Airegin," and Coltrane's "Liberia," "Dahomey Dance," and "Africa." All these pieces were written between 1953 and 1961. The rekindling of black solidarity with Africa, particularly among Black Bohemia, was not just a matter of bloodlines; on the contrary, it was a matter of blood spilled. Revolutionary political movements, combined with revolutionary experiments in artistic creation—the simultaneous embrace and rejection of tradition—forged the strongest physical and imaginary links between Africa and the Diaspora (Cruse 1968; Radano 1993; Weinstein 1993; Simone 1993; von Eschen 1996; Magubane 1987; Geiss 1974; Weisbord 1973; Esedebe 1982). Thus, it is not surprising that Harold Cruse, in one of his seminal essays on the coming of the new black nationalism, anticipated the importance of the style revolution and the place of the au naturel in it. As early as 1962, Cruse predicted that in the coming years "Afro-Americans … will undoubtedly make a lot of noise in militant demonstrations, cultivate beards and sport their hair in various degrees of *la mode au naturel*, and tend to be cultish with African- and Arab-style dress" (Cruse 1968: 73).

Of course, he was right. By the mid-1960s, however, the Afro was no longer associated with downtown chic but with uptown rebellion. It was sported by rock-throwing black males and black-leathered militants armed to the teeth. Thus, once associated with feminine chic, the Afro suddenly became the symbol of black manhood, the death of the "Negro" and birth of the militant, virulent black man.[1] The new politics led to new narratives that sought to explain the symbolic significance of the Natural style. The power of the text and oral narratives, the power of political movements themselves, allowed militants and hairstylists alike (often one and the same) to invest the Afro with new political meanings.

During the late 1960s and early 1970s, dozens of books, dissertations and manuals appeared that literally rewrote the history of the Afro—erasing its roots in the au naturel fashion movement. Several of these books were written by black barbers and hairdressers who had been politicized or were longtime advocates of Natural hair. One such author insisted that "The Afro was a serious setback for the perpetrators of Anglo-Saxonism." Another described the Afro as "a matter of reclaiming our soul" (Morrow 1973: 87; Jones and Jones 1971). In virtually all of these narratives, the Afro either originated in the mid-1960s (during or after the Watts uprisings) or could be traced to precolonial Africa and was then resurrected in the mid-1960s. However, contrary to many contemporary cultural studies scholars who assume that all black nationalist constructions of culture automatically assume a singular "blackness," the authors of most of these books emphasized the diversity of African hairstyles and hair textures, and some even admitted that various African ethnic groups used mud to slick down their hair. In a fascinating book titled *400 Years Without a Comb*, barber Willie Morrow (who is also the author of two additional small books, *Curly Hair* and *Curly Hair and Black Skin*), talks at length about the diversity of styles: the common use of flowers, braids, clay to create a sculpted, matted look. The book itself, he tells us, grows out of his "desire to expose the black man's struggle for identity through his hair." Likewise, in *All About the Natural*, written by Lois Liberty Jones and John Henry Jones and published by Clairol, the diversity of the African past is a central theme. They discuss dyeing and beadwork and braiding, but insist that "Nowhere was seen the attempt to artificially straighten or change the natural flow of the hair. Why? Because here at the scene of humanity's birth, traditions were established long before white men came to divide and enslave the unsuspecting people, long before Africa had ever seen a white man" (Morrow 1973: 4; Jones and Jones 1971).

For Willie Morrow, the tragic event which led to the "bondage" of black hair was the loss of the comb. Like the drum, the African comb or pick was an essential part of African culture. It was not only the most important tool for hair grooming; the comb was a work of art, hand-carved for the individual and a crucial part of one's identity.

Morrow even argued that the lack of proper hair grooming tools was a major source of black self-hatred. Not only did slaves use harmful products like axle grease and lard on their hair and scalp, but the small-toothed comb of the master damaged many heads.

> Black children learned early in life that the [European] comb hurt and got tangled in curls. So painful was this experience to black boys and girls, that they avoided getting their hair combed whenever possible; they were satisfied to let their hair stay matted forever. The eagerness to avoid this necessary grooming was passed on from generation to generation of children to this day. The truth was never told to them—that the comb, the European comb, was not designed for them.

The justification for the Natural, therefore, was driven as much as by health concerns as by identity politics. All of these books discuss in great detail the damage caused by straighteners and other chemicals (Morrow 1973: 49–80; see also Sagay 1983; White and White 1995: 45–76).

Of course, as cultural critic Kobena Mercer points out, no hairstyle is really "Natural," since they all require some degree of "cultivation" or "artificial techniques to attain their characteristic shapes and hence political significance" (Mercer 1990: 252, 256). Yet part of the impetus behind the Afro was to enable African-Americans to jettison unnatural chemicals and withdraw from the marketplace altogether. African or not, the Natural was, for some, an act of self-determination. However, even before the Afro reached its height of popularity, the haircare industry stepped in and began producing a vast array of chemicals to make one's Natural more natural. One could pick up Raveen Hair Sheen, Afro Sheen, Ultra Sheen and Head Start vitamin and mineral capsules, to name a few (Van Deburg 1992: 201–2). The Clairol Corporation (whose CEO supported the Philadelphia Black Power Conference in 1967) did not hesitate to enter the Natural business (Alien 1969: 163). Listen to this Clairol ad published in *Essence Magazine* (November 1970):

No matter what they say ... Nature Can't Do It Alone!
Nothing pretties up a face like a beautiful head of hair, but even hair that's born this beautiful needs a little help along the way ... A little brightening, a little heightening of color, a little extra sheen to liven up the look. And because that wonderful natural look is still the most wanted look ... the most fashionable, the most satisfying look you can have at any age ... anything you do must look natural, natural, natural. And this indeed is the art of Miss Clairol.

Depending on the particular style, the Afro could require almost as much maintenance as the process. And for those women (and some men) whose hair simply would not cooperate or wanted the flexibility to shift from straight to nappy, there was always the Afro wig. For $9.00 or $10.00, one could purchase a variety of different wig styles, ranging from the "Soul-Light Freedom" wigs to the "Honey Bee Afro Shag," made from cleverly labeled synthetic materials such as "Afrylic" or "Afrilon" (Van Deburg 1992: 201–2).

By the early 1970s, on the eve of the Afro's ultimate demise, the whole Natural movement took another turn. First, the Afro began to lose its specific political meaning, or at least the connection to black nationalist politics seemed to fade into the background. Although it was stripped of its imaginary connection to Africa and urban rebellion, the Afro continued to linger on the heads of young men into the middle to late 1970s since it coincided with the dominant aesthetic of male beauty—light-skinned (pronounced "skin-did"), bowlegged, with a big 'fro. The look laid bare the retreat from the original conception of the style as a celebration of *blackness*. At the time, some may recall, there was a real love affair with popular R&B groups like the Sylvers or The Brothers Johnson (though by then the Jacksons and their most famous brother had traded in their own famous Afros for the more treacherous world of the gheri curl). Second, the masculinization of the Afro in the aftermath of its depoliticization contributed to a backlash against black women with Natural hair. The age of Angela Davis and an Afro-coiffed Pam Grier (the diva of blax-ploitation films) was over. By the second half of the 1970s, actress/model Jayne Kennedy's long brown hair and light skin emerged as the era's most prominent representations of black female beauty. The December 1970 issue of *Essence Magazine* suggested that "getting straight" might be the wave of the future:

> The pressure to "go Natural" is almost overwhelm-ing, but the real question is, what is "natural" for you? For many black women, the honest answer to that is curly, wavy or even straight. For others, the straight route is a definite choice . . . Without apol-ogy, secure in where she's at politically (after all, it's what's under that head of hair that really matters), the woman who goes straight is clearly liberated enough to do her own thing in the fullest sense of that shopworn phrase.

Leading stylists such as Lois Liberty Jones (backed by Clairol, no less) tried to keep the Afro alive by diversifying the look in such a way as to emphasize both femininity and refinement. "We can all wear the Natural," she wrote, "but remember at its best it is not a do-it-yourself thing. There is the "primitive" Natural and there's the well-groomed coiffure. Some merely stop straightening their hair. Good! But you can't beat the professional care of a licensed beauti-cian to help you make the change." Although its nationalist moorings remained pretty much in-tact, Jones's explicit appeal to middle-class black women suggests a throwback to the au naturel days. For example, the "Egyptian Exotica" and the "Delta Magic" combined the Afro style with bands of braided hair. The latter was unusually complicated, and probably looked pretty silly. As Jones described it, the hair is not only "burst-ing into freedom above a band of braids," but it called for "one looping [braid] under the chin adding excitement for that special occasion." The "Freedom Burst" was a kind of "double bouffant look" created by two cornrow braids, each one braided back from the eyebrow. Other styles in-cluded "Soul Love," "Miss Zanzie" (most likely for "Zanzibar"), "Basic Black," and "Respect" (Jones and Jones 1971).

In some ways, the transformation of the Afro marked the beginning of the end. It is treated in contemporary popular culture as a relic of the 1960s or a key element of the 1970s retro style. Yet what the Afro represented, the debates it engendered, still lay at the heart of the politics of black hair. After all, the Afro was deeply em-bedded in a larger racial and gendered discourse about the black body under racism and sexism. For black women, more so than black men, go-ing Natural was not just a valorization of black-ness or Africanness, but a direct rejection of a conception of female beauty that many black men themselves had upheld. Indeed, the resur-gence of black feminism in the 1970s was partly sparked by the lack of self-determination black women had over their image. They sought new definitions of beauty that celebrated diversity within blackness and challenged the dominance of the haircare and cosmetic industries. These discussions and debates over hair, skin, facial features, the shape of one's body found voice in political movements such as the National Black Feminist Organization, in Toni Cade Bambara's essential anthology *The Black Woman* (1970), in the prose and poetry of the decade's leading black feminist writers, including Toni Morrison, Ntozake Shange, Alice Walker, Gloria Naylor, June Jordan, Michelle Wallace, bell hooks, Paula Giddings, Barbara Smith and Cheryl Clarke, to name a few. And singers such as Abbey Lincoln, pioneer of the au naturel, and Sweet Honey and the Rock continued to write and sing about black women's natural beauty.

The post-Black Power generation of black feminists carved out a new radical aesthetic that built upon the previous era's celebration of "nat-uralness" and African ancestry, but emphasized autonomy, sisterhood, and alternative sexualities. Many women turned to very close-cut Naturals and African-style braids (long before Bo Derek popularized the cornrow braids that became her signature too in *10*). While the close-cut 'fro did not carry as much explicit political baggage as the big 'fro, conditions rendered the style oppo-sitional. It not only challenged gender conven-tions in a world where long hair was a marker of femininity, but it was often interpreted [*as*] a sign of militancy: some employers saw the style in terms of racial militancy, while others (often black men) regarded the close cut as a sign of so-called "man-hating" feminism. Black women who chose to wear braids in the late 1970s and early 1980s paid the greatest price. Across the country dozens of black women, from TV news anchors to airline flight attendants, were banned from wearing braids or lost their jobs because they refused to comply. Employers regarded braids as distasteful, threatening or inappropriate statements of ethnic pride—and the courts, in most cases, upheld workplace policies banning African-style braids (Caldwell1991: 365–96).

No matter what we might think about culture and style as a terrain of struggle, hairstyle politics, particularly in the black community, reveal a great deal about power—the power of white over black, men over women, employers over workers, the state over citizens. But to understand the impact and meaning of this power struggle we must go beyond "reading" the form. As I have tried to emphasize throughout this brief essay, certain oppositional styles—most notably the Afro—were accompanied by "texts" that set out to establish meaning. The political contexts in which the Afro reached popularity and the particular meaning that black political activists, hairstylists, and ordinary proud black folks gave the Afro led to a rewriting of the history of black hair, a new narration of style politics that required omissions, revisions, and new myths. Even beyond the well-worn symbolism of the Afro, "hair activists" like Willie Morrow characterized it as a direct challenge to the dominant culture. Not only were manufacturers of European-style combs and hair straighteners losing money, but " [n]ursing caps didn't fit, airline caps didn't fit, military headgear didn't fit ..." (Morrow 1973: 87).

In other words, hairdressers, writers, activists, defenders of the 'fro, created their own counter hegemony, not simply by wearing the style but by fighting for control over its meaning. And for a brief moment, they even beat Clairol at their own game of appropriation.

NOTE

1. As Linda Roemere Wright's research reveals, ads and other images of Afro-coiffed women in *Ebony* magazine declined around 1970, just as images of black men with Afros were steadily rising (see Wright 1982: 24–5).

29

SUSAN BORDO

"Material Girl": Madonna as Postmodern Heroine

From S. Bordo, (1993), "'Material Girl': The Effacements of Postmodern Culture," in Unbearable Weight: Feminism, Western Culture and the Body *(Berkeley: University of California Press), 268–75.*

This celebration of Madonna as postmodern heroine does not mark the first time Madonna has been portrayed as a subversive culture-figure. Until the early 1990s, however, Madonna's resistance has been interpreted along "body as battleground" lines, as deriving from her refusal to allow herself to be constructed as a passive object of patriarchal desire. John Fiske, for example, argues that this was a large part of Madonna's original appeal to her "wannabes"—those hordes of middle-class preteeners who mimicked Madonna's moves and costumes. For the "wannabes," Madonna demonstrated the possibility of a female heterosexuality that was independent of patriarchal control, a sexuality that defied rather than rejected the male gaze, teasing it with her own gaze, deliberately trashy and vulgar, challenging anyone to call her a whore, and ultimately not giving a damn how she might be judged. Madonna's rebellious sexuality, in this reading, offered itself, not as coming into being through the look of the "other," but as self-defining and in love with, happy with itself—an attitude that is rather difficult for women to achieve in this culture and that helps to explain, as Fiske argues, her enormous appeal for preteen girls (1987: 254–90). "I like the way she handles herself, sort of take it or leave it; she's sexy but she doesn't need men ... she's kind of there all by herself," says one. "She gives us ideas. It's really women's lib, not being afraid of what guys think," says another (Skow: 1985: 77).

Madonna herself, significantly and unlike most sex symbols, has never advertised herself as disdainful of feminism or constructed feminists as man-haters. Rather, in a 1985 *Time* interview, she suggests that her lack of inhibition in "being herself" and her "luxuriant" expression of "strong" sexuality constitute her brand of feminist celebration (Skow 1985: 81). Some feminist theorists would agree. Molly Hite, for example, argues that "asserting female desire in a culture in which female sexuality is viewed as so inextricably conjoined with passivity" is "transgressive":

Implied in this strategy is the old paradox of the speaking statue, the created thing that magically begins to create, for when a woman writes—self-consciously from her muted position as a woman and not as an honorary man—about female desire, female sexuality, female sensuous experience generally, her performance has the effect of giving voice to pure corporeality, of turning a product of the dominant meaning-system into a producer of meanings. A woman, conventionally identified with her body, writes about that identification, and as a consequence, femininity—silent and inert by definition—erupts into patriarchy as an impossible discourse. (Hite 1988: 121–22)

Not all feminists would agree with this, of course. For the sake of the contrast I want to draw here, however, let us grant it, and note as well, that an argument similar to Fiske's can be made concerning Madonna's refusal to be obedient to dominant and normalizing standards of female *beauty*. I am now talking, of course, about Madonna in her more fleshy days. In those days, Madonna saw herself as willfully out of step with the times. "Back in the fifties," she says in the *Time* interview, "women weren't ashamed of their bodies." (The fact that she is dead wrong is not relevant here.) Identifying herself with her construction of that time and what she calls its lack of "suppression" of femininity, she looks down her nose at the "androgynous" clothes of our own time and speaks warmly of her own stomach, "not really flat" but "round and the skin is smooth and I like it." Contrasting herself to anorectics, whom she sees as self-denying and self-hating, completely in thrall of externally imposed standards of worthiness, Madonna (as she saw herself) stood for self-definition through the assertion of her own (traditionally "female" and now anachronistic) body type.

Of course, this is no longer Madonna's body type. Shortly after 1987 marriage to Sean Penn she began a strenuous reducing and exercise program, now runs several miles a day, lifts weights, and developed, in obedience to dominant contemporary norms, a tight, slender, muscular body. Why did she decide to shape up? "I didn't have a flat stomach anymore," she has said. "I had become well rounded." Please note the sharp about-face here, from pride to embarrassment. My goal here, however, is not to suggest that Madonna's formerly voluptuous body was a non-alienated, freely expressive body, a "natural" body. While the slender body is the current cultural ideal, the voluptuous female body is a cultural form, too (as are all bodies), and was a coercive ideal in the fifties. My point is that in terms of Madonna's own former lexicon of meanings—in which feminine voluptuousness and the choice to be round in a culture of the lean were clearly connected to spontaneity, self-definition, and defiance of the cultural gaze—the terms set by that gaze have now triumphed. Madonna has been normalized; more precisely, she has self-normalized. Her "wannabes" are following suit. Studies suggest that as many as 80 percent of nine-year-old suburban girls (the majority of whom are far from overweight) are making rigorous dieting and exercise the organizing discipline of their lives (*Wall Street Journal*, February 11, 1986). They do not require Madonna's example, of course, to believe that they must be thin to be acceptable. But Madonna clearly no longer provides a model of resistance or "difference" for them.

None of this "materiality"—that is, the obsessive body-praxis that regulates and disciplines Madonna's life and the lives of the young (and not so young) women who emulate her—makes its way into the representation of Madonna as postmodern heroine. In the terms of this representation (in both its popular and scholarly instantiations) Madonna is "in control of her image, not trapped by it"; the proof lies in her ironic and chameleon-like approach to the construction of her identity, her ability to "slip in and out of character at will," to defy definition, to keep them guessing (Texier 1990: 31). In this coding of things, as in the fantasies of the polysurgical addict (and, as I argue elsewhere in this volume, the eating-disordered woman), *control* and *power*, words that are invoked over and over in discussions of Madonna, have become equivalent to *self-creating*. Madonna's new body has no material history; it conceals its continual struggle to maintain itself, it does not reveal its pain. (Significantly, Madonna's "self-exposé," the documentary *Truth or Dare*, does not include any scenes of Madonna's daily workouts.) It is merely another creative transformation of an ever-elusive subjectivity. "More Dazzling and Determined Not to Stop Changing," as *Cosmopolitan* describes Madonna: "... whether in looks or career, this multitalented dazzler will never be trapped in *any* mold!" (July 1987). The plasticity of Madonna's subjectivity is emphasized again and again in the popular press, particularly by Madonna herself. It is how she tells the story of her "power" in the industry: "In pop music, generally, people have one image. You get pigeonholed. I'm lucky enough to be able to change and still be accepted ... play a part, change characters, looks, attitudes" (Ansen: 1990: 311).

Madonna claims that her creative work, too, is meant to escape definition. "Everything I do is meant to have several meanings, to be ambiguous," she says. She resists, however (in true postmodern fashion), the attribution of serious artistic intent; rather (as she told *Cosmo*), she favors irony and ambiguity, "to entertain myself" and (as she told *Vanity Fair*) out of rebelliousness and a desire to fuck with people (Ansen: 311; Sessums 1990: 208). It is the postmodern nature of her music and videos that has most entranced academic critics, whose accolades reproduce in highly theoretical language the notions emphasized in the popular press. Susan McClary writes:

> Madonna's art itself repeatedly deconstructs the traditional notion of the unified subject with finite ego boundaries. Her pieces explore ... various ways of constituting identities that refuse stability, that remain fluid, that resist definition. This tendency in her work has become increasingly pronounced; for instance, in her recent controversial video "Express Yourself" ... she slips in and out of every subject position offered within the video's narrative context ... refusing more than ever to deliver the security of a clear, unambiguous message or an "authentic" self. (McClary 1990: 2)

Later in the same piece, McClary describes "Open Your Heart to Me," which features Madonna as a porn star in a peep show, as creating "an image of open-ended *jouissance*—an erotic energy that continually escapes containment" (McClary: 12). Now, many feminist viewers may find this particular video quite disturbing, for a number of reasons. First, unlike many of Madonna's older videos, "Open Your Heart to Me" does not visually emphasize Madonna's subjectivity or desire—as "Lucky Star," for example, did through frequent shots of Madonna's face and eyes, flirting with and controlling the reactions of the viewer. Rather, "Open Your Heart to Me" places the viewer in the position of the voyeur by presenting Madonna's body as object, now perfectly taut and tightly managed for display. To be sure, we do not identify with the slimy men, drooling over Madonna's performance, who are

depicted in the video; but, as E. Ann Kaplan has pointed out, the way men view women *in* the filmic world is only one species of objectifying gaze. There is also the viewer's gaze, which may be encouraged by the director to be either more or less objectifying (Kaplan 1983: 309–27). In "Open Your Heart to Me," as in virtually all rock videos, the female body is offered to the viewer purely as a spectacle, an object of sight, a visual commodity to be consumed. Madonna's weight loss and dazzling shaping-up job make the spectacle of her body all the more compelling; we are riveted to her body, fascinated by it. Many men and women may experience the primary reality of the video as the elicitation of desire for that perfect body; women, however, may also be gripped by the desire (very likely impossible to achieve) to become that perfect body.

These elements can be effaced, of course, by a deliberate abstraction of the video from the cultural context in which it is historically embedded—the continuing containment, sexualization, and objectification of the female body—and in which the viewer is implicated as well and instead treating the video as a purely formal text. Taken as such, "Open Your Heart to Me" presents itself as what E. Ann Kaplan calls a "postmodern video": it refuses to "take a clear position vis-à-vis its images" and similarly refuses a "clear position for the spectator within the filmic world ... leaving him/her decentered, confused" (Kaplan 1987: 63). McClary's reading of "Open Your Heart to Me" emphasizes precisely these postmodern elements, insisting on the ambiguous and unstable nature of the relationships depicted in the narrative of the video, and the frequent elements of parody and play. "The usual power relationship between the voyeuristic male gaze and object" is "destabilized," she claims, by the portrayal of the male patrons of the porno house as leering and pathetic. At the same time, the portrayal of Madonna as porno queen-object is deconstructed, McClary argues, by the end of the video, which has Madonna changing her clothes to those of a little boy and tripping off playfully, leaving the manager of the house sputtering behind her. McClary reads this as "escape to androgyny," which "refuses essentialist gender categories and turns sexual identity into a kind of play." As for the gaze of the viewer, she admits that it is "risky" to "invoke the image of porn queen in order to perform its deconstruction," but concludes that the deconstruction is successful: "In this video, Madonna confronts the most pernicious of her stereotypes and attempts to channel it into a very different realm: a realm where the feminine object need not be the object of the patriarchal gaze, where its energy can motivate play and nonsexual pleasure" (McClary 1990: 13).

I would argue, however, that despite the video's evasions of clear or fixed meaning there *is* a dominant position in this video: it is that of the objectifying gaze. One is not *really* decentered and confused by this video, despite the "ambiguities" it formally contains. Indeed, the video's postmodern conceits, I would suggest, facilitate rather than deconstruct the presentation of Madonna's body as an object on display. For in the absence of a coherent critical position telling us how to read the images, the individual images themselves become preeminent, hypnotic, fixating. Indeed, I would say that ultimately this video is entirely about Madonna's body, the narrative context virtually irrelevant, an excuse to showcase the physical achievements of the star, a video centerfold. On this level, any parodic or destabilizing element appears as cynically, mechanically tacked on, in bad faith, a way of claiming trendy status for what is really just cheesecake—or, perhaps, soft-core pornography.

Indeed, it may be worse than that. If the playful "tag" ending of "Open Your Heart to Me" is successful in deconstructing the notion that the objectification, the sexualization of women's bodies is a serious business, then Madonna's *jouissance* may be "fucking with" her youthful viewer's perceptions in a dangerous way. Judging from the proliferation of rock and rap lyrics celebrating the rape, abuse, and humiliation of women, the message—not Madonna's responsibility alone, of course, but hers among others, surely—is getting through. The artists who perform these misogynist songs also claim

to be speaking playfully, tongue-in-cheek, and to be daring and resistant transgressors of cultural structures that contain and define. Ice T, whose rap lyrics gleefully describe the gang rape of a woman—with a flashlight, to "make her tits light up"—claims that he is only "telling it like it is" among black street youth (he compares himself to Richard Wright), and he scoffs at feminist humorlessness, implying, as well, that it is racist and repressive for white feminists to try to deny him his indigenous "style." The fact that Richard Wright embedded his depiction of Bigger Thomas within a critique of the racist culture that shaped him, and that *Native Son* is meant to be a *tragedy*, was not, apparently, noticed in Ice T's postmodern reading of the book, whose critical point of view he utterly ignores. Nor does he seem concerned about what appears to be a growing fad—not only among street gangs, but in fraternity houses as well—for gang rape, often with an unconscious woman, and surrounded by male spectators. (Some of the terms popularly used to describe these rapes include "beaching"—the woman being likened to a "beached whale"—and "spectoring," to emphasize how integral a role the onlookers play.)

My argument here is a plea, not for censorship, but for recognition of the social contexts and consequences of images from popular culture, consequences that are frequently effaced in postmodern and other celebrations of "resistant" elements in these images. To turn back to Madonna and the liberating postmodern subjectivity that McClary and others claim she is offering: the notion that one can play a porno house by night and regain one's androgynous innocence by day does not seem to me to be a refusal of essentialist categories about gender, but rather a new inscription of mind/body dualism. What the body does is immaterial, so long as the imagination is free. This abstract, unsituated, disembodied freedom, I have argued in this essay, glorifies itself only through the effacement of the material praxis of people's lives, the normalizing power of cultural images, and the continuing social realities of dominance and subordination.

30

GRAHAM LAWTON

Extreme Surgery

From **New Scientist,** *October 30, 2004: 54–6.*
Reprinted by permission of **New Scientist.**

Unhappy with your body? Join the club. And I don't mean the gym or health club. Exercise and diet, it seems, are too much like hard work. These days, cosmetic surgery is the way to go.

In the US, surgeons carried out 1.8 million cosmetic procedures in 2003, the largest number ever recorded and nearly double the 1997 figure. The numbers considering surgery were also at record levels—not just among adult women but also men and teenagers. And as acceptance of cosmetic surgery grows, costs fall and techniques improve, the chances are that having our bodies tweaked to make them more to our liking will become increasingly common.

The list of body alterations we can choose from is growing ever more extensive and radical. A few years ago, it was all about fixing one or two irregular features with a nose job or facelift. These days, it focuses on "harmonizing" the "aesthetic units" of your face and body by working on them all at the same time. Some surgeons are happy to perform four or five procedures at once. At the extreme end of this trend is a controversial practice known as the total body overhaul.

In the past, such radical reshaping would have taken months or years. Now cosmetic surgeons are getting the job done in weeks. Two American TV networks ran reality shows this year about cosmetic surgery, both promoting the idea of rapid, radical transformation. Fox Broadcasting's *The Swan* took seventeen "average girls"—"ugly ducklings" presumably being a bit too near the knuckle—and turned them into beauty queens in six weeks. ABC's *Extreme Makeovers* transformed twenty-four men and women in a similar time.

Thirty-two-year-old Cindy from San Diego in California was a typical *Swan* contestant. At school she was teased because of her droopy nose; as a grown-up with two children she felt unattractive and frumpy. Sex happened with the light off. Not any more. For the first time Cindy feels beautiful. She has a new nose, built from cartilage that used to be in her ear, plus a facelift, chin refinement, breast implants, tummy tuck, liposuction, lip augmentation, a brow lift and laser surgery on her eyes, not to mention nonsurgical treatments including laser hair removal and cosmetic dentistry, all in the space of a few weeks. If you were an old friend of Cindy's, you might be forgiven for not recognizing her in the street. And that, presumably, is the point.

Cindy is clearly happy with her new look, as are the majority of people who have cosmetic surgery. But the extent of the TV makeovers has whipped up a controversy. The shows' producers claim they are only reflecting what many people and their cosmetic surgeons are already doing, but many other surgeons are horrified. The very idea of a total body overhaul is wild exaggeration, they warn. In fact, it is positively dangerous. "Someone will die," warns Norman Waterhouse, a London-based surgeon and former president of the British Association of Aesthetic Plastic Surgeons (BAAPS).

But is there really a trend toward this sort of radical makeover, or is it just a TV phenomenon? It's hard to be certain. Statistics compiled by the American Society for Aesthetic Plastic Surgery (ASAPS) and other professional bodies record only the number of operations performed, not on whom and in what combination. But anecdotally, some practitioners in the US confirm that combination surgeries are on the increase. "There is a trend toward multiple procedures," says Michael McGuire, associate professor of plastic surgery at the University of California, Los Angeles. "There's an increasing realization that it's not just one aspect of your appearance that is inadequate. Unattractive teeth will still ruin your face even if you have a nose job."

The watchword is "harmony." A facelift that improves matters above the chin might make a sagging neck more obvious, so many surgeons now do a neck lift at the same time. Another popular combination is facelift, brow lift and eyelid surgery. And for new mothers who want to get back into shape quickly, tummy tuck plus breast lift is the must-have combo. Some surgeons have even taken to working in pairs, one taking on the face while the other handles the body. And with big improvements in the safety of anesthesia over the past ten years, surgeons are increasingly prepared to keep patients under for longer in order to make time for extra procedures.

"In seven hours you could get a facelift, eyelid surgery and an eyebrow lift plus a chemical peel, collagen injection or Botox," McGuire says. With a second surgeon working on your body at the same time, you are looking at a sizeable alteration in appearance. It's not exactly a total body overhaul. And it's not quite overnight; even the most minor cosmetic surgery takes days to heal. But it will be a noticeable and rapid change nonetheless.

So what is the limit? "I wouldn't exceed seven or eight hours," McGuire says. "After that you are not getting the surgeon's best work." Some surgeons go longer, he says, driven by competition or patients' demands. "It's not emergency surgery," McGuire points out, "but some people think it is."

Despite the increasing popularity of multiple procedures, most surgeons dispute the idea that a patient can walk into a clinic as an ugly duckling and walk out as a swan. "It's not possible, it's not safe and it's misleading," McGuire says. Waterhouse is more forthright. "I feel strongly that this trivializes and sensationalizes surgery. It grotesquely distorts perceptions of what aesthetic surgery is about." He also considers it potentially dangerous. If you prolong operation time there is a massive increase in the risk of deep-vein thrombosis and blot clots in the lungs, which can be life-threatening, he says.

Surgeons also worry that the promise of an as-seen-on-TV makeover distorts people's expectations. According to Stanley Klatsky, editor-in-chief of *Aesthetic Surgery Journal,* increasing numbers of would-be patients are turning up at clinics asking to be made over from head to toe overnight. Adam Searle, current president of the BAAPS, says the same is happening in the UK. People are starting to see cosmetic surgery as equivalent to a trip to the salon. "This is a major surgical procedure, not a hairdo," he points out.

According to an ASAPS survey this year, 34 percent of women in the US and 14 percent of men were considering having cosmetic surgery. If the rest of us are tempted to sneer at such vanity, it is also important to remember that cosmetic surgery can have real benefits. Ted Grossbart, a psychologist at Harvard Medical School, says the majority of patients are pleased with the results and consequently feel happier and more self-confident. "It can change lives," Searle says.

ANNOTATED GUIDE TO FURTHER READING FOR PART VI

The theoretical concepts most used in research on fashion and the body can be found in *The Fashioned Body* by Joanne Entwistle and *The Face of Fashion* by Jennifer Craik. *Body Dressing* edited by Joanne Entwistle and Elizabeth Wilson also examines theory in one section and has research articles in two sections. In addition to these books, the journal *Fashion Theory* publishes articles that place the body at the center of the interpretation; see these special issues: *Hair*, 1997; *Fashion and Eroticism* 1999; and *Dress and Gender* 2005. *The Body and Society* is Bryan S. Turner's 1984 treatise that first argued for sociology to place the body at the center of research. Chapter 4, "The Body in Context" in Susan B. Kaiser's textbook *The Social Psychology of Clothing* provides an excellent overview of types of research from the social/psychological field.

Two articles in the journal *Body and Society* examine contemporary body modifications: "The Possibility of Primitiveness: Towards a Sociology of Body Marks in Cool Societies" by Bryan S. Turner and "Anchoring the (Postmodern) Self? Body Modification, Fashion and Identity" by Paul Sweetman. *Tattoo: Bodies, Art and Exchange in the Pacific and the West edited by Nicholas Thomas, Anna Cole, and Bronwen Douglas is a scholarly book with extensive new illustrations of historical tattoos. It also covers contemporary practice in the Pacific.*

Naomi Wolf's *The Beauty Myth: How Images of Beauty Are Used Against Women* and Karen Peiss's *Hope in a Jar: The Making of America's Beauty Culture* treat the marketing of beauty as a commodity. Debra L. Gimlin's *Body Work: Beauty and Self-Image in American Culture* uses interviews with women to demonstrate what American women do and their expectations from working on their bodies. *Flesh Wounds: The Culture of Cosmetic Surgery* by Virginia Blum is a cultural study of the plastic surgery phenomenon.

Dorothy Ko's *Every Step a Lotus: Shoes for Bound Feet* is complemented by Judy Yung's *Unbound Feet: A Social History of Chinese Women in San Francisco*.

Among her books, Valerie Steele has written three specifically on fashion and the body. *The Corset: A Cultural History* examines the corset in fashionable dress. *Fashion and Eroticism: Ideals of Feminine Beauty from the Victorian to the Jazz Age*, treats femininity, beauty ideals and their interconnected nature to sexual allure. *Fetish: Fashion, Sex, and Power* provides a history of fetishism, which involves dress. Jane Farrell-Beck and Colleen Gau's *Uplift: The Bra in America* relates the history of the bra, partly through a review of patent history.

Extreme Beauty: The Body Transformed by Harold Koda was published in conjunction with an exhibition of that name at the Costume Institute in the Metropolitan Museum of Art in New York City in 2002. The well-illustrated book covers examples of extreme dress across the centuries and the globe.

PART VII
*F*ashion and Art

LINDA WELTERS

Introduction

Is fashion an art form? Art critics and fashion writers have debated this question for decades. Those on the "pro" side claim that fashion is indeed art because it is a visual medium whose creators respond to the same stimuli as painters and sculptors. Like art, it involves immense creativity as well as mastery of techniques and materials. The "con" side argues that fashion is fleeting, frivolous and feminized, and that ultimately it is commercial. Also, the fashion business is seasonal, which is not true of the art world. Artists supposedly are not concerned with selling. They are consumed with creating works of art, not producing a collection for regularly scheduled showings.

In addition to its commercial nature, features that distinguish fashion from art, according to its critics, are *medium*, *function* and *rarity*. The traditional *media* in which artists work include oil, watercolor and pencil (for paintings and drawings), and stone, metals and wood (for sculpture). Art made from fiber—tapestries, for example—has long been relegated to the category of "minor" or "decorative" art. Thus, textiles manipulated for the human body are categorized as decorative art too. Critics claim that "pure" art is not *functional*. It is art for art's sake. In the last century, however, the canon of what is considered art expanded to include photography, glass, ceramics and architecture, all of which are created with function in mind. Architecture, especially, has encountered little resistance in the academy. No one argues that

I. M. Pei's glass pyramid addition to the Louvre, one of the world's great art museums, is not art. Another argument against fashion being art is that it has no *rarity* value. It is not one of a kind, like an oil painting or a sculpture. (The limited-edition print, however, is accepted as art.) Today almost all clothes are made in multiples, negating any uniqueness. The more copies in circulation, the less artistic a fashion is perceived to be.

Regardless of which position one accepts, there is a clear relationship between art and fashion. Some of these relationships are elucidated below.

FASHION DESIGNERS AS ARTISTS

Considering the requirement that art is rare, one could argue that the couture designer is an artist. He or she creates a line from which individual copies may be ordered, much like the limited-edition print. Haute couture is exclusive, made of beautiful materials, and executed mostly by hand. While the commercial aspect is still present, the level of innovation is extremely high among the world's great couturiers, past and present. Madeleine Vionnet, for example, manipulated the qualities of supple fabrics, cutting on the bias to make extraordinarily beautiful clothes that look like liquid coverings for the body. Presently, art critics follow the creations of dozens of fashion designers for their artistic expressions of modernity. Some of these designers present their work as theatrical productions, akin to performance art. These costly, innovative fashion shows are part of the designer's vision for how to clothe the modern man or woman. Alexander McQueen's shows have been particularly notable in this regard.

Designers also appropriate images from well-known artworks for their fashion products, which seems to lend more credibility to their work. Piet Mondrian's color-block paintings, Pablo Picasso's cubist shapes, and Van Gogh's irises inspired Yves Saint-Laurent. Franco Moschino used pop art images for his creations. Designers also collaborate with artists, and are inspired by artistic movements. Elsa Schiaparelli, for example, worked with Salvador Dalí and Jean Cocteau to create Surrealist-inspired clothes.

Some fashion designers find expression in art media. Paul Poiret painted after he no longer designed apparel. Ralph Rucci experimented with watercolors and acrylics before deciding to become a fashion designer (Bissonnette 2005). Karl Lagerfeld is a published photographer.

ARTISTS AS CREATORS OF CLOTHING

Artists have, at times, tried their hand at creating clothing. In the twentieth century, Gustav Klimt, Wassily Kandinsky and Sonia Delaunay each designed dresses that expressed their artistic vision (Stern 2004). The Russian Constructivists and Italian Futurists designed menswear. Menswear is often omitted in the discussion of fashion as art.

In the late 1960s, during the height of the hippie era, a group of students at the Pratt Institute of Art in New York City chose fiber as their medium, creating sculptural forms for the body. Janet Lipkin, Jean Cacicedo, and Sharron Hedges crocheted, embroidered, hand-painted, appliquéd, and knitted one-of-a-kind "wearable art" sold in galleries rather than apparel stores. They based their clothing on the traditional, simply cut clothes of Asian cultures such as the Japanese kimono or the Turkoman coat. Their creative process struck a chord with thousands of craftspeople across the United States, giving birth to the art-to-wear movement. Many of these artisans now stage their own sales events outside the traditional retail system.

FASHION IN ART MUSEUMS AND GALLERIES

Many of North America's great art museums collect and exhibit fashion. The Metropolitan Museum of Art's Costume Institute in New York City houses over 75,000 costumes and accessories, and its curators regularly organize major exhibitions in a dedicated space. The Museum of Fine Arts in Boston, the Los Angeles County Museum of Art, the Cincinnati Art Museum, and the Royal Ontario Museum in Toronto also house important collections. While most art museums in major cities outside North America do not have costume collections, some cities have museums dedicated solely to costume, such as the Kyoto Costume Institute (Fukai 2002) or have decorative art museums with significant costume collections, such as the Victoria and Albert Museum in London. In Paris, the Musée de la Mode et du Textile is in a separate facility, but is affiliated with the Louvre.

Museums that feature retrospectives of living fashion designers earn criticism from the art world, citing the commercial nature of the fashion business. The Costume Institute's retrospective of Yves Saint-Laurent in 1983 was among the first to feature a living designer, and was viewed as a promotional tool for his business. Seventeen years later, an exhibition of Giorgio Armani's work at the Guggenheim received similar negative press.

Some galleries show the work of contemporary fashion designers as art. An example is "Fashioning Art: Handbags by Judith Leiber," a traveling exhibition of 160 handbags organized by the Corcoran Gallery of Art in 2003. The numerous press releases described the hand-beaded handbags as "remarkable works of art," an "extraordinary artistic achievement," and "melding the realms of art and fashion." It helps that her work features images borrowed from artists such as Henri Matisse and Georges Braque.

Paintings depicting fashion are often used to study fashion history. This can be problematic, as artists sometimes used studio props, draped fabrics, or allegorical dress to costume their sitters. Viewers must be aware of which paintings show sitters in "costume," and which show them in the fashions of the period. Of course, paintings offer the potential for rich analysis of fashion's importance, whether the sitters are depicted in "costume" or in contemporary dress.

FASHION PHOTOGRAPHY AND ILLUSTRATION

The fashion vs. art debate comes to a head when art museums show the work of photographers who sometimes work in fashion. Photography itself is "suspect" as an art form: at its most basic level, it involves pointing a camera and shooting a picture. When the Museum of Fine Arts, Boston opened a major retrospective of Herb Ritts's photographs in 1996, the critics complained that his commercial work was not art. Eight years later, when New York's Museum of Modern Art (MOMA) mounted *Fashioning Fiction in Photography since 1990*, which featured the work of thirteen contemporary fashion photographers, the critics were kinder, possibly because the exhibition was held in a temporary facility. Interestingly, MOMA had never before touched the subject of fashion prior to this show even though its first curator of photography was Edward Steichen, an early photographer of fashion. All of the exhibited photographs had been commissioned by, and published in, fashion magazines, raising the troublesome issue of commerce. One enthusiastic critic noted that "the art world has

been notoriously afflicted with an allergy to fashion" (Valdez 2004).

Illustrators also come under fire because their work is for hire. Illustration preceded photography as a way to depict fashion, beginning with the fashion plate, which was the format for disseminating fashion news until the birth of fashion photography around 1911. While most fashion plates are not considered art, some illustrators' work is highly collectible, such as images by George Lepape, Paul Iribe, and Georges Barbier in the 1910s and 1920s, and those of Ruben Toledo today.

FASHION AND ARCHITECTURE

In the past decade, architecture has developed a relationship to the retailing of fashion. Fashion houses hire internationally renowned architects to create retail spaces: Prada hired the Dutch architect Rem Koolhaas to design the flagship store in New York City in 2001 and Swiss architects Jacques Herzog and Pierre de Meuron for the Tokyo store in 2003. Increasingly, cutting-edge fashion is linked to architecturally interesting spaces.

Included in this section are four extracts that address the relationship of fashion to art. Michael Boodro's piece for *ArtNews*, the world's oldest international art magazine, discusses the main points in the debate over fashion as art. Richard Martin's extract from *Cubism and Fashion* compares the formal stylistic aspects of fashion drawing to works of cubist art. Olivier Zahm, the co-founder of the pioneering French art/fashion magazine *Purple*, is represented in an extract on fashion photography. Finally, Andrew Bolton discusses the work of Viktor & Rolf, the Belgian designers who often show in galleries.

31

MICHAEL BOODRO

Art and Fashion

From M. Boodro (1990) "Art and Fashion: A Fine Romance," in ArtNews September 1990: 120–7. Reprinted by permission of the author.

Art is art and fashion is an industry. Forget for a moment the multimillion-dollar auction market, the network of international dealers, the thousands of people—from museum guards to art book publishers—whose livelihoods depend on the creation, sale, and dissemination of art. There is a longstanding, genteel tradition—an ideal, at least—that art is the creation of individuals burning bright with lofty inspiration, that art is above commerce, that art, for its own sake or for any other reason, is the big, important thing. That's why we refer to the art world and not, more cynically, the art industry. Whereas fashion, or the rag trade, as it is affectionately called, comes with no such illusions attached. Fashion is not art. Fashion is frivolous and unimportant, except to a few hundred of its more addicted followers, thousands of people who make their living from it, and millions more who just like to shop.

And never the twain shall meet. Except that they do. In fact, the association between art and fashion is a long one and is only growing more intense. The depiction of elaborate clothes, rich embroideries, subtle colors, and shimmering, sumptuous fabrics has been an irresistible challenge and a joy for painters since the days of anonymous medieval manuscript illuminators. Holbein and Pisanello, Goya and Velázquez, Watteau and Ingres all expressed the high status and wealth of their sitters, as well as their own bravura techniques, in paintings that create brilliant illusions of silks and velvets and satins.

Where would Gainsborough's "Blue Boy" be without his blue suit? One of the most famous, and scandalous, dresses ever depicted in paint is the black velvet, low-cut gown worn by *Madame X* (Mme Gautreau) when she was portrayed by John Singer Sargent in 1884. That dress is still inspiring designers such as Carolyne Roehm, who says that she continues to refer back to the painting when she thinks about the ever-popular little black dress.

Of course, painters have occasionally gone beyond merely recording what was worn in front of them. Gustav Klimt, in his portraits of women, "designed" dresses that are more prominent than his subjects' faces—as we see in perhaps his most famous image, *The Kiss* of 1907–8, with its lavish gold pattern interspersed with colorful renderings of birds and fish. It is certainly not beside the point that Klimt's longtime lover, Emilie Flöge, was a dress designer.

Fashion has been no less abashed at using art for its own purposes. Mariano Fortuny, the great early twentieth-century Italian designer, created flowing, clinging dresses in silk that freely called up the elegant lines of classical Greek statuary. And the pull of art as a source is equally strong in our own time. After his couture showing last year, Yves Saint-Laurent told the press that he had been influenced by the palette of Botticelli. Valentino has taken black-and-white geometric motifs from the Viennese artists Josef Hoffmann and Koloman Moser and embroidered them in couture collection for Chanel recreated the tight Empire bustline and flowing Grecian folds seen in Jacques-Louis David's famous portrait, *Madame Recamier* (*c.* 1800), while Christian Lacroix has taken a Spanish turn, roused by retrospectives of Zurbarán and Velázquez—even replicating the voluminous line of the dress in Zurbarán's *Saint Elizabeth of Portugal* (*c.* 1630–35).

Yet designers don't only quote from works of art. Increasingly they are turning to artists and to the art scene to provide cachet for their enterprises. Avant-garde Japanese designer Rei Kawakubo has used photographs of painter Francesco Clemente and of photographers Doug and Mike Starn to advertise her Comme des Garçons line. (The Clemente portrait in turn appeared on the cover of a European art magazine.) Young artist Izhar Patkin, who showed his sculpture *Don Quijote, Segunda Parte* in New York at the Holly Solomon Gallery and in this summer's Venice Biennale, had an exhibition of the same work in Milan, not at a gallery but at the lavish retail complex of designer Romeo Gigli, with whom he has created fabric patterns. One of Calvin Klein's most famous ad campaigns, photographed by Bruce Weber in 1984, was shot in and around the ranch of Georgia O'Keeffe in the Arizona desert; O'Keeffe even allowed herself to be photographed as part of the series of black-and-white images.

Of course, in an industry noted for that sincerest form of flattery, the practice of knock-offs, as it's known in the business, it's not surprising that designers should turn to art for ideas. But the art and fashion connection is more complex than mere thievery and inspiration. Because of the transitory nature of clothing styles and the speed with which fashion absorbs whatever is new (an innovation shown on runways in October can be on the streets by December), fashion often reflects or even predicts a common mood or desire, a yearning for change, a nostalgia for a more glorious past, a need for a new and improved future.

Surely it was not coincidental that the 1960s' sleek, futuristic miniskirt sheaths and white vinyl go-go boots of Courrèges and Pierre Cardin,

Figure 59. Madame X (Madame Pierre Gautreau), 1883–84. John Singer Sargent (1856–1925). Oil on canvas; 82⅛ x 43¼ in. (208.6 x 109.9 cm). Arthur Hoppock Hearn Fund, 1916 (16.53). Image © The Metropolitan Museum of Art.

sequins on dresses. Gianni Versace, too, turned to the Secessionists as a source some years ago. Lately, in a series of short dresses, he evoked the colorful geometry of Sonia Delaunay's watercolors, and an Eiffel Tower he showed, done in sequins, was worthy of her husband, Robert's, paintings. (Sonia Delaunay designed dresses and textiles herself.) Meanwhile, Karl Lagerfeld's the metal-disc dresses of Paco Rabanne, and the extreme, geometric hairstyles of Vidal Sassoon all came to the fore at the same time that kinetic art, pop art, op art, and hard-edge geometric abstract painting were the rage, when the Apollo spacecraft were orbiting the globe and technology seemed to promise exciting new advances for art as well as for society.

It was certainly not happenstance that in the mid-1980s Christian Lacroix made his sensational debut as a couturier, with concoctions of pouf skirts of satin and brocaded velvets, at the same time that there were major touring retrospectives of the eighteenth-century painters Boucher and Fragonard, who presented sensuality as a froth of ruffles and ribbons. As Paul Audrain, chairman of the house of Lacroix, stated at the launching of the first new couture line in twenty-five years: "New social and cultural trends have put the values of the 1970s into reverse. Ten years ago, any kind of personal expression was at a low point. All that has changed. People with new money want to express their success and there was no new couturier to capitalize on this particular trend." The impulse that caused the fashion press to swoon and led thousands of women to temporarily abandon severe, modern black for frills and bustles in the midst of the Reagan era was similar to the spirit of the times that Boucher fancifully documented in his canvases done during the height of the French monarchy.

The inspiration and motivations of both artists and clothing designers can be strikingly similar. At the same time that such artists as Sherrie Levine, Mike Bidlo, and Richard Prince became famous for appropriating and re-presenting icons of the modernist canon, ranging from photographs by Walker Evans to the paintings of Jackson Pollock, the more adventurous fashion designers, including Karl Lagerfeld, Franco Moschino, and Patrick Kelly, were doing precisely the same to *the* modern fashion icon, the Chanel suit. By shearing its skirt to mini proportions, inverting its pockets, attaching big bright plastic buttons, and draping it with enough chains to make it comical, fashion proved that it too could appropriate its own past—not only mocking a

classic but showing its continuing versatility and relevance.

We owe a debt to painters for preserving fashion whole in their pictures. But the time came toward the end of the nineteenth century when all of that changed: photography became a widespread medium and fashion photography was born. Ironically, just when photography usurped the role of painting in documenting clothing, clothing came to play a different role in art. The Impressionists, with their break from the approved, classical subject matter of the academy and their radical concern with the everyday events of the middle class, portrayed passersby and gallerygoers, hat shoppers and picnickers, giving unprecedented importance to ordinary clothes, and a shock of recognition to viewers.

Claude Monet's 1866–67 *Women in the Garden,* Edouard Manet's *Reading* (1868), and Pierre-Auguste Renoir's 1876 *The Swing* all show the artists' delight in portraying simple white summer frocks in shimmering daylight. Gustave Caillebotte's *Paris; A Rainy Day,* of 1876–77, with its umbrellas and black-suited men, was as surprising for its straightforward realism as for its tilted ground plane and looming foreground figures. The clothes, and therefore the lives, depicted in these canvases were not so different from the viewer's own, and that meant art was no longer a rarefied, removed, or spiritual pursuit. Seeing their skirts and jackets, top hats and waistcoats must have been nearly as striking to contemporary art lovers as it would have been to see their own faces staring back at them from the canvas.

Still, what this meant as time passed was everyday clothes and the people who wore them became an acceptable and unshocking subject. Fashion's practice of rapidly changing clothing styles became a mass-market phenomenon by the beginning of our [20th] century, and photography only multiplied the effect of fashion as a universal experience in which everyone took part—be it humble or grand. Shock, in fact, was replaced by allure in fashion images.

Many great photographers have worked in fashion, including such undisputed masters as Edward Steichen, André Kértész, Man Ray, Diane Arbus, Richard Avedon, and Irving Penn.

[...]

It's a sign of the art world's more conservative side, however, that their fashion work has almost always been considered by the critics as secondary to their "art" photography, as if these images—no matter how elegant or innovative—were forever tainted by commerce.

When the focus of modern art shifted from realism to abstraction around 1910, with the birth of Cubism, the illustration of clothing fell away as a commonplace subject. Still, artists were never content simply to record clothing designs, and there is a long history of artists becoming directly involved with fabrics, with cut and drapery. Matisse, finding himself dissatisfied with the current fashions in women's hats, created an old-style feathered bonnet for one of his most famous series, the 1919 "Plumed Hat" pencil drawings and the related painting *White Plumes* of the same year. And the artists of the Bauhaus, the Wiener Werkstätte, and Russian Constructivism, all working during the early decades of this century, saw clothing and textile design as part of their utopian projects to create a new society with a new aesthetic order. Geometric forms, as symbols of preeminent human rationality, figured as a main element in many of their designs.

Yet perhaps the most intimate connection between art and fashion occurred during the heyday of Surrealism, when rationality was decidedly not the point. Part of the success of this movement's flirtation with fashion was no doubt due to the fact that it had no broad agenda and made no effort to awaken or elevate mass taste. Surrealist fashion was created in a spirit of fun, to amuse, to shock—and like so much else invented by the Surrealists—to question the basis on which judgments about art are made.

The designer most closely allied with the Surrealists was Elsa Schiaparelli, known for her amusing and outrageous attacks on the idea of conventional fashion. In 1937 Jean Cocteau collaborated with her, creating drawings to be embroidered on the back of an evening coat (twin profiles, forming the outline of a vase with pink silk roses) and on the front of a jacket (a woman's head and shoulders, with a cascade of golden hair of beads down the right sleeve). That same year Salvador Dalí designed a hat for her in the shape of a high-heeled shoe, a sort of Surrealist tricorne, and created the fabric for her "Tear Dress," which featured the illusion of numerous holes. (Forty years later, fashion history repeated itself when Rei Kawakubo introduced sweaters strewn with ready-made holes.) The 1938 Paris Expo, which was largely a celebration of Surrealism, featured mannequins dressed by Man Ray, Dalí, and André Masson. In the late 1930s and 1940s, the Surrealists were frequent contributors to the pages of *Vogue* and *Harper's Bazaar*, and they continued to use the imagery of their art in fashion items and accessories.

The effect of this ongoing collaboration has not, of course, always been wholly salutary. Critics, from time to time, ridiculed the Surrealists for their involvement with fashion. And the resistance still crops up now and again. The late Keith Haring, who first came to prominence in the early 1980s for his lively graffiti figures that decorated the New York subways, is one such case. His populist bent was celebrated until he opened his Pop Shop in SoHo, which sold not only posters and prints but T-shirts, bags, jackets, and hats bearing his distinctive cartoonlike imagery. At that point, some critics complained that he'd gone too far and become too populist. He stated in one of his last interviews, "My work was starting to become more expensive and more popular within the art market. Those prices meant that only people who could afford big art prices could have access to the work. The Pop Shop makes it accessible. It was all about participation on a big level."

These criticisms of artists have been mirrored almost exactly in the fashion world. When Yves Saint-Laurent showed his "Mondrian" dresses in 1965, and the following year brought out his "Pop Art" dress with an outline of a nude body that closely resembled pop artist Tom

Wesselmann's painting series "Great American Nudes," some critics thought that he had become too slavishly "artistic." Yet it can surely be argued that when, say, Bill Blass styles a Matisse painting on the back of a woman's jacket, as he did two years ago, he is affirming a century-long sentiment that designers are not denigrating but celebrating art. And artists who are attracted to fashion recognize not only its chic but its ability to participate in mass culture, as Haring said, on a big level.

In any case, the art and fashion connection continues, and not without artists' willing participation. French painters Jean-Charles Blais and Ben (Vautier) have both hand-painted dresses for their compatriot, designer Jean-Charles Castelbajac. Ben's was emblazoned with the tongue-in-cheek phrase, "Je suis toute nue en dessous," that is, "I'm completely naked underneath"; Blais featured one of his characteristic lumbering bodies with a very tiny head. In 1988 Saint-Laurent used a bird motif by Georges Braque, combined with a Cubist guitar design, on an evening gown. Japanese designer Issey Miyake, in a recent collection, used a stiffened pleated fabric that evokes the Winged Victory of Samothrace. And Jean-Paul Gaultier has picked up on the splash-and-drip paintings of Jackson Pollock, merging them with businesslike chalk stripes for women's suits.

A sideline to all of this collaborative verve, incidentally, is the creation of window displays for clothing and jewelry stores, which has become a virtual tradition among twentieth-century artists: Man Ray, Dalí, Robert Rauschenberg, Jasper Johns, and Andy Warhol are the most famous among the many artists who have been tempted by the offering of a continual, if casual, audience of viewers. Julian Schnabel has gone one better by designing an entire boutique, in New York, for the French designer Azzedine Alaïa, including benches and clothing racks that look very much like his sculptures. And when, in 1983, *New York* magazine asked such artists as Alex Katz, David Salle, Red Grooms, and Jean-Michel Basquiat to create backdrops for a series of fashion spreads, it was following a line that goes back at least to 1937, when *Vogue* commissioned fashion "photo-paintings" from Dalí, Pavel Tchelitchew, and Giorgio de Chirico.

With fashion and art both becoming more pervasive elements of contemporary life, it is inevitable that they will continue to cross over each other's boundaries. Stories on art and artists are regular features in today's fashion magazines. In museums, costume and fashion exhibitions are becoming increasingly popular.

[...]

And fashion photography, despite some critical rebuffs, is appearing on gallery and museum walls throughout America and Europe. Indeed, the time it takes for an image to jump from a magazine's pages to the walls of an exhibition is constantly shrinking, as proved by recent gallery shows of Herb Ritts and Bruce Weber in New York.

Though the connection has grown closer, there are still inevitable differences between the two. Art is typically private, the creation of an individual. Fashion is public, a collaboration between designer, manufacturer, and wearer and then between wearer and viewer. Art requires time, contemplation, and thought. Fashion is instantaneous—a flash of color and shape on the street; a new idea to be mocked or embraced; a surprise, a temptation, a flirtation.

Both art and fashion can reflect and distill the concerns of the moment in potent and surprising ways. But while most of us are not artists, we all get dressed every day—and fashion, by default, becomes our creative outlet. For many of us, dressing is our one opportunity to express ourselves visually, to exhibit flair, to demonstrate our mood, to add color to our days. Fashion designers understand this. They give us this opportunity to vent our creativity. Despite the hype and verbiage of overenthusiastic fans and the press, fashion designers don't usually speak of themselves as artists. They have too much respect for art to believe that. They know that art is eternal and that fashion designs are, on the whole, ephemeral. But then so is life.

32

RICHARD MARTIN

Fashion Rendering

From R. Martin (1998), **Cubism and Fashion** *(New York: Metropolitan Museum of Art), 126–9. © The Metropolitan Museum of Art, New York, 1998. Reprinted with permission from the Metropolitan Museum of Art.*

No one would be surprised that Cubism had an influence on the way fashion is represented, in both fashion photography and fashion illustration. Concerning the former, the specific effects were negligible, since photography was still coming of age for the fashion magazine and the considerable influence of artistic photography still prevailed. Concerning fashion illustration, the same Cubism that arguably constructed (and deconstructed) the forms of a previously representational fashion established new ways of seeing through the pictorial frame of Cubism.

Most importantly, the picture plane was fractured. Cubism's most easily imitated pictorial device was almost immediately taken up in fashion illustration. Graphically, fashion illustration as an abbreviating, essentializing system of notation had always eliminated or merely suggested some of the determinants of space and perspective with the assumption that these would be understood within pictorial convention. When Cubism offered another pictorial convention, the adumbrated forms of the illustration began to float in space and to take on the new, less gravity-prone aesthetic. In particular, high-style fashion advertising, including that of the house of Vionnet, accepted such a floating world. In this instance, the decision was not merely that of an after-the-fact illustrator; it was also an official sanction from the fashion house. Reticence made much fashion advertising very traditional, but no such timidity was observed by Vionnet, who perceived an integrity among all the expressive parts of the fashion house. Poiret would have claimed likewise, but his advertising image was far less progressive than his otherwise avant-garde styles and his novel uses of display and presentation.

Of course, it would not be long before the American fashion magazines would benefit from European modernism under the art direction of M. F. Agha at *Vogue* and Alexei Brodovitch at *Harper's Bazaar*. These two graphic designers understood that modern fashion could only be embraced within the graphic design of modernism. The elegance, simplicity, and energy that these magazines expressed in the 1930s was indebted to Cubism. These two popular magazines propagated not only the Surrealism that *Harper's Bazaar* so admired in the 1930s and 1940s but even more importantly, the reduced, abstracted forms derived from Cubism. We cannot imagine our modern fashion image without these magazines.

But Cubism went through important stages along the way, before it became so mainstream in design in the 1930s. Central in that period is the work of Thayaht (palindrome artistic name for Ernesto Michahelles, 1893–1959). Thayaht seized not only Cubism's lashing line but its energy as well; he transformed the segmenting slices of a Cubist surround into the dynamic lines of force that would put a model into swirling motion suggesting an automaton of the runway. Thayaht's matrix in Futurism would explain the presence of these lines and vortex as well as the proclivity to motion; he never let fashion appear static but instead placed it within an implied energy field. Thus it was that Thayaht's sophisticated artistic journey, as associated with the fine arts as it is with the applied arts, influenced his imagery. That Thayaht placed his prodigious talent chiefly in the service of Vionnet was no small

accident; he recognized the compatible sensibility and the possibility that he could suitably represent her work.

Thayaht was no ordinary illustrator. In fact, he saw himself as a fashion inventor with specific reference to his collaboration with his brother toward the development of a utopian system of clothing for men, which was issued as one of many Futurist manifestos. Thus, a designer more than a subservient illustrator, Thayaht conceptualized illustration. As much as his lines of forces suggest motion and eternity in the utopian forms of clothing that included asymmetrical vests and jackets for men with Futurist prints, his 1920s illustrations for Vionnet suggest at least an exalted ephemerality for fashion. Vionnet dresses shown with twists and complexity are often difficult to identify in illustrations; Thayaht's illustrations are especially perplexing and suggest a generic rather than a specific similarity. How ironic that some of Thayaht's most effective images depict the sports of golfing, swimming, and skating that capture real motion through Cubist devices. These are not Cubist or Futurist masterpieces or the kinds of fashion that will foster a more perfect, utopian future. They are therefore perhaps less than Thayaht's highest aspirations. They are merely the most practical form of fashion and lifestyle. They became lifestyle images precisely because Cubism was by the 1920s able to achieve lifestyle.

But Thayaht was not alone. Fashion illustrators selectively borrowed from Cubism, coveting its association with the progressive and modern and responding to its uses of the part to indicate the whole that fashion illustration had always known as a principle. Cubism was a second-generation presence for fashion illustrators, entering that realm only in the 1920s, long after the first wave of Cubist invention. But Cubism would be destined to maintain a long presence in illustration and in graphic design, a fashion not utopian but one that would last for decades to suggest style, sports, energy, and the new in synthesis.

UNE ROBE DE MADELEINE VIONNET

Figure 60. "Une Robe de Madeleine Vionnet," Thayaht, *Gazette du Bon Ton*, 1922. Collection of Linda Welters.

33

OLIVIER ZAHM

On the Marked Change in Fashion Photography

From O. Zahm (2003), "On the Marked Change in Fashion Photography," in **Chic Clicks: Creativity and Commerce in Contemporary Fashion Photography** *(Boston and Ostfildern-Ruit, Germany: Institute of Contemporary Art and Hatje Cantz Publishers), 28–35. Reprinted by permission of the author.*

Fashion photography is everywhere. The fashion image is a meta-image that totally transcends its object (clothing design) and specific context (fashion magazines) and, as such, has its circumference everywhere and its center nowhere. Flexibility, furtiveness, adaptability, mobility: the fashion image is not an *imaginaire* but an operational matrix. It becomes a global icon, which deciphers the semiotic chaos characteristic of our time even as it contributes to and extends that chaos.

1. GLOBAL ICON

The hegemony of the fashion photograph in the field of representation takes multiple and convergent forms.

On the artistic level, fashion photography is, justifiably or not, no longer regarded as a minor or essentially commercial genre but as a cultural value in its own right. It is shown in places reserved for art and published in sumptuous journals, and it has begun to be treated as a subject suitable for conceptual theorization.

On the cultural level, fashion photography now functions in a manner comparable to the alternative rock counterculture as a result of the proliferation of new magazines, iconic models, designers, and young photographers. Owing to the simplicity of its production (the revolution of the snapshot), its immediacy, and its relation to the body and to attitudes, fashion photography is a narcissistic and instinctual mirror for the younger generation. The fashion image, blurring the boundaries not only between genres but also of art itself, represents a dynamic, flexible model in phase with the permanent need to redefine the aesthetic and corporeal standards that characterize generational immanence.

On the semiotic level, the fashion image has gradually freed itself from its representational codes in order to infiltrate everywhere and exploit all other forms of representation from architecture to film and contemporary art.

The fashion photo is a hybrid icon of the present, an image compounded of all other possible images, at once amnesiac and invasive. The fashion image in a sense represents the monstrous reign of simultaneity in the aesthetic field and as such is the equivalent of information in the economic or political field. It is the world of images synchronized to its own aesthetic synchronization (the eternal return of the new as special effect), just as the news is the world of information synchronized to real time. Accordingly, this hybrid image is better suited to grasp new rhythms—the circulations and mobilities as well as the polysemy—of the present. Hence the fashion image may be better suited than any

Figure 61. "Versace Dress, Back View, El Mirage," Herb Ritts, American, 1952–2002. Gift of Herb Ritts. 2000.854. Photograph © 2007 Museum of Fine Arts, Boston.

other to capture or reveal its time—a veritable documentation of the contemporary, combining and compounding a variety of issues and referents symptomatic of the present.

This extension of the realm of fashion photography makes precise analysis of this area of creation difficult. Fashion photography is an especially fragmentary, disparate, and confused genre. Within this category one finds brilliant technicians of the glamour image (from Steven Meisel to Nick Knight and Inez Van Lamsweerde), true innovators (from Guy Bourdin to Juergen Teller), and occasionally great artists (such as Richard Prince, Cindy Sherman, Takashi Homma, and Nan Goldin). But the majority of the output consists of industrial images devoid of any kind of sensibility or polysemy or meaning. These images merely reproduce the codes of the fashion photo, articulating the three basic signifiers (clothing, models, location or studio). In fact, it is impossible to judge a fashion image apart from the context in which it was produced: specifically, the magazine for which it was shot, the date, and the time. For a fashion image is above all a commissioned image, a circumstantial image, a controlled and controlling image (desire, narcissistic investment). This is at once its limitation and its central characteristic, which confers meaning on it and is the source of both its strength and its weakness. That is why it is misleading to evaluate the work of a photographer on the basis of his "personal book," which rather defines the space of his creativity, when the whole art of a fashion photographer is precisely to circumvent the rules of fashion photography by introducing a personal vocabulary (which generally has no interest apart from this conflict with the norm).

Even the best fashion photography is still an industry in service of industry. It is an industry of images in service of a specialized industry (ready-to-wear, accessories, cosmetics) that is itself on the cutting edge of a global capitalism increasingly dominated by the system of fashion (the acceleration of cycles, the imperative of the new, the aestheticization of consumption, etc.). Hence most fashion photography is applied art, commercial art, interchangeable art destined for the trash can along with the magazines in which it appears. What is more, fashion photography is not especially well liked. It is indeed astonishing to learn from market surveys that the readers of women's magazines are quite wary of fashion photographs, which they instinctively suspect of superficiality, inauthenticity, and gratuitousness. People have always been suspicious of fashion photographs. They are disturbing in their very seductiveness, in their mimetic capacity, in the ease with which they copy and hyper-aestheticize

the quotidian and conceal the world of consumption behind a glamorous surface that fools no one. In fact, apart from a few famous names, fashion photography is an anonymous stylistic and visual enterprise. The sheer variety and number of fashion photographs makes it virtually impossible for the average person to identify the photographers who produce them. Hence an exhibition of fashion photographs could be presented as exhibitions of ancient or primitive art are presented: as an indicator of the cultural state of a society.

If, in spite of this, one tries to single out "names" that is, to identify "true artists," from this vast and disparate output, the question of value judgment immediately arises—how is a fashion photographer to be evaluated? On the basis of what aesthetic criteria? This is a delicate question, and one that I confront daily in the choices I make as a magazine editor. It is not simply a question of taste, of subjective appreciation, or even of preference for some particular subgenre (glamour as opposed to realism, say, or academicism as opposed to spontaneity, etc.). The choices are as much political as they are aesthetic. True, fashion images effectively participate in an increasingly familiar industry, and in so doing they participate in the extension of what Guy Debord has called the integrated spectacle, which is another way of saying the development of the immaterial aspect of capitalism. Nevertheless, it is totally arbitrary to assimilate fashion photography *in toto* to the "empire of signs." To do so would be as stupid as to assimilate the *cinéma d'auteur* to commercial Hollywood cinema, or every new CD to the recording industry as a whole. What interests us in fashion photography is precisely those photographers who are exceptions to the rule: those who are capable of breaking the commercial rules of the fashion photo and the relations it imposes and who can escape from the strict logic of consumerism in such a way as to implicate existence as a whole (as an aesthetic prize).

If more than 99 percent of fashion photography is commercial and wants rules (that is, consumption), the problem is to identify the exceptional. What is exciting about the exceptional is that it wants life, that is, destruction of the alienating forms of communication in order to root out those forms of existence, desire, and subjectivity of which fashion photography at its most demanding (though not necessarily its most technically sophisticated) can be the instigator. And this takes place right in the heart of blatant consumerism, collective amnesia, and the global project of desubjectification of mass individualism.

2. THE VAMPIRISM OF COMMERCIAL FASHION PHOTOGRAPHY

On the level of vocabulary, the fashion photo was for a long time shaped by pictorialism (Baron de Meyer, Edward Steichen). Later it drew on the vocabularies of the aesthetic avant-garde: abstraction, Surrealism, Abstract Expressionism, geometric art, op art. In the 1960s and 1970s, the outdoor naturalism of Richard Avedon, Frank Horvat, and William Klein took fashion photography into the street, abandoning the fabricated studio backdrop in favor of real social and urban settings. In fact, fashion photography ventured onto new terrain throughout the twentieth century in an endless process of externalization and hybridization. Today, fashion photography no longer has any specifically artistic or sociological referent. It is constantly reinventing its foundations and its origins and drawing on all sorts of existential influences and territories. It is a model open to all other realms, whether aesthetic or not: sports, film, television, music, architecture, landscape design, etc. The fashion photo falls within what the young French philosopher Mehdi Belhaj Kacem calls the "paradigm of cannibalism and vampirism" (Kacem 2001).

Fashion photography is a vampirism of representation, or representation in its vampiric form. It is an essentially impure and hybrid form of communication that assimilates, integrates, and fuses with all possible territories of reference, ruthlessly hijacking, recycling, and absorbing

their characteristic signs in a manner not unlike what is called "sampling" in electronic music. The vampirism of fashion photography is the most powerful, up-to-the-minute version of the decomposed, destructured, fragmented state of representation today (deprived as it is of any stable referent).

Barthes believed that the final object of fashion photography, its ultimate referent, was first clothing and second attractiveness or elegance, that is, in the final analysis, the body in the setting in which it is shot. In reality, it has no ultimate physical referent. The physical referent is constantly shifting, fleeing, and vanishing from view. Things have been turned around since fashion photography lost its autonomy and specificity. The fashion photo is no longer the body's mode of appearance, its factitious ontology, in the sense of nakedness of being; rather, it is the body's mode of disappearance, disintegration, execution, and fragmentation. This calls for explanation, and I shall do my best to provide it.

This disappearance is in part related to the idealization of the body, which vanishes behind the ambiguous system of artistic referents that stage its display. But it is also of an ontological order, or, to put it another way, it belongs to the order of the event at work in fashion photography and, beyond, in our mechanisms of representation, which originate in the endless destruction of referents. Fashion photography has a lethal psychedelic aspect: all those exploded, exploited, exposed bodies atomize the lost referent (the human figure made in the image of the divine). A commercial fashion photo disintegrates the figure of the human body (always singular, unique, and personal) and transforms it into what Deleuze calls the organless body, the desubjectified, anonymous, and artificial figure of the fashion model (which in the final analysis is the spectacular form of merchandise in Debord's sense). It is this dissociated form of the human figure that commercial fashion photography delivers to social cannibalism for everyone to devour with their eyes, assimilate, and appropriate, all at the instigation of a fraudulent desire to exist.

That is why commercial fashion photography has to be situated at the precise point where two distinct registers of expression intersect: namely, advertising and pornography. From advertising (which seeks to incite desire for the object) it retains the imperative of legibility and ease of decoding its fashion referent. From pornography (which seeks to incite the desire of the subject) it learns to ritualize sexual desire, to fetishize the relation to the body, and to aestheticize the sexual act in an impossible prostitutional exchange, a "non-site" of symbolic exchange amply analyzed by Jean Baudrillard (1976).

It is in relation, moreover, to this disappearance of the body, this impossible symbolic exchange, that fashion photography must be evaluated. How does a fashion photographer capture the murderous fantasy that haunts today's market economy? How does he conceptualize his photography in relation to the cannibalism of representation that he unleashes and actualizes? Can he resist this process of destruction? Or, more precisely, where does he take it? Can he divert its course? Can he take it down a path other than that programmed by the material, capitalistic, market forces that paradoxically provide him with his means of action, his photographic act? Questions such as these ought to enable us to construct a micro-genealogy of the fashion photo, a typology of fashion photography, and a preliminary evaluation of photographers. To borrow the terms of Kacem's analysis, which goes beyond that of Baudrillard, how can a "phenomenology of this impossible exchange" be achieved photographically? Because, paradoxically, such a thing is possible.

3. THE GLAMOUR STAGE OF THE INTEGRATED SPECTACLE

It is perhaps necessary to step back a bit in order to see how strictly commercial fashion photography fits into Guy Debord's theory of the "society of the spectacle."

Commercial fashion photography undeniably participates in the realm of the spectacle, not because it directly sells a stylish product (as advertising does) but because it endows that product with a supplementary "image." In other words, it adds value to the product, confers on it a "soulful supplement," an artistic interpretation. To be sure, this distinction is losing its pertinence today, as advertising has become so subject to the influence of photography that in some cases it is nothing other than fashion photography in its pure form. It is clear to everyone that commercial fashion photography is the most aesthetically advanced form of the social relations of the spectacle in the service of capitalist domination.

Extending Debord's analysis of the spectacle, Giorgio Agamben derived the concept of "unremarkable singularity" from his study of advertising to the DIM brand of stockings in France in the 1960s. Here, the figure of the human body was freed from its theological underpinnings and presented as "neither generic nor individual, neither an image of divinity nor an image of animality: the body has become unremarkable" (Agamben 1990). The unremarkable singularity of the model in the ad is unremarkable in the sense that it is "a resemblance without an archetype, that is, an idea." The fashion photograph captures neither the uniqueness of an individual (like the portraits of Wolfgang Tillmans and Thomas Ruff, for example) nor the generic quality of social identity characteristic of the use of photography in contemporary art (Beat Streuli or Andreas Gursky, for example).

This observation, while plausible, is ideological in nature. It flattens all fashion images into a single image (the coded, stereotyped commercial photograph). It also turns fashion photography into a separate continent (of alienation, loss of identity, the impossibility of experience) wherein postmodern man is driven to surrender, emptiness, boredom, and death by the power of the integrated spectacle. It would be stupid, however, not to acknowledge that the vast majority of commercial fashion photographs extend and reinforce the deadening effects of advertising, pornography, and the media in general.

But this Agamben-inspired indictment of fashion photography leads nowhere but to hatred of all images and rejection of the world as it is, to a radical but sterile critique of Empire and bio-power (of which fashion photography constitutes the most advanced aesthetic vocabulary)—unless we take Agamben (1990) at his word when he says that "the spectacle still contains something in the nature of a positive possibility, which can be turned against it."

4. TURNING FASHION PHOTOGRAPHY AGAINST ITSELF

One has to begin with particular photographers who exemplify the belief that, in the realm of appearances, the world need not be regarded as a place dedicated to death and the loss of all possibility of experience, that in fact such dispossession may be regarded as a starting point from which we must begin to reconstruct everything. The prerequisite for this is a certain minimal reflectiveness about the medium of photography. The aim is to identify those fashion photographers and magazines that resist the dissociative trend (that is, the tendency to regard glamour as a world apart) and are sufficiently aware of the vampiric nature of their medium to use it in a bio-aesthetic and not bio-political way (here I am using "bio-political" to refer to the spectacular domination of the body in the industrial world). Mehdi Belhaj Kacem (2001) defines the bio-aesthetic paradigm that has the potential to transform any noncommercial fashion photograph into a conscious poetic form of subjective resistance in the following terms: "In the world of impossible experience, where the ersatz of creation is nothing but the formal transcription of non-experience, all experience becomes, must be, will be, is a form of creation, an artistic poesis, an aesthetic work, a resolute elaboration." This is what is at stake in fashion photography that is the exception to the rule. And to be an exception is to want life and not death and the destruction of all experience, knowing that the medium (the fashion photograph) is, paradoxically, the vampiric language of the forces from which one must sooner or later sever oneself.

This is the heart of the matter. How can fashion photography get behind the glorious mask of the spectacular body to restore the fragile, singular human body in its precarious existence and refusal to be dispossessed, isolated, and subjected to the alienation of the market? What kind of fashion photography can accomplish this? The search, moreover, is not limited to the world of appearances or to the magazines themselves. The German philosopher Peter Sloterdijk is categorical on this point: "The will to artificiality takes precedence over the propensity to conform to a definite nature or a normative Antiquity." Furthermore, "This explains why, in the most intellectually advanced core of modernity, only inventors, artists, and entrepreneurs are still able to play a key role" (Sloterdijk 2000). We are definitively condemned to an exodus out of being and into the world of appearances. Artists and fashion photographers cannot turn the clock back, even if certain nostalgic and academic forms of photography can still be appealing (Paolo Roversi, for example). Yet there is a real danger of a return of fascism, a violent return of the repressed in the form of religious tradition, in large parts of the globe. In this respect, fashion photographers are children of nothingness and catastrophe. Here, too, the clock cannot be turned back. "The aesthetic and theory of technology, placed under the auspices of Being, always and necessarily lead to more or less explicit denunciations of the world of appearances, as an extended sphere of no use to an older and worthier reality" (Sloterdijk 2000).

For our generation, caught in the middle of this contradiction, the question arises daily: Must we go along with capitalism toward extension of the spectacle, toward ever greater glamorization and consumption? Or should we turn back, stop the movement, oppose it with violence or metaphysical protest, or resist, isolate ourselves, disappear, and leave the fight to others in the hope that we may escape, safe and sound, before everything becomes permanently polluted, factitious, artificial, reconstructed, fake, etc.?

For, in the realm of appearances, and especially in fashion photography, nothing can be accepted or deplored; everything remains to be done. It is up to us, acting independently, experimentally, and tentatively, to create journals and magazines (such as *Purple,* for example, but also *Dazed and Confused, i–D*, and others) to provide fashion photography with new possibilities for expression. The goal should be to produce fashion photography that does not reproduce the rules of spectacular domination but is, once again, an exception to those rules. In this sense, a fashion photography liberated from itself, a "bio-aesthetic" photography in Kacem's sense, can be seen as an attempt to reappropriate the separate sphere of synthetic images. This would be a fashion photography detached from the illusory, alienated world of consumerist glamour, which asks no questions as it accompanies subjectivity on its way to death, vitrification, and disappearance.

For instance, Anders Edström's fashion photographs are simple, affectless images of individuals close to him, shot without makeup or pointless artifice. They capture an instant, a fragile, all but imperceptible moment of life but in a way that allows existence to permeate the image. Banu Cennetoglu's fashion photography avoids using landscape and architecture as empty, purely plastic backdrops. It restores their concrete particularity and vital force, transforming them into a territory that coexists with his work. Similarly, Laetitia Benat's light, subtle photographs portray relations among models in a way that demonstrates genuine closeness with her subjects. There are no rules,

only exceptions. These are photographers who are trying to resist the models imposed on them by the magazines for exhibiting the body and the other. And beyond the magazines is a whole system of dependence on ad buyers, established codes, and the logic of the marketplace. The point is not to produce "beautiful" images, since beauty, purity, and aesthetics are precisely the rule in fashion photography. Nor is the point to produce antifashion: to accentuate truth, the naturalism of the situation, and the pseudo-integrity of relationships (which are merely one more photographic effect). A fashion photograph can be a vital form of resistance to subjective destruction if it manages to transform the vampirism inherent in all representation into a form of coexistence, of shared, inspirational, communicable existence, if its devouring of signs and images is used in the service of an intensely subjective, poetic, biological experience. These resources are not decorative effects, moreover, owing to the way in which they are photographed. For example, Mark Borthwick shoots models in frontal poses, but each pose is the site of a real presence of the individual being photographed. Such poses are subjective intensities.

One could multiply examples. They would nevertheless represent only a small part of the output of a visual industry that aims to achieve formal aestheticization and alienating desubjectification, deadening disembodiment, for the purpose of dominating bodies, controlling them, cloning them, and subjecting them to a slow but programmed death defined by a matrix of signs whose power is constantly being extended.

34

ANDREW BOLTON

Viktor & Rolf

From A. Bolton (2005), "Viktor & Rolf" in Cooper-Hewitt National Design Journal 2: 16–17. Reprinted with permission.

As if to put an end to the "art or fashion?" debate that has dogged their career trajectory, Dutch designers Viktor Horsting and Rolf Snoeren have asserted unequivocally, "We have always seen ourselves as fashion designers, even when we showed our work in museums and galleries. At those occasions, our work was about fashion" ("Viktor & Rolf: Self-Portrait" 2004: 280). Since they presented their first collection at the Salon Européen des Jeunes Stylistes in Hyères, France, in 1993, Viktor & Rolf have staged a number of "fashion" installations in a variety of "art" galleries, including *Winter of Love* at le Musée d'Art Moderne, Paris, in 1994, and *Designer's Dream* at the Torch Gallery, Amsterdam, in 1996. As well as being the subject of two major exhibitions, at the Groninger Museum (2000) and le Musée de la Mode et du Textile (2004), they guest-curated the exhibition "Fashion Colors: Viktor & Rolf & KCI" at the National Museum of Modern Art, Kyoto, and the Mori Art Museum, Tokyo, in 2004. In presenting their work in art galleries and museums, Viktor & Rolf strive to equate, or at least reconcile, art and fashion by emphasizing fashion's centrality to modern culture.

Although Viktor & Rolf believe that art and fashion share a similar impulse to reform our aesthetic perceptions, they understand that fashion is irrevocably commercial. As the journalist Amy Spindler has noted, "Commercial success is part of their underlying art project" (2000: 11). However, Viktor & Rolf's design philosophy is characterized by playful, knowing meditation on the "art or fashion?" conundrum. This meditation began with their debut collection, which introduced several features that have remained consistent in their work—layering, exaggerated silhouettes, and the replication of clothing elements. The designs, which were made from fragments of existing garments, were never intended to go into production, but rather were meant to function as a showcase for the designers' creative impulses. Such designs established Viktor & Rolf's reputation for stylistic as well as conceptual experimentation, a reputation that was reinforced by their radical and poetical haute couture presentations. Their first haute couture collection (spring/summer 1998), an analysis of components and composition of the couture, mixed statuary with the kinetic dynamism of the runway. Models walked out into the room as if on a catwalk, but then mounted a pedestal. In a protest of what the designers considered an unmerited emphasis on accessories in the fashion industry, a model in a white silk dress took off her hat and necklace, made of porcelain, and threw them on the floor, where they lay in fragments.

Defined by their theatricality and noninstrumentality, such elaborate showpieces figured prominently in Viktor & Rolf's haute couture collections. Their third couture collection (spring/summer 1999), which was made up entirely of showpieces, was an inventory of the

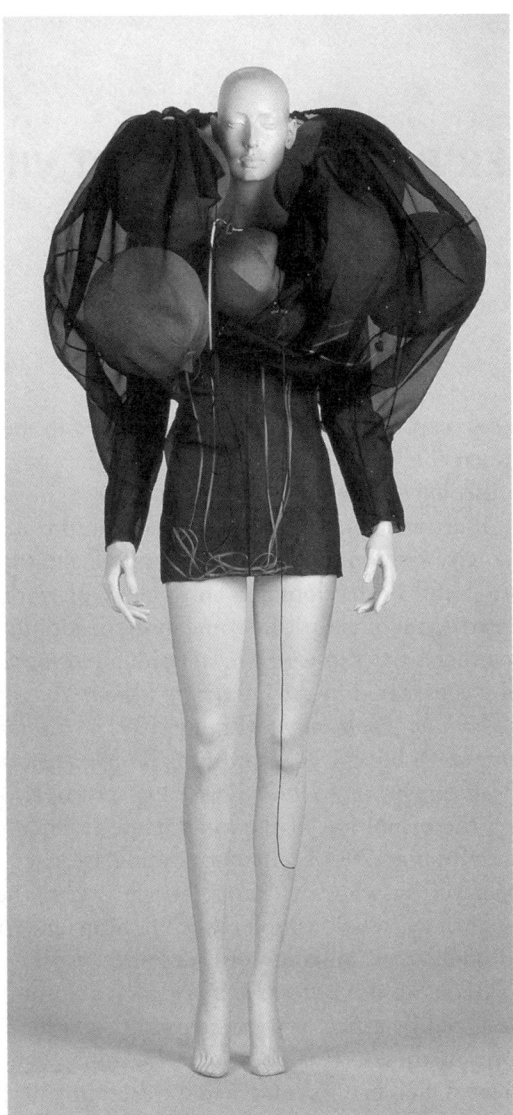

Figure 62. "Balloons" dress, Viktor & Rolf, The Netherlands, 1998. Silk organza, silk taffeta. Collection of the Groninger Museum.

details on which Viktor & Rolf had been working since the start of their career—bows, frills, ruffles, and ribbons. As the cultural historian Caroline Evans points out, "They intended it to be their last spectral collection before they launched themselves in the real world of embodied fashion and commerce, making clothes to go into production to be sold in the shops" (2003: 43). A year later, Viktor & Rolf presented their first prêt-à-porter collection (autumn/winter 2000–2001). Acknowledging their anxiety about how their move from the edge to the center of mass production might be received by their detractors, Viktor & Rolf dedicated the collection, which used stars-and-stripes-patterned material, to the "art of the commercial sellout." Typical of their ironic approach to fashion, an approach that combines cynicism with optimism, the collection, while more commercial, was no less conceptual than their one-off couture creations.

Viktor & Rolf have managed to expand the repertoire of fashion through their conviction that art and fashion share similar motivations and aspirations. As the dress historian Richard Martin has argued, "The underlying principle of consonance among the visual arts is evident in the work of Viktor & Rolf. In their pursuit in concept and practice, this creative team make us believe, as they do, in an art without embarrassing hierarchies or demeaning classification, but filled with contemporary visuality" (R. Martin 1999: 111). For Viktor & Rolf, art and fashion are united by their openness and magnanimity, a unison that not only explains the duo's appeal to both art and fashion curators, but one that questions the very relevance of the "art or fashion?" opposition.

ANNOTATED GUIDE TO FURTHER READING FOR PART VII

Art/fashion historians have explored the depiction of fashion in art over the last thirty years, creating a rich body of literature. Anne Hollander's pioneering work *Seeing Through Clothes* (1978) investigates pictorial art as it represents the human image, clothed and unclothed; she demonstrates how clothes in art have contributed to idealized visualizations of the human body. In *Sex and Suits* (1994), Hollander proposes the suit as an emblem of modernity. Aileen Ribeiro's many books and articles on fashion in art— ranging from *The Art of Dress: Fashion in England and France 1750 to 1820* to *Ingres in Fashion: Representations of Dress and Appearance in Ingres's Images of Women*—look at how artists depicted fashion in paintings. This sometimes complicated subject is explored in *Dress* 29 (2002), which includes papers selected from "Conversations About Costume and the Visual Arts," a conference at Winterthur Museum in 2001. Alice Mackrell's *Art and Fashion* provides a survey of art history and fashion history in modern times.

An interesting study on a single painting that has inspired fashion designers is Deborah Davis's *Strapless: John Singer Sargent and the Fall of Madame X* (see Figure 59).

The late Richard Martin, trained as an art historian, presented fashion as art in numerous exhibitions at the Fashion Institute of Technology (FIT), and later at the Metropolitan Museum of Art in the 1980s and 1990s. Catalogs authored by Martin, sometimes in collaboration with Harold Koda, accompanied the exhibitions, such as *Fashion and Surrealism* (1987). Fiona Anderson's

essay explores the symbiotic relationship between the "new" fashion history and the "new" museology (2000).

Illustrated books on individual couture designers, fashion photographers and illustrators are useful in developing a chronology of works created, but offer little interpretation. In addition to other articles in *Chic Clicks*, fashion photography is explored in *The Idealizing Vision: The Art of Fashion Photography* (Erving 1991), *Fashion Spreads* (Jobling 1999), and *Fashioning Fiction in Photography Since 1990*, the catalog accompanying the exhibition of the same name (Kismaric and Respini 2004). An outstanding treatise is Nancy Troy's *Couture Culture*, which goes to the heart of the relationship between fashion and art through an examination of Paul Poiret's work.

Radu Stern's *Against Fashion* explores clothing designed by artists as a counterpoint to fashion. One of these artists was Sonia Delaunay, who created her first "simultaneous" dress in 1913 (Albritton 2005). The first definitive book on the art-to-wear movement was Julie Schafler Dale's *Art to Wear* (1986).

Fashion and architecture, a recent area of scholarly inquiry, has been investigated by Hanisch (2006), Pawley (2000), Quinn (2003) and Wigley (1995). The fashion show as performance art has been explored by Alix Browne (2001), and by Ginger Gregg Duggan, Caroline Evans and others in a special issue of *Fashion Theory* (2001).

For a critical analysis of fashion aesthetics, see Sung Bok Kim's article in *Fashion Theory*, "Is Fashion Art?"

PART VIII

*F*ashion in the Media

LINDA WELTERS

Introduction

Of the many options presented by the fashion industry, some styles take off while others go unnoticed. The role the media plays in introducing fashion to the consumer is explored in this section. The media's influence on fashion consumption can be divided into two categories: the first is media used by the fashion business to promote fashion to consumers (e.g., magazines, Internet style websites and television style shows); the second is media in which certain people capture the imagination of the public, whose signature styles are then appropriated by the fashion business and repackaged for consumers.

MEDIA USED BY THE FASHION BUSINESS

Magazines are a vital part of the fashion industry. Most fashion magazines are published by large corporations. Condé Nast, the major player, publishes *Vogue*, one of the world's leading women's fashion magazines. Editions are published in America, the United Kingdom, France, Italy, Brazil, Australia, China, and soon India. The parent organization also owns *Teen Vogue*, *Vogue Man*, *Lucky*, *GQ* and *Glamour*. Hearst Publications is Condé Nast's main competitor with *Harper's Bazaar*, *Cosmopolitan*, *Esquire* and *Seventeen*. French publications include *L'Officiel*, *Elle* and *Marie Claire*. Since the 1980s, alternative magazines such as *i-D* and *Wallpaper** have grown in importance.

Fashion magazines are owned by publishing houses, which ultimately control the direction of the publication. Each magazine has its own editorial staff, who select clothes by specific designers/brands for its features. Editors can make or break a designer by featuring (or ignoring) his or her work in the magazine. The editor-in-chief is enormously influential in interpreting the direction of fashion for the consumer. Legendary women in fashion journalism are Edna Woolman Chase, Carmel Snow, Diana Vreeland and Anna Wintour. Carmel Snow, for example, championed Balenciaga in the pages of *Harper's Bazaar*; currently *Vogue* showcases talented young American designers through an annual contest launched in 2003. It is called the Council of Fashion Designers of America (CFDA)/Vogue Fashion Fund Award and supports the creative and business development of emerging designers. The editorial team contracts the photographers and models. Whereas fashion photographers, most of whom are male, enjoy long careers, models are not so fortunate. Models are the public face of fashion; taste in models changes rapidly as fashion constantly searches for the new. The popularity of childlike models in the late 1960s was eclipsed by healthy, natural types in the early 1970s; the faces of supermodels graced magazine covers in the 1990s, but were replaced by actresses in the new millennium. Models have generated controversy in recent years. Critics claim that the tall, willowy bodies of models set unrealistic expectations for personal appearance among young women, resulting in cases of bulimia and anorexia.

A majority of the pages in any fashion magazine are paid advertising rather than editorial content. Magazines earn their profit through advertising, not subscriptions. Advertisements take up a great number of pages in the average fashion magazine; it is important for designers, manufacturers and retailers to get the right message across to consumers through choice of model and photographer. Advertising can draw lots of attention to a name. Presentation of fashion in a shocking manner is often successful because of the publicity it generates. Consider Calvin Klein's provocative advertising for such basic items as jeans and cotton briefs. Many magazine subscribers cannot afford to buy the clothes they see in the magazines; but by purchasing a magazine like *Vogue* or *Harper's Bazaar*, they are participating in fashion. This is particularly true in developing countries such as China, where young people spend approximately $2.50 for a single fashion magazine (Wu 2006). This is a considerable sum in a country where only 18 percent of the population is considered middle class; to be designated as middle class in China, one must earn the equivalent of $602 per month (Rothrock 2006).

Fashion found another media outlet in 1980 when CNN television featured a program called *Style with Elsa Klensch*, which was devoted to fashion, decorating and beauty. Elsa reported Monday through Friday from the world's fashion capitals, with a special show on Saturday morning. Since the 1990s, fashion information has been available quickly on the web. Fashion-Zines from all over the world are available with the click of a mouse (<www.fashionangel.com>). Now podcasts are available on MP3 players, PDAs and cell phones. At no time in history has the consumer been so bombarded with fashion news. This proliferation of fashion information has made it difficult to determine where fashion is headed. Hence, we are experiencing a growth in interest in what fashion leaders are wearing.

MEDIA THAT INFLUENCE FASHION

Fashion leadership is presented to consumers in various media: newspapers, magazines, television and the Internet. Although thousands of faces come to the public's attention every year, only a few personalities have the components to set fashion trends. What are these components? First, the individual must be in the public eye and have the opportunity to be photographed. Second, the person must be attractive and embody characteristics that the public admires. Third, he or she must have the time and money to follow fashion. The fashion look need not be cutting-edge fashion, but it must be stylish.

Given these prerequisites, those who have the potential to set fashion trends include royalty, politicians, socialites and entertainers. Diana, the Princess of Wales, inspired many a bride to wear puff-sleeved gowns like the one she wore for her marriage to Prince Charles in 1981 (Emanuel 2006). Jacqueline Kennedy, the wife of US President John F. Kennedy, inspired a generation of American women to wear bouffant hairdos and pillbox hats. Kathleen Craughwell-Varda's extract explains Jackie's evolvement into a legendary fashion icon. Sports figures, such as former National Basketball Association star Michael Jordan, earned the admiration of fans who wanted to wear the "Air Jordans" manufactured by Nike. Movie stars have produced scores of legendary images, from Rudolf Valentino in *The Sheik* (1921) to John Travolta in *Saturday Night Fever* (1977). Marlene Dietrich has been an enduring icon of androgynous chic during and after her years as an actress. Sybil DelGaudio's work analyzes Dietrich's costumes in the movie *Morocco* (1930). Television is a later entry to the style influence game, but it came into its own in the 1980s with shows such as *Dallas*, *Dynasty* and *Miami Vice* (Cunningham 2003). More recent series such as *Absolutely Fabulous!*, *Sex and the City* and *Project Runway* appeal to viewers interested in fashion. The fashion adventures of Carrie Bradshaw and friends from *Sex and the City* are discussed in Anna König's extract.

The music industry has long had a symbiotic relationship with fashion. Black and Latino performers have been especially influential in setting trends, as role models for minority races are lacking in other media. Jazz musicians and performers who influenced fashion include Josephine Baker, who took Paris by storm in the 1920s, and Dizzy Gillespie, who inspired fans to wear sunglasses and berets in the 1940s. Since the 1960s, rock stars have inspired youth styles; this influence increased after the introduction of Music Television (MTV) in 1980, enabling millions to see what their favorite musicians were wearing in music videos. Music subcultures emerged with their own appearance codes. Punk, grunge and rap each began as new music genres with distinctive clothes, shoes, hairstyles and makeup that eventually influenced mainstream fashion. The reading by Daniel Wojcik examines the punk phenomenon.

Museums began connecting to fashion when Diana Vreeland, former editor of *Vogue*, guest-curated costume exhibitions at the Metropolitan Museum of Art's Costume Institute in the 1970s. By the 1980s, the influence of these exhibitions on the business of fashion became apparent. Bloomingdale's, a fashion-forward Manhattan department store, tied promotional themes to the Costume Institute's annual exhibits, as discussed in the extract by Debora Silverman. Often fashion businesses sponsor the exhibits. For example, Burberry sponsored "AngloMania: Tradition and Transgression in British Fashion" in 2006. The opening galas for these exhibitions have become New York's "party of the year," featuring designers, models, socialites, actresses and benefactors dressed to complement the exhibition's theme. The partygoers' attire is reported in the media, in a never-ending cycle of fashion-watching.

In the United States, no show is as closely watched for the glamour and style it exudes as the Oscars. What the stars are wearing is reported in newspapers, on television and on the Internet. Nominated actresses are gifted gowns by leading designers and lent diamond necklaces and earrings by the world's most famous jewelers. (The designers write off the costs as advertising.) With their stylists, the actresses select a look to make them stand out from the dozens of other actresses and celebrities at such events. The gowns that receive the best press are knocked off and in stores within days. The public's enthusiasm for news about what the stars are wearing has spread to other awards shows: the Golden Globes, the Grammies, the People's Choice Awards, the Country Music Awards, and so on. Now the simple phrase "red carpet" signifies this type of style-watching, which has become a form of entertainment in itself. Everyone can have an opinion of who's hot and who's not, regardless of whether or not they wear much more than jeans and sweatshirts themselves.

35

CHRISTOPHER BREWARD

Fashion on the Page

From C. Breward (2003), **Fashion** *(Oxford: Oxford University Press), 122–9.*
Reprinted by permission of Oxford University Press.

Though never a straightforward representation of real garments, the published fashion image during the first 200 years of its evolution was clearly primarily intended to function as a fairly reliable record of the coming mode. This role was subtly redefined in the twentieth century both by the growing importance of photography as the magazine's medium of choice (and a concurrent valorization of the photographer, the art director, and latterly the stylist as influential *auteurs*) and an increasing emphasis in the fashion industry on the imaginative potential of "lifestyle" and "art" as promotional tools in which the magazine came to play a central role. The growing autonomy of the fashion press and the dissolution of a singular Parisian fashionable lead gave rise to a modern visual language of fashion that valued symbolism over materiality and surrendered the fashion illustration over to the creative realm of "the dream." In this sense mass-reproduced fashion imagery can no longer be read as a direct commentary (if ever it really could) on the political economy of style as it is manufactured and worn (Crowley and Jobling 1996).

No other publication has been so closely associated with the visible effects of this shift as *Vogue.* Launched in the United States in 1892 as an elite society journal, it reoriented itself toward the world of high fashion in 1909 under the ownership of Thomas Condé Nast and the editorship of Edna Woolman [Chase]. British, French, and Italian editions were launched in 1916, 1920, and 1950 respectively This significantly underpinned the modern idea of fashion as a global phenomenon and pushed the products of its advertisers to a market much broader than those on America's social register who could actually afford the gowns described in its editorial content. More important than its international reach and increasingly formidable sales profile was the strength of its aesthetic direction. *Vogue* capitalized on design innovations introduced in the production of European art magazines at the turn of the century, repackaging the fashion magazine as a desirable object in its own right, a harmonious and authoritative style guide that functioned as a bible for the fashion-conscious. Setting his horizons beyond the more parochial concerns of the old-style woman's magazine, Condé Nast looked to the philosophical and moral ideals of high modernism as a means of energizing the pages of his journal. During the first thirty years of *Vogue's* existence photographers including Edward Steichen, George Hoyningen-Huene, Lee Miller, and Horst P. Horst incorporated the techniques of Surrealism in the creation of images which abstracted and fetishized the surfaces of fashionable life. Their work offered a luminous framework through which the reader might negotiate a more complex relationship between clothing, identity, image, and desire than that allowed by the more literal registers of the descriptive fashion plate.

This is not to suggest that the graphic tools of drawing and lithography immediately declined. Following Poiret's encouragement of artists such as Paul Iribe, illustrators such as Erté and Barbier pioneered a luxurious style of fashion illustration in the 1910s and 1920s. This took its references from the theater and the rarefied world of the decorative arts (drawing imaginative connections between interiors, furniture, costumes, and bodies in an idealized representation of fashionable life as a totalizing art form) and found an apposite home in the pages of *Vogue* and the *Gazette du Bon Ton*. Though the impact of illustration on the magazine lessened from the 1930s to the 1970s, notable painters including Dalí, Cocteau, de Chirico, and Bérard, Botero, and Hockney made regular contributions. Indeed the fashion drawing has continued to thrive as a distinctive genre enjoying something of a renaissance in the late 1990s, when ironic homage was paid by a new generation of illustrators, working in magazines such as *Wallpaper**, to the imagery and mood of earlier decades.

In the postwar period American *Vogue* flourished under the art direction of Alexander Liberman. Its sparse and clean-cut layouts played host to the cool and attenuated photographic images of Irving Penn, Jerry Schatzberg, and William Klein whose appreciation of the formal qualities of Abstract Expressionist painting and its connections with jazz music and Afro-American culture engendered an electrifying synergy between the formal world of high fashion and the dissonant New York art scene. *Vogue* was not alone in pioneering this new vision. At *Harper's Bazaar*, the art director Alexey Brodovitch encouraged an emphasis on documentary techniques and an understanding of the fashion magazine as a kinetic, continuous sequence of textual and pictorial information which complemented photographer Richard Avedon's filmic approach to the recording of style (Triggs 1995). In Britain during the same period the self-important grandeur of the American publishing house (typified by the figure of famously terrifying editor Diana Vreeland and lampooned in the Hollywood musical *Funny Face*) was challenged by a more radical social and sexual agenda. In *Vogue* of the late 1950s and 1960s (as well as in new titles such as *Queen* and *Nova,* the Sunday color supplements, and nascent lifestyle journals such as *Man About Town* aimed at young urban men) working-class photographers including Terence Donovan and David Bailey worked alongside bohemian members of the aristocracy such as Anthony Armstrong-Jones and an older generation of urbane dandies like Cecil Beaton and Norman Parkinson in promoting a reconfigured representation of English style. This substituted the Parisian salon and the landscape of uptown Manhattan with a quirky London scene, inflected by ironic class stereotypes, seething with sexual possibilities, and bristling with an irreverent disdain for traditional expectations.

A tendency toward a sexual objectification of the body also surfaced in the output and personal myths of the new generation of photographers and models. Bailey, for example, maintained a relationship with the model Jean Shrimpton that clearly endowed his images of her with a palpable sexual frisson. Such permissiveness was at odds with the icy hauteur favored in the previous decade. The mature (often married) models of the 1950s had been replaced by much younger women whose childlike attractiveness necessarily held a shorter shelf-life than that enjoyed by their forebears. The charged and predatory atmosphere which arose was replicated in the fictional representation of the phallic photographer in the contemporary Antonioni film *Blow Up.* A relaxation of sexual mores was also magnified through the imagery published by *Vogue* and its competitors in the 1970s and 1980s. Its genealogy can be traced through Helmut Newton's darkly provocative scenes of suggested lesbianism and sadomasochism, the homoerotic celebration of the muscular male physique and the camp retro-stylization of the supermodel that characterized the glossy work of Herb Ritts, Steven Meisel, and Bruce Weber, and the supposed flirtations with drug culture, anorexia, and pedophilia ascribed by critics to the abject vision of early 1990s "new realist" photographers Corinne Day, Wolfgang Tillmans, and Juergen Teller. All signified the ever more complex networks established between the magazine, its (contracted) creative staff, its advertisers, shifting readership demographics, and a broader context in which the creators and audience for such images now engaged with a ubiquitous and indiscriminate popular culture where distinctions between art and pornography, commerce, and fashion were deliberately blurred (Rogers and Williams 1998).

The increasing engagement of fashion photography with the subcultural interests of the urban young and the gradual exposure of such genres in the pages of established titles like *Vogue* also point to the importance of the independent style magazine as a generator of innovative aesthetic commentaries on fashion culture in the late twentieth century. Beyond the distinctive high cultural rhetoric of *Vogue* and *Harper's Bazaar*, journal readers had always had recourse to more popular or niche-marketed titles which appeared to respond directly to their economic and social circumstances and their intimate aspirations. Suburban housewives, unmarried stenographers, shopworkers and adolescent schoolgirls in early twentieth-century Britain and America had access to a wide range of cheap magazines like *Mab's Weekly* and *Woman's Own* which offered dress patterns, beauty tips, movie star exposés, and scaled-down interpretations of the latest Paris look alongside the romantic serializations, problem pages, and cake recipes. However, it was not until the experimental publishing ventures of the 1960s that more discerning British readers were able to locate a challenging visual code that equated with desires not catered for by the conservative presses of Fleet Street. The embracing of consumer culture by a newly enriched teenage constituency, whose immediate concerns oriented around clothing and pop music, provided the context for fan magazines like *Fabulous* and *Rave* through which many trainee fashion photographers passed, honing their distinctive documentary or avant-garde styles. During the later years of the decade, countercultural publications such as *Oz* offered a forum for political iconoclasm and graphic experimentation

which, whilst not naturally disposed towards the commercial concerns of the fashion business, nevertheless pioneered a space in which the nature and representation of popular culture could be contested and legitimated (Sabin 1996).

Table 1 Significant Fashion Magazines

Launch	Title
1798	The Lady's Monthly Museum
1806	La Belle Assemblée
1830	Godey's Lady's Book
1852	The Englishwoman's Domestic Magazine
1861	The Queen
1867	Harper's Bazaar
1873	The Delineator
1875	Myra's Journal of Dress and Fashion
1876	McCall's
1886	Woman's World
1890	Woman
1892	Vogue
1894	Woman's Own
1913	Vanity Fair
1931	Apparel Arts—later GQ
1931	Esquire
1939	Glamour
1945	Elle
1945	Ebony
1949	Modern Bride
1953	Playboy
1963	Cosmopolitan
1970	Harper's & Queen
1980	i-D
1981	The Face
1986	Arena
1991	Dazed and Confused
1991	Visionnaire

It was from this blurring of mainstream and underground categories that the distinctive style journalism of the 1980s and 1990s emerged, particularly in London and other British cities. The intervening energies of punk fanzines fed into the hybrid concern with music, film, politics, dance, and fashion that characterized influential titles like *The Face*, *Blitz*, and *i-D*, all of which were founded around 1980 (recognizing the high number of male readers among the audience for such magazines, these were followed by a rash of men's style titles including *Arena*, *FHM*, *GQ* in the mid-1980s, and latterly the more reactionary *Loaded* and *Maxim*). In their pages the commodification of radical street styles whose genesis can be traced back to the late 1950s found its apotheosis and a kind of dead end in the concept of "lifestyle." Here the minutiae of subcultural dressing were recorded in the blankly anonymous, full-length street and club portraits which have become the trademark of the genre (taken up with gusto in Japanese style publications), or pastiched and bricolaged by photographer/stylists Nick Knight, Ray Petri, and Marc Lebon. Any residue of authentic social allegiances as expressed through clothing was somehow lost in a celebration of the potential fluidity of fashion's surface signifiers. Thus at the height of this postmodernist and very Thatcherite practice during the late 1980s, a single spread in *The Face* might include borrowed references from New York rap culture, the traditional dress of Hasidic Jewish communities and the kitsch extravaganzas of Bollywood, combined with graphic layouts reminiscent of Russian constructivism (Hebdige 1988; Jobling 1999).

At the time of writing, this play with the autonomous social and aesthetic references of the fashion photograph has found a home inside the covers of independent titles such as *Dazed and Confused*, or the avant-garde showcases *Purple* and *Visionnaire* (two titles produced for and by fashion industry creatives). Such a development implies an apparent divorce from those traditional assumptions regarding the relationship of style and commerce, dress, and body which governed the production of images in the heyday of postwar *Vogue*. Now the gritty "hyper-real" contemporary fashion image, as purveyed by Elaine Constantine, Robert Wyatt, or Hannah Starkey is much more likely to critique and question the industry which supports it; to the extent that the pictorial rendering of desire for fashionable clothing takes second place to an exploration of the alienation and neuroses that inevitably attend the purchase and display of dress, but generally remain unspoken. While the fashion image has always operated as a benchmark of standards of taste and beauty, rarely has its message so challenged the very premise upon which fashion culture is built.

36

JENNIFER CRAIK

Supermodels and Super Bodies

From J. Craik (1994), **The Face of Fashion**
(London and New York: Routledge), 85–91.
Reproduced by permission of Taylor & Francis Books UK.

Whereas models had been an adjunct to the fashion industry, by the 1960s they were synonymous with it.[1] The status of modeling reached a zenith. Individual models became household names and international personalities. Twiggy, for example, was named "Woman of the Year" in 1966, an unthinkable occurrence previously. By the 1970s, models had become superstars, a trend that continued into the 1980s and 1990s. Supermodels were well-paid, high-profile, international jet-setters.

Their changing status was reflected in their earning power. American models earned about $25 a day in the 1940s. This had increased to $5,000 a day for a top model in the 1970s, and to between $15,000 and $25,000 a day by 1990. Highly successful models earned $250,000 a year, while about thirty earned $500,000, and a handful $2.5 million annually (Rudolph 1991: 72). Despite the potential earning power, most models have difficulty sustaining a regular income. Not only must potential models conform to criteria about their bodies, they must develop a distinctive trademark in their work. Crucial to the model is an updated portfolio of studio shots, "tear sheets" (from jobs they have done) plus a "head sheet" that includes vital statistics and rates. Modeling jobs are usually contracted through agencies that send out details of suitable models. Although models emphasize their individual attractions, they are usually chosen for jobs depending on whether they are "the right type" for the client and the clothes. Even top models endure "go-sees" and rejections (Hartman 1980: 64). The body becomes an all-consuming obsession for models and their coworkers. Models are judged on the "perfection" of their body, yet are considered unintelligent because of it. Lauren Hutton commented:

> I've met people who apparently felt that by virtue of being attractive, I was dumb. It's still a prevalent cliché. Unfortunately by being attractive, women can get what they want; they don't develop their personalities or sense of humor. But it's a stifling way to live. Who wants to just sit around and be vacuous? (quoted by Hartman 1980: 64)

Naomi Campbell has also described the frustration of being taken at "face value"—as being no more than her image as a model:

> Part of the problem is that people only take models at face value. In a way, what we do is like acting, except that we don't speak. Because we don't speak, we don't have anything to say. What we try to do is project all our emotion and personality through our faces, but that can be misconstrued. These pictures are poses, that is not what we are like in real life at all. We are women too; we have feelings. When you have a very visual job, your appearance is taken to be the most important thing about you. There is no defence. (quoted by L.-A. Jones 1992: 10)

Moreover, the ideal body changes and models can be displaced overnight should their "look" go out of fashion. [Jean] Shrimpton discovered on a shoot in Portugal that she was becoming a has-been when the other model, the Dutch-born Willie, was given the best clothes and more shots because she was younger and fresher. Shrimpton's reaction was one of powerlessness: "Even today I am not totally free of the sense of being a has-been" (Shrimpton 1990: 161). Modeling is a risky and transient business.

Each decade becomes associated with a particular image of femininity and of particular models who capture that look. Sometimes the look is associated with national images. Katie Ford of the Ford Agency identified German models with the 1960s, Italians with the 1970s, and English and Australians with the 1980s (Sheehan 1986: 64). These caricatures do not reflect the employment patterns in the industry as much as the encapsulation of successive idealized "looks." Even so, most of the successful models have conformed to Western stereotypes of beauty because "in every country, blond hair and blue eyes sell" (Rudolph 1991: 72). Although the majority of models are still white, the supermodels include some diverse looks and ethnicities. Even so, non-white models still experience ambivalence toward them within the industry. English-born black model Naomi Campbell suspected that many resented the fact that she has succeeded as a "black tulip" rather than a "typical English rose":

I should think that the people who really care about those things despise having me, a black tulip! Things are changing, of course, but will always be slow. Not a lot of ethnic girls—Hispanics, blacks, Japanese—do the endorsements, get awarded the big cosmetic contracts. We're good enough to model clothes, do the pictures, but that's it. (quoted by L.-A. Jones 1992: 10)

As the status of models has changed, so too has the profession. The dissolution of the distinction between runway and photographic models requires models who are flexible, have diverse skills and are more competitive. Successful models maintain a disciplined regime of body rituals to maximize their attributes, including constant dieting, exercise, massages, saunas, manicures and pedicures. At the Miss Venezuela Academy, which has produced four Miss Worlds, three Miss Universes and countless runners-up in the past decade, selected applicants are offered free aerobics training, diet advice, dental work, makeup applications, hairstyling, and "the latest range of cosmetic surgery"—a popular option (Perrottet 1993). "Getting the look" is one thing; keeping it is another. Elle MacPherson attributes her success to discipline—diet, exercise and punctuality—starting each day with 500 sit-ups and three liters of water (Lyons 1992: 12).

Despite, or perhaps because of, the enormous investment in their bodies, few models admit to being beautiful. Rather, they seem to be chronically dissatisfied with their looks. Even supermodel Cindy Crawford said: "It's hard doing a runway show. You're surrounded by forty of the most beautiful women in the world. You see all your own imperfections and none of theirs" (quoted by Rudolph 1991:74). Models separate their "professional" bodies from their "lived-in" ones, regarding them as alien. One fourteen-year-old model commented on her first photographs for *Elle:*

There was a lot of mucking around. You never really know how it's going to turn out. I was pleased with the pictures. But it's hard to relate them to being me. There's me at school and there's me in the magazine—they're completely different. (Safe 1990: 24)

Even top models are not immune from this sense of alienation and dissatisfaction. Although dubbed by *Time* magazine as "The Body of Our Time," Elle MacPherson has said:

I don't particularly like the way I look, to tell you the truth ... I often think I'm smarter than I look ... When you're trying to sell how beautiful you are and you don't think you're that beautiful, it's a bit scary. I have an image that's approachable to the public and it sells. That's great but it's different from being the most beautiful woman in the world. I know damn well what I see. (quoted by Wyndham 1990: 23–4)

The obsession with their looks breeds extreme insecurity. Shrimpton recalled:

> I was bored, and we must have been exceedingly boring to others. I found life trivial then, and looking back I do not understand why I stuck with it. We were so vain that we continued to dress ourselves up and go out to be looked at ... I was so insecure that I was always fiddling in the bathroom or running to the ladies to check my appearance. It was pathetic! Here I was, at the height of my fame, behaving like this. I was just an accessory. (Shrimpton 1990: 102)

Yet modeling continues to attract many young girls as a potentially glamorous and lucrative career. Many models are starting in their early teens. Photographers like them because they are still thin with perfect skin and clear eyes (Safe 1990: 26). Moreover, they are "fresh" and untrained in the conventional poses and gestures of experienced models. Their attraction is their youth and naivety. As Vivien Smith, of Vivien's Model Management, observed:

> They want a brand-new face so people will ask, "Who is this wonderful girl?" Another reason is that young girls don't have lines on their faces. They're like a fresh canvas and the makeup artists and photographers can create on them. (quoted by Safe 1990: 26)

The youth of up-and-coming models contrasts with the desire of the older top models to stay in the business. Ten years used to be considered the career span of a model. After that, they would get married or try to enter a related field, such as establishing their own agency, doing fashion design, photography or consultation, joining a public relations firm, or acting (Hartman 1980: 63). Increasingly, models are extending their modeling careers in other ways, through product endorsements, personalized calendars, and modeling for niche markets. The demand for older models (in their thirties and forties) has also

grown. At the age of forty, Lisa Taylor was reemployed by Calvin Klein, after she chided him for employing young models to promote clothes aimed at older women. The ploy was highly successful, reestablishing Taylor's career, selling Klein's clothes, and prompting public pressure to see more "role models of women when they're women, not children" (Sherrill 1992: 88). In other words, models are becoming career professionals.

Whereas models were at the beck and call of agents who discovered them, clients and designers who gave them work, stylists who decided on their look, and photographers who constructed their image, successful models have become tough negotiators. This shift in the power relations in the industry has created tensions between the old guard and the new "Cool Club" of supermodels. They have become hard-nosed businesswomen, demanding higher fees, and negotiating the conditions of their contracts. As advertising has become more competitive and international, the supermodels have become "one of the few reliable sales tools. Their beauty is a global ideal, as desirable in Tokyo as in Prague, Manila or Buenos Aires" (Rudolph 1991: 71). Equally, models are often better known than the designers of the clothes they wear, and attracting top models to show the seasonal collections has become an industry priority. According to Eileen Ford of the top New York agency, models are actively resisting being treated as "this cute plaything or this airhead" (*Mode,* September 1991: 72).

One of the most lucrative deals for models is an exclusive contract with a cosmetics or fashion designer or manufacturer, since it guarantees an income and exclusive work. It brought fame for Cindy Crawford (through Revlon), Paulina Porizkova (through Estée Lauder), Isabella Rossellini (Lancôme), and Claudia Schiffer (through Guess?). The contracts for these deals are comprehensive, detailing the responsibilities of the model to the employer. A contract between American designer Calvin Klein and model Jose Borain, to promote the perfume Obsession for a million dollars over three years, specified the following services:

all broadcast advertising, promotion and exploitation (e.g., network, local, cable and closed circuit television, AM and FM radio and cinema), print advertising, promotion and exploitation (e.g., printed hang-tags, labels, containers, packaging, display materials, sales brochures, covers, pictorial, editorial, corporate reports and all other types of promotional print material contained in the media including magazines, newspapers, periodicals and other publications of all kinds), including but not by way of limitation, fashion shows, runway modeling, retail store trunk shows, individual modeling and other areas of product promotion and exploitation which are or may be considered to be embraced within the concept of fashion modeling. (quoted by Faurschou 1987: 90)

For her part, Borain was required to maintain her "weight, hairstyle and color and all other features of ... physiognomy and physical appearance as they are now or in such other form as CK may, from time to time, reasonably request" (quoted by Faurschou 1987: 90). The contract also specified that her personal lifestyle should:

be appropriate and most suitable to project an image and persona that reflect the high standards and dignity of the trademark "Calvin Klein" and that do not diminish, impair or in any manner detract from the prestige and reputation of such trademark. (quoted by Faurschou 1987: 91)

The contract could not be terminated by Borain, but Calvin Klein could do so should Borain be disfigured, disabled, suffer illness or mental impairment; should she "come into disrepute or her public reputation [be] degraded or discredited." It could also be terminated on the death of Borain or bankruptcy of Klein (Faurschou 1987: 91). Thus, the contract specified precise bodily features as well as the personal attributes of the model deemed to reflect the qualities associated with the product. Product endorsement has also become an important sideline for Elle MacPherson. Launching her "Down-Underwear" line of lingerie for Bendon, she described herself as "a saleswoman": "As a model I sell products. I'm a very good saleswoman. It's very nice to have been

a consumer, to be a salesperson and now to be a creator and a ... realizateur" (Elle MacPherson, quoted by Wyndham 1990: 23).

Changes within the modeling profession have mirrored changes in the fashion industry as well as reflecting new ideas of femininity and ideals of the female body. Above all, modeling has placed a premium on particular constructions of beauty and female body shapes. Models currently epitomize the ideal female persona in Western culture, making top models highly desirable companions:

If you're an egomaniacal celebrity who doesn't consider the person on your arm to be a person rather than an accessory, what do you go for? You go for the accessory that is most sought after in that world. If what you are looking for is a good-looking woman, you naturally go looking in the modeling catalog. (*Mode* September 1991: 74)

Modeling epitomizes techniques of wearing the body by constructing the ideal technical body. Through those techniques, the body is produced according to criteria of beauty, gender, fashion and movements. These change as codes of prestigious imitation alter. The emphasis in modeling is on self-formation through the body to the exclusion of other attributes. As the model Moncur said: "It's an addiction, because you exist through others' eyes. When they stop looking at you, there's nothing left" (quoted by Rudolph 1991: 75). Models are trapped in their images. The increase in the use of male models suggests that the equation of femininity with appearance and bodily attributes has been a historical moment; constructions of masculinity are now undergoing a similar process of redefinition.

[...]

Techniques of masculinity are highlighting the body as the site of discipline, labor and reconstitution in the production of a social body that articulates the self and fits its cultural milieu, and where "the look" says it all.

EDITORS' NOTE

1. Earlier in the chapter from which this reading is extracted, Craik gives a short history of modeling. The use of models to display fashion designs commenced in the 1860s with haute couture. Initially modeling was not considered to be a reputable job. Gradually it was recognized as a profession in England and America with the advent of modeling agencies, although the pay was poor and conditions were unstable. Most girls modeled for a short time before "settling down." Finally in the 1950s, modeling became a major industry, developing into two branches: runway and photographic.

37

KATHLEEN CRAUGHWELL-VARDA

Jacqueline Kennedy Onassis

From K. Craughwell-Varda (1999), **Looking for Jackie: American Fashion Icons**
(New York: Hearst Books), 15–32. Reprinted with permission.

Jacqueline Kennedy Onassis had a sense of fashion that revolutionized the way women looked at clothes. Her confident style encouraged women to embrace the joy of wearing fine clothes and creating an elegant, aristocratic appearance. The formula was simple: tailored clothes with an air of simplicity, fabrics in flattering shades and patterns, accessories used to complement a look, and eye-catching details. Only Jackie's star quality could take such a simple formula and invest it with the power to alter permanently the direction of women's fashion.

[...]

Jacqueline Bouvier was still living at home with her mother and stepfather when she met Congressman John Fitzgerald Kennedy [aka "Jack"] at a dinner party in Georgetown in May of 1951. Even though guests thought they detected a mutual attraction between the two, nothing came of this initial meeting. Then, in 1952, they met again. This time, romance blossomed between Jackie and the recently elected US senator, and they were married on September 12, 1953, in Newport, Rhode Island. Although the bride and her family wanted a small affair, the groom's father, Joseph Kennedy, intervened. More than three thousand spectators watched as the 750 guests filed into the church for the nuptial mass. Afterward, 1,300 guests returned to Hammersmith Farm for an outdoor reception.

The Newport wedding would catapult the former Debutante of the Year from the society page to the front page around the world. For this momentous occasion, Jackie wanted to wear a sleek, modern gown, in keeping with the pared-down style she preferred for both day and evening, but Jack persuaded her to select something more traditional and old-fashioned.

The bride's mother hired Ann Lowe, an African-American dressmaker who catered to society women, to make her gown. An ivory silk taffeta was chosen to coordinate with an antique veil of rosepoint lace which both Jackie's mother and grandmother had worn. The gown had a portrait neckline with off-the-shoulder cap sleeves and a multitude of ruffles and tucks on the full skirt. Lowe had also been hired to make the bridesmaids' gowns: pale pink taffeta with wine-colored satin sashes.

[...]

Jacqueline Bouvier Kennedy married into one of America's wealthiest families, and she began to buy the clothes she had always longed to wear but had been unable to afford. With society friends reporting back to her on the latest styles in New York, Paris, and Rome, Jackie was soon spending as much as twenty thousand dollars a year on clothes. These exorbitant bills drove Jack to distraction, but her response was simple and seductively pragmatic: "I have to dress well,

Jack, so I won't embarrass you. As a public figure, you'd be humiliated if I was photographed in some saggy old housedress. Everyone would say your wife is a slob and refuse to vote for you." Indeed, Jackie's investment would soon yield a dividend that few—not even the shrewd Mrs. Kennedy herself—could clearly foresee. With Jack on his way to the nation's highest office, and with Jackie by his side, the tone was set: it would soon become de rigueur for the wives of public figures to pay meticulous attention to their attire and public image.

As the presidential election of 1960 drew near, John F. Kennedy's political advisers were wary of the effect his glamorous wife would have on voters. Jackie was not the average American homemaker, and many feared that her expensive clothes and aristocratic lifestyle would alienate America's burgeoning middle class. The opposite proved to be true. Jackie was young, fresh, and new—a welcome change from the typical politician's wife. After years of traditional hausfraus such as Bess Truman and Mamie Eisenhower, the public was ready for an exciting presence in the White House: crowd size doubled at campaign stops when Jackie was present. "It turned out that the voters loved her," noted campaign organizer Charles Peters. "She was perceived as the princess, and they basked in her glamour rather than being offended by it." Joseph Cerrell, who later became the executive director of the Democratic Party in California, recalled, "I remember her causing a considerable stir because it was the first time Californians had seen anybody sporting a hemline above the knee. Her glamour and her unconventional beauty attracted attention and enticed the news media, for whom the couple had become a symbol of youth and vitality—a new symbol of a New Age."

During the presidential campaign, Republicans turned Jackie's French couture clothes, and their price tags, into a campaign issue. Pat Nixon's "good Republican cloth coat" was held up as a mark of solidarity with the average American housewife. The attack backfired. Asked by reporters about her spending on clothes, Jackie responded, "That's dreadfully unfair. They're beginning to snipe at me about as often as they attack Jack on Catholicism. I'm sure I spend less than Mrs. Nixon on clothes. She gets hers at Elizabeth Arden, and nothing there costs less than two hundred or three hundred dollars." Apparently, Jackie's famous red cloth campaign coat was merely a copy of a Givenchy original and had been purchased at Ohrbach's department store. Despite Jackie's attempts to downplay her wardrobe, however, the following update appeared in *Women's Wear Daily* in September of 1960, just two months before the election: "Now it can be told—Mrs. John F. Kennedy, wife of the Democratic presidential candidate, has been diplomatically told that for political expediency—'No more Paris clothes, only American fashion.'"

In spite of the public hand-wringing over Jackie's cosmopolitan wardrobe, the Kennedy campaign was receiving strong support from clothing manufacturers and retailers across the country who anticipated the impact her clothes would have on the nation's consumers. *Women's Wear Daily* predicted that Jacqueline Kennedy would be "the most photogenic, fashion-conscious and chic occupant of the White House since Dolley Madison." Setting fears of a middle-class backlash aside, America's fashion industry was ready to gamble that Jackie's wardrobe would become a bellwether for the tastes of thousands of potential consumers.

Shortly after her husband's victory, Jackie gave birth to her son, John. During her recuperation she began to plan her White House wardrobe. Only thirty-one years old, Jacqueline Kennedy was the third-youngest First Lady in American history. As a President's wife and mother of two young children—three-year-old Caroline and newborn John—the pressures and responsibilities were enormous. Her first priority was maintaining a degree of normalcy in her family routine. She recognized the need for appropriate clothes and the importance her mode of dress would play in her husband's presidency. The elegant grandeur that would characterize the Kennedy administration was in fact carefully crafted. The Kennedys set out to represent the perfect American family, and photographers were hired to take meticulously arranged photographs of the first family at "informal" moments. While Jackie protested at this invasion of their privacy, the technique succeeded in establishing an unprecedented intimacy between the American public and the office of the President.

In what would become one of many relationships with leading figures of the fashion world, Jackie consulted with Diana Vreeland, then editor of *Harper's Bazaar* (and a formidable doyenne of style in her own right), on her White House wardrobe. As First Lady of the United States, Jackie knew that the politically expedient strategy would be to wear only American-manufactured clothing. As a disciple of French couture, she would of course have to redirect her fashion selections. In turning her focus to her own backyard, however, Jackie unwittingly brought attention to all that was beautiful and stylish in America, reinvigorating a nation's pride in its own rich tradition in the decorative arts. This attentiveness extended famously beyond the world of fashion and design to include the bohemian domain of the cultural elite: artists, writers, and dancers were invited into this new White House, the redecoration of which Jackie had carefully researched and overseen.

Designers from around the country sent letters and sketches, offering their services. Oleg Cassini, a descendant of Russian aristocracy who had designed clothes for many Hollywood celebrities, had been creating and selling his own line of fashions since the 1950s. Cassini was a friend of Jack Kennedy and his father, Joseph, and he sent a note to Jackie asking to be considered for selection as her personal designer. Cassini was allowed to meet with Jackie while she was still recuperating in the hospital after John's birth, and he brought with him several new designs created exclusively for her, including one for a gown for the inaugural ball. "I want you to be the most elegant woman in the world," Cassini told her. "I think that you should start from scratch with a look—a look that will set trends and not follow them."

Cassini's sales pitch worked (thanks in part to Joe Kennedy's offer to pay for all his daughter-in-law's clothes if she chose Cassini). The look the designer proposed was unlike his typical work and borrowed heavily from Givenchy. Together, Cassini and Jackie discussed the impact they wanted her clothes to have. Beneath that famous whispery voice was a woman with an iron will: Jackie knew exactly how she wanted to appear. Working closely with Cassini, she helped craft her image as the best-dressed woman in the world. No detail was too small to escape discussion, and together they scrutinized everything from color and cut to accessories. The style was to be simple, youthful, and elegant, the lines clean and uncluttered, setting off the First Lady's lithe figure. The look they created was the first purely American style to meet with enthusiastic acceptance on the international fashion scene, and it single-handedly boosted the US fashion industry's worldwide stature.

Soon after she appointed Cassini as her personal designer, Jackie sent him a letter outlining the wardrobe she would require:

What I need are dresses and coats for daytime, dresses suitable to wear to lunch. I don't know if you design coats, but I now see that will be one of my biggest problems, as every time one goes out of the house, one is photographed in the same coat.

Then for afternoon, cocktail dresses suitable for afternoon receptions and receiving lines—in other words, fairly covered up. Also, one or two silk coats to wear over them when I go out in the late afternoon. Any suggestions for accessories you have to wear would also be appreciated.

Then some pretty long evening dresses suitable for big official dinners. You know the kind I like: a covered-up look. Even though these clothes are for official life, please don't make them dressy as I'm sure I can continue to dress the way I like—simple and young clothes, as long as they are covered up for the occasion.

A fashion purist, Jackie insisted that all her dresses be originals and that any designs intended to be shown as part of Cassini's collection be altered from those of her exclusive commissions. She particularly wanted to avoid seeing "fat little women hopping around in [my] gown[s]."

A problem arose shortly after Cassini was hired. For the inaugural ball, Jackie had already ordered a gown of her own design from Ethel Frankau, the head designer of the fashion salon at Bergdorf Goodman. But Jackie adored the white satin gown Cassini had proposed when they first met. Jackie's solution was to wear Cassini's creation to the inauguration eve gala that was being orchestrated by Frank Sinatra, reserving the Bergdorf's gown for the balls on the night of the inauguration itself.

In the end, the outfit that truly announced the definitive "Jackie look" to the world was the Cassini dress and coat she wore to the inauguration ceremony on the Capitol steps. The ensemble was deliberately understated to highlight Jackie's youth and natural beauty. Cassini designed a fawn-colored wool coat with a sable collar and matching dress. Since every politician's wife would be huddled in furs, Jackie's outfit would create the perfect contrast. Diana Vreeland suggested that Jackie carry a matching sable muff. The now-legendary pillbox hat she wore that day was created by Halston, who was then the custom-design milliner at Bergdorf Goodman's renowned hat department (Jackie had been wearing Halston hats for years). The hat was inspired by a pillbox created by the Hollywood designer Adrian for Greta Garbo in the 1932 film *As You Desire Me*. Halston's version was purposely oversized to accommodate Jackie's bouffant hairstyle, which measured twenty-four inches in diameter when fully coiffed.

The hat was an immediate success. When asked later about its impact, Halston recalled that the day of the inauguration was cold and windy. Met with a gust of wind as she stepped from the limousine, Jackie grabbed her hat, putting a small dent in the crown. News photos picked up this image, and women and milliners began to put dents in their pillbox hats in imitation of the First Lady. Within a few weeks, the pillbox hat was the most popular style in the country. As an Ohrbach's buyer noted in April of 1961, "It's amazing how many women ask for the Kennedy hat. Even older women. They put the hat on the back of their heads, look in the mirror, and you can just see what's going through their minds. They're having the time of their lives seeing themselves as Jackie Kennedy. Naturally, we don't do anything to break the spell."

As First Lady, Jacqueline Kennedy's initial impact on American culture was unequivocally

Figure 63. Jacqueline Bouvier (Mrs. John F.) Kennedy, December 5, 1962, White House Diplomatic Reception Room. Robert Knudsen, White House/John Fitzgerald Kennedy Presidential Library and Museum, Boston.

in the realm of fashion. Women were immediately drawn to her chic, elegant appearance and began to emulate her. Clothing manufacturers responded to the demand by having copies of Jackie's clothes in stores within six weeks of their debut. She did not always originate fashions as First Lady, but she had the uncanny ability to detect a stylish trend just as it was emerging and put her stamp on it. Her less-is-more approach to dressing was a refreshing change from the typical fashions of the day. The "Jackie look" derived much of its popularity from its remarkable simplicity, and its components can be easily broken down:

The Shift Dress—Ranging from simple, sleeveless, knee-length linen frocks to more luxurious silk versions, usually with matching, unstructured jackets, the shift dress was a comfortable yet flattering garment that accentuated Jackie's regal posture and narrow hips. She favored boat necklines with bows or buttons as accents.

The Plain Cloth Coat—Sometimes fitted, sometimes cut to the fashionable A-line, Jackie's coats had youthful flair and interesting collars that drew attention to her face. Cassini's designs were made in solid colors, and were often unadorned except for oversized buttons and tassels in the same fabric.

The Pillbox Hat—This hat became a Jackie trademark and was reinterpreted by Manta O'Connor of Bergdorf Goodman's custom hat department in a variety of materials, including wool, silk, fur, and straw. Ironically, neither Jack nor Jackie was fond of hats, although most men and women in the 1950s and 1960s wore them in public. But the presidential couple realized that going hatless would have a negative impact on the millinery industry, and the pillbox and the other millinery creations that Jackie sported were worn to encourage the hat trade. While Jackie chose several flattering styles to wear in her official capacity, Jack elected to carry a hat rather than wear one. "Oh dear it was so pleasant when I didn't have to wear hats," Jackie once wrote to O'Connor. "They will pauperize me and I still feel absurd in them!"

The Bouffant Hairdo—The style that came to define the 1960s was created by Jackie's New York hairdresser, Kenneth Battelle, who soon became the most popular hairstylist in the country. He was flown down to the White House for special occasions. The rest of the time, maintaining Jackie's hairdo was left to her Washington hairdresser, whom she saw four times a week.

In addition to these basic signature components, Jackie also influenced the popularity of low-heeled pumps, one-shoulder evening gowns, tapered, slim-fitting pants, and English riding clothes. (Her sunglasses didn't appear until after her marriage to Aristotle Onassis in 1968, when she increasingly sought shelter from staring eyes.)

Jackie Kennedy's overall impact on the American popular imagination was enormous. A 1960 article in *Life* magazine said. "Fashion ads twinkle more mischievously with Jackie's unmistakable wide eyes. Her bouffant hairdo is becoming a by-word in beauty salons. All in all, the shy, beautiful First Lady's fashion followers are building up quite a bandwagon ... Despite herself, she is becoming the nation's #1 fashion influence." Her image was commercially exploited, too.

A Danish firm introduced Jackie mannequins. There were Jackie dolls and cutouts, and her face appeared on a host of kitschy items, including hot plates and planters. A Jackie look-alike opened *The Jack Benny Program* in 1962; the character Jackie Kennelrock soon appeared on *The Flintstones;* and in 1961, Miss America expressed a desire to "be more like Jackie." During her first year in the White House, Jackie received between six thousand and nine thousand fan letters a week, many from young girls.

Jackie's worldwide appeal became further apparent when the Kennedys went to Canada for their first official state visit in May of 1961. Jack Kennedy saw his wife in a new light as he witnessed her tremendous diplomatic skills and the easy manner with which she charmed foreign dignitaries and the public at large. The trip gave Jackie a needed boost of self-confidence, and it became increasingly obvious that she was a political asset to her husband and his administration on both the domestic and international scenes.

By the time the Kennedys made their state visit to France in 1961, Jackie was already hailed as an international sensation, but the ovation she received upon landing outstripped all expectations. More than a million Parisians lined the parade route, chanting "Jacqui! Jacqui!" as the Kennedys entered Paris. "From the moment of her smiling arrival at Orly Airport," *Time* magazine reported, "the radiant young First Lady was the Kennedy who really mattered."

The wardrobe Cassini created for the trip to France was designed with two objectives—to make Jackie look like a queen, and to prove that American fashion was the equal of French couture. It worked liked a charm. The normally taciturn Charles de Gaulle was completely enchanted with the First Lady, and the two spent a great deal of time discussing, in French, his country's history. As a courtesy to the French couture industry, Jackie wore a gown designed for her by Hubert de Givenchy to the state dinner given at Versailles in honor of the President and the First Lady.

Jackie's trip to Europe galvanized her international reputation as one of the world's best-dressed women. She regularly appeared on the covers of international magazines, including many published behind the Iron Curtain. Her projects to promote the arts and her spectacular restoration of the White House prompted Robert Frost to muse, "There have been some great wives in the White house—like Abigail Adams and Dolley Madison—so great you can't think of their husbands, Presidents, without thinking of them. It looks like we're having another one now."

The Kennedys were already making plans for their next four years in the White House when it all came to an abrupt end in Dallas in 1963. Amid the grainy footage, chaotic newsreels, and breathless sound bites that comprise our collective memory of that horrible day, Jackie's calm, iconic presence stands out. The image of the stunned widow in her pink wool suit, a copy of a Chanel original, is as familiar to us as that of the black limousine and the grassy knoll. For the next four days, her stoicism in the face of personal tragedy and national crisis would unite the country. Here was her chance to instill a sense of history as the living representative of her husband's presidency, and to leave an indelible impression on a generation. "Jacqueline Kennedy has today given her country the one thing it has always lacked, and that is majesty," a British journalist noted.

38

SYBIL DELGAUDIO

Dressing the Part: Sternberg, Dietrich, and Costume

From S. DelGaudio (1993), **Dressing the Part: Sternberg, Dietrich, and Costume** *(Teaneck: Fairleigh Dickinson University Press), 100–10.*

The notion of Sternberg's style as camp is extremely helpful in analyzing his use of costume.[1]

[...]

More generally, camp is about incongruity and irony (Babuscio 1977: 40). Incongruity works well in Sternberg's resistance strategy, since it is a notion that suggests the inappropriateness to which he was so attracted, an incompatibility that often took the form of extravagance and outrageousness. Additionally, incongruity serves as another expression of Sternberg's attention to the contrast between surface and underlying truth—a theme often expressed in costume signs throughout the Dietrich cycle.

[...]

For Sternberg, incongruity-as-camp surfaces in androgynous costume, i.e., cross-dressing, which occurs in *Blonde Venus*, *The Blue Angel*, *Dishonored,* and *The Scarlet Empress*. In *Morocco*, particularly, campy incongruity acts as a filmic second skin, a cloak that mystifies the audience and impedes realism. It is a structural principle for the film's narrative and thematic design, and a restatement of a favorite Sternberg theme. In highlighting difference, incongruity becomes another way of suggesting that things are not as they seem. Cross-dressing disguises one's sexual identity and presents an outer appearance that does not match the inner reality of one's sexual self.

Morocco begins in a typically exotic locale, foregrounding the idea of foreignness through costume and behavior. While military music and rhythms are heard on the soundtrack, the natives of the Moroccan city prepare to welcome their heroes. Dressed in the emblematic costume of the Arab, i.e., white burnouses, the natives prepare for the return of the foreign legionnaires, whose uniforms accommodate customary native dress in only one minor way: the caps (kepi) they wear contain a piece of fabric presumably added to protect them from sand and sun. Other than this minor detail, the soldiers are presented as foreigners, both in terms of their costume difference and in the way in which they are regarded and welcomed by the native men and women. The Foreign Legion itself has its own connotations of incongruity and dislocation, since it is an armed force comprised of European volunteers, many of whom have joined out of a sense of disconnection from their own society. Incongruity is further highlighted by Sternberg's introduction of the waiting women, some of whom lift their veils in a gesture of teasing accommodation and seduction. While the legionnaires are given orders about "behaving themselves" and "acting like gentlemen," Sternberg cuts to a shot of Arabs engaged in religious custom (kneeling and praying), again foregrounding incongruity and the difference between the two cultures. Legion-naire Tom Brown (Gary Cooper) flirts with an unveiled native woman, tossing a bracelet to her in a gesture that, for the first time, links the two cultures. Here, in the film's first scene, Sternberg has presented his major theme, i.e., incongruity, through a series of visual images that emphasize the central character's foreignness and dislocation, using costume to signify his concerns.

Morocco's second scene is concerned with an-other arrival, that of Amy Jolly (Marlene Diet-rich). As she emerges from the darkness of Lee Garmes's misty *mise-en-scène*, she is immediately noticed by La Bessiere (Adolphe Menjou), who offers his assistance and his business card. Like some of the native women in the previous scene, Amy also wears a veil (this one European, how-ever), but she does not lift hers, and the contrast to the earlier scene foregrounds her inaccessibil-ity. Her dark costume, in contrast to the light-er costumes of the Arab passengers on the ship on which she has arrived, conveys her foreign-ness. She is later described by the ship's captain as a "suicide passenger," a "one-way ticket" who never returns. She is also identified as a vaudeville actress, another of Sternberg's favorite professions (cf. *The Blue Angel, Blonde Venus, Macao),* since the performer acts as a vehicle for typical Stern-bergian tensions centered around impersonation and display. Both La Bessiere and Amy Jolly are travelers, foreigners in an exotic locale, and Stern-berg links them in this introduction. He will elab-orate on this comparison throughout the film, a comparison that will act as a thread for the con-tinuation of the theme of incongruity-as-camp. As Andrew Sarris has suggested, La Bessiere and Amy are analogues of each other and she is often presented, through their similar costumes, as a representation of the male who seeks to seduce her (Sarris 1966: 31). *Morocco's* next scene, the cabaret performance which introduces the for-eign Amy to a rather difficult audience comprised of both natives and Europeans, is the scene which unites all thematic and character elements of the two earlier scenes, as well as develops the notion of incongruity-as-camp through costume signs.

To advance the analogy between La Bessiere and Amy, Sternberg presents the French bach-elor in black-tie and tails. He makes the rounds throughout the cabaret, and, with great charm and civility, greets people he has not seen for a while. Later, Amy table-hops in much the same way, charming various members of the audience. For her first song, she wears a black tie, tails and top hat similar to La Bessiere's: sexual ambiguity is conveyed by both dress and behavior. Stern-berg is here using androgyny, characterized by cross-dressing, to convey campy incongruity through sexual masquerade. As Jack Babuscio states:

> To explain the relationship of Sternberg to camp it is necessary to return to the phenomenon of passing for straight. This strategy of survival in a hostile world has sensitized us to disguises, imper-sonation, the significance of surfaces, the need to project personality, the intensities of characters, etc. Sternberg's films—in particular the Dietrich films—are all camp insofar as they relate to those adjustment mechanisms of the gay sensibility. (1977: 50)

Babuscio's point is important in understand-ing Sternberg's attraction to sexual masquer-ade and disguise and in elaborating further on Sternberg's "ironic attitude toward his subject matter"(Babuscio 1977: 50). Irony, an essential element of camp sensibility that stresses styliza-tion over content, contributes further to the no-tion of incongruity-as-camp. In Sontag's words:

> Camp is a vision of the world in terms of style—but a particular kind of style. It is a love of the exaggerated ... of things being-what-they-are-not. (Sontag 1961: 277)

Sexual masquerade (i.e., cross-dressing) here becomes a kind of Otherness. Its incongruity is somewhat different from the incongruity of the Otherness of the foreigner suggested by the first two scenes, but similar in its presentation through stylization of something-that-is-what-it-is-not.

Sternberg's history as a frequenter of the German cabaret scene may account for his fascination with cross-dressing (Sternberg 1965: 228), since the German cabaret tradition was responsible for many nightclub acts that presented women as men or men as women (Bell-Metereau 1985: 103). In addition, Sternberg had seen Dietrich dressed in trousers at a social event, and was clearly intrigued with the prospect of dressing her in similar garb in his film (Sternberg 1965: 247).

In a blatant expression of directorial arrogance, Sternberg demonstrates his desire to control even the erotic connection between viewer and viewed (spectator and object) by concealing the well-known legs (the fetishized objects) from view, reshaping the erotic connection to produce a being, an Other, who appears to be what she is not.

Apparently, Sternberg's stubbornness served him well in a confrontation between himself and studio officials, who, upon seeing a brief trailer displaying Dietrich in formal male garb, rejected the idea as unrealistic (their wives wore "nothing but skirts") and impractical (a pair of trousers "could not be lifted"). But Sternberg stood his ground and got his way, later marveling immodestly at a creation that had actually influenced women to wear slacks (Sternberg 1965: 247).

Adolph Zukor, Paramount's studio chief, spoke of how the trend had begun.

> Marlene's indifference to publicity was a major reason why millions of Americans today wear slacks. At one point our publicity department decided that new press photographs of Dietrich were needed. "I'm loafing around in slacks," she told Blake McVeigh, the publicity man assigned to get the pictures. "If you want to shoot me this way, all right"... she posed in her trousers and ... the photographs were in great demand by the press. All over the country the stores were raided for their small supplies of women's slacks. The rage was on. (Zukor as quoted in Morley 1976: 1976)

Here is an example of how a star's extrafilmic life can reinforce her star presentation through promotion and publicity, extending the notion of incongruity (i.e., sexual ambiguity expressed through cross-dressing) beyond the limitations of the individual film.

In fact, Dietrich's appearances in slacks, both in her film roles and in her private life as well, began a real fashion trend for women in the 1930s. Hollywood's time schedule for film releases and the unavoidable lag behind fashion worried studio executives. Their fear that the costumes worn in films would appear dated by the film's release date encouraged an attempt to make Hollywood, rather than Paris, the fashion trendsetter (Head and Calistro 1983: 19). Relying on movies for advice about fashion, the public looked to studio designers as the fashion experts, and countless articles and photo layouts appeared in movie magazines such as *Photoplay* and *Screenland,* setting fashion standards more trusted than even those of *Vogue* or *Harper's Bazaar.*

Margaret Bailey sees the acceptance of slacks into public life as one of the major innovative fashion occurrences of the 1930s, attributing the trend to Dietrich's star power:

> She was the first to wear slacks in public in 1931 in Hollywood, although everyone wore them on the studio lot. It is ironic that a woman renowned for her femininity would launch a new vogue of fashionable masculinity. (Bailey 1982: 247)

Rebecca Bell-Metereau attributes the fashion for slacks to sociological factors. The stock market crash allowed more women to enter the workforce, and looking masculine was considered an asset.

> Perhaps film directors and critics celebrated the masculine aspect of woman in an unconscious attempt to reconcile audiences to the economic realities of the day, when an increasing number of women were usurping the role of provider for the family. (Bell-Meterau 1985: 70)

Dietrich's androgynous appeal, both in her private life and in her screen personae, was a quality seized upon by Sternberg, who frequently

Figure 64. Left: Greta Garbo in her famous slouch hat. Right: Marlene Dietrich in androgynous look. *Vanity Fair*, 1932. Historic Textile and Costume Collection, University of Rhode Island.

used sexual ambiguity teasingly, in an attempt to make ambiguous and incongruous the relationship between outward appearance and inner reality.

Cross-dressing can also be viewed as a political statement that utilizes costume to redefine the female self (Gubar 1981: 478). Simone de Beauvoir suggests that the definition of woman as female and man as human being forces woman into a position of male-imitation at those times when she most wants to be viewed as a human being (as quoted in Gubar 1981: 479). And Susan Gubar suggests that the rise of "masculine" clothing as a pervasive political issue in the suffrage movement might support de Beauvoir's suggestion that women could actually seek a kind of self-definition by imitating men (as quoted in Gubar 1981: 479).

Feminist film theorists Laura Mulvey and Claire Johnston view Dietrich's sexual masquerade as an indication of the absence of woman in male-dominated Hollywood cinema. Since woman is presented only in terms of what she represents for man, she becomes a manifestation of male narcissism, representing, through a process of displacement, the male phallus (C. Johnston 1977: 410). Further, the image of woman as sign within a sexist ideology is subject to the law of verisimilitude, the determinant of the impression of realism. Johnston blames this characteristic of Hollywood cinema for the repression of woman-as-woman and the celebration of her nonexistence (C. Johnston 1977: 410).

Johnston's argument is particularly interesting when applied to Sternberg's resistance to realism. Sternberg's style challenges accepted notions of reality by "breaking the illusion of realism," (C. Johnston 1973: 28) a strategy Johnston advocates as necessary for feminist filmmakers who seek to challenge audience assumptions and expose the falseness in traditional, capitalist representations of a so-called reality. His resistance makes Sternberg more of a revolutionary than he has heretofore been given credit for, and while his resistance has more to do with an assertion of power than with a declaration of consciousness, the result is a questioning of cinematic representation and its adherence to verisimilitude.

Sternberg's work also provides many examples of what Laura Mulvey interprets as fetishistic scopophilia in its transformation of the represented figure (Dietrich) into a fetishized object, making it reassuring rather than, as a castration threat, potentially dangerous. Fetishistic scopophilia "builds up the physical beauty of the object, transforming it into something satisfying in itself" (Mulvey 1977: 422). Mulvey claims that:

> Sternberg produces the ultimate fetish, taking it to the point where the powerful look of the male protagonist is broken in favor of the image in direct erotic rapport with the spectator ... woman is ... the direct recipient of the spectator's look. (Mulvey 1977: 422)

Mulvey further notes that there is no "mediation of the look through the eyes of the male protagonist." She locates the film's most highly emotional and dramatic moments as times when Dietrich is alone. For Mulvey, the most important absence is that of the controlling gaze within the screen space (Mulvey 1977: 423).

While it is true that Sternberg reveled in photographing Dietrich alone, ejecting most crew members from the set during the long close-up sessions and presenting her as a fetishized object in many scenes, Mulvey has failed to mention important instances in which the male protagonist does look directly at Dietrich. In both *Shanghai Express* and *Blonde Venus,* for example, Dietrich is the object of the male gaze, evidenced by close-ups and cutting, and is the source of men's changes of heart. In *Morocco,* both Cooper

and Menjou exercise fetishistic scopophilia— Cooper as a member of the audience at Amy's performance and Menjou on board the ship in the opening scene.

While feminist theorists such as Mulvey and Johnston provide an essential challenge to traditional Hollywood cinema and its representational system, their analysis of Dietrich's masculine attire works better in support of their theory rather than as a help in understanding Sternberg's schema. As Bill Nichols has suggested: "Clothing weaves another strand in Sternberg's ideolect; it is another code contributing to the plurality of meaning..." (Nichols 1981: 123). The analysis of one costume sign, i.e., Dietrich in male attire, isolates the sign from Sternberg's schema. Costume, for Sternberg, is a major narrative/thematic structural device in the complex textual system of his oeuvre, and consequently requires an analysis that considers it as such.

Dietrich's appearance in top hat, tie and tails in the film's cabaret scene, besides its stylization of incongruity-as-camp, serves to extend the idea of sexual ambiguity beyond the mysterious figure of Amy Jolly. In this scene, Sternberg introduces the idea of the double by presenting Amy and La Bessiere dressed in the same formal attire (Sarris 1966: 29).

Sexual ambiguity is further highlighted by Amy's flirtation with a female member of the audience and its gestural repetition with Tom Brown. Amy removes a flower from behind the woman's ear, sniffs it, kisses the woman (a move partially concealed by Amy's top hat), and tosses it to Tom, who mirrors Amy's gestures by sniffing the flower and placing it behind his ear. In a later scene in Amy's apartment, Tom kisses Amy, a move concealed here by a fan, and Amy removes the flower from Tom's ear, tossing it away with a gesture that completes a complex circle of sexual crisscrossing.

While sexual ambiguity and reversal are recurring motifs in many of Sternberg's films (see, for example, *The Shanghai Gesture, I, Claudius* and *Jet Pilot* among the non-Dietrich cycle), their appearance in *Morocco* serves the film's thematic purpose. The reversal here is a sign of Sternberg's understanding of woman's position as both soldier and victim within a male-dominated society. Amy describes herself as a member of the Foreign Legion of Women and one who has come to Morocco to do as Legionnaire Brown has tried to do, i.e., to "ditch the past." But, as she explains, women "wear no uniforms—no flags—no medals when they are brave," so the struggle is one of constant self-definition. The expression of discomfort is not so much with the denial of woman's presence, as feminist theorists suggest, but with the lack of any satisfactory definition of woman either by society or by mainstream artists. Sternberg's vision of discomfort remains, as it does in so many of his films, more radical than sexist.

Cross-dressing can also be viewed as masquerade, an extension of an idea advanced by psychoanalyst Joan Rivière. Rivière believed that femininity or womanliness was a mask worn by women who needed to hide their essential masculinity so as to avoid personal anxiety and social pressure (Rivière 1966: 210). Primarily interested in the intellectual, professionally successful woman, Rivière suggests that for such a woman, the public display of intellectual proficiency signified an exhibition of herself in possession of the father's penis, thus resulting in guilt for having castrated him. Fearing horrible retribution for such a deed, the woman masqueraded as guiltless and innocent by "disguising herself" as a castrated woman, which often required some form of "feminine" behavior, such as a display of ineptitude concerning typically "male" skills or choosing typically feminine clothing.

EDITORS' NOTE

1. This extract discusses Josef von Sternberg's use of stylization as a means of distancing in Morocco (1930), in which he experiments with campy artifice.

39

ANNA KÖNIG

Sex and the City in the British Fashion Press

*From A. König (2004), "Sex and the City: A Fashion Editor's Dream," in K. Akass and J. McCabe (eds.), **Reading Sex and the City** (London: I. B. Taurus), 130–43. Reprinted by permission of I. B. Taurus.*

Anyone familiar with the British style press will be aware of the fashion-page presence of *Sex and the City* in recent years. While one cannot literally measure *Sex and the City's* influence in fashion column inches, it is nonetheless useful to look at some examples of journalistic text, as this illustrates the frequency with which the show is referenced and highlights specific uses of language and tone.

The extracts cited below have been drawn from the online archives of British broadsheet newspapers including *The Daily Telegraph*, *The Independent*, *The Guardian* and *The Observer* as well as British *Vogue*, and cover the period April 2000 to February 2003. All are mainstream publications with high circulation numbers, so reflect a wide readership, albeit with a significant skew toward the higher end of the socioeconomic scale.

As early as September 2000, the impact of *Sex and the City* was acknowledged in the British fashion press, although initially it was presented as a stateside style phenomenon: "Sarah Jessica Parker and her costars in HBO's hit TV show *Sex and the City* are without doubt having a fashion moment. The whole of New York wants to dress like *Sex and the City*. In fact, the whole of America wants to dress like *Sex and* the *City*" (Cartner-Morley 2001).

By 2002 the show had established a presence within British fashion circles, and was seen to

have widespread appeal: "Channel 4's hit sitcom *Sex and the City* has inspired a slew of fashion imitations. It seems we just can't get enough of the antics of those New York dames—or their stunning wardrobes" (Anon. 2002).

Elsewhere it has been suggested that "*Sex and the City* is the only TV show that has made much of an impact on what we wear" (Freeman 2002). These extracts reflect the fact that British fashion press interest in *Sex and the City* is not based around a particular designer or brand; rather it is concerned with an overall look that is present in the show. One consequence of this has been the notable press attention devoted to the show's costume designer and stylist, Patricia Field.

While those connected with the fashion industry have long been familiar with the role of the stylist, the combination of *Sex and the City's* success and the growing trend for snippets of "insider" style information has given journalists a reason to introduce the concept to readers: "A stylist's work can involve many things. Working for *Sex and the City* means initiating trends" (Forrest 2001). Described as "architect of the signature *Sex and the City* style" (Vernon 2001: 36), Field has become a potent symbol of fashion kudos, with the power to bestow kooky New York fashionability on any item featured on the show. Indeed, in recent years she has become a celebrated fashion celebrity in her own right, and her "hip West Broadway boutique" (36) undoubtedly does brisk business as a consequence of her iconic status.

Having established that *Sex and the City* style appeals to British fashion writers, it is useful to identify the constituent ingredients of this influential look. Even within the limited scope of this study, examples were found linking *Sex and the City* to a plethora of fashion labels including Balenciaga (*Vogue* August 2002: 43), Jean-Charles de Castelbajac (Curry 2001), Matthew Williamson (Porter 2002), Pierrot (Limnander 2002: 212), Christian Dior (Cartner-Morley 2001), Emanuel Ungaro (I. Phillips 2001: 116), Alice & Olivia (Coulson 2002) and Narciso Rodriguez (Porter 2002). While designer labels such as Christian Dior and Balenciaga are well known and represent classic European style, even very fashion-literate readers would regard some of the others as fairly obscure. The strange and elaborate knitwear designs of New York label Pierrot, for example, would only be familiar to very dedicated, fashion-forward viewers and readers.

Above all, the *Sex and the City* look is epitomized by an eclectic approach to fashion that pushes boundaries and tests the style credulity of viewers, as this extract from *Vogue* illustrates: "Outfits … can be drop-dead sexy or [can] 'ironically' assimilate nerdy and ghetto-fabulous elements, such as dungarees and a faux-tacky nameplate necklace and earrings" (MacSweeney 2001: 171).

Field's quirky, individual approach to combining clothes and accessories draws together items as diverse as one-off couture garments, thrift store finds (often linguistically reclassified as "vintage," presumably to make them sound rather more exclusive and desirable) and the sample collections of young fashion graduates. Yet somehow this rag-bag style works, as it is always topped off with a generous helping of immaculate stateside grooming: even the most fastidious Brit would struggle to look quite as polished as the *Sex and the City* cast.

The show has effectively, therefore, become shorthand for a complex and often ambiguous set of fashion imagery. Fashion journalists tend to favor punchy, high-impact descriptions, and yet the outfits worn on the show are frequently complicated and sometimes downright odd. Thus the language of fashion becomes a mediator, a conduit that sorts new visual ideas into categories that are familiar and aesthetically digestible. As viewers and readers have become increasingly familiar with the distinct styling of the show's characters, there has been less of an imperative to explain the individual elements of the overall look, and it becomes sufficient to describe someone's appearance as "very *Sex and the City*" (Holgate 2001: 47).

However, as far as British style commentators are concerned, all are not equal among the cast of *Sex and the City*. Although the four main characters all have significant storylines, engage in interesting sexual encounters and deliver witty quips, only Carrie Bradshaw consistently excites the fashion appetite of the style press. Ultimately, therefore, the star of the show has also become the fashion journalist's darling, as Field always reserves the most fashion-forward, jaw-dropping outfits for Sarah Jessica Parker. Yet at times it is hard to differentiate between Carrie Bradshaw and Parker, for actor and character have melded into a single all-purpose fashion entity: if an item of clothing has been in the vicinity of Parker, it is newsworthy.

Importantly, the characters of the show have all evolved in such a way as to facilitate diverse audience identification. So while Carrie has come to epitomize all that is fashionable, Miranda has become the pragmatic careerwoman, Charlotte the sweet traditionalist, and Samantha the predatory sex bomb. Press citations reflect the fact that Carrie has the monopoly on fashion glory, a prime example being, "It's been no Manolos for Miranda—just baggy T-shirts [and] terrible hair" (Gibson 2003). Similarly, Kristin Davis has struggled to escape her prim on-screen persona, transforming herself into "a vampy sex goddess" for the men's magazine *FHM* (Foxe 2003). Interestingly, one of the few fashion press examples that is not about Carrie focuses on a pearl G-string worn by Samantha (Alexander 2002), a "fashion" item that says rather more about autoerotic excitation than it does about directional style.

While the examples cited earlier reflect the fact that many designer labels have been linked to *Sex and the City* or Parker, none has elicited as much fashion-page interest as Manolo Blahnik. Moreover, the media attention devoted to this prohibitively expensive brand of shoes warrants closer examination, as it highlights the importance of product placement in successful prime-time TV shows such as *Sex and the City.* At one time Jimmy Choo appeared to be the show's favorite shoe brand, making the label "such a big name, in fact, that an episode of the new series of *Sex and the City* revolves around Sarah Jessica Parker's Jimmy Choos" (O'Donnell 2001: 182). Yet in later episodes Manolo Blahnik shoes are given a prominent role within the show, raising the brand profile to vertiginous new heights and eliciting fashion press statements such as: "Carrie Bradshaw is a Manolo girl and her shoes play far more than a walk-on part in the series" (Singer 2002: 193).

Having ascertained that the fashion press regularly incorporates *Sex and the City* into editorial copy, one has to address the processes that have helped sustain such a constant presence on the fashion pages. Certainly, from the perspective of designers and PR companies, Carrie's wardrobe provides a far better showcase than any number of catwalk shows or advertising campaigns. This is high-profile, value-added marketing, as the following extract from the show's companion book indicates: "In the beginning, designers were cooperative, but we now have huge access, especially when it comes to the couture. The designers are great to us. Sarah Jessica is like a supermodel, and for her to wear the clothing on the show is important to the designers" (Sohn 2002: 68).

Clothes that are editorially interesting but which might otherwise be seen as odd or unwearable attain instant validation. Fashion copy invariably resounds with the discomforting question "Would you really wear it?" By making high fashion such a strong element within the show, *Sex and the City* provides the evidence that it can indeed be worn. Carrie and her friends are successful, intelligent (albeit fictional) women with busy, interesting lives; they are not empty-headed fashion junkies. One might view this, therefore, as a golden opportunity for the fashion press to persuade even the most skeptical reader of the benefits of high-cost, directional fashion.

In turn, editorial copy of this nature encourages fashion companies to place advertisements in newspapers and magazines. Given that advertising revenue has become an increasingly important issue for print publications in recent years (Cozens 2002), it is hardly surprising that the style press has eagerly embraced the fashion element of *Sex and the City.* The series may attract an audience from a broad socioeconomic spectrum, but it is the high-earning readership of broadsheet newspapers and glossy magazines that is of most interest to fashion editors and advertisers, for these are the women most likely to spend a proportion of their incomes on the products featured on the show.

Yet clearly press attention has also been beneficial to the series itself. Most TV shows are happy to receive sporadic attention from TV critics, but *Sex and the City* has, at least theoretically, doubled its press coverage by consistently securing column inches on the fashion pages. Moreover, it can be argued that the fashion press has been far more influential in terms of expanding the audience than TV reviews could ever be. As indicated in the first section, popular culture, and celebrity culture in particular, currently has a huge presence, both in fashion publications and women's magazines generally. By creating and subsequently maintaining a foothold in such publications, *Sex and the City* has rather cleverly established the potential to convert readers into viewers.

40

DANIEL WOJCIK

Punk and Neo-Tribal Body Art

From D. Wojcik (1995), **Punk and Neo-Tribal Body Art** *(Jackson: University Press of Mississippi), 7–21. Reprinted by permission of University Press of Mississippi.*

It was in the summer of 1976 that punk rock made its debut in the popular media, primarily as the result of the scandalous antics of the British band the Sex Pistols. Much of the attention focused on their style of body adornment, their loud and "obnoxious" music, their "self-mutilation" (burning their arms with lighted cigarettes and scratching their faces with needles), and their obscene behavior (cursing on a nationally televised talk show and performing a "spitting and vomiting act" at Heathrow Airport). It was not long before a variety of other punk rock bands appeared, the members of which often had little or no prior musical training. Like the Sex Pistols, initial groups such as The Damned, Buzzcocks, The Clash, X-Ray Spex, and The Adverts, among others, emphasized a raw, amateur musical style and a self-effacing, "anti-rock star" approach. In small clubs and squalid spaces, these punk musicians screamed their condemnations of the status quo at ear-shattering decibel levels, implicating the pretentious conventions of corporate rock music in the process.

This early punk subculture was characterized by anticommercialism, antiromanticism, and a lack of distinction between musicians and fans. It also quickly became renowned for a style of adornment calculated to disturb and outrage: dyed hair, studded leather jackets, torn clothing, bondage wear, profaned religious articles, tattooing, clothing defiled with obscenities and swastikas, and safety pins piercing the nose, lips, and cheeks. Claiming to be anarchists and nihilists, punks offended as many people as they could: some were distressed by the punk use of sexually "deviant" paraphernalia; others were disturbed by the profanation of religious objects and the use of swastikas; activists were irritated because punks had no articulated political views; and arbiters of social propriety were disgusted by the emphasis on the sordid and obscene.

[...]

The punk subculture flourished in England because it captured the mood of the time and gave expression to many of the frustrations and concerns of urban youth, such as the high unemployment rate, dismal economic conditions, and a pervasive attitude of desperation and futility. The punk motto "No future," a summation of the sense of hopelessness inherent in the early punk ethos, comes from the Sex Pistols' song "God Save the Queen" (1977).

[...]

The Sex Pistols' condemnation of all authority, their disdain for societal conventions, and their pessimistic appraisal of the future immediately appealed to disaffected youth around the world, and punk quickly became a global phenomenon.

[...]

Punks expressed their alienation through communal rituals of symbolic negation and personal acts of self-abuse. Presenting themselves as symbols of a society in a state of crisis and disintegration, punks enacted their own drama of societal cataclysm, creating the overall impression that they were sacrificing their bodies on the altar of postmodern despair.

PUNK BODY ART AND ADORNMENT

Punks, like previous postwar youth subcultures such as the Teddy Boys, the mods, the rockers, the skinheads, the beats, the zoot-suiters, and the hippies, created a coherent and elaborate system of body adornment that expressed their estrangement from mainstream society and that horrified the general public. Having little access to dominant means of discourse, punks displayed their disaffiliation and their subcultural identity through such adornment, which was for them an accessible and direct channel of communication. By manipulating the standard codes of adornment in socially objectionable ways, punks challenged the accepted categories of everyday dress and disrupted the codes and conventions of daily life.

[...]

Tattooing was another widely embraced form of adornment that transgressed conventional notions about the proper appearance of the body. Although believed to be the oldest and most pervasive type of permanent body modification, tattooing in Western culture until recently has been associated with deviance and marginality—the indelible badge of bikers, sailors, prisoners, prostitutes, savages, and circus freaks. Punk tattoos, inspired by the aesthetics of bikers and rockers, as well as by the Teddy Boys and rockabillies, served to stigmatize the bearer as someone existing outside of societal conventions. Unlike other forms of punk ornamentation which were temporary, however, tattooing signified one's commitment and allegiance to punk identity.

Initially, most punks were wary of established tattoo artists, whom they dismissed as too old, too mainstream, too expensive, or too conservative to administer the designs they desired. Therefore, many punks tattooed themselves or were tattooed by friends, the result being somewhat crude designs that reflected the punk do-it-yourself ethos and its emphasis on an amateur, unpolished aesthetic. Later, as some punks became trained in the art of tattooing, punk tattoos became more sophisticated, with designs more complex and diversified. Tribal designs, for example, appealed to some punks who valued the bold features, unique patterns, and exotic connotations of ancient tattoo imagery from Borneo, Polynesia, and Micronesia.

Punks borrowed motifs from Western tattoo tradition, but they were also innovative in developing their own unique designs, which expressed their personal and subcultural aesthetics. Unlike traditional Oriental-inspired tattooing, which involves covering an entire area of the body, such as the arm, with one design, punks seemed to prefer a pastiche aesthetic that resulted in a composite of designs. Like the decorations on punk jackets, early punk tattoos frequently dealt with the subject of human mortality. Skulls, crossbones, figures of death, and macabre imagery were common (grinning skulls with mohawks or spikes were ubiquitous). Spiders, spiderwebs, bats, snakes, crosses, and punk symbols for anarchy were popular as well. Other motifs included names of punk bands or a particular style of music, song lyrics, artwork from record covers and fanzines, political slogans, and images of favorite punk performers. After Sid Vicious of the Sex Pistols died of a heroin overdose, for instance, a number of his fans had his portrait tattooed on their bodies. Some males got tattoos of nude or scantily clad punk women with mohawks, a variation on a traditionally popular design among men. Punk women were also tattooed, an even more substantial violation of accepted codes of adornment than tattooing among men.

Tattooed women were relatively uncommon in the 1970s, and a woman with a visible tattoo was generally stigmatized as deviant or promiscuous. Although some tattooed female punks embraced macabre imagery, many seemed less interested in grisly and aggressive designs, preferring symbols of their favorite bands, "gloomy" designs (i.e., bats, spiderwebs), floral motifs (often in black), or personal insignias.

The use of body piercing, or what was referred to as "mutilation" by the mass media, had particularly powerful symbolic connotations (deviance, pain, masochism, self-destruction) and seemed to disturb non-punks more than all the other styles—hair, leather jackets, clothing, and tattoos—combined. Safety pins or razor blades dangling from ears were common, as were skeletons, crucifixes, swastikas, the hammer and sickle, iron cross, skulls, and other incongruous symbols or shocking objects. Rings, safety pins, or studs worn in the lip, cheek, nose, or eyebrow proved even more unsettling. Occasionally objects such as bones were displayed as nose or ear ornaments, but mass-produced commodities were more frequently used. Punks literally skewered and lacerated themselves with the mundane debris of daily life. The stereotyped image of a punk with a safety pin through a cheek became an icon of deviant youth, a media symbol of the punk folk devil that intensified a sense of moral panic in the wider population.

[...]

POST-PUNK BODY ADORNMENT

Despite commercialization and co-optation, punk aesthetics and ideology were never completely incorporated into mainstream society. Stereotypical depictions of punks continue to evoke connotations of deviance and are still used to represent the embodiment of dangerous youth. The punk subculture did not "die" immediately after its inception (a death that has been debated and refuted periodically in punk fanzines for nearly two decades). There are still many individuals who consider themselves punks, "post-punks," or "alternatives" (as well as many who refuse such labels altogether), and who continue to be inspired by the legacy of early punk in some way.

41

DEBORA SILVERMAN

Selling Culture: Bloomingdale's, Diana Vreeland, and the New Aristocracy of Taste in Reagan's America

From D. Silverman (1986), **Selling Culture** *(New York: Pantheon Books), 3–11.*
Reprinted by permission of the author.

In the year preceding the 1984 presidential election, 1 million people viewed a lavish exhibition at the Metropolitan Museum of Art [the Met] in New York: a retrospective entitled "Twenty-Five Years of Yves Saint-Laurent." Organized by Diana Vreeland, editor for over thirty years at *Harper's Bazaar* and *Vogue* and now special consultant to the Met's Costume Institute, the Saint-Laurent show celebrated the "genius" of "haute couture." Galleries filled with mannequins in gilded tunics, embroidered ball gowns, and flowing cocktail dresses were presented to the public as exceptional works of art, divested of all commercial imperatives. Vreeland glorified Saint-Laurent as the "dauphin," the rightful inheritor of the noble craft of the couturier, whose sumptuous creations originally graced the forms of French queens and aristocrats. The Met exhibit was a tribute not only to the visionary designer but also to his illustrious customers, whose names, as lenders of the lavish outfits, were inscribed on labels in front of each clothing display. As Saint-Laurent was hailed as the scion of the great aristocratic French dressers, so too were his affluent clients touted as the natural successors to the Old Regime elites.

Visitors to the Saint-Laurent show found the museum exhibition curiously indistinguishable from the same designer's displays at fashionable department stores such as Bloomingdale's and Neiman Marcus. The galleries at the Met were not organized according to a chronological development, befitting an artist's "retrospective." Nor did the show instruct us about the way Saint-Laurent's opulent ensembles were actually made, or about the position of these haute couture productions within the complex YSL fashion empire devoted to designer mass-marketing. Instead the galleries were arranged by color schemes, and by the "timeless" divisions that structure a certain type of woman's day: "day-wear" suits for strolling and shopping; "cocktail hour" dresses in black and white; and lavish "evening clothes" from ball gowns to ruffled "gazar" capes. Vreeland's Saint-Laurent show succeeded, not as museum education, but as a giant advertising campaign for French haute couture, as a public testimonial to the loyal patrons of the "dauphin" of fashion, and as a glorification of woman as an *objet d'art*, for whom life is an interminable round of changing from one luxurious outfit to another.

The triumph of French distinction, opulent fashion, and extravagant femininity in the Metropolitan Museum of Art in 1984 was not an isolated or an accidental phenomenon. Indeed, the Saint-Laurent show was part of an important movement of aristocratic posturing in American culture and politics. The movement is centered in New York, with direct links, in both personnel and themes, to the center of political power in the White House of Ronald and Nancy

Reagan. Though the movement originated before Reagan's arrival, the 1981 inauguration of a president dedicated to visible wealth and an unchecked "new luxury" solidified its ranks and gave it political meaning and significance.

The affiliates of the aristocratic movement span the worlds of politics, the media, fashion design, the department store, and the museum. Their aristocratic self-image and group identity are perpetuated by Reagan's economic policies, which benefit a small minority and distance them more and more from the majority of Americans. At the center of the aristocratic movement is a fundamental contradiction typical of Reaganism. While styling themselves an exclusive elite of wealth and cultivation, the aspirants to a new American nobility are dependent for their success and values upon the mass-market and leveling consumerism.

A gala party launching the Saint-Laurent exhibit at the Metropolitan Museum offered a group portrait of this amalgamated elite.

On December 5, 1983, 800 guests paid US$500 each to dine and dance in the Met's main hall in honor of the Saint-Laurent show's opening. For the evening's festivities, Saint-Laurent's fabric supplier, Gustav Zumsteg, swathed the main hall in fifteen thousand yards of fuchsia and orange silk. The dinner alone cost $80,000; the total cost for the event was underwritten by Saint-Laurent's perfume licensee, Charles of the Ritz. With few exceptions, the distinguished female guests arrived in Saint-Laurent evening dresses and seemed like live counterparts of the YSL mannequins arrayed in the galleries below. Nancy Kissinger, sheathed in a black Saint-Laurent ensemble with glittering jewel trim, arrived with Henry; others from the world of politics included Evangeline Bruce, widow of the ambassador and dowager of Washington social circles; Mercedes Kellogg, whose husband was a recent Reagan ambassadorial appointee; Houston socialite Lynn Wyatt, wife of Oscar, a major Reagan contributor; and Pat Buckley, who was the social chairperson responsible for organizing the entire evening. Media celebrities attending the gala included Bill Paley, chairman

of CBS; Linda Grey of *Dallas*; and Carol Burnett. Fashion designers also came to celebrate Saint-Laurent's triumphal entry to the Met: Bill Blass, Oscar de la Renta, Jacqueline de Ribes, and Carolina Herrera. Department-store heads included the chairman of Saks Fifth Avenue. Marvin Traub, the chairman of Bloomingdale's, was unable to attend the party, though he served as an adviser to the Met. Betsy Bloomingdale, out of town, sent her close friend and confidant Jerome Zipkin, the real estate heir who is also a frequent guest and close friend of Nancy Reagan's.

The peculiar combination of fashion, politics, high culture, and consumerism visible at the Met's Saint-Laurent show suggested something about the essential qualities of Reaganite political culture. The same group of people featured at the 1983 Met Saint-Laurent gala had had their photos splashed across the pages of *Interview* magazine and the *Washington Post* as they flocked, in splendid designer costumes, to the opulent presidential inaugural festivities of 1981. Designer Bill Blass sat in the Reagans' own box at one Kennedy Center inaugural party, where he could survey Nancy's friends Betsy Bloomingdale, Mary Jane Wick, and Estée Lauder shimmering in his signed creations. The Kissingers, Buckleys, de Borchgraves, Wyatts, and Bill Paley were also prominent personages at the Reagan galas, where they joined the Reagans' inner circle of longtime California friends—the Deutsches, Annenbergs, Tuttles, Wicks, Smiths, Jorgensons, Bloomingdales, and Stewarts—in an inaugural extravagance unparalleled in American history. Nancy's wardrobe alone cost $25,000; the cost of an entire week of brunches, lunches, and balls totaled close to $16 million.

Before and after the 1980 elections, the aristocratic tendency was detectable in two centers, whose promoters and ideology were inextricably interrelated. One center was consumerist, spearheaded at Bloomingdale's, where two major marketing campaigns of aristocratic themes were staged. In 1980 Bloomingdale's concentrated on the exotic riches of Chinese emperors, and then turned, in 1983, to the aristocratic crafts of

France's Old Regime. The second center of aristocratization was within a bastion of elite culture, the Metropolitan Museum of Art. Under the spell of Diana Vreeland, the Met's Costume Institute offered four exhibitions after 1980 whose subject and forms glorified the luxurious refinements of aristocratic traditions. Translating into high culture the Bloomingdale's sales campaigns, the Met devoted 1980 to "Chinese Imperial Robes," which displayed the palace garb and palace furniture of the Ch'ing dynasty (1644–1912). In 1981 Vreeland shifted to France, staging a celebration of decorative, aristocratic femininity: "The Eighteenth-Century Woman." In 1982 she organized a tribute to the last hurrah of aristocratic womanhood: "La Belle Epoque." Next, in 1983, came a vision of the modern successors to elite female ostentation: "Twenty-Five Years of Yves Saint-Laurent." In 1984 Vreeland glorified English gentry and equestrian apparel and ownership in "Man and the Horse," presented by Polo/Ralph Lauren.

The significance of these twin centers of aristocratic invocation, and the national and historical illusions they promote, extends beyond the confines of culture and consumerism to a consideration of its political meaning and resonance. Vreeland's projects glorifying social distinction and female decoration coincide with the reign of a political First Lady devoted to a new luxury, a woman whose passion in life, according to Laurence Leamer, is collecting exclusive designer clothes and never wearing the same ensemble twice. Nancy Reagan's aggressive amassing of china tableware, White House jewel collections, and twelve double closets full of designer regalia has its advocate in Diana Vreeland, who once claimed that "We mustn't be afraid of snobbism and luxury." Nancy Reagan invited Mrs. Vreeland to dine at the White House, and she shares her passion for the color red—what Vreeland has called "the great clarifier." Her preferred social circle of socialites and fashion designers—including Jerry Zipkin, Betsy Bloomingdale, James Galanos, and Bill Blass—also comprises the social world that Vreeland inhabits.

Yet the conjuncture between politics and the aristocratic cultural movement transcended these individual personalities and social influences. There was a deeper correspondence between the political program of the Reagan White House and the emergence of an aristocratic consumer culture at Bloomingdale's and the Metropolitan Museum. The idealization of non-American nobilities provided the elements of a new cultural style concordant with the politics born at the first Reagan inauguration: a style aggressively dedicated to the cult of visible wealth and distinction, and to the illusion that they were well earned; a style that adopted the artifacts of Chinese emperors, French aristocrats, and English noblemen as signs of exclusivity and renunciation; a style of unabashed opulence, whose mixture of hedonism, spitefulness, and social repudiation was captured in the slogan "Living well is the best revenge." The cast of characters sponsoring the Vreeland and Bloomingdale's spectacles is composed of corporate fashion designers, rich socialites, and mass-media moguls, who constitute a consumerist power elite, the new Reagan elite. The cultural projects they participate in are tied to the big business of illusion making and are perfectly suited to the politics of theater practiced in the White House. Reagan's politics and the aristocratic fashion culture share a fundamental inauthenticity, a reliance on fabrication, and a glaring disparity between symbolism and reality.

ANNOTATED GUIDE TO FURTHER READING FOR PART VIII

Fashion and photography was the theme of a special issue of *Fashion Theory* in 2002, which evolved in response to the Victoria and Albert Museum's exhibition "Imperfect Beauty: The Making of Contemporary Fashion Photography." In that issue, Carol Tulloch states: "The body of theoretical work on fashion photography is very small when compared with other areas of fashion theory such as gender or modernity" (Tulloch 2002: 1). This is also true of other media through which fashion is promoted. Paul Jobling's studies on photography and advertising are an exception to this generalization, as are a handful of other works mentioned in Part VII, Fashion and Art. Additionally, Suzanne Baldaia (2005) shows how photographers who worked for *Harper's Bazaar* used space age imagery in the 1960s to promote modernity in fashion.

Fashion in film has fared better in academia. Several lengthy studies have appeared in the last decade (Berry 2000; Massey 2000; Bruzzi 1997). Patricia Warner shows how Hollywood helped popularize American sportswear in the movies of the 1930s (Warner 2005).

Fashion and music is explored in *Zoot Suits and Second-Hand Dresses: An Anthology of Fashion and Music* (McRobbie 1988).

Advertising and marketing have their own academic journals, for example *Journal of Consumer Research*, *Journal of Advertising* and *Journal of Marketing Research*, which report both qualitative and quantitative research. Chapter 10 "Fashion Communication" in Michael Solomon and Nancy Rabolt's textbook entitled *Consumer Behavior in Fashion* (2004) provides background for this area of research. See also Malossi's *The Style Engine*.

Regarding celebrities and fashion media, there are many books on famous faces of the past. Some of these include sections on fashion. *Jacqueline Kennedy: The White House Years* (Bowles *et al.* 2001) focuses on how the former First Lady selected her wardrobe, thus introducing readers to the inside story of her success at appearance management. Similar books exist for Princess Diana (Emanuel and Emanuel 2006). The topic of celebrity and fashion could use deeper analysis than we have seen to date. Only Grant McCracken has addressed the issue in *Culture and Consumption II* (2005).

Breward's chapters in *Fashion* (2003) entitled "The Promotion of Fashion," "Disseminating Desire," and "Fashion and Film" are useful introductions as is the full chapter "Fashion on the Page" from which the reading in this section is extracted. Jennifer Craik's *The Face of Fashion* (1994) also covers aspects of the media presentation of fashion. Gilles Lipovetsky in *The Empire of Fashion* (1994) takes a socio-philosophical approach, arguing that the superficiality of fashion fosters tolerance in democratic societies; fashion media are discussed as they create ephemeral desire. Caroline Evans treats the manner in which fashion is portrayed in the media in *Fashion at the Edge*.

PART IX

From Haute Couture to the Street

LINDA WELTERS

Introduction

For approximately a century, from 1860 to 1960, new styles for women originated with Paris designers. Men's clothes were not "designed" as such, but subtly styled by tailors, most notably those on London's Savile Row. These luxurious clothes inspired dressmakers and tailors in cities and towns throughout the developed world to dress their own clients in the new styles. During the second half of the nineteenth century, the capacity of mass manufacturers to produce ready-to-wear clothing, especially for men and children, increased. The contribution of the paper pattern industry to the production of fashionable clothing at home should be mentioned as well (Burman 1999). This system of style innovation—trickling down from elite designers and tailors to ready-to-wear and home sewers—broke down in the 1960s, largely due to sociocultural changes. The theories behind these shifting patterns of style innovation and fashion adoption were discussed in Part II. In this section, the production and consumption of haute couture is explored along with examples of fashions inspired by looks that came from the street.

HAUTE COUTURE

Charles Frederick Worth is recognized as the Father of Couture. British by birth, he trained in London and moved to Paris in 1845. After finding employment at Maison Gagelin where he met his future wife, Marie, he honed his creative skills. In 1858 he left Gagelin and started his own dressmaking firm with Otto Bobergh. He succeeded in securing a "celebrity" client—the beautiful Empress Eugénie—and became a major influence on fashion until his death in 1895. How did his business differ from that of other dressmakers of the day? While the typical dressmaker sewed clothes to the customer's specifications, Worth went beyond this limited protocol, becoming the *creator* of the style. He designed a seasonal line to be presented to customers on live models at showings, after which customers ordered individual copies. He also sold models to be copied in England and America. Anne Hollander explains how Worth, the man, succeeded in a woman's business during a time when Paris reigned as the world's cultural capital.

Worth's success spawned a number of designers—Drecoll, Doucet, Pingat—whose luxurious styles were snapped up by the growing clientele for expensive, elitist apparel. Rich Americans, titled Europeans, and the *demimonde* (e.g., kept women) soon flocked to Paris couture houses. Transatlantic travel, coupled with favorable exchange rates, made the Paris trip affordable for upper-middle-class Americans. Thérèse and Louise Bonney explained the rules to novice "millionaire *américains*" in *A Shopping Guide to Paris*. Their book was published in 1929 when the vogue for buying custom-made clothing from a named Parisian designer hit its pinnacle. Shopping tourism was a concept not lost on Paris, where fashion-conscious visitors contributed greatly to the French economy.

The "Made in Paris" label was so desirable that copies of Paris originals constituted a significant part of the women's apparel business until the 1960s. Leading manufacturers from England and America attended the Paris shows, buying models for copying purposes. In the mid-1950s, the House of Dior alone counted for 5 percent of French exports (Palmer 2001). Alexandra Palmer explains how couture designs came to Toronto, Canada in *Couture and Commerce* (2001). Her study of Paris couture houses, Toronto retailers and couture customers in the 1950s informs us who bought these designer outfits, how they were sold and worn, and the positions of couture customers in Toronto society.

Palmer's extract requires some definitions and explanations. A *vendeuse* is a saleswoman at a French couture house; a *bonded model* is an original couture garment sold to manufacturers and retailers who used it for promotion and as a source for line-for-line copies; a *toile* is a muslin pattern sold by couture houses for copying purposes. After manufacturers in New York had finished with bonded models, they often sent them to Canada for resale. In Toronto, Eaton's, Holt Renfrew, Simpson's, and Joan Rigby were the elite stores that sold bonded models in addition to importing couture from Paris. In the postwar period, manufacturers and department stores were the bread and butter of French couture, not the private clients. Thus, Toronto customers were able to purchase beautifully made couture clothes that could be altered to fit without leaving their own city.

The hegemony of Paris slipped during the Second World War, when London and New York began recognizing their own designers out of necessity during the Nazi occupation of Paris. After the war, the Marshall Plan helped Italy reconstruct its textile industry, which in turn fed the developing fashion industry in Milan, Florence and Rome. The "youthquake" in England in the 1960s added London to the list of fashion cities. That decade also saw the entry of the designer into the menswear business. In the 1970s and 1980s, Japanese designers entered the scene. Now Paris is just one of many cities where fashion designers create beautiful clothes for both men and women.

At the same time, couture shrank to a tiny percentage of the overall designer fashion business. Few could afford the cost of the hand-worked clothes. Additionally, women of the "jet set" did not have time for numerous fittings, preferring instead to buy off the rack. French couturiers responded by opening prêt-à-porter divisions, which offered designs suited to machine assembly at more affordable prices. Designer ready-to-wear quickly became the center of the fashion business. Yves Saint-Laurent was one of the first couturiers to shift attention to ready-to-wear with the founding of his Rive Gauche label in 1966.

Recently a new category has emerged. It is called "demi-couture" and features the same handmade techniques one typically finds in haute couture, but is sold off the rack. The prices range from the low four figures into six figures (American dollars). The type of customer who purchases such clothes prizes their rarity (Holgate 2006).

STREET STYLE

A more fundamental phenomenon began surfacing in the 1950s and 1960s, which ultimately dissipated the old fashion system. This was the emergence of subcultures with specific styles that served as badges of identity, some of which inspired designers to create luxe versions of the styles. Now we call this "street style." The inspiring of designers by street style is the process described in Part II as "trickle up."

Isolated examples of subcultural style influencing high fashion existed prior to 1960. To wit: in the 1910s, bohemians in New York's Greenwich Village bobbed their hair and dressed in peasant embroideries, sandals, and other "anti-fashion" attire that evolved into the high-fashion looks of the 1920s (Saville 2005). During the postwar era, subcultural styles proliferated: dandified

Teddy Boys in Britain, leather-jacketed rebels in the US, and black-clad Beat Generation poets in France and America are a few examples. Ted Polhemus's extract "Bubble Up" addresses this change in fashion dissemination by examining the "Perfecto" brand leather jacket.

Subcultural style inspired Yves Saint-Laurent when he created the 1960 fall-winter collection for Dior based on Beat Generation styles (Welters 2005). Dior's couture customers rejected the look, claiming that it looked too much like the hooligans in the Latin Quarter of Paris. Meanwhile, American hippies started decking themselves out in all manner of costume-y looks: jeans, peasant blouses, tie-dyed T-shirts, old Army or Navy jackets, and secondhand clothes.

Now Pandora's box was open. Out flew punks, grunge rockers, goths, rappers and Rastafarians. Since the 1960s, fashion history has provided an almost infinite number of examples of how street style has influenced mainstream fashion. Zandra Rhodes, based in London, is an example of a designer who has successfully translated styles from subcultures into mainstream fashions, most notably with her safety-pinned, punk-inspired dresses and her own vividly colored and spiked hair. Rhodes also drew inspiration for her designs from ethnic dress, Western dress, and a host of other nontraditional sources in the 1970s

and 1980s (Rhodes and Knight 1985). Her work is emblematic of the new, postmodern fashion designer.

McRobbie's classic piece introduces the secondhand market, which used to be anathema to a "fashionista." Rummage sales, fleamarkets and secondhand shops became popular shopping venues among consumers of many income brackets, not just the poor. Now it is not uncommon to read about celebrities trying to distinguish themselves on the red carpet by wearing "vintage" (e.g., secondhand) dresses. Likewise, fashion leaders are mixing it up, wearing expensive designer pieces with mass-market or vintage pieces. Such widespread sources for design inspiration are an expression of our fractured postmodern life.

Sonnet Stanfill's piece on the Victoria and Albert Museum's recent acquisition of Vivienne Westwood designs addresses the client/designer relationship; the Costiffs purchased and wore Westwood from the mid-1970s until 1994. The section concludes with Yuniya Kawamura's observations of Japanese youth culture and the fleeting styles with which they preoccupy themselves. It is just one example of a constantly changing kaleidoscope of looks. Kawamura proposes the notion of these teens *producing* fashion to be *consumed* by others, which is an intriguing consideration.

42

ANNE HOLLANDER

When Worth Was King

From A. Hollander (1982), "When Worth Was King," in Connoisseur, *December, 114–21. Reprinted by permission of the author.*

Worth is a resonant name in fashion history—the only name dominating Parisian fashion during the last third of the nineteenth century, and a potent one until well after the First World War. The name stands for the founding of the great haute couture business in France, an enterprise that was to contribute powerfully both to modern French economic security and to the luster of French couture in the modern world. If today Worth's name has been largely forgotten, it has nonetheless endured.

Charles Frederick Worth came to Paris from his native England in 1845, when he was nineteen, driven by a keen ambition. He had been working in a fashionable London dry-goods firm, knew no French, and had no money. After a few false starts, he was hired by Gagelin, an elegant firm that sold dress fabrics, trimmings, and a number of made-up cloaks, mantles, and shawls. He stayed twelve years, becoming a leading salesman in charge of his own radical innovation, a dressmaking department inside the shop.

Those twelve years were essential to his future. Worth came to understand how elegance could be expressed through textiles; he learned French, and from his position behind the counter he learned to understand the women of his time.

Armed with his specialized awareness and native talent, Worth opened his own dressmaking shop in 1858 when he was thirty-two. He had by then a lovely young wife, who had been a cloak model at Gagelin and who served as his initial inspiration and mannequin. Within a decade this young Englishman became absolute king of French fashion and the only dressmaker famous on four continents. How did he do it? Most important, he established a completely new kind of shop specializing in the *design* of women's clothes, not just their construction. For two centuries, Parisian women's apparel had been made by other women. Before that, throughout the Middle Ages and the Renaissance, male tailors had made all the clothes for both sexes using women only as seamstresses. But in 1675 the sewing women broke away from the tailors' guild and got the legal right to be the exclusive makers of women's dress and to form their own guild. Consequently, during the whole of the eighteenth century and much of the nineteenth, the frivolous female craft of dressmaking was separate from the masculine art of tailoring for men. Although "fashion" was a long-standing Parisian specialty and Paris was renowned for its high standards of taste and inventive craftsmanship in women's clothes, dress designing was not a recognized occupation. Women studied fashion plates, bought their own material in fabric shops, and designed their own effects, relying on the suggestions and handiwork of deft milliners and dressmakers.

It was the well-established world of French female theater that swiftly capitulated to Worth's overmastering male eye and made him its sole director and producer. Worth dealt directly with the silk merchants and designed clothes in superb fabrics of his own choosing. His constant use of rich materials gave a needed boost to the silk manufacturers of Lyon, who wove more and more interesting textiles to Worth's order and gradually came to supply the whole couture business he had founded. Worth provided his customers with everything—the conception, the fabrics, the details, the execution. He was the first to design a "collection," to make up a range of dresses for every occasion. He worked with important clients to set them off to particular advantage, to individualize the costume according to his own creative view of the lady.

Because during his ascendancy Worth was unique, his was the first and perhaps the only true fashion dictatorship. At a crucial time in French cultural history, it was he alone who shifted the responsibility for a woman's appearance from the taste of the lady herself to that of her male couturier. In his own sphere, Worth crystallized the Romantic myth of woman as man's creation, the creature of his vision and imaginative power, the projection of his longing and his fear. During this same period, Flaubert created Emma Bovary, Tolstoy created Anna Karenina, and Dumas *fils* created *La Dame aux Camelias*. Living ladies who lacked a great novelist to invent them could now find a great designer for the task.

A MAN MUST DRESS A WOMAN

Since a woman's designer was now the arbiter of her appearance, "Fashion" came to be viewed as a blind and stupid force to be despised, something that trapped the gullible into looking ridiculous and the multitude into looking alike. Now only the fashion designer could save one from Fashion; in his hands and under his gaze the true self would find its right adornments. And it was at around this time that the playwright Feydeau is supposed to have said, "One must be a man to know how to dress women." As a man, Worth automatically made the enterprise seem serious:

a man in a woman's business was looked upon as an artist, whose imaginative vision transcended the mode.

Worth's customers delighted in being "created" by him, to the occasional uneasiness of their husbands, lovers, and fathers, who, of course, were footing the bills. That he was English undoubtedly contributed to his success: as a foreigner he was classless, able to deal intimately with ladies of high station without seeming presumptuous; the English, moreover, had long been highly regarded in France for their skillful handling of cloth. Indeed, all Worth's dresses enhanced women's looks through clever cutting and superb fitting. His designs were simple and clear, with flattering lines and unfussy embellishments. They emphasized the sweep of the whole figure and clarified the outline of the head and neck, or of the arms and waist. His early evening dresses, described in various memoirs, were often of simple white tulle, perhaps shot with pure silver thread or caught up with a few clusters of violets.

In the 1840s and 1850s, just before Worth appeared on the scene, a stasis characterized fashionable feminine costume. The crinoline reached its hugest size—a great dome supported by a hooped petticoat. Sleeves opened wide at the bottom to show very full undersleeves. The bonnet, completely surrounding the face with a curtain in the back to hide the hair, boxed in the head and rendered the neck invisible. Shawls were obligatory outdoors. They obscured the lines of the upper body and spread out over the big skirt so that a woman walking on the street became a vast cone of fabric with only her face visible at the top.

A dress might have its bodice, skirt, and sleeves all trimmed separately, but in the same way: three small ruffles above the waist, three large ruffles below it, three ruffles on each sleeve—a leaden scheme, allowing for many variations on only one idea. Ball gowns were very décolleté all the way around and bared the shoulders, but deep flounces encircling the neckline tended to veil the upper torso. The matching flounces around the vast skirt further emphasized the encircling character of the costume. A woman stood in the center of her clothes, a nearly invisible column supporting a huge, festooned tent.

During the 1860s, the decade of Worth's rise to fame, a new look of forward movement and activity overtook female dress. The domed skirt was narrowed at the top to show the shape of hips and stomach, and swelled out in back as if in a stiff breeze. The bonnet was sharply reduced in size, lost its curtain, and sat high on the back of the head, where the hair was swept up into a big, visible chignon. The neck emerged, sleeves narrowed, and shawls were abandoned in favor of fitted outer garments. The skirts of ball gowns swept backward into exuberantly puffed-out drapery and flowing trains. Trimming lost its staid, compartmentalized quality, as rows of flounces fell out of favor and flat, applied ornament began to sweep over the whole costume. Colors deepened and contrasts were sharpened. Vitality and zest with a little daring exaggeration of the figure were the signs of the new mode. While he didn't start it, Worth contributed a great deal of impetus to this trend. He urged it forward with inspired taste, as though eager to expose the feminine shape, to model the female body and then propel it into graceful motion.

CLOTHES MAKE THE WOMAN

Worth could never have succeeded so quickly without the favorable situation that prevailed in France. In 1852, after decades of civil unrest, Bonaparte's nephew Louis Napoleon became emperor. A new court, financed largely by merchants and bankers, had instant need for the obvious marks of imperial status and power. Louis had a beautiful Spanish wife, who unlike much of her court, was noble, and, indeed, she looked every inch an empress in her exquisite clothes. It was Eugénie who became Worth's patron, not only establishing his prestige but also encouraging his use of sumptuous fabric and his lavish designs for court functions. Worth designed sober traveling costumes and restrained walking

suits, but his genius was for the luxurious public garments so necessary to the ladies of the new empire. In 1859 the racetrack at Longchamps was opened, and the *haut monde* flocked there with no other purpose than to see and be seen, to confirm the importance of the new Napoleonic age, if only through the imposing elegance of its women.

But times had fundamentally changed. A bourgeois puritanism had crept into the rebuilt society of France. Sexual mores, which had reached a state of refined depravity under the *ancien régime*, were now founded upon a strict, essentially middle-class code: there were virtuous women, and there were whores; there was society, and there was the *demimonde*. The famous courtesans of this period all seem to have existed only for the purpose of providing a cause for the truly destructive extravagance of noblemen and gentlemen who also had to maintain costly legitimate establishments. Unlike the courtesans of Athens, Venice, or Versailles, these *grandes cocottes* were not known for their witty conversation and cultural influence, or even for amorous technique and superior erotic gifts. Their skill was visible expenditure, the more vulgar the better. For the men who supported them, they satisfied what seemed an urgent need for public evidence of potency in the form of wealth, rather than for private sources of pleasure. They embodied the complex fantasies of sex and money generated by such a materialistic and prudish world.

Wives meanwhile had the task of displaying legitimate status. The game of society was to keep the two worlds apart. The wives in their elegant finery and carriages did not acknowledge the existence of mistresses, who stayed on the other side of the racetrack in their even more dashing dress and equipage. Society closed its ranks against the *demimonde*, which was nevertheless ubiquitous, notorious, and highly conspicuous.

Worth dresses appeared on both sides of the track. The new creator of the female image had as much scope for his talents among gaudy courtesans as among dignified bankers' wives and stately princesses; in all cases, the desired effect was that of no expense spared. One result was that Worth became immensely rich, richer than any other dressmaker before him. Since he dressed public figures, his fame and clientele reached far beyond Paris to the royal courts of other nations, where ladies hoped to rival the exquisite chic of Eugénie and her circle, and to the democratic shores of the United States, where immense fortunes were being made by enterprising men and spent by their energetic women, in Paris if possible. The designer's prices, like his prestige, were nearly double those of other dressmakers. His clients found them well worth it.

An important movement underway in Paris during Worth's career was the early development of modern French painting. "Art for the sake of art" was a new countercultural slogan among the painters of the avant-garde, who opposed the formulae of official art and the careers it assured. Beautifully rendered salon paintings on mythological themes were being challenged by scenes of uncompromising reality executed with a painterly directness that showed respect for the importance of the medium and the subject. The independent artist, who was scornful of any success that smacked of artistic compromise, became a new hero. As in any commercial and conventional age, creative imagination was a rare commodity.

Worth capitalized on this. In calling himself an artist he invoked the new authority of the artist as revolutionary prophet and pure-minded visionary, when in fact he functioned as an official decorator paid to produce delicious confections for the rich. His photograph in later life shows him in a soft velvet cap and fur-lined robe, a costume worn (like Wagner's similar outfit) in imitation of Rembrandt, the great hero of artistic self-determination. Worth had come a long way from the dry-goods counter.

In fact, as an artist, Worth was a wonderful designer. He worked in a new medium—the complete image of the dressed woman, not just her dress. Far from ordering him to come to them, the great ladies often went to his atelier before the ball to put on their gowns, receive the

Figure 65. "A Worth Evening Dress," *Harper's Bazar*, April 11, 1891. Historic Textile and Costume Collection, University of Rhode Island.

final touches, and submit to his approval, confident that his eye was clearer than their own. He had a gift not just for good tailoring and for embellishing feminine looks but also for understanding advanced trends in modern design. Although he had no part in the revolutionary new vistas opened up and illuminated by Manet and Degas, his works do bear the unmistakable flavor of what was to become art nouveau during the decade in which he died. His mature designs show a sinuous harmony among all elements of each costume, a rhythmic clarity of applied decoration, a new and dynamic asymmetrical use of old motifs.

When Charles Frederick Worth died, in 1895, he was almost imperceptibly succeeded by his two devoted sons, Gaston and Jean-Philippe—the latter a gifted designer and sympathetic disciple of his father, the former a shrewd businessman. Jean-Philippe followed the aesthetic paths laid out by his father, continuing to create rich and sleek new arrangements of Renaissance and rococo themes. Although they demonstrate the radical changes in feminine shape and style inaugurated at the turn of the century, Jean-Philippe's designs are indistinguishable in spirit from those of his father. They show a similar respect for the authority and beauty of richly woven silk, and an equal sense of the drama of the female figure—a feeling for "presence."

Other couturiers of the new generation that had risen on the tide of Worth's success were exploring different avenues. Some stressed the delicacy of lace and fragile embroidery; others, the crisp, tailored look of active modernity; and still others, the inventive fall of drapery. Among its competitors, the House of Worth stayed true to an ideal of dignity and broadly displayed wealth until it was finally driven into the shade by the social modes of the twentieth century. Society changed its character, and women their forms of display. Royal and imperial courts had by then rapidly dwindled in number and power, and custom-made presentation robes were no longer required.

END OF THE DYNASTY

Neat suits, amusing but useful little dresses, and brisk sportswear, alternating with festive expressions of ephemeral fantasy, all drove out the elaborate ostentations that had been so important for Charles Frederick Worth's original clientele. Nevertheless, the reign of Jean-Philippe and Gaston Worth continued to prosper and was smoothly followed by that of Gaston's two sons, Jean-Charles, the designer, and Jacques, the business director, who took over the house in the 1920s. This great fashion dynasty ended finally only in 1952, on the retirement of Roger Worth, the eldest son of Jacques and the fourth generation of Worths in couture.

Worth was the first dressmaker to demonstrate publicly—and force others to acknowledge—the importance of control over the way clothes look. For centuries that principle had been well understood ("The apparel oft proclaims the man," said Polonius), but the wearer had to take his or her own risks. Worth was the first to offer such control as a service to the female public—at a price, of course. Although he owed his first success to the empress, he was no captive court dressmaker. He was the first to profit personally from the fact that a flair for style and taste in dress, like beauty, are no respecters of social status or good morals. Unlike all the tailors and milliners who worked for Queen Elizabeth I and Marie Antoinette, he made his name, not that of his clients, a synonym for elegance.

43

THÉRÈSE BONNEY and LOUISE BONNEY

The Dressmaking World

From T. and L. Bonney (1929), A Shopping Guide to Paris
(New York: Robert M. McBride & Co.), 1–8.

What—another book about Paris?

No wonder you ask, for each year recently has brought its quota. Books that take you sightseeing, some laboriously, others pleasantly. Books that take you slumming in strange quarters of this romantic city. Books that lead you by the hand and brazenly "crash the doors" of shrinking celebrities. Books that tell you how to recognize the wine when it is red, and when it is white!

Still we have the presumption to offer another, because no one else has thought to write about shopping. More thousands of American dollars are spent in this activity than in any other by visitors to Paris. It is a difficult thing to spend them wisely in a city that offers so much. Hence, these words suggesting ways of "making both ends meet." Even if you are not planning a Paris trip, much of this book may make shopping in America more interesting and satisfactory and exciting, now that the ocean is really getting smaller every day. Whether you go to France or stay at home, there are few of you who are not interested in Paris clothes and Paris dressmakers. So we shall start with this world, which represents one of the largest industries of France, as well as one of its most important art expressions.

Any American woman trained by the monthlies, the dailies, and the rotogravure knows the leading dressmakers and milliners of Paris by name at least. If she is discerning and interested she knows rather well the points that distinguish one from another. She can tell a Vionnet dress

from a Poiret, and an Agnès hat from a Reboux. She is probably living in the dream that when she goes to Paris she will have one Paris gown at least,

Figure 66. "Madeleine Vionnet personally creates her costumes on doll-models," *A Shopping Guide to Paris* by Thérèse and Louise Bonney, 1929.

and as many more as her budget allows, possibly squeezing the budget a little! But when she arrives she finds that she cannot walk easily into a dressmaking establishment and buy a dress. This world has its etiquette. It serves best those who follow its ways. It is obliged to surround itself with safeguards, for the copyist is always alert. What may seem like positive ungraciousness is usually only an intolerance of some intrusion in its harmoniously ordered life, or a protective interest in knowing who you are and why you are there. At the entrance of every stranger this question is in the dressmaker's mind, and it must be answered satisfactorily if the stranger enters again. Then too there are times when strangers are less welcome, especially at the beginning of seasons when the houses are showing to journalists and transatlantic and European buyers. Usually there are two such openings, one the last week in July or the first in August; the other the last week in January or the first in February; the August one coinciding with the summer influx of Americans.

You will want to decide this important matter of the dress first, whether it be one or a dozen that you are selecting. It is the foundation of your shopping, and unto it must be added hats, gloves, shoes, bag, fur, scarf, handkerchiefs, stockings, jewelry, if you follow the smart Parisian woman in the emphasis she places on the ensemble. *Where* you will go for it depends on your taste and your pocketbook, but your shopping experience in any one house will be much the same as in any other, and quite different from the Fifth Avenue formula. So perhaps you will be saved time and confusion if you know the technique of this kind of buying.

The price is of first importance! If the prices of the *grands couturiers* are beyond your range it will be best not to go, for no house is interested in giving some three hours or more of personal attention to a client who has no intention of buying. One experience of "eye-shopping," and your welcome may be less warm next time. The prices range from seventy-five dollars[1] for the simplest sport dress to thousands of dollars for something magnificent in the way of a fur coat.

There are, however, few models at this minimum and not every large house has such a minimum. The houses really in vogue during any season are apt to have a low price of one hundred and twenty-five dollars. Do you want to pay this? If you do, very well—start out on one of the thrilling experiences of your life. If you do not, my advice is this: (1) buy at the semi-annual sales of the big houses when the models are disposed of cheaply; (2) find a good dressmaker who, with many of the resources of Rodier, Bianchini, and the other fabric creators at her command, a searching eye, and nimble fingers, can do very well by you inexpensively; or (3)—and this may surprise you—buy some of the many good copies of French models in American department stores and shops! There are smaller houses, to be sure, myriads of them—Alice's, Germaine's, Madeleine's, Marie's. They are usually the result of the superior imagination and initiative, or the good fortune of a *première*, a *vendeuse* (saleswoman), or a designer from a big house. Sometimes, of course, they "grow up" into establishments of the first class. This type of house between the *grand couturier* and the less pretentious dressmaker, this book will not attempt to cover. There are too many, their standards are not easily determinable, and their prices are not low enough to make purchases a bargain. Still we do not want to discourage you completely from experimenting with them. If you have a friend with admirable taste who has been well pleased with one, follow in her footsteps by all means if you want to. For myself I see little point in paying more for a gown than I should pay for one of like quality in New York and not enjoying the distinction of having one from a well-known creator.

The sales we have mentioned are held by most of the houses once or twice a year just before the showing of the new collection, to dispose of three types of models: (1) model gowns from the last collection; (2) model gowns which have been made for special exhibitions in other European cities; (3) new gowns, sometimes unfinished, ordered by a client but not delivered because of a precipitate departure or some other reason. Sometimes a house will sell these models throughout the year to clients whom it knows well. If your figure is an average one you will often find wonderful bargains. In many houses alterations will be made so that you can be fitted perfectly. Expect to find better bargains in street and sport clothes than in the more perishable dinner and evening gowns. If you become rather well known in a house, don't hesitate to say to your vendeuse as you are seeing an original collection—"Save that model for me, please, at the end of the season." If she likes you she will! And you will have the model for half price or less, depending on its condition.

[...]

The "little dressmaker" is a big figure in the average American woman's mind! She can buy many of her fabrics from the big houses. She follows style movements through all the avenues known to the clever Parisienne. She is "tricky" with her needle, or rather her little midinettes are tricky with *their* needles. There are hundreds of her in the city to a few of whom we shall introduce you in another chapter.

Now if you have decided that you really want to shop in the high world of fashion you will want to know something of its etiquette. The collections of the big houses are shown once or twice daily, at the appointed hour, always ten-thirty or eleven in the morning, and two-thirty or three in the afternoon. The order of showing is usually from sport dresses on through to evening gowns, following the activities and the interests of a woman's day. The collection is shown only once although individual models may be repeated. There are from one hundred and twenty-five to four hundred models depending on the policy of the house. Patou, for instance, designs prolifically, discarding the less popular models after the first week or two. These models, incidentally, often appear as exceptional bargains in the sales. The models are presented on mannequins, who have more graces than "bathing beauties," sometimes the more obvious ones which mark the mannequin, again the more subtle ones due

to the training of the house or the background of the individual mannequin, for some of these girls are well born. You must not always expect to find facial beauty of a startling order. Their greatest asset is a well-proportioned body and a sense of this particular kind of drama which lies perhaps in an abstraction approaching art. Symbols of beauty, not flesh-and-blood beauty; mannequins, not individuals!

The models are either named or numbered, and the names will be a joy to you if you understand French! Although you are usually given a program it is well to have your own memorandum book and pencil for note-taking. The parade is a little bewildering and your ideas of the gowns you liked best may be rather vague at the end. Your entry into a house will be less embarrassing and confusing if you know the name of a vendeuse or of a friend who has purchased there. If you do not, ask the directrice to be assigned one. She will usually speak at least "dressmakers' English." Her role is to stand by, to answer questions about name, price, material, and to note your favorites if you ask her. Do not hesitate to call the mannequin to you, and to inspect any details of the gown which may interest you. After the collection has been exhibited, you can ask to have any model reshown, either "in hand," or on the mannequin. As a rule it is best to insist on the mannequin, as it is impossible to know the values of a gown, the subtlety of line, the flow of material, and the relation to the figure, unless you see it on a model.

If now you find yourself really interested in buying, either order immediately or leave your name and address as is the custom, and return the next day, when the collection is not being shown to discuss the order with your vendeuse, and possibly with the head of the house. Consider well color, line, material. You can change the color if you feel sure of your taste; you can change the line somewhat to adapt it to peculiarities of taste or figure; but—you won't change the material unless you are particularly courageous or particularly foolish! This involves a very real risk since a model is practically always created around the texture values of a fabric. As a rule the fewer the changes, the greater the success. Changes too involve special handling in the workrooms and special fittings. If the model is materially changed in spite of all this advice, think to ask the price, as it may be quite different, one way or the other! Perhaps it will be well to give you one more piece of advice here—do not "bargain" as a rule. It is not the thing to do. These houses have artistic and commercial integrity, and unless you are an old customer or are ordering extensively, it is best not to question the established price.

Your fitting will be assigned to you. Be on time! Otherwise your fitter and your vendeuse may be required for another fitting before yours is over, and it does not pay to take chances with this new gown. The vendeuse takes charge of the fitting, advising minor changes if you are not interested in directing matters yourself. Sometimes she does very well, sometimes *not* so well! So do not hesitate to make suggestions if you are not satisfied and are one of those fortunate people who know what they can and what they cannot wear. I strongly advise a final trying-on, although most houses do not provide for it. But to guard against disappointment if you have set your heart on wearing this particular gown for some special occasion, or are leaving the city immediately, *insist* upon it, even if attempts are made to discourage you. A little nip under the arm, an inch more of freedom in the belt may make all the difference between a successful and an unsuccessful evening!

If you are not an old customer, arrange to pay at this last fitting or have the money ready in the hotel office when the garçon delivers the gown. It is the custom of the country to send a bill legalized by the stamp, with the delivery. Your response should be to pay. It is in no sense a reflection on your credit.

This—the technique of the order. The houses vary slightly in methods of presentation and control, but the principles are the same. Now the question is—where is this important gown to be bought? Out of the dozens of dressmakers in Paris, which will you choose? Obviously a difficult question for you or me to answer, given different tastes and different pocketbooks. So in the following discussion I shall try only to make you feel at home with certain of the dressmakers, and to save you from going to Poiret if you have a Vionnet soul!

Now and then someone springs into print with a list of the ten leading dressmakers of Paris, the ten highest of the high! I shall not presume to do that. The finest house in the city will not interest you if the spirit of its creations does not appeal to you. The house which boasts a startling success this year may not be so popular next, due to any one of a number of factors: a change of important designers, a change in management, the loss of a fine fitter, the failure of the season's materials to inspire the head of the house as happily as last year's. You should know enough of the personalities and the policies of a house to decide for yourself whether it will interest you. An unexpected detail may convince you more than any starred list or special recommendation. The well-dressed woman, no matter how she accomplishes this end, attends to the matter herself. So I shall leave the ratings to you.

NOTE

1. US$75 in 1929 is equivalent to US$810 in 2005 <www.westegg.com/inflation/>.

EDITORS' NOTE

The authors discuss the houses of Jenny, Chantal, Louiseboulanger, Poiret, Lanvin, Lelong, Vionnet, Callot, Jane Regny, Champcommunal, Rochas, Patou, Suzanne Talbot, Molyneux, Nicole Groult, Myrbor, Chanel, Worth, Paquin, Cheruit, Premet, Martial et Armand, O'Rossen, Doucet et Dœuillet, Beer et Drecoll, Redfern, Mary Nowitzky and Schiaparelli.

44

ALEXANDRA PALMER

Torontonian Taste in Couture

From A. Palmer (2001), **Couture and Commerce: The Transatlantic Fashion Trade in the 1950s** *(Vancouver: University of British Columbia Press),* **282–92.** © *University of British Columbia Press, 2001.* **All rights reserved by the publisher.**

> To be at all outstanding in dress now requires distinct originality and exceptional taste.
>
> Pringle 1949

The interplay of factors that determined the market for couture reveals a distinctly Torontonian taste. Canadian taste was regulated and filtered by professionals—Paris *vendeuses*, store buyers, and sales assistants—who exerted a considerable influence on what fashions were ultimately seen, purchased, and worn. Commercial choices of couture were made for two audiences: private clients; and the general public, which was kept up to date with current design trends through elaborate fashion shows. Couture was marketed as the height of advanced style, serving as a role model for all fashion design. Theatrical, attention-getting designs were chosen for fashion shows to show off the cosmopolitan sophistication of the store. Canadian retailers were acutely aware of the cultural value of displaying couture within fashion shows that were seen by thousands of women. Their interpretation of couture designs and presentation of coordinated ensembles unquestionably acted as a barometer for a feminine, English-Canadian standard of approved good taste and demonstrated correct Canadian etiquette. By contrast, store purchases for a private client were considered in terms of the individual and her role in society.

Local merchants' comprehension of a Canadian, and specifically Torontonian, taste has been illustrated throughout this book [i.e., *Couture and Commerce*]. The example of Eaton's fashion coordinator, Dora Matthews, ordering Paris designs in fabrics more suited to Canadian taste, not the "itchy doormat" fabric, testifies to her identification of a taste very distinct from that of Paris. Analogously, Holt Renfrew ordered a Dior cocktail dress in a colorful blue taffeta instead of in black as shown on the runway model, and thought it necessary to move the pockets on a Balenciaga suit from the skirt to the jacket, resulting in a more conservative look. In 1955, fashion reporter Olive Dickason (1955: 17) remarked that Canadian manufacturers were "Canadianizing the new fashions ... as Canadians prefer toned-down versions of extreme Paris styles ... more casual than what is found in originals." This was in contrast to American consumers, who were inclined to buy copies that were closer to the Paris design. Emily Post wrote that Americans tended to overdress and that to be overdressed "is to be vulgar and merely conspicuous" (1945: 455), while *Vogue's Book of Etiquette* put it more bluntly, saying, "It is in extremely bad taste to wear clothes in public that depart wildly from the accepted norm" (Fenwick 1948: 11). By contrast, Canadian understatement was a recognized characteristic. It was discussed on national television when Rosemary Boxer asked Harold Sniederman, owner of a sportswear shop, to compare the style of Canadian and American women. Sniederman said of Canadian women, "I think they are more conservative; I think they dress better" (*Tabloid* 1953).

Finally, the Toronto consumer imposed her own taste on all these preselected goods. Her taste was formed in conjunction with the requirements of the social season and Canadian cultural notions of value. To make the decision to buy a garment, a woman would want to feel flattered by the design and to have the requirements of appropriateness, longevity, and value met in terms of price, exclusivity, and design. The Canadian taste for understatement and long-term value is demonstrated by Catherine Elliott's wardrobe. She did not shop in Paris but relied on the preselected taste of Toronto buyers, and especially on the local specialty shop Joan Rigby, as well as patronizing local dressmakers. She was an active committee woman, serving as a member of the Garden Club and the Girl Guide Council. She was also a member of the old Toronto society and had inherited the tradition of her mother, who had dressed in leading designers' fashions.[1] Her taste embraced tailored suits, such as a Sybil Connolly. She wore her second wedding dress— a taupe wool dress and jacket ensemble by Hardy Amies—for years. She preferred British designers, who were not known for dramatic styles, and this extended into her choice of evening wear by Norman Hartnell. Her taste was for well-made, conservative styles that would last, reinforcing the importance of serviceability and longevity for Torontonians.

Joan Rosefield Lepofsky's wardrobe was composed of a quantity of imported bonded couture models and did embrace some lavish designs. The 1948 Dior bustle dress that she wore to the races was a bonded model and certainly one of the more striking Paris models produced at the time. Her very dramatic Jean Dessès evening gown, "Sciabe," she only wore once or twice as it was so noticeable and also because the hobble skirt design made it difficult to walk in.[2] Her bonded Chanel suits were much worn,

however, demonstrating Torontonian taste for understatement.

The couture wardrobe of Toronto socialite Signy Eaton reveals many typical aspects of couture worn in Toronto. She was an important member of the old elite Toronto circle, playing a prominent sociocultural role as wife of the president of Eaton's department store, a member of the Junior League, and an active member of the Art Gallery of Toronto. She was keenly aware of the impact of her dress, which was often reported in the press. Her constant nomination to the best-dressed lists and place within the Hall of Fame established by the *Toronto Telegram* testify to the correctness of her taste and also to the certainty that she was a role model for other Canadians, though she told me she dressed for herself. Mrs. Eaton first dressed in Paris couture in 1955 and continued to do so into the 1960s, when she would travel to Europe with her husband, who was conducting business. The bulk of her extant wardrobe in the Royal Ontario Museum, though predominantly evening wear, demonstrates her selections from the top European couturiers— Balmain, Dior, Fath, Givenchy, and Hartnell— as well as from more obscure names such as the Italian house Villa & Co. and the Spaniard Rodriguez. She also purchased bonded models, even though she did not recall doing so.[3] The nuances of Canadian clothing etiquette are clearly reflected in Mrs. Eaton's many comments on appropriate dress for different occasions. The social importance of wearing "good" and "correct" clothes cannot be overstated, and its significance was directly reflected in the time spent shopping, dressing, and maintaining a couture-based wardrobe, an important point that has been largely disregarded and unvalidated, as scholar Daniel Miller (1995) has noted.

Margaret Maynard, in her work on Australian dress, discusses the balancing act of being fashionable, but not too fashionable, which was also encountered by the Australian elite in the nineteenth century. She writes of the "constant tension between the concern for maintaining a suitable stylish appearance and trying to avoid the shame of vulgarity," and the "extremely

narrow line marking the difference between being finely dressed, thus achieving social visibility, and seeming to be overdressed" (Maynard
1994: 100). Insecurity in dress and etiquette,
and particularly the fear of appearing in public
in an overly dressy costume, seems to have been
a constant and recurring colonial anxiety. Canadians consistently chose a conservative tack that
emulated British sartorial taste, summed up by
the English couturier Hardy Amies, who said,
"It has always been rather bad taste in England
to be obviously expensively dressed, especially
among society people" (Glynn 1972).

There was an informal Canadian consensus that to be too fashionable was, in fact,
un-Canadian. This self-effacing stance was cau-
tioned against in 1954 by a "British expert … a
professor of political science at Cambridge University" who was visiting Canada and thought
that "a lack of extravagant self-esteem is all to
the good—there is enough of that for all North
America on constant tap south of the border.
But it can be overdone. There is a danger that a
modest man or a modest nation may be taken at
face value" (Brogan 1954: 23).

By the early 1960s, however, a change was
evident. Canadians accepted styles that were increasingly interchangeable with European and
American models. Not only had the importance of couture originals drastically dwindled,
but English-Canadian taste in couture had become less distinct, replaced by an emerging international taste in fashion. It also needs to be
remembered that during the 1950s, American
manufacturers and stores influenced elite Canadian taste indirectly by reselling bonded models and directly by widely disseminating copies
adapted for the North American market. There
were certainly some similarities in the two markets, as demonstrated by sales of Christian Dior–
New York models in both countries. The 1950
Christian Dior–New York model "Avenue Mon-
taigne," for example, sold 121 copies throughout
North America and was considered perfectly appropriate for Canadian taste.

The couture dress of elite Toronto women
from 1945 to 1960, however, can be seen as part

of the development of English-Canadian postwar
cultural identity. Historically, there has been no
iconographic form of dress to represent Canada,
or Canadianness, despite regional symbols of
English-Canadian dress such as Scottish tartans
and kilts and Québécois habitant dress, as exemplified by the *capote* and *ceinture fléchée*. Yet during the 1950s, couture clothing worn in Canada
did act as a recognizable form of "national" dress
for elite women and was also what the majority
of women aspired to wear. Dressed in couture,
elite women moved in international circles as
cultural ambassadors, and through their dress
achieved what the 1949–51 Massey Report, a
study of Canadian culture, called for: "the promotion abroad of a knowledge of Canada that is
not a luxury but an obligation" (Canada 1951:
254). Canadian women wearing couture served
the nation in this capacity.

A European model of couture suited English
Canadians, as it reinforced their distance from
American customs and aligned them with their
traditional European and English roots. Couture was the most desirable form of dress, as it
provided a visual social entrée into elite social
circles. It was easily recognized and instantaneously accepted as beyond reproach, as long as it
conformed to the occasion. Couture was one of
the clearest symbols that the wearer understood
codes of behavior.

During the 1950s, the roles of the elite were
clearly based on gender and class. Men dominated public and political life, while women orchestrated the private lives of their families and their
social circle. Couture wardrobes symbolized and
highlighted the status of the social elite and implied that the wearers were knowledgeable cultural and social professionals who practiced con-
noisseurship in many fields. Couture operated as
a professional working uniform. Couture provided a standard for national sartorial taste, influencing large numbers of Canadian women at
far wider social levels than the small number of
couture clients. Elite Torontonian women were
not avant-garde in their couture dress. Their
consumption simply conformed to an internationally accepted standard, adjusted to national

and then personal taste. Distinguishing their dress was a uniquely Canadian discrimination imposed on their selections at all stages of design, production, merchandising, and purchase. Understatement, discretion, and notions of socioeconomic value epitomized Toronto women's couture style and consumption patterns in the postwar years.

In 1952, British fashion journalist Alison Settle wrote, "Fashion is, after all, the most successful ... I'd be inclined to say, the only really successful ... form of internationalism." Couture signified European elitist sociocultural economic power and values to an international constituency. This book [i.e., *Couture and Commerce*] has set out to study couture consumption in a way that treats it as a continually evolving aspect of modern culture rather than as a fixed and universal social function (D. Miller 1987: 157). Consumption is a central element of contemporary societies and must play an important role in attempts to understand their nature. I hope that my work has both problematized and illuminated the designs and the lives of those who participated in the production, reception, and consumption of couture during the 1950s—when these beautifully designed and crafted clothes were worn and enjoyed by so many North American women.

NOTES

1. During the 1930s, Catherine Elliott had a dressmaker, Mrs. Jarvis, went to Vassallo and Maria, Ruth McDougal, Meme Dystée, Creeds, Holt Renfrew, Eaton's, and Simpson's, and favored Joan Rigby (interview with Flavia Redelmeier). The Royal Ontario Museum has several pieces from the family, dating from the 1890s onward.

2. A turn-of-the-century Paris custom-designed dress for Mrs. Sheldon Stephens of Montreal was never worn; the basting stitches are still in the garment at the McCord Museum of Canadian History. Perhaps this was another instance of a design being "too French," or flamboyant.

3. Signy Eaton was on the 1952 best-dressed in Toronto list, published by *Liberty* magazine, and the first *Toronto Telegram* best-dressed list in 1952. She was also voted onto the Hall of Fame list published by the *Toronto Telegram* in 1962 (interview with Signy Eaton). The Royal Ontario Museum has a Henry à la Pensée from her with a bond tag inside.

45

TED POLHEMUS

Trickle Down, Bubble Up

From T. Polhemus (1994), **Streetstyle: From Sidewalk to Catwalk**
(London: Thames and Hudson), 8–12. © 1994 Ted Polhemus.
Reprinted by kind permission of Thames and Hudson Ltd., London.

Styles which start life on the street corner have a way of ending up on the backs of top models on the world's most prestigious fashion catwalks. This shouldn't surprise us because, as we have seen, the authenticity which streetstyle is deemed to represent is a precious commodity. Everyone wants a piece of it.

But it is more than the price tag which distinguishes the genuine article from its chic reinterpretation. It's a question of context. And when fashion sticks its metaphorical gilt frame around a leather motorcycle jacket, a hippie kaftan, a pair of trainers, of a ragga girl's batty-riders, it transforms an emblem of subcultural identity into something which anyone with enough money can acquire and wear with pride.

However much streetstyle and fashion might superficially resemble each other, they are actually poles apart. Fashion is trendy. It celebrates change and progress. Change, because This Year's New Look always elbows aside Last Year's New Look in a perpetual pursuit of novelty. Progress, because of the implicit assumption—one which characterizes modern society—that The New is also—by definition, *ipso facto*—The Improved. Both a product of modernism and its ultimate expression, fashion faces resolutely toward the future. It has the capacity to generate the new and fresh, a capacity which has always made it appealing to those who subscribe to the view that change is preferable to the status quo and that tomorrow holds more promise than yesterday. (And when in the 1980s there was a widespread swing toward postmodernism which cast doubt on such progressive assumptions, this was reflected in a corresponding shift away from ever-changing fashion and toward classic, anti-trendy style.)

In its heyday (for example, in the 1950s and 1960s, fashion managed to get practically everyone to fall in line behind the particular look which it decreed to be the trend. As Peter York puts it in *Modern Times*:

Fashion had its own establishment, a kind of Vatican, in the 1950s and 1960s and in this setup they had dictators who set the lines for everybody to follow.

The lines were set like edicts in the way of the old world ... They were set by magazine editors for magazine readers. *Vogue* used to announce the color of the season and up and down the land shops presented clothes in banana beige or coral red or whatever.

In the 1950s there were actually lines for fashion. Dictates about [what] the shape [of] a woman's clothes should be, irrespective of the shape of her. And then came the 1960s. Remember the mini ...

And the point was that everyone wore it, your sister, your auntie, the gym mistress, everyone.

For truly THERE WAS NO ALTERNATIVE (York 1984: 10).

We find an even more illuminating example of the fashion system in action if we turn the clock back just a little further, to 1947, when Christian Dior launched his "New Look" on a world still waiting for the dust to settle on the Second World War. If ever there was a time when people yearned to catch a glimpse of a promising future, this was it, and the New Look, though actually a reworking of an old look, certainly seemed fresh and novel compared to the dress women had been obliged to wear throughout the war.

Using extravagant amounts of fabric in its long, full skirts and cinching in women's waists in a way which some saw as unliberated, Dior's design raised many an eyebrow and prompted many a politician to rail against its profligacy. But such opposition was, of course, doomed to failure. For here was the spirit of The New at a time when everyone was desperate to be rid of The Old.

Of course only a tiny minority of women were in a position to purchase one of Dior's creations, but the years following 1947 saw the New Look "trickle down" (indeed, in this case, cascade down) to the department stores and, very quickly, to patterns which could be run up at home. However difficult it was to accomplish, women from Paris to Los Angeles and all points in between struggled to fall in step with the march of fashion. For, as Peter York correctly says, in those days THERE WAS NO ALTERNATIVE.

This classic example illustrates the three principal characteristics of fashion: its celebration of The New, its singularity (*the* New Look) and its diffusion from high society to mass-market. But today, while stories of the death of fashion (my own included) may have been exaggerated, all three of these characteristics seem much less in evidence than they were only a few decades ago.

Firstly, as one might expect in a "Postmodern Age," a growing number of people seem dubious about the proposition that what is new is necessarily improved. Such distrust in progress is hardly surprising at a time when environmental, economic and social realities cast such a dark shadow on the future. This shift in attitude has influenced developments in interior and furniture design, as well as in architecture—most notably in a renewed emphasis on "Reconstruction." Likewise, in the sphere of clothing and accessory design, "timeless classics" have gained in popularity. Indeed, those who jump uncritically on the latest bandwagon have been branded "fashion victims," while the word "trendy" has often become a put-down rather than a compliment.

Secondly, instead of the authority of *the* fashion, one is today more likely to see pluralism, with different designers proposing radically conflicting New Looks. While some fashion pundits may strive to reduce this cacophony of different colors, shapes, hemlengths and so on, into a consistent trend—a single "direction"—anyone viewing the photographs of the Paris, Milan, London or New York shows can appreciate that difference, rather than consensus, is the order of the day.

Such multiplicity of "direction," coupled with an apparently growing inclination on the part of many simply to wear what suits them rather than to swallow fashion's prescription, has brought a variety of dress and adornment styles which is arguably without equal in history. The homogeneity of appearance which Peter York (in the quote above) sees as characteristic of, for example, the 1960s ("everyone wore it, your sister, your auntie, the gym mistress, everyone") is no longer typical. Today, when you look at what people are actually wearing on the street, in the office and at nightclubs, what is obvious is that now there *is* an alternative. Indeed, lots and lots of alternatives, as the "edicts" of yesteryear are pushed aside by the demands of personal choice.

Finally, do new looks still begin life within high fashion and "trickle down" for mass consumption? It is undoubtedly true that the mass-market "mainline" fashion industry continues to take a lead from the more exclusive, highly priced designers. But do the creations we see on those exclusive, camera-flashlit catwalks all originate in the minds of the world's top designers?

Not on the evidence that I see. To my eyes an increasingly frequent chain of events goes like this. First there is a genuine streetstyle innovation. This may be featured in a pop music video and streetkids in other cities and countries may pick up on the style. Then, finally—at the end rather than the beginning of the chain—a ritzy version of the original idea makes an appearance as part of a top designer's collection.

Instead of trickle down, *bubble up*. Instead of the bottom end of the market emulating the top end, precisely the reverse.

If Dior's New Look illustrates the traditional trickle-down process, then the "Perfecto"

motorcycle jacket (also known as the "Bronx" jacket) may serve to illustrate the bubble-up process in action. Based on a Second World War design, the Perfecto jacket as made by the Schott Brothers Company of New York became the symbol of rebellious youth when Marlon Brando wore one in *The Wild One*. With its sinister black sheen and its zips like knife slashes, this garment embodied an attitude and lifestyle which directly challenged "normal society."

Figure 67. "Perfecto" black leather jacket (2000.03.01). Historic Textile and Costume Collection, University of Rhode Island.

In the suburban American community in which I grew up in the 1950s and 1960s, the only kids who wore such jackets hung out at the pool hall "looking for trouble." This was *Rumble Fish* territory—deep on the wrong side of town.

While I can recall secretly admiring these jackets early in the 1960s, it would be well into the 1970s before I actually got up the nerve to buy one. Nor was such hesitancy based entirely on unjustified paranoia. As shown in *American Graffiti*'s portrayal of teenage life in the USA of the early 1960s—where the hero's madras sports jacket contrasts tellingly with his tormentors' Perfecto-style jackets—this garment marked a very real subcultural (and often socioeconomic) boundary.

In Britain, a similar jacket was made by Lewis Leathers. Mick Farren, a braver soul than myself, got it together to buy himself one when he was only fifteen:

> I bought the jacket in a small, backstreet men's clothing store, hard up against a railway bridge in a medium-sized seaside town in southern England. It was hardly the concrete jungle but it passed at the time. The store specialized in tacky, juvenile delinquent fashions—polka dot shirts, stardust peggies, dayglo socks and lurid suits that usually fell apart after a couple of weeks ... I stood in front of the store's full-length mirror and slipped off whatever jacket I was wearing. (It isn't part of the memory. It was probably some flaky tweed sports coat of which my mother totally approved.) I struggled into what was going to be my first cool garment ... The jacket came from D. Lewis Ltd. of Great Portland Street, London. It was the Bronx model. As I stared into the mirror, I couldn't believe myself. Admittedly the mirror was tilted up to produce the most flattering effect, but I looked great. My legs seemed longer, my shoulders seemed broader. I flipped the collar up. I looked so damned cool. Mother of God, I was a cross between Elvis and Lord Byron. (Farren 1985)

Only very gradually, throughout the 1970s and into the 1980s, did the black leather motorbike jacket become accepted as everyday, "normal" apparel. Arguably the most potent indicator of how streetstyle in general has gradually

become an accepted part of our culture, its wider appeal was guaranteed when it became de rigueur for serious rock musicians. From Gene Vincent to Jim Morrison, from Lou Reed to The Clash, from Bruce Springsteen to George Michael, the black leather jacket is there to assure us of a musician's authenticity.

What makes the Perfecto The Real Thing is its Bad Boy/Girl, wrong-side-of-the-tracks image. That and the fact that it is a classic, antifashion garment, virtually unchanged in its design for some five decades.

But what is true of the genuine article as made by the Schott Brothers or Lewis Leathers is not true of the countless imitations which began appearing on high-fashion catwalks in the 1980s. First it was the "street cred" designers like Katharine Hamnett, Pam Hogg and Jean-Paul Gaultier who produced their own jazzed-up versions. But when, by the mid-1980s, high-fashion designers like Claude Montana, Thierry Mugler, Gianni Versace and Sonia Rykiel showed versions of the Perfecto, the bubble-up process was well and truly complete.

The transformation of the Perfecto-style jacket from subcultural emblem to high and mainstream fashion is hardly unique. Most of the dozens of streetstyles dealt with in this book have at some time, in some way, provided inspiration for a wide range of fashion designers. Indeed, we have come to expect that styles which begin life on dead-end, mean streets will almost instantaneously and with ever-increasing regularity make an appearance on even the most prestigious of fashion catwalks. And, in the process, the pages of *Vogue* and *Elle* have often come to resemble those of *The Face* and *i-D* (but with the difference that the former's "punks," "raggamuffins," "travelers" and so forth are actually highly paid models styled in some fantasized imitation of The Real Thing),

On one level this inversion of the socioeconomic order is all very admirable. Who wants to return to a time when the social elite were so full of themselves that they refused to believe that anything of value could come from those further down the ladder? It was the 1960s which at long last recognized that culture is not the prerogative of the upper classes—a realization which revitalized our society with creative talent and new blood.

The bubble-up process has made us a fully fledged creative democracy in which talent isn't thought to be limited by class or race or education or how much money you've got in the bank. For our culture as a whole it is surely all for the best that the full spectrum of creative energy in our society has been tapped.

However, those who are actually members of such stylistically influential subcultures may not share this enthusiasm for the bubble-up process. Both in 1977, when Zandra Rhodes presented her ripped and safety-pinned "Punk Look," and, more recently, when Versace and other high-fashion designers produced similarly derivative styles, genuine punks of my acquaintance usually categorized such imitation as "insult" rather than flattery. Likewise, Johnny Stuart, author of the definitive book on rockers, recently commented that:

It is irritating to see how the leather jacket has become just a fashion garment. I can remember how back in the days when rockers were far, far outnumbered by mods, to wear your leathers was a risky business indeed. If you weren't careful, if you didn't stay on your bike and keep moving, your leather jacket could get ripped off your back and you could get a real beating. The fancy fashionable versions of the Perfecto which you see all over the place these days water down the significance of the thing, taking away its original magic, castrating it. (conversation with the author, 1994)

Even within the fashion industry there is concern at what is seen as "exploitation" of street-style creativity. According to British designer Joe Casely-Hayford (1994):

The fashion world has become so hungry that people are scouring—they come from all over the world to London, taking aspects of different groups and using it, consuming it and moving on to the next thing. But the fashion world will continue to miss the essence and will continue to exploit and will continue to rape and will continue to move on in a very superficial and trivial way.

Strong words. But then the implication and effects of the bubble-up process cannot be taken lightly. Imitation may be the sincerest form of flattery, but just as the counterfeiting of fashion designers' own designs undermines their value, something similar occurs when fashion copies streetstyle. That authenticity and sense of subcultural identity which is symbolized in street-style is lost when it becomes "this year's latest fashion"—something which can be purchased and worn without reference to its original subcultural meaning. In this sense, what may begin as a designer's genuinely felt desire to celebrate "the street" as a wellspring of fresh ideas may have the inadvertent effect of undermining the "street value" of these styles for the very people who originally created them.

46

ANGELA McROBBIE

Secondhand Dresses and the Role of the Ragmarket

From A. McRobbie (1997) "Second-hand Dresses and the Role of the Ragmarket" in K. Gelder and S. Thornton (eds.), **The Subcultures Reader** *(London and New York: Routledge), 191–199. Originally published in A. McRobbie (ed.),* Zoot Suits and Second-hand Dresses *(Boston: Unwin Hyman), 1988. Reprinted by permission of the author.*

Several attempts have been made recently to understand "retrostyle." These have all taken as their starting point that accelerating tendency in the 1980s to ransack history for key items of dress, in a seemingly eclectic and haphazard manner. Some have seen this as part of the current vogue for nostalgia while others have interpreted it as a way of bringing history into an otherwise ahistorical present. This [essay] will suggest that secondhand style or "vintage dress" must be seen within the broader context of postwar subcultural history. It will pay particular attention to the existence of an entrepreneurial infrastructure within these youth cultures and to the opportunities which secondhand style has offered young people, at a time of recession, for participating in the fashion "scene."

Most of the youth subcultures of the postwar period have relied on secondhand clothes found in jumble sales and ragmarkets as the raw material for the creation of style. Although a great deal has been written about the meaning of these styles little has been said about where they have come from. In the early 1980s the magazine *iD* developed a kind of vox pop of street style which involved stopping young people and asking them to itemize what they were wearing, where they had got it and for how much. Since then many of the weekly and monthly fashion publications have followed suit, with the result that this has now become a familiar feature of the magazine format. However, the act of buying and the processes of looking and choosing still remain relatively unexamined in the field of cultural analysis.

One reason for this is that shopping has been considered a feminine activity. Youth sociologists have looked mainly at the activities of adolescent boys and young men and their attention has been directed to those areas of experience which have a strongly masculine image. Leisure spheres which involve the wearing and displaying of clothes have been thoroughly documented, yet the hours spent seeking them out on Saturday afternoons continue to be overlooked. Given the emphasis on street culture or on public peer-group activities, this is perhaps not surprising, but it is worth remembering that although shopping is usually regarded as a private activity, it is also simultaneously a public one and in the case of the markets and secondhand stalls it takes place in the street. This is particularly important for girls and young women because in other contexts their street activities are still curtailed in contrast to those of their male peers. This fact has been commented upon by many feminist writers, but the various pleasures of shopping have not been similarly engaged with. Indeed, shopping has tended to be subsumed under the category of domestic labor with the attendant connotations of drudgery and exhaustion. Otherwise it has been absorbed into consumerism where women and girls are seen as having a particular role to play. Contemporary feminism has been slow to challenge the early 1970s orthodoxy which saw women as slaves to consumerism. Only Erica Carter's work (1979) has gone some way toward dislodging the view that to enjoy shopping is to be passively feminine and incorporated into a system of false needs.

Looking back at the literature of the late 1970s on punk, it seems strange that so little mention was paid to the selling of punk, and the extent to which shops like the Sex shop run by Malcolm McLaren and Vivienne Westwood functioned also as meeting places where the customers and those behind the counter got to know each other and met up later in the pubs and clubs. In fact, ragmarkets and secondhand shops have played the same role up and down the country, indicating that there is more to buying and selling subcultural style than the simple exchange of cash for goods. Sociologists of the time perhaps ignored this social dimension because to them the very idea that style could be purchased over the counter went against the grain of those analyses which saw the adoption of punk style as an act of creative defiance far removed from the mundane act of buying. The role of McLaren and Westwood was also downgraded for the similar reason that punk was seen as a kind of collective creative impulse. To focus on a designer and an art-school entrepreneur would have been to undermine the "purity" or "authenticity" of the subculture. The same point can be made in relation to the absence of emphasis on buying subcultural products. What is found instead is an interest in those moments where the bought goods and items are transformed to subvert their original or intended meanings. In these accounts the act of buying disappears into that process of transformation. Ranked below these magnificent gestures, the more modest practices of buying and selling have remained women's work and have been of little interest to those concerned with youth cultural resistance.

[…]

THE ROLE OF THE RAGMARKET

Secondhand style owes its existence to those features of consumerism which are characteristic of contemporary society. It depends, for example, on the creation of a surplus of goods whose use value is not expended when their first owners no longer want them. They are then revived, even in their senility, and enter into another cycle of consumption. House clearances also contribute to the mountain of bric-à-brac, jewelry, clothing and furniture which are the staple of junk and secondhand shops and stalls. But not all junk is used a second time around. Patterns of taste and discrimination shape the desires of secondhand shoppers as much as they do those who prefer the high street or the fashion showroom. And those who work behind the stalls and counters are skilled in choosing their stock with a fine eye for what will sell. Thus although there seems to be an evasion of the mainstream, with its mass-produced goods and marked-up prices, the "subversive consumerism" of the ragmarket is in practice highly selective in what is offered and what, in turn, is purchased. There is in this milieu an even more refined economy of taste at work. For every single piece rescued and restored, a thousand are consigned to oblivion. Indeed, it might also be claimed that in the midst of this there is a thinly veiled cultural elitism in operation. The sources which are raided for "new" secondhand ideas are frequently old films, old art photographs, "great" novels, documentary footage and textual material. The apparent democracy of the market, from which nobody is excluded on the grounds of cost, is tempered by the very precise tastes and desires of the secondhand searchers. Secondhand style continually emphasizes its distance from secondhand clothing.

The London markets and those in other towns and cities up and down the country cater now for a much wider cross-section of the population. It is no longer a question of the *jeunesse dorée* rubbing shoulders with the poor and the down-and-outs. Unemployment has played a role in diversifying this clientele, so also have a number of other less immediately visible shifts and changes. Young single mothers, for example, who fall between the teen dreams of punk fashion and the reality of pushing a buggy through town on a wet afternoon, fit exactly with this new constituency. Markets have indeed become more socially diverse sites in the urban landscape. The Brick Lane area in London, for example, home to part of the Bangladeshi population settled in this country, attracts on a Sunday morning, young and old, black and white, middle-class and working-class shoppers as well as tourists and the merely curious browsers. It's not surprising that tourists include a market such as Brick Lane in their itinerary. In popular currency, street markets are taken to be reflective of the old and unspoilt; they are "steeped in history" and are thus particularly expressive of the town or region.

The popularity of these urban markets also resides in their celebration of what seem to be pre-modern modes of exchange. They offer an oasis of cheapness, where every market day is a "sale." They point back in time to an economy unaffected by cheque cards, credit cards and even set prices. Despite the lingering connotations of wartime austerity, the market today promotes itself in the language of natural freshness (for food and dairy produce) or else in the language of curiosity, discovery and heritage (for clothes, trinkets and household goods). There is, of course, a great deal of variety in the types of market found in different parts of the country. In London there is a distinction between those markets modeled on the genuine fleamarkets, which tend to attract the kind of young crowd who flock each weekend to Camden Lock, and those which are more integrated into a neighborhood providing it with fruit, vegetables and household items. The history of these more traditional street markets is already well documented. They grew up within the confines of a rapidly expanding urban economy and played a vital role in dressing (in mostly secondhand clothes), and feeding the urban working classes, who did not have access to the department stores, grocers or other retail outlets which catered for the upper and middle classes. As Phil Cohen (1979) has shown, such markets came under the continual surveillance of the urban administrators and authorities who were concerned with "policing the working-class city." The street markets were perceived by them as interrupting not only the flow of traffic and therefore the speed of urban development, but also as hindering the growth of those sorts of shops which would bring in valuable revenue from rates. These were seen as dangerous places, bringing together unruly elements who were already predisposed toward crime and delinquency; a predominantly youthful population of costermongers had to be brought into line with the labor discipline which already existed on the factory floor.

The street market functioned, therefore, as much as a daytime social meeting place as it did a place for transactions of money and goods. It lacked the impersonality of the department stores and thrived instead on the values of familiarity, community and personal exchange. This remains the case today. Wherever immigrant groups have arrived and set about trying to earn a living in a largely hostile environment, a local service economy in the form of a market has grown up. These offer some opportunities for those excluded from employment, and they also offer some escape from the monotony of the factory floor. A drift, in the 1970s and 1980s, into the microeconomy of the street market is one sign of the dwindling opportunities in the world of real work. There are now more of these stalls carrying a wider range of goods than before in most of the marketplaces in the urban centers. There has also been a diversification into the world of new technology, with stalls offering cut-price digital alarms, watches, personal hi-fis, videotapes, cassettes, "ghetto-blasters" and cameras. The hidden economy of work is also supplemented here by the provision of goods obtained illegally and sold rapidly at rock-bottom prices.

This general expansion coincides, however, with changing patterns in urban consumerism and with attempts on the part of mainstream retailers to participate in an unexpected boom. (In the inner cities the bustling markets frequently breathe life and color into otherwise desolate blighted areas. This, in turn, produces an incentive for the chain stores to reinvest, and in places such as Dalston Junction in Hackney, and Chapel Market in Islington, the redevelopment of shopping has taken place along these lines, with Sainsbury's, Boots the Chemist and others, updating and expanding their services. The stores flank the markets, which in turn line the pavements, and the consumer is drawn into both kinds of shopping simultaneously. In the last few years many major department stores have redesigned the way in which their stock is displayed in order to create the feel of a market place. In the Top Shop basement in Oxford Street, for example, there is a year-round sale. The clothes are set out in chaotic abundance. The rails are crushed up against each other and packed with stock, which causes the customers to push and shove their way through. This intentionally hectic atmosphere is heightened by the disc jockey who cajoles the shoppers between records to buy at an even more frenzied pace.

Otherwise, in those regions where the mainstream department stores are still safely located on the other side of town, the traditional street market continues to seduce its customers with its own unique atmosphere. Many of these nowadays carry only a small stock of secondhand clothes. Instead, there are rails of "seconds" or cheap copies of high-street fashions made from starched fabric which, after a couple of washes, are ready for the dustbin. Bales of sari material lie stretched out on counters next to those displaying makeup and shampoo for black women. Reggae and funk music blare across the heads of shoppers from the record stands, and hot food smells drift far up the road. In the Ridley Road market in Hackney the hot bagel shop remains as much a sign of the originally Jewish population as the eel pie stall reflects traditional working-class taste. Unfamiliar fruits create an image of color and profusion on stalls sagging under their weight. By midday on Fridays and at weekends the atmosphere is almost festive. Markets like these retain something of the preindustrial gathering. For the crowd of shoppers and strollers the tempo symbolizes time rescued from that of labor, and the market seems to celebrate its own pleasures. Differences of age, sex, class and ethnic background take on a more positive quality of social diversity. The mode of buying is leisurely and unharassed, in sharp contrast to the Friday afternoon tensions around the checkout till in the supermarket.

Similar features can be seen at play in markets such as Camden Lock on Saturday and Sunday afternoons. Thousands of young people block Camden's streets so that only a trickle of traffic can get through. The same groups and the streams of punk tourists can be seen each week, joined by older shoppers and those who feel like a stroll in the sun, ending with an ice cream further along Chalk Farm Road. Young people go there to see and be seen if [not] for any other reason than that fashion and style invariably look better worn than they do on the rails or in the shop windows. Here it is possible to see how items are combined with each other to create a total look. Hairstyles, shoes, skirts and "hold-up" stockings; all of these can be taken in at a glance. In this context shopping is like being on holiday. The whole point is to amble and look, to pick up goods and examine them before putting them back. Public-school girls mingle with doped-out punks, ex-hippies hang about behind their Persian rug stalls as though they have been there since 1967, while more youthful entrepreneurs trip over themselves to make a quick sale.

SUBCULTURAL ENTREPRENEURS

The entrepreneurial element, crucial to an understanding of street markets and secondhand shops, has been quite missing from most subcultural analysis. The vitality of street markets today owes much to the hippie counterculture of the late 1960s. It was this which put flea-markets firmly back on the map. Many of those which had remained dormant for years in London, Amsterdam or Berlin, were suddenly given a new lease of life. In the years following the end of the Second World War the thriving black markets gradually gave way to the fleamarkets which soon signaled only the bleakness of goods discarded. For the generation whose memories had not been blunted altogether by the dizzy rise of postwar consumerism, markets for old clothes and jumble sales in the 1960s remained a terrifying reminder of the stigma of poverty, the shame of ill-fitting clothing, and the fear of disease through infestation, rather like buying a secondhand bed.

Hippie preferences for old fur coats, crêpe dresses and army greatcoats, shocked the older generation for precisely this reason. But they were not acquired merely for their shock value. Those items favored by the hippies reflected an interest in pure, natural and authentic fabrics and a repudiation of the man-made synthetic materials found in high-street fashion. The pieces of clothing sought out by hippie girls tended to be antique lace petticoats, pure silk blouses, crêpe dresses, velvet skirts and pure wool 1940s-styled coats. In each case these conjured up a time when the old craft values still prevailed and when one person saw through his or her production from start to finish. In fact, the same items had also won the attention of the hippies' predecessors, in the "beat culture" of the early 1950s. They too looked for ways of bypassing the world of ready-made clothing. In the rummage sales of New York, for example, "beat" girls and women bought up the fur coats, satin dresses and silk blouses of the 1930s and 1940s middle classes. Worn in the mid-1950s, these issued a strong sexual challenge to the spick and span gingham-clad domesticity of the moment.

By the late 1960s, the hippie culture was a lot larger and much better off than the beats who had gone before them. It was also politically informed in the sense of being determined to create an alternative society. This subculture was therefore able to develop an extensive semi-entrepreneurial network which came to be known as the counter-culture. This was by no means a monolithic enterprise. It stretched in Britain from hippie businesses such as Richard Branson's Virgin Records and Harvey Goldsmith's Promotions to all the ventures which sprang up in most cities and towns, selling books, vegetarian food, incense, Indian smocks, sandals and so on. It even included the small art galleries, independent cinemas and the London listings magazine *Time Out*.

From the late 1960s onward, and accompanying this explosion of "alternative" shops and restaurants, were the small secondhand shops whose history is less familiar. These had names like "Serendipity," "Cobwebs" or "Past Caring" and they brought together, under one roof, all those items which had to be discovered separately in the jumble sales or fleamarkets. These included flying jackets, safari jackets, velvet curtains (from which were made the first "loon" pants) and 1920s flapper dresses. These secondhand goods provided students and others drawn to the subculture, with a cheaper and much more expansive wardrobe. (The two looks for girls which came to characterize this moment were the peasant "ethnic" look and the "crêpey" bohemian Bloomsbury look. The former later became inextricably linked with Laura Ashley and the latter with Biba, both mainstream fashion newcomers.) Gradually, hippie couples moved into this secondhand market, just as they also moved into antiques. They rapidly picked up the skills of mending and restoring items and soon learnt where the best sources for their stock were to be found. This meant scouring the country for out-of-town markets, making trips to Amsterdam to pick up the long leather coats favored by rich hippie types, and making thrice-weekly trips to the dry-cleaners. The result was loyal customers, and if the young entrepreneurs were able to anticipate new demands from an even younger clientele, there were subsequent generations of punks, art students and others.

The presence of this entrepreneurial dynamic has rarely been acknowledged in most subcultural analysis. Those points at which subcultures offered the prospect of a career through the magical exchange of the commodity have warranted as little attention as the network of small-scale entrepreneurial activities which financed the counterculture. This was an element, of course, vociferously disavowed within the hippie culture itself. Great efforts were made to disguise the role which money played in a whole number of exchanges, including those involving drugs. Selling goods and commodities came too close to "selling out" for those at the heart of the subculture to feel comfortable about it. This was a stance reinforced by the sociologists who also saw consumerism within the counterculture as a fall from grace, a lack of purity. They either ignored it, or else, employing the Marcusian notion of recuperation, attributed it to the intervention of external market forces. It was the unwelcome presence of media and other commercial interests which, they claimed, laundered out the politics and reduced the alternative society to an endless rail of cheesecloth shirts.

There was some dissatisfaction, however, with this dualistic model of creative action followed by commercial reaction. Dick Hebdige (1979) and others have drawn attention to the problems of positing a raw and undiluted (and usually working-class) energy, in opposition to the predatory youth industries. Such an argument discounted the local, promotional activities needed to produce a subculture in the first place. Clothes have to be purchased, bands have to find places to play, posters publicizing these concerts have to be put up … and so on. This all entails business and managerial skills even when these are displayed in a self-effacing manner. The fact that a spontaneous sexual division of labor seems to spring into being is only a reflection of those gender inequalities which are prevalent at a more general level in society. It is still much easier for girls to develop skills in those fields which are less contested by men than it is in those already occupied by them. Selling clothes, stage-managing at concerts, handing out publicity leaflets, or simply looking the part, are spheres in which a female presence somehow seems natural.

While hippie style had run out of steam by the mid-1970s, the alternative society merely jolted itself and rose to the challenge of punk. Many of those involved in selling records, clothes and even books, cropped their hair, had their ears pierced and took to wearing tight black trousers and Doctor Marten boots. However, the conditions into which punk erupted and of which it was symptomatic for its younger participants were quite different from those which had cushioned the hippie explosion of the 1960s. Girls were certainly more visible and more vocal than they had been in the earlier subculture, although it is difficult to assess exactly how active they were in the do-it-yourself entrepreneurial practices which accompanied, and were part of, the punk phenomenon. Certainly the small independent record companies remained largely male, as did the journalists and even the musicians (though much was made of the angry femininity of Poly Styrene, The Slits, The Raincoats and others). What is less ambiguous is the connection with youth unemployment, and more concretely, within punk, with the disavowal of some of the employment which was on offer for those who were not destined for university, the professions or the conventional career structures of the middle classes.

Punk was, first and foremost, cultural. Its self-expressions existed at the level of music, graphic design, visual images, style and the written word. It was therefore engaging with and making itself heard within the terrain of the arts and the mass media. Its point of entry into this field existed within the range of small-scale youth industries which were able to put the whole thing in motion. Fan magazines (fanzines) provided a training for new wave journalists, just as designing record sleeves for unknown punk bands offered an opportunity for keen young graphic designers. In the realm of style the same do-it-yourself ethic prevailed and the obvious place to start was the jumble sale or the local fleamarket. Although punk also marked a point at which boys and young men began to participate in fashion unashamedly, girls played a central role, not just in looking for the right clothes but also in providing their peers with a cheap and easily available supply of secondhand items. These included 1960s cotton print shifts like those worn by the girls in The Human League in the early 1980s (and in the summer of 1988 "high fashion" as defined by MaxMara and others), suedette sheepskin-styled jackets like that worn by Bob Dylan on his debut album sleeve (marking a moment in the early 1960s when he too aspired to a kind of "lonesome traveler" hobo look), and many other similarly significant pieces.

This provision of services in the form of dress and clothing for would-be punks, art students and others on the fringe, was mostly participated in by lower middle-class art and fashion graduates who rejected the job opportunities available to them designing for British Home Stores or Marks and Spencer. It was a myth then, and it is still a myth now, that fashion houses were waiting to snap up the talent which emerges from the end-of-term shows each year. Apart from going abroad, most fashion students are, and were in the mid-1970s, faced with either going it alone with the help of the Enterprise Allowance Schemes (EAS), or else with joining some major manufacturing company specializing in down-market mass-produced fashion. It is no surprise, then, that many, particularly those who wanted to retain some artistic autonomy, should choose the former. Setting up a stall and getting a licence to sell secondhand clothes, finding them and restoring them, and then using a stall as a base for displaying and selling newly designed work, is by no means unusual. Many graduates have done this and some, like Darlajane Gilroy

and Pam Hogg, have gone on to become well-known names through their appearance in the style glossies like *The Face*, *Blitz* and *iD*, where the emphasis is on creativity and on fashion-as-art.

Many others continue to work the markets for years, often in couples and sometimes moving into bigger stalls or permanent premises. Some give up, retrain or look round for other creative outlets in the media. The expansion of media goods and services which has come into being in the last ten years, producing more fashion magazines, more television from independent production companies, more reviews about other media events, more media personalities, more media items about other media phenomena, and so on, depends both on the successful and sustained manifestation of "hype" and also on the labor power of young graduates and school-leavers for whom the allure of London and metropolitan life is irresistible. For every aspiring young journalist or designer there are many thousands, however, for whom the media remains tangible only at the point of consumption. Despite the lingering do-it-yourself ethos of punk, and despite "enterprise culture" in the 1980s, this bohemian world is as distant a phenomenon for many media-struck school-leavers as it has always been for their parents. "Enterprise subcultures" remain small and relatively privileged metropolitan spaces.

47

SONNET STANFILL

Punks and Pirates: The Costiff Collection of Vivienne Westwood

Michael and Gerlinde Costiff's collection of nearly three hundred Vivienne Westwood garments is evidence of the designer's cult-like appeal. Purchased in London over a twenty-year period, the clothes are also indicative of the long-term, delighted devotion of two of Westwood's most loyal clients. The Costiffs, as vintage collectors, fashion connoisseurs, club owners and King's Road residents, celebrated dressing up, with Westwood as their designer of choice, from the punk days of the mid-1970s until Gerlinde's death in 1994.

The Victoria and Albert Museum (V&A) purchased the Costiff Collection in 2002.[1] The museum considers Westwood a designer of excellence and one who has remained a fearless, groundbreaking creator for over three decades. Awarded an Order of the British Empire (OBE) in 1992, Dame Commander (DBE) in 2006 and twice voted British Designer of the Year, Westwood has achieved near oracular status in British fashion. In 2004, the V&A honored her influence by staging a retrospective of her prolific, provocative career. While the Costiff Collection does not chronicle her entire career, for the V&A it represented a rare opportunity to obtain twenty years' worth of designs with a single acquisition. In addition, it provides evidence of some of the designer's most intriguing sources of inspiration. The fruits of Westwood's study of historical dress (the corset, the crinoline, the seventeenth-century fabric-slashing technique) and art and design history (the paintings of eighteenth-century French artist François Boucher, eighteenth-century porcelain and marquetry patterns) are evidenced in the Costiffs' purchases. Further, the collection's provenance was nearly as compelling as the clothes. A dynamic and fashionable couple, the Costiffs' personal histories, both as Westwood's clients and contemporaries, corresponded in fascinating ways with the designer's own.

Michael and Gerlinde came to London separately in 1968: Michael at age twenty-one from the village of Grindleford in the Peak District National Park, and Gerlinde at twenty-six from Regensburg in Bavaria, Germany. Their meeting and courtship coincided with Westwood's emergence as a designer. In 1970, Westwood and her husband and design partner Malcolm McLaren began selling rock and roll memorabilia and clothing at their first shop, Let it Rock, at 430 King's Road. This was the year before Michael and Gerlinde married and moved to the bottom end of the same street. Westwood and McLaren reopened 430 King's Road in 1972 as Too Fast to Live Too Young to Die and again, after refurbishment, under the name Sex in 1974. Sex offered, among other things, rubber and leather fetish gear, much of it customized by Vivienne herself. Michael and Gerlinde (at this time running a stall of 1950s and 1960s kitsch in London's Antiquarius antique market) then started shopping there, sparingly at first: only one garment from 1974 survives in their collection.

In 1977, McLaren and Westwood reopened their shop under the name of Seditionaries. According to Claire Wilcox, Senior Fashion Curator at the V&A, this latest incarnation provided the sartorial identity for the punk movement (Wilcox 2004: 13). The Costiffs responded to London's punk explosion and to Westwood and McLaren's Seditionaries clothing with amused enthusiasm. They bought a number of key looks including two bondage suits for Michael and, for Gerlinde, a "God Save the Queen" T-shirt, mohair jumpers and several pairs of dauntingly high-heeled shoes. Michael Costiff had this to say about the punk movement, "We were almost thirty—we were too young to be hippies, too old to be punks. It was all a sort of a pose, which I couldn't go along with. But then I didn't want to be an anarchist or overthrow anything. I like the Queen!"[2]

Michael and Gerlinde bought even more looks from "Pirate," the Autumn/Winter 1981–82 collection. They attended the catwalk presentation (Westwood's first) and purchased many full outfits (fifteen survive) as well as individual garments and accessories. Michael said of the "Pirate" show, "It was the most extraordinary thing you'd ever seen. It was just so luxurious. There was the glitter of gold, clothes that were swashbuckling, heroic … it was MAGICAL." The pleasure of wearing these early collections resulted in the Costiffs' particular loyalty to McLaren and Westwood and later, when the couple and design duo parted ways, to Vivienne as she struck out on her own. Acknowledging the importance of the Costiffs' patronage, Westwood said, "The Costiffs must have been best customers from punk times until the terrible day of Gerlinde's sudden death."[3] Michael Costiff, in describing the frisson caused by wearing early Westwood, said:

> The wonderful thing about it was, because we were traveling quite a lot then, if you wore anything of Vivienne's you'd just meet people at the airport, or people would approach you all the time and comment. We were in Khartoum, and somebody came up to us in the hotel and said, "Excuse me, are you English?" because we were wearing Westwood.

The Costiffs bought Westwood most consistently from 1976 to 1986 with at least a few significant pieces, usually more, from most seasons. They bought widely from "Pirates," "Buffalo" (A/W 1982–83), "Punkature" (S/S 1983), "Witches" (A/W 1983–84) and "Mini Crini" (S/S 1985). Michael also purchased several key outfits from "Cut and Slash" (S/S 1991) and Gerlinde bought several important examples from "Portrait" (A/W 1990/91). There are a few Westwood collections that did not hold great appeal for the Costiffs. For example, there is very little of the stunning tweed suiting, tailoring and fine knitwear from "Harris Tweed" (A/W 1987–8). Also missing are good representations from "Pagan I" (S/S 1988), which featured Greek-inspired drapery. Additionally, there are only a few garments from "Pagan V" (S/S 1990).

Although the Costiffs did buy full Westwood outfits, they did not always wear the designer's clothing head-to-toe. A rare instance of Gerlinde wearing all Westwood is captured in a photograph taken of her in London's Battersea Park in full "Buffalo" regalia at an Easter parade in 1982 (Figure 68). More often the Costiffs mixed Westwood pieces with other garments. Michael Costiff said, "That was quite Gerlinde really. With anything that looked sort of expensive she would wear something else really cheap and cheesy so it didn't look too sort of grand." Michael too liked to mix his Westwood in unexpected ways, for example wearing his bondage trousers and boots with a tailored jacket and tie to give them a subversive look. As these anecdotes suggest, the Costiffs not only bought hundreds of Westwood garments, they, like many of her loyal clients, wore them over decades with undiminished enthusiasm. According to Michael, "Gerlinde was wearing 'Pirates,' particularly for holidays, up until the day she died." Further proof of the longevity of Westwood's designs is that for years the basis of Gerlinde's wardrobe was the Vivienne Westwood corset. The corset was another Westwood garment whose construction was based on historical study, for the designer examined eighteenth-century examples in the V&A's archives. Westwood's diverse modern

Figure 68. Left: Gerlinde Costiff in head-to-toe Vivienne Westwood at Battersea Park, London, 1982. Right: Gerlinde and Michael Costiff wearing Vivienne Westwood at Elton John's birthday party, 1991. Michael is also wearing an eighteenth-century frock coat. Victoria and Albert Museum, Department of Textiles and Dress.

interpretations, with their zip fastenings, unusual textiles and even removable sleeves, are well represented in the Costiff collection—seventeen survive. Michael recalled:

> Gerlinde wore a corset like other people wore a T-shirt. It was really a foundation for her look for a while. She had terrible scabs from the boning that used to dig into her. But you quite liked that for fashion … suffering! Things that hurt! Because you were aware of it all the time. It forced you to consider your presence and you knew you were dressed up and felt fabulous.

The Costiffs' love of clothing, dressing up and going out eventually had a bespoke venue. In 1989 they established Kinky Gerlinky, their monthly London club nights, which attracted an eclectic crowd of, as Michael put it, "men, women and everything in between." With

Michael as organizer and Gerlinde as hostess, the club's popular events were often themed and featured ever more outrageous costume contests. Gerlinde hosted these occasions with panache and chose Vivienne Westwood to design some of her more elaborate ensembles. During this period Gerlinde placed a number of what Westwood called "special orders": existing looks in special fabrics chosen specifically for the client. One memorable example is an outfit consisting of red satin corset, codpiece-accented underpants, boots and gloves based on a design from "Cut, Slash and Pull" (S/S 1991). Westwood also made the same look for Gerlinde in a bold leopard print (Figure 68).

The Costiffs' and Westwood's paths occasionally crossed socially and professionally. Michael and Gerlinde invited the designer to judge several of the Kinky Gerlinky costume contests.

Westwood said about the club, "There has never been anything like the nights of Kinky Gerlinky, the entire ballroom filled with thousands having the time of their lives, looking like you never saw before on the flood tide of their fantasy of fabulous, over-the-top, fun dressing."[4] In addition to everyday wear and clothes for their club nights, the Costiffs often relied on Westwood when dressing for social events. For a night out dancing at New York's Studio 54 in the late 1970s, Michael chose his Westwood bondage suit. On a later trip to New York, Gerlinde wore "Witches" and "Punkature"—their heavy wool and sheepskin materials made them ideal (warm as well as stylish) for the fashionable city's cold winters. To attend Elton John's birthday party in 1991, Gerlinde wore her outlandish Westwood leopard print ensemble, complete with matching over-the-knee platform boots. On this same evening Michael sported gold Vivienne Westwood jeans along with an eighteenth-century frock coat that was, as he put it, "having one last wear." The photograph in Figure 68 shows them on that occasion.

Michael Costiff's evocative accounts of wearing Westwood help explain the couple's impulse to amass such an extraordinary inventory of her designs. Further insight into Westwood's allure can be found in the words of her long-time-associate, Murray Blewitt, who declared:

I think that when someone has bought something of Vivienne's, has had the courage or the inclination to, often you find that they become a loyal customer. They come back because there's something about the clothing that appeals to them—whether it be the asymmetric things that pull and push against the body or a corset that made you aware of yourself. They return because they feel ennobled by the clothes.[5]

Michael Costiff summed up his own feelings about wearing Westwood by saying simply, "To tell you the truth, if someone asks you who your clothes are by, there's something very nice about saying 'Vivienne Westwood.'"

NOTES

1. The V&A acquired the collection thanks to the generous assistance of the National Art Collections Fund, the Friends of the V&A, the Elspeth Evans Trust, the Monica Barnett Bequest and the Dorothy Hughes Bequest.
2. All quotes from Michael Costiff are taken from an interview with the author in February 2003.
3. Letter from Vivienne Westwood to the V & A, September 3, 2002.
4. Ibid.
5. Interview with Murray Blewett, February, 2003.

48

YUNIYA KAWAMURA

Japanese Street Fashion: The Urge To Be Seen and To Be Heard

INTRODUCTION

Fashion in postmodern times often emerges out of youth culture and is then commercialized by the industry to reach a wider audience to spread it as "fashion." By using Japanese street subculture as a case study, we can understand the group affiliation of Japanese teen girls who walk around the streets of Tokyo.[1] A strong social connection and a sense of belonging exists among these teen girls, who dress themselves in unique and original outfits, some of which may be outrageous, radical and extraordinary. These teens are not simply consumers, but also producers of fashion.

Since the early 1990s, Japan has faced the longest and the worst economic recession in its history. Japanese society is known to be extremely cohesive and conformist, but as John Nathan (2004) explains, this may be fracturing under the strain of economic stagnation. Fathers are losing jobs for the first time in their lives,[2] mothers who used to be full-time homemakers now have to look for part-time jobs to supplement their household income, and children find no hope in future Japan. As a result, statistics show that violence in schools has risen dramatically. Since 1998, teens aged between fourteen and nineteen have been involved in 50 percent of all felony arrests, including murder (Nathan 2004). A feeling of helplessness, disillusionment,

alienation, uncertainty and anger has permeated throughout society, from adults to children. A gradual breakdown of family, social and economic systems has occurred. The entire society's value system, especially that of the teens, is going through a major transition. The previous generations' traditional Japanese beliefs, such as selfless devotion to employers, respect for seniors and perseverance, are collapsing (Ijiri 1990). A shift from old ideology and ways of life is evident in today's Japan.

Fashion expresses the prevailing ideology of society. The teens see the assertion of individual identity as more important and meaningful than that of family or school identity, which used to be the key affiliations in Japanese culture, so they seek ways to oppose mainstream ideology. They are in search of a community or a group where they are accepted, welcomed and feel comfortable. Such behavior is reflected in their norm breaking and unconventional, yet commercially successful styles that have emerged out of different street subcultures.

Ironically, it is under these social and economic conditions that Japanese street fashion has become increasingly creative and innovative, as if the teens were looking for ways to rebel against the traditional values and to challenge and redefine the existing notion of what is fashionable. They go against the grain of the normative standard of every aspect of society.

JAPANESE STREET FASHION AND SUBCULTURE

For many Japanese teens, life centers around the Shibuya 109 Department Store near Shibuya Station in Tokyo. The teens unconsciously and unintentionally create a subculture, which according to Dick Hebdige (1988: 35), forms in the space between surveillance and the evasion of surveillance, and that translates the feeling of being under scrutiny into the pleasure of being watched. Furthermore, Hebdige explains (1988: 27) that girls have been relegated to a position of secondary interest within both sociological accounts of subculture and photographic studies of urban youth, and masculine bias still exists in the subcultures themselves. But it is the girls who play a major role in Japanese subcultures.

The first major street subculture that appeared in the mid-1990s, and which helped fuel this sector of the fashion industry, is known as *Ganguro*—which literally means face-black or black face.[3] A common sight on the streets of Tokyo at the time was groups of young girls between the ages of fifteen and eighteen with long hair, dyed brown or bleached blonde, tanned skin, heavy makeup, brightly colored miniskirts or short pants, and high platform boots. A designer in my fieldwork study who used to be a *Ganguro* said: "I was a hardcore *Ganguro* when I was in high school. I had to be. Otherwise, I wouldn't have been accepted by the other kids. I would have been totally out of place if I'd looked normal. We all want to fit in when we are teenagers. But it becomes embarrassing if you still look like a *Ganguro* by the time you go to college."[4] There is a time limit as to how long they remain in the *Ganguro* subculture. Then they move on to form another subculture.

Ganguro led to *Amazoness*, which was more extreme than *Ganguro*, with very heavy makeup, but according to some industry professionals, it was so extreme that it did not last long. Instead, in the late 1990s, *Yamamba*, which refers to a mountain witch in Japanese mythology, replaced the *Ganguro* look. More recently, *Yamamba* has evolved into *Mamba*, which is already beginning to fade away. Multiple interactions occur simultaneously on the streets of Tokyo, and the subcultures with specific appearances have branched out into so many different sub-subcultures that it is almost impossible to track down all the existing groups as each subculture comes up with a distinctive style. For example, if one claims to be a *Celemba,* one must dress in LizLisa brand from head to toe. If one is a *Cocomba*, one wears Cocolulu brand, one of the most popular street fashion brands among teens.

On the bridge near Harajuku Station, another fashion district in Tokyo, the *Gothic Lolita* subcultural group is found (Figure 69). The *Gothic Lolita* fashion has been one of the most popular looks in the Harajuku area since 1999, and it is part of the *Lolita* subculture. This style can be seen as a counter-reaction to the *Ganguro* style

Figure 69. Gothic Lolitas on the bridge near Harajuku Station. Photograph by Yuniya Kawamura. Reprinted by permission of Sage Publications Ltd. from Yuniya Kawamura, "Japanese Teens as Producers of Fashion," *Current Sociology* (©International Sociological Association/ISA, 2006).

and others that evolved out of it. It is popular among those who think *Mamba, Yamamba* or *Ganguro* is too outrageous and unfeminine. Like other subcultures, *Gothic Lolita* is dominated by girls. The image is that of a Victorian doll, which appears to be an exaggerated form of femininity with pale and fair skin, curly hair, knee- or mid-thigh-length Victorian-style dresses with laces and frills, pinafores, bloomers, stockings and shoes or boots.

Gothic Lolita sub-styles include *Elegant Gothic Lolita*, with a monochromatic palette, *Classical Gothic Lolita*, with pastel colors, and *Punk Gothic Lolita*, with punk elements such as leather, zippers and chains. Other *Lolitas* include *Ama-Loli*, with a basic *Lolita* look using mostly white. If pink is used, it is called *Pink-Loli*. When two girls wear exactly the same *Lolita* style, it is called *Futago-Loli*, which means "Twin Lolitas."

Many of the subcultural groups have created website communities. There are rules as to what kind of topics can be posted on the Internet so that they can maintain the subcultural identity of the site. Discussions on specific brands for their members, questions about how to put together a particular look, and instructions on making items to create a particular look are typical. They exchange, auction, buy and sell their own fashion items. The enthusiasts create and use their own language and abbreviations, which outsiders cannot comprehend, such as *LoliBra*, which means a *Lolita* brand or a *Cardi*, which means a cardigan.

The distinctive look functions as a visible group identity for the teens and becomes a shared sign of membership affiliation; it is also used to communicate their ideas, intentions, purposes and thoughts. The intended meaning and the interpretation of the look varies, and the teens are aware of this uncertain communication. Therefore, these styles are functional and purposeful only within the specific territory of Harajuku and Shibuya, among particular groups of people. These teens rely on a distinctive appearance to proclaim their symbolic subcultural identity, which is not political or ideological. It is simply fashion that determines their group affiliation, and it is very innovative. They have the desire to be seen and to be noticed by society and thus standing out becomes important.

CONCLUSION

Fashion is a collective activity that arises out of particular social relationships among the members of a subculture. Within every subculture, there are common values, attitudes and norms that bind members together. They are frequently expressed visually through distinctive clothes, makeup, accessories and jewelry, which are used to signify identity. Fashion today cannot be dictated solely by professional designers. The junior high and high school students who represent Japanese street culture and fashion have the potential to influence other teens. They not only consume and diffuse fashion but also guide industry professionals as to what the next trends will be. Particular styles imply which and what level of social groups are involved. In this context, the teen consumers, who are at the same time the producers, have dominance, although not completely, over the production and dissemination of fashionable looks, resulting in a complementary relationship between the production and consumption of fashion.

NOTES

1. A sociological discussion of fashion looks at the macro-structural analysis of the social organization of fashion and also the micro-interactionist analysis of the individuals involved in the production of fashion, which is different from the production of clothing, dress or costume (Kawamura 2004b). It also investigates the interaction and interdependence between organization and the individuals involved in the world of fashion (Crane 2000).
2. Japanese men have had a strong belief in lifetime employment. It used to be against their cultural norm to change jobs.
3. Editors' note: The label *Ganguro* is related to the look of tanned skin.
4. Kumiko Okuma interviewed on July 22, 2005, in Tokyo, Japan.

ANNOTATED GUIDE TO FURTHER READING FOR PART IX

One of the best books on Parisian couture is Elizabeth Ann Coleman's *The Opulent Era,* written to accompany an exhibition of the same name at the Brooklyn Museum. In it, she discusses the business, designs and clients of Charles Frederick Worth, Jacques Doucet and Emile Pingat. Valerie Steele's *Paris Fashion* (1998) treats the unique culture of Paris and the way it fostered the design business.

British design is detailed in *The Cutting Edge,* a catalog edited by Amy de la Haye for an exhibition at the Victoria and Albert Museum. For a case study of the premier Savile Row British tailoring firm, see Stephen Howarth's *Henry Poole: Founders of Savile Row.*

Regarding American fashion design, see Caroline Rennolds Milbank's *New York Fashion: The Evolution of American Style* (1989). An in-depth study of the dressmaking business of two Italian-American sisters is presented in *From Paris to Providence: Fashion, Art, and the Tirocchi Dressmakers' Shop, 1915–1947,* edited by Susan Hay.

The rise of Italian fashion is ably laid out by Nicola White (2000). Yuniya Kawamura, author of the extract on Japanese street fashion, wrote on the entry of Japanese designers in Paris in *The Japanese Revolution in Paris Fashion* (2004). In it, she explains the categorization of fashion by the French industry: haute couture, demi-couture, and ready-to-wear.

Charlotte Seeling's *Fashion: The Century of the Designer 1900–1999* provides a thorough, beautifully illustrated history of the designers of the twentieth century. More than just a picture book, it addresses cultural changes too.

Zandra Rhodes, one of the first to be inspired by the styles of subcultural groups and ethnic groups (the Ukraine, Mexico), published what could be considered an "autobiography of design" in 1985. It is titled *The Art of Zandra Rhodes.*

For background on subcultural styles, see Ted Polhemus's *Street Style,* which gives the history of "style tribes" from the 1940s to the 1990s. His categorization of subcultures as "tribes" marked a new understanding of how dress contributes to formation of identity. For a book-length study of one of Polhemus's style tribes, see *Goth: Identity, Style and Subculture* by Paul Hodkinson.

Several essays in *Twentieth-Century American Fashion,* edited by Linda Welters and Patricia Cunningham, deal with subcultural style. These include Deborah Saville's work on Greenwich Village bohemians, Linda Welters's chapter on the Beat Generation, and the essay on hip-hop style by Robin Chandler and Nuri Chandler-Smith. The promotion of American designers during the Second World War is discussed by Sandra Buckland.

The secondhand clothes market, patronized by consumers for individualized looks and by designers for inspiration, is discussed in a book of essays edited by Alexandra Palmer and Hazel Clark, *Old Clothes, New Looks* (2004).

PART X
The Fashion Business

LINDA WELTERS

Introduction

Fashion is, above all, a business. Even the most creative designer will close up shop if the bottom line is red. This is what happened to American designer Isaac Mizrahi in 1998 when, just six months after showing his spring collection, he went out of business. Mizrahi had been the darling of the fashion media, garnering high praise for his luxurious styles; he was the star of *Unzipped* (1995), a documentary film that followed the creation of his 1994 fall/winter collection. After a "sabbatical" during which Mizrahi pursued other creative endeavors, he reemerged in 2004 as the high-profile designer of a collection of women's clothes for Target, the Minneapolis-based mass-merchandiser. This successful venture not only breathed new life into the designer's career, but also raised the profile of Target, which has since contracted with other designers to fulfill its mission of "Design for All." Now the giant Wal-Mart is attempting to go upscale too, with its own faux designer collections.

Fashion is a complex, multi-layered, highly competitive business. Successful companies sell the right merchandise at the right time and at the right price. To get it "right," people in the fashion business must understand their market as well as how to create products that meet consumer demand. The path from design concept to the consumer is divided into three categories: textiles and other materials, fashion design and manufacture, and retailing. Marketing—advertising and promotion—occurs at all levels. Each level is discussed below.

TEXTILES AND OTHER MATERIALS

Textiles are the raw materials for most fashion products, but leather, fur, jewelry, cosmetics and beauty products are also part of the fashion business. Textile production begins with the fiber, the smallest unit of a fabric. For millennia, all fibers came from nature, with the major fibers being cotton, flax, wool and silk. Over the course of the twentieth century, chemical companies researched and developed many manufactured fibers, which now make up approximately 50 percent of US apparel. These manufactured fibers include rayon, polyester, acrylic, nylon and spandex among others. Whether natural or manufactured, fibers are spun or twisted into yarns; yarns are made into fabrics through weaving, knitting, or other methods; and fabrics are finished. Color can be added at any stage, depending on the desired effect. Textiles are tested by quality control to ensure that they meet performance and safety standards. A host of marketing/merchandising support systems exist to facilitate production of fashionable textiles that will appeal to the consumer.

Certain natural fibers are associated with particular countries. China dominates the silk trade; India is the world's oldest cotton grower; Egypt is known for its long-staple cotton; and Australia is the source for merino wool.

Textiles inspire fashion designers, and vice versa. Often designers work with textile manufacturers to develop unique fabrics. Europe and

Japan have strong reputations for making luxurious fashion fabrics. Italy, in particular, is known for fine wools and silks; England, Ireland and Scotland for woolens; and Switzerland for cottons. The major textile trade shows are Première Vision, held outside Paris, and Interstoff in Frankfurt, Germany.

Textile manufacturers continually search for the cheapest place to manufacture their goods. This means that countries with low labor costs, low taxes and few environmental regulations attract business. The trend has been to move production to developing countries with large, poor populations and few environmental restrictions, such as China and India. Setting up a textile plant requires greater financial investment and technical knowledge than establishing an apparel-manufacturing operation. Most textiles for apparel come from Asia: Korea, for example, produces runs of 10,000+ yards for women's suitings.

DESIGN AND MANUFACTURE

Ever since the birth of couture in the mid-nineteenth century, the media has focused on the role of the designer in creating fashion; but most fashion design is a team effort. It would be more accurate to call the design of today's clothing "product development." The focus is on the *brand*, which in some cases is the name of a designer, but may also be a store name or a manufacturer's name. The brand may produce non-apparel fashion goods, such as bed linens, furniture or even wall paint.

Whether Nicolas Ghesquière is designing a collection for the House of Balenciaga, Coach is creating new handbag styles, or Zara is working on its fall line, the creative team comes up with a concept. Usually working nine to twelve months in advance of the product appearing in stores, the team presents concepts for approval. After receiving the "OK," the teams proceed with creating the styles: fabrics are sourced, patterns are made, and samples are sewn and fitted. Designers and manufacturers show the next season's offerings to buyers through highly publicized fashion shows during market weeks, but lines may also be viewed in company showrooms in major cities or at regional markets. Manufacturers' representatives also travel to small stores to show buyers the latest offerings. After orders have been placed, it takes about four to six weeks until the product is delivered.

Producing fashion has become a global enterprise, thanks to rapid communication via Internet, fax and express delivery service. Cheap labor is the key to earning greater profit in this highly competitive, narrow-margin industry. More often than not, apparel factories do not own the goods; they are contracted only to cut and sew. China, Bangladesh and Vietnam are some of the Asian countries that offer the cheapest labor to assemble apparel. Their low labor costs help negate the time it takes to deliver finished goods to the US and Europe by ship, which is just under two weeks.

The structure of apparel companies ranges from sole proprietorships to partnerships to large corporations. Apparel manufacturers face many challenges: late deliveries, cancelled orders, excess inventory, charge-backs and overdue payments from retailers. While sole proprietorships offer the potential for great creativity, a large corporation can better weather financial setbacks.

Apparel is designed with various price points in mind. Couture offers the most creativity, and the highest prices. Couture designers show their collections in Paris twice a year, in January and July. Couture is a very small percentage of the apparel business, but generates huge publicity for the brand's ready-to-wear lines. The most prominent ready-to-wear, or prêt-a-porter, designers show their collections during market weeks held sequentially in Paris, London, Milan and New York. For decades most ready-to-wear designers have shown four collections annually: Spring, Summer, Fall I and Fall II. Resort/cruise is sometimes a fifth collection. Spring and Fall I are the most important collections. Manufacturers are now moving toward more frequent roll-outs of new styles.

"Shopping the market" to see the competition's products is a common practice in the industry. Sometimes this results in copies, or "knockoffs." It is difficult to prosecute design piracy, particularly with globalization of production.

RETAILING

Fashion is sold to the consumer through a variety of retail outlets, depending on the product's price point. One of the older retail categories is the department store, which developed in the mid-nineteenth century. Department stores greatly influenced middle-class consumers throughout the twentieth century, but have been challenged by other retail categories in recent decades including mass-merchandisers, discounters, off-price, outlet stores, vintage, catalog, television shopping channels and e-tailing.

Buyers hold a lot of power in the fashion adoption process because they are preselecting for the consumer. They are constantly on the lookout for the next new thing so their stores are well stocked when consumers want to make purchases. Their selections determine how fashion-forward the retailer is.

Malls have been a fixture of middle-class American culture since the era after the Second World War. Every American city has one or more malls, and shopping has become entertainment. In the 1990s, mega-malls superseded older malls, providing restaurants, theaters, even theme parks. The geographical nature of the United Kingdom's old towns and cities preserves "High Street" downtown shopping districts. Malls have begun appearing elsewhere in the world, such as Canary Wharf in London's Docklands district. The mall concept is flourishing beyond Europe. China opened the Golden Resources Mall (6 million square ft.) in Beijing in 2004. The Mall of Arabia (10 million square ft.) is scheduled to open in Dubai in 2006.

For top designers, high-profile retail space is part of the business. Internationally known designer brands are sold in their own stores or in top-end stores such as Brown's in London or Barney's in New York. Store locations are critical—big-name designers and retailers must be in trendy locations in the world's fashion cities as the store must reinforce the designer's image. Hence the recent trend for hiring architects to create cutting-edge retail space—the store itself becomes a destination.

Some retailers are vertically integrated, designing and manufacturing their own merchandise to sell in their own specialty chain stores. Examples include Gap, Marks & Spencer, Next, Zara and H&M. Vertical integration streamlines the supply chain, bringing goods to consumers quickly and at reasonable cost. The introduction of bar codes, laser technology and computer chips sewn into tags has revolutionized inventory control and replenishment, and is often called "quick response" or "lean retailing."

At all levels of the fashion business, the pressure to beat the previous year's numbers is constant. The cycle is speeding up. The advent of the digital age brings instant fashion information to the consumer; consequently, fashion-forward customers expect to see these goods at their favorite retailers instantly, resulting in the "pre-show." Designers show the line to their best retail customers in advance of fashion week so that goods can be ordered and in the stores prior to the publicity generated around the runway shows.

The capacity to produce clothes cheaply, and the fast-moving nature of fashion, has created a new twist to the fashion business. Americans and Europeans are discarding used clothing more quickly than in the past. This has resulted in a burgeoning secondhand trade in the developing world, particularly in Africa.

The readings in this section vary from a case study of the design and production of an Alexander McQueen dress to the secondhand market in Africa. Readers will learn about finishing premium jeans, the Mall of America, and Islamic consumers, as well as how India is growing its own fashion industry.

49

KATY CHAPMAN

Inside Design: A Look at the Method Behind the Madness

Originally published in AATCC Review 2, 2 (February 2002): 21–4. Reprinted with permission from the copyright holder, AATCC <www.aatcc.org>.

The pressure on soft-goods companies to compete in today's marketplace with new and innovative product concepts has never been greater. Changes in global communications and sourcing have lead to a broader exchange of ideas at a much more rapid speed than a few years ago. Combined with the challenges of keeping prices low and quality high, what may be a consumer's dream is now a designer's worst nightmare.

Challenges faced at the front end of the process are often passed down through the supply chain, creating more issues later in production and quality assurance. Understanding what makes designers tick may be the first step in recognizing how to balance marketing concerns with production issues, so that the entire supply chain may exist more harmoniously.

THE BIRTH OF AN IDEA

Each season is met with a new array of fashions that speak to the trend of the moment. Last fall it was the Victorian look, while this coming spring promises an updated version of the ethnic-folk craze. How do designers decide what looks will be favored by consumers and (more importantly) fashion editors, and when?

Trend Services

For corporate designers, the first glimpse at a future fashion may come from a trend forecasting service. For a fee, these services predict color, silhouette, fabrication, and print design themes, often as much as two years in advance. Trend services are comprised of design and marketing experts who look at economic and cultural influences to take a barometric "reading" of consumer preferences in seasons to come.

They shop global markets to gather fabrics, sample garments, colors, art, and ideas from various cultures that speak to a particular trend or mood. They also look at the performance of trends in the past to gather insight into future behaviors. For example, hemlines have been historically lower in times of economic recession and shorter when the stock market is up. If several seasons are dominated by softer, more neutral color palettes, then the cycle of fashion may dictate a trend toward brighter, more saturated colors.

Media Influences

Other areas where trend mavens and designers gain inspiration are from current events and the media. Art exhibits featured at major city museums will often spark new interest in the looks of a particular time or culture. Television continues to be a great messenger of fashion trends to the masses, whether it's what Carrie is wearing on *Sex and the City*, *Entertainment Tonight*'s coverage of what stars are wearing on the red carpet, or the ever-increasing coverage of runway fashion shows on cable channels such as "E!"

And let's not forget the influence movies have on trends. Remember the Ray-Ban Wayfarer craze of the late 1980s, sparked by films such as *Risky Business* and *The Blues Brothers*? Once only the focus of consumer magazines, fashion interest now permeates all aspects of our media-rich lives.

Necessary Direction

Yet with so many ideas to pull from, are the predictions made by trend services always right on target? Sometimes not, so most companies will subscribe to more than one trend service and take a cross-section of the best ideas from which to form a seasonal direction. They often back this information up with further trend research and shopping expeditions of their own, to customize a direction for their brand or target audience.

Most designers use trend services as a point of inspiration to begin designing for a season, rather than relying on them as the final word. Trend services provide the necessary direction that helps designers stay "on the same page," so there is uniformity to the look and color of goods at retail in any given season. In other words, the proliferation of a trend in stores is no happy accident.

KEEPING UP WITH THE TREND CYCLE

Caught in the revolving door of fashion, trends at retail are turning faster than ever before. Due to the accessibility of fashion over the Internet and television, today's consumer is much closer to trends as they emerge. With the touch of a mouse they can see what's happening in the Far East or Europe, markets that were once the best-kept secret source of ideas for American designers. Websites such as <www.Style.com>, a joint project between *Vogue* and *W* magazines, offer fashion news and runway reports along with an array of product offerings that echo the trends they promote. Armed with more knowledge and less cash to spend, today's consumer is apt to make more careful selections.

This means that fashion companies must use innovation at the right time and price to please this wise and choosy consumer. Once a trend is reported in a fashion magazine, it has often neared its peak in terms of popularity. Where companies could once design well over a year in advance of a season, they are now forced to bring products to market within only a few weeks of conception.

Fighting Fire with Fire

How do designers keep up with this quest for fashion brilliance? For one, they fight fire with fire by using the Internet for their trend information—much like their consumer counterparts. However, the trend information available only to professional designers on the Web is much farther ahead on the fashion curve. For an annual fee, Web-based trend services such as Worth Global Style Network (<www.WGSN.com>) and <www.FashionInformation.com> offer a one-stop-shop for fashion news, forecasting, runway reports, and street trends from around the world.

Service bureaus and original print houses are also getting into the game by offering trend reporting online to help their customers decide what looks of the season to develop. One example of this is The Style Council (<www.thestylecouncil.com>), which complements its trend pages with a password-protected design collection, enabling customers to search and purchase original print ideas online. Many trend services may not post their forecasts and shopping reviews on the Internet, but will make this information available to customers via e-mail and digital photos.

In the old days, trend services would shop the international markets, attend runway shows, and then compile the information into a slideshow presented to designers at a scheduled time and place. With the help of the Internet, designers can now research information 24/7, download images and photos, and compose storyboard concepts much faster than ever before.

PULLING IT ALL TOGETHER

Once trend information has been gathered, the race begins to pull it all together into a cohesive seasonal line. The first step for many designers is to create storyboards of overall trend directions, which are presented to internal teams and customers, such as product managers, merchandisers, salespeople, buyers, etc. Storyboards usually include a collage of photos and images gathered from trend services, magazines, and the Internet, all depicting the mood of a trend.

These trend boards are accompanied by sample garments purchased at retail from competitors or shopping trips abroad, original artwork for print inspiration, and skeins of yarns or paint chips for color direction. Trend boards are presented to those in an organization who will impact design decision-making later in the process, so that all may weigh in with their thoughts on a season's overall direction before the real work begins. More often than not, representatives from production are not included in these trend reviews.

While design teams are pulling together trend boards, they may simultaneously begin to send color chips out to dyers for lab dips. They often do this before final trend approvals to get a jump on the season, realizing that it takes time to create, "tweak," and approve lab dips. Concerned about having the right color selection for a season, there is a tendency for designers to overdevelop, leading to more lab dips than will actually make it into a line.

MAKING CONCEPT INTO REALITY

Once trend directions have been agreed upon, the real work begins in applying concept to actual product. In addition to lab dips, artwork is created for the various prints, knits, wovens, or any other surface details that add interest to the garment or home fashion product.

Idea to Artwork

Ideas for surface designs often begin from original prints and antique fabric swatches purchased from outside agents, or competitive garments purchased from retail. These design references are developed into actual artwork that can be reproduced in production, with the correct repeat sizes, colors, number of screens, thread count, yarns, knit stitch, etc.

While several years ago in-house artists used paint to create designs and repeats, most have now gravitated to the use of computer-aided design (CAD) instead. CAD systems improve the efficiency of creating designs, enabling more flexibility for multiple versions, and an interface with production machinery for faster sampling. However, working on a computer does not necessarily replace fluidity of painting by hand, so some in-house studios employ both CAD and paint artists.

Artwork to Specs

As surface designs are being created, garment silhouettes and details are being worked on simultaneously. Working from either purchased garments or a past season's silhouette, "technical designers" create black and white flat sketches of each garment that will be represented in a line including stitches, plackets, buttons, zippers, and other important details. These flat sketches may later be combined with prints, patterns, and solid colors to form "mini-bodies" of the complete product idea, to be used in presentations and sales efforts.

Flat sketches are also an important element in creating specifications, or "specs," which give detailed measurements of the various garment components by size or grade, and are sent to production along with fabric details for sampling and final product. Some companies employ in-house patternmakers to create first patterns that are sent along with the specs for sampling; while more often than not specs are sent alone, requiring further translation by the supplier.

Outside Help

To keep costs low, most in-house design studios do not employ enough artists or technical designers to keep up with all of the work that needs to be done during peak periods of development. Therefore, companies tend to send a percentage of the design work out to independent service bureaus for development. Many of these bureaus offer a full range of services, including painted artwork, garment sketches, CAD work, and digitally printed fabric samples.

Once a design is sent outside for development, some control over its outcome may be lost, so companies combat this by bringing in freelance design help to work alongside in-house designers. While freelance designers help buffer crunch times and are available for more immediate feedback on design issues, they bring with them varying experiences that can either help or hinder the development process.

Managing Creative Resources

As we have seen so far, the design process is implemented by several individuals and resources, each adding a bit of their own experience and flair to the product. In addition, product managers, sales teams, merchandisers, sourcing managers, and buyers may all have a say in the shape a product line is taking.

Keeping it all in check is a design director or design vice-president, who not only manages the team of individual designers creating products, but also serves as a liaison for ideas and opinions flowing from outside of the design team.

Good design is a combination of aesthetic, trend, retail statistics, price points, quality, and good marketing sense. So to keep the balance, ideas must be compromised and designs must be reworked over and over until the mix is right.

WHEN THE REAL FUN BEGINS

Once designs are completed and approved, they are sent to mills and factories for sampling and (hopefully) production. This is where the frustration begins. With little technical training, designers will send what they feel best represents their design idea, not knowing that it will require major translation on the receiving end.

Doing Their Best

A tiny skein of yarn serves as a color standard from which to create a lab dip; a twelve-color tonal design may need to be reproduced in eight flat colors; an intricate sample garment purchased from Gucci may need to be "knocked off" at discount price points. Or, worse still, the designer has overcompensated for his or her lack of knowledge by including detailed instructions that serve more to confuse than help the mill understand what he or she wants. Whatever the case may be, mills do their best and send back samples that are often rejected by the designer, requiring rework and new submittals.

Getting it Right

This is not entirely the designer's fault. Often designers don't know what information mills need, and so they take their best shot. They may not know what questions to ask in advance and therefore don't get feedback that would help improve a process until it is too late.

Unfamiliar with a mill's capabilities, they send a design reference that cannot possibly be duplicated by that particular manufacturer, only to see the integrity of their art severely compromised when samples come back. Ultimately this final outcome is perceived as a direct reflection on the designer's capabilities, so under pressure a designer will push harder on production to "get it right," regardless of the cost. Inevitably this push and pull causes friction on both sides.

Education and Experience

Lack of technical education or experience is a contributing factor to issues designers face in understanding production parameters. While there are many textile and design schools in the nation that teach varying degrees of technical skills, many designers in the market did not attend these schools or classes. In fact, many designers in fashion found their way here from other disciplines: interior design, graphic design, buying or merchandising, to name a few.

Most of what today's designers learn comes from experience on the job. Therefore, they are only as good as the processes and capabilities presented to them at the various companies they have worked for. The more experienced the designer, the better their dialog with production and the faster the results.

ROOM FOR IMPROVEMENT

With a lot of back and forth and trial and error, designs eventually make it from the conceptual stage to final product. However, the design process is riddled with many obstacles that stand in the way of efficiency.

The Challenge

While designing might seem like a fun job, it is 90 percent perspiration and 10 percent inspiration. Designers are continuously challenged to come up with better products to meet market demands, yet at price points that allow the best possible profit margins. Competition is putting a squeeze on lead times, which means designers must turn around ideas faster than ever and with fewer resources.

Many companies are cutting back on their design forces yet expect the same amount of creativity and volume in shorter amounts of time. Designers are faced with multiple opinions and directions from others outside of the design team, which impacts their ability to develop rapidly with few revisions. And their lack of knowledge of production parameters can often lead to delays in sampling, adding further friction to the entire process.

So what can be done to remove some of these obstacles? Certainly in today's economy, market demands and competition to stay afloat will not lessen. Nor can the creative process be attacked head-on, which may stifle innovation and result in stale product offerings. However, the most obvious and accessible area of improvement would be in the design to production interface.

Teamwork is Key

Ask any designer and he or she will tell you— designers need more education in the production process. And most are willing to learn if management will provide them time. Designers need more back and forth dialog with production. They need their design direction to be heard, and they need to understand better how their ideas can be achieved at a given manufacturing level. They need to be presented with production parameters and options that help them solve design problems earlier in the process, without stifling their creativity. In turn, it would be helpful if designers would include production in some of the early discussions on trends and design development, so that capabilities and lead times can be discussed before a lot of time and money is wasted.

In short, design and production need to act as more of a team, so that the conversations are two-way and problems are solved together. There is a lot designers can learn from their production counterparts that will inevitably help them design a better product. Through a better appreciation of the design effort, production may just help them get there.

50

JOHN ANDREWS

Business Sense: It Takes a Lot More than Individual Flair to Stay at the Top

Extracted from "Rags to Riches: A Survey of Fashion," in **The Economist,** *March 6, 2004: 6–8. © 2004 The Economist Newspaper Ltd. All rights reserved. Reprinted with permission. Further reproduction prohibited <www.economist.com>*

"It's the capacity to make opposing forces work a bit like fire and water," says Bernard Arnault. It's not enough to have a talented designer, the management must be inspired too. The creative process is very disorganized; the production process has to be very rational."

Mr. Arnault as chairman and controlling owner of LVMH, the world's biggest fashion and luxury-goods group, knows what he is talking about. He also knows that the history of fashion is littered with great designers who turned out to be commercial disappointments. America's Isaac Mizrahi, for example, had enjoyed a decade of ecstatic reviews from the fashion press, yet had never managed to make a profit for his backers at Chanel when he left in 1998. Zandra Rhodes, a pink-haired British designer with a magical command of fabric, has never made the money her talent deserves, even though in the 1970s and 80s she had a client list that ran from Bianca Jagger to Princess Anne.

Ralph Toledano, the chief executive of Chloé in Paris, argues that disappointments are inevitable when a designer has to cope alone with the pressures of business. "Creativity is essential: this is the essence of our business, our main asset. But, and this is where business comes in, fashion is not an art—it is creation applied to garments and accessories which must be successfully sold."

Rather like a pop star, the designer needs a good manager. "There is almost no example of a success story in our industry that is not based on a foundation of two people," says Mr. Toledano. In France, Christian Dior had Jacques Rouët, and Yves Saint-Laurent had Pierre Bergé. Chanel is now identified with Karl Lagerfeld, a 65-year-old multilingual German instantly recognizable by his silver ponytail and ever-present dark glasses; but it is Alain Wertheimer, says Mr. Toledano, who "is discreetly running the business." In Italy, Miuccia Prada has Patrizio Bertelli; the late Gianni Versace had his brother Santo; even Giorgio Armani, a rare case of someone successful both as a designer and a businessman, started with a business partner, Sergio Galleotti. In America, Calvin Klein had Barry Schwartz, and Ralph Lauren worked with Peter Strom.

The difficulty is to sustain the relationship. Virtually every designer leaves college dreaming of establishing his or her own label, so to work for an existing label is a detour on the way to the dream. On the other hand, not to work for a famous fashion house might consign you to poverty and irrelevance. One solution is to allow a designer his own label while still working for the established brand. Karl Lagerfeld has his own label while still designing for Chanel; similarly John Galliano at Dior. Even so, the world of fashion remains extraordinarily fluid. Mr. Lagerfeld once worked for Chloé, as did Stella McCartney. Both are now with the Gucci Group.

Clearly, then, loyalty should not be taken for granted. As Mr. Toledano puts it, in a successful relationship the designer "respects the brand, and the brand trusts the designer's interpretation of its DNA." If the designer rejuvenates the brand, "he becomes the figurehead, and the house that wants to secure his collaboration will find it crucial to allow this new designer to share the company's profits." In other words, loyalty will have to be bought.

Mr. Arnault would probably agree with that. Certainly LVMH's designers have for the most part prospered within his empire. But there is more to the Arnault formula than simply hiring talented managers, such as Sidney Toledano (no relation to Ralph, though they were schoolmates in Morocco) at Dior. Nor is it enough for such managers to hire talented designers such as John Galliano. What also counts is keeping control of the brand. For Mr. Arnault, this means selling mostly through directly owned stores; limiting the licensed use of the brand name by others; and, through constant acquisitions in different parts of the business, making sure that your eggs are not all in one luxury basket.

BIG EGGS, MANY BASKETS

LVMH, created in 1987, has far more eggs than anyone else, many with long-standing credentials. Its initials stand for Louis Vuitton, a maker of high-quality leather luggage founded 150 years ago; Moët, a champagne company founded in 1743; and Hennessy, which has been making fine cognac since 1765. Add watchmakers, such as TAG Heuer, and retailers such as DFS (which started in duty-free shopping in Hong Kong in 1961), and Mr. Arnault's empire adds up to more than fifty companies and brands and employs more than 56,000 people, two-thirds of them outside France. Whatever the economic vicissitudes that may afflict the world of luxury, some parts of the empire are bound to be making money.

Mr. Arnault's formula is not unique; he has simply developed it more highly than his closest competitors have done. They are the Swiss-based Richemont group and the Gucci Group, a Dutch-registered company controlled by Pinault-Printemps-Redoute, a French department-stores-to-high-fashion conglomerate headed by François Pinault. All three mix "hard" goods, i.e., watches and jewelry, with "soft" goods such as clothing, scarves, perfumes, shoes and leather goods. Like everyone else in the luxury-goods market, all three face the challenge of maintaining "brand integrity"—analyst-speak for that indefinable aura that convinces a consumer to pay a lot of money for something he, or more likely she, could buy much more cheaply elsewhere.

The destroyer of brand integrity is "brand dilution," which is the perverse reward for popularity. If too many people have a supposedly exclusive Fendi handbag or Hermès scarf, it is no longer exclusive, and therefore, in the customer's view, no longer worth its vertiginous price. It is this logic that explains the luxury sector's constant efforts to limit counterfeiting and copying. Designers admit to a certain pride that they are being copied. But their corporate backers are not so relaxed: piracy means an inferior product that too many may mistake for the real thing. And even if the consumer knows that the product is pirated and inferior, he or she may still decide it is better value than the real thing: a woman's "Lacoste" polo shirt can be had in a Bangkok street market for $5, whereas the genuine article will cost $70 in Saks.

But what if the product is absolutely genuine, and is merely being sold at a bargain price? "Parallel importing," meaning retailers taking advantage of cross-border price differences to undercut regular prices, "creates confusion" to use the delicate phrase of Ferruccio Ferragamo, head of the Italian luxury-goods company founded by his shoe-making father, Salvatore. The logical response for a fashion house is to control its own distribution.

That means two things: having exclusive stores, and limiting licenses. Louis Vuitton, for example, has more than 300 stores in fifty countries. The New York "flagship" is on Manhattan's Fifth Avenue; the Hong Kong equivalent is in the Landmark building, with a constant queue of Japanese visitors outside. Gucci's huge Manhattan store is on Madison Avenue. Armani is opening a flagship store on Shanghai's Bund to add to the 290-odd it has around the world. Louis Vuitton makes about 80 percent of its sales in its own stores; Gucci more than 50 percent; Armani about 40 percent.

The rationale is simple. Instead of selling at wholesale prices to a department store, the fashion house can use its directly owned store to sell at retail prices to the consumer. It can also control its prices, get to know its customers better and promote its brand image through chic, exclusive shops. Over the past decade almost every luxury brand—one exception is Ralph Lauren—has concentrated on developing sales through its own stores.

The downside is the burden of fixed costs such as rent and employees. As the department stores put it, you need "footfall" to make a profit—which is why they always put their cosmetics counters on the ground floor to lure customers in. For the luxury labels in their own stores, it is hard to make money with expensive dresses occupying a lot of precious retail space. Expensive shoes and handbags are a safer bet, so almost everybody does them too.

Nonetheless, it seems unlikely that Shanghai Tang will ever sell enough to make financial sense of its shop on Madison Avenue, so it may be just as well that Hong Kong's ebullient David Tang in 1998 sold his creation to the Richemont group. It may be equally unlikely that Stella McCartney, part of the Gucci Group, will cover the costs of her recently opened London flagship, just off Bond Street. The trouble is that less exalted locations will not do: in the fashion world image is everything.

That image can take a battering when licensing goes awry. In the short term a license is a guarantee of profit: the designer grants someone else the right to produce and sell a product under his name, and in return receives an up-front fee followed by a royalty of 3–8 percent of gross sales. The licensee bears the risk and the designer reaps a reward.

The problem is in the long term. If a licensee sells the product at a discount, or lowers its quality, or sells it in the wrong place, or bundles it together with low-quality products, the "brand integrity" will be harmed, perhaps permanently. The best-known example is Pierre Cardin, whose licensing operations proliferated so much that by the 1980s he had lent his name to up to 800 products, including toilet-seat covers. In the end, despite his talents as a couturier, he became too common for many high-fashion customers.

Mr. Cardin, rolling in his royalties, did not seem to care. By contrast, Calvin Klein, who had licensed the manufacture of his jeans and underwear, cared a lot: in 2000, enraged by seeing his jeans on sale in cut-price outlets such as Costco, he sued Warnaco, his licensee, for breach of contract.

The trend now is for labels to buy back their licenses. When Kim Winser and her Hong Kong business partner, Kenneth Fang, took over Pringle of Scotland in 2000, one of the first things Mrs. Winser did as chief executive was to get back the ailing label's sixty-four licenses. "We only had to pay for one," she explains. "The other sixty-three had broken the rules." With the licenses revoked, Mrs. Winser can now concentrate on restoring the upmarket image of a brand that is more than 180 years old. Gone is the emphasis on golf and the sponsorship contract with Nick Faldo; in has come a new flagship store on Bond Street, a new designer and an emphasis on more interesting versions of the high-quality knitwear that made Pringle's reputation in the first place.

Similarly, one reason for the recovery of Burberry's image—and profits—is that Rose Marie Bravo, an American wooed away from Saks Fifth Avenue in 1997 to become the quintessentially British company's chief executive, quickly bought back many of its licenses.

Nonetheless, licenses have their uses. Being a dress designer does not mean you know how to make sunglasses or women's tights or produce a perfume, so why not hire out your name to those who do, such as Luxottica in eyewear or Estée Lauder and Procter & Gamble in cosmetics and fragrances? Dior Couture, for example, still has eyeglasses, jewelry, lingerie and hosiery made under license, though most of its other 300 or so licenses have been taken back.

Betsey Johnson, whose sexy, fun dresses have inspired a cult following among the baby-boomer generation that loves the Rolling Stones, is negotiating her first licenses this year, for shoes, hosiery, lingerie and jeans. Chantal Bacon, Miss Johnson's business partner, explains: "Before, we felt we could do it ourselves, and we tried with jeans for three or four years—but we could never get it quite right." Nor could Donna Karan, who insisted on doing her own fragrance launch in the early 1990s, and managed to lose US$5.9m on sales of $4.1m within six months.

GROW TALL

But leave the last word on business to Giorgio Armani, a man who has had three decades' experience with his own label and inspires admiration throughout the industry, not least because he manages to make money even from his couture

range. "It's really very straightforward," says Mr. Armani. "I design for real people. I think of our customers all the time. There is no virtue whatsoever in creating clothing or accessories that are not practical." So much for the fireworks on the catwalk.

Just as important, Mr. Armani says, be sure to be consistent, even as you diversify from high fashion into cheaper "diffusion" ranges, or into non-fashion areas such as home furnishings. Mr. Armani's range goes "with a consistent Armani thread that links everything together" from the very expensive Giorgio Armani line to the affordable Armani Exchange.

And, most of all, keep control of your brand. Licensing and franchising can help a business develop: Armani had a manufacturing agreement with Italy's GFT for twenty-one years. "However, no one looks after your name as you do yourself. My view is that a vertically integrated approach, where we control all aspects of design, production, distribution and retail, is ultimately the correct strategy for the long-term prosperity of the brand."

But first you have to establish the brand. That is the problem facing the next generation of designers.

51

LISA ARMSTRONG

The Diary of a Dress: Alexander McQueen Shares the Saga of How One of His Inspirations—A Peter Arnold Orchid Photograph—Evolved from Simple Sketch to Production Nightmare to a Stunning Gown Fit for Supermodel Naomi Campbell

From Harper's Bazaar (August, 2004): 136–9. Reprinted by permission of the author and Hearst Communications.

Alexander McQueen, who has been called many things in his thirty-five years—troubled genius, master of menace, inventor of modern armor—doesn't do flowers. He does precise geometry that rises and swoops over the human form, tracing its contours with the steely precision of a laser and, in the process, magically makes the body look better. And yet there those orchids were, luminescent, voluptuous, caught in an icy spotlight as they quivered on the draped silk evening dresses that capped his fall 2004 show. Imagine Strindberg writing an episode of *Will & Grace* and you'll come close to the surprise element of these gowns in his collection.

The orchids are huge—literally. That was McQueen's masterstroke; anyone could have done small blooms. Big had to be McQueen. He discovered the orchids among his extensive collection of books, in a coffee-table tome by Peter Arnold, a renowned photographer who shoots flowers all over the world. "Everything I do is connected to nature in one way or another," explains McQueen, whom friends call Lee. "These were so striking and strange that they leaped out at me." The images that McQueen subsequently enlarged on three dresses were photographed at an orchid farm in California and in Thailand.

Naomi Campbell loves the orchids. "The way Alexander uses color is just extraordinary. The way he constructs. His eye for detail," says Campbell, as she stands patiently while the designer fits onto her an Empire-waist, orchid-patterned dress that she's planning to wear to the American Express party he's hosting in London, her eyes shimmering behind turquoise contact lenses. "In that respect, he reminds me of Azzedine [Alaïa] and Gianni [Versace]. There's something very pure about his work."

The orchids weren't the only surprise in that show. After the finale, a barefoot and white-suited McQueen tiptoed across his vast raised stage and paid homage to Domenico De Sole. The departing Gucci Group president and CEO, seated in the front row, was responsible, along with Tom Ford, for bringing McQueen into the Gucci stable four years ago and putting him on the path to global superstardom. It was a tremendously indiscreet moment in a world where poker faces are the norm.

"The bare feet were my way of showing how humbled I felt by what was happening," McQueen says, rubbing his nose ruminatively. It is two months since he presented his fall line, a month after Tom Ford threw a dinner for some

Figure 70. Portrait of Alexander McQueen with Naomi Campbell wearing the orchid dress. *Harper's Bazaar*, August 2004. Used with permission of photographer Sean Cunningham.

of the designers and cohorts he was leaving behind at Gucci Group. Internally, there is no sense of a company unraveling, even though there have been departures of some key Gucci people, and McQueen's world has been rocked, as have those of Stella McCartney, Balenciaga's Nicolas Ghesquière and Tomas Maier (who heads Bottega Veneta), the designers behind three of Gucci Group's other key brands.

"The worst part was that the whole Tom/Domenico thing was out of my power," reflects McQueen, who hates feeling powerless. (It reminds him of his upbringing in a fairly violent neighborhood.) "In a way, I felt betrayed by

Domenico. It wasn't his fault, but he'd become a father figure to me. It was hard watching him and Tom leave. They really enhanced my vision of commerciality and fashion."

Against that backdrop came the orchid dresses, some of the most serene that McQueen has ever designed, although their conception was anything but. After his initial sketches, the orchid images had to be transferred onto silk by laying down each color separately, in an undertaking that got unbelievably complicated and technical. Suffice it to say, the dresses almost didn't happen—it was a difficult time, the whole collection was late, stuck in Italy until two days before the show in Paris, and the labor of transferring the orchids from their original photographic medium onto silk turned out to be even trickier than McQueen had imagined. The whole process nearly drove the specialists at the Gucci factory in Italy to distraction.

Not even McQueen had envisioned it would take around a half-dozen attempts to get the damn things right. Most of the audience couldn't envision McQueen's making flowers at all. The rest of the collection featured a procession of intergalactic warriors, striding out of their spacecraft in beige-pink jersey jumpsuits and twisty dresses, or molded hourglass suits in pale tweeds. Combined with the models' fetal-like white skin and shorn hair, the show offered a strange kind of beauty. "It's weird. I don't know if the press liked the collection much," says McQueen, "but commercially it has been selling phenomenally, and now everyone's photographing it."

Coming on the heels of all the stark angularity (and its polar opposite, the strange, draped jersey that hung from the models like skeins of loose skin), the deceptively simple orchid dresses looked almost like an afterthought from a long-forgotten Talitha Getty or Haight-Ashbury collection. When I mention this, McQueen acquires the pained look of a teacher faced with a particularly dense pupil. "Sometimes it amazes me how little the people get the shows," he says. "It was inspired by *Signs* [the Mel Gibson movie about crop circles, aliens and lost faith—classic

McQueen territory], and those orchid dresses were pivotal. It was very important to have a natural element to the presentation." He adds, "And I knew they would surprise." Evidently, so did Arnold, the photographer of the orchids, who had no qualms about licensing his artwork to McQueen: "He's an amazing craftsman. I had full confidence in him."

McQueen has sourced art references before, most notably when, for his spring 2001 show, he used one of Joel-Peter Witkin's extraordinary and disturbing photographs, *Armor*, as the inspiration for a tableau that had Kate Moss, among others, pony-stepping around a glass box. At the end of the show, a masked, naked, portly model, lying on her side, who had apparently been breathing through an apparatus, emerged from a box within the box. The clothes, by the way, were ravishingly polished—gorgeous suits and dreamy eveningwear.

But that's McQueen for you—from his first show, "Jack the Ripper Stalks His Victims," in 1992, and including his four-year stint as creative director of Givenchy, he has repeatedly used unsettling imagery as a backdrop to showcase his elegant clothes. McQueen concedes that nowadays the menace in his shows is sometimes a device. The orchid dresses, for example, looked almost eerie on that cavernous runway, yet they couldn't have been more conventionally lovely. It's certainly hard to imagine him producing anything so lyrical in his early days. "I used to use a lot of bondage allusions and hard-edged clothes. Because I was coming out as a gay man, they reflected what I felt and what I was seeing in gay clubs. It wasn't always nice. It could be very dark and ugly. When you wear one of my dresses, whether it's got elements of bondage or orchids, you're getting me, 100 percent."

Cathartic? Definitely. "The shows aren't instead of a shrink," he says with a wry laugh.

"They're what come out of the sessions. It's never about feeling *I must do a 1930s collection, I must do beige dresses, or I must do a flower.* The 'They Shoot Horses, Don't They?' spring 2004 collection came directly from the [1969] Jane Fonda film [of the same name], which said everything I had been feeling about America at that moment—it's in a scary place. This fall show was about purity, about focusing on the clothes. I wanted something to counteract all the feathers and the flounces of the pirate collection last spring."

Actually, right now, as he helps Campbell into a different outfit that he has designed for her, McQueen is back with feathers—and flames. In addition to being fitted for the orchid dress, Campbell has asked McQueen to design a dress for the final night of her three-day thirty-fourth birthday party in Saint-Tropez. "I wasn't that inspired by her fire-and-ice party theme," he says laconically. She slips into a dazzling red dress with a feather-print border lapping at her feet. "I'm not a psychologist, but I try to dress the inner person. Naomi wants a wasp waist, corset and lots of tulle." He sighs diplomatically. "I felt she should look ethereal, like a phoenix rising from the ashes." In the feather-print dress, she looks incredible. "It's a balance," says McQueen of his couture work. "You're giving them what they want and at the same time trying to see beyond what they want to what they need." Campbell accepts this with good humor; perhaps it's the two-week diet of hot water, cayenne pepper and maple syrup she has been following. A cerulean sky the color of Campbell's eyes floods the East London studio with uncharacteristically golden rays, casting a mellow glow on everyone. "Lee's an artist—very mature," she says rapturously. "He makes you look beautiful. That's all you need to know."

52

NICHOLAS COLERIDGE

The Islamic Factor

Extracted from N. Coleridge (1988), **The Fashion Conspiracy** *(New York: Harper and Row), 195–204. Copyright © 1988 by Nicholas Coleridge. Reprinted by permission of HarperCollins Publishers.*

The delay in the distribution of British and French *Vogue* to the bookstalls of the Hyatt Regency hotel in Riyadh is seldom less than six weeks, although the copies reach the port of Jeddah only nine days after publication. On arrival, the bundles of magazines are winched out of their container bins and driven to a warehouse to fester for a fortnight. In due course they are scrutinized, like all foreign titles, by the Committee for the Propagation of Virtue and the Suppression of Vice. Originally set up by the fundamentalist Imam Muhammad ibn Abdul Wahhab, it is the committee's task to remove from fashion magazines photographs liable to charges of immodesty. This procedure involves three censors, who frisk the issues page by page, marking offending pictures with a black felt pen. When they have finished, the specimen magazine is passed on to an office of clerks who tear from every copy the marked pages. Since magazines are printed on both sides of the paper, they rapidly shrink in size. The 272-page June 1986 issue of British *Vogue* had been trimmed to scarcely a hundred pages by the time that Claus Wickrath's white suit fashion story (with exposed bosom), Patrick Demarchelier's Gaultier corset feature and Alex Chatelain's "Wilder Shores of Summertime" had been expunged.

However, the time in which the new *Vogue* can reach private customers in Riyadh, via King Khaled International Airport, is less than twenty-four hours. Flown in by private jet, packages for the wives of the princes of the House of Saud bypass customs. An indication of how rapidly magazines do get through is evident in the response to merchandise.

"Often we are telephoned from Saudi Arabia for this dress or that only a few days after it has appeared in *Vogue*," says Pierre Cardin. "Perhaps it is because they have more time than Europeans to read magazines that Arab women are so aware of what is for sale." Courier firms near the Faubourg Saint-Honoré are forever dispatching frock boxes to anonymous box numbers in Riyadh. "Take a collection by any of the important European designers—the French and Italians anyway—and break it down into composite parts," says an assistant fashion buyer for Bonwit Teller. "You will find two or three outfits playing to the gallery, you know, outrageous stuff for the newspapers next day; then there's the commercial core of the collection; and then there's a gaudy passage in the second half of the show—usually between cocktail and evening gowns—when you think the designer has lost his way…. Afterward you realize that you weren't *meant* to like those gaudy outfits—they aren't designed for you—and they're not ever going to be worn where you'll see them—because they are intended for the Arab market."

Ask almost any designer where his clothes end up, and you are told, in one of twenty-five possible permutations, New York, Paris, Milan, London and Tokyo. This is misleading. The Gulf is an equally significant destination. Nine Middle Eastern cities have sufficient traffic with the West for it to constitute the sixth fashion terminus, the submerged 11 percent of the fashion industry. These are Riyadh and Jeddah, Kuwait, Amman, Dubai, Shahjah and Ajman (United Arab Emirates), Bahrain and Abu Dhabi. Of the nine, Kuwait is the most important, followed by Dubai, Riyadh and Jeddah in that order. In terms of export volume, the Gulf is a more restricted market than, say, Tokyo, but this is to ignore the particular shopping habits of rich Arab women. Because they are more mobile than their counterparts in the core fashion capitals—traveling more, owning property abroad (or at the very least having recourse to cousins in the West), much of their spending is done outside the Gulf.

Turnover at the Salhiya shopping complex on Fahd al-Salem, Kuwait's principal outlet for Ungaro, Lagerfeld, Basile and Gianfranco Ferre, falls short of Isetan in Tokyo, but the power of the dirham [a unit of currency] is spread across the malls and airport boutiques of the world, producing a fashion momentum of its own. Between 1976 and 1986 Islamic taste has first embraced Western high fashion and then, in a most striking way, modified and in some respects even undermined it.

"I've been at Valentino when they've packed off almost a whole boutique for a wedding, 150 pairs of shoes, just buying and buying, the way you'd buy if you were buying seeds for the garden," says André Leon Talley of *House and Garden*. "They took me to a room and it was hung all the way round with clothes going to Kuwait. They were crating them up. Mountains of tissue paper. Valentino and Scherrer cornered that Arab market for eight or nine years. Scherrer dressed all the Kuwaiti royalty and it spread downward."

When the British designer Alistair Blair was training in Paris he became conscious of the dirham's insidious potential to subvert. "Much of the time it was cash coming across the counters

at the couriers—French and Swiss francs or dollars—and of course people couldn't resist designing for the market, everything beaded to the hilt and lined in mink ... They were selling wedding dresses at Scherrer for $100,000. It was never actually printed anywhere, that price, but one got feedback from the embroidery houses. When I started at Dior and Givenchy, the Middle East were the biggest customers and so much that was designed had the Middle East in mind."

It is somehow typical of the Paris couturiers, who were largely bankrolled by Middle East money during the dark days of the mid-1970s, that they should now depreciate its significance. With the sole exception of Queen Noor of Jordan, who is in any case American-born, no Arab customer is ever mentioned in the rather important House List of Famous Clients. You are told at length about minor French starlets and the wives of Italian industrialists, but nothing at all of the spouse of the Bahrain import-export merchant, whose international money order for 15,000 francs is awaiting clearance in the accounts office.

You might reasonably imagine, at this advanced stage of the fifteenth Islamic century, that oil riyals [Saudi Arabian currency] would carry similar prestige to American petrodollars, but this is not so. When challenged, the Paris couturiers say that Arabs expect privacy, but this is only half true. Valentino in Rome seldom mentions his Arabian customers by name, while acknowledging the importance of OPEC sales. "Clearly," says an American client, "it is the classic blend of French snobbishness and xenophobia. All I can say is whenever I go to my couturier the showroom is crawling with Saudi princesses, looking very chic too, with their bodyguards waiting outside on the sidewalk."

Arab money first made an impact on the couture in the mid-1970s. "Before that they were still in their tents or downgrade rooms at the Hilton," says Suzy Menkes, fashion editor of the *International Herald Tribune*. Initially it was the Kuwaitis who hit Paris, gravitating to Nina Ricci and Jean-Louis Scherrer. These were followed by customers from the United Arab Emirates, in particular Dubai and Shajah, and then from Bahrain. Finally, in the early 1970s, the Saudis became a serious prospect.

"Two or three seasons ago I was sitting next to Bernadine Morris at Saint-Laurent," says Menkes, "and there was the usual line-up of Rothschilds at the front. Then we noticed two women covering their faces up to their eyes with their programs. The room was very hot and we thought at first they were fanning themselves. Gradually we realized they were Saudi princesses, using their programs as yashmaks. That was the first time I'd seen Saudis at a press show. Usually they go to the private clients' show, or are given their own."

With the riyal came terrible temptations. The least successful houses, up to their ears in debt, saw the Arabs as cash cows and milked them mercilessly. Capitalizing on their taste for expensive beading, dresses were beaded from neck to ankle.

[...]

The couture houses became predatory. "Knocking on desert doors" became the ribald euphemism for drumming up orders in the Gulf. These were giddy days, still too early to estimate the potential size of the Arab market. Couturiers sent agents to the Gulf to solicit clients. Most returned, frustrated and bemused, having spent six frosty weeks in the coffee shop of the Kuwait Hilton, while the elusive clients skied at the Palace Hotel, St Moritz. By January 1983, however, most Arabs who wished to wear couture had chosen their atelier, and the market was seen to be a volatile, impulsive one—with women buying heavily for a few seasons, then missing a few—rather than the steady flow of American orders.

[...]

"I did an interview recently with one of the big American TV stations and they were surprised and thrilled that I'd talk about my Arab clients," says Beauchamp Place couturier Bruce Oldfield.

They'd come on from Paris where no one would mention them. Although they're high in the buying stakes they're deemed low on prestige. I have fantastic Arab clients ... well-educated women who look after their figures. Arab women are far more savvy about the way they want to look than the English. Quite often they'll ring up from Jeddah and say 'Please send me a few sketches,' or else they'll come in with a copy of *L'Officiel* or some other magazine which shows the couture and they'll point at a picture and say 'I want that.' You might wonder why they haven't gone direct to Balmain, instead of asking me to do something along his lines, and you know the answer is that at Balmain it would cost £10,000 and here it might be between three and four.

Contracted into barely fifteen years of international shopping, Islamic taste has two separate levels of Western fashion awareness. The richest Saudis and Kuwaitis—spending less than three months a year at home in the Gulf—are now so completely acclimatized to designer labels that their gaudier instincts have mellowed. It is this quite small nomenclature of Arabs who are clustering to Ralph Lauren's Rhinelander Building on Madison Avenue, or buying the more subdued Italian designs. The second wave are the cash-rich wives of import-export merchants and contractors for the new Gulf ports. It is largely for their custom that the workrooms of Paris have been transmuted by the crescent of Islam.

[...]

Arab women, especially Saudi women, dress mostly to impress each other. Since it is considered too raunchy to wear a backless Nina Ricci in front of a man who is not your husband, the airing of clothes is restricted. The clothes-conscious Saudi woman dresses not for power breakfasts, but for video teas. These take place between noon and four o'clock in the afternoon, when several dozen wives will congregate in the women's quarters of a particular sheikh to eat dates and *kulwushkur*, sticky pine kernel and cashew-nut pastries. Afterward, in salons decorated part Louis-Quatorze, part Louis Armstrong, they watch videos again. Much of the success of the French couturiers has been in sending videos of their shows to Saudi Arabia with instructions in Arabic over the credits on how to order by telephone. A couturier's assistant described the call.

"Sometimes," she says, "we take orders from six or more women at the same time. They come on the telephone one after the other from the same house, giggling and laughing like schoolgirls and having such fun. Always they are friendly, the Saudis, but I am a little sorry for them. It is a little sad, I think, to have such beautiful clothes and nowhere to wear them. But we are not complaining, it is good for the seamstresses."

Like Westerners arriving in a strange foreign city, and making straight for an American chain hotel to impose a measure of order out of chaos, the Arab client is loyal to the designers she knows about. New designers have not generally been successful in breaking into the Middle East. Label snobbery is strong. "In the same way that Arab men debate the merits of cars ('Rolls-Royce good, Mercedes very good') by reverently intoning their names, so their wives attach extraordinary prestige to certain labels," says a high-fashion boutique owner with shops in Beirut and Kuwait. What is available in the shops is an entirely arbitrary mixture of famous and idiosyncratic labels. At Kuwait's Salhiya fashion complex with its half-mile shopping mall, there is an Ungaro boutique selling stark Kansai Yamamoto, a Valentino shop (owned by something called the Dinar Trading Co.), Parfums Paloma Picasso and a shop called Elegance, specializing in tea towels.

At the other side of town at the Khaleejia department store, a five-storey downmarket Selfridges stranded on the edge of a flyblown building site, there is the same arbitrariness: tulle evening dresses by Caroline Charles and Murray Arbeid (both good but really quite small English designers), plastic sandals from Taiwan, gilt carriage clocks shaped like harps, and little black see-through cocktail numbers by Jacques Azagury.

[...]

Why do Arab women like couture so much? "Because of their figures," says a Paris seamstress ... "Couture after a certain age is the only thing that fits." And for its quality: "They've certainly got a need to show their wealth by the intricacy of the work," says Bruce Oldfield. "They're very, very *au fait* with workmanship around the fashion capitals. They've looked around and seen the best—not in terms of design, but quality—and they want that quality and that richness."

It is difficult to name the best-dressed Arab women, because so much of their shopping is done collectively: mothers choosing for their daughters, cousins buying two dozen pieces on their last afternoon in Paris as presents for the family in Shahjah. A dozen or so names, however, recur season after season on the racks of couture clothes awaiting dispatch from Paris. These are Al Nuaimi, the family of the ruler of Ajman; Al-Bahr and Al-Marzouq, Kuwaiti merchant families; Al Shaikh, the family name of the Saudi Arabian Minister of Justice, His Excellency Ibrahim Ibn Mohammed Ibn Ibrahim Al Shaikh; Al Mansouri, the rambling family of the Deputy Minister of Foreign Affairs, Sheikh Abdul Rahman Al Mansouri; Abdul Aziz, the family of the Crown Prince Abdullab of Saudi Arabia; and Queen Noor of Jordan.

[...]

The future of Arab taste for Western clothes is as much a question of politics and religion as money. Already, report some couturiers, a new conservatism is discernible. Islamic fundamentalism is provoking a taste for more demure, less heavily beaded dresses. "It is often the husband who is imposing limits and insisting on necklines two inches below the throat," says Oldfield. "Recently I've noticed everything becoming less relaxed, and I'm sure it is the indirect influence of the Ayatollah. We're selling fewer wedding things plunging to the waist or slit to the crotch. I don't pretend to understand it. They divide the men from the women at Muslim weddings in any case, so all this promiscuity is only seen by the other girls."

EDITORS' NOTE

Arab patronage of fashion has continued, and the fashion world has taken notice. According to a May 6, 2006 Agence France press release, the Middle East accounts for 40 percent of the clientele for haute couture, which is why Valentino, Ungaro, Givenchy and Calvin Klein sent their latest designs, along with thirty-six models, to Abu Dhabi for a four-day exhibition. And at least one Arab woman has been internationally recognized for her sense of style. Kuwait-born Queen Rania of Jordan, one of the world's best-dressed women, was compared to Princess Diana and Jackie Kennedy in an exclusive profile published in the March 2003 issue of *Harper's Bazaar*.

TIFFANY WEBBER-HANCHETT

Dorothy Shaver: Promoter of "The American Look"

*From T. Webber-Hanchett, "Dorothy Shaver: Promoter of the
'The American Look,'" Dress 30 (2003): 83–7.
Reprinted by permission of the Costume Society of America.*

[Dorothy] Shaver's ideas about institutional branding, imaginative promotion and fashion forecasting provide a context for the storewide support of American designers—her best-known innovation. In the spring of 1932, the first year of her vice presidency [of the New York department store Lord & Taylor], Shaver launched Lord & Taylor's "American Fashions for American Women" campaign (Shaver Papers). This promotion helped pave the way for bringing American designers out of obscurity. The campaign came at a time when Paris was the center of the fashion world and many New York designers worked anonymously for manufacturers and retailers, copying or interpreting Parisian fashions for the American market. It also came at the height of the Great Depression, which for Shaver produced the "right psychological moment" to boost store sales and stimulate New York industry (Shaver Papers).

Other industry leaders had made attempts in the 1910s and 1920s to advance American designers.[1] For example, Best & Company featured American fashions in 1929 and, in fact, coined the phrase "The American Look" for their in-house promotions. But as one journalist, writing in 1933 on the Lord & Taylor promotion, pointed out, it was "sensational that anyone should base a strong campaign on [American designers]. Who could sell a dress admittedly designed by an *American*?" (Shaver Papers).

The "American fashions" campaign was a comprehensive, well-coordinated merchandising plan that had been in development since 1929. The idea behind it was to create a cult of personality around American fashion designers similar to that surrounding French couturiers. Shaver and her staff hoped that the campaign would generate prestige around Lord & Taylor for having forecasted a "new trend," as well as sell dresses. They scouted young American designers not widely known outside of the industry and purchased their samples for mass manufacture. They hosted publicity luncheons to introduce the designers to the public, showcased their designs in the Fifth Avenue windows and advertised them by name just as the French couturiers were advertised (Shaver Papers).

For the April 1932 promotion, the store featured the work of Elizabeth Hawes, Annette Simpson and Edith Marie Reuss.[2] An advertisement that ran in the *New York Times* on April 17, 1932, lists the designers' names next to illustrations of their designs; excerpts from the ad read:

Lord & Taylor recognizes a new trend toward clothes of, by and for the American Woman, as created by Three Young American Designers. Lord & Taylor ever eager to sponsor a new idea, recognized in the work of three young designers a new expression in clothes created for the American woman. Clothes that understand American life, as she lives it … These young women began designing clothes for their acquaintances, typical American girls. One designs fabrics only—prints—because she knows that prints are an American fashion. Each of them has gathered a clientele so large that she has become a HOUSE. In presenting these collections we believe that you will discover a new satisfaction in buying, and wearing clothes that understand you.

Hawes's "sports and dance frocks" were sold in the Young New Yorkers' Shop, which housed junior misses' fashions. Simpson's more upscale fashions were sold in the higher-end Little Salon for misses (Shaver Papers). A sign in the Fifth Avenue window that displayed Simpson's models explained why her designs were featured: "Young women these days want to look feminine but not obviously so. And Miss Simpson is particularly happy in giving the most demure of her frocks that sure touch of sophistication" (Lord & Taylor Archives).

Reuss's printed fabrics were made into moderately priced dresses and were sold by the yard in the store's fabric department (Shaver Papers). A second Fifth Avenue window displayed her prints against a backdrop of larger-than-life illustrations, paintbrush and paint bottles. The window display copy reads: "American women will always wear prints and the Women's dress shop has chosen these delightful Reuss designs for some of its most charming fashions. You'll want one of these prints the minute the thermometer begins to rise" (Lord & Taylor Archives).

According to Shaver's account, the store fared very well from the first promotion:

Women came into the store, advertisements in hand, asking for specific models by name. We sold 50 of one number and 150 of another in just a few days. We were convinced that we had planned correctly and that American designers were at last coming into their own … Here was a promotion that was justified by its results. (Shaver Papers)

Fabric and dress manufacturers reported that the promotions "quickened trade more than had been anticipated" ("American Styles for Americans," 1932: 18). Hawes mentioned that the promotion increased the number of manufacturers knocking on her door (1938: 195). In the months following the April promotion, her designs for the Young New Yorkers' Shop again appeared in Lord & Taylor advertisements, and Muriel King was added to the store's list of featured designers.

By April of 1933, another three designers were showcased: Alice Smith, Ruth Payne and Clare Potter.[3] An ad in the Sunday, April 9, 1933, edition of the *New York Times* is headlined, "From Behind the Scenes"; an excerpt reads:

Lord & Taylor, the first to arouse interest in Young American designers, believes that the young women responsible for some of the smartest, most wearable sports clothes seen in America, should emerge from obscurity and receive the plaudits they so richly deserve.

The advertisements and store displays for this group differed from the first; they included photographs and signatures of the designers, as well as descriptions of their work in their own words. Alice Smith described her fashions as the perfect weekender outfits, and Clare Potter said that her outfits were perfect for town or country wear. This promotion emphasized the increasing popularity of sportswear; all three designers' fashions were sold in the Sports Shop, outside of which a prominent display featured the designers.

The collections once more were well received and "sold like mad" (Shaver Papers). June Hamilton Rhodes, publicist for the Fashion Group in the 1930s, wrote in 1933 that she had heard talk about not only the newest Chanels, Vionnets and Schiaparellis, but also the latest "Hawes and Potter model" or "Reuss print" (Shaver Papers). Press coverage for both the 1932 and 1933 promotions referred to them as tremendous steps in fashion history and called Shaver a pioneer (Shaver Papers).

Praise, however, did not come without competition or criticism. Best & Company ran an ad taking credit for many of the innovations that Lord & Taylor claimed. This ad rhetorically asks among other things, "Who was first to accord recognition (as long ago as 1929) to American designers?" (Best & Company advert 1932: 7) Others accused Shaver of concocting a "deep dyed plot against the Parisian world of fashion, in which Lord & Taylor exploded the bomb" (Shaver Papers). Shaver released a statement defending the store's promotion. She called the campaign "sound and constructive" and "the logical outcome of two years of thought, and study, not only of developments in fashion, but of customer demand." She said that she had "no illusion that American Designers will in any way dim the light that has burned so brightly in Paris for centuries. Rather, we feel that there is a definite place in the American woman's wardrobe for styles conceived by American Designers and executed by American makers."

In the following 2–3 years, the store repeated its promotion of Clare Potter, whose fashions had sold well in the Sports Shop, and sportswear designers Vera Maxwell and Helen Cookman were featured in the College Shop (Kirkland 1985: 35). By 1935 the press had dubbed the "American Fashions" campaign "The American designers' movement," a phrase that the store used in its subsequent advertisements.

Other retailers joined in the movement, although Paris still held sway throughout the 1930s (Shaver Papers). The Fashion Group and similar trade associations organized shows of both French and American fashions. Publicist Eleanor Lambert took on American designers as clients, and in 1938 *Vogue* launched its Americana issue. That same year, Tom Brigance came on board as Lord & Taylor's in-house designer, and Shaver inaugurated the store's Rose Awards, which recognized the contributions of American talent in textile and apparel design. Recipients of the award included Clare Potter, Nettie Rosenstein, Adrian and textile designer Dorothy Liebes among others.

The American designers movement climaxed in 1940 with the outbreak of the Second World War and the subsequent cut-off of the United States from French couture. Industry leaders made a concerted effort during the war to promote American fashion and to establish New York as the new fashion capital.[4] One way in which Lord & Taylor participated in this was to open a Designer's Shop in September of 1940. An advertisement in the *New York Times* on September 8, 1940, lists the designers by name and touts the exclusivity of Lord & Taylor's promotion, as had been done in the past. In the ad, the Designer's Shop is called a "revolutionary new kind of dress shop"; it sold the fashions of ten designers working for seven competing manufacturers. Karen Stark and Charles Cooper are probably the best remembered of the group.[5] The Fifth Avenue windows contained mannequins wearing the fashions of the ten designers along with photographs and press clippings about the shop (Lord & Taylor Archives).

That same year, Lord & Taylor buyer Marjorie Griswold purchased Claire McCardell's first line of samples from manufacturer Townley Frocks. Her highly original sportswear designs became synonymous with "The American Look," a phrase that Lord & Taylor copyrighted in 1945. Shaver launched the American Look campaign by boldly predicting that the Look was to be "the most important fashion trend in the world" (Shaver Papers). American fashion had come into its own during the war and offered a healthy rival to the newly reinstated French couture.

For Lord & Taylor, the campaign was the culmination of over ten years of actively promoting designers; it also demonstrated the extent of Shaver's promotional prowess. The quintessential Look had as much to do with American designers and fashionable sportswear as it did with generating pride in American industry and speaking to the complex roles of women during and just following the war (Yohannan and Nolf 1998: 8).

The advertisements, beautifully illustrated by Dorothy Hood, describe the Look in terms of overall appearance and American ideals. An excerpt from an ad that appeared in the May 1945 issue of *Vogue*, featuring a dress designed by Adele Simpson, reads: "You can thank your ancestors for the American Look; the way you carry your head high and proud; it's because you share in

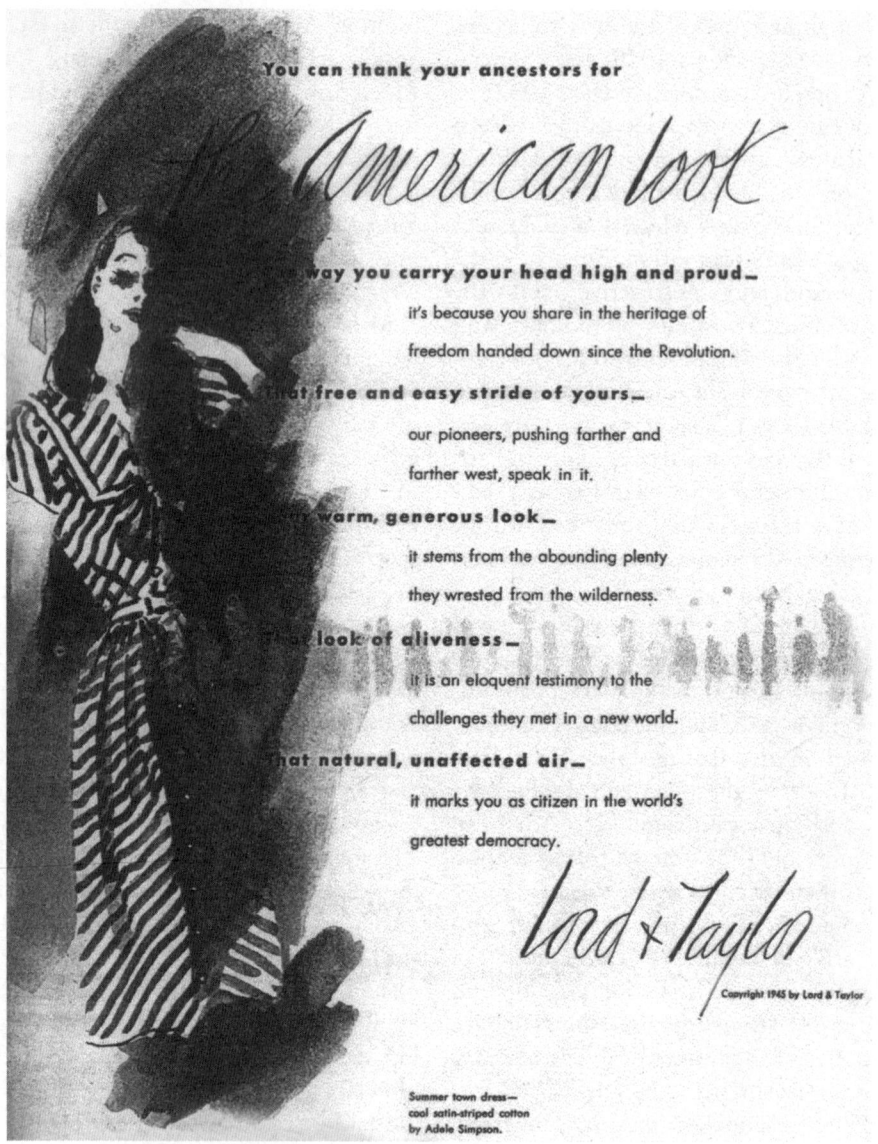

You can thank your ancestors for

american look

...way you carry your head high and proud...

it's because you share in the heritage of

freedom handed down since the Revolution.

...that free and easy stride of yours...

our pioneers, pushing farther and

farther west, speak in it.

...warm, generous look...

it stems from the abounding plenty

they wrested from the wilderness.

...look of aliveness...

it is an eloquent testimony to the

challenges they met in a new world.

...that natural, unaffected air...

it marks you as citizen in the world's

greatest democracy.

Lord & Taylor

Copyright 1945 by Lord & Taylor

Summer town dress—
cool satin-striped cotton
by Adele Simpson.

Figure 71. The American Look, advertisement, *Vogue*, May 1945. Reprinted with permission of Lord & Taylor, a division of Federated Retail Holdings, Inc.

the heritage of freedom handed down since the Revolution." According to a photographic essay that appeared in *Life*, also in May 1945, the Look consisted of "cleanliness and good grooming, simplicity and naturalness, glamour and domesticity, confidence and agelessness, and long legs" ("What is the American Look?" 1945: 88).

An advertisement from the August 5, 1945, edition of the *New York Times* asks, "Who is She?" The text reads, "She is America's own product ... She's a paradox." She is both successful businesswoman "in a man's world" and a homemaker; she is cultivated, imaginative, socially active, a trendsetter: "She's so American."

Several American Look advertisements and the Fifth Avenue windows link the Look to specific fashions, such as sportswear sold in the College Shop and/or particular designers. Although Claire McCardell's fashions became most identified with the Look, numerous sportswear designers were promoted through this campaign, including Tom Brigance, Clare Potter, Philip Mangone, Jo Copeland, Tina Leser, Carolyn Schnurer, Anne Fogarty, Bonnie Cashin and Joset Walker, among others. The campaign lasted into the 1950s and weathered the immense popularity of Christian Dior's New Look, which stores, including Lord & Taylor, copied line-for-line. The American Look campaign was so successful that other retailers referred to it in their advertisements to promote their own products.[6]

The American Look campaign solidified Dorothy Shaver's reputation as a trailblazer and champion of American fashion. Her hope that American fashion would be on par with Paris—that a separate but equal place existed for both—came to fruition, and she helped pave the way for this to happen. Robert Riley said that those who worked for her understood the importance of what she was doing, as did she. She once remarked:

> When you and I are long put away, people who chart the flow and history of international styles will say that right there, in that April of 1932, the stream of clothes from Paris met the stream of clothes from New York, and spread out all over the country in two valuable interpretations of fashion. (The Fashion Group International Records)

Shaver's movement to recognize American designers also enhanced the image of Lord & Taylor as one of the country's premier, trendsetting department stores in the first half of the twentieth century; over fifty years later, the store's tagline is still "The Signature of American Style." Shaver raised the bar in retailing through the store's witty and provocative advertising and promotion, use of fashion forecasting and the expansion of the store into the suburbs; she also opened new opportunities for women in the fashion business

through her outstanding example. The Shaver Touch left an indelible mark both on Lord & Taylor and on the American fashion industry.

NOTES

1. See Whitney Blausen, "Textiles Designed by Ruth Reeves" (Master's thesis, Fashion Institute of Technology SUNY, 1992); Buckland, "Promoting American Fashion"; Daves, *Ready-Made Miracle*; Booten Herndon, *Bergdorf's on the Plaza: The Story of Bergdorf Goodman and a Half-Century of American Fashion* (New York: Alfred A. Knopf, 1956); Kidwell and Christman, *Suiting Everyone*; Lauer, *Fashion Power*; Leach, *Land of Desire*; Levin, *The Wheels of Fashion*; Milbank, *New York Fashion*; Shaw, "American Fashion"; Lauren Whitley, "Morris de Camp Crawford and American Textile Design" (Master's thesis, Fashion Institute of Technology SUNY, 1994).

2. Hawes was a New York couturiere who owned her own shop at the time and was chosen for her "capricious, whimsical New York costumes"; Simpson, who was living and designing in Paris, making one hundred models a month on direct order from American manufacturers, was chosen for her "sophisticated salon interpretations"; and Reuss, a New York-based textile designer, was selected to design printed fabrics for "the American woman of excellent taste and limited means" (Shaver Papers).

3. Potter worked for manufacturer Charles Nudelman at the time and is best remembered of the three; very little biographical information exists about Payne and Smith.

4. Sandra Buckland in her dissertation, "Promoting American Fashion, 1940 through 1945: From Understudy to Star," has discussed in detail efforts made during the war to promote American fashion and to establish New York as the new fashion capital.

5. The group of ten designers included Vera Jacobs, Zelma Golden, Karen Stark, Pat Warren, Vera Host, Will Saunders, Bertha Altholz, Frances Troy Stix, Charles Cooper and Fritzie Hannah.

6. The specialty store Straus and the cosmetics company Dorothy Gray referred to the Look in their advertisements.

MICHELLE LEE

McFashion is Entertaining

As the sun rises and sets in Bloomington, Minnesota, more than twenty thousand ladybugs flutter about in the Mall of America. Crews released the legions of cutesy insects into the mall's seven-acre amusement park, Camp Snoopy, as a natural means of pest control in the indoor garden. The undertaking was the product of creativity: some imaginative employee had evidently been thinking outside the box. And here, at America's most visited destination (around forty-two million visitors each year—that's more than Disney World, Graceland, and the Grand Canyon combined), creativity counts for extra brownie points.

The Mall, a pristine 4.2 million sq. ft fortress located fifteen minutes from downtown Minneapolis, is not only a marvel of enormity but also a symbol of where McFashion has brought us.[1] The Mall's management loves its massiveness, boasting in press materials, "If a shopper spent ten minutes browsing at every store it would take them more than eighty-six hours to complete their visit to Mall of America." With all that leasable space, though, it's somewhat surprising that its big draw isn't some grand selection of unique stores. In fact, the shops are the typical mall offerings: Limited, Gap, Victoria's Secret, Structure, Casual Corner, Ann Taylor. Its true selling point is entertainment—too many attractions to list. Among them: a twenty-six-ride amusement

park with Ferris wheel and roller coaster, bowling alley, shark tank, eight nightclubs, eighteen-hole mini golf course, a college campus, and twenty-seven fast-food restaurants. It even has its own chapel, where more than twenty-five hundred couples have been married since opening day. By the end of 2010, the Mall will complete a billion-dollar Phase II expansion, which will add hotels, offices, condos, a spa and fitness center, business conference centers, theaters, and a high-end specialty retailing district, expanding the behemoth to a whopping 9.7 million sq. ft.

Although two of McFashion's basic principles are its quickness and ease, most consumers don't just buy clothes; they *shop* for them. Buying is deliberate; shopping is aimless. Buying is work: shopping is leisure. Buying is boring; shopping is entertaining. If shopping is a religion, the Fashion Victim, particularly in the States, is a devout disciple. The US already has more than forty-two thousand malls, where nearly two-thirds of America's retail trade takes place. Although most of us complain that there aren't enough hours in the day to take care of what we need to, we still take an average of three or four clothes-shopping trips per month. According to Harvard professor Juliet Schor, Americans spend three to four times as many hours per year shopping as Western Europeans. We do spend slightly less time per visit than we used to—about an average of seventy-three minutes, down from ninety minutes in 1984. But quicker shopping doesn't mean we're buying less. Between 1995 and 1997, the average mall customer's spending rose 13 percent, to US$67 dollars per visit, according to the International Council of Shopping Centers.

We're crazy for shopping, and twelve states rank malls among their top three tourist attractions. Between 1972 and 1992, the annual rate of new shopping-center construction outpaced the growth in population and potential consumers, according to Frederick Abernathy and his colleagues in the book *A Stitch in Time.* The number of independent department stores declined dramatically in the 1980s, but specialty shops blossomed. In 1964, there was enough retail space in the US to give each person 5.3 sq. ft. all to themselves. By 1996, it had risen to 19 sq. ft. per person—that's enough space to build a comfortable studio apartment in New York. In comparison, per capita retail space in Mexico is estimated at 0.3 sq. ft.

With so much competition for consumers' dollars, vendors need to make themselves stand out. Entertaining malls—those with games, rides, shows, and other attractions—have left smaller, "non-entertaining" ones in the dust. Retail prognosticators estimate that during the next decade somewhere on the order of 8,600 malls, more than 1 billion sq. ft of leasable space, will go bankrupt or be adapted for another use. Mall developers worry that the time spent shopping will continue to wane, and have been forced to think of different ways to attract people, pouring billions of dollars into attractions to set themselves apart from the thousands of competing shopping centers. As a result, there are two types of new malls that have popped up around the country in the past three decades: the pseudo-luxe fashion center and the mega mall.

The pseudo-luxe fashion center caters to the bourgeois adult. It has a puffed-up name—like the Arboretum at Great Hills, Towne West Square, or The Shops at Willow Bend—that avoids the use of the word *mall,* which would conceivably suggest a lack of sophistication.

Common areas are filled with mahogany coffee tables, burgundy rugs, and dark leather couches, the type of decor you might expect at a posh private club. Even the tenants are different, usually described in publicity material as "fine shops" or "better stores." In addition to the mall mainstays like Gap and Banana Republic, there are stores like Gucci, Burberry, and Prada, anchored by swankier department stores like Saks Fifth Avenue and Neiman Marcus. The pseudo-luxe fashion center has a few "better" restaurants and cafes scattered throughout, but rarely a formal food court (the scent of Panda Express wafting in front of the Louis Vuitton store would surely turn off some customers).

The mega mall, on the other hand, panders to children—the young and the old ones. Common areas look like the bedrooms of spoiled rich kids: bright splashes of color, big letters, giant playthings hanging from towering ceilings, proprietary talking animated characters. Corridors are designed to look like slightly more modern versions of Disney World's Main Street. At Florida's Sawgrass Mills, a giant wooden alligator head greets you at every parking entry. Entryways with names like the Pink Flamingo Entrance and Yellow Toucan Entrance broadcast multilingual greetings. Walk inside, through the lively corridors with thousands of colorful banners festooning the ceiling, and eat at the Hurricane Food Court. You can dine at a theme restaurant with the whole family, catch a film, sit down and watch a cooking demonstration, attend a baseball card show, or get the autograph of one of your favorite soap-opera stars. At the mega mall, the catchphrase is: shoppertainment.

The concept of so-called "shoppertainment," years in the making, didn't truly come into its own until the early 1980s. In 1981, Canada's West Edmonton Mall opened with more than eight hundred stores and a hotel, amusement park, miniature golf course, church, a water park for sunbathing and surfing, a zoo, and a 438-foot-long lake. After witnessing the success of this soon-to-be rival, Mills Corporation, a mall developer based in Arlington, Virginia, set out to spread shoppertainment around the US. "We see ourselves more as a Disney-type venture than a mall," Mark J. Rivers, executive vice president at Mills, told *Businessweek* in 1999. The concept of mixing shopping and attractions has been further fueled by several studies, including a 1996 survey conducted for direct-mail company Metromail, which found that 34 percent of shoppers said they are driven more by emotional factors such as fun and excitement than by "logical" factors such as price, quality, and convenience.

The mega mall is conceived as a biosphere, a self-contained metropolis where we could conceivably survive cooped up for the rest of our lives. It is our town square, our church, our theater, our general store, our saloon, our cobbler, our tailor, our park, our zoo. Even the lingo has changed: shoppers are now "guests," shopping is an "experience," and malls are "entertainment centers." The shoppertainment idea has spread all over the world, from Korea's Lotte World, which has a shopping mall, deluxe hotel, folklore center, indoor theme park, and sports center to Japan's Torius Mega Mall, the country's first American-style mall, which opened in 1999 with an amusement park, karaoke bar, petting zoo, and bathhouse. Its developer, Torius, Inc., plans to open ten more mega malls throughout Japan by 2010.

Sometimes, it's not even necessary for people to use the mall's exciting bells and whistles—it's enough that they just *know* about them. The Mall at Short Hills once offered helicopter rides to bring people from New York City to its New Jersey locale. "Actually, nobody ever really rode in it," says Rosemary McCormick, president of the Shop America Alliance, a national consortium of shopping malls and retailers who market themselves as tourist attractions, and former marketing director for the Mall of America. "It was a PR gimmick but it was a great PR gimmick. The media loved it in New York City."

In some cases, attractions aren't added solely for the purpose of entertaining shoppers. Many shoppertainment malls have become massive billboards for companies. Corporate sponsorship is not only acceptable, it's highly encouraged. American sports fans rolled their eyes as stadium after stadium was renamed to promote some company: Staples Arena, Bank One Ballpark, Qualcomm Stadium, PacBell Park. Inside the malls you'll see plenty of similar corporate canoodling, from the Mall of America's Pringles Snack Stacks Showdown to the General Mills Cereal Adventure with the Cheerios Play Park and Cocoa Puffs Chocolate Canyon. In 2000, credit card company Discover Financial Services bought the naming rights to Sugarloaf Mills, a 1.3-million-square-foot outlet mall in Gwinnett County, Georgia, to rename the center Discover Mills. The unprecedented naming-rights deal is unlikely to be the last of its kind.

The amusement park/McDonald's Playland feel of many malls has also seeped into the stores themselves, with retailers realizing that they too can set themselves apart by offering touches of fun. The Old Navy flagship store in San Francisco features a DJ booth, mechanized mannequins, and a giant television playing Old Navy ads. In-store DJs spin bass-heavy house and techno at some Diesel stores. The one in the Mall of America has its own sit-down deli, Torpedo Joe's. Even the luxury market is getting in on the fun. Prada's 24,500 sq. ft. flagship store, opened in December 2001 in Manhattan's SoHo district, includes a towering auditorium where shoppers can sit on long wooden steps with their well-groomed terriers, high-resolution TV screens in the fitting rooms to replace mirrors, and touch-screen computers that allow shoppers to search the store's inventory. Dressing rooms have sheets of liquid-crystal glass that become opaque or transparent at the push of a button. It may not be a Ferris wheel, but it's amusing nonetheless.

Rents at shoppertainment malls are generally higher, but the retail dog and pony show pays off. Clothing sales in this type of environment are simply more successful. For instance, the average store at the highly entertaining Mall of America takes in about $540 per square foot annually, compared to the national average of $341 per square foot. Good for business: yes.

Good for the overall state of fashion: no. When it comes down to it, the whole concept of shoppertainment is a sad commentary on what McFashion has done—the clothes themselves are so lackluster that their surroundings have to be jazzed up to make them look appetizing to the public. But it works. It gets people into the mall and, as a result, into the stores. Today, when people make lists of their favorite hobbies, many, disturbingly, include shopping. McFashion has helped make the act of browsing and buying a national pastime. And the retailers reap the rewards.

EDITORS' NOTE

1. In Chapter 4 of *Fashion Victim*, Michelle Lee compares mass-market clothing retailers to fast food chains, such as McDonald's, because they both dish out familiar, predictable products. She contends that mass-market fashion is fast to purchase, easy for consumers to integrate into their wardrobes, carefully planned and well marketed by retailers, unintimidating, and disposable. Yet it relies on "knocking off" (i.e., copying) successful designer styles rather than offering innovative fashion design. Furthermore, it homogenizes culture. Here she discusses shopping as entertainment.

55

JULIA FEIN AZOULAY

Born in the USA: The Growing Premium-Denim Market Goes Global

Originally published in AATCC Review 6, 3 (March 2006): 25–6, 28–30.
Reprinted with permission from the copyright holder, AATCC <www.aatcc.org>.

At retail prices that can easily reach US$350 and beyond for a pair of jeans, high-end denim has become a category unto itself. Distinguished by design, weave, construction, attention to detail, intentional imperfections, and advanced textile treatments, premium denim is now a powerful force and a major factor in the fashion trade.

Consumer loyalty is avid, and has as much to do with aesthetics and high-quality production as brand image. Premium denim applies couture aesthetics and standards of integrity to a classic, American institution that was born in working-class practicality. The result is a subtle mix of craftsmanship and respect for natural defect that is taking over and taking off.

Although Levi's offers a vintage line that qualifies for premium status (Levi's premium jeans collection starts at around $150 retail, and sells for as much as $550 for vintage reproductions), most premium labels may be unfamiliar territory to long-time members of the apparel and textile trade establishment. True Religion; Earnest Sewn; 7 For All Mankind; Citizens for Humanity; Lucky Brand; Adriano Goldschmied; Paper, Denim, & Cloth; and Joe's Jeans are the heavyweight domestic stars, while Diesel (Italy) and Evisu (Japan) are also premium contenders. Rock & Republic, Antik Denim, and Paige Denim are quickly edging in to find a spot in the premium stratosphere as well.

The names may not sound familiar (although there isn't a fashion-conscious teenager in America who doesn't know them in her sleep) but the numbers speak for themselves. "The premium-denim market has grown in the last five years by about 5 percent a year," says Robert Passikoff of the brand and customer-loyalty research and strategic-planning consultancy, Brand Keys Inc. Globally, he adds, "Denim jeans sales are probably around $15 billion [per year]."

ARTISAN CREATIONS AND TECHNICAL EXPERTISE

Behind the impressive numbers lies an equally impressive level of technical expertise and an innovative network that includes laundries, mills, and chemical R&D. Earnest Sewn, for example, launched by Paper, Denim, & Cloth founder and premium-denim star Scott Morrison, is a "highly concept-driven product. Everything—from our twice-sewn sewing process, to our specialized hand-sanding techniques which are worked on by one expert artisan per jean, to our coffee-stained hang tags and our individually wrapped craft paper packaging—lends itself to the overall concept of mixing denim's Americana past with the Japanese beauty aesthetic of Wabi-Sabi, which looks to find perfection in

Figure 72. New "Lucky Brand" jeans that show abrasion on pocket edges achieved through finishing processes. Hangtag states "Handle With Care." Photograph by Linda Welters.

imperfection." According to Morrison, in addition to combining attention to detail with an amazing fit, "We've also ensured that only a limited number of units are produced in each style, and only the world's finest retailers/stockists will carry the collection."

Japanese Aesthetic

Wabi-Sabi stitching, the company explains, refers to the ancient Japanese style aesthetic, which recognizes an artisan approach to beauty that doesn't require perfect, mechanical consistency. "We asked our factory to remove the guides on our sewing machines in an effort to recreate the beauty of hand-sewn garments," says Morrison. "What you'll notice is imperfect, slightly askew stitching around areas with curves in the patterns (i.e., pocket openings). The idea is that every pair of Earnest Sewn jeans is unique and

the individuality of each jean needs to be referenced and admired."

Indeed, many consider Japanese denim to be the ultimate mix: blending natural vegetable indigo and classic loop dyeing (which feeds a rope of cotton through indigo dye, allows the indigo to oxidize, and then heads back through the dye vats for up to sixteen dips or more) with modern technology, computers, and instruments to monitor pH levels, chemistry, and dye bath temperatures. Japanese denim is often woven on narrow-shuttle looms and consciously recreates a vintage look complete with flaws and slubs. Mechanical looms, which make denim look too perfect and mass-produced, are shunned. Other highly valued qualities are the attention Japanese mills devote to the shape of the yarn, the indigo dye formula and dyeing techniques, the speed of the looms, and the warp tension during weaving—producers create denim running as high as $20 and even $50 per yard.

The aesthetic, in other words, is based on vintage denim production techniques. Evisu, for example, was launched in 1988 by Hidehiko Yamane, who had an extensive collection of his own jeans from the 1950s, was something of a "vintage jeans connoisseur," and reportedly wanted to recreate the vintage feel of the jeans in his collection. His denim is strictly Japanese, his traditional production methods are labor-intensive, and his jeans are therefore expensive.

Nevertheless, the brand is sold in more than four hundred of the top stores in the world and—worn by such celebrities as David and Victoria Beckham—is considered a must-have by denim connoisseurs.

Authentic Americana

True Religion, launched by denim guru Jeff Lubell in 2003, predicted fourth quarter 2005 sales to hover comfortably around $25 million, with net sales for 2005 reaching over $102 million. Sold in the United States, Japan, Canada, Mexico, the United Kingdom, Europe, South Africa, and Australia, the brand hangs domestically [the United States] at such higher-end retailers as Nordstrom, Neiman Marcus, Saks Fifth Avenue, Bloomingdale's, Barney's, and Henri Bendel. "We've created some specialty denims that incorporate pima [long staple cotton] yarn," Lubell says. "And we're running a pima warp with a pima fill."

Noteworthy is Lubell's observation that:

All the denim mills in the world are trying to reproduce a denim that existed at one point in time—the Double X fabric from Levi Strauss in the 1930s, 40s and 50s. Everybody—in Italy, Japan, everywhere. Cone Mills was the primary source for Levi Strauss—ninety-nine out of a hundred times, it was a Cone fabric. They make the best denims in the world, and I do 96 percent of my business with Cone.

That authentic vintage denim the premium labels are all trying to recreate starts with the cotton fiber and type of cotton seed itself, Lubell

explains. In possession of this highly prized proprietary information, Cone Mills can spin cotton yarns from the very formula used in the denim fabrics it produced as far back as 1878—a formula that would constitute a veritable gold mine on the open market. "I'm a purist," Lubell reveals, "and I believe in Made In America. The success of True Religion has been our fit and our styling," he adds, "but I give all the credit to Cone Mills."

"We've always done nice denims and beautiful ring-rings," says Kara Nicholas, of Cone Mills. "Competing on an innovative level for high-end denim with Japan and Europe hasn't been a focus of ours in the past," she notes. "But in the past few years, Cone has been experimenting with new fibers, new techniques, and focusing on creating new denims. Certainly in terms of the fly shuttle looms and the narrow, selvage denims, Cone has always been an important supplier. We've been making denim for a hundred years, so we have archives, and we can recreate our vintage look. Any shrink-to-fit vintage Levi's 501 jeans, manufactured from the 1920s to 2003, would be made of Cone denim."

With its main White Oak plant in Greensboro, NC, Cone also maintains two plants in Mexico and has broken ground for another plant in Xia Xing, China. The denim source for Earnest Sewn, True Religion, Levi's and LVC (Levi's Vintage Collection) in 1982, Cone came ironically close to selling off its fly shuttle looms—now such a valuable resource. With today's bustling premium market, Cone uses novelty fill yarns such as pima fibers, organic fibers, cotton-linen, and hemp, and experiments with a vibrant R & D department for loyal high-end denim customers.

There's a great deal of prestige surrounding Japanese denim, says Nicholas, but Levi's Japan works with Cone. On their hang tags, their Japanese jeans proudly boast that they are made in perhaps the most authentic denim plant of all—Cone Mills. "There's a mystique in the United States for Japanese denim," she notes wryly, "but there's a mystique in Japan for American denim."

PREMIUM PROCESSING NETWORK

This mystique is partly due to an innovative network that includes laundries, mills, and chemical R & D. Much of the premium market revolves around special treatments, including stonewashing, sandblasting, hand-sanding and distressing, whiskering, overdyeing, and chemical and enzyme washes. Sanforizing minimizes shrinkage, while mercerizing already woven denim increases luster. A newer, environmentally friendly way to stonewash jeans without pumice stones involves applying organic enzymes to the surface of the denim fabric. Once the desired shade is achieved, the enzyme action is stopped by changing the alkalinity of the bath, or its temperature. The denim then needs to go through a final rinsing and softening cycle. Acid washing—first introduced in Italy during the late 1980s—involves soaking pumice stones in bleach, tumbling them with the jeans, and then neutralizing.

ENZYMES CREATE THE SOUGHT-AFTER LIVED-IN LOOK

One of the most important enzyme suppliers to the premium-denim industry is Genencor International, reportedly the second largest developer and manufacturer of industrial enzymes in the world. Genencor rolled out its first cellulase product [natural protein products that accelerate cellulose degradation]—IndiAge 44L—in 1990. This past September, the company launched a high-concentrate, high-contrast neutral cellulase for the textile processing industry that specifically offers superior denim-processing performance in a wide variety of pH and temperature conditions.

IndiAge Excel has shown strong performance in a pH range of 6 to 7.5 at 55°C, the industry standard, and a range that is gentle enough not to impact fiber strength. In addition, this range is optimal for the efficiency of surfactants—meaning that less surfactant needs to be used in denim processing, increasing cost-effectiveness. Another advantage: less back-staining with this

product means high blue and white contrast on the outside of the garment is achieved, while inside pockets will stay white.

"The first users of cellulase enzymes were denim processors," explains Anna-Liisa Auterinen of Genencor. "Every denim laundry in the world that's doing stonewash today uses enzymes, and their use has extended to the bio-finishing of other fabrics as well."

In 2005, in deference to the important role denim processing plays in the enzyme industry, Novozymes—the world leader in providing enzymes to the fashion trade—organized its laundry products into three brands: the high-end grouping of denim treatment products called Denimax, the lower-priced Valumax, and Novo-tech (high-concentrate products for formulation).

SPECIAL TREATMENTS DEFINE PREMIUM DENIM

Premium-denim lines owe their worn-out, faded look to enzymes—but this isn't the only feature that makes premium denim ... "premium." Other techniques include fraying, slashing, and other hand-worked customization.

For example, Earnest Sewn's Limited Edition Rollo 64, which retails for $350, features Japanese selvage denim made of 100 percent cotton, and comes packaged in a Japanese twill bag, hand stamped and numbered. Stonewashed and treated with pigment to achieve a vintage look, this premium jean also boasts patched and mended knee repair, intense sanding on the thighs, and manual damage and nicking throughout pockets and hem. It is resin-baked to seal in the whiskers, as well.

"I think Earnest Sewn has become a concept and a lifestyle that our consumers appreciate and believe in," says Morrison, "because of the references to authentic vintage denim, the attention to detail in our sewing, and the handmade feel of Wabi-Sabi stitching. All of these things contribute to our success, but most importantly, as with any denim company, the quality of the product and the fit is what stands the brand apart."

While Earnest Sewn concentrates on the detail of sewing and a subtle level of manual distressing, Joe Dahan of Joe's Jeans (launched in 2001, and carried at 1,500 stores coast to coast, including such prestigious shops as Fred Segal) concentrates on precise fits, clever, slimming silhouettes offered in both stretch and rigid denim, and hand-crafted treatments like topstitching, appliqué, and embroidery. Worn by an endless parade of celebrities including Nicole Richie, Drew Barrymore, Lindsay Lohan, Cameron Diaz, Alicia Keys, and Catherine Zeta Jones, Dahan is considered a gifted denim artisan who enjoys a uniquely creative relationship with the textile.

Laundries—The Unsung Heroes

Celebrity endorsements may help, but all of the premium-denim lines rely equally on the industry's unsung hero: the laundries. One important player is Sights Denim Systems in Kentucky, which Earnest Sewn's Morrison calls "a leader in terms of development innovation and authentic washed product."

No simple laundromat, this family business, founded eighteen years ago, invents processes, and process or finish categories, "births" brands, and creates new products by applying a variety of finish treatments to American fabrics (Avondale, Swift, and Cone are all customers), as well as Japanese and Italian textiles. "A lot of our finish inventions come from old-world textile techniques, which we put a new spin on," says Bart Sights. "We actually borrowed resin from the twill industry. People were using it to prevent wrinkles, and we decided to use it to create wrinkles. We originally started using stones and abrasives on denim, and then we applied it to twill."

Pointing out that stonewashing is used in just about every pair of denim jeans today, Sights reveals that "the premium denim is mostly involved with finishing." Sights should know. Washing about 25,000 units a week, his business handles a million pairs of jeans each year, taking them through anywhere from five to fifteen steps, which can include washers, ovens, and hand-sanding—each a number of times.

ON A ROLL

"Denim is perhaps the hottest category in clothing right now," says Earnest Sewn's Scott Morrison, "and it has very few barriers of entry ... meaning, just about anyone can try to start a denim brand, and in most cases, retailers are willing to listen to newness. Right now is an interesting time in the denim market due to the over-saturation of brands. I do not think that the marketplace can sustain the number of labels that are currently available. Eventually, the ones that will remain after the wave dies down are the brands that lead the market in direction, innovation, and imagination. With the over-saturated denim market creating a more sophisticated consumer, retailers and consumers alike have to differentiate more and more between brands. Quality, innovation, and fit—these three factors are perhaps the most important in determining the survival of all the new denim products coming into the market."

Commanding high price points and growing 5 percent a year, the premium-denim market is on a roll. The best labels, however, *earn* those high prices—a single pair of jeans goes through a number of steps and stages, many of which are labor-intensive and require high levels of technical textile expertise. Combining modern technology with vintage aesthetic, premium denim has carved out a niche of its own. At the same time, with its homage to the vintage American blue jean of the early to mid-twentieth century and shuttle-loom-woven denims, the premium-denim market is returning the global focus to an American textile heritage.

56

SIMONA SEGRE REINACH

Four Models of Fashion Relationships

From S. Reinach (2005) "China and Italy: Fast Fashion Versus Prêt-à-Porter. Towards a New Culture of Fashion," **Fashion Theory, 9(1): 50–6.**

When we try to summarize the elements that define the relationship between Italy and China in matters of fashion, things do not seem to be terribly complicated.

China is still mainly a production base for Italy. The more traditional side of the Italian textile industry would prefer things to stay that way, with China as a huge resource of low-cost skilled workers and artisans.

China, on the other hand, intends to free itself from a situation where it is only a producer, by developing quality, adding more profitable phases, and moving toward verticalization, until it is able to launch proper brands at an international level, using its capacity for speed to full advantage. An example of this is the British Creative Fashion Network (CFLN) in Shanghai, a recently opened UK fashion consultancy, which operates at different levels and has various functions: a licensing service for European brands, products, and concept shops (Marks & Spencer and Benetton, for example). It is now helping the Chinese who wish to enter and export to new European markets. Styling Bureau, CFLN's most recent office, opened in Milan, offers assistance to those Chinese who wish to develop fashion brands capable of competing on the international market.

So, even if China appears to be chasing international and, in particular, Italian prêt-à-porter, in reality the situation is somewhat more complex. The whole of China can be considered as an enormous textile laboratory in which new concepts of fashion take shape and stand out more visibly, a vast territory in which various types of producers and textile workers have been operating for many decades, and with China's entrance into the WTO, it has all become more visible and fast-changing.

Even if Italy remains the model China follows, and regards [Italy] as the quintessence of quality and communications, in many ways it is really their vision of fashion that is at the vanguard.

In order to understand this complex state of affairs, we can try to classify the relationship between Italy and China as far as textiles and fashion are concerned, according to the amount of influence and exchange occurring between the two sides.

There is a level, which I would call "Traditional," where the exchange between the two sides is low and the relationship is characteristic of that between a poor country and a rich one. China produces raw materials under commission and sells them to Italy, which transforms them into a product with a high added value. A prototype of this relationship is the silk industry. A complex relationship binds the Chinese silk industry to that of Como, Italy, which abandoned silkworm culture many years ago, typical of poor agricultural economies, in favor of other silk-processing phases, of which the most delicate is perhaps dyeing—a field in which the Italians are still unsurpassed, notwithstanding Chinese efforts.

However, as we have already pointed out, this too is rapidly changing. For years Como has been world leader for high-quality silk. Now the Chinese industries are trying to improve the quality of their silk production both in regard to adding one of the most delicate phases in processing, dyeing, and in attempting to go the fashion route—their model for this is an Italian company, namely, Walter Mieli of Jiaxing.

At a second level, which I would call "Dangerous Games," lies the sale of Italian textile machinery in China. The same companies that sell textile machines to the companies in Como, also sell to the Chinese. Thus, the Chinese go from being competitors to clients. In fact, one-fifth of exported Italian textile machines go to China. China has now become a reference point as the leading foreign market for Italian companies producing textile machinery. In 2002 exports to Beijing more than doubled, moving from 199 to 414 million euros (+108 percent) and almost the whole of the increase in Italian production is due to the exploits of the Chinese.

Often the Chinese combine the importation of machinery with the "importation" of retired Italian artisans, whom they recruit in Italy and employ for a few years, in order to absorb their "love of the product," namely all those little secrets of Italian productivity traditions that a machine alone could never reveal.

At a third level, we can place the production of finished garments. We could call this the "Melting Pot." There is a little bit of everything here; there is a lot of influence and contamination. Italy commissions clothing of all kinds in China, which it then sells both in Italy and at an international level. Thus, there is a very wide spectrum: from extremely organized *joint ventures* or WFOEs [wholly foreign-owned enterprises] to individual entrepreneurs who work as mediators. The Chinese learn how to make a product from the Italians, but they also learn how to build a brand and a brand image. Chinese companies are also beginning parallel production, as in the case of a Chinese company whose core business is producing women's garments for a leading Italian brand and that has now started up its own very

similar production, branded Elegant.Prosper —now in joint venture with Italian textile group Miroglio—that currently boasts forty-five stores in China and hopes to start exporting at an international level. Then there is the case of the Chinese sports brand Li-Ning aiming to challenge Nike, employing in its team the Italian designer Max Zago, who counts among his clients Nike, Fila, Diadora, and Champion.

There is, finally, a fourth level, similar to the first in the low level of exchange between the sides and the elevated rituality expressed in their relationship, but of a different type and, unlike the first, in continual growth. We could call this level "Parade." This represents the sales of leading Italian brands in China.

At the celebration events organized for Italian fashion and its lifestyle models, which are supported by organizations such as ICE [Italian Institute for Foreign Trade] and most modern media, one can witness in the main Chinese cities such as Shanghai, Beijing, and Shenzhen, the so-called "experimental town," new malls displaying Italian luxury products destined for the Chinese nouveau riche. One significant example is Zegna: "When we got here more than ten years ago, we were the only ones," says Paolo Zegna. "Today, in this country we have thirty-five sales points (twenty-four wholly-owned and six franchised out), for a turnover which was around 25 million dollars in 2001, and took the Zegna company to top brand in Chinese men's fashion" (Verga 2003). Other famous brands include Benetton, Ferragamo, Max Mara, Furla, Prada, Armani, Bruno Magli, Gucci, and Versace.

But perhaps the most interesting sector, for the purpose of our debate on the changes in fashion culture, is the low-end sector, the mass-market, to be found in the third model. The Fashion China Fair in Shanghai is the place to observe everything in ferment in fast fashion today. This is a fashion textile fair that is somewhat overlooked by ICE and also by the leading names in prêt-à-porter. Here, one can witness the many underground movements and new configurations that global fashion produces. The Italian companies present at the fair are all small and largely unknown. They are, however, flanked by designers from China, Hong Kong, and Asia. This is the fast fashion and imitation fair. When I visited the September 2002 edition I was struck by the fact that only one of the Italian companies present was looking for a Chinese producer, as was usual practice. Instead, they all wanted to export their low-cost products and viewed China as an interesting new outlet for market-stall fast fashion. Right next to them were Chinese producers of fake Italian brands with ambiguous names, such as Forence Italy—Chinese brands registered in Italy, courtesy of the Chinese people who live there, and produced and sold in China as if "made in Italy."

CONCLUSIONS

Prêt-à-porter is above all a sphere of cultural production. The models of production are cultural and consumption models: "As a privileged site of production, fashion—particularly 'high fashion' or haute couture—is a powerful sphere of cultural production" (Niessen *et al.* 2003: 19).

Presented until now as a "gated commodity" to protect it from a reality and paradox that descended from it: prêt-à-porter is a mass-produced product and can now be easily copied by fast fashion, imitated by fake brands, endangered by the counterfeiting of goods and brands, and subjected to all kinds of transformations that compromise its glamour and embodiment of luxury goods.

This is the reason why designers today are moving toward personalization and fashion is offering unknown "small brands" as an antidote to the standardization and globalized omnipresence that retail policies have stamped on high fashion.

The huge variety of fashion styles present in China, the contradictory reality emerging from the breakdown of a simple low-cost model, yet involving skilled production, reveals the sweeping changes and substantial contradictions that globalization stamps upon fashion.

According to Lise Skov (2003: 240):

This should prompt some self-critical reflections in anyone who still believes in privileged links between modernity and the West. The modernist dialectics of disembodying and re-embodying can be staged in infinite ways in fashion, and while some ways are quite conventional, others have the potential to question received notions of cultural fixity.

Furthermore:

We have moved beyond a naive assumption that fashion designers and other cultural producers are unproblematic representatives of their culture. Their work needs to be situated in the context of the global fashion system that is highly segmented at the same time as its global manufacturing networks provides intimate links between East Asia and the West. Global industrial structures have to be included as an integral part of cultural analysis.

Imitation is the heart of fast fashion that is gradually winning over consumers of all ages and buying power throughout Europe. It is in fact production and the new distribution schedule of fast fashion that best responds to the social transformation, with its practices of extemporary and unpredictable consumption that, in turn, influence the pattern of production and distribution of the fashion system.

China, by definition, is fast fashion, just as Italy is prêt-à-porter par excellence. In Italy this is a hot issue. There are those who insist, like the entrepreneur Carlo Guglielmi, member of the association of brand industries, Centro Marca, and President of Indicam, the institute that fights against counterfeiting, that "We are now one step away from commercial war with China." Even the former Italian Minister of Finance, Tremonti, is convinced that it is a matter of a price war and a problem of protecting Italian products, or rather of protecting IPR. "We have Article 18 and they (the Chinese) have slaves" ("China, Putting the Brakes on Our Exports" in *La Repubblica*, October 6, 2003).[1]

But there are also different views. I quote from an article by another entrepreneur, Carlo

De Benedetti, once again from the Italian daily newspaper *La Repubblica* ("Who's Afraid of the Chinese Giant?" October 3, 2003):

> The Chinese phenomenon is feared by many. But in the debates held over the last few weeks, which focused upon the matter of duties and monetary aspects, one notices a minimalist and trivializing approach, almost as if one is unable or does not wish to understand the magnitude of the phenomenon we are witnessing. On the contrary, I believe we are coming to a new crossroads in the history of civilization—quite similar to that described by Braudel—with the world's axis once again on the move, this time passing from the Atlantic to the Pacific, thus Europe is facing the danger of the decline of an era. After two centuries of absolute planetary domination, European civilization seems to be helplessly witnessing its marginalization and just as it happened between Athens and Rome over two thousand years ago, the finest fruits of its culture may just ripen elsewhere.

NOTE

1. Article 18 of the Italian Labor Statute, Italian Law 300/1970 "The reintegration of workers" obliges companies with over fifteen employees to reemploy employees who have been made redundant "without a justified cause."

57

VANDANA BHANDARI

Fashion in India

The Indian fashion industry has grown rapidly since 1990 and has become serious business today. India's tradition of textile handicrafts; growing media influence; and the Indian government's liberalization, privatization, and globalization program (LPG), begun in 1990, have contributed to this growth. Deeply embedded textile and dress traditions provide a basis of artisanal skills and a unique garment repertoire. India's long-established movie industry and star system has shaped a vital celebrity culture poised to transmit fashion information to the public through the media. These two cultural sub-systems, however, were not enough for the Indian economy to develop a modern fashion industry. The LPG program, instituted to rectify India's economic conditions, was critical in modern fashion's blossoming.

FOUNDATION IN TRADITION

India's rich and varied textile and dress heritage enjoys world renown. Some of the most prominent historical elements of the textile heritage are decorative textiles traded on the ancient Silk Road, the luxurious silk and exquisite jewel-embedded embroideries of the Mughal Empire (1483–1757), and the dyeing, weaving, and decorative techniques of various subgroups. This heritage has influenced the modern fashion industry through colorations, fibers, weaves, embellishments and garment styles. Today the essential qualities of Indian traditions merge with modern fashion.

The Textile Ministry, non-government organizations (NGOs), and fashion designers have reinvigorated India's traditional textile crafts. The Textile Ministry and numerous NGOs—including Dastkar (in New Delhi), Kala Raksha Trust (in Kutch), and the Rehwa Society (in Maheshwar)—sustain traditional crafts by supporting the people who make them. They have assisted textile craftspeople in capitalizing on their traditional skills by exhibiting their work, facilitating collaboration and providing outlets for products. Fashion designers have built bridges between the worlds of traditional craft and modern fashion by catering to the contemporary consumer sensitive to these textile traditions. Designer Ritu Kumar is widely recognized for her work in textile revival, especially with *zardozi,* a sumptuous form of metal embroidery that flourished in the great workshops of the Mughal Empire. Today Kumar's bridal and eveningwear lines, often based on traditional garment forms, showcase *zardozi* and thus are permeated with traditional Indian dress aesthetics. Her retail business, first begun in Delhi in 1966, now has two production sites and thirteen boutiques across India. Through efforts of the aforementioned entities and many others, Indian traditional textile arts—*ikat* (fabric woven from yarns tie-dyed before weaving), *patola* (double-ikat fabric), *bandhini* (tie-dye in patterns), block printing, *shisha* (mirror embroidery), and others—survive and thrive as part of the global fashion industry.

Until recently, women in India were expected to remain connected to the domestic sphere.

Today Indian women often complete university degrees and are professionally employed. The primary traditional dress for Indian women has been the sari (a wrapped and draped garment) worn with the *choli* (a short, tight blouse). Saris continue to be common for weddings and celebrations, but increasingly the shalwar kameez (a trouser and tunic combination, originally from North India) and *dupatta* (long stole) replace the sari for work. The shalwar kameez, worn in South Asia for over a century, translates easily into modern styles and several designers have developed variations fusing the traditional forms with modern tastes.

MEDIA

Movies are the dominant entertainment form in India. Bollywood (the Mumbai-based Hindi movie industry), and other Indian movie sectors, bring Indian stars to the South Asian diaspora around the world. Fashion inspired by these movies is big business. Styles worn by movie stars dictate fans' taste. The public's romance with movie fashion started with Indian independence in 1947. The puffed-sleeve blouses worn by Devika Rani in the early 1950s were revived when Sharmila Tagore reintroduced them in the movie *Amar Prem* (1971). It was in this decade that the shalwar kameez gained universal appeal. When Bhanu Athaiya designed the tight, short kameez and an equally tight *churidar* (trousers) with a chiffon *dupatta* for movie heroine Sadhna, the nation followed the style. Other trends transmitted by movie stars include white shalwar ensembles worn with colored *dupattas* after the release of the movie *Chandni* (1989) and short *kurtas* (short, loose upper garment) after a style worn by Rani Mukherjee in *Bunty and Babli* (2005). Indian men follow movie fashion just as women do. In the 1970s, style statements of movie star Rajesh Khannasafari—safari suits and loose *kurtas*—were widely worn. Dev Anand's hair-flicking and scarves, Salman Khan's vest, and Amir Khan's stylized beard all transferred from the screen to the street.

Neeta Lulla, a movie fashion designer, summed up the role of the Indian movie industry in fashion when she said that, "The onus on the designers is greater. Your appeal has to be global, every detail has to be in keeping with international trends … Bollywood is a fashion catalog and trend forecaster …" (*The Economic Times*, October 15, 2005). Movie and fashion designers cross over between the two industries. Capitalizing on the symbiotic relationship of movie celebrity culture and fan taste, designers produce their own retail fashion lines. For example, designer Manish Malhotra is building a super-umbrella brand for men and women while also focusing on the glamour world of movie stars and high-end gowns.

Fashion magazines have been popular in India for decades. In the 1950s *Eve's Weekly* and *Trends* were the top magazines. In the 1960s *Femina* became important. Lately, *Elle* and *Couture* have been influential. In 2006 *Vogue* announced plans to publish an Indian edition. The *GFQ* (*Gentlemen's Fashion Quarterly*) began publication in 1982. Home-shopping catalogs such as *Burlington* appeared a decade later. *Glad Rags,* and other locally produced fashion magazines, report fashion news. National dailies followed the local papers' lead in fashion reporting; and *The Times of India, Indian Express* and *Economic Times* started regular fashion columns in the late 1990s. In the last fifteen years textile and apparel trade magazines such as *Clothesline, Apparel Online, Apparel View* and *Images* reported on the industry in India.

Fashion marketing in India uses lifestyle identities. The new generation of urban teenagers, who are in sync with the latest international styles, is enmeshed in a visual culture supported by postmodern imagery offered by MTV, Channel V, and Fashion TV. The influence of models has exploded. Models have started to endorse fashion products and are gaining celebrity status. Today, models such as Fleur Xavier have become fashion icons whose every word and move is covered by the media.

Just as elsewhere in the world, the boom in lifestyle publications and electronic media in

India has played a significant role in the transmission of fashion trends. Fashion news, both international and within India, are reported on web pages such as <www.fdci.org>. In India's techno-savvy environment, the new medium for transmitting fashion is the Internet.

INDUSTRY INFRASTRUCTURE

Although not globally competitive in 1990, an Indian textile and apparel manufacturing sector existed to serve the world market. The LPG improved the general economic and physical infrastructure of India, and this assisted the textile and fashion industry's global competitiveness. Improved telecommunications and transportation led to increased productivity and growth. Outsourcing from the United States and Europe resulted in higher employment in India. In 2005–06, India's textile and apparel industry "contributes about 14 percent to industrial production, 4 percent to GDP, and 16 percent to the country's export earnings" (Annual Report 2005–2006). Textile exports contributed US$13 billion in 2004–5, and the size of the domestic market is estimated at $25 billion.

Globalized markets in textiles and apparel resulted from an initiative of the WTO (World Trade Organization) called the Agreement on Textiles and Clothing (ATC). The ATC defined a ten-year transitional program—from 1995 through 2004—to bring the trade in this sector in line with WTO open global market principles. It reduced or lifted most longstanding quota restrictions on textiles and apparel in the global marketplace. India was already the preeminent provider for embroidered, beaded and sequined work. Open access to export markets encouraged the Indian industry; in the post-quota regime, Indian manufacturers supply an even wider range of fashion products in the international market. Aided by the national LPG program and the full implementation of ATC, Indian vendors such as Orient Craft and Gokuldas Images have built capabilities in product development and logistics for the global

apparel market. Manufacturing in sportswear, outerwear, infant's wear and other garment lines continues to develop.

To remedy specific structural deficiencies of the Indian textile and apparel sector, the Ministry of Textiles established the National Institute of Fashion Technology (NIFT) in 1986. By 2006, campuses in seven key cities around the country were training fashion professionals in design, management and technology. In turn, these new professionals enter the increasingly globalized industry.

The Fashion Design Council of India (FDCI), established in 1998, serves related retailers and manufacturers, and promotes Indian fashion designers, nationally and globally. The FDCI produces India Fashion Week in New Delhi, a fashion extravaganza presenting and marketing Indian designers and manufacturers. In 2006 eighty designers from all over the country participated. Manish Arora (trained at NIFT) presented an unconventional collection in kaleidoscopic shades. Empire-line trapeze shapes, layering, embellishments and detailing created an avant-garde collection bringing him, once again, status as one of the leading designers from India.

RETAIL

A new generation of professionals, equipped with the education and skills to compete on the world stage, emerged in India. Families now earn multiple incomes. A large middle class, one that is expected to continue to grow—India's 1.06 billion population is second only to China's 1.29 billion (US Census Bureau, 2004)—enjoys increased discretionary spending. Thus, interest in consumer products, including fashionable apparel, is expanding among elite and middle-class consumers.

In the mid-1980s, Indian designers focused on couture. A small number of designers, such as Rohit Bal, were creating handmade garments for the elite. Just as in the West, evolving dynamics of market prices, consumer tastes, and buying

Figure 73. Left: Arjun Khanna menswear. Right: Design by Manich Arora. Wills Lifestyle India Fashion Week, New Delhi, India, 2006. Source: Fashion Design Council of India.

patterns necessitated growth in prêt-à-porter and appropriate retail outlets to cater to wider target customer groups.

Consumers exposed to internationalized markets through increased imports, travel, and use of the Internet want smart luxury. In India as in the rest of the world, they willingly pay the prices of luxury goods. As a result, an influx of international luxury brands has occurred. In 2006 it is possible to buy the latest collection of luxury brands, such as Christian Dior, Cartier, Moschino and Chanel.

Beyond the luxury sector, international brands such as Marks & Spencer, Guess, Esprit, Mango and Tommy Hilfiger have strategic linkages with Indian companies and are retailing in India. Other companies, like UCB, have set up both manufacturing units and retail stores in the country.

The global industry builds on consumers' love of variety by providing new fashions frequently. Indian "fast fashion" apparel retailers—FabIndia, Anokhi, Bandhej and Gurjari—also market modern designs with traditional elements.

FUSION STYLE

For much of the late twentieth century, Indian attire has mixed traditional dress items with Western ones, especially in men's dress: in small towns a man's conventional shirt is worn with a draped *dhoti*, and at weddings a turban appears with a man's formal suit. In the rapid flow of style change, modern fashions based on a fusion of Indian and Western styles have emerged. Whereas for a few decades before the 1980s ethnic menswear was restricted largely to use as nightwear and for ceremonial occasions, in the 1980s a new stylish formal look emerged for fashionable Indian men. The *kurta-pyjama* got the designers' stamp and now Indian men use the *kurta-pyjama* with draped *dupattas* for casual and formal wear. The *achkan* (knee-length, coat-like garment), *churidar* and jodhpurs (riding breeches) have become popular among fashion leaders. Arjun Khanna, who has worked with intricate detailing to create wearable couture, is well known for his clean lines in Indian wear. Designers such as Rohit Bal and Rajesh Pratap create looks that incorporate Indian ethnic elements in Western garment styles.

While Western styles have become more acceptable in India, traditional Indian styles have infiltrated Western fashion. Indian fashion has fused its styles and textiles with Western ones to provide contemporary fashions for Indians, as well as for the global marketplace. Today, the *kurta* is a style statement from New York to New Delhi and from London to Lucknow. While the sari and shalwar kameez continue to be prominent for a majority of urban women throughout India, Indo-Western looks, or fusion styles, for example *kurta* worn with jeans, are also fashionable.

Clearly, fashion is big business in India. India's unique textile and dress heritage, coupled with recent economic changes, has given it a competitive edge in the globalized market.

58

PIETRA RIVOLI

"Two for a Penny"

From P. Rivoli (2005) The Travels of a T-Shirt in the Global Economy (Hoboken, NJ: John Wiley & Sons, Inc.), 190–6. Copyright © 2005 John Wiley & Sons. Reprinted with permission of John Wiley and Sons, Inc.

The Manzese market in northern Dar es Salaam is the largest mitumba market in Tanzania.[1] The market runs along busy Moragora Road for more than a mile and contains hundreds of tiny stalls. Like a suburban shopping mall, different stalls gear their products to different customers. Stalls specialize in baby clothing or blue jeans, athletic wear or Dockers, or even curtains. The higher-end stalls boast this year's fashions, tastefully displayed, but the perfect Dockers are priced at $5.00, far out of reach for the poor and accessible only to Tanzania's upper classes. Blue jeans, too, are high-end items, and the shoppers poring over the blue jeans are discerning consumers, often with a better sense of what is in (how many pockets? how much flare?) than the original purchaser. The young people in Dar es Salaam are as fashion-savvy as young Americans, with a flawless sense of the hip and unhip.

The market mechanism is considerably more flexible than in an American department store. The Dockers with waist sizes in the low 30s sell for more than those with sizes in the 40s, as Tanzanians in general lack Americans' paunches. Otherwise identical polo shirts can vary in price as well, with more popular colors and sizes commanding a premium. Prices trend up at the end of the month when many workers get paid, but drift lower during periods between paychecks.

Perhaps the most interesting pricing behavior is evident in the divide between men's and women's clothing, as both supply and demand influences lead to significant price discrimination against the men. First, because Western women buy many more new clothes than men, they throw away many more clothes as well. Ed Stubin estimates that the bales arriving from the Salvation Army contain between two and three times as much women's clothing as men's. Women are also more particular about the condition of their clothing, so about 90 percent of what is cast aside by women is still in good condition. Men, however, not only buy less clothing but wear it longer, so only half of the clothing received by the used clothing exporters is in good condition. On the supply side, the bottom line is that world supply contains perhaps seven times as much women's clothing in good condition than it does men's. African demand exacerbates this imbalance, as African women's clothing preferences exclude much of Western fashion while men clamor for the limited supply of T-shirts, khakis, and suits that are in good condition. The end result of this supply and demand dynamic is that in the Manzese market, similar clothing in good condition may cost four to five times as much for men as it does for women.

Geofrey Milonge runs a T-shirt stall near the center of the Manzese market. Geofrey stands tall and shiny black, with the languid pride and gentle manner that seem to be the national

Figure 74. Bale of used clothing from Savers, Fall River, Massachusetts, May 2005. Photograph courtesy of the Haffenreffer Museum of Anthropology.

traits of the Tanzanians. Geofrey arrived from the countryside more than ten years ago, hoping to escape the rural poverty of his village in the interior. Today, he is a mitumba trade success story, having started out on the sidewalk with just a single fifty-kilo bale of clothing, which he had purchased on credit. Geofrey buys and sells about a hundred bales of clothing per month, and runs three mitumba stalls in the Manzese market, each catering to different types of consumers. His T-shirt stall is neatly laid out, with hundreds of T-shirts lining the walls on hangers. Geofrey sells between ten and fifty T-shirts per day, usually for between 50 cents and $1.50. Almost all of Geofrey's T-shirts are from America.

The labels show that most of the T-shirts were originally born in Mexico, China, or Central America, and most of the T-shirts also reveal something about their life in America. The college and professional sports team shirts (Florida Gators, Chicago Bulls) are ubiquitous, and winning teams' shirts fetch higher prices. Washington Redskins shirts move slowly, but Geofrey had earlier in the morning received $2.00 for the Pittsburgh Steelers. US sportswear logos are popular, too—Nike, Reebok, Adidas—but Geofrey's customers can easily tell the fakes (cheaper, coarser cotton) from the genuine. Middle American suburbia hangs neatly pressed as a backdrop to the more valuable sports logos. Across the back of the stall is a Beaver Cleaver caricature of America: weekend activities (Woods Lake Fun Run 1999), family vacations (Yellowstone National Park—Don't Feed the Bears), social conscience (Race for the Cure), and neighborhood teams (Glen Valley Youth Soccer) are some of the customers' choices.

Geofrey buys his T-shirts in fifty-kilo bales, and, because of the snowflake challenge, he is very careful about where he buys from.[2] The sellers can hide all kinds of garbage in the middle of a bale, so it pays to know your suppliers and to make sure that they know that if they give you garbage you won't be back. Geofrey prefers to buy bales that have been sorted in the United States, rather than in Africa. The US-sorted bales cost a bit more, but the jewels are less likely to have been skimmed off and you get a lot less junk. In the world of mitumba, an unbroken US-sorted bale is a high-end luxury good.

In her study of the secondhand clothing trade in Zambia, anthropologist Karen Hansen found perverse manifestations of the preference for castoffs fresh from American bales (Hansen 2000). In the world of mitumba, Hansen found, consumers seek out "new" clothing that is wrinkled and musty-smelling. A fresh-pressed or clean-smelling garment cannot possibly have spent weeks or months in a compressed bale in a warehouse or shipping container; therefore, it is the more wrinkled and musty clothing that is likely to be "new" from America, while the fresh-pressed and clean-smelling clothing is more likely to be "old"—that is, worn or presorted in Africa.

Mitumba dealers told me repeatedly that 90 percent of a bale's value comes from 10 percent of the items. For every GAP shirt in perfect condition that might fetch $3.00 there will be a dozen pieces that will be hard to unload even at 50 cents. Once the few jewels have been skimmed, the bale's market value drops dramatically. As a result, successfully plying the mitumba trade is about keeping track of jewels. A bale consisting only of suburban activities will be a losing proposition for Geofrey. If the sports teams, GAPS, and Nike snowflakes have been pilfered, the fun run and family vacation T-shirts that are left will not allow him to cover his costs. In Dar es Salaam, just as in Brooklyn, the business is all about snowflakes.

When Geofrey gets the chance to skim for jewels himself he takes it. Many importers order clothing in larger bales, say 500 or even up to 1,500 pounds, which are too large for a single dealer to purchase. In these cases, the importer or wholesaler hosts a party of sorts, to which Geofrey and his peers will try to cadge an invitation. Sometimes, the dealers will pay 1,000 to 2,000 schillings ($10 to $20) to be invited. There are refreshments and a competitive camaraderie leading up to the highlight of the party: the breaking open of the bale. The bale-breaking is a highlight because only if mitumba dealers can see the breaking with their own eyes can they be sure that the jewels have not been skimmed, and in a large bale from the United States, the chances of valuable jewels are high. The mood is festive and raucous because of the surprise to come: you just never know what the Americans will throw away, and to be invited to the party to get first crack at the jewels can mean a windfall for the week.

The wholesaler breaks the bale and the melee begins. A 1,000-pound bale might contain up to 3,000 articles of clothing, and almost every bale will contain surprises. The dealers begin a competitive rummaging and quickly pull out the jewels. Multiple mini auctions for the jewels take place simultaneously. The spotless Nike attracts offers of $1.00, which quickly rise to $1.50 and then $2.00. The baby overalls with the tags still attached draw bids of 50 cents, then 75, and finally $1.25. A special find is to uncover a group of identical items—six matching yellow sweaters, say, or a dozen blue twill shirts—the matching clothing has a ready and profitable market as uniforms for businesses.

The mini auctions at the bale-breaking parties are close to a perfectly competitive market. There are many buyers; there is perfect information; there is, as an economist might say, excellent price discovery. And there is good fun. The element of surprise keeps it a fun market as well as a functioning one, and the party is a treasure hunt as well as a market. The hunt for treasure does not stop with the clothing but extends to the pockets, as Americans throw away not just perfectly good clothing but perfectly good money as well. US dollars, no less.

The most valuable jewels will never make it to the crowded Manzese market. Instead, the top-of-the-line jewels hang from trees in the commercial area near the harbor, close to Dar es Salaam's only office tower, its handful of banks, and its second-floor walkup stock exchange. These jewels—a perfect suit, say, or a like-new prom dress—hang like solitaires from the trees on the main boulevard, away from the pedestrian hubbub of the Manzese. A trader lucky enough to nab such a jewel will hire a helper to sit under the tree and guard the jewel until it is purchased, or until nightfall, whichever comes first.

The middle and upper classes often do not enter the crowds at the Manzese market, though they too are dressed in mitumba. Just as a wealthier family might have help to shop for food, many Tanzanians also have relationships with mitumba dealers who know their size and style preferences, and keep a watch for just the right suit or dress shirt. Such personal shoppers make house and office calls when just the right jewels turn up in the bales.

When Geoffrey Milonge emerges from the competitive market as a buyer he almost immediately joins another perfectly competitive market as a seller. There are hundreds of stalls and thousands of T-shirts in the Manzese market, and the consumers have nothing if not choices. At the other end of the spectrum from the jewels are the dregs, the clothing that is hard to unload at any price. Most mitumba dealers have a card table or two in the middle of their stall that is piled high with clearance items that haven't sold. While the vendors' better offerings will neatly line the stall on hangers, the dregs are simply piled up, mitumba's answer to the clearance table at Wal-Mart.

Most stalls have a worker with a microphone who drones on in a mesmerizing chant to entice shoppers to stop. As evening approaches, the competition intensifies because the shopkeepers would much rather unload a few more garments than pack them until the next day. The voices from the microphones form a cacophony that gets louder and louder as the afternoon wears on. The stall owners like Geofrey Milonge are especially loath to pack up the clearance table items as darkness approaches. The Swahili chants ring out as the prices for items on the clearance table drop like a sharp curve along with the sun. By the end of the day the clothing on the clearance table that sold for a dime at noon might go for two for a penny.

For Geofrey Milonge, the day ends in a seller's competition as intense as the buyer's competition with which he started the morning. If he rests in the morning the competition will snag the jewels, and if he rests in the evening the competition will snag his customers. The markets at the center of Geofrey's livelihood are more flexible—and closer to a "real" market—than anything the T-shirt has experienced before. With no barriers between himself and the market, Geofrey must adjust his selling prices by men's or women's, by size, by color, by weather, and by time of day and time of month, and he must adjust his buying prices at the bale-breaking party, by trying to predict who will happen by that morning, what they will want, and what they will pay.

EDITORS' NOTES

1. "Mitumba" is the Swahili word for used clothing.
2. The use of the term "snowflake" to describe items in a bale of used clothing means that each item is unique, like a snowflake. However, some snowflakes are much more valuable than others.

ANNOTATED GUIDE TO FURTHER READING FOR PART X

Because the fashion business is so fast-moving, practitioners tend to watch for new titles from publishers who cater to the industry. In the United States, Fairchild Publications services both the trade and the college textbook market. Founded in 1892, the company has expanded and now publishes five consumer fashion magazines—three of which are aimed at the bridal market—and eight trade papers including *Women's Wear Daily* (WWD), the "bible to the rag trade." Retailers, designers, journalists and fashion students are among those who subscribe to *WWD, DNR, Footwear News* and *WWD Beauty Report International. W Magazine* is aimed at affluent consumers who want to follow the latest lifestyle trends. Fairchild's book division publishes textbooks for university courses in design, production and marketing of fashion products as well as textile science and costume history. Visit the website (<www.fairchildpub.com>). Most authors approach their topics in a straightforward manner to address the practical realities of the industry. Although written for an American audience, these textbooks are excellent for anyone attempting to learn the ropes of the business.

Prentice Hall also publishes a range of textbooks aimed at filling the needs of typical university textile/fashion curriculums. Like Fairchild, the titles parallel the curriculum in major American universities with textiles and/or fashion programs including basic textiles, pattern-making, draping and fashion history. Prentice Hall publishes *Textiles* (Kadolph and Langford 2007), one of the oldest titles for the study of fabrics, now in its tenth edition.

Berg's entries address the culture of the textile and apparel business as well as its practical application. *The Fashion Business: Theory, Practice, Image* (White and Griffiths 2000) developed from a collection of essays from a series of lectures by practitioners and educators at Kingston University. *The Textile Book* (Gale and Kaur 2002) provides an overview of the textile industry and introduces career opportunities. *Fashion and Textiles: An Overview* (Gale and Kaur 2004) deals with both textiles and apparel, including chapters on consumers and the future. New titles can be seen at <www.bergpublishsers.com>.

Supply chain management has changed the way textile and apparel manufacturers do business. *A Stitch in Time* (Abernathy *et al.* 1999), written by a team at Harvard's Center for Textile and Apparel Research Center, addressed the potential for use of computers, bar codes, and laser technology by retailers to swiftly replenish goods to achieve "lean retailing."

The fortunes to be made in fashion have inspired new titles in marketing including *Markets in Fashion: A Phenomenological Approach* (Aspers 2005), and *Mastering Fashion Marketing* (Jackson and Shaw 2006). For the story of how Louis Vuitton became Japan's luxury brand of choice, see Hata Kyojiro's *Louis Vuitton Japan: The Building of Luxury* (2004).

The business of fashion now encompasses the burgeoning secondhand trade, courtesy of the growing amount of post-consumer waste. The first to examine this phenomenon from a scholarly viewpoint was Karen Hansen in *Salaula* (2000), a study of the secondhand clothing trade in Zambia.

Many publishers are trying to get in on the fascination with fashion, producing a surfeit of reading material ranging from glossy magazines to beautifully illustrated coffee-table books to academic studies. Keeping up with the fashion business means being aware of all that's new in the publishing world.

PART XI
*F*uture of Fashion

LINDA WELTERS

Introduction

Predicting fashion is important to the industry for the obvious reason that designers, manufacturers and retailers must produce goods that consumers will want to buy in the not too distant future. Culture watchers also have an interest in the future of fashion because it is a bellwether of modernity (or postmodernity). Fashion, however, is mercurial and notoriously hard to predict. Companies exist for the sole purpose of forecasting trends for the fashion industry. Yet fashion depends on many fluid components, some of which have been presented in this book: identity, geography, politics, art, media and the economy. Although no one can predict fashion's future with any degree of certainty, theories of fashion as well as fashion history provide tools to contemplate the future.

If history has taught us anything, it is that fashion means change. For over a century we have seen a trend toward casual attire. The historical essays in Part I reported that styles introduced as informal daywear gradually became accepted for more formal occasions. For example, the mid-nineteenth century sack coat evolved from informal daywear into the tuxedo, accepted formal attire, by the early twentieth century. In our time, clothing intended for participation in active sports is worn by all ages for many types of activities besides sports. Many young men don't even own suits. The inescapable progression to casual clothes and other trends have caused some observers, such as Teri Agins, to question whether or not fashion still exists. In the extract

from her book, Agins outlines four mega-trends that spell the "end of fashion."

In *Street Style*, Ted Polhemus suggested that postmodernism has resulted in a "shift away from ever-changing fashion and toward classic, anti-trendy style" (1994: 8–9). In the extract in this section he lists ten implications for the fashion industry gleaned from his keen observations of cultural shifts in appearance. He considers style as an "identity badge" that is "instantly re-programmable" by surfing "the style universe for a different presentation set." It is "an infinitely generative signification system that is powerful and subtle enough to transmit between those distant, self-contained parallel universes that we all now inhabit" (1994: 78). This signification system is spreading beyond the population of young adults in Western countries, another indicator of where fashion is heading. As we have demonstrated in the selection of extracts for this book, fashion is now a global phenomenon. Permutations of fashion have spread to Africa, the former Soviet bloc countries, India and China. A recent National Public Radio broadcast reported that young people in Kabul, Afghanistan were wearing Western fashion, much to the chagrin of conservatively dressed villagers who view fashion as an indicator of foreign and immoral behavior.

Although teenagers and young adults will continue to drive fashion changes, interest in appearance will stretch well past middle age as the baby boomers born after the Second World

War grow old. Fashion is not just for the young anymore; it will be a lifelong interest. Since people are living longer, the market for fashionable products among older consumers will increase too. The cyclical nature of fashion will continue to influence other consumer products such as cell phones, cars, and restaurant menus.

Fashion is being marketed to the very young, creating consumers for life (Cook 2004). Juliet Schor, in the extract of her recent work, tells us that American children recognize logos by the tender age of eighteen months. Schor also wrote *The Overspent American* (1999), a critique of middle-class American consumerism. Middle-class America's large closets, generous credit card limits, and off-site storage units help them deal with the overabundance of consumer goods.

Sustainability has become an important issue. Recycling plastic soda bottles into polyester fiber for fleece products is one solution. Another is reworking old clothes into new, high-cost creations. The New York designer collective Imitation of Christ consider themselves "social engineers" who "transform undesirables into desirables."

New technological developments always impact fashion. History has shown us how manufactured fibers, synthetic dyes and the sewing machine have changed the sartorial landscape. Today a host of new technologies—the Internet, cell phone cameras and podcasts on MP3 players—allow new fashion ideas to be transmitted across the globe instantly. Digital technology also brought us mass customization, three-dimensional manufacturing, digital printing and anti-counterfeiting controls. "Smart" clothes that sense heart rate and body temperature through computerized cloth are on the horizon. Although not yet commercially available, the research and development projects introduced in "Dreamweavers," the piece from *National Geographic*, show what the future can bring.

As world power is shifting east, some are calling the twenty-first century the "Chinese Century." Arthur C. Mead discusses trade policies in relation to China, and what it means for world apparel production. China has become the world's apparel factory. Signs point to the Chinese wanting to own the whole supply chain from product design to shipping. What will China's growing wealth mean? Chinese consumers are showing great interest in Western fashion after years in dull Mao suits. Fashion magazines that report trends in neighboring Asian countries such as Japan and Korea are much sought after. Promotional activities—runway shows, model contests and fashion design contests—are wildly popular. The Chinese are as celebrity crazy as England, the US, and India. Chinese actresses Gong Li and Ziyi Zhang appear on the Hollywood red carpet wearing designer gowns. The Giorgio Armani retrospective at the Shanghai Art Museum in the spring of 2006 reveals a trend toward elevating fashion to the status of art, an unthinkable concept during the Mao years.[1] Shanghai, with its history as a cultural capital, is on its way to becoming a world fashion city. All the cards are in place for Chinese fashion to become the visible expression of the "Chinese Century."

How exactly Chinese fashion will play out is the question. Will wealthy Chinese consumers lap up Western luxury brands, as many companies hope who are making significant investments in China? Will Wal-Mart, with its low prices, succeed in winning over the majority of Chinese consumers as they have American consumers? Or will China's nascent fashion industry respond to the world's growing curiosity about the emerging superpower with a new global aesthetic that appeals to Western European and American taste? Already Blanc de Chine, a company based in Hong Kong, is designing "cultured" clothes based on the "eight disciplines" of Eastern thought. To further accentuate China's growing position in the world, Beijing is hosting the 2008 Summer Olympics.

One way to develop a fashion industry is to educate young people who want to become designers, manufacturers and retailers. For decades, British and American universities have taught textile scientists from around the world, particularly India and China. Over the last decade, interest has shifted from textiles to design and merchandising. Countries all over the world have been developing fashion degree programs. The Institute of Textiles and Clothing at Hong Kong Polytechnic University, for example, offers bachelor, master and PhD degrees. The UK alone offers over seventy programs, many of which are attended by international students. There will be an educated workforce designing, producing and marketing fashion products at the local, regional, national and global levels.

While corporations are betting that fashion's future lies in inexpensive, mass-produced styles sold through homogenous department stores and specialty chains, individualists search out boutiques that sell fashion-forward styles from young designers, trade in indigenous products from Third World countries, or mix vintage styles with new merchandise for a fresh look. The constantly evolving throng of aspiring designers and merchandisers may find employment with large corporations, or march off on their own, sparking a thousand new ideas for discerning customers to negotiate the perfect "look of the moment."

NOTE

1. To reiterate points made earlier, fashion is a business despite its longing to be considered "art." In 2006, Giorgio Armani had thirty-nine free-standing stores in China. The exhibition raises the Giorgio Armani brand to the level "art," increasing its desirability.

59

TERI AGINS

What Happened to Fashion?

From T. Agins (1999) **The End of Fashion: The Mass Marketing of the Clothing Business** *(New York: William Morrow and Company, Inc.), 7–16. Copyright © 1999 by Teri Agins. Reprinted by permission of HarperCollins Publishers.*

For all of its glamour and frivolity, fashion happens to be a relevant and powerful force in our lives. At every level of society, people care greatly about the way they look, which affects both their self-esteem and the way other people interact with them. And it has been true since the beginning of time that people from all walks of life make the effort to dress in style.

Yet fashion, by definition, is ephemeral and elusive, a target that keeps moving. A clothing style becomes fashionable when enough people accept it at any given time. And conversely, fashions go out of style when people quit wearing them. Traditionally, the fashion system has revolved around the imperative of planned obsolescence—the most familiar examples being the rise and fall in skirt lengths, and for men the widening and narrowing of trousers and neckties. Every few years, when the silhouettes change, women and men have been compelled to go shopping and to rebuild their wardrobes to stay in style.

In America's consumer society, which burgeoned after the Second World War, apparelmakers, designers, retailers, and their symbiotic agents, the fashion press, were the omnipotent forces pushing fashion's revolving door. They have been responsible for creating new fashion trends and inducing people to shop until they dropped, to scoop up the novelties the industry promoted. This order was a mighty mandate that prevailed throughout the 1980s, a system which established a consensus that kept millions of consumers moving in lockstep. Perhaps that's what William Shakespeare foresaw when he wrote: "Fashion wears out more apparel than the man."

But in recent years, a number of circumstances caused a revolutionary shift that upset the old order and wrested control away from the forces in the fashion industry. In 1987, designers missed the boat when they failed to sell women on short skirts. They misfired again, a few seasons later, with the somber "monastic" look and other fads, resulting in millions of dollars of losses to the industry. By the mid-1990s the forces of fashion had lost their ability to dictate trends. Increasingly, the roles have reversed. The power now belongs to us, the consumers, who decide what we want to wear, when we buy it, and how much we pay for it. And nowadays, consumers are a lot savvier and more skeptical when it comes to fashion.

Four megatrends sent fashion rolling in a new direction.

WOMEN LET GO OF FASHION

By the 1980s, millions of baby-boomer career women were moving up in the workplace and the impact of their professional mobility was monumental. As bank vice presidents, members of corporate hoards, and partners at law firms, professional women became secure enough to ignore the foolish runway frippery that bore no connection to their lives. Women began to behave more like men in adopting their own uniform: skirts and blazers and pantsuits that gave them an authoritative, polished, power look.

Fashion's frothy propaganda no longer rallied the troops. The press beat the drums for a decade, but the name Isaac Mizrahi still drew a blank with millions of American women who hadn't bothered to notice.

A defining moment in high fashion occurred in 1992 with the closing of Martha, the venerable dress salon on Park Avenue. Starting in the 1930s, Martha Phillips, a feisty entrepreneur with impeccable taste, began her reign as one of America's leading standard-bearers for snob appeal and Paris originals. And for nearly six decades, elegant women beat a path to the pink-walled emporium on shopping trips that took hours as Phillips and her attentive staffers put their clients together in head-to-toe perfection. Such was the drill during an era when rich women derived much of their self-worth from wearing the best couture labels.

Martha's demise was the latest casualty in a rash of salon deaths, coming just months after the closing of such salons as Loretta Blum in Dallas, Amen Wardy in Beverly Hills, and Sara Fredericks in Boston. Martha Phillips and her exquisite counterparts couldn't hack it any more because the pacesetting socialites who once spent a fortune on their wardrobes no longer devoted so much time and money to getting dressed up. Park Avenue style maven and decorator Chessy Rayner, who used to be a front-row regular at the Paris fashion shows, was among those who had made the conversion from clothes horse to fashion renegade. In 1992, she recalled: "Today my style is totally pared down and non-glitz."

As such salons folded, many of their suppliers, namely the couture houses in Paris, faced a precarious future. For most of the twentieth century, Paris designers had set the standard, introducing the full-skirted "New Look" after the Second World War, the "sack" silhouette of the 1950s, the "space age" sleek of the 1960s, and the "pouf" party dress in the 1980s. Such were the trends that Seventh Avenue manufacturers slavishly copied and adapted for the mass-market. But by the 1990s, most Paris designers couldn't set the world's fashion agenda anymore. Styles were no longer trickling down from the couture to the masses. Instead, trends were bubbling up from the streets, from urban teenagers and the forces in pop music and counterculture with a new vital ingenuity that was infectious. The powers in Paris were taken aback when their captivated clients awoke from the spell of couture and defected in droves. And thus, the fortress of French fashion came tumbling down.

PEOPLE STOPPED DRESSING UP

By the end of the 1980s, most Americans were wedded to jeans, loose knit tops, and Nike shoes, which became the acceptable standard of everyday dress even in offices. Leading the charge for informality were men, in their rejection of the business suit, which since the start of the industrial age had been the symbol of masculine authority and the uniform of the corporate workplace.

Starting in the 1980s, the bespectacled computer nerds at the helms of America's buoyant high-tech industries broke the pattern of stuffed-shirt formality in business. Microsoft Corp. founder Bill Gates emerged as the world's wealthiest man—and the personification of the Internet-set look, dressed for success in chinos and sports shirts.

In America's more traditional corporations, the men's fashion revolt first erupted in Pittsburgh, of all places. In the fall of 1991, Pittsburgh-based Alcoa, the giant aluminum concern, became the first major corporation to sanction casual office attire. The move came about after Alcoa had allowed employees who contributed to the United Way to dress casually during a two-week fund drive. The perk proved so popular that Alcoa decided to give its employees the option of never having to dress up again. Even Alcoa's top honchos stopped suiting up. One typical weekday morning in March 1992, Ronald Hoffman, an Alcoa executive vice president, was working in his suite on the thirty-seventh floor wearing a yellow V-neck sweater, an open-neck shirt, and slacks. "There used to be a time when a white shirt went with your intelligence," Hoffman told *The Wall Street Journal.* "But now there's no reason to do this anymore."

Before long, the rest of corporate America had shifted into khakis and knit shirts at least one day of the week, which became known as "casual Friday." Computer giant IBM went so far as to go casual every day, starting in 1995. Levi Strauss & Co., the world's biggest apparel-maker, caught the wave in the early 1990s with its loose-fitting Dockers casual pants, which quickly became a popular wardrobe staple for men. It took less than five years for Dockers to explode into a US$1 billion-a-year business.

Without enough suit buyers to go around, many of America's fine haberdasheries and boutiques suffered the fate of Martha. Charivari, a flashy New York chain known for its dressy and expensive European designer imports for men and women during the 1980s, planned to ride out the dress-down trend. In 1991, Charivari plastered on billboards: "Ripped jeans, pocket tees, back to basics. Wake us when it's over. Charivari." Instead, seven years later, it was Charivari that was over—and out of business.

Indeed, it seemed as though not only dress-up clothes, but good taste, had fallen by the wayside as millions of Americans sank into sloppiness, wedded to their fanny packs, T-shirts, jeans, and clunky athletic shoes. "Have We Become a Nation of Slobs?" blared the cover headline of *Newsweek,* February 20, 1995. The accompanying article provided a mountain of evidence that people were no longer dressing to impress, including a Boston funeral director who said that some families were now asking for their loved ones to be buried without a coat and tie.

PEOPLE'S VALUES CHANGED WITH REGARD TO FASHION

Most people used to put "fashion" on a pedestal. There was a sharp delineation between ordinary clothes from Casual Corner and Sears amid true "fashion" from Paris couturiers and boutiques like Charivari and Martha. But such a divide existed before so many options for fashion became widely available at every price level. Stores like Ann Taylor, The Limited, Gap, Banana Republic, and J. Crew turned out good-looking clothes that deflated the notion that fashion belonged exclusively to the elite. In effect, designer labels started to seem like a rip-off. Increasingly, it became a badge of honor to be a bargain hunter, even among the well-to-do. Discounter Target stores struck the right chord with this tagline in its ads: "It's fashionable to pay less."

Many people like Deirdre Shaffer, a 31-year-old part-time psychotherapist from a New Jersey suburb, learned this lesson quite by accident. In 1994, Shaffer and her husband attended a cocktail party at their local country club to which she wore a black dress from Ann Taylor and $12.99 black suede sandals that she had just purchased from K Mart. Earlier that day, Shaffer didn't have enough time to comb the upscale malls where she usually bought her clothes. So, while she was shopping in K Mart for paper towels and toothpaste, she wandered over to the shoe racks, where she found the sandals. That evening, Shaffer was feeling quite satisfied with her budget find. "I got more compliments on the shoes than my dress," she recalled, noting that her friends were "impressed when I told them they came from K Mart."

Indeed, seeing was believing for Shaffer and millions of folks who wised up. It was akin to a Wizard of Oz discovery: behind the labels of many famous name brands was some pretty ordinary merchandise. Increasingly, the savviest shoppers started paying closer attention to details like fabric, workmanship, and value—and thus became less impressed with designer labels. *Consumer Reports,* which is best known for its evaluations of kitchen appliances and cars, helped millions of shoppers see the light when the magazine began testing different brands of clothes for durability, fiber content, and wear. The truism "You get what you pay for" was proven false. In a 1994 test of chenille sweaters, *Consumer Reports* concluded that a $340 rayon chenille sweater from the upscale Barney's New York "was only a bit higher in quality" than a $25 acrylic chenille sweater from K Mart. In another trial in 1997, the magazine gave its highest ranking for men's polo knit shirts to Honors, a store brand that sold for only $7 at Target, but whose quality scored well above those versions by Polo Ralph Lauren at $49, Tommy Hilfiger at $44, Nautica at $42, and Gap at $24.

Marketing analysts describe consumers' new embrace of the most functional and affordable clothes as the "commoditization" of fashion. Beginning in the 1980s, more apparel-makers shifted most of their manufacturing from the US to low-cost factories in the Far East, where they were able to provide more quality at an attractive price: good-looking polo shirts and other apparel that were perfectly acceptable to most people—with no sustainable difference between one brand or another. As more people had no reason or burning desire to dress up anymore, they had no qualms about buying their clothes wherever they could get the best deal—just as Deirdre Shaffer did at K Mart.

The commoditization of clothes coincided with the most popular clothing trends of the 1990s: the "classics," "simple chic," and "minimalism." This comes as no surprise. Such mainstream styles are far easier for designers to execute on a commercial scale, in that they are cheaper and safer to produce, with less margin for error in the far-flung factories in China, Hong Kong, Korea, and Mexico, where much of today's apparel is made.

Furthermore, there's a whole generation of people under forty who don't know how to discern quality in clothes. Generation X-ers born in the 1970s didn't grow up wearing dresses and pantyhose in high school, nor did they own much in the way of "Sunday clothes." These young people are largely ignorant of the hallmarks of

fine tailoring and fit. Jeans, T-shirts, stretch fabrics, and clothes sized in small, medium, large, and extra-large are what this blow-dry, wash-and-wear generation have worn virtually all of their lives. While their mothers and grandmothers donned slips and girdles—and pulled out the ironing board before they got dressed—these young people had already formed the habit of wearing comfortable, carefree clothes.

TOP DESIGNERS STOPPED GAMBLING ON FASHION

Isaac Mizrahi mistakenly believed that there were enough fashion mavens still willing to put their trust in his taste level. But the best-selling designers nowadays know better. Liz Claiborne, Polo Ralph Lauren, and Tommy Hilfiger are among the fashion houses that grew into billion-dollar empires of apparel, handbags, cosmetics, and home furnishings. Such fashion houses just also happen to be publicly traded companies, which must maintain steady, predictable growth for their shareholders. The upshot: The big guns can't afford to gamble on fashion whims. Fashion as we have known it requires a certain degree of risk-taking and creativity that is impossible to explain to Wall Street. Even though the leading designers tart up their runways with outlandish, crowd-pleasing costumes, they are grounded in reality. The bulk of the actual merchandise that hits the sales floor is always palatable enough for millions of consumers around the world, thus generating the bottom line that Wall Street expects.

With so much consumer rejection of fanciful fashions, will the world turn into a sea of khakis and T-shirts? Will Paris couture and the likes of Mizrahi and Charivari ever rise again? And moreover, will fashion ever matter as it used to?

"The fact is that women are interested in clothes, but the average consumer isn't interested in the 'fashion world,'" observes Martha Nelson, the editor of *In Style* magazine. Women want attractive clothes that function in the real world, "not something that is impossible to walk and drive in. You know, clothes that fit into your life."

So, that's why we've come to the end of fashion. Today, a designer's creativity expresses itself more than ever in the marketing rather than in the actual clothes. Such marketing is complicated, full of nuance and innovation—requiring far more planning than what it takes to create a fabulous ballgown, as well as millions of dollars in advertising. In a sense, fashion has returned to its roots: selling image. Image is the form and marketing is the function.

Nowadays, a fashion house has to establish an image that resonates with enough people—an image so arresting that consumers will be compelled to buy whatever that designer has to offer. The top designers use their images to turn themselves into mighty brands that stand for an attitude and a lifestyle that cuts across many cultures. Today's "branding" of fashion has taken on a critical role in an era when there's not much in the way of new styling going on—just about every store in the mall is peddling the same styles of clothes. That's why designer logos have become so popular; logos are the easiest way for each designer to impart a distinguishing characteristic on what amounts to some pretty ordinary apparel.

Having burnished his image through millions of dollars of advertising, Calvin Klein towers as a potent brand name and leverages his CK logo across a breadth of categories—$6.50 cotton briefs, $1,000 blazers, and $40 bath towels—even though there are plenty of cheaper options widely available.

Image, of course, works in conjunction with the intrinsics—the style, quality, and price of each actual item—and image comes from everywhere: the ambiance of the location where the clothes are sold, the advertising, the celebrities who wear the clothes, and so forth. Image is how the Gap sells a $12.50 pocket T-shirt, how Ralph Lauren pushes a $40 gallon of wall paint, and how Giorgio Armani moves $1,500 blazers.

These designers assault the American public with their ubiquitous advertising, most typically seen in the fashion press. But the roles have reversed there as well. Fashion publications like *WWD*, *Vogue*, *Harper's Bazaar*, *GQ*, and the rest have lost their power in their editorial pages to make or break fashion trends—the same power designers have lost to the consumer. Nowadays, the mightiest fashion brands, by virtue of their heavy-duty advertising, take their message directly to the public—unfiltered by the subjectivity of the editors: Ralph Lauren's ten-page advertising inserts in the front of *Vogue* and *Vanity Fair* are more arresting than any fashion spread featuring his clothes in the editorial pages of the magazine.

It was always confounding, this business of selling fashion. And now the industry has become fragmented into so many niches in which scores of companies churn out more and more merchandise at every price range, season after season. The fashion industry powers at the head of the class prevail because they swear by retailing's golden rule: The consumer is king.

[…]

Fashion, which began in the hallowed ateliers of Parisian couture, now emanates from designers and retailers from around the world, reaching the masses at every level. In today's high-strung, competitive marketplace, those who will survive the end of fashion will reinvent themselves enough times and with enough flexibility and resources to anticipate, not manipulate, the twenty-first-century customer.

60

TED POLHEMUS

Implications for the Appearance-alteration Industries

From T. Polhemus (1998) "Beyond Fashion" in G. Malossi (ed.), The Style Engine: Spectacle, Identity, Design, and Business: How the Fashion Industry Uses Style to Create Wealth (New York: Monacelli Press), 78–9. Reprinted by permission of the author.

1. Within the appearance-alteration industries I include clothing, hat, footwear, jewelry, eyewear, and sportswear designers; hairstylists and make-up artists; exercise and bodybuilding specialists; body piercers and tattooists, among others. Altering appearance is not and never has been simply a matter of covering the body with garments. While different industries draw on different techniques and expertise, all (or many) are integrated into a total look. As in the production of, for example, an automobile, the appearance-alteration industries should be working together rather than separately. The product is a look, and fabric, leather, feathers, chemicals, and so forth are only a means to this end.

2. People today buy clothes, cosmetics, etc., on the basis of what these products "say." Semiotics rather than aesthetics is the *raison d'être* of today's fashion industry. The more packed with reference, allusion, and symbolism, the more valuable and desirable the product. Such signification can be achieved either by the use of color, cut, design motif, fabric, etc., or by value added by marketing and advertising. The consumer wants and needs to buy a new vocabulary rather than a new dress, necklace, lipstick, or haircut.

3. What is being said by appearance grows ever more complex. If in the past a look was intended to say: "I'm rich," "I'm respectable," "I'm sexy"; a look today is intended not only to say "I'm interesting" but to specify in precisely what way that person is interesting. The juxtaposition of opposing—even completely contradictory—styles and meanings is one way of accomplishing this. Irony is another. The more multifaceted, layered, and downright confusing a look, the more likely it is to be perceived as authentic.

4. In order to make a unique, idiosyncratic appearance statement, a person must assemble the component parts (the adjectives) that will work together to express just how that person is "interesting." As with music, appearance today is "in the mix."

5. The day when the designer or stylist could (and was expected to) dictate a "total look" is long gone. This is not, however, to suggest that designers are less important than before—just that their role has changed. Designers are now semiological component manufacturers for a self-assembly product (the "style statement").

6. Seasonal fashion change for its own sake is no longer valued by the majority of consumers. (Indeed, it risks signifying a lack of personal integrity.) This is especially true when fashion journalists strive to cram many looks from different designers into a singular direction (mistakenly thinking that is how they should do their job). Brown is not the new black—every color is. The

consumer wants to have information about the full and glorious range of what is available. The "next big thing" is that there will not be a next big thing.

7. The importance of the designer as visionary grows ever greater. Realized in the form of fantasy garments, which could never be worn in real life, or in extraordinary photography for advertisements, these visions of how life might be are what the consumer wants to buy into. (The signified—the dream, the vision of how life might be—rather than the signifier—the shirt, pair of shoes, eye shadow, etc.—is the product.) Compressed into a logo, these visionary signifiers can be sold in the form of accessories, T-shirts, perfumes, and wearable garments. That people are buying a logo rather than, say, a dress is not at all to devalue the process, it is simply to underline the extent to which appearance is a communication business. A logo that radiates the right lifestyle messages is a valuable product in and of itself—that is, valuable for the consumer who wishes to incorporate it into their presentation of self. (Thus, insofar as one can put these things into words, the Benetton logo gives its wearers the possibility of communicating that they are socially responsible, non-racist practitioners of safe sex, while the Diesel logo gives its wearers the possibility of communicating that they are wacky, fun-loving, off-the-wall, ironic, surreal, psychedelic, knowing sort of people.)

8. Nothing sells like signification. But at the same time no properly postmodern person would want to be seen wearing just one signification. It is much more interesting to juxtapose oppositional meanings within one presentation set. (For example, a Benetton sweater worn with Diesel trousers, suggesting a personal identity that balances social responsibility with an off-the-wall sense of fun—e.g., a person who uses condoms and ecstasy.) Designers who refuse to allow their work to be shown (for example, in editorial magazine photography) with work from other sources give the impression that their work is not amenable to do-it-yourself sampling and mixing—thereby devaluing it in the eyes of today's postmodern consumers. (For the same

reason, the importance of the catwalk show where the work of only one designer is on display needs to be questioned. Just as furniture manufacturers now use catalogs to show their products in use in a "real" situation, so those in the appearance industries must display their products in use in the "real" world.)

9. It used to be that being able to afford someone to style your appearance (or to decorate your home) was a mark of status. Now to do so just signals a lack of authenticity. To be real is to do it yourself. Those involved in the business of fashion must now take this on board. The appearance industries are more important than ever before, but to be successful the professionals need to let their creations became a starting point for something else and not a fait accompli. The consumer wants to be treated like a creative partner rather than like a mannequin.

10. Whether we call it fashion or style (or whatever) is not as important as recognizing that what people want from their clothes and accessories has radically changed. Fashion is not what it used to be because the world we live in is not what it used to be, and appearance alteration has an almost magical ability to express and shape itself to the Zeitgeist of an era. In the 1950s or 1960s (as in the Renaissance), people wanted clothes to say "I'm avant-garde." Now that modernism has given way to postmodernism a key change is our attitude toward change—namely, like our tribal ancestors we fear change at least as much as we welcome it. Instead, our postmodern age is focused on exploring all the possible parallel universes that can and do exist within the here and now. Such pluralism and heterogeneity, however, make it ever more important to find a way to cut through the buildup of alternative white noise to proclaim "I am here." This is what people today need their clothes to do: to signal where they are in an ever more confusing world. Luckily, appearance is a rich, multifaceted, subtle, powerful, and instantaneous communication system that is fully capable of saying anything we want it to.

What do you want to say today?

Here's looking at you.

61

JULIET B. SCHOR

Born to Buy

From J. Schor (2004) **Born to Buy: The Commercialized Child and the New Consumer Culture** *(New York: Scribner), 19–20, 25–7. Reprinted with the permission of Scribner, an imprint of Simon & Schuster Adult Publishing Group. Copyright © 2004 Juliet Schor.*

The typical American child is now immersed in the consumer marketplace to a degree that dwarfs all historical experience. At age one, she's watching *Teletubbies* and eating the food of its "promo partners" Burger King and Mc-Donald's. Kids can recognize logos by eighteen months, and before reaching their second birthday they're asking for products by brand name. By three or three and a half, experts say children start to believe that brands communicate their personal qualities, for example, that they're cool, or strong, or smart. Even before starting school, the likelihood of having a television in their bedroom is 25 percent, and their viewing time is just over two hours a day. Upon arrival at the schoolhouse steps, the typical first grader can evoke 200 brands. And he or she has already accumulated an unprecedented number of possessions, beginning with an average of seventy new toys a year.

By age six and seven, girls are asking for the latest fashions, using nail polish, and singing pop music tunes. The day after the dELIA*S clothing catalog arrives in the mail, marketers report that "everyone brings their catalog to school" to talk about the products in it. (When I wrote those words, dELIA*S was hot; when they appear in print, who knows? Trends move at the speed of light in this world.) Eight-year-old boys are enjoying Budweiser commercials (the consistent favorite ad for this age group), World Wrestling Entertainment, and graphically violent video games. Schools routinely ban the toy fads that

Figure 75. A young shopper trying on summer sandals with the help of her mother. Photograph by Linda Welters.

sweep the market, from Power Rangers to Poké-mon, on the grounds that they lead to fights, antisocial behavior, and disruption. The average eight- to thirteen-year-old is watching over 3.5 hours of television a day. American children view an estimated 40,000 commercials annually. They also make approximately 3,000 requests for products and services each year.

As kids age, they turn to teen culture, which is saturated with violence, alcohol, drugs, and guns. Teen media depict a manipulated and gratuitous sexuality, based on unrealistic body images, constraining gender stereotypes, and, all too frequently the degradation of women. The dominant teen culture is also rife with materialism and preaches that if you're not rich, you're a loser. Adolescents are subjected to unremitting pressure to conform to the market's definition of cool. MTV has been the global leader in promoting these values, and its worldview has become pervasive among youth. And now, teen culture has migrated down to younger children. Eight- and nine-year-olds watch MTV and BET (Black Entertainment Television), reality shows, and other prime-time fare ostensibly aimed at teens and adults. Marketers are deliberately investing children's culture with the themes and sensibilities that have worked with teens. As Betsy Frank, head of research for MTV Networks, explained, "If something works for MTV, it will also work for Nickolodeon." It's a widespread process, known as tweening.

[…]

BONDED TO BRANDS

These days, when kids ask, they ask for particular brands. A 2001 Nickelodeon study found that the average ten-year-old has memorized 300–400 brands. Among eight- to fourteen-year-olds, 92 percent of requests are brand-specific, and 89 percent of kids agree that "When I find a brand I like, I tend to stick with it." A 2000 Griffin Bacal study found that nearly two-thirds of mothers thought their children were brand-aware by age

three, and one-third said it happened at age two. Kids have clear brand preferences, they know which brands are cool, they covet them, and they pay attention to the ads for them. Today's tweens are the most brand-conscious generation in history.

The increased salience of brands is a predictable outcome of kids' greater exposure to ads. Companies spend billions to create positive brand associations for their products, attempting to connect them with culturally valued images, feelings, and sensibilities. This is especially true in the youth marketplace, where so many of the products are hardly differentiable without the labels. There's a copycat sameness to sodas, fast food, candy, athletic shoes, jeans, and even music and films. And in light of that, companies have to work overtime to establish brand identity and loyalty. They turn brands into "signs," pure symbolic entities, detached from specific products and functional characteristics. This has been a winning strategy and youth have eagerly embraced an ethic of labels and logos. But brand value is a hard quality to sustain, especially in today's super-competitive environment. The intensification of what scholars Robert Goldman and Stephen Papson have dubbed "sign wars," that is, corporate competition centered on images, has led to an ever-accelerating spiral of changing symbolism and brand vulnerability. And that vulnerability fuels marketing innovation and sometimes desperation.

In what industry insiders call the "kidspace," much of the action has been in what is called brand extension. Products are inserted into a vast matrix of other products. There's the Pokémon TV program, the collectible cards, the handheld electronic game, Pokémon toys at the fast food outlet, Pokémon versions of classic board games, Pokémon clothing, school supplies, plastic cups, backpacks, Pokémon everything and anything. Indeed, the process of extensive branding has become a profoundly normalized part of children's lives. It's now a lack of branding that's out of the ordinary. One of my friends explained to me that her son, a five-year-old with sophisticated musical tastes, was baffled by the fact that there was no "Talking Heads stuff"—no show, no toys, no logo, no nothing. What was going on, he wondered, with this band he liked so much?

Increasingly the brands kids want aren't just any brands. They crave designer duds and luxury items. By the mid-1990s, parents and buyers reported a sea change as girls aged six to ten became more fashion- and label-conscious. They wanted trendy styles like platform shoes and black clothing. They started asking for Hilfiger and Donna Karan labels. The designers claim that "kids are driving the trend," but they have been advertising heavily to them. Meanwhile, children's lines have sprung up at fashion houses such as Armani and Calvin Klein. Burberry opened Burberry Kids, and Abercrombie & Fitch, the current bad boy of youth apparel, became tweens' favorite brand. Upscaling has gone beyond designer clothes. By the end of the 1990s, Marianne Szymanski, founder of the Toy Research Institute, reported that: "Kids are starting to want more expensive toys like computer software, cell phones, VCRs, e-mail, stereos, bedroom microwaves (for making popcorn while they watch movies in their own 'bedroom theater'). And guess what? Parents are buying all these items." Kids are also amassing far more toys than ever

before. The number of toys sold annually rose 20 percent between 1995 and 2000. The United States, despite having only 4.5 percent of the world's population, now consumes 45 percent of global toy production.

Consumer experiences are also going luxe, and they're often more adult-like. The London salon MiniKin Kinder offers eight-year-olds its "Princess Treat" with haircut, manicure, and minifacial. Even cosmetic surgery has begun to reach down into childhood, according to journalist Alissa Quart, who reports that the year between elementary and middle schools is becoming a popular time for aesthetic enhancement for eyes, lips, chins, and ears. For those seeking the ultimate experience, FAO Schwartz offered birthday sleepover parties at a price of $17,500, and they were booked solid. Restaurateurs report that, "Crayons just won't do it anymore." Now they're providing menus attached to Magna Doodle sets, watercolor paint boxes, and Chinese carryout boxes with chopsticks, fortune cookies, and toys. In perhaps the most dramatic example of restaurant upscaling to come along yet, in 2000, McDonald's gave away Madame Alexander dolls, full-sized versions of which go for $50, with its Happy Meals.

62

CATHY NEWMAN

Dreamweavers: Weaving the Future

Extracted from **National Geographic 203, 1 (January 2003): 50–70.**
Reprinted with permission.

For quite some time I have had a recurrent dream of floating in air. So when I read about Alex Soza's antigravity jacket, I wondered if my fantasy could, so to speak, sprout wings.

Soza, a young Danish designer, agreed to take me to his studio in Valby, a Copenhagen suburb, to see the jacket, which had just been returned from being exhibited in a museum. Midway through the train ride from my hotel to his studio, his eyes turned heavy behind his fender-thick black-rimmed glasses, and his body slumped. Shortly, he shook himself awake and apologized. "I daydream," he said. "That's how I get ideas."

The antigravity jacket had materialized from such a daydream, he explained. "I was on the subway, and this picture of a floating jacket popped into my mind," he said. "I envisioned a beautiful woman stepping out of a jacket and the jacket remaining suspended."

Unfortunately, my fantasy of floating was not part of the picture; although the jacket itself could float, Soza made it clear it could not levitate the wearer.

In his studio he opened a cardboard box and pulled out the jacket, which looked like a beached jellyfish shriveled by sun. The jacket is made out of two layers of polyurethane membrane quilted into channels into which chemicals can be introduced that react to form helium.

"Could I try it on?" I asked.

Horror crossed his face. "It's too fragile. But it works. I can show you pictures." He handed me a photograph showing the jacket suspended like a bit of ectoplasm in the air.

When I said there didn't seem to be much practical use for a jacket that just floated and couldn't support the weight of the wearer, he gave me a pitying look.

"It's about imagination!," he said, with the gleam of a visionary. "It's a beautiful dream! It's turning science fiction into scientific fact!"

To be a dreamer like Alex Soza is to be sensitive to sights and sounds invisible and inaudible to the rest of us. Soza—like many dreamers scattered around the globe—happens to dream about new textile systems. But not all flights of fancy get off the ground. Though some soar into reality, others crash-land. Even so, the dream world of high-tech textiles is an exciting place to be these days.

Ever since our ancestors flung a pelt over themselves to shelter against the cold, textiles have protected us from the slings and arrows of weather, war, and much else. At first textiles were made from natural materials like silk and wool. With the invention of rayon at the end of the nineteenth century, fibers became increasingly sophisticated and versatile.

Now the field is poised on the edge of a new era. The newest generation of textiles may be so high-tech and smart that they take you into outer space, allow you to communicate (by wearing your phone, not just your heart, on your sleeve), and even save your life.

The story of high-tech textiles is about creating fabric strong enough to float a building from one place to another or a camouflage suit that can—with the aid of fiber optics—allow a soldier to disappear into changing terrain. But it is also a story about dreamers who get ahead of themselves and sometimes slip over the edge.

Once upon a time all fibers came from natural sources: wool from the hair of sheep; cotton from a plant with a downy, fiber-filled pod; silk from the secretions of a caterpillar, *Bombyx mori*.

"I have often thought, that probably there might be a way found out to make an artificial glutinous composition, much resembling ... that excrement ... out of which, the Silk-worm wire-draws his clew," wrote Robert Hooke, the father of microscopy, in the seventeenth century. But the first true synthetic fiber would not appear until 1935, when scientists at the DuPont Company invented nylon.

Synthetic fibers are polymers, molecules based on carbon and linked in long chains, typically with hydrogen, nitrogen, and oxygen added on. Polymers can be melted or dissolved and drawn into a thread, and herein lies a difference between synthetic and natural fibers.

"If I tried to melt cotton, it would disintegrate, whereas a synthetic like nylon can be melted and shaped into any form I want," said Jim Romine, director of material science and engineering at the DuPont Experimental Station in Wilmington, Delaware. DuPont is the biggest manufacturer of synthetic fibers in the world.

Synthetics can do things beyond the reach of natural fibers. Take Kevlar, an early high-tech textile. Pound for pound stronger than steel, Kevlar belongs to a class of carbon fibers called aramids, used in high-strength applications such as antiballistic vests and astronaut tethers. Other high-tech fibers like Nomex and Zylon have high-temperature resistance, perfect for firefighters and race-car drivers.

For the record, Romine was wearing a silk tie, gray wool pinstripe pants, and a blue shirt that was 60 percent cotton, and when I pointed out the predominance of natural fibers in his clothes, it didn't throw him a bit.

"It's a matter of aesthetics," he said. "I may want the material I wear to drape or look a certain way." He fingered his tie. "I may want the fabric to rustle. And there is an elite factor."

"On the other hand," he continued, "if you're a race-car driver, forget cotton or silk. You will put on that Nomex suit."

"You just wouldn't believe what we're working on," a colleague of Romine's at DuPont told me with a knowing smile as we sat around a table at the research center. "It'd knock your socks off." As I waited for the sock-knocking revelation, he added, "Unfortunately we can't talk about it." The curtain of proprietary rights and nondisclosure had descended—and not for the last time, as it would turn out.

The closed-mouth syndrome is, at heart, a matter of money. Textiles are labor-intensive. Much of the textile-manufacturing business has shifted to Asia and Eastern Europe where labor is cheaper. High-tech textiles are seen as a way to resurrect a flagging sector in the United States and Western European countries. Competition is fierce and global in scope. Why give away secrets?

In London I visited Philips Design, a design laboratory run by the European manufacturer Philips Electronics. The studio is a dream-tank for wearable electronics. Among the dreams spun by Philips are an intelligent apron ("This linen apron with integrated power circuit and built-in microphone allows for hands-free operation of kitchen appliances. Turn down a hot plate. Recall a recipe on the screen") and the Queen of Clubs outfit ("Here's an outfit for the girl who's really into clubbing. Sensors hidden in her clothes allow her to affect the lights and beat of the music ... So that she can make contact with other people across the dance floor, she has pageable pants with lights that flash when someone is trying to get in touch"), but these, it was explained, were prototypes rather than off-the-rack buyables.

The only market item so far hit stores a few years ago, when Philips collaborated with denim-maker Levi Strauss to produce what was billed as the first wearable electronics jacket. The jacket, called the ICD+, sold for about a thousand dollars. The ICD+ was equipped with an MP3 audio player and cell phone. Headphones were built into the hood, and a microphone was embedded in the collar, but to me at least, it seemed little more than a snazzy-looking jacket with sewn-in wires and pockets.

When I expressed disappointment, Clive van Heerden, director of Intelligent Fibres, pointed out that it was an early first step and a conservative one. "We want to make the jacket that makes the coffee and picks up the kids and keeps track of the shopping list, but it's not going to happen overnight."

Van Heerden explained that Philips was working on other products like the jacket, but with advanced technology that actually incorporated the electronics into the fabric itself. Pressed for details, he balked and invoked the shroud of corporate secrecy.

"I would love to tell you more" van Heerden said, "but our client is absolutely paranoid."

In a larger sense, high-tech textiles like jackets wired for sight and sound may redefine what clothes are all about. "In the past, clothing protected us from the elements," said Ian Scott, head of technology for womenswear at British retailer Marks & Spencer. "Then clothing became about fashion. The future is about clothing that can do something for you. It's no longer passive. It's active." In the next few years, M&S hopes to introduce an "intelligent bra," a sports bra that can sense stress and adjust its dimensions to give perfect support. "We're not divulging how it works," Scott said. Somehow, I was not surprised.

Jeff Wolf, head of a small start-up called Sensatex in New York City, enthused about a smart T-shirt with conductive fibers that feed into a small transmitter that can monitor vital signs like heartbeat, blood oxygen, respiration, and body temperature—and that's just for starters. He showed me a prototype, which looks pretty much like an ordinary T-shirt, but of thicker material—similar to an Ace bandage—with several ports for phone-jack-like connectors. Down the road, he explained, sensors that carry light and video can be incorporated into the shirt, as can a GPS signal.

Its inventor, Sundaresan Jayaraman, a professor at the Georgia Institute of Technology, envisions applications such as monitoring babies at risk for sudden infant death syndrome, keeping tabs on postsurgical geriatric patients at home, and making sure firefighters on the job don't suffer from heat or other physical stress. "I call the shirt a wearable motherboard," Jayaraman said. "There's no limit. We can plug in as many sensors as you want." The information travels via conductive fibers woven into the shirt to a small wireless transmitter, which will send the information to be interpreted wherever you specify—say your doctor's office or hospital monitoring station.

In the future, clothes won't just sit there. They'll be primed to do something. Though the potential of a product like Jayaraman's smart shirt is impressive, just how active and garrulous we'll want our street wear to be is another matter.

"Do you really want your clothes to talk to you?," I asked Katharine Hamnett, a forward-thinking London designer noted for no-holds-barred opinions.

"Absolutely not," she said. "Imagine what they'd say. Things like: 'You liar.' Besides, there's enough chatter in the world."

"I'm opening my box of toys," Hugues Vinchon promised. Vinchon is an executive with Dubar-Warneton, a manufacturer of technical textiles in Wattrelos, a French town near the Belgian border. As we sat in a conference room in the company offices, he pulled out samples of his inventory like a magician pulling scarves from a hat.

First it's a swatch of oil-eating textile, which absorbs five times its weight in oil (the perfect mop for petrochemical spills); then a fabric that absorbs vibrations ("Can you imagine a motorboat you can't hear?" he said); finally an ordinary-looking cloth bag. "Completely water-soluble," he said. "It's strong enough to carry heavy objects. But if I dip it in boiling water it disappears. Unfortunately I am a little ahead of myself. I only have one potential customer for this vanishing fabric."

"Who?," I asked.

"The French Atomic Energy Commission. But they won't tell me how they intend to use it."

On the other hand, the US Army Soldier and Biological Chemical Command center in Natick, Massachusetts, is happy to play show-and-tell (within limits). At Natick, as the center is known, researchers develop materials needed to clothe and shelter military personnel. "I take frostbite personally," a scientist in the textile division told me. "My son-in-law is a marine, and he suffered frostbite on a mission once."

High-tech textiles are everywhere at Natick. There are research projects focused on air beams, inflatable high-strength fabric tubes that would allow a team to erect an airplane hangar in a fraction of the time a conventional metal structure would take. The largest air beams, about 30 inches in diameter and 80 feet long, are so strong you can hang a fully armored Humvee from one. Yet they pack down into the back of a truck. "We have a team of guys who run around the world setting up metal-frame maintenance hangars," said Jean Hampel, the engineer in charge of the project. "It takes ten people five days to set one up. We can set one made of air beams up with six people in two days."

In another building, Quoc Truong worked on an amphibious suit for Navy SEALs that can take them from water to land and back to water again. SEALs on a mission have to wear a wetsuit and then carry and change into clothes for use on land, Truong explained. "So the Navy came to us and asked us to develop a single suit that does both." The answer, he believes, is a paper-thin membrane made out of a material manufactured by the Japanese company Mitsubishi Heavy Industries that is sandwiched between two layers of stretchable polyester fleece. On land the membrane opens up, allowing heat to escape. In water the membrane closes down, retaining body heat and minimizing heat loss. The suit is currently being tested.

In the lobby of Natick's headquarters I could view a life-size model of the Future Warrior 2025, a soldier mannequin dressed to kill. The body-hugging black suit and helmet combine the sleekness of a racing skater with the menace of RoboCop. Future Warrior 2025 is a military wish list for what the well-dressed combat soldier will wear by the end of the first quarter of the twenty-first century. Among other marvels, the suit will incorporate communications hardware, monitor the wearer's physical condition, tell commanders the location of every soldier, be able to sense light from the environment and adjust camouflage patterns accordingly, and protect against ballistics, radiation, and chemical and biological agents.

"Someday we may have robots, but right now the soldier is the most important thing on the battlefield," said Tom Tassinari, a Natick scientist. "Men and women fire weapons, fly planes, and drive tanks. Protecting that individual is one of our key missions—and I mean not just protection from bullets, but from climate, flame, lasers, biologicals, chemicals, and radiation."

"It's a grim business you're in," I said.

"Just the opposite. I'm trying to prevent death. I don't think I could handle the other end of it."

At Natick, scientists are also playing with the idea of an instant suit. "It's blue-sky stuff," admitted Carole Winterhalter, a textile expert. To make the suit, she suggested, you'd have a machine (and these already exist) that would scan your body with lasers and calibrate your dimensions. The heads of the lasers would be combined with a nozzle that would spray and wrap a polymer fiber around your contours to create an instantly fabricated, formfitting uniform ready for the battlefield or mess hall. "Instead of making a fiber, spinning it into yarn, weaving it into fabric, cutting and sewing it into clothes, you'd go from fiber to garment with none of the steps in between," she said.

Of course, when you think about it, that kind of system has been in operation for eons. A spider goes directly from polymer fiber (spider silk) to application (a web). As usual, nature was there first.

"My company is based on the lessons of the spider," said Jeff Turner, as he picked up a plush spider toy the size of a dinner plate, started to show it to me, then stopped as concern flashed across his face.

"You're not arachnophobic, are you?" Turner, forty-two, heads a start-up biotech company in Montreal called Nexia Biotechnologies, whose big-bet project is the production of spider silk. Spider silk is the ultimate fiber dream. It is five times as strong as steel, yet has tenacity, or stretch, making it ideal for many applications. Turner, whose energy level resembles one of those Quebec mega-hydro dams, was leaping with excitement as he explained the concept in Nexia's offices.

"Spiders are making high-impact materials right before your eyes," he said. "And it only took them 400 million years to get there. Nature is a series of solutions to questions of survival. In looking at a web, we're looking at the end point of a life-and-death game that has been playing for years. The game rules say you only have what is on this table—twenty different amino acids. The spider has taken the same amino acids that are in your hair, skin, body and has put them together to make a beautiful continuous filament with perfect crystallinity. And it's truly biological; no high temperatures or noxious chemicals needed for manufacturing."

Unfortunately, spiders can't be farmed. They're cannibalistic. So Turner's group has come up with an alternative. Introduce the spider-silk-protein gene—which only affects the mammary gland—into the genetic makeup of a goat. Take the spider-silk-protein out of the milk. Process the protein. Spin it. *Voilà!* Spider silk by way of goat milk.

So what does a goat that has a spider-silk-protein gene look like? Like any other goat, it turns out. After all, Turner said, the genetically modified goat has 70,000 ordinary goat genes and a single spider-silk-protein gene. As for the ethics of tampering with a goat's genes, Turner pointed out that the goats aren't harmed. "Why are people afraid?" he asked rhetorically, then answered his question: "People fear newness; people fear change."

Production of spider silk is at least eighteen months away, but already Turner envisions applications for the new material, called BioSteel. First on the market, he said, would be suture thread for eye surgery finer and stronger than today's nylon, then antiballistic vests and biodegradable fishing lines. In the far-out future-applications department, Turner proposes a space elevator. "Why use rockets to lift objects into orbit? Why not do something different? Why not have a honking big satellite and dangle a rope down to the Earth and pull them up? OK—so it's 200 miles, and there's not a rope that will hold its weight at that length—but spider silk with its high strength-to-weight ratio could."

"Civilizations define themselves by the materials they use," Turner said. "The industrial revolution came about because of steel. Computers came from silicon. We are about to enter the age of bio-mimicry. It's back to nature."

EDITORS' NOTE

As of this writing, Nexia has abandoned the spider silk project after attempts to spin the protein into a usable fiber failed.

ARTHUR C. MEAD

Made in China

Apparel is a comparatively small industry with 3.9 percent of world trade in manufactures, which makes it about the same as the iron and steel industry and less than a quarter of the office machines and telecommunications sector, but it has an importance far exceeding its size. Apparel is important because it's mobile, and as such it functions much like the canary in a coal mine, as a leading indicator. While all industries "scour the planet for the lowest-cost production, as well as places that are free from government regulation, environmental constraints, and pressure from independent labor movements" (Appelbaum et al. 2005), the apparel industry is quicker at responding to changing incentives, and thus this question is on the minds of many business leaders, workers, politicians and policy-makers around the world: Is the apparel industry on the move again? It is, and to understand the nature of the impending shift we need to look at the primary driver of those changes—the rise of China. In July 2005, *The Economist* suggested that "China is behind almost everything"—housing and oil prices, profits and wages, inflation and interest rates and wages, and certainly the same is true of the apparel industry ("From T-shirts to T-bonds" 2005). China is at the center of the forces that will determine the future of fashion, but because China's future is tied to its past, that is where we begin our search for the future of the apparel industry.

THE PAST AND PRESENT

Three fateful decisions altered China's economic history and greatly affected its relationship with the world. The first was in the fifteenth century, when China chose to isolate itself from the world, a decision that triggered a monumental economic collapse. As the world's superpower, with an economy that was one-third larger than all of Western Europe's and accounted for 25 percent of the world's GDP in 1500 (Maddison 2001, 2006), China chose to reign in Admiral Zheng's fleet of nine-masted, 150-meter treasure ships that ruled the Indian Ocean just as the Portuguese were sailing their 30-meter caravels into the Indian Ocean. What followed was a redistribution of world economic power from East to West. By 1913, China had been humiliated by the English in the Opium War and Japan in the Sino-Japanese war, and its economy had shrunk to one-quarter of Western Europe's, about 9 percent of the world's GDP. The foundation had been laid for the communist revolution that would establish Mao Zedong as leader of the world's most populous communist nation in 1949.

The second decision was Mao's decision, following the lead of the Soviet Union and the overwhelming majority of the newly independent countries, formerly European colonies, in South America, Africa, and South Asia, to choose isolation from the world as a development strategy.

Mao's promise of a better tomorrow was built on agrarian reform that ended land ownership, five-year industrial plans driven by state- and community-owned businesses, the Great Leap Forward of 1958 and the Cultural Revolution of 1966. In the West, meanwhile, the decision was made that a third world war would best be avoided by reviving the international trade decimated by two world wars and the Great Depression, and in 1947 the General Agreement on Tariffs and Trade (GATT) was established to guide the dismantling of existing quotas and tariffs, which in 1995 morphed into the World Trade Organization (WTO). The result was that in the West international trade exploded, with the value of manufacturing exports rising 11 percent annually, three times faster than world GDP (1950–2004) as suppliers shifted production closer to markets, critical resources, or lower labor costs, and consumers in the two biggest markets, Europe and the US, got lower prices (World Trade Organization 2005). Unfortunately for China, the Great Leap Forward will be most remembered for the great famine it produced. Mao's decision to sit on the sidelines as trade took off, coupled with his success in promoting population growth, will be remembered for furthering China's slide. By the time Mao died in 1976, China's share of the world's population had fallen to 5 percent, one-fifth the size of Europe's and one-quarter the size of the US, and by 1981 there were 633 million people in China living on less than $1 a day—which represented about 63 percent of China's population and 43 percent of the world's poor.[1]

The third decision was that of Deng Xiaoping to open China to the world in 1978, with the creation of four Special Economic Zones located near Taiwan and Hong Kong. Deng had seen firsthand the economic miracles of Japan and the four Asian tigers (Hong Kong, Korea, Singapore, Taiwan) that had chosen to build their economies around an export sector selling to Europe and the US. Between 1950 and 1980, growth in GDP per person in those five countries averaged 440 percent, three times as fast as China, and now it was China's turn to grow (Maddison

2006). The engine would also be exports. Deng, whose favorite phrase was "I don't care what color the cat is, as long as it catches the rat," embedded a few peculiarities. Deng had inherited a country of nearly one billion, far bigger than any of those Asian success stories, and since productivity and not people would fuel the growth, Deng launched his one-child policy in 1979, which left China with today's demographic issues—an undersupply of females, a surplus of children with no siblings and a shortage of workers to support a rapidly aging population. Deng, a victim of the purges of the Cultural Revolution, knew all too well of China's history of political unrest and regional factionalism, so political freedom was not an option, as the Chinese saw in 1977 with the closing of the "Democracy Wall" and the world saw in 1989 in Tiananmen Square. China's growth would also be different because it would be based on foreign direct investment (FDI) of multinationals that would act as a magnet for firms looking for access to those one billion potential consumers and low labor costs. This gave China access to important technology transfers, but left it without its own world-famous brands such as Korea's Samsung or Japan's Sony.

The results were remarkable. China's entry into the world trading system increased the world's labor supply by a third (Zeng 2005). Given that the average hourly compensation for manufacturing workers in China was estimated to be 3 percent of US and EU (15) costs and 25 percent of costs in Brazil and Mexico (Banister 2005), this drove down the price of labor around the world as firms relocated operations to China because of their inability to compete with "The China Price." Chinese exports of manufactures began flooding the world market, enough to increase six-fold China's share of world manufacturing exports between 1980 and 2000. Exports also generated economic growth averaging 10 percent a year, which would lift 422 million people in China above the $1 a day poverty level, the largest such improvement in history (Zeng 2005).

The impact of China on the apparel industry, however, was muted by two developments in international trade policy—quotas and regional trade preferences—that were triggered by the mobility of the textile and apparel industries. The relocation of textile and apparel production from North America, beginning in the 1950s in Japan and then moving to Hong Kong, Taiwan, Singapore, and Korea, happened quickly, and this triggered a series of protectionist agreements. The Long-Term Agreement Regarding International Trade in Cotton Textiles (LTA) in 1962 established quotas on the imports of cotton goods, and in 1974 the Multi-Fiber Agreement (MFA) extended this to other materials. In 1994, during the Uruguay round of GATT negotiations for further cuts in tariffs and quotas, the decision was made to replace GATT with the WTO, which did not include China, and to replace the MFA with an Agreement on Textiles and Clothing (ATC) that established a four-stage quota liberalization schedule to eliminate all quotas on apparel and textiles by January 1, 2005.

Regional trade policies, meanwhile, became a component of the US's national security strategy when President Reagan, worried about communism's threat in Central America and the Caribbean, created the Caribbean Basin Initiative (CBI) in 1982 to provide duty-free access to the US market. The idea, also behind President Clinton's support for NAFTA a decade later, and more recently popularized by Thomas Friedman in *The Lexus and the Olive Tree*, was simple: keep people busy at work and not at war. The apparel industry was perfect since it was mobile and required limited capital investment, so it could be relocated to the desired locations. What followed were a number of additional regional trade agreements that opened US and European markets to neighboring countries and an array of the world's poorest countries.

The effect of the quotas and regional trade agreements can clearly be seen in three features of apparel's geography in the 1990s. First, apparel production did survive in Europe and the US, but it did not thrive. In the 1990s in the US, employment in apparel fell 49 percent as the industry shed 413,000 production workers (Bureau of Labor Statistics 2006). Second, apparel production moved to some of the world's poorest nations, which had been given access to the EU and US markets in the regional trade deals, explaining why four of the top fifteen apparel exporters (India, Pakistan, Indonesia, and Bangladesh) were classified as low-income by the World Bank, while for all manufactures only one (India) was low-income (World Trade Organization 2005). The industry thrives in environments found in poor agricultural countries; thus, apparel became viewed by many as the first step on the economic development ladder. The "proof" was that East Asia had so successfully used apparel to move into the ranks of the world's wealthiest countries. At this time, though, many of the poor, apparel-producing countries have failed to take that next step. In the 1990s more than 90 percent of the increase in manufacture exports in Bangladesh and Macao was in apparel, while in El Salvador, Peru, Dominican Republic, Sri Lanka, and Tunisia it exceeded 50 percent. By the year 2000 apparel accounted for at least half of the earnings from manufacturing in Lesotho and Mauritius in Africa, El Salvador and the Dominican Republic in the Americas, and Bangladesh, Cambodia, Sri Lanka and Macao in Asia. And not to be overlooked is the role apparel plays in the emancipation of women, a way out of the informal economy. In Bangladesh, Cambodia and Sri Lanka, females accounted for more than 80 percent of the workforce, while in Guatemala, Mauritius, Morocco and Romania their share exceeded 50 percent (Ernst et al. 2005). The third feature was a pattern of regional specialization that appeared in apparel production in the 1990s. The EU and US, accounting for about three-quarters of the world's clothing imports, became centers of low-cost producer networks, those in South and Central America serving the US, and those in Africa, Eastern Europe, and the Middle East serving Europe. As a result, in the 1990s exceptional growth rates in apparel exports were seen in Mexico (1,370 percent); and El Salvador, Honduras, Costa Rica, and Canada (all 500+ percent) serving the US; and Romania 541 percent, Morocco 232 percent, Bahrain 1,115 percent, and Jordan 951 percent serving Europe. The traditional, but aging, industry leaders—Singapore (–50 percent), Korea (–33 percent), and Taiwan (–25 percent)—were the biggest losers. And finally China was beginning to exert its influence on the market. Apparel exports rose 243 percent in the decade, enough to double its share of world exports to 18 percent. The stage was set for the first step into the future when China gained entry into the WTO in 2001 (World Trade Organization 2005).

THE FUTURE

The apparel industry received two big shocks soon after the passing of the millennium—China's entry into the WTO (2001) and the end of the MFA (2005). How much the industry responds, and how fast, will depend upon future developments in trade policies and China. What we do know is that the wave of Chinese imports, as well as their low price, that flooded the EU and US markets quickly got the attention of policy-makers in the EU and US. The US moved to restrict some product categories, the most widely publicized being bras and socks, and the EU moved to analyze import data. Once the preliminary, mind-boggling, post-MFA numbers arrived, both the EU and US rushed to exercise the "safeguard" loophole in the original ATC agreement. In the EU in the first quarter of 2005, apparel imports from China in nine monitored categories were up 221 percent from the year earlier, driving their market share from 20 to 35 percent, while the average price fell 18 percent (Nathan Associates 2005). The response was the EU-China Memorandum of Understanding on Textile Trade signed in 2005, which reinstated quotas on ten categories through the end of 2007.

In the US it was a similar picture. In three apparel categories —cotton trousers, underwear, and knit shirts—the US sought quota protection in mid-2005. US imports from China rose an average of 1,025 percent, which increased China's market share from 1 to 10 percent (Nathan Associates 2005). The US followed the EU's lead

and as of January 2006, quotas were reinstated on thirty-four product categories, which would remain in effect through the end of 2008. The breadth of China's advance in the US, as well as the effect of the new quotas, can be seen in more recent data on year-to-date sales for April 2004, 2005, and 2006, which covers the end of the MFA and the reinstitution of quotas. In April 2005, apparel imports from China for each of the seventeen apparel categories rose faster than the total, giving China an annual increase of 46 percent and a global market share that rose from 17 to 24 percent. China has been slowed, however, by the new quotas. Imports from China fell 8 percent between 2005 and 2006, four times faster than all apparel imports (US Census Bureau 2006).

As for the future effects of the quotas and regional trade agreements that succeeded at distorting the industries' pattern of trade in much of the era after the Second World War, the existing quota extensions running through 2007 in the EU and 2008 in the US are not likely to be extended again. The main beneficiaries of existing policies are the workers in a number of very poor countries who are underrepresented in policy-making international agencies and workers in the already gutted US and EU industries. At the time of the initial trade restrictions in the early 1960s, almost 2 million production workers were employed in the US but, by 2006, fewer than 350,000 were employed, not enough to exert the same influence over trade policy in the US. This will most likely hurt the smaller and poorer countries in sub-Saharan Africa and South and Central America, which relied heavily on apparel. There also appears to be a shift in the textile and apparel industries underway that favors emerging Southeast and South Asia. Between 2004 and 2006, imports from Cambodia and Bangladesh rose more than 50 percent, and in India, Indonesia, Vietnam, and Pakistan they rose more than 25 percent. The only other countries with increases exceeding 25 percent were Egypt and Jordan. This growth came at the expense of the US, where employment in textile and apparel dropped about 50 percent from

2000 to 2006 (Bureau of Labor Statistics 2006). It has also hurt more affluent Asia, where import losses from Taiwan and Korea both exceeded 25 percent, the Americas, with El Salvador (–31 percent), Dominican Republic (–18 percent), Mexico (–18 percent), Canada (–14 percent), and Honduras (–10 percent) all experiencing double-digit losses, and Turkey (–23 percent) and Italy (–14 percent). One of the more surprising results was the sharp fall in imports from Macao and Hong Kong in 2005, and then their revival in 2006.

Many of the same countries hurt by the end of quotas and China will also be hurt by changes in the apparel industry's structure, which Pietra Rivoli outlined in *The Travels of a T-Shirt in the Global Economy*. China has become a key link in a global production chain extending from the farms to the factories to the final consumers. China has become the factory in a buyer-driven value chain where the BIG money and power is in the marketing, branding and design stages because the barriers to entry are highest there; the power of international conglomerates who own the brands will only grow with their size and increasing concentration in the industry (Gereffi 1999). Once freed of the distortions imposed by quotas, these large buyers will downsize and consolidate their supply sources, which favors producers that can ramp up production and deliver full-package production. This one-stop shopping that delivers everything from cutting and sewing to shipping favors the rising power in the industry: the giant transnational contractors based mainly in East Asia who direct buyers' orders to their factories scattered across low-cost regions (Appelbaum et al. 2005). Also favoring these contractors is the move toward lean retailing, which rewards reliable supply-chain partners, and countries that have good communications and transportation infrastructures.

The clear winners given all of these industry trends are China and India with their long history in textiles, and Pakistan with its current capacity for textile production. After that it gets a bit less certain, but Vietnam, which benefits from both its location and cheap labor, Bangladesh, which will be limited by a weak infrastructure, and possibly Sri Lanka, a beneficiary of high quotas, appear to be best positioned to grow their industries. The regional suppliers close to the EU and US markets, where wages tend to be higher than in China, will lose market share, but they should be able to focus on niches that favor their sole competitive advantage, time-to-market, which is increasingly important with lean manufacturing. Included here would be Mexico and a few Central American countries supplying the US, and Egypt, Romania, Turkey, and Morocco for the EU. The countries that are overwhelmingly seen as losing are the smaller, higher income countries and sub-Saharan Africa (Ernst et al. 2005).

What remains uncertain, however, is the extent to which China's competitive advantages are sustainable in the longer term, which is undoubtedly why "sustainable" was one of the three guiding principles in China's eleventh five-year plan. In 2006 stories were already appearing about labor shortages and wage increases in China, exactly the pattern experienced in the earlier Asian success stories, but China may prove to be different (Bradsher 2006). It has a virtually endless supply of labor—it is just not located where the jobs are, along the coast and in its cities. In 2005, nearly 800 million Chinese were living in rural areas where incomes were low and jobs scarce, and the disparities between rural and urban China have been growing. Income per capita in coastal Guangdong Province in 1978, as China turned outward, was twice that in central Guizhou Province, but by 1999 it was almost eight times higher (Catin et al. 2005). This inequality is the driving force behind the world's largest rural-urban migration in history. The UN projects the migration will add 340 million people to China's cities between 2005 and 2030 (Catin et al. 2005), which has created a "floating population" with no residency permits to live in urban areas that may number 150 million, about the size of the entire US labor force. Add to this the millions of workers a year displaced by the closing of the state-owned enterprises, and labor will have little to no power to negotiate wage increases, but there will be a need to generate possibly 8–10 million jobs a year (Zeng 2005). For apparel, this should translate into increased state support, since China will desperately need labor-intensive industries. What will change though, will be that there will be increasing pressure to move operations inland, and this will raise transportation time and costs and reduce China's competitive advantage. This may prove to be less of a problem in the future, however, as the geography of demand changes.

The growth of China, combined with the stagnation in Europe and the overextended consumer in the US, suggests that China and India may be the growth centers in the market for apparel. It has been estimated that the Chinese middle class numbers 110 million (Yellen 2005), about the size of Japan, and it is certainly growing faster there, which is why in 2006 you could not pick up a business magazine without a story of a new industry "discovering" the market. Factories in China and Asia are benefiting from the demand. What we may be close to seeing is the emergence of Chinese international brands such as Shanghai Tang, which will allow China to earn more of the profit from apparel.

Limiting China's market share in the longer term will be the environmental degradation and resource demands that have accompanied its breakneck growth. The US Energy Information Administration reported that of the ten most polluted cities in the world, seven were in China, and that was before a decade of 10 percent a year growth. It is unlikely that China will be able to continue its industrialization without regard for environment and resource demands, and this could increase costs and regulations. The potentially biggest negative effect on China's cost-effectiveness will be adjustments in the exchange rate, which in mid-2006 was generally accepted as being held at an unsustainably low level. While we may not have the "meltdown" forecast by Fallows (2005), there is no question that the yuan will rise relative to the US dollar and this will reduce China's cost advantage. A

final limiting factor would be the potential for social unrest and political instability. China's authoritarian government has delivered on Mao's initial promise of a better life as compensation for the hard work and hardship associated with the growth and restructuring of China's economy; this has allowed it to maintain order and peace in a country with a long history of unrest. As we move forward, though, if China's economic growth rate slips below that needed to absorb the dislocated, and if the downsides of that growth, such as the highly publicized chemical spill on the Songhua River in 2004 that closed down water to a city of nearly 4 million, become more visible, then political stability will be jeopardized and the 74,000 instances of social unrest reported in 2004 will grow to a point that FDI will be discouraged.

As we head into the post-MFA world, many in the apparel industry wish the world had heeded Napoleon's warning: "Let China sleep. For when China wakes, it will shake the world." China has awoken, and it has begun to shake the world, and as so often in the past, the effects were felt early in the labor-intensive apparel industry. Indeed, the "canary in the coal mine" is gasping for breath in many countries with fading apparel industries.[2]

NOTES

1. This is a generally accepted measure of poverty; see Chen and Ravallion 2004.
2. Additional data sources for this paper included:
   United Nations (2004), World Population Prospects: The 2004 Revision Population Database, United Nations <esa.un.org/unpp/>.
   International Monetary Fund (2006), World Economic Outlook Database, April.
   US Department of Commerce, International Trade Administration, Office of Textile and Apparel, Preliminary Import Data—US Imports of Certain Textiles and Apparel <otexa.ita.doc.gov/prelimadmin/prelimdata.htm>.

ANNOTATED GUIDE TO FURTHER READING FOR PART XI

It is difficult to recommend what to read for the future of fashion. By the time this book is in print, the near future already will have passed into memory. To get a grasp on fashion's future, it is imperative to stay abreast of current events. Major newspapers that report on fashion as a cultural phenomenon and as a business are a good place to start. Many of these newspapers are viewable online: Cathy Horyn's and Guy Trebay's columns at the *New York Times*, Robin Ghivens at the *Washington Post* (who received the 2006 Pulitzer Prize in Criticism for her fashion reporting), and Suzy Menkes at *International Herald Tribune*. *The Economist* regularly reports trends in the textile and apparel industry worldwide.

For technical advances, see publications where new developments in textiles are reported. The *AATCC Review*, published by the Association of Textile Chemists and Colorists, offers articles on new developments. Formerly a journal that published technical papers and industry news only, since 2001 *AATCC Review* has been publishing insightful "C2C" (Concept to Consumer) reports.

For information about technological advances in textiles, see *Extreme Textiles* (McQuaid 2005), published to coincide with an exhibition of the same name at the Cooper-Hewitt National Design Museum. Sarah Braddock (now Clarke) wrote two books—*Techno Textiles* and *Techno Textiles 2*—that are also informative.

Two articles by a team of researchers in Britain explain their investigations toward an "Emotional Wardrobe" (Goulev et al. 2004; Stead et al. 2004). They have created a prototype for a system of sensors, a computer interface, and a specifically designed garment incorporating a colored light display. The wearer's emotions translate into colored light on the garment's surface.

Regarding the historic shift of power and capital to Asia, and to gain insight on how it affects the future of fashion, read Thomas Friedman's *The World is Flat*. Since its publication, this landmark book has alerted business leaders and government officials to the realities of a global marketplace. Other titles specifically about China are Oded Shenkar's *The Chinese Century* (2005), Ted Fishman's *China Inc.* (2005) and Clyde Prestowitz's *Three Billion New Capitalists* (2005). *Fashion in Asia* by Douglas Bullis offers a view into the aesthetic ideas of designers from Indonesia, Singapore, Malaysia, Thailand, the Philippines, Taiwan, Hong Kong and China.

BIBLIOGRAPHY

Abernathy, F. H., Dunlop, J. T., Hammond, J. H., and Weil, D. (1999), *A Stitch in Time: Lean Retailing and the Transformation of Manufacturing Lessons From the Apparel and Textile Industries*, Oxford: Oxford University Press.

Abraham, N. and Torok, M. (1994), *The Shell and the Kernel*, Vol. 1, trans. N. T. Rand, Chicago and London: University of Chicago Press.

Agamben, G. (1990), *La Communauté qui vient*, Paris: Seuil.

Agins, T. (1999), *The End of Fashion*, New York: William Morrow.

Albritton, A. (2005), "'She Has a Body on Her Dress': Sonia Delaunay-Terk's First Simultaneous Dress, 1913," *Dress* 32: 3–13.

Alcott, W. A. (1834), *The Young Man's Guide*, Boston: Lilly, Wait, Colman and Holden.

Alexander, H. (2002), "Pants Too Good to Keep Under Wraps," *The Daily Telegraph*, September 19 <www.telegraph.co.uk>.

Alexandrian, S. (1985), *Surrealist Art*, New York: Thames and Hudson.

Alien, R. L. (1969), *Black Awakening in Capitalist America: An Analytic History*, Garden City, NY: Doubleday.

"American Styles for Americans" (1932), *New York Times*, June 24.

Anderson, B. (1986), *Imagined Communities,* London: Verso.

Anderson, F. (2000), "Museums as Fashion Media," in S. Bruzzi and P. Church-Gibson (eds.), *Fashion Cultures: Theories, Explanations and Analysis*, London: Routledge, pp. 371–85.

Anderson, S., Lee, T., and Cavanaugh, J. (2005), *A Field Guide to the Global Economy*, New York: Norton.

Annual Report, 2005–2006, Ministry of Textiles, Government of India.

Anomaly (1948), *The Invert and His Social Adjustment*, London: Ballière, Tindall and Cox.

Anon. (2002), "Getting the *Sex and the City* Look," *The Independent*, April 15 <www.independent.co.uk>.

Ansen, D. (1990), "Magnificent Maverick," *Cosmopolitan* 311 (May).

Appadurai, A. (1990), "Disjuncture and Difference in the Global Cultural Economy," *Theory, Culture and Society* 7: 295–310.

Appadurai, A. (1996), *Modernity at Large: Cultural Dimensions of Globalization*, Minneapolis, MN: University of Minnesota Press.

Appelbaum, R. P., Bonacich, E., and Quan, K. (2005), "The End of Apparel Quotas: A Faster Race to the Bottom?," Center for Global Studies, Paper 2, February 5 <repositories.cdlib.org/isber/cgs/2>.

Apter, E. (1992), "Masquerade," in E. Wright (ed.), *Feminism and Psychoanalysis: A Critical Dictionary*, Oxford and Cambridge, MA: Basil Blackwell.

Armour, S. and D. Leinwand (2003), "Wal-Mart Cleaners Arrested in Sweep," *USA Today*, October 24 <www.usatoday.com/money/industries/retail/2003-10-23-walmart-arrests_x.htm>.

Arnold, J. (1964), *Patterns of Fashion: Englishwomen's Dresses and Their Construction c. 1660–1860*, London: Macmillan.

Arnold, J. (1988), *Queen Elizabeth's Wardrobe Unlock'd*, Leeds: Maney.

Ash, J. and Wilson, E. (eds.) (1992), *Chic Thrills: A Fashion Reader*, London: Pandora.

Ashley, S. (1964), "The 'Other' Homosexuals," *One* XII (2).

Aspers, P. (2005), *Markets in Fashion: A Phenomenological Approach*, Routledge Studies in Business Organization and Networks, London: Routledge.

Attfield, J. (2000), *Wild Things: The Material Culture of Everyday Life*, Oxford: Berg.

Babuscio, J. (1977), "Camp and the Gay Sensibility," in R. Dyer (ed.), *Gays and Film*, London: British Film Institute.

Bailey, M. (1982), *Those Glorious, Glamour Years*, Secaucus, NJ: Citadel.

Baizerman, S., Eicher, J. B. and Cerny, C. (1993), "Eurocentrism in the Study of Ethnic Dress," *Dress* 20: 19–32.

Bakhtin, M. (1984), *Rabelais and His World*, Bloomington and Indianapolis: Indiana University Press.

Baldaia, S. (2005), "Space Age Fashion," in L. Welters and P. A. Cunningham (eds.), *Twentieth-Century American Fashion*, Oxford: Berg.

Baldwin, E., Longhurst, B., McCracken, S., Ogborn, M. and Smith, G. (1999), *Introducing Cultural Studies*, Athens: University of Georgia Press.

Bambara, T. C. (ed.) (1970), *The Black Woman: An Anthology*, New York: New American Library.

"Ban on Freak Suits Studied by Councilmen" (1943), *Los Angeles Times*, June 9.

Banerjee, M. and Miller, D. (2003), *The Sari*, Oxford and New York: Berg.

Banister, J. (2005), "Manufacturing Earnings and Compensation in China," *Monthly Labor Review*, August.

Banner, L. (1983), *American Beauty*, New York: Alfred Knopf.

Barber, B., and Lobel, L. (1953), "'Fashion' in Women's Clothes and the American Social System," in R. Bendix and S. M. Lipset (eds.), *Class, Status and Power*, New York: The Free Press.

Barboza, D. (2004), "In Roaring China, Sweaters Are West of Socks City," *New York Times*, Sec. A, 1, December 24.

Barnard, M. (2002), *Fashion as Communication*, 2nd ed., London: Routledge.

Barr, J. (1982 [1950]), *Quatrefoil*, Boston: Allyson Publications.

Barthes, R. (1969), *The Fashion System*, trans. M. Ward and E. Howard, Berkeley: University of California Press.

Barthes, R. (1972), *Mythologies,* trans. A. Lavers, London: Jonathan Cape.

Barthes, R. (1983 [1967]), *The Fashion System,* trans. M. Ward and R. Howard, New York: Hill and Wang.

Barthes, R. (1985), *The Fashion System*, London: Cape.

Baudelaire, C. (1964 [1863]), *The Painter in Modern Life and Other Essays*, New York and London: Phaidon Press.

Baudot, F. (1997), *Paul Poiret*, London: Thames and Hudson.

Baudot, F. (1999), *Fashion: The Twentieth Century*, New York: Universe.

Baudrillard, J. (1976), *L'Echange symbolique et la mort*, Paris: Gallimard.

Baudrillard, J. (1981), *For a Critique of the Political Economy of the Sign*, St. Louis, MO: Telos Press.

Baumgarten, L. (2002), *What Clothes Reveal: The Language of Clothes in Colonial and Federal America*, Williamsburg, VA: Colonial Williamsburg Foundation.

Baumgarten, S. A. (1975), "The Innovative Communicator in the Diffusion Process," *Journal of Marketing Research* 12 (February 1): 12–18.

Bayly, C. A. (2004), *The Birth of the Modern World, 1780–1914: Global Connections and Comparisons*, Blackwell: Oxford.

Beaton, C. (1954), *The Glass of Fashion*, London: Weidenfeld and Nicolson.

Beaton, C. (1982), *Self-Portrait With Friends: The Selected Diaries of Cecil Beaton 1926–1974*, ed. R. Buckle, Harmondsworth: Penguin.

Becker, E. (2004), "Textile Quotas to End Soon, Punishing Carolina Mill Towns," *New York Times*, Sec. C, 1, November 2.

Becker, H. S. (1982), *Art Worlds*, Berkeley: University of California Press.

Bell, D. and Valentine, G. (1995), "The Sexed Self: Strategies of Performance, Sites of Resistance," in S. Pile and N. Thrift (eds.), *Mapping the Subject: Geographies of Cultural Transformation*, London and New York: Routledge.

Bell, Q. (1976), *On Human Finery*, London: Hogarth Press.

Bell-Metereau, R. (1985), *Hollywood Androgyny*, New York: Columbia University Press.

Benhamou, R. (2001), "Who Controls This Private Space? The Offense and Defense of the Hoop in Early Eighteenth-Century France and England," *Dress* 28: 13–22.

Benjamin, W. (1973 [1939]), "On Some Motifs in Beaudelaire," in *Illuminations*, trans. H. Zohn, London: Fontana/Collins.

Benjamin, W. (1985), *One Way Street and Other Writings*, trans. E. Jephcott and K. Shorter, London: Verso.

Benjamin, W. (1999), *The Arcades Project* (written 1927–40, first published 1982), trans. H. Eiland and K. McLaughlin, Cambridge, MA: Harvard University Press.

Berman, M. (1983), *All That is Solid Melts Into Air: The Experience of Modernity*, London: Verso.

Bernier, O. (1981), *The Eighteenth-Century Woman*, New York: The Metropolitan Museum of Art.

Berry, S. (2000), *Screen Style: Fashion and Femininity in 1930s Hollywood*, Minneapolis: University of Minnesota Press.

Bérubé, A. (1990), *Coming Out Under Fire: The History of Gay Men and Women in World War Two*, New York: Free Press.

Best and Company advertisement (1932), *New York Times*, May 29.

Bhachu, P. (2000), "It's Hip to Be Asian: The Local and Global Networks of Asian Fashion Entrepreneurs," paper presented at the Annual Conference of American Geographers, Pittsburgh, April.

Bhachu, P. (2003), *Dangerous Designs, Asian Women Fashion the Diaspora Economies*, London and New York: Routledge.

Birnbach, L., (ed.) (1980), *The Official Preppy Handbook*, New York: Workman Publishing.

Bissonnette, A. (2005), *Chado Ralph Rucci*, Kent, OH: Kent State University Museum.

Blausen, W. (1992), "Textiles Designed by Ruth Reeves," Master's thesis, Fashion Institute of Technology.

Blomfield, P. (2002), "The Designer Fashion in New Zealand," Industry New Zealand Scoping Study, available from <www.industrynz.govt.nz/about-us/publications/reports>.

Blum, D. (2003), *Shocking!: The Art and Fashion of Elsa Schiaparelli*, Philadelphia: Museum of Art; and New Haven, CT: Yale University Press.

Blum, S. (1982), *Eighteenth-Century French Fashion Plates in Full Color: 64 Engravings from the "Galerie des Modes," 1778–1787*, New York: Dover.

Blum, V. L. (2003), *Flesh Wounds: The Culture of Cosmetic Surgery*, Berkeley: University of California Press.

Blumberg, P. (1974), "The Decline and Fall of the Status Symbol: Some Thoughts on Status in a Post-Industrial Society," *Social Problems* 21 (April 4): 480–98.

Blumer, H. (1968), "Fashion," in D. Sills (ed.), *International Encyclopedia of the Social Sciences* 5, New York: Macmillan Co., pp. 341–5.

Blumer, H. (1969a), "Fashion: From Class Differentiation to Collective Selection," *Sociological Quarterly* 10: 275–91.

Blumer, H. (1969b), *Symbolic Interactionism: Perspective and Method*, Englewood Cliffs, NJ: Prentice Hall.

Bogatyrev, P. (1976), "Costume as a Sign," in L. Matejka and I. R. Titunik (eds.), *Semiotics of Art*, Cambridge, MA: MIT Press, pp. 13–19.

Bonacich, E., Appelbaum, R. P., and Chin, K. (2000), *Behind the Label: Inequality in the Los Angeles Apparel Industry*, Berkeley: University of California Press.

Bordo, S. (1993), *Unbearable Weight: Feminism, Western Culture and the Body*, Berkeley: University of California Press.

Born, G. and D. Hesmondhalgh (eds.) (2000), *Western Music and its Others: Difference, Representation and Appropriation in Music*, Berkeley: University of California Press.

Boucher, F. (1967), *20,000 Years of Fashion: The History of Costume and Personal Adornment*, New York: Harry N. Abrams.

Bourdieu, P. (1983), *La distinzione. Critica sociale del gusto*, Bologna: Il Mulino.

Bourdieu, P. (1984), *Distinction: A Social Critique of the Judgement of Taste*, London: Routledge.

Bourdieu, P. (1989), *Outline of a Theory of Practice*, Cambridge: Cambridge University Press.

Bowles, H., Schlesinger Jr., A. M., and Mellon, R. L. (2001), *Jacqueline Kennedy: The White House Years—Selections from the John F. Kennedy Library and Museum*, New York: Bulfinch.

Braddock, S. and O'Mahony, M. (1999), *Techno Textiles: Revolutionary Fabrics for Fashion and Design*, New York: Thames and Hudson.

Bradsher, K. (2004), "Bangladesh Survives to Export Again; Competition Means Learning to Offer More Than Just Low Wages," *New York Times*, Sec. C, 1, December 14.

Bradsher, K. (2006), "Rising Yuan Pushes China Upmarket," *New York Times*, April 20.

Brand, J. and Teunissen, J. (2005), *Global Fashion Local Tradition: On the Globalisation of Fashion*, Warnsveld: Terra.

Brannon, E. L. (2005), *Fashion Forecasting*, New York: Fairchild Books.

Braudel, F. (1973), *Capitalism and Material Life 1400–1800*, trans. M. Kochan, London: Weidenfeld and Nicolson.

Breward, C. (1995), *The Culture of Fashion: A New History of Fashionable Dress,* Manchester: Manchester University Press.

Breward, C. (1999), "Sartorial Spectacle: Clothing and Masculine Identities in the Imperial City, 1860–1914," in F. Driver and D. Gilbert (eds.), *Imperial Cities*, Manchester: Manchester University Press.

Breward, C. (1999), *The Hidden Consumer: Masculinities, Fashion and City Life 1860–1914*, Manchester, Manchester University Press.

Breward, C. (2003), *Fashion* (Oxford History of Art), Oxford: Oxford University Press.

Breward, C. (2004), *Fashioning London: Clothing and the Modern Metropolis*, Oxford: Berg.

Breward, C. and Evans, C. (eds.) (2005), *Fashion and Modernity*, Oxford: Berg.

Breward, C. and Gilbert, D. (2006), *Fashion's World Cities*, Oxford: Berg.

Breward, C., Conekin, B., and Cox, C. (eds.) (2002), *The Englishness of English Dress*, Oxford: Berg.

Brighton Ourstory Project (1992), *Daring Hearts: Lesbian and Gay Lives of 50s and 60s Brighton*, Brighton: QueenSpark Books.

Brogan, D. W. (1954), "Is Canada Ready for Greatness?," *Mayfair*.

Brooke, J. (2004), "Down and Almost Out in Mongolia; End of Garment Quota System Signals Tough Times Ahead," *New York Times*, Sec. C, December 29, p. 1.

Browne, A. (2001), "Amazons of the Avant-Garde," *ARTNews* (November): 168–70.

Brownmiller, S. (1984), *Femininity*, New York: Linden Press, Simon and Schuster.

Bruzzi, S. (1997), *Undressing Cinema*, London: Routledge.

Bryant, M. W. (2004), *WWD Illustrated: 1960s–1990s*, New York: Fairchild Publications.

Brydon, A. and Niessen, S. (eds.) (1998), *Consuming Fashion: Adorning the Transnational Body*, Oxford and New York: Berg.

Buck, A. (1961), *Victorian Costume and Costume Accessories*, London: Barrie and Jenkins.

Buck, A. (1979), *Dress in Eighteenth-Century England*, New York: Holmes and Meier.

Buckland, S. S. (1996), "Promoting American Fashion, 1940 through 1945: From Understudy to Star," PhD dissertation, Ohio State University.

Buckland, S. S. (2005), "Promoting American Designers, 1940–44: Building Our Own House," in L. Welters and P. A. Cunningham (eds.), *Twentieth-Century American Fashion*, Oxford: Berg.

Buck-Moss, S. (1991), *The Dialectics of Seeing: Walter Benjamin and the Arcades Project*, Cambridge, MA and London: MIT Press.

Budd, M., Entman, R. and Steinman C. (1990), "The Affirmative Character of US Cultural Studies," *Critical Studies in Mass Communication* 7: 169–84.

Bullis, D. (2000), *Fashion in Asia*, New York: Thames and Hudson.

Bureau of Labor Statistics (2006), *National Employment Statistics* <www.bls.gov/data/home.htm>.

Burleigh-Evett Report, July (2001), "Textile and Clothing Industry Preliminary Report, Part A: Breaking Patterns With the Past," prepared for Industry New Zealand.

Burman, B. (ed.) (1999), *The Culture of Sewing: Gender, Consumption and Home Dressmaking*, Oxford: Berg.

Butler, J. (1990), *Gender Trouble: Feminism and the Subversion of Identity*, New York: Routledge.

Butler, J. (1993), *Bodies that Matter: On the Discursive Limits of "Sex,"* New York: Routledge.

Butler, J. (1997), *Excitable Speech: A Politics of the Performative*, London: Routledge.

Buxbaum, G. (ed.) (1990), *Icons of Fashion: The 20th Century*, Munich: Prestel.

Byrde, P. (1979), *The Male Image: Men's Fashion in England 1300–1970*, London: B. T. Batsford.

Byrde, P. (1992), *Nineteenth-Century Fashion*, London: B. T. Batsford.

Caldwell, P. M. (1991), "A Hair Piece: Perspectives on the Intersection of Race and Gender," *Duke Law Journal* 365: 365–96.

"California Governor Appeals for Quelling of Zoot Suit Riots" (1943), *Washington Star*, June 10.

Callahan, C. R. and Paoletti, J. B. (1999), *Is it a Girl or a Boy? Gender Identity and Children's Clothing*, exhibition catalog, Richmond, VA: Valentine Museum.

Calzini, D., Odden, J., Tsai, J., Hoffman, S., and Tran, S. (1997), *Nike Inc.: Survey of Vietnamese and Indonesian Expenditure Levels*, Dartmouth: The Amos Tuck School.

Canada (1951), *Report of the Royal Commission on National Development in the Arts, Letters and Sciences, 1949–51* (Massey Report), Ottawa: King's Printer.

Cannon, A. (1998), "The Cultural and Historical Contexts of Fashion," in A. Brydon and S. Niessen (eds.), *Consuming Fashion: Adorning the Transnational Body*, Oxford and New York: Berg, pp. 23–38.

Carlyle, T. (1987 [1833]), *Sartor Resartus*, eds. K. McSweeney and P. Sabor, Oxford: Oxford University Press.

Carnegy, V. (1990), *Fashions of a Decade: The 1980s*, New York: Facts on File, Inc.

Carter, E. (1979), "Alice in Consumer Wonderland," in A. McRobbie and M. Nava (eds.), *Gender and Generation*, London: Macmillan.

Carter, M. (2003), *Fashion Classics from Carlyle to Barthes*, Oxford and New York: Berg.

Cartner-Morley, J. (2001), "Riding High," *The Guardian*, February 16 <www.guardian.co.uk>.

Cartner-Morley, J. (2002), "From Front Room to Front Row," *The Guardian*, September 25 <www.guardian.co.uk>.

Casely-Hayford (1994), speaker, an episode of *Reportage*, BBC 2, January 26.

Castells. M. (1991), *The Informational City*, Oxford: Blackwell.

Catin, M., Luo, X. and Huffel, C. V. (2005), "Openness, Industrialization, and Geographic Concentration of Activities in China," World Bank Policy Research Working Paper, September.

Chace, R. (2003), *The Complete Book of Oscar Fashion*, New York: Reed Press.

Chalmers, M. (1983), "Politics of Crisis," *City Limits*, August 19–25.

Chandler, R. M. and Chandler-Smith, N. (2005), "Flava in Ya Gear: Transgressive Politics and the Influence of Hip-Hop on Contemporary Fashion," in L. Welters and P. A. Cunningham (eds.), *Twentieth-Century American Fashion*, Oxford: Berg.

Chauncey G. (1994), *Gay New York: Gender, Urban Culture and the Making of the Gay Male World, 1890–1940*, New York: Basic Books.

Chen, S. and Ravallion, M. (2004), "How Have the World's Poorest Fared Since the Early 1980s?" World Bank Policy Research Working Paper No. WPS 3341.

Chenoune, F. (1993), *A History of Men's Fashion*, Paris: Flammarion.

Chibnall, S. (1985), "Whistle and Zoot: The Changing Meaning of a Suit of Clothes," *History Workshop* 20: 56–81.

Cicolini, A. (2005), *The New English Dandy*, London: Thames and Hudson.

Clancy, D. (1996), *Costume Since 1945: Couture, Street Style and Anti Fashion*, New York: Drama Publishers.

Clark, C. E., Jr. (1976), "Domestic Architecture as an Index to Social History: The Romantic Revival and the Cult of Domesticity in America, 1840–1870," *Journal of Interdisciplinary History* 7 (Summer): 33–56.

Clark, R. W. (1853), *Lectures on the Formation of Character, Temptations and Mission of Young Men*, Boston: John P. Jewett and Co.

Clarke, J. (1976), "Style," in S. Hall, J. Clarke, T. Jefferson, and B. Roberts (eds.), *Resistance Through Rituals*, London: Hutchinson.

Clarke, J., Johnson, T., Hall, S., and Roberts, B. (1992), "Subcultures, Cultures and Class," in T. Bennett, G. Martin, C. Mercer, and J. Woolacott (eds.), *Culture, Ideology and Social Process: A Reader*, Milton Keynes: Open University Press.

Clarke, S. B. and O'Mahony, M. (2006), *Techno Textiles 2: Revolutionary Fabrics for Fashion and Design*, New York: Thames and Hudson.

Cohen, P. (1979), "Policing the Working-Class City," in B. Fine *et al.* (eds.), *Capitalism and the Rule of Law*, London: Hutchinson.

Cohen, S. (1972), *Folk Devils and Moral Panics*, London: MacGibbon and Kee.

Cohen, S. (1980 [1973]), *Folk Devils and Moral Panics*, Oxford: Martin Robertson.

Cole, S. (2000), *"Don We Now Our Gay Apparel": Gay Men's Dress in the Twentieth Century*, Oxford: Berg.

Coleman, E. A. (1982), *The Genius of Charles James*, Brooklyn: Brooklyn Museum.

Coleman, E. A. (1989), *The Opulent Era: Fashions of Worth, Doucet and Pingat*, London: Thames and Hudson.

Commons, J. R. (1964 [1909]), "American Shoemakers: 1648 to 1895," in *Labor and Administration*, Reprints of Economic Classics, New York: Augustus M. Kelley, pp. 219–66.

Commons, J. R. (1977 [1901]), "The Sweating System," in L. Fink (ed.), *Out of the Sweatshop*, New York: Quadrangle.

Comstock, T. G. (1892), "Alice Mitchell of Memphis," *New York Medical Times*, No. 20.

Conlan. F. F. (1995), "Dining Out in Bombay," in C. A. Breckenridge (ed.), *Consuming Modernity: Public Culture in a South Asia World*, Minneapolis: University of Minnesota Press, pp. 90–127.

Constantino, M. (1997), *Men's Fashion in the Twentieth Century*, London: B. T. Batsford.

Cook, D. T. (2004), *The Commodification of Childhood: The Children's Clothing Industry and the Rise of the Child Consumer*, Durham, NC: Duke University Press.

Cory, D. W. (1953), "Can Homosexuals Be Recognized?" *One* 1 (September).

Cosgrave, B. (2000), *The Complete History of Costume and Fashion from Ancient Egypt to the Present*, London: Octopus Publishing Group.

Cosgrove, D. and Jackson, P. (1987), "New Directions in Cultural Geography," *Area* 19, 95–101.

Cosgrove, D. E. (2000), "Cultural Geography," in R. J. Johnston et al. (eds.), *The Dictionary of Human Geography*, 4th ed., Oxford: Blackwell, pp. 134–8.

Cosgrove, S. (1984), "The Zoot Suit and Style Warfare," *History Workshop Journal* 18: 77–91.

Cosmopolitan (1987), cover, July.

Coulson, C. (2002), "Who What When Where Why?" *The Daily Telegraph*, May 17 <www.telegraph.co.uk>.

Cozens, C. (2002), "Wanted: A Patient, Diplomatic Media Executive with Rhino Skin," *The Guardian*, July 2 <www.guardian.co.uk>.

Craik, J. (1994), *The Face of Fashion: Cultural Studies in Fashion*, London and New York: Routledge.

Crane, D. (2000), *Fashion and Its Social Agendas: Class, Gender, and Identity in Clothing*, Chicago: The University of Chicago Press.

Crane, L. (1963), "How to Spot a Possible Homo," *Daily Mirror*, April 28.

Craven, L. (1814), *Letters from the Right Honourable Lady Craven, to his Serene Highness The Margrave of Anspach, During her Travels Through France, Germany, and Russia in 1785 and 1786*, London: A. J. Valpy.

Crewe, L. and Beaverstock, J. (1998), "Fashioning the City: Cultures of Consumption in Contemporary Urban Spaces," *Geoforum* 29 (3): 287–308.

Crewe, L. and Forster, Z. (1992), "Markets, Design and Local Firm Alliances in the Nottingham Lace Market: Possibilities and Problems," Final Research Report to the University of Nottingham.

Crewe, L. and Forster, Z. (1993), "Markets, Design and Local Agglomeration: The Role of the Small Independent Retailer in the Workings of the Fashion System," *Environment and Planning D* 11: 213–29.

Crewe, L. and Lowe, M. (1995), "Gap on the Map: Towards a Geography of Consumption and Identity," *Environment and Planning A* 27: 1877–98.

Critic (pseudonym) (1947), *New Statesman and Nation* XXXIV (September 20).

Crossley, N. (1995a), "Body Techniques, Agency and Inter-corporality: On Goffman's Relations in Public," *Sociology* 129: 1, 133–49.

Crossley, N. (1995b), "Merleau-Ponty, the Elusive Body and Carnal Society," *Body and Society* 1 (1): 43–63.

Crossley, N. (1996), "Body/Subject, Body/Power: Agency, Inscription and Control in Foucault and Merleau-Ponty," *Body and Society* 2 (2): 99–116.

Crowley, D. and Jobling, P. (1996), *Graphic Design: Reproduction and Representation since 1800*, Manchester: Manchester University Press.

Cruse, H. (1968), *Rebellion or Revolution?* New York: Morrow.

Csordas, T. (1993), "Somatic Modes of Attention," *Cultural Anthropology* 8 (2): 135–56.

Csordas, T. (ed.) (1996), *Embodiment of Experience: The Existential Ground of Culture and Self*, Cambridge: Cambridge University Press.

Cunningham, P. (2003), *Reforming Women's Fashion, 1850–1920: Politics, Health and Art*, Kent, OH: Kent State University Press.

Cunnington, C. W. (1990), *English Women's Clothing in the Nineteenth Century*, New York: Dover reprint.

Cunnington, C. W. and Cunnington, P. (1951), *History of Underclothes*, London: Faber and Faber.

Cunnington, C. W. and Cunnington, P. (1952), *Handbook of English Mediaeval Costume*, London: Faber and Faber.

Cunnington, C. W. and Cunnington, P. (1954), *Handbook of English Costume in the Sixteenth Century*, London: Faber and Faber.

Cunnington, C. W. and Cunnington, P. (1955) *Handbook of English Costume in the Seventeenth Century*, London: Faber and Faber.

Cunnington, C. W. and Cunnington, P. (1957), *Handbook of English Costume in the Eighteenth Century*, London: Faber and Faber.

Cunnington, C. W. and Cunnington, P. (1959), *Handbook of English Costume in the Nineteenth Century*, London: Faber and Faber.

Cunnington, C. W. and Cunnington, P. (1960), *A Dictionary of English Costume: 900–1900*, London: Adam and Charles Black.

Cunnington, C. W. and Cunnington, P. (1966), *Handbook of English Costume in the Nineteenth Century*, 2nd ed., London: Faber and Faber.

Cunnington, C. W. and Cunnington, P. (1992), *The History of Underclothes*, New York: Dover reprint.

Curry, H. (2001), "The Fabulous Mr. Castelbajac," *The Guardian*, October 26 <www.guardian.co.uk>.

D. H. Evans and Co.'s Handy Guide to London for the Use of Americans Tourists (1902), London: D. H. Evans and Co.

D'Aureville, J. B. (2002), *Who's a Dandy? Dandyism and Beau Brummell*, trans. George Walden, London: Gibson Square Books.

Dale, J. S. (1986), *Art to Wear*, New York: Abbeville Press.

Damhorst, M. L., Miller-Spillman, K. A. and Michelman, S.O. (eds.) (2005), *The Meanings of Dress*, New York: Fairchild.

Daves, J. (1967), *Ready-Made Miracle*, New York: G. P. Putnam's Sons.

Davidoff, L. (1973), *The Best Circles: Society Etiquette and the Season*, London: Croom Helm.

Davis, D. (2003), *John Singer Sargent and the Fall of Madame X*, New York: Jeremy P. Tarcher/Penguin Group.

Davis, F. (1985), "Clothing and Fashion as Communication," in M. R. Solomon (ed.), *The Psychology of Fashion*, Lexington, MA: Lexington Books, pp. 15–77.

Davis, F. (1992), *Fashion, Culture, and Identity*, Chicago: University of Chicago Press.

de la Haye, A. (ed.) (1997), *The Cutting Edge: 50 Years of British Fashion, 1947–1997*, London: Overlook.

de la Haye, A. and Tobin, S. (1994), *Chanel: The Couturière at Work*, London: Victoria and Albert Museum.

de Marly, D. (1985), *Fashion for Men: An Illustrated History*, London: B. T. Batsford.

Dean, C. (1992), *The Self and Its Pleasures: Bataille, Lacan and the History of the Decentered Subject*, Ithaca, NY and London: Cornell University Press.

Delpierre, M. (1997), *Dress in France in the Eighteenth Century*, trans. Caroline Beamish, New Haven, CT: Yale University Press.

Derrida, J. (1994), *Spectors of Marx: The State of Debt, the Work of Mourning, and the New International*, trans. P. Kamuf, New York and London: Routledge.

Derrida, J. (2004 [1967]), *Writing and Difference*, trans. A. Bass, London and New York: Routledge.

Diamond, I. and Quimby, I. (1988), *Feminism and Foucault: Reflections on Resistance*, Boston: Northeastern University Press.

Dickason, O. (1955), "Paris and London Fashions are Quickly Copied Here," *Globe and Mail*, September 8.

Dicken, P. (2000), "Globalization" in R. J. Johnson, D. Gregory, G. Pratt, and M. Watts (eds.), *The Dictionary of Human Geography*, 4th ed., Oxford: Blackwell, pp. 315–16.

Dickens, C. (1861), *The Life and Adventures of Martin Chuzzlewit*, Vol. 1, Boston: Fields, Osgood and Co.

Dollimore, J. (1998), *Death, Desire and Loss in Western Culture*, London: Allen Lane, Penguin.

Dominguez, V. (1986), "The Marketing of Heritage," *American Ethnologist* 13 (3): 546–5.

Domosh, M. (1998), "Those 'Gorgeous Incongruities': Polite Politics and Public Space on the Streets of Nineteenth-Century New York City," *Annals of the Association of American Geographers* 88: 209–26.

Douglas, M. (1970), *Purity and Danger*, Harmondsworth: Penguin.

Douglas, M. (1973), *Natural Symbols, Explorations in Cosmology*, London: Barrie and Jenkins.

Douglas, M. (1979), "Do Dogs Laugh: A Cross-Cultural Approach to Body Symbolism," in M. Douglas (ed.), *Implicit Meanings: Essays in Anthropology*, London: Routledge and Kegan Paul.

Douglas, M. (1984), *Purity and Danger: An Analysis of the Concept of Pollution and Taboo*, London: Routledge.

Duberman, M. (1994), *Stonewall*, New York: Dutton.

Duggan, G. G. (2001), "The Greatest Show on Earth: A Look at Contemporary Fashion Shows and their Relationship to Performance Art," *Fashion Theory*, 5 (3): 243–70.

Dwyer, C. and Jackson, P. (2001), "Commodifying Difference: Selling EASTern Fashion," paper presented at the Annual Conference of American Geographers, New York, February.

Dwyer, C. and Jackson, P. (2003), "Commodifying Difference: Selling EASTern Fashion," *Environment and Planning D: Society and Space* 21: 269–91.

Eco, U. (1986), *Lumbar Thought, Travels in Hyperreality*, Orlando, FL: Harcourt Brace Jovanovich.

Eicher, J. B. (ed.) (1999), *Dress and Ethnicity*, Oxford and New York: Berg.

Elias, N. (1983), *The Court Society*, Oxford: Blackwell.

Ellis, H. (1936), *Sexual Inversion, Studies in the Psychology of Sex*, Vol. 2, Part 2 [Vol. 1], New York: Random House.

Ellison, R. (1947), *Invisible Man*, New York: Random House.

Eluard P. (1933), *Food for Vision*, n.p.: Editions Galliard.

Emanuel, D. and Emanuel, E. (2006), *A Dress for Diana*, New York: CollinsDesign.

Encyclopedia of American Regional Cultures (2004), 8 vols, Westport, CT: Greenwood Press.

Entwistle, J. (1997), "Power Dressing and Fashioning of the Career Woman," in M. Nava *et al.* (eds.), *Buy This Book: Studies in Advertising and Consumption*, London: Routledge.

Entwistle, J. (2000), "Fashioning the Career Woman: Power Dressing as a Strategy of Consumption," in M. Talbot and M. Andrews (eds.), *All the World and Her Husband: Women and Consumption in the Twentieth Century*, London: Cassell.

Entwistle, J. (2000), *The Fashioned Body. Fashion, Dress and Modern Social Theory*, Cambridge and Malden, MA: Polity Press and Blackwell Publishers.

Entwistle, J. and Wilson, E. (1998), *The Body Clothed, 100 Years of Art and Fashion*, London: Hayward Gallery.

Entwistle, J. and Wilson, E. (eds.) (2001), *Body Dressing*, Oxford and New York: Berg.

Erlmann, V. (1996), "The Aesthetics of the Global Imagination: Reflections on World Music in the 1990s," *Public Culture* 8 (3): 467–87.

Ernst, C., Ferrer, A. H., and Zult, D. (2005) "The End of the Multi-Fibre Arrangement and its Implication for Trade and Employment," International Labor Organization Employment Strategy Papers.

Erving, W., O'Brian, G., Steele, V., Wiles, A., Hollander, A., and Martin, R. (1991), *The Idealizing Vision: The Art of Fashion Photography*, New York: Aperture Foundation.

Escobar, A. (2001), "Culture Sits in Place: Reflections on Globalism and Subaltern Strategies of Localization," *Political Geography* 20: 139–74.

Esedebe, P. O. (1982), *Pan-Africanism: The Idea and Movement, 1776–1963*, Washington, DC: Howard University Press.

Evans, C. (1999), "Masks, Mirrors and Mannequins: Elsa Schiaparelli and the Decentered Subject," *Fashion Theory* 2 (1): 3–31.

Evans, C. (2001), "The Enchanted Spectacle," *Fashion Theory* 5 (3): 271–310.

Evans, C. (2003), *Fashion at the Edge: Spectacle, Modernity, and Deathliness*, New Haven, CT: Yale University Press.

Ewing, E. (1992), *History of Twentieth-Century Fashion*, 3rd ed., New York: Costume and Fashion Press.

Fallers, L. A. (1961), "A Note on the 'Trickle Effect,'" in S. Lipset and N. Smelser (eds.), *Sociology: Progress of a Decade*, Englewood Cliffs, NJ: Prentice Hall.

Fallows, J. (2005), "Countdown to a Meltdown," *The Atlantic Monthly*, July/August.

Farrell-Beck, J. and Gau, C. (2002), *Uplift: The Bra in America*, Philadelphia: University of Pennsylvania Press.

Farren, M. (1985), *The Black Leather Jacket*, London: Plexus.

"Fat or Not, 4th Grade Girls Diet Lest They Be Teased or Unloved," (1986), *Wall Street Journal*, February 11.

Faurschou, G. (1987), "Fashion and the Cultural Logic of Postmodernity," in A. and M. Kroker (eds.), *Body Invaders: Panic Sex in America*, New York: St Martin's Press, pp. 78–93.

Feldman, E. (1992), *Fashions of a Decade: The 1990s*, New York: Facts on File.

Fenwick, W. (1948), *Vogue's Book of Etiquette*, New York: Simon and Schuster.

Field, G. A. (1970), "The Status Float Phenomenon: The Upward Diffusion of Innovation," *Business Horizons* 13 (August 4): 45–52.

Fields, J. (2003), "Erotic Modesty: (Ad)dressing Female Sexuality and Propriety in Open and Closed Drawers, USA, 1800–1930," in B. Burman and C. Turbin (eds.), *Material Strategies: Dress and Gender in Historical Perspective*, Malden, MA: Blackwell.

Finch diary (n.d.), Kinsey Institute for Research in Sex, Gender, and Reproduction Library, Indiana University, Bloomington, quoted in G. Chauncey (1994), *Gay New York: Gender, Urban Culture and the Making of the Gay Male World, 1890–1940*, New York: Basic Books.

Fischer, G. V. (2001), *Pantaloons and Power: A Nineteenth-Century Dress Reform in the United States*, Kent, OH: Kent State University Press.

Fishman, T. C. (2005), *China Inc.: How the Rise of the Next Superpower Challenges America and the World*, New York: Scribner.

Fiske, J. (1987), "British Cultural Studies and Television," in R. C. Allen (ed.), *Channels of Discourse*, Chapel Hill: University of North Carolina Press, pp. 254–90.

Fiske, J. (1988), *Understanding Popular Culture*, Boston: Unwin Hyman.

Flügel, J. C. (1930), *The Psychology of Clothes*, London: Hogarth Press.

Flügel, J. C. (1971 [1930]), *The Psychology of Clothes*, New York: International Universities Press.

Forrest, E. (2001), "Madonna? She Looks So Dated…," *The Daily Telegraph*, July 11 <www.telegraph.co.uk>.

Foster, H. (1996), *The Return of the Real: The Avant-Garde at the End of the Century*, Cambridge, MA: MIT Press.

Foster, V. (1984), *A Visual History of Costume: The Nineteenth Century*, London: B. T. Batsford.

Foucault, M. (1973), *The Order of Things: An Archaeology of the Human Sciences*, trans. A. M. Sheridan-Smith, New York: Vintage.

Foucault, M. (1977), *Discipline and Punish*, London: Penguin Books.

Foucault, M. (1978), *The History of Sexuality, Volume One*, London: Penguin Books.

Foucault, M. (1980), *Power/Knowledge. Selected Interviews and Other Writings 1972–1977*, ed. C. Gordon, Brighton: Harvester Press.

Foucault, M. (1984), *The History of Sexuality, Volume Two: The Care of the Self*, trans. R. Hurley, New York: Pantheon.

Foucault, M. (1984), *The History of Sexuality, Volume Three: The Uses of Pleasure*, trans. R. Hurley, New York: Pantheon.

Fox, R. W. and Lears, T. J. J. (eds.) (1983), *The Culture of Consumption: Critical Essays in American History, 1880–1980*, New York: Pantheon Books.

Foxe, D. (2003), "Time to Sex up her City," *The Daily Telegraph*, March 14 <www.telegraph.co.uk>.

Fraser, K. (1981), *The Fashionable Mind*, New York: Knopf.

Freeman, C. (1993), "Designing Women: Corporate Discipline and Barbados's Offshore Pink-Collar Sector," *Cultural Anthropology* 8: 2, 164–85.

Freeman, C. (2000), *High Heels and High Tech in the Global Economy: Women, Work and Pink-Collar Identities in the Caribbean*, Durham, NC: Duke University Press.

Freeman, H. (2002), "Beyond the Kaftan," *The Guardian*, January 11 <www.guardian.co.uk>.

French Fashion Plates in Full Color from the Gazette du Bon Ton (1912–1925), (1979), New York: Dover Publications.

Friedman, T. L. (2005), *The World is Flat: A Brief History of the Twenty-First Century*, New York: Farrar, Straus and Giroux.

"From T-shirts to T-bonds," (2005), *The Economist*, July 30.

Fukai, A. (1989), "Rococo and Neoclassical Clothing," in J. Stariobinski et al. (eds.), *Revolution in Fashion: European Clothing, 1715–1815*, New York: Abbeville Press.

Fukai, A. and Suoh, T., Iwagami, M., Koga, R., and Nii, R. (2002), *Fashion: The Collection of the Kyoto Costume Institute*, Cologne: Taschen.

Gale, S. and Kaur, J. (2002), *The Textile Book*, Oxford: Berg.

Gale, S. and Kaur, J. (2004), *Fashion and Textiles: An Overview*, Oxford: Berg.

Garfield, S. (2000), *Mauve: How One Man Invented a Colour that Changed the World*, London: Faber and Faber.

Garland, R. (1995 [1954]), *The Heart in Exile*, Brighton: Millivres Books.

Garratt, S. (1998), "Who's Sari Now?" *The Sunday Times* (Style section), August 23, p. 4.

Geertz, C. (1964), "Ideology as a Cultural System," in D. E. Apter (ed.), *Ideology and Discontent*, London: Free Press.

Geiss, I. (1974), *The Pan-African Movement*, London: Methuen.

Gereffi, G. (1999), "International Trade and Industrial Upgrading in the Apparel Commodity Chain," *Journal of International Economics* 48.

Gershon, R. (1999), "A Life in Clothes," *Granta* 65: 77–102.

Gibson, J. (2003), "Miranda, My Hero," *The Guardian*, February 21 <www.guardian.co.uk>.

Giddens, A. (1991), *Modernity and Self-Identity: Sled and Society in the Late Modern Age*, Cambridge: Polity Press.

Gidlow, E. (1980), "Memoirs," *Feminist Studies*, No. 6.

Gilbert, D. (1999), "*London in all its Glory—or How to Enjoy London*: Guidebook Representations of Imperial London," *Journal of Historical Geography* 25: 279–97.

Gilbert, D. (2000), "Urban Outfitting: The City and Spaces of Fashion Culture," in S. Bruzzi and P. Church-Gibson (eds.), *Fashion Cultures*, London: Routledge.

Gillespie, M. (1995), *Television, Ethnicity and Cultural Change*, London: Routledge.

Gimlin, D. L. (2003), *Body Work: Beauty and Self-Image in American Culture*, Berkeley: University of California Press.

Ginsburg, M. (1982), *Victorian Dress in Photographs*, London: B. T. Batsford.

Gladwell, M. (2000), "The Young Garmentos; The T-shirt Trade Becomes a Calling," *New York Times*, April 24, pp. 70–84.

Glennie, P. and Thrift, N. (1992), "Modernity, Urbanism, and Modern Consumption," *Environment and Planning D: Society and Space* 10: 423–43.

Glynn, P. (1972), "The Life and Hard Times of British Couture," *The Times* (London), January 18 [clipping].

Goffman, E. (1959), *The Presentation of Self in Everyday Life*, New York: Anchor Books.

Goffman, E. (1971), *The Presentation of Self in Everyday Life*, London: Penguin Press.

Goffman, E. (1972), *Relations in Public: Microstudies of the Public Order*, New York: Harper and Row.

Goodrum, A. (2001), "Producing Britishness: Globalisation and the Construction of National Identity in British Fashion," PhD dissertation, University of Gloucestershire, England.

Goodrum, A. (2005), *The National Fabric: Fashion, Britishness, Globalization*, Oxford: Berg.

Gorman, P. (2001), *The Look: Adventures in Pop and Rock Fashion*, London: Sanctuary Publishing.

Goulev, P., Stead, L., Mamdani, E. and Evans, C. (2004), "Computer-Aided Emotional Fashion," *Computers and Graphics* 28 (5): 657–66.

Greenhouse, S. (2004a), "In-House Audit Says Wal-Mart Violated Labor Laws," *New York Times*, January 13.

Greenhouse, S. (2004b), "Altering of Workers' Time Cards Spurs Growing Number of Suits," *New York Times*, April 4.

Greenhouse, S. (2004c), "Wal-Mart is Said to be in Talks to Settle Illegal Immigrant Case," *New York Times*, August 5.

Greenhouse, S. and Barbaro, M. (2006), "The Ugly Side of Free Trade: Sweatshops in Jordan," *New York Times*, May 3 <www.nytimes.com>.

Greenidge. T. (1930), *Degenerate Oxford?: A Critical Study of Modern University Life*, London: Chapman and Hall.

Grund, F. J. (1959), *Aristocracy in America*, New York: Harper Torchbooks.

Gubar, S. (1981), "Blessings in Disguise: Cross-Dressing as Re-Dressing for Female Modernists," *The Massachusetts Review* 22 (3).

Guenther, I. (2004), *Nazi Chic?: Fashioning Women in the Third Reich*, Oxford and New York: Berg.

Hall, L. (1992), *Common Threads: A Parade of American Clothing*, Boston, Toronto, London: Little Brown and Company.

Hall, S. (1977), "Culture, the Media and the 'Ideological Effect,'" in J. Curran, M. Gurevitch, J. Deverson, and J. Woollacott (eds.), *Mass Communication and Society*, London: Arnold.

Hall, S. and Jefferson, T. (eds.) (1976), *Resistance Through Rituals: Youth Subcultures in Post-War Britain*, London: Hutchinson.

Hall, S., Clarke, J., Jefferson, T., and Roberts, B. (eds.) (1974), *Resistance Through Rituals*, London: Hutchinson.

Halttunen, K. (1982), *Confidence Men and Painted Women: A Study of Middle-Class Culture in America, 1830–1870*, New Haven, CT: Yale University Press.

Hamilton, T. (1833), *Men and Manners in America*, Vol. 1, Philadelphia: Carey, Lee and Blanchard.

Hammack, D. (1991), "Developing for Commercial Culture" in W. Taylor (ed.), *Inventing Times Square: Commerce and Culture at the Crossroads of the World*, Baltimore: Johns Hopkins University Press.

Hancock, C. (1999), "*Capitale du plaisir*: The Remaking of Imperial Paris," in F. Driver and D. Gilbert (eds.) *Imperial Cities*, Manchester: Manchester University Press.

Hanisch, R. (2006), *Absolutely Fabulous! Architecture for Fashion*, Munich and London: Prestel.

Hannerz, U. (1989), "Notes on the Global Ecumene," *Public Culture* 1(2): 66–75.

Hannerz, U. (1991), "The Global Ecumene as a Network of Networks," in Adam Kuper (ed.), *Conceptualizing Societies*, London and New York: Routledge, pp. 34–56.

Hannerz, U. (1996), *Transnational Connections*, London: Routledge.

Hansen, K. T. (2000), *Salaula: The World of Secondhand Clothing and Zambia*, Chicago: University of Chicago Press.

Hansen, K. T. (2004), "The World in Dress: Anthropological Perspectives on Clothing, Fashion, and Culture," *Annual Review of Anthropology* 33: 369–92.

Haraway, D. (1997), *Simians, Cyborgs and Women: The Reinvention of Nature*, London: Free Association Books.

Harrington, C. (1999), "The Seams of Subjectivity and Structure: Women's Experience of Garment Work in Aotearoa, New Zealand and Fiji," PhD dissertation, University of Otago, New Zealand.

Harris, D. (1997), *The Rise and Fall of Gay Culture*, New York: Hyperion.

Harrison, M. (1991), *Appearances: Fashion Photography Since 1945*, London: Cape.

Hartman, R. (1980), *Birds of Paradise: An Intimate View of the New York Fashion World*, New York: Delta.

Harvey, D. (1990), *The Condition of Postmodernity*, Oxford: Blackwell.

Harvey, J. (1995), *Men in Black*, Chicago: University of Chicago Press.

Hata, K. (2004), *Louis Vuitton Japan: The Building of Luxury*, New York: Assouline.

Haug, F. (ed.) (1987), *Female Sexualization*, London: Verso.

Hawes, E. (1938), *Fashion is Spinach*, New York: Random House.

Hay, S. (ed.) (2000), *From Paris to Providence: Fashion, Art, and the Tirocchi Dressmakers' Shop, 1915–1947*, Providence: Rhode Island School of Design Museum of Art.

Head, E. and Calistro, P. (1983), *Edith Head's Hollywood*, New York: E. P. Dutton.

Hebdige, D. (1979), *Subculture: The Meaning of Style*, London: Methuen.

Hebdige, D. (1988), *Hiding in the Light: On Images and Things*, London: Routledge.

Heilbroner, R. (ed.) (1986), *The Essential Adam Smith*, New York: W. W. Norton.

Held, D. (ed.) (2004), *A Globalizing World? Culture, Economics, Politics*, 2nd ed., London: Routledge.

Helmer, W. J. (1963), "New York's 'Middle-Class' Homosexuals," *Harpers* 226 (March): 85–92.

Hendrickson, H. (ed.) (1996), *Clothing and Difference: Embodied Identities in Colonial and Post-Colonial Africa*, Durham, NC and London: Duke University Press.

Herndon, B. (1956), *Bergdorf's on the Plaza: The Story of Bergdorf Goodman and a Half-Century of American Fashion*, New York: Alfred A. Knopf.

Himes, C. (1943), "Zoot Riots are Race Riots," *The Crisis*, July 1943 [reprinted in Himes (1975), *Black on Black: Baby Sister and Selected Writings*, London: Joseph].

Hirsch, P. M. (1972), "Processing Fads and Fashions: An Organization-Set Analysis of Cultural Industry Systems," *American Journal of Sociology* 77 (January 4): 639–59.

Hirst, P. and Thompson, G. (1996), *Globalization in Question*, Cambridge: Polity Press.

Hite, M. (1988), "Writing—and Reading—the Body: Female Sexuality and Recent Feminist Fiction," *Feminist Studies* 14 (1): 121–2.

Hjelmslev, L. (1959), *Essays in Linguistics*, Copenhagen: Nordisk Sprog-og Kultuforlag.

Hobsbawm, E. and Ranger, T. (eds.) (1983), *The Invention of Tradition*, Cambridge and New York: Cambridge University Press.

Hodkinson, P. (2002), *Goth: Identity, Style and Subculture*, Oxford: Berg.

Hoffman, M. (1968), *The Gay World: Male Homosexuality and the Social Creation of Evil*, New York: Basic Books.

Holgate, M. (2001), "North Star," *Vogue*, August: 47–8.

Holgate, M. (2006), "Demi-Monde," *Vogue*, July: 60, 62, 64.

Hollander, A. (1978), *Seeing Through Clothes*, New York: Viking Press.

Hollander, A. (1994), *Sex and Suits: The Evolution of Modern Dress*, New York: Alfred Knopf.

Hollander, A. (2002), *Fabric of Vision: Dress and Drapery in Painting*, London: National Gallery.

Holson, L. M. (2005), "Gothic Lolitas: Demure vs. Dominatrix," *New York Times*, March 13.

Howarth, S. (2003), *Henry Poole: Founders of Savile Row*, Honiton, UK: Bene Factum Publishing Ltd.

Howe, B. (1967), *Arbiter of Elegance*, London: Harvill Press.

Howes, K. (1994), *Broadcasting It: An Encyclopedia of Homosexuality in Film, Radio and TV in the UK, 1923–1993*, London: Cassell.

Hughes, C. (2006), *Dressed in Fiction*, Oxford: Berg.

Ijiri, Kazuo (1990), "The Breakdown of the Japanese Work Ethic," *Japan Echo* XVII (4): 35–40.

Ingham, R. (ed.) (1978), *Football Hooliganism*, London: Inter-action Imprint.

Iribe, P. (1908), *Les Robes de Paul Poiret racontées par Paul Iribe*, Paris: Société Générale d'Impression, Paris (in the collection of the Museum of Fine Arts, Boston, 1998.2).

Jackson, P. (2004), "Local Consumption Cultures in a Globalizing World," *Transactions IBG* 29 (2): 165–78.

Jackson, P., Thomas, N., and Dwyer, C. (2004), Consumer Culture in London and Mumbai: Exploring the Transnational Geographies of Food and Fashion, unpublished paper.

Jakobson, R. (1963), *Essais de linguistique générale*, Paris: Editions de Minuit.

Jackson, T. and Shaw, D. (2006), *Mastering Fashion Marketing*, New York: Palgrave Macmillan.

Jameson, F. (1998), *The Cultural Turn: Selected Writings on the Postmodern, 1983–1998*, London and New York: Verso.

Jivani, A. (1997), *It's Not Unusual: A History of Lesbian and Gay Britain in the Twentieth Century*, London: Michael O'Mara Books.

Jobling, P. (1999), *Fashion Spreads: Word and Image in Fashion Photography Since 1980*, Oxford: Berg.

Jobling, P. (2005), *Man Appeal: Advertising, Modernism and Menswear*, Oxford: Berg.

Johnson, K. P., Torntore, S. J., and Eicher, J. B. (eds.) (2003), *Fashion Foundations: Early Writings on Fashion and Dress*, Oxford: Berg.

Johnston, C. (1973), "Women's Cinema As Counter Cinema," *Notes on Women's Cinema*, London: Society for Education in Film and Television.

Johnston, C. (1977), "Myths of Women in the Cinema," in K. Kay and G. Peary (eds.), *Women and the Cinema*, New York: E. P. Dutton.

Johnston, L. (2005), *Nineteenth-Century Fashion in Detail*, London: V&A Publications.

Jones, J. (1996), "Coquettes and Grisettes: Women Buying and Selling in Ancien Régime Paris" in V. de Grazia with B. Furlough (eds.), *The Sex of Things: Gender and Consumption in Historical Perspective*, Berkeley: University of California Press.

Jones, L.-A. (1992), "Naomi: Supermodel, Superstar," *Sunday Mail Magazine*, July 26, pp. 10–11.

Jones, L. L. and Jones, J. H. (1971), *All About the Natural*, New York: Clairol.

Jouve, M. (1997), *Balenciaga*, New York: Universe/ Vendome.

Kacem, M. B. (2001), *Society*, Paris: Tristram.

Kadolph, S. J. and Langford, A. L. (2007), *Textiles*, 10th ed., Upper Saddle River, NJ: Prentice Hall.

Kaiser, S. (1998), "The Body in Context," in *The Social Psychology of Clothing*, New York: Fairchild, pp. 97–143.

Kaiser, S., Nagasawa, R. H., and Hutton, S. S. (1991), "Fashion, Postmodernity and Personal Appearance: A Symbolic Interactionist Formulation," *Symbolic Interaction* 14 (2): 165–85.

Kaiser, S., Nagasawa, R. H., and Hutton, S. S. (1995), "Construction of an SI Theory of Fashion: Part I: Ambivalence and Change," *Clothing and Textile Research Journal* 13 (3): 172–83.

Kaplan, E. A. (1983), "Is the Gaze Male?" in A. Snitow, C. Stansell, and S. Thompson (eds.) *Powers of Desire: The Politics of Sexuality*, New York: Monthly Review Press, pp. 309–27.

Kaplan, E. A. (1987), *Rocking Around the Clock: Music Television, Postmodernism and Consumer Culture*, New York: Methuen.

Kawamura, Y. (2004a), *The Japanese Revolution in Paris Fashion*, Oxford: Berg.

Kawamura, Y. (2004b), *Fashion-ology: An Introduction to Fashion Studies*, Oxford: Berg.

Kelley, R. D. G. (1979), "Nap Time: Historicizing the Afro," *Fashion Theory* 1 (4): 339–51.

Kelley, R. D. G. (1994), *Race Rebels: Culture, Politics, and the Black Working Class*, New York: The Free Press.

Khan, S. (1937), *Mentality of Homosexuality*, Boston: Meader Publishing.

Kidwell, C. B. and Christman, M. C. (1974), *Suiting Everyone: The Democratization of Clothing in America*, Washington, DC: Smithsonian Institution Press.

Kidwell, C. B. and Steele, V. (eds.) (1989), *Men and Women: Dressing the Part*, Washington, DC: Smithsonian Institution.

Kiernan, J. (1916), "Classification of Homosexuality," *Urological and Cutaneous Review*, 20.

Kim, S. B. (1998), "Is Fashion Art?" *Fashion Theory* 2 (1): 51–72.

King, C. W. (1963), "Fashion Adoption: A Rebuttal to the 'Trickle-Down' Theory," *Toward Scientific Marketing*: 108–25.

King, H. H. and Ogunbiyi, T. (1963), "Should Negro Women Straighten Their Hair?" *Negro Digest*, August: 65–71.

Kinsella, S. (1995), "Cuties in Japan," in L. Skov and B. Moeran (eds.) *Women, Media, and Consumption in Japan*, Honolulu: University of Hawaii Press.

Kirke, B. (1998), *Madeleine Vionnet*, San Francisco: Chronicle Books.

Kirkland, S. (1985), "Sportswear for Everyone," in R. Martin (ed.), *All-American: A Sportswear Tradition*, New York: Fashion Institute of Technology.

Kismaric, S. and Respini, E. (2004), *Fashioning Fiction in Photography Since 1990*, New York: Museum of Modern Art.

Kleinberg, S. (1978), "Where Have All The Sissies Gone?" *Christopher Street*, March 1978.

Ko, D. (2001), *Every Step a Lotus: Shoes for Bound Feet*, Berkeley: University of California Press.

Koda, H. (2001), *Extreme Beauty: The Body Transformed*, New York: Metropolitan Museum of Art.

Koda, H. and Bolton, A. (2005), *Chanel*, New York: Metropolitan Museum of Art.

Kondo, D. (1997), *About Face: Performing Race in Fashion and Theater*, London and New York: Routledge.

König, R. (1973), *The Restless Image: A Sociology of Fashion*, trans. F. Bradley, London: George Allen and Unwin.

Koolhaas, R. (2002), *Verso un'architettura estrema* (Conversations with students), Milano: Postmedia Books.

Kroeber, A. L. (1919), "On the Principle of Order in Civilization as Exemplified by Changes of Fashion," *American Anthropologist* 21 (3): 235–63.

Kron, J. (1983), *Home-Psych: The Social Psychology of Home Decoration*, New York: Clarkson N. Potter, Inc.

Kücher, S. and Miller, D. (2000), *Clothing as Material Culture*, Oxford: Berg.

Kuchta, D. (2002), *The Three-Piece Suit and Modern Masculinity: England, 1550–1850*, Berkeley: University of California Press.

Kunciov, R. (ed.) (1971), *Mr. Godey's Ladies: Being a Mosaic of Fashions and Fancies*, Princeton, NJ: Pyne Press.

Lang, K. and Lang, G. E. (1961), *Collective Dynamics*, New York: Thomas Y. Corwell.

Larimer, T. (1998), "Sneaker Gulag: Are Asian Workers Really Exploited?," *Time International*, May 11: 30–2.

Larner, W. (1998), "Hitching a Ride on a Tiger's Back: Globalisation and Spatial Imaginaries in New Zealand," *Environment and Planning D: Society and Space* 16: 599–614.

Larner, W. (2003), "Neoliberalism?" *Environment and Planning D: Society and Space* 21: 509–12.

Larson, V. (2001), "Fashion High," *North and South*: 48–55.

Lasch, C. (1979), *The Culture of Narcissism*, New York: W. W. Norton and Co.

Lauer, J. C., and Lauer, R. H. (1981), *Fashion Power: The Meaning of Fashion in American Society*, Upper Saddle River, NJ: Prentice Hall.

Laver, J. (1937), *Taste and Fashion*, New York: Harrap.

Laver, J. (1973), "Taste and Fashion Since the French Revolution" in G. Wills and D. Midgley (eds.), *Fashion Marketing*, London: George Allen and Irwin, pp. 379–89.

Laver, J. (1995), *Costume and Fashion: A Concise History*, London: Thames and Hudson.

Lawton, G. (2004), "Extreme Surgery," *New Scientist*, October 30: 54–6.

le Bourhis, K. (1989), *The Age of Napoleon*, New York: Metropolitan Museum/Harry N. Abrams.

Leach, W. (1993), *Land of Desire: Merchants, Power, and the Rise of a New American Culture*, New York: Pantheon.

Lee, S. T. (ed.) (1975), *American Fashion: The Life and Lines of Adrian, Mainbocher, McCardell, Norell, and Trigère*, New York: Quadrangle/New York Times Book Co.

Lefebvre, H. (1971), *Everyday Life in the Modern World*, London: Allen Lane.

Lefebvre, H. (1991), *The Production of Space*, Oxford: Blackwell.

Lehmann, U. (1999), "Tigersprung: Fashioning History," *Fashion Theory* 3 (3): 297–321.

Lehmann, U. (2000), *Tigersprung: Fashion in Modernity*, Cambridge, MA: MIT Press.

Lehnert, G. (2000), *A History of Fashion in the 20th Century*, Cologne: Könemann.

Lemire, B. (1990), "The Theft of Clothes and Popular Consumerism in Early Modern England," *Journal of Social History* 24 (2): 255–76.

Lemire, B. (1992), *Fashion's Favourite: The Cotton Industry and the Consumer in Britain, 1660–1800*, Oxford: Oxford University Press.

Lemire, B. (1997), *Dress, Culture and Commerce: The English Clothing Trade Before the Factory, 1660–1800*, New York: Palgrave.

Leroi-Gourhan, A. (1945), *Milieu et techniques*, Paris: Albin-Michel.

"Letter to the Editor" (1947), *New Statesman and Nation* XXXIV (October 4).

Levin, P. L. (1965), *The Wheels of Fashion*, New York: Doubleday.

Lévi-Strauss, C. (1966 [1962]), *The Savage Mind*, Chicago: University of Chicago Press.

Lévi-Strauss, C. (1969), *The Elementary Structures of Kinship*, London: Eyre and Spottiswoode.

Li, X. (1998), "Fashioning the Body in Post-Mao China," in A. Brydon and S. Niessen (eds.), *Consuming Fashion: Adorning the Transnational Body*, Oxford, New York: Berg, pp. 71–90.

Limnander, A. (2002), "The Apple Bites Back," *Vogue*, September: 209–12.

Linnell, A. (2001) "Fashion Statement," *Sunday Star Times*, May 6: D l.

Lipovetsky, G. (1994), *The Empire of Fashion: Dressing Modern Democracy*, trans. C. Porter, Princeton, NJ: Princeton University Press.

Lippard, L. (ed.) (1970), *Surrealists on Art*, Englewood Cliffs, NJ: Spectrum, Prentice Hall.

Lord and Taylor Archives, Lord and Taylor, New York.

Loughery, J. (1998), *The Other Side of Silence: Men's Lives and Gay Identities: A Twentieth-Century History*, New York: H. Holt.

Lowe, E. D. and Lowe, J. W. G. (1985), "Quantitative Analysis of Women's Dress," in M. R. Solomon (ed.), *The Psychology of Fashion*, Lexington: Heath/Lexington, pp. 193–206.

Lowe, J. W. G. and Lowe, E. D. (1982), "Cultural Pattern and Process: Stylistic Change and Fashion in Women's Dress," *American Anthropologist* 84 (3): 521–44.

Lowe, J. W. G. and Lowe, E. D. (1984), "Stylistic Change and Fashion in Women's Dress: Regularity or Randomness?" in T. C. Kinnear (ed.), *Advances in Consumer Research*, Provo, UT: Association of Consumer Research, pp. 731–34.

Lukey, R. J. (1970), "Homosexuality in Men's Wear," *Menswear*, February.

Lurie, A. (1981), *The Language of Clothes*, New York: Random House.

Lynn Linton, Eliza (1868), "The Girl of the Period," *Saturday Review*, March 14.

Lyons, J. (1992), "Elle and the Body Politic," *Sydney Morning Herald Good Weekend Magazine*, October 3: 10–21.

Lyotard, F. (1979), *The Postmodern Condition: A Report on Knowledge,* trans. G. Bennington and B. Massumi, *Theory and History of Literature*, Vol. 10, Minneapolis: University of Minnesota Press.

Mackrell, A. (2005), *Art and Fashion: The Impact of Art on Fashion and Fashion on Art*, London: B. T. Batsford.

MacSweeney, E. (2001), "A Girl Like You," *Vogue*, February: 168–72.

Maddison, A. (2001), *The World Economy: A Millennial Perspective*, Development Centre of the Organization for Economic Co-operation and Development.

Maddison, A. (2006), *World Population, GDP and Per Capita GDP, 1–2003 AD*, Development Centre of the Organization for Economic Co-operation and Development.

Magubane, B. M. (1987), *The Ties That Bind: African-American Consciousness of Africa*, Trenton, NJ: Africa World Press.

Malossi, G. (ed.) (1998), *The Style Engine: Spectacle, Identity, Design, and Business: How the Fashion Industry Uses Style to Create Wealth*, New York: Monacelli Press.

Mansveldt, J. (2005), *The Geographies of Consumption*, London: Sage.

Marcus, E. (1992), *Making History: The Struggle for Gay and Lesbian Equal Rights, 1945–1990: An Oral History*, New York: Harper Collins.

Margin, J. D. (1955), "The Margin of Masculinity," *One* III (5).

Martin, B. (1981), *A Sociology of Contemporary Cultural Change*, Oxford: Basil Blackwell.

Martin, R. (1987), *Fashion and Surrealism*, New York: Rizzoli.

Martin, R. (1996), *Christian Dior*, New York: Metropolitan Museum of Art.

Martin, R. (1998), *Cubism and Fashion*, New York: Metropolitan Museum of Art.

Martin, R. (1999), "A Note: Art and Fashion, Viktor and Rolf," *Fashion Theory* 3 (1): 109–20.

Martin, R. and Koda, H. (1989), *Jocks and Nerds: Men's Style in the Twentieth Century*, New York: Rizzoli.

Martineau, H. (1837), *Society in America*, Vol. 3, New York: Saunders and Otley.

Marx, K. (1970), *Capital*, London: Lawrence and Wishart.

Massey, A. (2000), *Hollywood Beyond the Screen: Design and Material Culture*, Oxford: Berg.

Mass-Observation Sex Survey, Sexual Behaviour, Box 4, File E, Appendix 1, Abnormality. 6.7.49, Brighton, UK: Mass-Observation Archive, University of Sussex Library.

Matsui, M. (2005), "Beyond the Pleasure Room to a Chaotic Street: The Transformation of Cute Subculture in the Art of the Japanese Nineties," in T. Murakami (ed.), *Little Boy: The Arts of Japan's Exploding Subculture*, New York and New Haven, CT: Japan Society and Yale University Press, pp. 208–39.

Mauss, M. (1973), "Technique of the Body," *Economy and Society* 2 (1): 70–89.

Maynard, M. (1994), *Fashioned from Penury: Dress As Cultural Practice in Colonial Australia*, Hong Kong: Cambridge University Press.

Maynard, M. (2004), *Dress and Globalization*, Manchester: Manchester University Press.

McClary, S. (1990), "Living to Tell: Madonna's Resurrection of the Fleshy," *Genders* 7 (Spring): 2.

McCracken, G. (1988), *Culture and Consumption*, Bloomington: Indiana University Press.

McCracken, G. (2005), "Celebrities" in *Culture and Consumption II: Markets, Meaning and Brand Management*, Bloomington: Indiana University Press, pp. 91–115.

McDowell, C. (ed.), (1998), *The Pimlico Companion to Fashion: A Literary Anthology*, London: Pimlico.

McDowell, L. and Court, G. (1994), "Missing Subjects: Gender, Power and Sexuality in Merchant Banking," *Economic Geography* 70: 229–51.

McIntyre, R. (2006), "Are Workers' Rights Human Rights and Would It Matter If They Were?" *Human Rights, Human Welfare* 6: 112, <www.du.edu/gsis/hrhw/volumes/2006/mcintyre-2006.pdf>.

McIntyre, R. and Ramstad, Y. (2002), "John R. Commons and the Problem of International Labor Rights," *Journal of Economic Issues* 36 (2): 293–301.

McIntyre, R. and Ramstad, Y. (2003), "Reasonable Value and the International Organization of Labor Rights," *Économie et Institutions* 1er Semestre: 83–109.

McIntyre, R. and Ramstad, Y. (2004), "Not Only Nike's Doing It: 'Sweating' and the Contemporary Labor Market," in D. P. Champlin and J. T. Knoedlerm (eds.), *The Institutionalist Tradition in Labor Economics*, Armonk, NY: M. E. Sharpe.

McIntyre, R. and Ramstad, Y. (2005), "Grab it if You Can! An Exploration of the Ethical Basis of Crony Capitalism," presented to Association for Evolutionary Economics, Philadelphia, PA, January 8.

McKendrick, N. (1983), "The Consumer Revolution of Eighteenth-Century England" in N. McKendrick, J. Brewer, and J. Plumb (eds.), *The Birth of a Consumer Society: The Commercialisation of Eighteenth-Century England*, London: Hutchinson.

McKendrick, N. and Brewer, J., and Plumb, J. H. (1982), *The Birth of a Consumer Society: The Commercialization of Eighteenth-Century England*, Bloomington: Indiana University Press.

McLuhan, Marshall (1962), *The Gutenberg Galaxy*, Toronto: University of Toronto Press.

McNay, L. (1992), *Foucault and Feminism: Power, Gender and the Self*, Cambridge: Polity Press.

McNay, L. (1999), "Gender, Habitus and the Field: Pierre Bourdieu and the Limits of Reflexivity," *Theory, Culture and Society* 16 (1): 95–117.

McQuaid, M., Beesley, P., Brown, S., Hanna, S., McCarty, C., Wilson, P., and Young, A. (2005), *Extreme Textiles: Designing for High Performance*, New York: Princeton Architectural Press.

McRobbie, A. (ed.) (1988), *Zoot Suits and Second-Hand Dresses: An Anthology of Fashion and Music*, Boston: Unwin Hyman.

McRobbie, A. (1989), "Second-Hand Dresses and the Role of the Ragmarket," in McRobbie, A. (ed.), *Zoot Suits and Second-Hand Dresses: An Anthology of Fashion and Music*, London: Macmillan.

McRobbie, A. (1997), "More! New Sexualities in Girls' and Women's Magazines," in McRobbie, A. (ed.), *Back to Reality? Social Experience and Cultural Studies*, Manchester: Manchester University Press.

McRobbie, A. (1998), *British Fashion Design: Rag Trade or Image Industry?*, London: Routledge.

Meikle, J. L. (1979), *Twentieth Century Limited: Industrial Design in America, 1925–1939*, Philadelphia: Temple University Press.

Mendes, V. and de la Haye, A. (1999), *20th-Century Fashion*, London: Thames and Hudson.

Menefee, S. (1943), *Assignment: USA*, New York: Reynal and Hitchcock.

Mepham, J. (1973), "The Structuralist Sciences and Philosophy," in D. Robey (ed.), *Structuralism: The Wolfson College Lectures 1972*, Oxford: Clarendon Press.

Mercer, K. (1990), "Black Hair/Style Politics" in R. Ferguson, M. Gever, T. T. Minh-ha and C. West (eds.), *Out There: Marginalization and Contemporary Cultures*, New York and Cambridge, MA: The New Museum of Contemporary Art and MIT Press, pp. 247–64.

Merleau-Ponty, M. (1976), *The Visible and the Invisible*, trans. A. Lingus, Chicago, IL: Northwestern University Press.

Meyersohn, R. and Katz, E. (1957), "Notes on a Natural History of Fads," *American Journal of Sociology* 62 (May): 594–601.

Mian, M. (2001), *Neve Oggetti del desiderio*, Turin: Einaudi.

Mihaly, E. (1998), "The Truth About Third World Workers," *The Providence Journal*, June 3.

Milbank, C. R. (1985), *Couture: The Great Designers*, New York: Stewart, Tabori and Chang.

Milbank, C. R. (1989), *New York Fashion: The Evolution of American Style*, New York: Harry N. Abrams.

Miller, D. (1987), *Material Culture and Mass Consumption*, Oxford: Basil Blackwell.

Miller, D. (1995), "Consumption and Commodities," *Annual Review of Anthropology* 24: 141–61.

Miller, D. (1995), "Consumption as the Vanguard of History: A Polemic by Way of an Introduction," in D. Miller (ed.), *Acknowledging Consumption: A Review of New Studies*, New York: Routledge.

Miller, D. (1998), "Coca-Cola: A Black Sweet Drink from Trinidad," in D. Miller (ed.), *Material Cultures: Why Some Things Matter*, London: UCI Press, pp. 169–87.

Miller, G. (2004), "Everyday Low Wages: The Hidden Price We All Pay for Wal-Mart," A Report by the Democratic Staff of the House Committee on Education and the Workforce, commissioned by Rep. George Miller (C-CA) Senior Democrat <edworkforce.house.gov/democrats/WALMARTREPORT.pdf>.

Millhauser, S. (2006), "A Change in Fashion," *Harper's Magazine*, May: 75–7.

Mitchell, A. (1983), *The Nine American Lifestyles*, New York: Warner Books.

Molloy, J. T. (1977), *The Woman's Dress for Success Book*, New York: Warner Books.

Monbiot, G. (2004), "The Fruits of Poverty," *The Guardian*, March 16.

Mooney, B. (1984), *The Sunday Times*, March.

Moore, J. W. (1978), *Homeboys: Gangs, Drugs and Prison in the Barrios of Los Angeles*, Philadelphia: Temple University Press.

Morgado, M.A. (1993a), "Animal Trademark Emblems on Fashion Apparel: A Semiotic Interpretation: Part I. Interpretive Strategy," *Clothing and Textiles Research Journal* 11 (2): 16–20.

Morgado, M.A. (1993b), "Animal Trademark Emblems on Fashion Apparel: A Semiotic Interpretation: Part I. Applied Semiotics," *Clothing and Textiles Research Journal* 11 (3): 31–8.

Morgan, R. (ed.) (1970), *Sisterhood is Powerful: An Anthology of Writings from the Women's Liberation Movement*, New York: Random House.

Morley, S. (1976), *Marlene Dietrich*, New York: McGraw-Hill.

Morrow, W. (1973), *400 Years Without a Comb*, San Diego: Black Publishers of San Diego.

Muggleton, D. (2000), *Inside Subculture: The Postmodern Meaning of Style*, Oxford and New York: Berg.

Mulvey, K. and Richards, M. (1998), *Decades of Beauty: The Changing Image of Women 1890s–1990s*, New York: Octopus Publishing Group.

Mulvey, L. (1977), "Visual Pleasure and Narrative Cinema," in K. Kay and G. Peary (eds.), *Women and the Cinema*, New York: E. P. Dutton.

Murakami, T. (2005), *Little Boy: The Arts of Japan's Exploding Subculture*, New York and New Haven, CT: Japan Society and Yale University Press.

Nag, D. (1991), "Fashion, Gender and the Bengali Middle Class," *Public Culture* 3 (2): 93–112.

Naisbitt, J. (1982), *Megatrends*, New York: Warner Books.

Narayan, U. (1995), "Eating Cultures: Incorporation, Identity and Indian Food," *Social Identities* 2: 63–86.

Nathan Associates, Inc. (2005), *Developing Countries and Textiles and Apparel Trade*, Arlington, VA, April <www.nathaninc.com/publications/index.asp?bid=751305>.

Nathan, John (2004), *Japan Unbound: A Volatile Nation's Quest for Pride and Purpose*, New York: Houghton Miffin.

Nava, M. (1996), "Modernity's Disavowal: Women, the City and the Department Store," in M. Nava and A. O'Shea (eds.), *Modern Times: Reflections on a Century of English Modernity*, London: Routledge.

Neal, L. (1974a), "Ellison's Zoot Suit," in J. Hersey (ed.), *Ralph Ellison: A Collection of Critical Essays*, Englewood Cliffs, NJ: Prentice Hall.

Neal, L. (1974b), "Malcolm X: An Autobiography," in L. Neal (ed.), *Hoodoo Hollerin' Bebop Ghosts*, Washington, DC: Howard University Press.

Nelson, K. L. (ed.) (1971), *The Impact of War on American Life*, New York: Holt, Rinehart and Winston.

Newton, Stella Mary (1974), *Health, Art and Reason*, London: J. Murray.

Nichols, B. (1981), *Ideology and the Image*, Bloomington: Indiana University Press.

Niessen, S. and Brydon, A. (eds.) (1998), *Consuming Fashion: Adorning the Transnational Body*, Oxford and New York: Berg.

Niessen, S., Leshkowich, A. M. and Jones, C. (eds.) (2003), *Re-Orienting Fashion*, Oxford: Berg.

O'Donnell, K. (2001), "Choo Polish," *Vogue*, March: 179–82.

O'Neal, G. S. (1998), "African-American Aesthetics of Dress: Current Manifestations," *Clothing and Textiles Research Journal* 16 (4): 167–75.

O'Sullivan, S. (1982), "Passionate Beginnings: Ideological Politics 1969–82," *Feminist Review* 11.

Ogborn, M. (1998), *Spaces of Modernity: London's Geographies 1680–1780*, London: Guilford Press.

Ogunnaike, Lola (2004), "SoHo Runs for Blue and Yellow Sneakers," *New York Times*, December 19.

Oxfam (2004), "Finding the Moral Fiber: Why Reform is Urgently Needed for a Fair Cotton Trade," Oxfam Briefing Paper, London: Oxfam <www.oxfam.org/en/>.

Painter, T. (1941), "The Prostitute," Kinsey Institute Library; 168–9, quoted in G. Chauncey (1994), *Gay New York: Gender, Urban Culture and the Making of the Gay Male World, 1890–1940*, New York: Basic Books.

Palmer, A. (2001), *Couture and Commerce*, Vancouver: UBC Press.

Palmer, A. and Clark, H. (eds.) (2004), *Old Clothes, New Looks: Second-Hand Fashion*, Oxford: Berg.

Partington, A. (1992), "Popular Fashion and Working-Class Affluence," in J. Ash and E. Wilson (eds.), *Chic Thrills: A Fashion Reader*, London: Pandora.

Paulicelli, E. (2004), *Fashion Under Fascism: Beyond the Black Shirt*, Oxford: Berg.

Pawley, M. (2000), *Fashion + Architecture*, New York: Wiley-Academy.

Payne, B., Winakor, G., and Farrell-Beck, J. (1992), *The History of Costume*, New York: Harper Collins.

Paz, O. (1967), *The Labyrinth of Solitude*, London: Penguin Press.

Peacock, J. (1993), *20th-Century Fashion: The Complete Sourcebook*, London: Thames and Hudson.

Peacock, J. (1996), *Men's Fashion: The Complete Sourcebook*, London: Thames and Hudson.

Peiss, K. (1998), *Hope in a Jar: The Making of America's Beauty Culture*, New York: Metropolitan Books.

Perrottet, T. (1993), "Inside Miss Universe Inc.," *Sydney Morning Herald Good Weekend Magazine*, January 9: 18.

Pexton, M. (1989), *Changing Styles in Fashion: Who, What, Why*, New York: Fairchild Publications.

Phillips, I. (2001), "The Frill of It," *Vogue*, April: 115–18.

Phillips, R. B. (1989), "Native American Art and the New Art History," *Museum Anthropology* 13 (4): 5–13.

Pile, S. and Thrift, N. (eds.) (1995), *Mapping the Subject: Geographies of Cultural Transformation*, London: Routledge.

Piponnier, F. and Mane, P. (1997), *Dress in the Middle Ages*, New Haven, CT: Yale University Press.

Plant, S. (1997), *Zeros and Ones: Digital Women and the New Technoculture*, London: Fourth Estate.

Plummer, D. (1965 [1963]), *Queer People: The Truth About Homosexuals in Britain*, New York: Citadel.

Polegato, R. and Wall, M. (1980), "Information-Seeking by Fashion Opinion Leaders and Followers," *Home Economics Research Journal* 8 (May 5): 327–38.

Polhemus, T. (1994), *Street Style: From Sidewalk to Catwalk*, New York: Thames and Hudson.

Polhemus, T. (1996), *Style Surfing*, London: Thames and Hudson.

Polhemus, T. and Proctor, L. (eds.) (1978), *Fashion and Anti-Fashion*, London: Thames and Hudson.

Porter, C. (2001), "Sexual Heeling" *The Daily Telegraph*, November 4 <www.telegraph.co.uk>.

Porter, C. (2002), "Flying Visit Takes the Shine Off Designer's US Debut," *The Guardian*, February 15 <www.guardian.co.uk>.

Porter, K. and Weeks, J. (eds.) (1992 [1991]), *Between the Acts: Lives of Homosexual Men, 1885–1967*, London: Routledge.

Post, E. (1945), *Emily Post's Etiquette: The Blue Book of Social Usage*, New York: Funk and Wagnalls.

Prestowitz, C. (2005), *Three Billion New Capitalists*, New York: Basic Books.

Pringle, G. (1949), *Etiquette in Canada: The Blue Book of Canadian Social Usage*, 2nd ed., Toronto: McClelland and Stewart.

Proust, M. (1913–1927), *Remembrance of Things Past*, 3 vols., New York: Vintage.

Pulos, A. J. (1983), *American Design Ethic: A History of Industrial Design to 1940*, Cambridge, MA: MIT Press.

Purdy, D. L. (ed.) (2004), *The Rise of Fashion: A Reader*, Minneapolis: University of Minneapolis Press.

Purvis, S. (1996), "The Interchangeable Roles of the Producer, Consumer and Cultural Intermediary: The New 'Pop' Fashion Designer," in J. O'Connor and D. Wynne (eds.), *From the Margins to the Centre: Cultural Production and Consumption in the Post-Industrial City*, Aldershot: Arena.

Quinn, B. (2002), *Techno Fashion*, Oxford and New York: Berg.

Quinn, B. (2003), *The Fashion of Architecture*, Oxford and New York: Berg.

Rabine, L. W. (2002), *The Global Circulation of African Fashion*, Oxford and New York: Berg.

Rabinow, P. and Rose, N. (eds.) (2003), *The Essential Foucault*, New York: New Press.

Radano, R. M. (1993), *New Musical Figurations: Anthony Braxton's Cultural Critique*, Chicago: University of Chicago Press.

Radcliffe Richards, J. (1980), *The Sceptical Feminist*, London: Routledge and Kegan Paul.

Reade, B. (ed.) (1970), *Sexual Heretics: Male Homosexuality in English Literature from 1850 to 1900*, London: Coward-McCann.

Rhodes, Z. and Knight, A. (1985), *The Art of Zandra Rhodes*, Boston: Houghton Mifflin.

Ribeiro, A. (1983), *A Visual History of Costume: The Eighteenth Century*, London: B. T. Batsford.

Ribeiro, A. (1983), *Dress and Morality*, London: B. T. Batsford.

Ribeiro, A. (1988), *Fashion in the French Revolution*, London: B. T. Batsford.

Ribeiro, A. (1995), *The Art of Dress: Fashion in England and France 1750 to 1820*, New Haven, CT: Yale University Press.

Ribeiro, A. (1999), *Ingres in Fashion: Representations of Dress and Appearance in Ingres's Images of Women*, New Haven, CT: Yale University Press.

Ribeiro, A. (2002), *Dress in Eighteenth-Century Europe, 1715–1789*, London: Yale University Press.

Richardson, J. and Kroeber, A. L. (1940), "Three Centuries of Women's Dress Fashion: A Quantitative Analysis," *Anthropological Records* 5 (2): 111–53.

Rider, F. (ed.) (1924), *Rider's New York City. A Guide-book for Travelers*, London: George Allen and Unwin.

Ritzer, G. (1993), *The McDonaldization of Society*, London: Pine Forge Press.

Ritzer, G. (1998), *The McDonaldization Thesis: Explorations and Extensions,* London: Sage.

Rivière, J. (1966), "Womanliness as a Masquerade," in H. M. Ruitenbeek (ed.), *Psychoanalysis and Female Sexuality,* New Haven, CT: College and University Press.

Rivière, J. (1989 [1929]), "Womanliness as a Masquerade," in V. Burgin, J. Donald and C. Kaplan (eds.), *Formations of Fantasy*, London: Routledge.

Roach-Higgins, M. E., and Eicher, J. B. (1992), "Dress and Identity," *Clothing and Textile Research Journal* 10 (4): 1–8.

Roach-Higgins, M. E., Eicher, J. B., and Johnson, K. K. P. (eds.) (1995), *Dress and Identity*, New York: Fairchild.

Roberts, M. (1992), " 'World Music' and the Global Cultural Economy," *Diaspora* 2(2): 229–42.

Robinson, D. E. (1975), "Style Changes: Cyclical, Inexorable, and Foreseeable," *Harvard Business Review* 53 (6): 121–31.

Roche, D. (1989), *La Culture des apparences: Une histoire du vêtement (XVIIe-XVIIIe siècle)*, Paris: Librairie Arthème Fayard.

Roche, D. (1994), *Dress and Fashion in the Ancien Régime*, Cambridge: Cambridge University Press.

Rogers, B. and Williams, V. (eds.) (1998), *Look at Me: Fashion and Photography in Britain 1960 to Present*, London: British Council.

Rogers, E. (1983), *Diffusion of Innovations*, 3rd ed., New York: The Free Press.

Root, R. A. (2005), *The Latin American Fashion Reader*, Oxford and New York: Berg.

Rosen, E. (2002), *Making Sweatshops: The Globalization of the US Apparel Industry*, Berkeley: University of California Press.

Ross, A. (2004), "The Making of the Second Anti-Sweatshop Movement," in *Low Pay, High Profile: The Global Push for Fair Labor*, New York: The New Press, pp. 32–50.

Ross, R. J. S. (ed.) (1997), *No Sweat: Fashion, Free Trade and the Rights of Garment Workers*, New York: Verso.

Ross, R. J. S. (2004), *Slaves to Fashion: Poverty and Abuse in the New Sweatshops*, Ann Arbor: University of Michigan Press.

Rossi, A. (1982), *The Architecture of the City*, Cambridge, MA: MIT Press.

Rothrock, V. (2006), "Homegrown Brands Battle for Market Share," China in Depth, *Women's Wear Daily*, March.

Ruark, J. (2001), "A Second Look at the Big Squeeze," *Chronicle of Higher Education*, November 23: 48, 13.

Rubin, W. (ed.) (1984), *"Primitivism" in 20th Century Art: Affinity of the Tribal and the Modern*, 2 vols, New York: Museum of Modern Art.

Rudolph, B. (1991), "The Supermodels," *Time* 6 (37) (September 16): 70–6.

Rushing, A. B. (1988), "Hair-Raising," *Feminist Studies* 14 (2): 325–35.

Sabin, R. (1996), *Comics, Comix and Graphic Novels*, London: Phaidon Press.

Safe, M. (1990), "Model Children," *Sydney Morning Herald Good Weekend Magazine*, June 16–17: 20–7.

Sagay, E. (1983), *African Hairstyles: Styles of Yesterday and Today*, London: Heinemann Educational Books.

Said, E. (1994 [1979]), *Orientalism*, London and New York: Vintage.

Sapir, E. (1931), "Fashion," in E. R. A. Seligman (ed.), *Encyclopedia of the Social Sciences* 6, New York: Macmillan Co., pp. 139–44.

Sarbin, T. R. (1943), "The Concept of Role-Taking," *Sociometry* 6: 273–84.

Sarbin, T. R. (1954), "Role Theory," in G. Lindzey (ed.), *Handbook of Social Psychology, Vol. I, Theory and Method*, Cambridge, MA: Addison-Wesley, pp. 223–58.

Sarbin, T. R. (1983), "Place Identity as a Component of Self: An Addendum," *Journal of Environmental Psychology* 3: 337–42.

Sargeant, W. (1949), *Life*, XXVI, April 11, 1949.

Sarris, A. (1966), *The Films of Josef von Sternberg*, New York: Museum of Modern Art.

Sassen, S. (1991), *The Global City: New York, London, Tokyo,* Princeton, NJ: Princeton University Press.

Saussure, F. de (1974), *Course in General Linguistics*, London: Fontana.

Saville, D. (2005), "Dress and Subculture in Greenwich Village," in L. Welters and P. A. Cunningham (eds.), *Twentieth-Century American Fashion*, Oxford and New York: Berg.

Schneider, G. and ElBoghdady, D. (2003), "Stores Follow Wal-Mart's Lean In Labor," *Washington Post*, November 6: 1.

Schneider, J. (1978), "Peacocks and Penguins: The Political Economy of European Cloth and Colors," *American Ethnologist* 5 (3): 413–47.

Schoeffler, O. E. and Gale, W. (1973), *Esquire's Encyclopedia of Twentieth-Century Men's Fashion*, New York: McGraw-Hill.

Schor, J. B. (1999), *The Overspent American: Why We Want What We Don't Need*, New York: HarperCollins.

Scott, L. (2004), *Fresh Lipstick: Redressing Fashion and Feminism*, New York and Houndmills: Palgrave Macmillan.

Seeling, C. (1999), *Fashion: The Century of the Designer: 1900–1999*, Cologne: Könemann.

Seltzer, M. (1998), *Mortal Lessons: Death and Life in America's Wound Culture*, New York: Touchstone.

Sessums, K. (1990), "White Heat," *Vanity Fair*, April: 208.

Settle, A. (1952), *Radio Times* [typescript], L50.6, January, Alison Settle Archives, University of Brighton.

Severa, J. (1995), *Dressed for the Photographer: Ordinary Americans and Fashion 1840–1900*, Kent, OH: Kent State University Press.

"Sexual Identity" (television program) (1981) quoted in K. Howes (1994), *Broadcasting It*, London: Cassell.

Shaver Papers, Archives Center, National Museum of American History, Washington, DC.

Shaw, M. (2000), "American Fashion: The Tirocchi Sisters in Context," in Susan Hay (ed.), *From Paris to Providence: Fashion, Art, and the Tirocchi Dressmakers' Shop, 1915–1947*, Providence, RI: Museum of Art, Rhode Island School of Design.

Sheehan, P. (1986), "Why Were We Born So Beautiful?" *Sydney Morning Herald Good Weekend Magazine*, November 29: 62–5.

Shenkar, O. (2005), *The Chinese Century*, Upper Saddle River, NJ: Wharton School Publishing.

Sherrill, M. (1992), "The Once and Future Model," *Allure*, June: 88–9, 114.

Shogun, R. and Craig, T. (1964), *The Detroit Race Riot: A Study in Violence*, Philadelphia and New York: Chilton Books.

Shrimpton, J. (1990), *Jean Shrimpton: An Autobiography*, London: Ebury Press.

Silverman, D. (1986), *Selling Culture: Bloomingdale's, Diana Vreeland, and the New Aristocracy of Taste in Reagan's America*, New York: Pantheon Books.

Simkins, A. A. (1982), "The Functional and Symbolic Roles of Hair and Headgear Among Afro-American Women: A Cultural Perspective," PhD dissertation, Greensboro: University of North Carolina.

Simmel, G. (1904), "Fashion," *International Quarterly* 10: 130–55.

Simmel, G. (1957 [1904]), "Fashion," *The Journal of American Sociology* LXII (6): 541–58.

Simmel, G. (1971 [1903]), "The Metropolis and Mental Life," in D. N. Levine (ed.), *On Individuality and Social Forms*, Chicago: University of Chicago Press.

Simone, N. with Cleary, S. (1993), *I Put a Spell on You: The Autobiography of Nina Simone*, New York: Da Capo Press.

Simpson, M. (ed.) (1996), *Anti-Gay*, London: Freedom Editions.

Sinfield, A. (1998), *Gay and After*, London: Serpent's Tail.

Singer, S. (2002), "Manhattan Rhapsody," *Vogue*, February: 192–5.

Sketel, W. (1930), *Sexual Aberrations: The Phenomenon of Fetishism in Relations*, New York: Liveright Publishing Corporation.

Skov, L. (2003), "Patterns of Culture in Global Fashion: Production, Representation and Agency," *Scandinavian Journal of Design History* 13: 7–24.

Skov, L. (2003), "Fashion Nation: A Japanese Globalization Experience and a Hong Kong Dilemma," in S. Niessen, A. M. Leshkowich and C. Jones (eds.), *Re-Orienting Fashion: The Globalization of Asian Dress*, Oxford and New York: Berg.

Skow, J. (1985), "Madonna Rocks the Land," *Time*, May 27: 77–81.

Sloterdijk, P. (2000), *L'Heure du crime et le temps de l'oeuvre d'art*, Paris: Calmann-Lévy.

Smart, B. (ed.) (1999), *Resisting McDonaldization*, London: Sage.

Smith, A. (1937 [1776]), in E. Cannan (ed.), *An Inquiry Into the Nature and Causes of the Wealth of Nations*, New York: Modern Library Edition, Random House.

Smith, A. (1976 [1759]), in D. D. Raphael and A. L. Macfie (eds.), *The Theory of Moral Sentiments*, New York: Oxford University Press.

Snitow, A., Stansell, C. and Thompson, S. (1984), *Desire: The Politics of Sexuality*, London: Virago.

Sohn, A. (2002), *Sex and the City: Kiss and Tell*, New York: Pocket Books.

Solomon, M. R. and Rabolt, N. (2004), *Consumer Behavior in Fashion*, Upper Saddle River, NJ: Pearson.

Sontag. S. (1961), "Notes on Camp," *Against Interpretation*, New York: Dell.

Sowell, T. (1996), *Migrations and Culture*, New York: Basic Books.

Spar, D. and Burns, J. (2000), *Hitting the Wall: Nike and International Labor Practices*, Harvard Business School Case #9-700-047, Boston: Harvard Business School.

Spencer, H. (1966 [1879]), "Ceremonial Institutions," in *The Principles of Sociology*, Vol. II, Part IV, in *The Words of Herbert Spencer*, Vol. VII, Osnabrück: Otta Zeller.

Spindler, A. (2000), "Viktor and Rolf," *Viktor and Rolf Haute Couture Book*, Exhibitions International.

Sproles, G. B. and Burns, L. D. (1994), "A Theory of the Fashion Process" in *Changing Appearances*, New York: Fairchild.

Starobinski, J., Duboy, P., Fukai, A., Kanai, J., Horii, T., Arnold, J., and Kamer, M. (1989), *Revolution in Fashion: European Clothing, 1715–1815*, New York: Abbeville Press.

Stead, L., Goulev, P., Evans, C., and Mamdani, E. (2004), "The Emotional Wardrobe," *Personal and Ubiquitous Computing* 8: 282–90.

Steele, V. (1985), *Fashion and Eroticism: Ideals of Feminine Beauty from the Victorian to the Jazz Age*, New York: Oxford University Press.

Steele, V. (1988), *Paris Fashion*, Oxford: Oxford University Press.

Steele, V. (1996), *Fetish: Fashion, Sex and Power*, Oxford: Oxford University Press.

Steele, V. (1997), *Fifty Years of Fashion: New Look to Now*, New Haven, CT: Yale University Press.

Steele, V. (1998), *Paris Fashion: A Cultural History*, rev. ed., Oxford and New York: Berg.

Steele, V. (2000), *Fifty Years of Fashion: New Look to Now*, New Haven, CT: Yale University Press.

Steele, V. (2000), "Fashion: Yesterday, Today and Tomorrow," in N. White and I. Griffiths (eds.), *The Fashion Business: Theory, Practice, Image*, Oxford and New York: Berg.

Steele, V. (2001), *The Corset: A Cultural History*, New Haven, CT: Yale University Press.

Steele, V. (2003), *Fashion: Italian Style*, New Haven, CT: Yale University Press.

Steele, V. and Major, J. S. (1999), *China Chic. East Meets West*, New Haven, CT: Yale University Press.

Stern, R. (2004), *Against Fashion: Clothing as Art, 1850–1930*, Cambridge, MA: MIT Press.

Sternberg, J. (1965), *Fun in a Chinese Laundry*, New York: Collier.

Steward, S. M. (1982), quoted in J. Barr (1982 [1950]), *Quatrefoil*, Boston: Alyson Publications.

Stitziel, J. (2005), *Fashioning Socialism: Clothing, Politics and Consumer Culture in East Germany*, Oxford and New York: Berg.

Stone, G. (1962), "Appearance and the Self," in A. M. Rose (ed.), *Human Behavior and the Social Processes: An Interactionist Approach*, New York: Houghton Mifflin, pp. 86–116.

"Strong Measures Must be Taken Against Rioting" (1943), *Los Angeles Times*, June 9.

Summers, L. (2001), *Bound to Please: A History of the Victorian Corset*, Oxford and New York: Berg.

Sweetman, P. (1999), "Anchoring the (Postmodern) Self? Body Modification, Fashion and Identity," *Body and Society* 5 (2–3): 51–76.

Symonds, J. A. (1881), "*A Problem* in *Modern Ethics*," quoted in B. Reade (ed.) (1970), *Sexual Heretics*, London: Coward-McCann.

Tabloid (1953), CBC Canada, NFA V1 8204 043-2, NFT7SA, February 27, National Archives of Canada, Moving Image and Sound Archives, Ottawa.

Talsman, W. (1966 [1958]), *The Gaudy Image*, London: Olympia Press.

Tarlo, E. (1996), *Clothing Matters: Dress and Identity in India*, Chicago: University of Chicago Press.

Taylor, L. (2002), *The Study of Dress History*, Manchester: Manchester University Press.

"Tenney Feels Riots Caused by Nazi Move for Disunity" (1943), *Los Angeles Times*, June 9.

Tesnières, L. (1959), *Eléments de syntaxe structurale*, Paris: Klincksieck.

Texier, C. (1990), "Have Women Surrendered in MTV's Battle of the Sexes?," *New York Times*, April 22: 31.

The Economic Times, October 15, 2005.

The Fashion Group International Records, Manuscripts and Archives Division, New York Public Library.

The New Zealand Herald (2002), "NZ Designers Upstage Hosts at Australian Fashion Week," May 10.

"The Riots," (1943), *The Crisis*, July.

Thomas, N., Cole, A. and Douglas, B. (eds.) (2005), *Tattoo: Bodies, Art and Exchange in the Pacific and the West*, Durham: Duke University Press.

Thornton, S. (1997), "The Social Logic of Subcultural Capital," in K. Gelder and S. Thornton (eds.), *The Subcultures Reader*, London: Routledge.

Tickner, L. (2000), *Modern Lives and Modern Subjects*, New Haven, CT: Yale University Press.

"Time for Sanity" (1943), *Los Angeles Times*, June 11.

Tocqueville, A. de (1945), *Democracy in America*, Vol. 2, New York: Vintage Books.

Todd, J. (1850), *The Young Man: Hints Addressed to the Young Men of the United States*, Northampton, MA: n.p.

Tortota, P. G. and Eubanks, K. (2005), *Survey of Historic Costume*, 4th ed., New York: Fairchild Publications.

TradeNZ Press Release, (1999), "NZ Designers to Return to London Fashion Week," August 3, available from <www.tradenz.govt.nz>.

Trebay, G. (2003), "Taking Hip-Hop Seriously. Seriously," *New York Times*, May 20.

Trevor-Roper, H. (1983), "The Invention of Tradition: The Highland Tartan in Scotland," in E. Hobsbawm and T. Ranger (eds.), *The Invention of Tradition*, Cambridge: Cambridge University Press, pp. 15–41.

Triggs, T. (1995), *Communicating Design: Essays in Visual Communication*, London: B. T. Batsford.

Troy, N. J. (2003), *Couture Culture: A Study in Modern Art and Fashion*, Cambridge, MA: MIT Press.

Tucker, A. (1998), *The London Fashion Book*, New York: Rizzoli International Publications Inc.

Tucker, A. and Kingswell, T. (2000), *Fashion: A Crash Course*, New York: Watson-Guptill Publications.

Tulloch, C. (2002), "Letter from the Editor," *Fashion Theory* 2 (1): 1–2.

Turner, B. (1984), *The Body and Society: Explorations in Social Theory*, Oxford: Basil Blackwell.

Turner, B. (ed.) (1990), *Theories of Modernity and Postmodernity*, London and Newbury Park, CA: Sage.

Turner, B. (1996 [1984]), *The Body and Society*, London and Thousand Oaks, CA: Sage.

Turner, B. (1999), "The Possibility of Primitiveness: Towards a Sociology of Body Marks in Cool Societies," *Body and Society* 5 (2–3): 39–50.

Turner, R. H. and Surace, S. J. (1956), "Zoot Suiters and Mexicans: Symbols in Crowd Behavior," *American Journal of Sociology* 62: 14–20.

US Census Bureau (2004), *International Database*, "Countries Ranked by Population: 2004" <www.census.gov/cgi-bin/ipc/idbrank.pl>, accessed March 15, 2006

US Census Bureau (2006), *International Database*, "Countries Ranked by Population: 2004" <www.census.gov/cgi-bin/ipc/idbrank.pl>, accessed March 15, 2006.

US Census Bureau (2006), Country and Product Trade Data Special Report: Textile Imports <www.census.gov/foreign-trade/statistics/country/sreport/textile.html>.

US General Accounting Office (1994), *Data on the Tax Compliance of Sweatshops, 1994* <www.unclefed.com/GAOReports/ggd94-210fs.pdf>.

Valdez, S. (2004), "Fashioning Fiction in Photography Exhibition" <www.lookonline.com/momaexhibition.html>.

Van Deburg, W. L. (1992), *New Day in Babylon: The Black Power Movement and American Culture, 1965–1975*, Chicago: University of Chicago Press.

Vanhaeren, M., d'Errico, F. Stringer, C., James, S. L., Todd, J. A. and Mienis, H. K. (2006), *Science*, June 23: 1785–8.

Veblen, T. (1899), *The Theory of the Leisure Class: An Economic Study in the Evolution of Institutions*, New York: Macmillan.

Veillon, D. (2002), *Fashion Under Occupation*, Oxford and New York: Berg.

Verga, D. (2003), "Cina: un nuovo mercato per l'alta moda" (China: A New Market for Haute Couture) <www.netmanager.it>, accessed April 9.

Vermorel, F. and Vermorel, J. (1978), *The Sex Pistols*, London: Tandem.

Vernon, P. (2001), "Sex Appeal," *Vogue*, July: 34–7.

Vidal, J. (2000), "Stay Off Catwalk, Oz Tells Kiwis," *The Evening Post*, August 23: 2 <www.kiwicareers.govt.nz/industry>.

Vigée-Lebrun, E. (1986), *Souvenirs*, ed. Claudine Herrmann, Paris: Des femmes.

"Viktor and Rolf: Self-Portrait" (2004), *Fashion in Colors: Viktor and Rolf and KCI*, Kyoto: The Kyoto Costume Institute, Kyoto.

Visweswaran, K. (1997), "Diaspora and Opportunity in the Plural City," in R. Waldinger and M. Bozorgmehr (eds.), *Ethnic Los Angeles*, New York: Russell Sage Foundation, pp. 445–70.

von Eschen, P. (1996), *Race for Empire: African-Americans, Anti-Colonialism, and the Cold War*, Ithaca, NY: Cornell University Press.

Walton-Roberts, M. and Pratt, G. (2005), "Mobile Modernities: One South Asian Family Negotiates Immigration, Gender and Class," *Gender, Place and Culture* 12 (2): 173–95.

Warner, P. C. (2005), "The Americanization of Fashion: Sportswear, the Movies and the 1930s," in L. Welters and P. A. Cunningham (eds.),

Twentieth-Century American Fashion, Oxford and New York: Berg.

"Warren Orders Zoot Suit Quiz; Quiet Reigns After Rioting" (1943), *Los Angeles Times*, June 10.

Warren, C. A. B. (1974), *Identity and Community in the Gay World*, New York: Wiley.

Waterbury, J. B. (1852), *The Voyage of Life; Suggested by Cole's Allegorical Paintings*, Boston: Massachusetts Sabbath School Society.

Waters, M. (1995), Globalization, 2nd ed., London: Routledge.

Watson, J. (ed.) (1998), *Golden Arches East: McDonald's in East Asia*, Stanford, CA: Stanford University Press.

"Watts Pastor Blames Riots on Fifth Column" (1943), *Los Angeles Times*, June 11.

Watts, M. J. (1996), "Mapping Identities: Place, Space and Community in an African City" in P. Yeager (ed.), *The Geography of Identity*, Ann Arbor: University of Michigan Press, pp. 59–97.

Waugh, C. F. (1999), "'Well-Cut through the Body:' Fitted Clothing in Twelfth-Century Europe," *Dress* 26: 3–16.

Waugh, N. (1964), *The Cut of Men's Clothes 1600–1900*, London: Faber and Faber.

Waugh, N. (1968), *The Cut of Women's Clothes 1600–1930*, London: Faber and Faber.

Webber-Hanchett, T, (2003), "Dorothy Shaver: Promoter of 'The American Look,'" Master's thesis, University of Rhode Island.

Webber-Hanchett, T, (2006), "Art Deco Textiles" and "Postwar Couture," in *MFA Highlights: Textile and Fashion Arts*, Boston: MFA Publications.

Weeden, P. (1977), "Study Patterned on Kroeber's Investigation of Style," *Dress* 3: 8–19.

Weeks, J. (1990), *Coming Out: Homosexual Politics in Britain from the Nineteenth Century to the Present*, London: Quartet.

Weinstein, N. C. (1993), *A Night in Tunisia: Imaginings of Africa in Jazz*, New York: Limelight Editions.

Weisberger, L. (2004), *The Devil Wore Prada*, New York: Broadway Books.

Weisbord, R. (1973), *Ebony Kinship: Africa, Africans, and the Afro-American*, Westport, CT: Greenwood Press.

Welters, L. (2005), "The Beat Generation: Subcultural Style," in L. Welters and P. A. Cunningham (eds.), *Twentieth-Century American Fashion*, Oxford and New York: Berg.

Welters, L. and Cunningham, P. A. (eds.) (2005), *Twentieth-Century American Fashion,* Oxford and New York: Berg.

"What is the American Look" (1945), *Life*, May 21.

White, N. (2000), *Reconstructing Italian Fashion: America and the Development of the Italian Fashion Industry*, Oxford and New York: Berg.

White, N. and Griffiths, I. (eds.) (2000), *The Fashion Business: Theory, Practice, Image*, Oxford and New York: Berg.

White, S. and White, G. (1995), "Slave Hair and African-American Culture in the Eighteenth and Nineteenth Centuries," *Journal of Southern History* 61 (1): 45–76.

Whitley, L. (1994), "Morris de Camp Crawford and American Textile Design," Master's thesis, Fashion Institute of Technology.

Wigley, M. (1995), *White Walls, Designer Dresses: The Fashioning of Modern Architecture*, Cambridge, MA: MIT Press.

Wilcox, C. (2004), *Vivienne Westwood*, London, V&A Publications.

Wildeblood, J. and Brinson, P. (1965), *The Polite World: A Guide to English Manners and Deportment from the 13th to the 19th Century*, London: Oxford University Press.

Wilford, J. N. (2006), "Old Shells Suggest Early Human Adornment," *New York Times*, June 23, A1.

Williams, C. (2003), "Evaluating the Penetration of the Commodity Economy," *Futures* 35: 857–68.

Williams, C. and Windebank, J. (2003), "The Slow Advance and Uneven Penetration of Commodification," *International Journal of Urban and Regional Research* 27: 250–64.

Wilson, E. (1982a), "If You're So Sure You're a Feminist, Why Do You Read the Fashion Page?" *The Guardian*, July 26, and letters in response to Wilson, August 2.

Wilson, E. (1982b), *What is to be Done about Violence Towards Women?* Harmondsworth, UK: Penguin.

Wilson, E. (1985), *Adorned in Dreams: Fashion and Modernity*, London: Virago.

Wilson, E. (1992), "The Postmodern Body," in J. Ash and E. Wilson (eds.), *Chic Thrills: A Fashion Reader*, London: Pandora.

Wilson, E. (2003 [1985]), *Adorned in Dreams: Fashion and Modernity*. London and New York: I. B. Taurus.

Wilson, E. (2004), "Magic Fashion," *Fashion Theory* 8 (4): 375–86.

Wines, M. (2005), "Dollar's Fall Silences Africa's Garment Factories," *New York Times*, March 12, Sec. A, p. 1.

Wolf, E. R. (1982), *Europe and the People without History*, Berkeley: University of California Press.

Wolf, N. (1990), *The Beauty Myth: How Images of Beauty Are Used against Women*, London: Chatto and Windus.

Wolfe, T, (1970), *Radical Chic and Mau-Mauing the Flak Catchers*, New York: Farrar, Straus and Giroux.

Wollen, P. (1993), *Raiding the Icebox*, Bloomington: Indiana University Press.

Wollen, P. (2003), "The Concept of Fashion in the Arcades Project," *Boundary* 2 (Spring): 131–42.

Woodward, S. (2000), "Looking Good: Feeling Right—Aesthetics of the Self," in S. Kücher and D. Miller (eds.), *Clothing as Material Culture*, Oxford and New York: Berg, pp. 21–39.

World Trade Organization (2005), International Trade Statistics <www.wto.org/english/res_e/statis_e/its2005_e/its05_toc_e.htm>.

Wright, L. R. (1982), "Changes in Black American Hairstyles from 1964 through 1977, as Related to Themes in Feature Articles and Advertisements," Master's thesis, Michigan State University.

Wrigley, R. (2002), *The Politics of Appearances: Representations of Dress in Revolutionary France*, Oxford and New York: Berg.

Wu, J. (2006), "Chinese Fashion Industry and Trade Policies," lecture presented at the University of Rhode Island, Kingston, RI, March 22.

Wyndham, S. (1990), "The Business of Being Elle," *Australian Magazine*, April 14–15: 20–6.

Yellen, J. (2005), "Reflections on China's Economy," *FRBSF Economic Letter*, November 5.

Yeshiva University Museum (2005), *A Perfect Fit: The Garment Industry and American Jewry*, New York: Yeshiva University.

Yohannan, K. and Nolf, N. (1998), *Claire McCardell: Redefining Modernism*, New York: Harry N. Abrams.

York, P. (1980), *Style Wars*, London: Sidgwick and Jackson.

York, P. (1984), *Modern Times*, London: Futura.

Young, A. B. (1937), *Recurring Cycles of Fashion, 1760–1937*, New York: Harper and Row.

Yung, J. (1995), *Unbound Feet: A Social History of Chinese Women in San Francisco*, Berkeley: University of California Press.

Zakim, M. (2003), *Ready-Made Democracy: A History of Men's Dress in the American Republic, 1760–1860*, Chicago: University of Chicago Press.

Zelinsky, W. (2004), "Globalization Reconsidered: The Historical Geography of Modern Western Male Attire," *Journal of Cultural Geography* 22 (1): 83–134.

Zenderland, L. (1978), *Recycling the Past: Popular Uses of American History*, Philadelphia: University of Pennsylvania Press.

Zeng, D. Z. (2005), "China's Employment Challenges and Strategies after WTO Accession," World Bank Research Working Paper, No. 3352, February.

Zhou, W. (2001), *Shanghai Baby*, Glasgow: Pocket Books/Simon and Schuster.

"Zoot Suit Originated in Georgia" (1943), *New York Times*, June 11.

"Zoot Suit War Inquiry Ordered by Governor" (1943), *Los Angeles Times*, June 9.

"Zoot Suit Warfare Spreads to Pupils of Detroit Area" (1943), *Washington Star*, June 11.

"Zoot-Girls Use Knife in Attack" (1943), *Los Angeles Times*, June 11.

"Zoot-Suit Fighting Spreads On the Coast" (1943), *New York Times*, June 10.

"Zoot-Suiters Again on the Prowl as Navy Holds Back Sailors" (1943), *Washington Post*, June 9.

INDEX